THE BRITISH CABINET SYSTEM

AUSTRALIA
The Law Book Co. of Australasia Pty. Ltd.
SYDNEY   MELBOURNE   BRISBANE

CANADA AND U.S.A.
The Carswell Company Ltd.
TORONTO

INDIA
N. M. Tripathi Ltd.
BOMBAY

NEW ZEALAND
Legal Publications Ltd.
WELLINGTON

THE
BRITISH CABINET SYSTEM

By

ARTHUR BERRIEDALE KEITH,
D.C.L., LL.D., D.LITT., F.B.A.

SECOND EDITION

BY

N. H. GIBBS
*Fellow and Tutor of Merton College, Oxford,
and University Lecturer in Modern History*

LONDON
STEVENS & SONS LIMITED
1952

First Edition (1938) *by A. Berriedale Keith*
Second Edition (1952) *by N. H. Gibbs*

Published by
Stevens   &   Sons   Limited
of 119 & 120 Chancery Lane,
London   —   Law   Publishers
and   made   and   printed   by
William Clowes and Sons Limited
of London and Beccles

CONTENTS

v

Appendices

PREFACE

THE purpose of this new edition is to bring Keith's original work up to date, partly by including reference to events of the years since the book first appeared, and partly by using material on earlier events which has been published in the same period.

In some cases new material has been presented in completely new sections added to the text, such as that on the War Cabinet of 1939–45. Some additions have been incorporated in the original text, as in the section on the Committee of Imperial Defence and that on the Crown and the dissolution of Parliament. In yet other cases, for example the dismissal of ministers, Keith's original text has been rewritten and his arguments to some extent modified. These additions have been either too lengthy or too frequent to be indicated in footnotes or placed together in an additional chapter; but the editor has tried to make them in such a way that the spirit as well as the form of the original text should be retained. There is much to be said for a new approach to the history and working of Cabinet government, based on less formal and institutional grounds than those adopted by Keith and most other standard writers on the subject. But, so long as the author's traditional method of approach is accepted, nothing that has happened during the last thirteen years, either in the work of the Cabinet itself or in its relations with Parliament, can be taken to alter his main conclusions.

One substantial omission has been made, viz. Chapter 6 of the original work, 'The Privy Council and the Departments of State.' Although that chapter presented a great deal of useful information about ministers and their departments in a convenient form it seemed, in principle, wrong to leave it in the main body of a study devoted to the work of ministers in their corporate capacity. Other similar changes have not altered the form of the book. The section on 'The Cabinets from William IV.' becomes an appendix, together with a further appendix to illustrate the growth in size of the Cabinet during the last one hundred years. The chapter on 'The Constitution Under Strain,' virtually a postscript when the book was first published, has been taken into the relevant part of the main text.

A bibliography has been added.

N. H. G.

Oxford.   *February* 1952.

CHAPTER I

THE DEVELOPMENT OF CABINET GOVERNMENT

1. THE CONVENTIONAL BASIS OF CABINET GOVERNMENT

THE national government of Great Britain today is controlled by the Cabinet, who, indeed, are His Majesty's servants, but for all normal purposes servants whose advice the King must, and readily does accept. The Cabinet itself owes its unity to its selection by the Prime Minister, who is chosen by the sovereign. But the choice of the sovereign is conditioned by the consideration that it is imperative that his nominee should be able to command the votes of a majority of the members of the House of Commons. These members in turn are elected at intervals of not more than five years by an electorate, which in principle includes all persons, male and female, not under twenty-one years of age. The effective working of the system depends on the existence of political parties, through whose activities in organisation the electors in the constituencies, which all choose one member only, are presented with the opportunity of voting for one or other of candidates who profess allegiance to a distinct party and to the principles it professes. In practice the elector votes often, not so much for principles, as for the recognised leader or sometimes leaders of one party or another. He may feel himself incompetent to decide on measures to be taken in the future. He often thinks he knows in whom he may put his trust, and is prepared to accept what plans ultimately approve themselves in his leader's eyes.

Essentially the whole system of the supreme control of administration and legislation rests on the observation of certain practices, which are conveniently styled constitutional conventions. That this is so is admitted on every hand. Recognition of it was accorded by Article 2 of the Agreement for a Treaty between Great Britain and Ireland of 1921, when the law, practice, and constitutional usage governing the relationship of the Crown or of its representative, or of the Imperial Parliament to the Dominion of Canada, were made applicable to the Irish Free State, and in sect. 4 of the Status of the Union Act, 1934, of the Union Parliament, specific reference is made to the constitutional conventions regulating the use by the Governor-General of his legal power of summoning and dissolving Parliament and of appointing ministers.[1] It is essentially by the growth of conventions that the Cabinet system exists. Save for the most occasional allusion, as in the Ministers of the Crown Act, 1937, neither Prime Minister nor Cabinet is known to law, and one may still search in vain in the statute book for any recognition of the party system, and yet the essential control of British administration and legislation is vested in a Cabinet whose existence would be impossible in its present form without the co-operation of party organisation.

Convention alone provides for the essential rules of Cabinet government.[2] It demands that the will of the electorate at a general election, which under law must be held quinquennially at least, shall be reflected by the sovereign continuing in office or placing therein as Prime Minister, with power to choose his colleagues, the leader of the victorious party. It requires that the Cabinet shall maintain continuous touch with the Commons by meeting Parliament every year. It demands that, if the Commons withdraws its support, the Cabinet must either resign, or appeal to the electorate for a new mandate. If that is not accorded, the ministry must resign if the election has given a clear majority to the opposing party; but, if there are more opposing parties than one, and the result is not clear, it may meet Parliament and allow a vote to decide its fate, as the Conservative ministry did in January, 1924. But it cannot ask another dissolution, nor should the Crown concede it if it were asked. Convention again determines that the Cabinet is collectively responsible for the conduct of the executive government, and for appointments made, and that its duty is to initiate legislation. It requires a ministry in case of domestic crisis to exert all its powers to maintain law and order, but also to summon Parliament forthwith to consult with it. It equally demands that in conducting foreign affairs, which appertains in

[1] For some discussion on this see H. V. Evatt, *The King and his Dominion Governors*, Appendix, pp. 299–306.
[2] Ridges, *Constitutional Law of England* (ed. Forrest), p. 5; A. V. Dicey, *Introduction to the Study of the Law of the Constitution* (9th ed.), pp. 417–473.

law solely to the Crown, the ministry shall have full regard to the will of the Commons, and shall not declare war, or neutrality, or make peace, or enter into important treaties without securing as soon as possible endorsement by the Commons, which so far as is possible should be taken into counsel before the Crown is committed to any definite course of action.

The Crown again, by convention, is required to accept the advice of the Cabinet in all cases, unless it is prepared to find another ministry, which will justify to Parliament, and secure its approval of the refusal to accept the advice of the previous ministry. It must, therefore, in all normal circumstances, assent to any bill which is passed by the two houses of Parliament, or by the Commons, under the Parliament Act, 1911, and it must grant a dissolution to a ministry, again, in all normal circumstances, unless it has already been granted recently a dissolution without securing as a consequence a renewal of the confidence of the electorate.

It rests also on convention that the Cabinet depends for its existence on the lower house only, and may disregard the hostility of the upper chamber. The essential principle of the initiative in finance of the lower house, under the authority of the Cabinet, and of the subordination of the Lords rested solely on convention until the Parliament Act, 1911. The same Act rendered definite and greatly limited the power of the Lords to deal with general legislation, which, in theory absolute, had hitherto been regulated, as it proved inadequately, by convention only.

One of the fundamental principles which renders the operation of Cabinet government in Britain essentially different from its operation in France is purely conventional, the rule that the Commons will deal with financial proposals only on the initiative of the ministry, with which therefore rests the framing of the budget, the determination of expenditure, and the devising of taxation.[3] How essential this is for the British system of Cabinet government as opposed, for instance, to the French, can be seen from the fact that the adoption of the same rule necessarily accompanied the creation of Cabinet government in the British colonies.

It is again by convention only that the Commons do not attempt, by the creation of committees, to control in detail administration and legislative proposals, as is done in France.

3 Sir Thomas Erskine May, *Parliamentary Practice* (15th ed.), pp. 654, 668.

Conventions, as may be seen, are merely usages, and they are styled conventions, without any implication that they have the force of law. From law proper they differ in part in definiteness. When it was proposed on the grant of responsible government to the Australian colonies to lay down by law the cases in which the Crown might or might not disallow legislation, the decision in favour of abandoning the attempt, which had the support of Mr. Gladstone,[4] was largely based on the advantages of the flexibility of constitutional usage over law, which could only be altered by a fresh appeal to Parliament. When, on the other hand, the Parliament Act, 1911, was passed, it was because the Lords held wider ideas on the nature of the convention regarding acceptance by that chamber of legislation passed by the Commons, and the latter demanded more precise definition. No doubt this is not an invariable criterion. The rules of the Commons, as to initiation of legislation, are precise and explicitly formulated, and in the case of the relations of the Crown and ministers certain doctrines are equally clear, but in general the doctrine holds good.

Law, again, has one advantage over conventions in its categorical character. If it is formally enacted, a principle is felt to express the will of the country, and to command obedience from a people which still respects law as *primâ facie* the embodiment of the public will, as opposed to a convention which may be regarded as the expression of practical convenience, but without cogency, if other considerations arise. Moreover, in many cases law can be enforced in the sense that the Courts can be invited to pass judgment on actions declared to be contrary to law, and these judgments will normally be enforced by the administrative machinery appointed for that end. No Government can lightly face the feeling which is created by any declaration that it has acted illegally, for that would arouse against it, not merely the opposition, but the public opinion of a vast body of electors, who feel that it is imperative to uphold the validity of the law. Even a strong ministry cannot risk difficulties arising from this source. When it turned out that the ministry had made a mistake in arresting, and handing over to the Irish Free State, Mr. Art O'Brien,[5] the fact that its action might be morally justifiable, did not prevent the country being insistent, when it was ruled to be technically illegal, on the

[4] A. B. Keith, *Responsible Government in the Dominions* (1928 ed.), i. 24.
[5] *Home Secretary* v. *O'Brien*, [1923] A. C. 603.

grant of compensation to him and others in like position by the Restoration of Order in Ireland (Indemnity) Act, 1923. This psychological fact must be borne in mind, and it operates even where it would be impossible to enforce through the existing machinery a declaration by the Courts of law, or even to obtain a formal declaration of law, as when a Government expends money without due legislative sanction.[6] In such a case it may be impossible for a private person to secure a declaration that the act is illegal, but opinion will resent it. In the case of a convention it is always possible to argue that it is not established, that what has happened in the past is not a binding precedent, and that in new circumstances a new line should be struck out. This position is aided by the fact that, while writers of text-books on constitutional matters seldom disagree as to the law, they do disagree in the most marked manner as to the extent to which conventions exist and are binding, and their views necessarily change with each practical issue arising. The close state of parties in the House of Commons after the General Election of February, 1950, for example, gave rise to some discussion on the powers and duties of the Crown if asked for a dissolution in the early months of its life by the new Labour Government, a discussion in which authorities were quoted to support widely varying opinions.

Conventions, therefore, are really only usages in matters affecting the constitution, and an effort to distinguish between usages and conventions, on the ground that the latter are usages followed, because they are held to be binding, is really of minimal value. A usage in constitutional matters, it will be found on investigation, is normally based on some definite convenience or utility in relation to the constitutional system of the day, and with the passing of the years it is followed under the influence of the normal psychological principle of imitation and willingness to follow precedent. In England this attitude of mind has created for our Courts the rule of obeying precedents, a principle which is not by any means normally accepted by judiciaries, and which has opponents in distinguished legal circles. There can be no doubt that the judicial outlook has helped to encourage in constitutional matters the search for precedent, since it is a familiar and marked example of the putting into operation of a natural human tendency.

---

[6] *Dalrymple* v. *Colonial Treasurer*, [1910] T. P. 372 ; Keith, *Responsible Government in the Dominions* (1928 ed.), i. 186 ff.

When Queen Victoria died, the immediate reaction of the Office of Works was to look for the precedent of 1837,[7] and for each British coronation regard has been sedulously had to the precedents of the former. Lord Esher's work for the sovereign took largely the form of collecting the stores of precedent to be found among the royal archives, and of adducing thence such authority as he thought fit to guide the monarch in new emergent cases. Any usage, it may fairly be said, in England tends to gather to itself *ipso facto* authority, and this applied equally to any change of usage. This is the substantial justification for Lord Salisbury's declaration on the issue of the franchise on October 28, 1884: 'If the House of Lords reverses its course, under threats, because a majority of the House of Commons object to their policy, it will, by that very act, become Constitutional law that the House of Lords is bound to submit to the House of Commons. From that moment the Lords will have lost all power of resistance: and unchecked power will have passed to the Commons.'[8]

Lord Salisbury's view is justified because, though he put the matter too strongly, he was dealing with a real probability. If the Lords yielded on such an issue as that in question, it must create a precedent of grave importance, for it would indicate that the existing constitutional system had developed to a position in which it demanded that the House of Lords should definitely subordinate its views to those of the Commons. In the same way the importance of the selection of Mr. Baldwin in 1923, in lieu of Lord Curzon as Prime Minister, rests on the fact that, by passing over the man, who on existing precedents might well be deemed to have a superior claim, the King showed that he recognised that constitutional development demanded the presence of the Premier in the lower chamber to meet the Labour opposition.[9] The new usage, it may confidently be predicted, will endure, unless and until some alteration in other constitutional conditions renders it inappropriate. In like manner we can see the fundamental misunderstanding which induced Mr. Asquith to formulate the doctrine that the King would not be bound to give a dissolution to Mr. MacDonald, if that were

[7] *Journals and Letters of Reginald, Viscount Esher*, i. 274 f.
[8] *Letters of Queen Victoria*, 2 s., iii. 559 f.
[9] H. Nicholson, *Curzon : The Last Phase*, p. 355 ; Lord Ronaldshay, *Life of Lord Curzon*, iii. 352 ; B. E. C. Dugdale, *Arthur James Balfour*, ii. 359–362 ; L. S. Amery, *Thoughts on the Constitution*, p. 21, suggests that the precedence has been created *ex post facto* and that it was not in the minds of those who advised the King.

asked for, in view of the fact that there was in operation a three-party system. What he failed to remember was that the Crown must be wholly reluctant to refuse to give the electorate a chance to give a clear verdict in favour of one political party or another, and that that consideration would drive it forthwith to concede, as it in fact did in 1924 concede, a dissolution to the Labour leader.[10]

We must therefore set against the cogent force of any existing practice the argument that it may be departed from, because it no longer accords with the development of the constitution, when a new usage may be created, and itself be followed until circumstances alter. When a convention is claimed to be absolute, it will be found that it rests so essentially on our constitutional system that to break it would be fatal. Thus, to intermit the meeting of Parliament would result in the ministry having at no distant date no legal power to spend money, even though large sums might be in the Treasury; the Army and Air Force (Annual) Act could not be passed, and if already passed before the decision to avoid meeting Parliament would expire, and no coercion could be exercised. The Courts would vindicate the law, and the ministry would in the last resort be dismissed by the sovereign if it still clung to office. In fact, no doubt labour and general unrest would have driven it to resign if it could not face the Commons. Again, that a ministry must command the support of the Commons results from the necessity of securing finance and the Army and Air Force Act. It is true that the exercise of this control is normally not requisite, but in 1937 the Country Party in the Commonwealth of Australia, very wisely, by threatening to refuse supply, prevented the Premier from a premature dissolution of Parliament, and Mr. Aberhart in Alberta was similarly forced to concede the demands of his followers for a more intensive application of the social credit system.[11] The convention that the Crown will assent to a bill passed by Parliament is, indeed, very firmly established, by reason of the fact that ever since 1705 has the sovereign thus acted. But the reason is simply that, if the sovereign felt that the ministry was carrying legislation not approved by the country, and that he could obtain a ministry which would defend his action in preventing it becoming law, he would dismiss the ministry before the measure

10 A. B. Keith, *The King and the Imperial Crown*, pp. 169 ff. [This view, a slight modification of similar earlier statements by its author, has been strongly contested; Evatt, *The King and His Dominion Governors*, chap. viii.—Ed.]
11 A. B. Keith, *The Dominions as Sovereign States*, p. 165.

was actually presented for his assent. That a King should not dismiss a ministry, which still commands the approval of the Commons, is no doubt strengthened by the fact that dismissal, real or virtual, last occurred in 1783 and 1807,[12] before the Reform Act of 1832 gave power to the people, but it would be impossible to say that changed circumstances might not render exercise of such authority necessary.

Usages can easily be disregarded, on the other hand, when they rest merely on precedent and their reasons have clearly disappeared. Thus the omission from the coronation ceremonial of the banquet and the challenge of the King's champion were dropped without difficulty, as otiose and unmeaning.[13] With the creation of the new legislative machinery of the Church of England Assembly (Powers) Act, 1919, it became convenient to dissolve the Convocations without waiting, as was normally done, for the dissolution of Parliament, and it was done without hesitation.[14] In like manner, when in 1921 it was inconvenient for the King to hold a council in Scotland to approve the speech prepared for him by Cabinet, the formality, despite long usage, was readily dropped.[15] In 1868 Mr. Disraeli, on defeat at the general election, decided to resign without meeting Parliament.[16] No doubt, in a sense, this was revolutionary, for the old theory was that the Commons controlled the ministry, and that it should meet Parliament and receive thence its fate. But the Premier accepted the conclusion that the electorate was the true sovereign, and bowed to its will, and even Mr. Gladstone felt entitled to follow his example, despite his reverence for precedent and the authority of the Commons, while on both occasions the Queen assented to a course which had the great advantage of suiting her convenience.[17] In 1929 Mr. Baldwin carried the matter rather further, for the fact that there were three parties rendered it possible to doubt if either opposition party could form an effective Government, and suggested that it would be wholly constitutional for him to meet Parliament. But he treated the vote as a clear intimation that he was not acceptable as Premier.[18] Yet it cannot be said in this case that a binding precedent has been set. It will necessarily depend on the future

[12] In 1834 dismissal cannot now be admitted : *Melbourne Papers*, pp. 220 ff.
[13] A. B. Keith, *The King and the Imperial Crown*, p. 28.
[14] Sir Almeric Fitzroy, *Memoirs*, ii. 743 f., 751.   [15] *Ibid.*, ii. 756 f.
[16] *Letters of Queen Victoria*, 2 s., i. 556 ff.   [17] *Ibid.*, 2 s., ii. 316 ff.
[18] 261 *H. C. Deb.* 5 s., 535.

development of party relationships, as will also the experiment of a Cabinet in which a vital issue was not accepted by all members as in 1932.   In its actual working that effort broke down soon, but its failure, though suggestive, is naturally not definitive of the issue. Another example of a new usage is that the decision to dissolve, and of the time of dissolution, lies with the Prime Minister and not with the Cabinet.   It is not certain when this practice originated, although probably responsibility lies with Mr. Lloyd George during the war or with Mr. Baldwin in 1923.[19]   What is clear is that in October, 1935, Sir John Simon could write that 'The decision whether there shall be an immediate general election and, if so, on what date the country shall go to the polls, rests with the Prime Minister, and until the Prime Minister has decided, all anticipations are without authority.'[20]   It remains to be seen whether this practice survives the pressure which the Labour Party, more than the Conservative Party, seems likely to bring to bear upon its leaders.   The experience of 1931–2 suggested that the Labour Party was unwilling to accept dictation in this matter,[21] but in 1950 and 1951 Mr. Attlee appears to have adopted his predecessors' practice.

Moreover, precedents have the disadvantage that they are not easy to prove.   The sources whence they can be learned are unsatisfactory in the main.   The biographies of statesmen, even autobiographies, are restricted by considerations of the Official Secrets Acts[22] and by obligations of propriety.   Cabinet government is based on the duty of members to keep confidences, and publication of secrets, even long after, is not always felt to be proper.   The exceptional action of ministers, as regards the transactions up to and after the Great War, as in the works of Mr. Churchill[23] and Mr. Lloyd George,[24] has not passed without censure.   Moreover, constitutional niceties have often no meaning for popular biographers.   In many cases, again, the biographer is inclined to be a panegyrist and to view all that his subject did in a roseate light, which leads consciously or unconsciously to the suppression of facts, or even to invention.   Thus, Mr Lloyd

---

[19] Sir C. Mallet, *Life of Lord Cave*, p. 264.   [20] *The Times*, October 18, 1935.
[21] H. Finer, *The Future of Government*, p. 87, n. 15.
[22] Mr. Edgar Lansbury was fined in 1934 for publishing a memo. by his father on unemployment.
[23] Winston Churchill, *The World Crisis*, 6 vols.
[24] David Lloyd George, *War Memoirs*, 6 vols.

George[25] asserts that it is a matter of history that on December 6, 1916, all those present at the conference with the King at Buckingham Palace expressed their readiness to serve under Mr. Balfour, with the exception of Mr. Asquith, but the evidence of Mr. Asquith, as preserved by Lord Crew,[26] as well as that of Mr. Balfour,[27] irresistibly suggest that Mr. Lloyd George's memory has failed him. It is not then surprising if the informants of Mr. Greville often told him less than the whole truth.   We can see in his own record the kind of evidence he had to rely upon; he notes, not rarely, the contradictions in the versions of people who must have had first-hand knowledge.   The matter is complicated for writers at the present day, who may have knowledge given in confidence, which they cannot directly use, and who must content themselves with asserting that such and such a view is generally held, or is reasonably believed.   It is significant of the difficulties of definite ascertainment that no one can give for certain the cause of the precise period for resignation chosen by Lord Salisbury, though detailed accounts were in verbal circulation on the day when his resignation was made public.[28]   Nor even when actions are known does it follow that motives are comprehended; we may cite precedents as evidence, though in following previous action a Premier may have been actuated by very different considerations than those which moved his predecessors.

Precedent, however, is always useful for argument; Lord Esher, who regularly quoted it, though he recognised that it was rarely conclusive, was an adept in selecting those which he thought most apposite, as establishing that a course of action was constitutional.[29]   It is always of some value to represent your own position as conforming to the principles and precedents of the constitution, and there is a *primâ facie* case for holding that what was done before in similar circumstances by men of high standing and experience, should be done again, and that there is a case against change.   Thus, the argument that the Cabinet experiment of 1931 was unconstitutional, was not without weight, and so far as experience went the opposition to the change proved not unjustified. A similar issue arose in 1938, when the Labour Party demanded an

---

25 David Lloyd George, *War Memoirs*, ii. 997.
26 Spender, *Lord Oxford*, ii. 274.   27 Dugdale, *Arthur James Balfour*, ii. 177 f.
28 Sir Sidney Lee, *Edward VII.*, ii. 158 f.
29 Esher, *Journals and Letters*, ii. 77 f.

election on the score that in departing from the mandate in foreign affairs, asked for in 1935, the Government was straining its constitutional powers. The ultimate criterion of constitutionality is unquestionably the verdict of the electorate. Those who contended that the Balfour ministry outstayed its mandate and should have resigned or dissolved after the defection of Mr. J. Chamberlain in 1903, might be held to have been justified by the result of the election under the new ministry. Those who contended that the formation of the National Government in 1931 was a due exercise of the prerogative of the Crown, were plainly confirmed in that belief by the endorsement of the ministry in the general election. Thus the electorate has the power to confirm old or establish new usages as constitutional, and as constituting conventions of the working of the constitution on the realm.

The constitutional system, however, can work only by moderation on the part of all concerned with it. Majority rule, if it means that the majority considers itself entitled to administer and legislate in the interests of the majority, without regard to the feelings of the minority, is a dangerous system, as can be seen from the history of Spain, where moderation and respect for minority rights has been conspicuous by its absence. The British tradition is clearly that all administration and legislation should be governed by the ideal of serving the common interest, and this in practice means that differences between the parties should be confined within limits. The future of British government is largely bound up with the question whether, if the Labour Party seeks to effect a complete transformation of the social system from a capitalist to a non-capitalist basis, this can be made compatible with the former system of acceptance of certain fundamental doctrines, as binding on any party while in power. It is possible also that in a socialistic Commonwealth the system of Cabinet government, based on parties, would cease to be operable.

It is not unnatural that the question should have been raised, whether the time has not come to bring the present freedom of the Cabinet from legal control to a close; but public opinion still favours the policy of leaving complete liberty of development free from the difficulties inherent in written constitutions, and in attempts to place on the Courts the duty of passing legal strictures on matters of advice tendered to the sovereign regarding the use of legal powers. It is not without interest to note that two great Parliamentarians of very different types of mind were strongly opposed to judicial investigation of political action. The hopeless difficulties in which the judges on the Parnell Commission were placed were pointed out convincingly in 1890 by Mr. Gladstone,[30] and Mr. Asquith energetically opposed, in 1917 and 1918 alike, the proposal to set up judicial bodies to investigate the Mesopotamian fiasco and the issue of the charges made by Sir F. Maurice against Mr. Lloyd George.[31] He disliked the idea of the mixing of the political and judicial function, and thought it damaging to the Bench that it should be involved in controversies about policy or strategy. Nor is it any answer to these objections that the judicial enquiry, conducted in 1936,[32] into the leakage of information on the budget, was plainly far superior in effectiveness and conclusiveness to any enquiry by Select Committee, such as had taken place in the matter of the Marconi scandal in 1912.[33] In these cases what were involved were facts which could best be determined by the ordinary rules of common law.

2.   THE EVOLUTION OF THE CONSTITUTIONAL CONVENTIONS

THE conflicts of the Stuart kings with Parliament and the settlement after the revolution of 1688 left it impossible for the Crown to attempt to carry out a policy without regard to Parliament. The practice of legalising a standing army for a year only, though it conceded the possession of military forces, also rendered recourse to Parliament each year necessary, and the strict limitation of the sums granted to the Crown to amounts barely adequate for the conduct of the ordinary civil government rendered application to the legislature essential for any attempt to enter on a new course of policy. The fate of Danby proved that mere royal commands would not be accepted by Parliament as a defence for any acts, and the Act of Settlement forbade the grant of pardon before conviction to any person impeached. To enact legislation by prerogative, to raise taxes, to suspend Parliamentary legislation or dispense with its operation, had become illegal, and the King no longer could control the judges through the right of dismissal, so that they

30 John Morley, *Life of William Ewart Gladstone* (London, 1903), iii. 390 ff., 408 ff.
31 Spender, *Lord Oxford*, ii. 294 f., 303 f.   32 Cmd. 5184.
33 Spender, *Lord Oxford*, i. 361 ff.

steadily developed not merely independence of the King but the readiness to view with strict regard to legality any acts done by the executive. Nor was it easy now to control the Commons, for to create by prerogative new members had become impossible; James II. had used legal process or the threat thereof to remodel the constitutions of Parliamentary boroughs, but the oligarchies, who thus had the power of returning members, were now safe from capricious judicial action, and the Crown dare not attack the new corporations.

To achieve harmony between sovereign and legislature thus presented new difficulties. William III. had little idea of responsible government, and his ministries of 1689–96 were constructed without predominant party considerations.[34] But he gradually realised more or less clearly the advantages of having a relatively harmonious ministry, and his Whig ministry of 1697 was gradually transformed into a Tory ministry by 1700, as he appreciated that a change in the balance of power in the House of Commons in 1698 rendered advantageous a like change in the composition of his Government. Under Anne the position altered. The Queen herself was most anxious to assert her right to select ministers, independently of party and Parliament alike[35]; moreover, both under William III. and Anne the fact that a ministry of a definite party complexion was in power was a factor making for the return of members of that party to the Commons. Thus in 1695 the Whig successes at the polls were no doubt aided by the introduction of Whig ministers in lieu of Tories in the preceding year, and in 1701 the addition to Tory strength reflected the introduction prior to the election of Tory ministers. In 1702 and 1710 the choice before the elections of Tory ministers helped to procure strong Tory elements in Parliament. The reason for this result is obvious. Not only had the Crown itself a wide patronage and the power to grant pensions and honours, as well as to find the funds for direct bribery, but the magnates appointed to office had influence and power and could determine the fate of seats, especially when representation became more and more imperfect with the passage

34 After the election o1 1690 he strengthened the Tory element in the ministry ; but, perhaps on Lord Sunderland's advice, he altered its complexion to Whig, before the 1695 election, which gave a Whig majority ; C. S. Emden, *The People and the Constitution*, p. 102 ; G. N. Clark, *The Later Stuarts*, chap. vi.
35 *Historical MSS. Commission, 9th Report*, App. pp. 471 f. ; Emden, *loc. cit.*

of time and the change, through economic conditions, of the distribution of the population.

Yet Anne had difficulties. Marlborough and Godolphin, finding that the Tories were lukewarm in regard to the war on which they had set their hearts, were not enthusiastic for the Hanoverian succession, and by no means inclined to the doctrine of religious toleration, had to fall back on the Whigs, and the election of 1705 gave them a real majority. The Queen was then pressed to supersede the Tory Lord Keeper by the leader of the Whigs in the Commons, and later on parted with Harley at the demand of the still indispensable Marlborough and Godolphin. When she realised from the Sacheverell incident that the change of public feeling pointed to a possibility of successful action, she removed in 1710 her Whig ministry in favour of a Tory one.[36] Thus, and by no means readily, the Queen virtually admitted that party must play a considerable part in determining the composition of ministries.

But Anne, like her predecessors, still presided in Cabinet and took a definite part in the framing of policy.[37] George I., however, after 1717 ceased to attend.[38] He did not understand English, and Englishmen were not inclined to be sufficiently good courtiers to learn German. He could discuss foreign politics in French with the Secretaries of State, but even Lords Somers and Cowper knew no French. Robert Walpole and he tried to converse in bad Latin. This led inevitably to the development of the office of Prime Minister; for, once the King was removed from the Cabinet, the natural tendency was for some minister to take his place as a unifying influence. The importance of the Cabinet was also greatly enhanced, when the sovereign was unable even to understand fully the advice reported to him by the President of the Council.[39] The King thus naturally for a variety of reasons concerned himself but slightly with the internal government of the country. It was not his desire to part with power; he refrained

[36] In 1711 the Whigs, headed by Walpole in the Commons, appeared as akin to an opposition party. He had vainly suggested, in 1710, combined action in resignation on the evidence of the Queen's hostility.

[37] See E. R. Turner, *Cabinet Council, 1622–1784*, i. 350 ff., 376 ff., 409 ff., 432 ff., 443 ff.

[38] Later cases of attendance (Turner *op. cit.*, ii. 97–100) are almost wholly cases of final settlement of speeches to Parliament, or to consider judicial sentences. The latter usage ceased only in 1837.

[39] Wolfgang Michael, *England under George I.*, i. 92 ff.

from giving Lord Halifax the post of Lord High Treasurer, as possibly creating a power dangerous to his own, but, though Lord Halifax tried to assert his authority as First Lord of the Treasury, now put in commission, he did not succeed in establishing for himself effective primacy; that he endeavoured to do so shows how natural the evolution was.

But Robert Walpole succeeded where Halifax had failed, and it is significant that one source of his success lay in the fact that he was First Lord of the Treasury and in the Commons, where he was determined to remain, and which he was equally determined to control.[40] The favour of the King was of course essential, and this he maintained when George II. was on the throne, by the conviction of Queen Caroline that his policy of maintaining peace and keeping taxation low was more favourable to the security of the dynasty than a warlike policy, such as that which her husband would have liked to follow. The royal favour gave him the means by places, money, and honours to influence, directly and indirectly, the Commons, and the fact that he kept an effective majority there dominated the position. He entered the ministry at first in a position relatively inferior to that of Townshend, but he ended by achieving complete primacy and ousting from the Cabinet any who wished to dispute his place. His rejection of the title of Prime Minister was based not on repudiation of his power, but on acceptance of the fact that to the public the style connoted a royal favourite, not the chosen of the people.[41] His relations with the Commons led him to the decision to relinquish office in February, 1742, when it pronounced against him, after the general election of 1741. It is true that it is difficult to treat that election as fought on any definite principle, but we may take it that the result was influenced by his growing personal unpopularity on the score of his self-sufficiency and length of tenure of power, though the defeat did not result in any complete change in the administration and still less in the reversal of his chief policies in internal government.[42]

Walpole never attempted to raise the question of the possibility of the Commons imposing him on the King. We find, however, that after his retirement the party managers, who adopted his

40 W. R. Anson, *The Law and Custom of the Constitution*, vol. II (ed. Keith), i., pp. 50, 125–127.
41 For some suggestive remarks on this subject see *Studies in Anglo-French History*, ed. A. Coville and H. W. V. Temperley, chap. iii.
42 Emden, *The People and the Constitution*, pp. 105, 113, 160.

methods, were strong enough to compel the King to part reluctantly with Carteret in 1744, and to accept Pitt in 1746 as a minister. This they accomplished by resigning *en masse* and leaving the King unable to discover any minister who would be able to win the support of the Commons. In 1756 there occurred another precedent of importance. The resignation of the Duke of Newcastle can only be attributed to his feeling that he could not face the popular clamour against his management of affairs. A like example of the weight of popular feeling, despite the existence of a majority in the Commons, may be seen in Lord Bute's resignation in 1763.

George III., however, was so completely English as himself to enter into the business of securing for himself control of the method of persuasion which helped to keep ministries in power, of destroying parties, and of negativing collective responsibility among ministries, which plainly was a grave barrier to royal authority. His success was not slight, but it produced the evolution of a party, the Rockingham Whigs, which had definite ideas on resistance to royal control of ministries, and which held in theory the view that, if called upon to serve the King, it must do so as a unity under the control of its own chosen leader, a doctrine very much disliked by the King, and by no means generally current. When popular opinion once more drove Lord North to resign in March, 1782, an office which he had long held only to please the King, and Lord Shelburne, after the brief Rockingham ministry, was forming a Cabinet, the Duke of Grafton[43] explained that he did not regard him as Prime Minister, but only as holding the principal office in the Cabinet. When Shelburne fell in 1783, the new ministry had Fox and Lord North as the real controllers, while the Duke of Portland took the Treasury. It was only after the King's initiative in dismissing the coalition had won support from the electorate, largely no doubt owing to royal influence,[44] that Pitt became effectively Prime Minister from 1784 to 1801, enjoying the full confidence of the King and primacy in his Cabinet. His refusal in 1803 to consider the suggestion of Addington that he and Pitt might be Secretaries of State, without any real Prime Minister, marks the definite ending of controversy. Since then it may be taken as

[43] Grafton, *Autobiography and Political Correspondence* (ed. Anson), p. 361.
[44] Emden, *The People and the Constitution*, pp. 196–198; W. T. Laprade, E. H. R., vol. xxxi, 224 ff.

generally conceded that 'there should be an avowed and real minister, possessing the chief weight in the Council and the principal place in the confidence of the King.'[45]

But there was an obvious difficulty and defect in the system. The pleasure of the King remained the essential feature; under it the Prime Minister could secure that his Cabinet should be of one mind, as when Pitt was enabled to secure the removal of his Lord Chancellor in 1792, when he opposed in the Lords a Governmental policy.[46] But, if it failed, a successful Prime Minister might be compelled to resign office by a half-demented sovereign, though, as far as any ordinary judgment could go, he enjoyed the confidence of the people of his country. In like manner the same sovereign was able in 1807 to turn out the Grenville ministry and to substitute that of the Duke of Portland. No one doubted under the regency or the reign of George IV. of his power to have a ministry of his liking, and the Whigs were deeply disappointed that he did not fulfil their expectations by calling them to office. In 1807 and 1812 alike, authoritative voices declared the unquestionable right of the Crown to select its own ministers, as Pitt himself had done in 1801.[47]

The explanation of a state of things so curious at first sight, lies in the condition of Parliamentary representation, which allowed the control of seats by the Government or private persons. We know, as late as 1806, that the members attached to the Government, as such, might suffice to turn the balance in the Commons, though an Act of 1809 to prevent trafficking in seats seems to have had some result. Even under Charles II. we find Lord Shaftesbury declaring that the representation was unfair, as boroughs with a handful of voters had equal representation with great boroughs. It soon became natural to look to the results in the few boroughs, such as the City of London and Westminster, with male householder suffrage, and the counties where the forty shilling freeholder prevailed. This is attested by Swift in 1711,[48] and insisted upon in *The Craftsman* in 1734, when it claimed that the knights of the shire were three to one for the opposition. The same view was repeated in respect of the election of 1741. Moreover, Sir R. Peel in 1829, in justifying his conversion to Catholic emancipation, cited the votes

---

45 Lord Stanhope, *Life of Pitt* (1879 ed.), iii. 109 ff.
46 *Ibid.*, i. 435 ff.; see also D. G. Barnes, *George III. and William Pitt, 1783–1806*.
47 35 *Parliamentary History*, 962.
48 Emden, *The People and the Constitution*, pp. 188 ff.

of fifteen large counties and twenty most populous towns, a fact used effectively against his opposition to reform in 1831 by Lord J. Russell and Earl Grey alike.[49]   But even in the counties, aristocratic influences were powerful, and sometimes by agreement Whigs and Tories divided the representation.[50]   When Brougham attacked Lord Lonsdale's interest in Westmorland he was challenging— unsuccessfully in 1818, 1820 and 1826 alike—an authority not impugned since 1774.[51]   In the boroughs there were cases like Old Sarum, where the owner of some burgage land returned two members, and, taken on the whole, Charles Grey could assert that over half the Commons was sent there by 160 persons.[52]   Other calculations increase the figure, but the position is beyond all dispute.   In 1831, when the population of England was fourteen millions, 236 members were returned for ten southern counties with 3,260,000 people, while the six of the north with 3,594,000 had but sixty-eight, so that the industrial revolution had no corresponding authority in the Commons.   Birmingham and Manchester, each with more than 100,000 people, were without members, while in Cornwall there were forty-two seats for 300,000 people; of these twenty were controlled by seven peers, twenty-one by eleven commoners, and one only was free.   In these conditions it is easy to understand how bribery flourished, and how after the Reform Act of 1832 many voters were sulky because the good old practice had disappeared.

Parties existed, no doubt, rather by tradition than principle, and those interested in politics attached themselves to them according as family tradition or personal ambition directed.   There was no attempt, however, to organise the electors, naturally enough, since the cruder methods of bribery, influence, intimidation by mob violence, and treating were easier.[53]   Reform was checked by the excesses of the French revolution, while various efforts were made to answer the argument for it by specious retorts.   Burke, who had denied the doctrine of virtual representation when adduced by Lord Mansfield[54] in the case against the American colonies'

49 Emden, *The People and the Constitution*, p. 190.
50 For some eighteenth-century evidence on this point see L. B. Namier, *The Structure of Politics at the Accession of George III.*, vol. ii., chap. v.
51 A. Aspinall, *Lord Brougham and the Whig Party*, pp. 86 ff., 174.
52 See J. R. M. Butler, *The Passing of the Great Reform Bill* ; G. M. Trevelyan, *Lord Grey of the Reform Bill ;* E. and A. Porritt, *The Unreformed House of Commons.*
53 G. Kitson Clark, *Peel and the Conservative Party*, p. 217.
54 16 *Parl. Hist.* 172–7.

right to resist taxation, came in 1792[55] to defend it for Britain, and Pitt in 1783, as well as Sir R. Peel in the case of the Reform Bill stood up for it, though plainly there was no answer to Macaulay's argument that, if virtual representation really produced the same result as direct representation, there was no reason for denying the latter when it was wanted.[56]

The delay in achieving reform was remarkable. But the close of the war and the repression of public opinion and meetings by the ministry, as in the Six Acts of 1819, were followed by the scandal connected with Queen Caroline which exposed to public reprobation the private life of those connected with the Court.[57] At last there was some response to the propaganda which Cobbett had so long and so widely carried on against the unrepresentative character of Parliamentary institutions. In Ireland D. O'Connell formed the Catholic Association to seek to secure emancipation, and, despite efforts at repression by attacks on him and on the Association, his organisation of the voters at the elections of 1826 showed that they could, with the aid of the priests, be effectively detached from the great landowners who had seemed securely to control the votes in the counties.[58] The success of this effort led to the decision of the Duke of Wellington and Sir R. Peel to concede Catholic emancipation as a means of recalling the voters to their allegiance, and thus paved the way for the advent of the Whigs to power, with the support of the Canningites, who agreed with them on the issue of reform. Among the unenfranchised workers political unions were developed in 1831–32 to agitate and hold great public meetings, at one of which at Birmingham, in November, 1831, the threat to refuse to pay taxes was uttered. The Reform Act of 1832[59] only in part satisfied the agitators, for it gave a much less generous extension of the franchise than had been demanded, and open voting left much room for influence and bribery; but it was of fundamental importance as providing the necessary conditions for the operation of true Cabinet government by acknowledging an authority which, when consulted, could give a verdict which

---

55 *A Letter to Sir Hercules Langrishe.*
56 23 *Parliamentary History*, 831 ; 24 *H. C. Deb.* 2 s., 1243 ; 2 *H. C. Deb.* 3 s., 1197.
57 J. R. M. Butler, *The Passing of the Great Reform Bill*, p. 38.
58 D. Gwynn, *Daniel O'Connell* (1947), pp. 165 ff.
59 2 & 3 Will. IV. cc. 45, 65, 88.   The electorate was increased by 217,600, say, 49 per cent.

the Commons, Lords and King alike could not really ignore. Sir R. Peel showed his full appreciation of the position when, after dissolving Parliament, he recognised in 1835 that by failing to obtain a majority, though he had improved his position in the Commons, he had placed himself in a position in which he must resign, because he had not authority to carry on the administration.[60]   It is significant that Lord Melbourne[61] suggested that it would be impossible to carry on government without the rotten boroughs which the Act of 1832 swept away, so little could he realise the essential character of the new system which was being created.[62]   It is significant also that he never fully appreciated the new position; when he resigned in 1841 after an unsuccessful dissolution, regarded by him and the Queen as an appeal by the latter to the people to return her ministry to authority, he advised the Queen to state that she had only parted with her ministers in deference to the opinion of Parliament, though she still had confidence in them.[63]   Naturally she did not realise any more than her retiring Premier that in the nature of things the verdict of the electors deprived her of the right to feel confidence in ministers of whom the voters had disapproved, that it was no longer a question of personal integrity or sagacity in a minister, but of his right to represent the will of the people, as expressed by the suffrages of the electorate.

Even before the reform issue became urgent, the duty of the Crown to act against personal inclination on the advice of ministers had been established definitively by the action of George IV. in assenting to the Act to establish Catholic emancipation.[64]   The King made every effort to escape the duty, and he had the precedent of George III., who had consistently in the case of England denied his duty to break his coronation oath, as he held, by assent to such a measure.   Times, however, had changed, and the King found that no ministry would take responsibility for governing if he refused to accept emancipation.   This was soon followed by the issue of reform.   The King was most reluctant to agree to swamp the Upper House, but he promised to do so, when he found that no ministry could be

60 27 *H. C. Deb.* 3 s., 980 ff.
61 Charles Greville, *Memoirs: A Journal of the Reigns of King George IV., King William IV., and Queen Victoria* (1888 ed.), ii. 283.
62 'For Scotland it was political birth, the beginning of a duty and a power' : Morley, *Gladstone*, iii. 535.
63 *Letters of Queen Victoria*, 1 s., i. 321 ff.
64 A. B. Keith, *The King and the Imperial Crown*, p. 65.

found to replace that of Earl Grey.[65]   In both cases the position was plain.   The Commons, unreformed as it was, was so far responsive to the voice of the country as to refuse to support a ministry which was determined to govern against that voice.   The Reform Act made that voice more fully articulate and brought the member of Parliament under periodic control.

3. THE SEPARATION OF CABINET AND COUNCIL.

THE composition of the Cabinet was throughout this period of evolution in process of change as it became differentiated from the Council.   The term Cabinet under Charles I.[66] is not rare to denote either a Committee of the Council or a special group of advisers in the royal confidence.   Under Charles II. the position of the Council as the body which discusses and decides affairs of State is plain, but there are Committees of that body which deal with special aspects, especially foreign affairs, and report for final settlement to the Council.[67]   At the close of his reign, after the abortive experiment of a representative Council sponsored by Sir W. Temple,[68] we find mention of the Cabinet composed of those great officers and courtiers whom the King relied on for the interior despatch of his business,[69] and who had the transaction of most actions of government, foreign and domestic.   No doubt in its weekly meetings the policy which would finally be adopted in Council was determined.   William III. relied too much on himself to constitute a Cabinet with wide authority ;[70] we find him regarding the Cabinet as a rather formal body, while he consulted, not in Cabinet, with a few specially chosen ministers.   But Lord Sunderland in 1701 appears already with a clear conception of a Cabinet which the King should regularly consult, composed of the great officers of State, and in 1692 it was assumed in the Commons that one source of the unsatisfactory position of foreign relations was the fact that the Council accepted, without knowing the reasons, policies devised by the Cabinet.[71] Hence the attempt in the Act of Settlement, 1701, to remedy the situation by requiring that matters properly cognisable by the Privy

65 *Correspondence of William IV. and Earl Grey* (ed. Henry, Earl Grey), vol. ii, passim.
66 Turner, *Cabinet Council, 1622–1874*, i. 19 ff.
67 *Ibid.*, i. 52 ff., 94 ff., 113 ff.
68 *Ibid.*, i. 341 ff., ; cf. 109 ff., 113 ff.
69 Anson, *The Law and Custom of the Constitution*, vol. II (ed. Keith), i. 94 f.
70 *Ibid.*, i. 95 ff.
71 5 *Parliamentary History*, 731.

Council should be transacted therein, and all resolutions taken should be signed by the members assenting thereto. That provision and the equally injudicious effort to exclude not merely ordinary office holders, but ministers of State from the Commons never became operative.[72]   The fate of the Council was very different.   Under Anne the process already in operation under William III. became complete, or nearly so.   The Council, styled Privy Council or Great Council, met under the Queen for formal approval of business which had been worked through by a Committee of Council, at which the Queen might be present, while the Cabinet, wherein the Queen sat, took the essential decisions.   The Council, however, was destined to act once more in a deliberative capacity on July 30, 1714, when the Queen was dying.   Lord Oxford had indeed been dismissed, but his place as Lord Treasurer had not been filled, and until this was done he might be held to be legally in office, and thus on the Queen's death to be under the Act of Succession a member of the Regency Council.   But the Whig Dukes of Somerset and Argyll entered the Council Chamber unbidden, and took charge, with the Duke of Shrewsbury, of the situation.   Under their guidance the Council advised the appointment of the Duke of Shrewsbury as Lord Treasurer.[73]

Under George I., as already mentioned, the Cabinet soon became dissociated from the Council in form through the constant absence of the King, and the King also ceased to attend meetings of the Committees of Council.   Another formal distinction goes back probably to the initiation of the Cabinet system ; its members down to the creation of a Cabinet Secretariat in 1916 were summoned as His Majesty's servants by the instructions of the Premier or other leading minister, by a secretary,[74] while Council and Council Committee meetings were called on instructions by the Clerk of the Council.

The Hanoverian Cabinet, however, appears definitely to have been a comparatively large body, whose members were summoned mainly to approve decisions already taken by the inner Cabinet, which on occasion was composed merely of Robert Walpole, the Chancellor, and the two Secretaries of State.[75]   This division is attested under Grenville also, and formally the distinction was

[72] Anson, *The Law and Custom of the Constitution*, vol. I (ed. Gwyer), 85 ff.
[73] Michael, *England under George I.*, i. 52 ff.   See also Anson, *op. cit.*, vol. II, i. 104 ff.
[74] Turner. *Cabinet Council, 1622–1784*, ii. 71 ff.   [75] *Ibid.*, ii. chap. xxvi.

marked by the fact that the inner circle only had the circulation of important papers in Cabinet boxes, to which they had keys. In 1771 the Duke of Grafton, while accepting the Privy Seal, stipulated that he should not be summoned to meetings of the confidential Cabinet. The position was clearly explained by Lord Mansfield in 1775, when he repudiated responsibility for any action since the close of the Grenville ministry on the score that he had ceased since then to be a member of the efficient Cabinet, though he remained a member of the Cabinet.[76] This, of course, was a position wholly incompatible with collective responsibility, and one quite in keeping with the ideas of George III., who desired to destroy party, and who was glad to have Cabinet ministers whom he might consult, though they were not in harmony with the inner circle of ministers.[77]

The disappearance of this anomaly begins with the ministry of Lord Rockingham, composed of eleven members, each holding high office. In 1801 the principle that only a member of the efficient Cabinet is a true Cabinet member is asserted by Addington as against Lord Loughborough who, though no longer Lord Chancellor, retained his Cabinet key and attended Cabinet meetings.[78] A last survival of the older *régime* may be seen in the Grand or Honorary Cabinet, summoned in 1806 before the opening of Parliament, to hear the draft of the royal speech read, a function later dropped. The Archbishop of Canterbury, formerly a regular member of the greater Cabinet, then appeared presumably for the last time at a Cabinet.

The irresponsibility of Cabinet members for policy adopted by the Cabinet appears from Lord Camden's repudiation of responsibility for the measures taken against Wilkes in regard to the Middlesex election, and the imposition of the fatal tea duty in 1770 on the American colonies.[79] The Duke of Grafton, while complaining of the attitude of Lord Camden in respect of a matter to which the whole Cabinet consented, explained, quite inconsistently, that the tax was no measure of his; in fact he, as Premier, had been out-voted. How little Cabinet responsibility was understood in 1806 appeared in the discussion of the membership of the Cabinet given to Lord Ellenborough, the Lord Chief Justice, which was challenged

---

76 18 *Parliamentary History*, 274 f., 279.
77 For a summary of this subject see E. T. Williams, *The Cabinet in the Eighteenth Century*, 'History' vol. xxii, pp. 240 ff.
78 Lord John Campbell, *Lives of the Lord Chancellors* (3rd ed.), vi. 314.
79 Grafton, *Autobiography*, p. 246.

on the ground that as member of the Cabinet he might be responsible for the decision to take legal proceedings over which he would have to preside as judge.   But Lord Temple denied Cabinet responsibility, and Fox maintained the advantage of fixing it upon an individual minister as such.[80]   This point of view is clearly explained by the fact that legal responsibility was in the minds of those concerned. Impeachment of an individual was a living possibility, but it was difficult even for the judicious Hallam to conceive how an impeachment for sitting as a Cabinet councillor could be drawn.[81]

With collective responsibility was closely connected the restriction of membership of the Cabinet to ministers with administrative duties. The old Cabinet had contained members, such as the Archbishop, the Lord Chamberlain, and the Master of the Horse,[82] but Pitt's Cabinet in 1784 was composed of the Lord Chancellor, the Lord President, the Lord Privy Seal, whose position was assured by custom, the First Lords of the Treasury and Admiralty, and the two Secretaries of State, who in 1782 had stood out as ministers for home and foreign affairs, and not, as they once were, mere mouthpieces of the Council.   In 1801 to these members are added a third Secretary of State, whose creation the war had necessitated, and who dealt with war and the colonies, the Master of the Ordnance, the President of the Board of Control to represent Indian issues, a minister to deal with trade and the post office, and the Chancellor of the Duchy of Lancaster, a sinecure office.   The tradition was already becoming established that a Cabinet should contain just so many members as were desirable for the effective control of business, and that places must be found for the heads of the great administrative departments of State.

It remained, however, still possible for ministers in the Cabinet to differ in view on substantial issues, as when in Lord Liverpool's Government the Home Secretary opposed, the Foreign Secretary favoured, Catholic emancipation.   After the contact with the electorate was established by the Reform Act, such differences ceased to be tolerable, and we find Mr. Gladstone in 1868[83] telling an anecdote, showing how Lord Melbourne appreciated the necessity of unanimity towards the world.   Lord John Russell's famous letter

---

80 6 *H. C. Deb.* 1 s., 308 ff.
81 Henry Hallam, *Constitutional History of England* (7th ed.), iii. 183 ff.
82 Turner, *Cabinet Council, 1622–1784*, ii. 358 ff.
83 *Letters of Queen Victoria*, 2 s., i. 563.

on free trade from Edinburgh threatened to dissolve the Cabinet, when Lord Melbourne ended all discussion by saying : 'Well, gentlemen, there is no doubt that John Russell's letter is a d——d letter : but he has written it, and we must go through with it!' Although, of course, in opposition such unanimity is less essential, for attack can take varied forms not all consistent, without ceasing to be effective, Sir R. Peel, feeling that the Conservatives were hampered in their attitude to the Irish Municipal Corporations Bill by the divergence of view between the Lords' and the Commons' supporters of the Conservative faith, summoned the members of the late Cabinet to consider the like measure for Ireland.[84]

84 G. Kitson Clark, *Peel and the Conservative Party,* p. 345.

CHAPTER 2

THE FORMATION AND DISSOLUTION
OF THE CABINET

1. The Selection of the Prime Minister

It follows from the development of Cabinet government that the formation of a Cabinet depends essentially on the royal choice of a Prime Minister. Occasion for such action may arise on the death of the incumbent of the office, or on his resignation. In the latter case the ground of that resignation is necessarily a factor of prime importance. If it is occasioned by ill-health or the burden of age or tiredness, then normally no question arises of a change in the political complexion of the ministry. If, on the other hand, it is the outcome of defeat in the House of Commons or at a general election or the imminence of such a defeat, then a change of ministry involves normally recourse to the opposition in the House of Commons. But in every case the King has some measure of freedom of choice, though normally within very narrow limits. It is essential that the Prime Minister shall be able to form a Government which can secure a vote of confidence if need be from the Commons, and the sovereign must fix finally upon a politician thus qualified. But there may be more than one politician capable of such action, and it must always be remembered that the power to award high office gives the nominee of the Crown a considerable measure of power to secure support. It is significant that, when Mr. Asquith resigned in December, 1916, many Ministers, who had previously opposed the appointment of Mr. Lloyd George as Prime Minister, accepted office in the new administration.[1] On the other hand, party ties are often strong enough to resist such persuasion ; thus Mr. R. MacDonald in 1931 was unable to carry over to the new National Government which he formed the services of any of the able young men of the Labour Party, such as Mr. H. Morrison or the late Mr. W. Graham.

The royal choice prior to 1923 might fall on a peer or a commoner

[1] Spender, *Lord Oxford*, ii. 272 ff ; Lord Beaverbrook, *Politicians and the War*, vol. ii, chap. xxiv.

as circumstances might dictate. In the early days of democratic rule the arguments against a peer were of slight weight, even though the fact that the strife of parties was mainly carried on in the Commons, suggested to the Duke of Wellington his refusal to accept office in 1839, and his support for the appointment of Sir R. Peel instead.[2] It was only the growth of democracy and the fact that Parliament came to be deeply engaged in social problems which rendered the presence of the Prime Minister in the Lower House more and more desirable. There may be adduced in favour of the selection of a peer as Prime Minister the consideration that he is set free to concentrate on essential problems, as a result of detachment from the burden of constant attendance in the Commons. There is no reason to suppose that the arrangement worked badly in 1835–41 under Lord Melbourne, in 1852, 1858–59 and 1866–68 under Lord Derby, in 1865–66 under Earl Russell, or in 1876–80 under Lord Beaconsfield. It is true that Lord Rosebery proved a definite failure as Prime Minister in 1894–95, but that was due to personal defects of temperament coupled with the fact that Sir William Harcourt had hoped to succeed Mr. Gladstone, and accepted the refusal of his colleagues to admit his claims, not merely with a very bad grace, but also on conditions which resulted in rendering more than usually difficult the position of leader.[3] Mr. Gladstone himself in 1894 was not opposed to a peer as successor, and, if asked, would have recommended Lord Spencer for royal favour, nor would the choice have been unwise.[4] Lord Salisbury in his terms of office, 1885–86, 1886–92, and 1895–1902, was unquestionably not an ideal head of the Government, but it would be impossible to suggest that the control could better have been entrusted to other hands ; his nephew's tenure of office was far less successful, and ended in disaster in 1905. It was energetically contended in 1905 by Sir E. Grey, Mr. Haldane, and even by Mr. Asquith,[5] that it would be proper for Sir H. Campbell-Bannerman to lead the party and control the Government from the Upper House, and there is little doubt that his decision against medical advice and that of the King led to

2 *Memoirs of Sir Robert Peel* (ed. Stanhope & Cardwell), ii. 19. For Wellington's view of the constitutional position of the House of Lords see W. Bagehot, *The English Constitution*, chap. iv. ; also 47 *Parl. Deb.* 3 s., 1016.
3 A. G. Gardiner, *Life of Sir William Harcourt*, ii. 271 ff. ; *Letters of Queen Victoria*, 3 s., ii. 373, 375 f.
4 *Letters of Queen Victoria*, 3 s., ii. 369.
5 Spender, *Lord Oxford*, i. 172–174 ; J. A. Spender, *Life of Sir Henry Campbell-Bannerman*, ii. 188 ff.

his enforced resignation in 1908, when he was dying. In the controversy of 1916 the suggestion was pressed on Mr. Asquith himself that he should cease to attempt to combine the duties of final control of the war operations with that of leader of the Commons, on the ground that the burden was too great for any man[6] and Mr. Lloyd George as Prime Minister did not attempt to perform the usual functions of the leader of the Commons. His failure, however, to resume this function effectively after the close of the war proved to have reacted fatally on his hold on the Commons in 1922, when the Chanak episode undermined the position of the ministry, already menaced by the Irish settlement of 1921. The personal touch with members necessary to secure a rally to the Government in such an emergency was lacking, and the fall of the ministry became inevitable.

It was this precedent which partly determined the fate of Lord Curzon in 1923 when Mr. Bonar Law resigned through ill-health.[7] It is true that the position of a Prime Minister in the Upper House had become more difficult through the developments of the Parliamentary position even since 1902. The House of Lords had grown more and more Conservative since the split of the Liberal Party on Home Rule in 1886, while the extension of the franchise in 1867 and 1884, and, above all, 1918, had accentuated the democratic character of the Commons, whose supremacy over the Lords was established by the Parliament Act, 1911. It was certainly possible to base the refusal to appoint Lord Curzon on the plea that the official opposition was essentially in the Commons, and weight no doubt attached to this consideration ; it may be said that the head of the ministry should be prepared to fight his own contests against the adverse forces. But this argument must be taken with reserve. It is perfectly possible to hold that the burden of leadership in the Commons is too grievous to permit of the exercise of calm statesmanship, and that the head of the ministry ought to be to some extent detached from leadership of the party. But this is far removed from the spirit of party politics, and in Lord Curzon's case the scales were heavily weighted against him by his personality.

---

[6] Spender, *Lord Oxford*, ii. 252 ff. ; Mr. Asquith however, argued that such a division of responsibilities would be unworkable, *ibid.*, p 265. During the war of 1939–45, the Prime Minister ceased to lead the House of Commons after February, 1942, and, on the formation of the Labour Government in 1945, the Lord President of the Council became leader.

[7] Nicholson, *Curzon : The Last Phase*, pp. 353 ff. ; see also *ante*, p. 6, n. 9.

Whatever he might be to his intimates, to the outside world he presented an appearance of Olympian aloofness and conveyed the impression of overweening self-confidence, which rendered men unwilling to serve under him. No doubt, however, it was the earnest advice of Earl Balfour which determined the King to refuse him the office he deemed his services no less than his abilities marked as his due ; it is significant that Earl Balfour never revealed to his friend the part he had so deliberately played in destroying his ambition.[8] The precedent, however, must be regarded as decisive under any normal circumstances, for as matters stand there is slight probability that any peer will possess claims to preferment as then were Lord Curzon's. Moreover, it is significant that Earl Baldwin did not show the slightest desire to continue his Premiership with transfer to the Upper House, though such a decision would certainly have been popular enough in the country after he had established his reputation by his brilliant handling of the abdication of Edward VIII. None-the-less, it remains possible that a Prime Minister might retain that office after transfer to the Upper House, though the selection of a peer for that office would be abnormal.

In the circumstances of 1923 there can be little doubt that the King had a definite, if limited, possibility of selection ; if he had commissioned Lord Curzon, it is probable that he would have succeeded without great difficulty in securing colleagues. *Ex post facto* judgments on these issues are not of great value ; Mr. Lloyd George in 1916 found his way easy, once he had authority to offer posts. In many cases, no doubt, the sovereign has no alternative, for the choice may be definitely fixed for him by the fact that party favour determines who must lead. In 1859 Lord Palmerston was the obvious choice, but the Queen endeavoured to induce him and Lord John Russell to serve under Lord Granville, quite in vain.[9] On Lord Palmerston's death in 1865, Earl Russell was patently the only possible choice ;[10] three years later Lord Derby's resignation left Mr. Disraeli without a rival ;[11] no one doubted that Mr. Asquith in 1908 must replace Sir H. Campbell-Bannerman,[12] and

---

8 Dugdale, *Arthur James Balfour*, ii. 361. [The account given here hardly supports Keith's interpretation. See also Amery, *Thoughts on the Constitution*, p. 21.—Ed.]
9 H. C. F. Bell, *Lord Palmerston*, ii. 215 f. ; *Letters of Queen Victoria*, 1 s., iii. 438–440.
10 Lord Fitzmaurice, *Life of Earl Granville*, i. 486.
11 *Letters of Queen Victoria*, 2 s., i. 496 ff.
12 Spender, *Lord Oxford*, i. 228 ; Lee, *Edward VII.*, ii. 578

the transition from Mr. MacDonald to Mr. Baldwin in 1935 was as inevitable as Mr. N. Chamberlain's succession in 1937. The case was really as obvious in 1880, when Queen Victoria should, in accordance with the patent fact that Mr. Gladstone was the architect of the Liberal victory, have offered him the Premiership.[13] Unhappily by that time the Queen had imbibed a deep distrust of Mr. Gladstone from her late Premier, and she endeavoured therefore to obtain Lord Hartington for the office. It was clearly an unfortunate step, for it had not the excuse that Lord Hartington was in any sense the acknowledged head of the party. It is true that he was the leader of the party in the Commons by election, but the Queen had never thought of the doctrine that a leader should be in the Commons, and her late Prime Minister had been elevated to the Lords. Moreover, as Mr. Gladstone indicated, if the Queen did not care to face the necessity of offering him the office, she could properly have applied to Earl Granville, to whom Mr. Gladstone held that he had handed over the leadership of the party, and who was party leader in the Lords.[14] The unanimity of both possible leaders that Mr. Gladstone must be chosen compelled the surrender of the Queen, but not until relations between her Prime Minister and herself had been rendered difficult. The position was very different in 1894 ; it may be that the majority of the cabinet was anxious to see Lord Rosebery chosen in place of Sir W. Harcourt ; but Lord Spencer was highly esteemed, and, supported by Mr. Gladstone's recommendation, could easily have formed an effective ministry. The Queen, however, was personally attached to Lord Rosebery, and her choice, though it proved unlucky, was quite natural.[15]

Much more latitude is available to the Crown in cases where there are no clear cut party divisions, presenting the sovereign with nothing more than the choice of a leader from a party clearly entitled to hold office. It is not rare in British history for differing combinations to be possible, and for Governments to be formed and live without clear majorities, so that they are exposed to defeat, entailing the resignation of the Prime Minister, although the opposition has no clear plurality of votes. The Conservative split on protection entailed the fall of Sir R. Peel in 1846, and the Peelites long after added confusion to politics by the uncertainty of their

13 *Letters of Queen Victoria*, 2 s., iii. 80 ff. ; Morley, *Gladstone*, ii. 620–624.
14 It was assumed by almost all the Press that she would do so : *Letters of Queen Victoria*, 2 s., iii. 77.
15 *Ibid.*, 3 s., ii. 370 ; Spender, *Lord Oxford*, i. 90 f.

action. By combining with the Whigs in 1852 they defeated Lord Derby.[16] Personal feeling has also played a considerable part in the destruction of ministries ; it was Lord Palmerston's resentment at his removal from office by Lord John Russell that brought down the ministry of 1852,[17] while Lord John Russell was no doubt influenced by like sentiments when he acted so strangely in 1855 and compelled Lord Aberdeen to resign.[18] The defeat of Lord Palmerston in 1857 on the issue of his treatment of China led merely to his successful dissolution, but the self-confidence thence engendered came into conflict with unreasoning prejudice next year, when he endeavoured to make reasonable reparation for the impunity hitherto extended to plotters on British territory, by proposing a bill to penalise incitement to murder.[19] This led to minority government until 1859, and Earl Russell's unlucky reform proposals in 1866 saw a further two years of minority rule.[20] A period of comparatively strong Governments was ended in 1885–86 by Lord Salisbury's first term of office, but his second term was secured from interruption by the fact that the Liberal Unionists became rapidly, in all but name and organisation, Conservatives. From 1910 until coalition was formed in 1915 the Liberal Government was kept in office by the support of the Irish Nationalists, its independent majority disappearing at the election of January, 1910. The Labour Government of 1924 was frankly a minority ministry, supported during its brief existence by Liberal complaisance, and that of 1929–31 was in like case. From 1852 to 1855 Lord Aberdeen's ministry was a frank coalition, as was the ministry reconstructed by Mr. Asquith in 1915, and again altered by Mr. Lloyd George a year later. But the ministry of Lord Salisbury, followed by Mr. Balfour of 1895–1905, consisted of two elements, differing in no serious regard, and its dissolution had nothing to do with the fact that it included Conservatives and Liberal Unionists ; and the National Government of 1931, while in its origin a genuine coalition, soon passed over into virtually a Conservative ministry, supported by Conservative votes, a small number of ex-Liberals, and a handful of ex-Labour members.

When, as in these instances, ministries lack essential cohesion,

---

[16] *Letters of Queen Victoria*, 1 s., ii. 499 f. On their disturbing effect, see Morley, *Gladstone*, i. 551 f., 558, 567.
[17] *Letters of Queen Victoria*, 1 s., ii. 444–446 ; Bell, *Lord Palmerston*, ii. 58.
[18] Bell, *Lord Palmerston*, ii. 108 f. [19] *Ibid.*, ii. 180 ff.
[20] *Letters of Queen Victoria*, 2 s., i. 331 ff.

the fall of the Government inevitably creates a situation in which the sovereign must exercise personal judgment.　It is, however, obviously proper that the sovereign should ask the leader of the party which has brought about the fall of a ministry to take office, and the leader has a *primâ facie* obligation to assume the burden, for it is plainly contrary to the interests of the country that the Government should be one discredited by failure, and a defeated ministry cannot be expected to be willing to remain in office when their proposals are rejected.　It may, of course, prove impossible for the leader to form a ministry.　In 1851 Lord Stanley failed to do so, [21] with the result that Lord John Russell struggled on until 1852, when Lord Derby was more successful, though his ministry was in a minority. [22]　On Derby's failure to secure a majority at the general election the appointment of Lord Aberdeen was rendered obvious by the fact that both the Whigs and the Peelites were willing to serve under him.　But Lord Derby advised the Queen to send for Lord Lansdowne on tactical grounds, eliciting from her consort the contention that the matter was within her discretion and not a case for official advice. [23]　She secured, however, his concurrence in the proposal to consult the two peers together, but the plan miscarried through the ill-health of Lord Lansdowne, and Lord Aberdeen accepted office when this point was made clear.　On the collapse of his ministry, with the defection of Lord John Russell on Mr. Roebuck's demand for a Committee of Enquiry into the conduct of war in the Crimea, the Queen turned to Lord Derby, on the natural ground that he was the head of the largest party in the Commons, which by its vote for the motion had caused the resignation of the Government.　Lord Derby countered this claim by pointing out that his party had not sponsored the motion, nor arranged it with the mover, and, as he could not form a coalition, he refused to take office. [24]　Lord John Russell found it impossible to secure support [25] and Lord Palmerston had to be asked to re-unite the Whigs and the Peelites, which he did for the moment, though his determination to accept the duty of acting on Mr. Roebuck's demand cost him the services of the leaders of the Peelites immediately afterwards. [26]

The Queen's readiness to apply to the leader of the opposition was affirmed again in favour of Lord Derby in 1858 and 1866,

[21] *Letters of Queen Victoria*, 1 s., ii. 346 ff.
[22] *Ibid.*, 1 s., ii. 447 ff. ; Bell, *Lord Palmerston*, ii. 59 ff.
[23] *Letters of Queen Victoria*, 1 s., ii. 501.　　　[24] *Ibid.*, 1 s., iii. 101 ff.
[25] *Ibid.*, 1 s., iii. 111 ff.　　　　　　　[26] *Ibid.*, 1 s., iii. 122 ff.

though on both occasions the ministry which was formed had to be a minority Government, dependent for its existence on the inability of its opponents to unite to eject it from office. On Lord Derby's resignation, her selection of Mr. Disraeli, who had been the driving power of the ministry, as his successor was inevitable, and her regard for him led to her abortive offer in 1873 (discussed below), and her appointment of him to office in 1874. In 1880, as we have seen, Mr. Gladstone's effective leadership of the opposition was ignored in favour of the party leader in the Commons, a step quite properly disapproved by Mr. Gladstone as obviously motived by the desire to keep him out of office. In 1885 the selection of Lord Salisbury as Prime Minister was justified by the fact that, while not technically leader of the party, he was leader in the Lords, and his position was patently dominant, as compared with that of Sir S. Northcote, whom the Queen had recognised privately as leader in 1881.[27]

In 1886 the Queen should have offered power to Mr. Gladstone as the leader of the party whose support of the amendment of Mr. Jesse Collings, the advocate of the ideal of 'three acres and a cow,' had caused the defeat of the ministry in the Commons. But the Queen had already striven to keep Lord Salisbury in power by appeals[28] to such Liberals as Mr. Goschen, Mr. W. E. Forster, and Lord Hartington, and Lord Salisbury accepted responsibility for advising her that she might consult Mr. Goschen.[29] The Queen, in making this proposal, relied on the precedent of 1851 and 1855. In the former case the Queen had seen Lord Lansdowne before she sent for Lord Stanley, and Lord Lansdowne, who was leader of the House of Lords, and Lord John Russell discussed the situation with her before the latter formally resigned.[30] After Lord Stanley refused to accept office, the Queen consulted the Duke of Wellington, after informal discussion with the Prince Consort.[31] In 1855 the Queen at once sent for Lord Derby, in accordance with the opinion of Lord Aberdeen, and consulted Lord Lansdowne only after Lord Derby's intimation that he could not form a ministry.[32] It is, therefore, clear that the precedents relied on by the Queen lacked any close similarity to the situation as regards Mr. Goschen, but patently precedents are not of decisive value. The emergence of new situations justifies departure

---

27 *Letters of Queen Victoria*, 2 s., iii. 218 f. 28 *Ibid.*, 2 s., iii. 714 ff.
29 *Ibid.*, 3 s., i. 24, 26. 30 *Ibid.*, 1 s., ii. 346 ff. 31 *Ibid.*
32 *Ibid.*, 1 s., iii. 106 ff.

from precedent, and the Queen's action must be judged on its merits. On that ground the case was poor. Mr. Goschen virtually refused to visit the Queen, urging her to send for Mr. Gladstone, thus showing that he felt the duty of the Crown to be clear.[33]   Lord Salisbury, though he thought that Mr. Goschen should have visited the Queen, and that Sir H. Ponsonby should see him, nevertheless realised that, in the circumstances, the Queen could not withhold an offer, seeing that Mr. Gladstone had not publicly committed himself to a policy of Home Rule.[34]   Had he done so, he suggested that the matter might be open to consideration. In face of this opinion and the attitude of Mr. Goschen, the Queen naturally had no option but to offer office to Mr. Gladstone, very adroitly covering her position by asserting that she had understood that he was anxious to retire from public life, and that her offer left him free to accept or not as he thought best.

It is clear that, as matters stood, the Queen would have been well advised to make the offer forthwith to Mr. Gladstone, because her failure to do so conveyed inevitably the impression that she was not impartial in her attitude towards him, and in fact we know that she was not free from bias against his policy. The matter, however, might have presented a different appearance if Mr. Gladstone had actually announced his conversion to Home Rule. It could then have been argued, as recognised by Lord Salisbury, that the political situation was so uncertain that it was perfectly proper to consult Mr. Goschen to see whether a Government of a moderate character might be formed. Even so, no doubt it would have been better to make the offer to Mr. Gladstone in order to conform to the practice of the Queen in regard to Lord Derby. But it is safer in constitutional issues to insist on substance rather than on form, and to agree with Mr. Goschen that the Queen's duty to approach Mr. Gladstone was imposed by the realities of the political situation, as Lord Salisbury himself agreed.

In a brief period the Queen again consulted Mr. Goschen as to whether, on the resignation of Mr. Gladstone as the result of the general election, she should send for Lord Salisbury, and received his emphatic advice to that effect, showing that Mr. Goschen saw no objection to being consulted when this took place under circumstances precluding any idea of unfairness.[35]   In 1892 the question

---

[33] *Letters of Queen Victoria*, 3 s., i. 29–31, 33.   [34] *Ibid.*, 3 s., i. 27.
[35] *Ibid.*, 3 s., i. 161.

of sending for Mr. Gladstone caused anxiety to the Queen, who at one time had thought of sending for Lord Rosebery. Sir H. Ponsonby sounded Sir W. Harcourt and other minor lights of the Opposition, learning that they held Mr. Gladstone the only possible choice, a view which Lord Rosebery had earlier made quite clear to Sir H. Ponsonby himself.[36] In the result, the Queen abandoned the idea of seeing Lord Rosebery before acting, and sent for Mr. Gladstone, but her attitude shows clearly that she did not accept the view that she was not entitled to consider independently whom she should choose for office. No doubt, in her final decision she was influenced by the argument, pointed out by Sir H. Ponsonby, that if she selected Lord Rosebery and he refused she would be placed in the unpleasant position of seeming to have been compelled to resort to Mr. Gladstone. In fact nothing but success in securing a ministry would prevent the sovereign from being placed in a difficult position in such a case. But the difficulty must not be exaggerated, nor is it necessary to deny the right of the Crown to weigh possibilities. Mr. Balfour's view in 1904,[37] that in the event of his resignation the King should send for Sir H. Campbell-Bannerman in lieu of Lord Spencer, was simply in accord with common sense, for by that date Lord Spencer's position in the Liberal Party could not compare for a moment to that of Sir H. Campbell-Bannerman.[38] On the other hand, it is quite impossible to accept Lord Esher's claim that it would have been unconstitutional for the King to have sent for Lord Spencer and Sir H. Campbell-Bannerman, and to have discussed the issue with them together.[39] The duty of a sovereign is unquestionably not to take sides, and subject to that, the Crown must be free to make such enquiries as seem best calculated to ascertain who can form a ministry. To disapprove the Queen's soundings in 1892 is impossible, and the King in 1905 might quite properly have seen Lord Spencer with Sir H. Campbell-Bannerman, though, as matters turned out, he had already made social contacts with the latter abroad, and had no real doubt that he should send for him.

The principle that consultation is proper, provided that it is

---

36 *Letters of Queen Victoria*, 3 s., ii. 130 ff.   37 Esher, *Journals and Letters*, ii. 56.
38 Halévy's assertion that up to September, 1905, Lord Spencer was universally expected to be Premier is quite mistaken. In October he became incapacitated by illness. Elie Halévy, *Histoire du Peuple Anglais an XIXᵉ Siècle*, Epilogue, ii., p. 2.
39 Esher, *Journals and Letters*, ii. 77 f.

intended simply to ascertain who best can form a Government is in accordance with common sense, and is also exemplified by many instances, though these do not involve so directly the question of the preferential claim of the leader of the Opposition to a summons. An outgoing Prime Minister who retires voluntarily or from ill-health may naturally be expected to recommend his successor, and even if he resigns because of a defeat in the Commons or at the polls, he is the natural person to express an opinion.   It is perfectly true that he has no right to advise, because the right to advise, as the Prince Consort recognised in 1852, when Lord Derby was defeated in the Commons, is correlative to the taking of responsibility for the advice.[40]   But, though the Queen was fully within her rights when she refrained from asking Mr. Gladstone's advice in 1894, as he was within his rights in refusing to give it to Sir H. Ponsonby except at the royal request, that attitude was no doubt affected by the royal prejudice against the aged Premier.[41]   In 1868 Lord Derby recommended spontaneously Mr. Disraeli, and, if Lord Salisbury in 1902 did not formally recommend Mr. Balfour, that was doubt-less because such a recommendation was patently unnecessary.[42] It is not clear whether Mr. Balfour formally offered advice about his successor in 1905, but his views in favour of Sir H. Campbell-Bannerman were probably before the King.[43]   The King must also have known that Sir H. Campbell-Bannerman regarded Mr. Asquith as his obvious successor.[44]   Lord Esher indeed, insisted on principle that the King must make his own decision without learning the view of the Cabinet as desired by Lord Knollys, but Lord Esher's views on such topics were often too personal to be accurate.[45] Mr. Asquith naturally advised the formation of the first coalition under himself in 1915, after, by resignation, securing a free hand to reconstruct the ministry, and he repeated this action in the crisis of 1916, when it was still hoped to effect a reconstruction which would not mean his retirement.[46]   In the later stages of the issue it

---

40 *Letters of Queen Victoria*, 1 s., ii. 501.   Lord Salisbury advised in 1886 (*ibid.*, 3 s., i. 27).
41 *Ibid.*, 3 s. ii. 369 ; Morley, *Gladstone*, iii., 512–513.   The Queen sent a hand-some apology to Lord Salisbury for not offering him office at once.
42 This point is not recorded.   But cf. Bernard Holland, *Life of the Duke of Devonshire*, ii. 280 ;   also J. L. Garvin, *Life of Joseph Chamberlain*, iii. 611.
43 Esher, *Journals and Letters*, ii. 78.
44 Cf. his interviews with both on March 4, 1908.   Spender, *Lord Oxford*, i. 194 f.
45 Esher, *Journals and Letters*, ii. 272 ff.
46 Spender, *Lord Oxford*, ii. 164 ff., 265, 273 ff. ;   Beaverbrook, *Politicians and the War*, ii. 259.

is clear that the King had full opportunity to learn the views of
Mr. Asquith, Mr. Lloyd George and Mr. Bonar Law, and that
Mr. Asquith took the decision to recommend an offer of office to
Mr. Bonar Law seems certain, though Mr. Chamberlain seems to
have thought otherwise.[47]   It seems clear that in 1922 Mr. Lloyd
George could not avoid indicating that Mr. Bonar Law must be his
successor, for it was he who, issuing from retirement under the
influence of Lord Beaverbrook, had announced his attitude of
disapproval of the coalition at the decisive meeting of the party.
On the other hand, Mr. Bonar Law himself was too ill to be asked
for his advice; perhaps also he wished to avoid giving any lead
against Lord Curzon, and preferred to be exempt from any responsibility for the decision to pass him over.[48]

   The precedent of discussion in 1916 was clearly followed in
1931. The financial crisis induced by the financial policy of the
ministry, aggravated by the international financial situation,
threatened the ministry, a minority Government, with disaster from
the prospect of a calamitous failure to maintain the gold standard.
The Prime Minister advised the King to see Mr. Baldwin and Sir
Herbert Samuel, the leaders of the Opposition parties, on August 23,
on his return from Balmoral, and after they had done so, the
Prime Minister met his colleagues in Cabinet, and the decision was
taken to resign.   The general expectation was that this step would
be followed by the sending for the leader of the Conservatives, but
the result was different.   When he presented to the King the
resignation of the Cabinet, Mr. MacDonald recommended him to
send for the leaders of the Opposition on August 24, and the outcome
of that meeting was the Prime Minister's receiving authority to
create a new Government based on party co-operation.[49]   That
the King was active in procuring this result while limiting himself
entirely to his constitutional right of suggestion, is generally conceded, and, whatever judgment may be passed on the attitude of
Mr. MacDonald, the correctness of the royal attitude is clear.[50]
The new Government once established, the transit of power to
Mr. Baldwin in 1935, and thence with automatic precision to
Mr. Chamberlain in 1937, was automatic; in both cases it may

47 Sir Austen Chamberlain, *Down the Years*, p. 125.
48 Ronaldshay, *Life of Lord Curzon*, iii. 350 ; Dugdale, *Arthur James Balfour*, ii. 360.
49 Viscount Snowden, *An Autobiography*, ii. 947–954.
50 S. Webb, *Political Quarterley*, iii. 1 ff.; Keith, *The King and the Imperial Crown*,
pp. 130 ff.

be taken for granted that their predecessors advocated royal appointment.

A problem of great difficulty is raised by the question of the character and extent of the obligation created by the offer of office by the Crown.   No doubt politicians are specially interested in the necessity that the King's service must be carried on; their *métier* demands that they should be astute to promote the maintenance of orderly government on democratic lines; it is on the tacit assumption that this is their standpoint that they have been returned to Parliament.   Hence the political leader is bound to avoid anything pointing to the destruction of effective administration, but the responsibility is not confined to the Opposition.   The Government is equally bound so to order its policy as to prevent the country suffering from the *régime* of a discredited administration, lacking the power to act effectively in the interests of the State. Hence, it follows that neither Government nor Opposition should so direct its policy as to render probable such an outcome.

The issue arose in 1851, when the Government of Lord John Russell suffered defeat on a motion on the franchise by Mr. Locke King.   Lord Stanley was clearly not responsible for the motion of radical inspiration, and naturally he suggested to his sovereign that the true remedy was the forming of a coalition between the Whigs and the Peelites.   It must, however, be added that he felt it his duty as a loyal subject to risk everything, except his principles and his honour, to carry on the Government.[51]   His fortitude was not then tested, but his attitude explains his acceptance in 1852 of the duty of forming a Government when Lord Palmerston brought down the Government.   On the other hand, in 1855 the case for his taking office was stronger, for his party had provided the votes which carried Mr. Roebuck's motion and defeated the ministry. His attitude was decidedly open to criticism, for he attempted to evade responsibility, and though he tried to form a Government he speedily declared it impossible to do so.[52]   He was equally reluctant in 1858, when Lord Palmerston was defeated, but the Queen very reasonably pressed him to act on the obvious ground that the existing ministry felt, as a result of its defeat, discredited and unable to govern successfully, and that he controlled a party whence a Government acceptable to the country could be formed.[53]

[51] *Letters of Queen Victoria*, 1 s., ii. 351.   [52] *Ibid.*, 1 s., iii. 102 ff.
[53] *Ibid.*, 1 s., iii. 337 ff.; Bell, *Palmerston*, ii. 180 ff.

The issue was decisively raised in 1873 by Mr. Disraeli's refusal to take office after his party had defeated Mr. Gladstone on the Irish University Bill.[54]   Mr. Disraeli was motived by considerations of electoral advantage; he had no desire to take up the arduous task of finishing off current business and then going to the country on a policy of his own, realising acutely the advantages of forcing Mr. Gladstone to remain in office in difficult conditions, with the probability of suffering serious defeat when he went to the polls. His plea that having been in opposition he had no issues to frame was clearly untenable.   Mr. Gladstone naturally pressed the proposition that the logical sequel to a deliberate defeat of a major Governmental measure must be acceptance of the duty of forming a ministry, and cited as precedents Lord Grey's acceptance of office on defeating the Duke of Wellington in 1830, and the events of 1835, of 1841, of 1852, of 1858, of 1859, of 1866, and of 1868, in each of which the Opposition had accepted the duty of taking office.   He admitted exceptions in 1832, in 1851, and in 1855, but insisted that the Opposition failure then to form ministries had been due to inability, not reluctance, a statement rather exaggerated as regards 1851, but that, it must be remembered, was a case where the defeat of the ministry was incidental, not deliberately planned as in 1873.[55]   Mr. Disraeli conceded that it would be an act of recklessness and faction for an Opposition to throw out legislation when it knew it was not prepared to take office, if its aim was merely to destroy the Government.   But he insisted that the circumstances precluded his taking office forthwith, and that it was impossible to accept the proposition that an Opposition could be forced into acceptance of objectionable legislation by reason of the fact that the Parliamentary situation was such as to preclude its acceptance of office.[56]   The defence *in vacuo* might be deserving of serious consideration; in the actual instance it had little cogency, for the principle is sound that, if the opposition is unwilling to take office, with a view to an early dissolution, it should bear in mind that it is bound to great discretion in criticism, and of such discretion nothing whatever had been shown on the Irish Universities Bill. Mr. Gladstone reiterated the doctrine in 1880, when he advised

[54] P. Guedalla, *The Queen and Mr. Gladstone*, i. 395 ff.; Morley, *Gladstone*, ii. 450–452, 652–653; W. F. Monypenny and G. E. Buckle, *Life of Disraeli* (1929 ed.), ii. 548–557.
[55] Guedalla, *The Queen and Mr. Gladstone*, i. 399–402.
[56] Monypenny and Buckle, *Disraeli* (1929 ed.), ii. 555.

Lord Hartington, for whom the Queen had sent, that it was his duty either to take office or to advise the choice of another Premier, and that, if the latter refused, he would still be bound to undertake the formation of a ministry.[57]   In like spirit Lord Salisbury consented to take office in 1885, though he had a better excuse than Mr. Disraeli for reluctance to act, since, in view of the extension of the franchise and redistribution, an immediate dissolution was impossible.[58]   Naturally he would have preferred to avoid holding office in the circumstances, but after some delay the Queen persuaded him that he should accept on the giving by Mr. Gladstone of assurances as to financial business, which the Queen quite fairly thought sufficient, though they fell short of what was asked by Lord Salisbury.   In 1895 the duty of Lord Salisbury to take office was perfectly clear, and he wisely did not persist in his quite untenable effort to prove that it was the duty of Lord Rosebery to dissolve if he were not willing to carry on after his defeat on the cordite issue in the Commons.[59]   A party which defeats a Government with a small majority must realise that it is bound to take office if the ministry resigns.

There was in 1905 a stronger case for the refusal of the opposition, if it so desired, to accept office on the resignation of Mr. Balfour.[60]   The King was far from satisfied with Mr. Balfour's proposal to resign rather than dissolve, and Sir H. Campbell-Bannerman had the issue under his consideration.   Lord Ripon, however, pointed out that it was impossible to secure that by refusal to take office Mr. Balfour would have been compelled to dissolve; The King might instead have sent for Lord Lansdowne or Mr. Chamberlain.[61]   In any case Sir H. Campbell-Bannerman adopted the sound view, that policy dictated readiness to accept the obligations of office in view of the attacks which had been directed at Mr. Balfour for clinging to it, and a most successful dissolution attested the soundness of the decision.   The principle is reasonably clear.   An Opposition which knows that it is anxious to secure power is entitled to harass the ministry in every way, but such action is not proper, if the Opposition to the ministry is aware that it cannot attempt to form a Government.   In that case it must criticise with discretion.

57 Morley, *Gladstone*, ii. 623 f.   58 *Letters of Queen Victoria*, 2 s., iii. 663 f.
59 *Ibid.*, 3 s., ii. 524 ff.   60 Lee, *Edward VII.*, ii. 189 f.
61 L. Wolf, *Life of the First Marquess of Ripon*, ii. 273 f.

Normally and properly the arrangements for the appointment of a new ministry should be carried out in Great Britain, and preferably in London under modern conditions of convenience of travel. One remarkable exception must be recorded, the arrangement under which Mr. Asquith had to find time to go to Biarritz in order to kiss hands. It is true that the King mentioned to him on March 4, 1908,[62] that he would expect him to take this action, but, though Mr. Asquith's acquiescence then, and when Sir H. Campbell-Bannerman was driven by the hopeless character of his illness to resign, made him responsible for the error, it must be admitted, as Lord Esher asserts,[63] that the action was a *faux pas.* It was condemned on all sides contemporaneously by both political and non-political opinion, which, perhaps, did not make sufficient allowance for the failure of the King's health.

(2.) The Prime Minister's Formation of the Cabinet

With the selection of the Prime Minister the essential work of the Crown is completed, for it rests with the former to make up his list of ministers and to present it for the royal assent. That assent need not be a formality, though the position of the Prime Minister in this regard is very strong. It is always open to him to assure the Crown that his list represents the terms on which it is possible for him to carry on the Government, and it is plain that the position of the King then becomes very delicate. He cannot expect to find another member of the same party willing to attempt to form a ministry; in the nature of things to look elsewhere for a Premier is out of the question. On the other hand, *noblesse oblige;* to force on the Crown an unsatisfactory person would run counter to the deference due to the King, and, if it were known that the ministry was pressing any appointment unduly on the sovereign, it would be resented. On the other hand, with the growing power of democracy, the sovereign will naturally accept as of course ministers who in the Victorian epoch would have been impossible. Technically the last word rests with the King, because it is he who appoints.[64]

The essential principles of Parliamentary government demand that all officers of Cabinet rank shall be members of one or other House of Parliament. Exceptions are due only to special and

---

[62] Spender, *Lord Oxford,* i. 195.   [63] Esher, *Journals and Letters,* ii. 300 f.
[64] Ministers are both servants of the Crown and hold office under it. Cf. *Lewis v. Cattle* (1938), 54 T. L. R. 721.

2*

temporary circumstances. Mr. Gladstone in the office of Colonial Secretary (1845–46), was without a seat,[65] and Sir A. G. Boscawen, as Minister of Agriculture, was in like case in 1922–23.[66] But General Smuts' position, as member of the War Cabinet in 1917–18 without a seat in Parliament, was an anomaly excused by war conditions. In 1935 the disastrous defeat of Mr. MacDonald at Seaham must have entailed his resignation, had not an appeal to the Scottish Universities secured him a seat, while a peerage was conferred on a minor politician to secure a seat for Mr. M. Mac-Donald, whose own constituents had rejected him, though less decisively. Mr. MacDonald himself in 1931 vainly endeavoured to find a seat for Sir W. Jowitt as Attorney-General, but the attempt failed, and Sir W. Jowitt had to resign. Occasionally minor offices may be held out of Parliament. The Scottish law officers should find seats there, but in 1924 and 1929 the Lord Advocate in the Labour administrations was treated as a non-political officer. In 1923, on the other hand, it was found necessary to have the Solicitor-General in the Commons, though the Lord Advocate was not in either House in Mr. Bonar Law's ministry.

The allocation of ministers as between the Houses is now in part regulated by the Ministers of the Crown Act, 1937,[67] and subsequent Acts creating new ministries. No person holding the office of Chancellor of the Exchequer, Secretary of State, First Lord of the Admiralty, President of the Board of Trade, Minister of Agriculture and Fisheries, Minister of Education, Minister of Labour, Minister of Transport, Minister of Health, Minister of Supply [68] or Minister of Defence[69] is thereby disqualified from sitting in the House of Commons, but not more than sixteen of these may sit in the House of Commons at any one time. The Lord President of the Council, the Lord Privy Seal, the Postmaster-General and the Minister of Works[70] may also sit in the House of Commons, although only three of them may sit and vote there at any one time. This means, in effect, that if all the above offices are filled, the holders of three of them, in addition to the Lord Chancellor, will be in the House of Lords.[71] The First Lord of

65 Morley, *Gladstone*, i. 287 f.
66 H. A. Taylor, *Viscount Brentford*, p. 166 : he had fought two by-elections.
67 1 Ed. VIII. & 1 Geo. VI., c. 38.   68 Ministry of Supply Act, 1939.
69 Ministry of Defence Act, 1946.   70 Minister of Works and Planning Act, 1942.
71 The old tradition was aristocratic: Lord Salisbury had ten peers, Mr. Balfour eight, in his first ministry. Mr. N. Chamberlain, in June, 1937, had six. Mr. Churchill also had six peers in his original Cabinet in 1951.

the Treasury, the Minister of Town and Country Planning,[72] the Minister of National Insurance,[73] the Minister of Fuel and Power,[74] the Minister of Civil Aviation,[75] and the Minister of Pensions may also sit and vote in the House of Commons, as may, finally, not more than twenty-four persons holding the office of Parliamentary Under-Secretary.[76] The penalty for disregard of these rules is one not exceeding £500 a day for sitting or voting.[77]

The claim has often been made that any minister who is charged with important financial responsibilities should take his seat in the Commons, but the rule is by no means invariably followed. In the case of the Foreign Office a strong argument for presence in the Commons is afforded by the importance of the Commons keeping in close contact with the minister in charge of foreign policy, having regard to its vital importance to the national welfare. The argument has validity, and in the National Government, after its reconstitution, the office was successively held by Sir J. Simon, Sir S. Hoare, and Mr. Eden. The resignation of the latter on February 20, 1938, was followed by the appointment to the post of Lord Halifax. The attack, however, of the Labour Party on the change was met by the Prime Minister, who undertook to answer himself all questions of importance, leaving to the Under-Secretary only minor questions,[78] and Sir A. Sinclair supported the appointment, on the score that this procedure gave the Commons the reality of control. In the case of the Air Ministry the attack on Lord Swinton's tenure in 1937–38 was accentuated by accusations of failure to develop civil aviation. The Prime Minister countered the onslaught by the ingenious plan of adding to the Cabinet a minister without a substantive portfolio in the person of Earl Winterton, an Irish peer, Chancellor of the Duchy of Lancaster, who was appointed a member of the Air Council to act as deputy thereon to the Secretary of State, and to deal in the Commons with all major questions affecting air on the service side, leaving

---

72 Minister of Town and Country Planning Act, 1943.
73 Ministry of National Insurance Act, 1944.
74 Ministry of Fuel and Power Act, 1945.
75 Ministry of Civil Aviation Act, 1945.
76 The number specified in the Act of 1937 was twenty; this was temporarily increased to twenty-six in 1940 and subsequently amended; see S.R. and O., 1942, No. 1131.
77 Salaries of ministers are also regulated by the Ministers of the Crown Act, 1937.
78 Cf. Mr. Curzon's position as Under-Secretary (1895–98) to Lord Salisbury: Nicolson, *Curzon: The Last Phase*, pp. 35–40.

to the Under-Secretaty questions of civil aviation, which were to be his main care. But public feeling shortly compelled Lord Swinton's retirement in favour of Sir Kingsley Wood.[79] The difficulty, of course, is that it is extremely difficult for a minister in charge of a great department to find time for serious thinking on its problems when he has the Commons to attend and questions therein to answer. But the advantage gained in this way from the presence of the minister in the Lords is lessened by his failure to keep in touch with the feeling in that House, and by the fact that a minister of the highest calibre usually desires a chance to attain the Prime Minister-ship, and therefore cannot be expected to go to the Lords.

Something, of course, depends on the nature of the work to be done at any moment. When finance is specially concerned, it is desirable that a department should have its head in the Commons. The War Office was placed under Lord Derby in 1916, and Lord Hailsham kept it from 1931 to 1935, but Mr. Hore-Belisha was entrusted with it in 1937, when the question arose of securing better recruiting, and it became necessary for the minister to be able to secure funds from the Treasury and spend them to the satisfaction of the Commons, while making the service much more attractive in order to secure the necessary men.[80] The possibility of having a peer at the Admiralty was accepted, even by Mr. Gladstone, who had Lord Northbrook in 1880, Lord Ripon in 1886, and Earl Spencer in 1892; it is rendered possible by the readiness of the country to find funds for the navy.

Where the head of the department is in the Lords, there must be an officer of the rank of Parliamentary Under-Secretary in the Commons; as we have seen in the case of an important ministry like the Air Ministry, it may be necessary to have a special post to secure effective representation where controversial issues are likely to arise. On the other hand, the Upper Chamber must be content with such representation as can be given without undue incon-venience. In recent years that has been far from ungenerous, while the Lord President, the Lord Privy Seal, and the Officers of the Household, if peers, are available for dealing with business affecting departments without direct spokesmen in the Lords. The Paymaster-General has no actual duties; hence, if a peer is appointed, he can undertake systematically the representation of

[79] Viscount Swinton, *I Remember*, p. 146.
[80] Keith Feiling, *Life of Neville Chamberlain*, p. 317.

departments. The Chancellor of the Duchy of Lancaster and the Minister of Works are not usually officers with much work to do, and they can easily, if peers, be of service in the Lords.

Another expedient is the appointment of ministers without portfolio. The most famous instance of this is the case of the Duke of Wellington, when, in 1841–45, he led the Lords without office, and Lord Lansdowne performed a like service for the Government of 1855–58. Lord John Russell's insistence on leading the Commons, without portfolio, in the ministry of 1852, evoked objections of various kinds;[81] the point that he would thus seem to evade the necessity of re-election, could be met by the consideration that he could accept the Chiltern Hundreds and then be re-elected, but Lord Palmerston hinted that it was a rather dangerous precedent to set the example of the tenure of high office without emoluments.[82] Lord John yielded so far as to become Foreign Secretary for a few weeks, but then resigned that office and led the House without portfolio, until in June, 1854, he accepted the post of Lord President. Another anomalous case occurred in 1867, when Mr. S. Walpole remained in the Cabinet without office after resigning from the Home Office.[83] The anomalous War Cabinet evoked like results. From 1915 to 1921 ten cases occurred of ministers in the Cabinet without portfolio, eight drawing salaries, their appointments being made under legislation of 1917, permitting the suspension of the rule of re-election on acceptance of office. But the system ended in 1921 after a debate in the Commons, which showed its unpopularity.[84] The last minister without portfolio was Dr. Addison, who held the chairmanship of four Cabinet committees, and was member of six others, but who was not personally very popular.

After a lapse of fourteen years the system was revived in Mr. Baldwin's ministry of 1935, when Lord Eustace Percy and Mr. Eden received ministries. The former found the position anomalous and unsatisfactory, and resigned office, later leaving parliamentary life. The latter was given the duty of dealing with League of Nations' affairs, his legal position being clarified by the House of Commons Disqualification (Declaration of Law) Act, 1935, but on Sir S.

---

[81] *Letters of Queen Victoria*, 1 s., ii. 507; Bell, *Palmerston*, ii. 71 f.
[82] G. P. Gooch, *Later Correspondence of Lord John Russell*, ii. 119.
[83] *Letters of Queen Victoria*, 2 s., i. 425, n. 1. He disappeared in Mr. Disraeli's ministry (i. 509).
[84] 143 *H. C. Deb.* 5 s., 596–7, 1592 ff.

Hoare's retirement in December, 1935, Mr. Eden was appointed in his place, and no fresh appointment was made in lieu.[85]

The existence of ministries without substantial departmental duties, whether without portfolio or, as is normal, with one of the virtually sinecure offices, is useful mainly as a means of providing for men, whose capacity for departmental work has been lessened by passage of time, or who have no taste for administration, but whose counsel is of value, as in the case of the Duke of Wellington and Lord Lansdowne. More recent cases are those of Mr. John Bright, who proved a poor administrator at the Board of Trade in 1868, but was later valuable as Chancellor of the Duchy. Lord Morley, after Mr. Asquith had in 1910, in despair, accepted the latest of his constant resignations, was rescued from his unfortunate plight by the intervention of Mr. J. A. Spender, who found Mr. Asquith happy to give him an opportunity of useful service as Lord President.[86] The same office has been accorded at the last period of their careers to Lord Tweedmouth[87] and Lord Wolverhampton[88] respectively. Or such a post may console a minister for whom, despite youth and capacity, no place can be found in the ordinary ranks, as in the case of Lord Eustace Percy.[89] On the other hand such offices can, whether in war or peace, be usefully occupied by ministers who are entrusted with major responsibilities of a general rather than a Departmental kind. This is true of Sir John Anderson who was Lord President from 1940–43, and of Mr. Herbert Morrison who became Lord President in the Labour Government of 1945.

The Law Officers of the Crown are normally not included in the Cabinet, though Sir Rufus Isaacs was accorded that honour in 1912, and Sir D. Hogg, when induced to enter Parliament, was given a Cabinet seat (1924–29). The objections to such a step are

---

85 By Re-election of Ministers Act, 1919, and House of Commons (Declaration of Law) Act, 1935, ministers appointed to perform definite duties without being in charge of a Department may sit in the House of Commons, though not more than three such ministers may sit and vote at the same time. Salaried ministers without portfolio are also exempt from re-election.

86 Spender, *Lord Oxford*, i. 291 f.

87 For his short tenure and breakdown, see Fitzroy, *Memoirs*, i. 351 ff.

88 He was the first dissenter and solicitor to hold the office: *ibid.*, i. 363.

89 Lord Curzon was Lord President from 1915–19, latterly in the War Cabinet. Lord J. Russell pointed out in 1866 that a Chancellor of the Duchy not in the Cabinet was of no use: *Letters of Queen Victoria*, 2 s., i. 295. In the Cabinet of 1937 the Privy Seal was given to Earl De La Warr to represent National Labour.

obvious enough, and the fact that the Lord Chancellor occupies an equally or more anomalous position naturally forms no defence; the objections to the exercise of judicial powers of the highest importance by a member of the Cabinet are unanswerable, even though by prudent restraint the anomaly is in practice but slightly felt. There would, of course, be no insuperable difficulty in terminating the anomaly.

The Prime Minister must, in considering his list and in making new appointments, as occasion demands, consider his political position and the necessity of placating various interests. The Cabinet has no right to be consulted as to new appointments, and Mr. Gladstone was opposed to admitting any right of that body to determine its own membership;[90] but his view has not been invariably adopted. There is nothing in theory objectionable to asking the views of the Cabinet. There may be mentioned the incident in 1851, when the Queen resented the Cabinet's desire to have Lord Clarendon as Foreign Secretary;[91] in 1866, however, she asked Lord Russell to find out the view of the Cabinet upon the addition of Mr. Goschen to its numbers.[92] In 1847 and 1848 Lord John Russell consulted the Cabinet regarding the selection of Lord Clarendon as Lord Lieutenant of Ireland, and the offer of the Admiralty to Sir J. Graham.[93] Lord Palmerston made a rule of consultation,[96] he obtained its advice in 1855 to approach the Whigs, rather than the Tories, in order to fill the posts vacated by the Peelites, and asked its approval of the replacement of Mr. Gladstone by Sir G. C. Lewis and a successor to Sir W. Molesworth. Later records are few; but in 1923 Mr. Baldwin asked the Cabinet if he could add Mr. Chamberlain and Lord Birkenhead as ministers without portfolio, in preparation for the election of 1923, but the Cabinet was not united, and so the plan was dropped.[95]

Most of these cases are, however, exceptional, for there is little likelihood of consultation with a Cabinet that is still being made. More normal and indeed, inevitable, are consultations with other leaders of the Prime Minister's party. In Victorian days when the Upper Chamber was powerful, the leader in the Commons, if

90 Morley, *Gladstone*, iii. 101.
91 *Letters of Queen Victoria*, 1 s., ii. 419.
92 *Ibid.*, 2 s., i. 294 f.
93 *Ibid.*, 1 s., ii. 143; Greville, *Memoirs*, 2 s., iii. 259.
94 Duke of Argyll, *Autobiography and Memoirs*, i. 539, 590; ii. 77.
95 Earl of Birkenhead, *Life of Lord Birkenhead*, ii. 232.

commissioned, had to take counsel with the leader in the Lords, and *vice versâ* Sir R. Peel worked with the Duke of Wellington, Lord Lansdowne was the mentor of Lord John Russell, with whom Lord Aberdeen had to deal in his coalition of 1852–55. It is difficult to think of Mr. Gladstone or his great rival as subject to any great pressure; but Sir Charles Dilke and Mr. Chamberlain insisted on securing the latter a Cabinet seat in 1880.[96] On the other hand, despite a very determined effort made by Sir Edward Grey and Mr. Haldane in 1905 to secure Sir H. Campbell-Bannerman's acceptance of a peerage, his determined resistance renders it unlikely that he deferred unduly to their judgment in arranging his Cabinet. His choice, for instance, of Lord Elgin for the Colonial Office, and of Lord Loreburn as Lord Chancellor in place of Mr. Haldane, was purely based on personal considerations, and his handling of the other offices conveyed disappointment, both to Mr. Bryce and Mr. Morley. In the case of a coalition, need for consultation is obvious. We know that the coalition of 1915 was arranged between Mr. Asquith and Mr. Bonar Law and that of 1916 between Mr. Lloyd George and Mr. Bonar Law. We have some information of the making of the Labour ministries of 1924 and 1929. In 1924 Mr. MacDonald acted largely on his own authority.[97] On the latter occasion Mr. MacDonald still showed considerable independence, but consulted much more fully with Mr. Henderson, Mr. Snowden, Mr. Clynes, and Mr. Thomas.[98] The coalition of 1931 was determined by Mr. MacDonald, Mr. Baldwin, and Sir Herbert Samuel. In 1939, Mr. Churchill's representations affected the composition of Mr. Chamberlain's War Cabinet;[99] and, in May, 1940, when Mr. Churchill decided to make his own administration representative of all parties, he consulted Mr. Attlee and Mr. Greenwood about the distribution of offices.[1]

It must, of course, be remembered that, while the Prime Minister has the advantage of being able to offer posts at his discretion, politicians of standing can safely decline what is given, if they command so much support in the party as to make it unwise to dispense with their services. Lord Palmerston used to demand the

---

[96] Garvin, *Joseph Chamberlain*, i. 285 ff.
[97] Snowden, *Autobiography*, ii. chap. xliv; Princess Marthe Bibesco, *Life of Lord Lord Thomson of Cardington*, pp. 149–151.
[98] *Snowden, Autobiography*, ii. chap. lxi.
[99] Winston Churchill, *The Second World War*, i. 320.   [1] *Ibid.*, i. 526.

Foreign Office until his dismissal in 1851; thereafter he was content with other offices, but no one can doubt that even the Queen would have sanctioned his appointment to that post had he cared to press for it. As we shall see, in 1868, Lord Clarendon opposed a polite negative to the offer of anything but the Foreign Office. In 1852 Lord John Russell insisted, as the price of his adhesion to Lord Aberdeen's ministry, that he should have the leadership of the Commons without portfolio, and, though induced to accept for a time the Foreign Secretaryship, he soon demanded and obtained his own terms.[2] There are few cases of equal persistence of recent date on record. Lord Rosebery would only serve in 1892 as Foreign Secretary and even then only after much persuasion by royalty. Other ministers, as notably in Sir H. Campbell-Bannerman's Cabinet of 1905, have acquiesced in accepting ministries which they did not desire rather than be left out, and no doubt the like remark applies to the several forms of the National Government. But Mr. Lloyd George successfully demanded the Exchequer in 1908.[3]

In selecting Under-Secretaries the Prime Minister must plainly have regard to the wishes of the head of the department. Mr. Gladstone is an authority for the view that the appointment is made by the Secretary of State, as in the case of Lord Granville's appointment to the Foreign Office by Lord Palmerston, and of Mr. L. Courtney's appointment to the Home Office by Sir W. Harcourt.[4] But the position seems to be that the Prime Minister has the patronage, though he would not give the head of a department a colleague likely to be uncongenial. It was Sir R. Peel who appointed Mr. Gladstone in 1835 to the Colonial Office,[5] and Lord Palmerston who selected Lord de Grey for the War Office in 1859,[6] and it was Sir H. Campbell-Bannerman who placed Mr. Churchill under Lord Elgin, though the latter probably hardly appreciated what he was to suffer at the hands of his much too brilliant subordinate.

2 *Letters of Queen Victoria*, 1 s., ii. 507.
3 Esher, *Journals and Letters*, ii. 303. He had first ascertained Mr. Morley's acquiescence. Morley decided to remain at the India Office, provided he was given the usual Viscounty, which was readily conceded. Spender, *Lord Oxford*, i. 198.
4 Guedalla, *The Queen and Mr. Gladstone*, ii. 130 f. He resented the Queen's disapproval of Mr. Courtney's transfer in 1881 to the Colonial Office. 'I think this intolerable. It is by courtesy only these appointments are made known to H.M.' (*Ibid.* 165.)
5 Lady F. Balfour, *Life of Lord Aberdeen*, ii. 19.
6 Wolf, *Life of Lord Ripon*, i. 142.

Of royal control of appointments instances from Queen Victoria's reign are clear. Her right to criticise was asserted by Lord Melbourne in accordance with William IV.'s practice.[7] It is curious to note that in 1851, when Lord Stanley was trying to form a Cabinet, she yielded to his suggestion of Mr. Disraeli as a Secretary of State, only because of the difficulties under which Lord Stanley was working.[8] She insisted, when asking Lord John Russell to resume power, that Lord Palmerston must not remain Foreign Secretary, but, though Lord John Russell made promises on this score, he found he dare not keep them, and Lord Palmerston ceased to hold the office in question only when his intransigence drove the Premier to remove him later in the year.[9] She then successfully asserted her wish to have Lord Granville in his place, against the preference of the Cabinet for Lord Clarendon, though she permitted an offer to be made to the latter in the assurance that it would be rejected.[10] Her dislike of Lord Palmerston as Foreign Secretary prevented Lord Derby offering him that office in 1852, when he was seeking to strengthen his position by so valuable an acquisition, although Derby did consider Palmerston for the office of Chancellor of the Exchequer.[11] Her special interest in foreign affairs expressed itself in vetoing in 1852 Mr. Bernal Osborne for the Under-Secretaryship;[12] in 1861, however, she reluctantly accepted Mr. Layard.[13] In 1866 she was confronted by a delicate position, for she thought Lord Stanley insufficiently qualified for the office of Foreign Secretary, but found that she could not effectively impress this opinion of his son on her Prime Minister.[14] In 1868 she endeavoured to induce Mr. Gladstone to refrain from giving Lord Clarendon the Foreign Office, but though Mr. Gladstone would have deferred to her wishes if possible, the refusal of Lord Clarendon to accept any other office was decisive.[15] It was only after reference to the Cabinet that the Queen accepted Mr. Goschen as member of the Cabinet while holding in 1866 the Duchy of Lancaster,[16] and in 1872 the Duke of Somerset was vetoed for the Duchy.[17]

[7] *Letters of Queen Victoria*, 1 s., i. 339.   [8] *Ibid.*, 1 s., ii. 365.
[9] *Ibid.*, 1 s., ii. 354, 376–381.   [10] *Ibid.*, 1 s., ii. 415–420.
[11] *Ibid.*, 1 s., ii. 447   [12] *Ibid.*, 1 s., ii. 514.
[13] *Ibid.*, 1 s., iii. 567–570.   [14] *Ibid.*, 2 s., i. 352–3.
[15] *Ibid.*, 2 s., i. 555–566.   [16] *Ibid.*, 2 s., i. 294 f.
[17] Guedalla, *The Queen and Mr. Gladstone*, i. 348.

The Queen's attitude in 1880 was specially drastic.[18]   She
had been compelled to accept Mr. Gladstone, but she vetoed
Mr. R. Lowe, demanded assurances that Mr. Chamberlain had
not made republican speeches, and a recantation of Sir C. Dilke's
attacks on the civil list, as the condition of allowing him to become
Under-Secretary at the Foreign Office, while in 1882 she refused
him the Duchy of Lancaster, and relegated him to the Local
Government Board.[19]   She made a merit of accepting Mr. Childers
at the War Office, and Lord Selborne as Lord Chancellor, while
the Earl of Fife was ruled too young to be Lord Chamberlain.   In
1886 she refused to re-appoint Mr. Childers to the War Office,
but accepted him in the Home Office, an attitude due to the dislike
felt for the minister by the Duke of Cambridge;[20] Sir C. Dilke
she vetoed on the plausible ground of his appearance in a divorce
case.   This veto she reaffirmed in 1892,[21] and Mr. Labouchere
shared the same fate.   The position was rendered easier by the
fact that it was possible to evade difficulties by putting the matter
in the light that he would have had to sacrifice his connection with
his newspaper *Truth* if in the ministry.   More important was her
refusal to accept Lord Ripon at the India Office, which went to
Lord Kimberley, but she accepted the former at the Colonial Office.
It was of course possible to object to an ex-Viceroy receiving the
India Office.   Lord Salisbury sacrificed Mr. Matthews in 1895,
and kept Lord Cross in 1886–92 and 1895–1900 to please her.[22]

But the Queen's attitude was not merely one of criticism.   She
was quite willing to use her influence to aid in the formation of
ministries, notably in the securing of Lord Rosebery for the Foreign
Office in 1892, an undertaking in which she had the aid of her son.[23]
Of Edward VII. little is recorded; his illness at the time of the
remaking of the ministry of 1902 precluded his usual activity, and
in the personnel of the ministry of 1905 he showed ready acquiescence, though he rejected Lord Herschell as a lord-in-waiting on

---

18 *Letters of Queen Victoria*, 2 s. iii. 84 ff.; Guedalla, *The Queen and Mr. Gladstone*,
ii. 85–91.
19 *Letters of Queen Victoria*, 2 s., iii. 370 f., 378, 390.   S. Gywnn and G. M.
Tuckwell, *Life of Sir Charles Dilke*, i. 492–495.   Lord Derby had to take the
Colonial, not Foreign, Office (1882), and was refused the Garter: Guedalla,
The Queen and Mr. Gladstone, ii. 111, 221.
20 *Letters of Queen Victoria*, 3 s., i. 28, 38, 42.
21 *Ibid.*, 3 s., ii. 120, 150.
22 *Ibid.*, 3 s., ii. 529.
23 *Ibid.*, 3 s., ii. 144 f.

the score that he was to combine the post with that of private secretary to the Lord Lieutenant of Ireland.[24]   The office of Lord Chamberlain was given with his assent to Lord Althorp with a viscounty.   What was striking was that he overlooked the curious blunder by which the list of the Cabinet was published in *The Times* on December 8, before the King had finally approved.   In the subsequent changes in 1908 he seems to have been in agreement.[25] Later information is not available in any authentic form, but George V.'s constitutional theory precludes any probability of his pressing his views on appointments.[26]

To give a minister Cabinet rank is a simple procedure, since no new appointment is involved, and a mere invitation from the Prime Minister suffices.[27]   But, even if the minister is already sworn of the Privy Council, and so even that formality is not requisite, the Premier would doubtless inform the King of his intention to add to the Cabinet the minister in question.   In 1908 the King commented on the desire which Mr. Churchill was believed to have to be admitted to the Cabinet while still Under-Secretary, but demurred to such action, quoting the refusal of Lord Rosebery to accept a similar proposal when Sir E. Grey was Under-Secretary at the Foreign Office.[28]   It is significant that both agreed as to the desirability of Mr. Churchill's promotion, but the King insisted that he must wait until a Cabinet post was available.   That shortly happened, though whether this particular consideration weighed with the Premier in getting rid of Lord Elgin remains to be shown.

3.   The Formal Transfer of Office

The mode in which a new Cabinet comes into existence differs according to whether the ministry falls to be formed from the same political party on the resignation of its head, or represents the displacement of one party by another.

A ministry is as much dissolved by the resignation of the Prime Minister, and that is so, whether the other members wish resignation

---

[24] Lee, *Edward VII.*, ii. 444 ff.

[25] For an unnamed veto, see Spender, *Lord Oxford*, i. 195.

[26] Mr. MacDonald reduced to three the political posts in the royal household as a courtesy to the King.   See Anson, *The Law and Custom of the Constitution*, vol. II (ed. Keith), i. 157 f.

[27] Cf. the case of Mr. Goschen in 1866: *Letters of Queen Victoria*, 2 s., i. 294 f.

[28] Spender, *Lord Oxford*, i. 195.

or not. This was frankly admitted by Lord John Russell when Lord Melbourne determined to resign in 1841,[29] and Sir R. Peel insisted on it in 1846, with the result of Cabinet acquiescence.[30] It is now unquestioned, and the political implications of the doctrine will be considered later. But resignation is in law not a cessation of tenure of office. A Prime Minister and his colleagues by constitutional practice remain at their posts, pending the moment when a new ministry is constituted and is prepared to take over; should the Prime Minister die in office, the rest of the ministers likewise remain in office until the new Government is constituted. Moreover, if the new Prime Minister retains ministers in their existing offices, there is no need for re-appointment. They retain their offices with tenure unaffected by the fact that the ministry has been dissolved. On the other hand, each minister holds until asked to retain his post on the understanding that he will relinquish it at the moment when he is asked to do so. If he failed, he would forthwith be dismissed by the King on the advice of the Prime Minister. It is curious that so obvious a principle should have been mistaken by Mr. Lansbury in the Commons on the change of ministry in 1935, when Mr. Baldwin disposed of the issue by careful examination of the precedents of Pitt's resignation in 1761, the death of Mr. Canning and Lord Palmerston in 1827 and 1865, and the resignations of 1902, 1908, and 1923.[31]

Naturally as short a period as possible intervenes between the resignation of the ministry and the installation of its successor; it is bad for the country that there should be any prolonged period, when ministers are precluded by obvious considerations of fairness to their successors from arriving at important decisions. Formerly longer delays have been known, as in 1839, 1845, and 1851, where after resignation ministers had to resume office, as no successors could be found, and in 1855, when it took time to find a new Government. In 1839 a very odd incident occurred. The Queen was unable to agree with Sir R. Peel's demand that the ladies of the bedchamber should be changed on political grounds. The moribund Cabinet was resuscitated to consider the issue and advised the Queen that she need not concede the point, with the result that Sir R. Peel refused to proceed with the formation of a

---

29 Gooch, *Later Correspondence of Lord John Russell*, i. 36.
30 *Letters of Queen Victoria*, 1 s., ii. 94–95; Gladstone, *Gleanings*, i. 243.
31 304 *H. C. Deb.* 5 s., 337–349, 357–358.

ministry, and Lord Melbourne carried on for two years longer. The action was regarded by Greville as unconstitutional, on the ground that the Whigs could constitutionally tender no advice to the Queen 'until Sir Robert Peel had formally and finally resigned his commission into her hands.' Certainly we should now accept the view that the terms on which a new Government accepts office must be decided by that Government alone.[32]

The actual formal transfer takes place as regards the Lord Chancellor, the Lord Privy Seal, and the Secretaries of State and other ministers having seals, by the handing over of their seals of office to the King, who hands them to their successors.[33] In the case of the Lords of the Treasury, the First Lord of the Admiralty, the Chancellor of the Duchy of Lancaster, and the Postmaster-General fresh letters patent are issued, revoking the earlier appointments. It is now the rule that two Councils are held on the same day, the retiring ministers being received by the King and handing over their seals, while at the second the seals are given to ministers, and the King declares the Lord President

---

[32] *Letters of Queen Victoria*, 1 s., i. 210; Greville, *Memoirs*, 2 s., i. 207 ff.
[33] On the procedure in the case of those without seals, see *Letters of Queen Victoria*, 2 s., iii. 679. When the new Secretaryship of State for Air was created, Walter Long lent his seals: Fitzroy, *Memoirs*, ii. 668.

CHAPTER 3

THE PRIME MINISTER AND HIS COLLEAGUES

(1.) THE STATUS OF THE PRIME MINISTER

IT is a commonplace that Sir R. Peel was the model Prime Minister. It is claimed, and seemingly with truth, that he supervised and was genuinely familiar with the business of each department.[1] He himself, though his Chancellor of the Exchequer was able, introduced his budgets in 1842 and 1845. The War Office, the Admiralty, the Foreign Office, the administration of India and of Ireland felt his personal influence as much as the Treasury or the Board of Trade. Sir R. Peel[2] frankly claimed the duty to deal with these departments, and added that of exercising the then wide and unrestricted royal patronage, the whole of the communications with the sovereign, correspondence with persons of station on public business, the reception of deputations, and attendance for six or seven hours a day for five or six days a week when Parliament was sitting. It is plain that the days are gone when such a comprehensive view of the duties of a Prime Minister could be made actual; Mr. Gladstone or Mr. Disraeli in their best days could emulate without attaining his achievement; the extension of state functions today would render even their degree of control impossible; were the Prime Minister to undertake it, the result would no doubt be equally disastrous to him and to the country. Moreover, Sir R. Peel had the good fortune not to be troubled by subordinates of capacity comparable with his own; Sir J. Graham and Mr. Goulburn are dim shadows at the present day.

Lord Melbourne's essential love of peace precluded any effort to engross authority, and Lord John Russell's wayward and undependable spirit was unequal to the problem of dealing with Lord Palmerston. The latter had definitely limited interests,

---

[1] Lord Rosebery, *Miscellanies, Literary and Historical*, i. 197; cf. Morley, *Gladstone*, i. 248.
[2] *Report of Select Committee on Official Salaries* (1850), pp. 40 f.

and had no desire whatever to enforce the practice under Sir R. Peel by which measures were brought before him by all departments before consideration, in the form determined by him, by the Cabinet; hence the famous episode of 1860 when the Prime Minister did not conceal his indifference to the destruction by the Lords of Mr. Gladstone's Paper Duties Bill.[3]

There is abundant evidence that Mr. Disraeli did not care to adopt the rôle of controller of departmental affairs. His policy was to appoint a man he trusted to the headship of a department, and then to support him as long as he trusted him, even against criticism from the rest of the Cabinet. Thus he allowed Lord Carnarvon to annex the Transvaal without even the knowledge of the Cabinet, refused against his own better judgment to recall Sir Bartle Frere from South Africa in deference to the wishes of the Queen and Sir M. Hicks Beach,[4] and determined on the route for the Afghan campaign at the motion of Lord Cranbrook against the wishes of a majority of the Cabinet. Lord Salisbury's criticism[5] of this attitude is clear but not uncontested,[6] and it certainly cannot be said that the Prime Minister was willing to support a colleague against the Cabinet in the department in which, as was inevitable, he took special interest; he forced his foreign policy on the Cabinet despite the resistance of Lord Derby and his resignation.[7] The impression left is that the Premier preferred individual to Cabinet rule, and that was natural in view of his close relations with the Queen who looked to him to give effect to the policy on which they agreed, no doubt usually on his initiative. It would have been embarrassing to allow Cabinet intervention, and Lord Carnarvon bears testimony to the clever use made by the Premier of the royal authority to force through his foreign policy even by a hint of resignation of the throne.[8] This attitude was the more possible because Mr. Disraeli had no desire to promote legislation on social reform of a wide character which would have demanded combined consideration by the Cabinet; he remained in essentials content to deal with administration.

[3] *Letters of Queen Victoria*, 1 s., iii. 509–510; Bell, *Palmerston*, ii. 259 ff.; Morley, *Gladstone*, ii. 31–40.

[4] Lady V. Hicks Beach, *Life of Sir Michael Hicks Beach*, i. 130.

[5] A. J. Balfour, *Chapters of Autobiography*, pp. 113–114.

[6] For example, Hicks Beach regarded Disraeli's refusal to recall Bartle Frere as a sign of strength, not weakness.

[7] *Letters of Queen Victoria*, 2 s. ii. 583 f., 609, 611.

[8] Lord Gladstone, *After Thirty Years*, p. 141.

Of Lord Salisbury's attitude, we have sufficient evidence both from Lady G. Cecil[9] and from Sir M. Hicks Beach,[10] a candid critic.   He was engrossed in foreign affairs, his one real interest, and insisted on holding that office when Prime Minister up to 1900. Moreover, he was destitute of the desire or knowledge necessary to enable him to delegate authority to his subordinates in the Foreign Office.   His love of working at home rendered him little more than a stranger in his own department, and his mode of work left him without the necessary time to attempt any supervision of other departments.   He was content, therefore, to allow his ministers to work out their own problems, and to accept majority decisions of the Cabinet even against his own judgment, contrasting therein strongly with Mr. Disraeli's preference for his own judgment, based on that of a trusted subordinate or backed by the authority of the Queen.

The authority exerted by Mr. Gladstone in the ministry of 1868–74 was doubtless wide and far-reaching, and he made an effort to control departmental business in the manner of Sir R. Peel.[11] But he introduced a new element unknown to Mr. Disraeli or Lord Salisbury, belief in the duty of a ministry to press forward large measures of reform, such as the disestablishment of the Irish Church, or, later, electoral reform and the grant of self-government to Ireland.   In the ministry of 1880–85 he had a new rôle to play in mediating between the Whigs and the Radicals,[12] whose control by the restless ambition and genuine conviction of Mr. J. Chamberlain led to the growing discomfort of the Whigs, and prepared the way for the Whigs' desertion in 1886 of the Liberal cause, in conjunction, curiously enough, with the minister whose advanced social views had caused Gladstone so much anxiety, and had entailed the conciliatory intervention of the Premier to keep the peace.   Even when in 1892 a slight majority restored the Liberals to office rather than power, the leader had differences of importance to face; there had developed a spirit of Imperialism which was foreign to his nature.   This difference of outlook was fated to grow until it accelerated his departure from office, and presented his successor with a hopeless effort to preserve some semblance of unity when his own imperialism was contrasted sharply with the sentiments of the

9 Lady Gwendolin Cecil, *Life of Robert, Marquis of Salisbury*, iii. 167 ff.
10 Lady V. Hicks Beach, *Hicks Beach*, ii. 360 f.
11 Lord Oxford and Asquith, *Fifty Years of Parliament*, ii. 185.
12 Morley, *Gladstone*, iii. 2 ff.

leader of the House of Commons. There could be no idea of effective control of his Cabinet by Lord Rosebery.

Mr. Balfour's tenure of office has been variously judged.[13]   It is clear that his tactics completely failed to preserve unity as between the supporters of tariff reform and free trade, and the circumstances of the departure of the free trade ministers from office are not wholly creditable.   His new ministers were much inferior to him in capacity and were doubtless glad to be guided by his experience. But the view that he was the ablest Prime Minister of the present century, whether Mr. Lloyd George be excepted or not, seems impossible to defend.   His management of the parliamentary position, so as to remain in office without an effective programme, was justly censured by the overwhelming defeat which was meted out to the ministry in 1906.   His intellectual talent was superior to that of any other Premier of the century, but the Conservative Party was probably wise in ridding itself of his leadership in 1911, and in never restoring him to that position.[14]

Sir H. Campbell-Bannerman became Prime Minister suffering from health already impaired and full of domestic anxiety over the growing illness of his wife.[15]   He had also under him a Cabinet composed of men of divergent views, for the divergence of view between supporters of Imperialism and opponents was far from dead, and the ministry was deeply engaged in efforts to carry legislation against the solid opposition of the House of Lords.   In these circumstances he could intervene only in issues of first-class importance, but it was to him that the grant of responsible Government to the conquered Boer colonies was due in 1906–07.   Mr. Asquith had no easy task with Mr. Lloyd George and Mr. Churchill, eager to press social legislation at the expense of defence preparations, but his good natured and easy going treatment of the ministry was not unsuccessful.[16]   His defects, such as they were, appeared during the war years, and especially after the coalition forced upon him in 1915.   The Cabinet with its disparate elements required careful control and guidance, and, making all allowances for the

[13] Lee, *Edward VII.*, ii. 159 f., 173–191; Dugdale, *Arthur James Balfour*, i. 333 ff.
[14] Dugdale, *Arthur James Balfour*, ii. 81–92; Chamberlain, *Politics from Inside*, pp. 370 ff.
[15] Lee, *Edward VII.*, ii. 441–477.
[16] Lord Oxford and Asquith, *Fifty Years of Parliament*, ii. 186.

criticism by friends of Mr. Lloyd George or of Mr. Bonar Law,[17] it must be recognised that he failed in the crisis to impose leadership in adequate measure. It was very different with his successor. Mr. Lloyd George's creation of the War Cabinet left the Prime Minister in a unique position of authority, for Mr. Bonar Law, who alone was in a position to oppose him with authority, was convinced alike of his sincerity and capacity to win the war, and lent him invaluable and self-effacing aid.[18] If we may judge from his own record, his control must have been secured by his remarkable capacity to see with the utmost clarity the strong points of any argument which appealed to him, and to expound it, coupled with his not less characteristic ability to minimise, or wholly to ignore, important considerations telling against his point of view. It is the leading feature of his defence of his attitude in the long feud with Sir W. Robertson and Lord Haig that he ignores entirely in his polemic the real points of the case against him, and instead presents the views of his opponents in such a manner as to render them incapable of sustaining the onslaught directed against them.[19] It is easy to understand how completely he could carry with him a Cabinet when arguments so plausible were presented with all his genuine force of persuasion, for it is not to be supposed that the Premier was conscious in the least that he had failed to present to himself the real case on the opposing side.

In one respect Mr. Lloyd George undoubtedly went far beyond the duties of a Prime Minister, and it was his constant intervention in foreign affairs which earned him, not unjustly, the dislike of Lord Curzon, and induced the latter to rally to the side of Mr. Bonar Law, and thus to assure the destruction of the coalition ministry in 1922. To create a rival secretariat in the Cabinet Office, to decide issues of the highest importance behind the back of the Foreign Secretary, to receive Ambassadors without the presence of the minister, and even without prior notification were inexcusable acts. It is true that Lord Curzon showed both lack of self respect and of his duty to the country in acquiescing in such a position, but he no doubt consoled himself with the feeling that he could still do good service to his country, which later proved true, above all by his very genuine feat in regard to the negotiation of

17 Beaverbrook, *Politicians and the War*, chap. 16.
18 H. A. Taylor, *Andrew Bonar Law*, pp. 225–236.
19 *E.g.*, Lloyd George, *War Memoirs*, chap. 89.

peace with Turkey.[20]   No doubt Mr. Lloyd George never succeeded in realising the essential change brought about by the advent of peace, and the necessity of restoring the old practices of Cabinet government.   He delayed as long as he dared the restoration of the normal Cabinet, and he actually seems to have thought it possible that Mr. A. Chamberlain would accept office as Chancellor of the Exchequer without a seat in the Cabinet.[21]   When this idea was rejected with firmness, all that he would concede was a place in the Cabinet, but the restoration of the full Cabinet was further delayed, without, it seems clear, any public advantage.[22]

Mr. Bonar Law was from the first so unwell that it was not to be expected that he would seek to maintain the authority of his predecessor, nor had he any desire to do so.   Far from being anxious to retain the expanded office, which furnished his predecessor with ammunition and enabled him to intervene in administration, he contemplated even its abolition, and through his initiative its size was reduced.   Mr. MacDonald, like Lord Salisbury, in 1924, conceived it to be his duty to take the Foreign Office, and thus at once by reason of the complexity of the work disabled himself, even if he had desired it, from interference in the administration of other departments.   In the ministry of 1929, though the error of 1924 was not repeated, his interest in foreign affairs, and his desire to control Mr. Henderson as Foreign Secretary, was no doubt one of the causes of that estrangement between the two men which was so marked in 1931.[23]

Mr. Baldwin's ministries appear to reveal him as essentially a good Cabinet man, unwilling to intervene in the business of his colleagues, save to such extent as issues were inevitably brought before the Cabinet.   His tendency to trust his colleagues was marked most conspicuously in the acceptance by him and his Cabinet of the accord with M. Laval arrived at hastily and without proper consideration by Sir S. Hoare on a hurried visit to Paris in December, 1935.   It must have been patent on any serious consideration that the plan of action proposed, under which the Negus

---

[20] Nicolson, *Curzon: The Last Phase*, pp. 23, 56 ff.   [It should be noted that though the author here expresses a view frequently expressed then and since by other persons, Mr. Nicolson does not condemn Lloyd George in such sweeping terms for his interference in foreign affairs; indeed, he expressly denies that the Premier's interference was 'unwarrantable': *ibid.*, p. 59.—ED.]

[21] Austen Chamberlain, *Down the Years*, pp. 139 f.   [22] *Ibid.*, p. 142.

[23] See, however, Snowden, *Autobiography*, ii. 598.

would have been advised to make concessions to Italy, which must have formed a mere prelude to the complete control of that power over his dominions, was a definite breach of duty under the Covenant of the League. Its hasty repudiation under stress of public feeling showed Mr. Baldwin's sensitiveness to the will of the people, but the mischief had been done and could not be cured by Sir S. Hoare's retirement to save the face of the Government. Subsequently, Mr. Baldwin found a safer minister in Mr. Eden, but the advent of Mr. N. Chamberlain, bent on an accord with Italy at the expense of Ethiopia, led to the disappearance from the scene of the Foreign Secretary, and his replacement by Lord Halifax.[24]

From now on, and at least until the spring of 1939, British foreign policy remained under the control of one man, the Prime Minister. The Foreign Secretary, whatever his personal doubts or those of his Department, loyally followed his chief, while the latter gave his chief confidence in these matters to a permanent Civil Servant, Sir Horace Wilson.

Against these signs of the paramount importance of the Prime Minister there is little to set. The best known recent case of a Premier being overruled by a Cabinet majority on an issue of importance is that of Mr. Bonar Law on Mr. Baldwin's debt settlement with the United States.[25] Failing health, no doubt, explains why the Premier, convinced of the folly of a settlement on terms so onerous and so certain to be of grave disadvantage to European appeasement, determined to remain in office instead of throwing on Mr. Baldwin the onus of an action with which he so seriously disagreed.

It is clear, therefore, that the polite description of the Prime Minister as *primus inter pares*, which satisfied Lord Morley,[26] or the higher claim of Sir W. Harcourt[27] that he should rank as *inter stellas luna minores* is inadequate to describe the real position of the Prime Minister if by temperament he is willing to assert to the full the position which he can assert if he so desires.[28] The power of the Prime Minister grows, not diminishes, and this is inevitable when the sources whence it is derived are borne in mind. The root of the

---

24 February 20, 1938. The issue was debated on February 21 and 22.
25 Taylor, *Andrew Bonar Law*, pp. 270–272.   26 Morley, *Walpole*, p. 157.
27 Gardiner, *Life of Sir William Harcourt*, ii. 612.
28 Keith, *The King, the Constitution, the Empire and Foreign Affairs*, 1936–37, pp. 41 ff.

matter lies in the fact that since the Reform Act of 1832, the Prime Minister has become the choice of the electorate, and general elections have frequently been fought on personalities rather than on principles.   The reason for this lies in the fact that democracies find it easier and wiser to form judgments on men rather than on doctrines.   They feel, after a man has been before them in high office, that they can trust him or not to further the kind of views which will appeal to them, even when applied in novel settings. The Tamworth manifesto of 1834 in which Sir R. Peel appealed to the electors to support him in office which had been conferred on him by William IV., marks the beginning of the new epoch, and it was made absolutely clear by the election of 1857, when the issue was certainly nothing more or less than whether Lord Palmerston should be in power or not.[29]   In 1859, the contest was between Lord Derby and Mr. Disraeli in office and Lord Palmerston and Lord John Russell outside;[30] in 1865, Lord Palmerston's personality alone counted.[31]   Later the electors voted for Mr. Disraeli or Mr. Gladstone, and the addresses of these politicians to the electors in their own constituencies became palpably appeals to the nation.   Mr. Disraeli realised this in 1868 no less than Mr. Gladstone, in 1874, when he secured Cabinet approval for his chief projects and referred as a justification to Sir R. Peel's precedent.[32]   A further step was due to Mr. Gladstone himself, when no longer in name, though in reality, leader of the Liberal Party. His famous Midlothian campaign in 1879 against the policy of the government was successful in destroying the ministry, and the Opposition leaders were not slow to follow suit, even Lord Salisbury condescending to speak at public gatherings outside his constituency, a fact of which Mr. Gladstone reminded his sovereign when, in 1886, she called his attention to his allocutions to enthusiasts at such informal places as railway stations.[33]

Royal remonstrances could not stay an inevitable process.   The election of 1892 was carried for Mr. Gladstone by his personal appeal to many voters whose interest in Home Rule was negligible, a fact which helps to explain why in 1895 there was for once accord between Lord Rosebery and Sir W. Harcourt that the ministry should resign on the adverse vote on the cordite supply, and not

---

[29] Morley, *Gladstone*, i. 564.   [30] *Ibid.*, i. 622.   [31] Bell, *Palmerston*, ii. 414 ff.
[32] Morley, *Gladstone*, ii. 485–7; Guedalla, *The Queen and Mr. Gladstone*, i. 442.
[33] Morley, *Gladstone*, iii. 344.

ask for a fresh vote of confidence from the electorate.[34] The resounding Liberal victory of 1906 was much influenced by the loss of faith in Mr. Balfour engendered by the shifts and tactics of the years 1903–05, which placed him in an unfavourable light when contrasted with the simple downrightness of Sir H. Campbell-Bannerman, whose vast fund of acumen was little realised outside his immediate circle. It was in part the failure of Mr. Asquith in personal magnetism which left him with so poor a majority in 1910 as compared with that of 1905; respect for his substantial talents aroused none of the enthusiastic loyalty which assured Mr. Gladstone of strong support in Scotland. On the other hand, Mr. Lloyd George succeeded in conveying to the electors a firm belief in his rôle of victor in the World War; the vast majority of 1918 was a personal triumph. It took long for Mr. Baldwin to establish anything like a personal hold; the famous slogan of 'Safety First' definitely depressed his chances in 1929, and it was only six years later that his personality counted very definitely in the election of 1935. It may be noted also that the Labour and Liberal parties at that contest suffered gravely from lack of personality in their leaders, neither of whom was well known or appreciated outside narrow circles. No doubt this aspect may be exaggerated,[35] but it is safe to say that, having regard to the character of the electorate, especially since the establishment of full adult suffrage, personality plays a vitally important part in any election. It must be remembered that the Premier not merely sets the programme in his electoral address, which is therefore studied by all seriously interested in governmental problems. His voice is heard on the radio, he addresses vast gatherings of his constituents, and his speeches are reported at length. Between elections, interest is deliberately concentrated on him by the party press and organisations, and no by-election passes without his sending a cordial letter of support to a candidate, of whom he probably knows nothing, despite his assurance to the party that he is deserving of full support. His appeal, the electors know, is not really for support to the candidate as such, but for support to their chosen leader and a candidate who should stand without such endorsement could expect short shrift from the party followers.

---

34 Mr. Goschen, in 1895, attributed the Liberal debacle largely to the fact that it was not a Gladstonian election; *Letters of Queen Victoria*, 3 s., ii. 541 f.
35 The general election of 1945 is an outstanding example of the failure of a personal appeal and the triumph of a policy.

The Prime Minister's position is thus essentially bound up with the party system.   He is the head of the party, exercises a general control over it, and appoints the officials who exercise detailed control and handle the central funds thereof.   Without a party backing, the position of a Prime Minister is untenable.   Sir R. Peel split his party in 1845, and after his defeat in the following year his career was ended.   Mr. Lloyd George equally destroyed his party by the election of 1918, and in 1922 realised that with his party he had destroyed his own position.   Mr. R. MacDonald in 1931 betrayed, in the view of his party colleagues, the Labour Party, and nothing but the policy of Mr. Baldwin, who was willing to enjoy the substance without the form of power, and the general wish to maintain the appearance of non-party government, maintained him in office until 1935.   On the other hand, Mr. Gladstone recovered from the disaster of 1886 and regained power in 1892 because he had never left his position in the party.

(2) THE FUNCTIONS OF THE PRIME MINISTER

IT is clear that in modern conditions there is no possibility of the Prime Minister holding any other office with substantial duties, and the Ministers of the Crown Act, 1937, recognises this by giving him the salary of £10,000 a year as Prime Minister and First Lord of the Treasury.   Incidentally his office thus receives, as does the Cabinet, formal recognition of striking character, though the style was used by Lord Beaconsfield when he signed the treaty of Berlin, 1878, and precedence was conferred on the Prime Minister by royal warrant of 1905,[36] immediately after the Archbishop of York, while the Chequers Estate Act, 1917, provides for the use of Chequers by the incumbent of the office.   His unique position is further attested by the grant of a pension of £2,000 a year to ex-Prime Ministers.

Instances, therefore, of the tenure of other offices are largely of historic interest.   Sir R. Peel was Chancellor of the Exchequer in 1834–35.   Mr. Gladstone in 1873, when scandals in regard to the Post Office rendered it necessary to make changes in the ministry, took for a time the same office, thus starting a difficult controversy whether this action did not require re-election, though as he was also First Lord of the Treasury that claim was disputable.[37]   In

[36] Lee, *Edward VII.*, ii. 443 f.   [37] Morley, *Gladstone*, ii. 465 ff.

1880–82 he combined the tenure of both offices, and in 1923, when Mr. Baldwin became First Lord, he remained for a brief period also Chancellor. Though Mr. N. Chamberlain was Chancellor when he became Prime Minister in 1937, the burden of defending his impost on profits fell on Sir J. Simon, transferred from the Home Office to the Chancellorship.

Lord Salisbury, on the other hand, insisted in 1885–86, 1886–92, and 1895–1900 on holding the Foreign Office, and did not become First Lord, save for a brief period in 1886. From 1900 he was Lord Privy Seal. In 1885, in view of Lord Randolph Churchill's objections to serving under Sir Stafford Northcote as First Lord and leader in the Commons, the latter was translated to the Lords.[38] In 1886 Mr. W. H. Smith led the Commons as First Lord, as did Mr. Balfour in the ministry of 1895–1902. In 1924, however, Mr. MacDonald combined the Foreign Secretaryship and the office of First Lord,[39] a combination of offices which appears seriously to have overtaxed his strength. From 1940 to 1945 Mr. Churchill was also Minister of Defence; and though his second office carried with it no statutory duties and was supported by no department, it did symbolise an extremely active direction of the military side of the war effort and involved a constant work in addition to the normal duties of a Prime Minister. On forming his administration in 1951 Mr. Churchill again combined the offices of Prime Minister and Minister of Defence, this time with a department and statutory duties.

Apart from these exceptional cases the Premier's duties alone are onerous. They have been described thus by Mr. Gladstone.

'The Head of the British Government is not a Grand Vizier! He has no powers, properly so-called, over his colleagues: on the rare occasions when a Cabinet determines its course by the votes of its members, his vote counts only as one of theirs. But they are appointed and dismissed by the Sovereign on his advice. In a perfectly organised administration, such for example as was that of Sir Robert Peel in 1841–6, nothing of great importance is matured, or would even be projected, in any department without his personal cognisance; and any weighty business would commonly go to him before being submitted to the Cabinet. He reports to the Sovereign its proceedings, and he also has many audiences of the august occupant of the Throne.'[40]

[38] *Letters of Queen Victoria*, 2 s., iii. 663.   [39] Snowden, *Autobiography*, ii. 606.
[40] Gladstone, *Gleanings*, i. 242–243.

The Prime Minister, as we have seen, forms the Cabinet, and, as we shall see, can secure the removal of ministers in order to maintain Cabinet harmony.   He presides over its deliberations, and through the Secretariat supervises the punctual execution of Cabinet decisions.   He presides over the Defence Committee which has taken over the functions of the Committee of Imperial Defence,[41] and which has the vital function of preparing national defence.   In the Foreign Office business he is essentially concerned, and major issues in other departments should be brought to his notice, so that he may decide whether they should come before the Cabinet. Where departments differ in view he may decide, unless the dispute is so vital as to render Cabinet intervention desirable.   Questions of policy are discussed with those ministers immediately concerned, with a view to final decisions by Cabinet.   Major appointments of all kinds are made on his recommendation, and other appointments, which primarily appertain to the heads of the departments, are made with his concurrence.   For honours he recommends and approves departmental submissions to the King.

On all Cabinet matters he is the channel of communication with the King, and departmental ministers, though they have the right of direct communication with the Crown, keep him informed of matters of importance.

He has in the past, normally been the leader of the House of Commons, and as such, determines, subject to the guidance of the Cabinet, the vital question of priority in time, and the fate of private members' bills, which are often doomed to destruction, unless the ministry determines, as in the case of Mr. Herbert's measure to promote divorces,[42] to spare Government time.[43]   He is expected to answer questions on the business of the Commons, to reply to general interrogations not falling within the sphere of individual departments, and to intervene in debates of general importance, such as those on defence, foreign affairs, and domestic issues of prime character.   At the same time, as head of the party, he is concerned with all issues affecting its operations; he fosters promising young adherents and intervenes to prevent the development of fissures in its cohesion.

---

[41] Cmd. 6923–1946, §20.   [42] Matrimonial Causes Act, 1937.

[43] It should be noted, however, that Mr. Churchill ceased to lead the House after February, 1942, and Mr. Attlee appointed his Lord President to lead the House in 1945.   In 1951, again, Mr. Churchill refused the leadership.

He must also guide public opinion by receiving deputations and discussing issues, by public speeches at party conferences, and on other set occasions. He may occasionally appear at international conferences or meetings, as Lord Beaconsfield did at the Congress of Berlin, Mr. Lloyd George at the Peace Conference of Paris, Mr. Neville Chamberlain at the meetings in Germany preceding the Munich Agreement, and Mr. Churchill at several conferences of the 'Big Three' during the Second World War. He may receive foreign representatives, especially in a crisis. The Prime Minister also presides at the rare but important meetings of the Imperial Conference, when there is expected from him a declaration of the loyalty of the Commonwealth to the Crown and its attitude towards foreign affairs. He conducts relations in matters of Cabinet rank with the Dominions; an example of classical importance was afforded by the negotiations over the mode in which effect should be given to the abdication of King Edward VIII.[44]

Finally, it is to the Prime Minister that heads of departments turn in case of urgent emergency, where Cabinet sanction is normally needed, but where time forbids its being obtained. In such a case the Prime Minister has implied authority to decide, certain of homologation later by the Cabinet.[45]

In the execution of these duties, difficulties have most frequently arisen in the sphere of foreign affairs, because it will always be far from easy to adjust the necessary measure of independence of the minister and the control of the Prime Minister. No doubt the Cabinet must determine the broad lines of policy, but that leaves many important and urgent issues to be disposed of as they arise. In the history of Lord Palmerston's connection with the Foreign Office, friction with his chief was seldom long absent, and the position was aggravated, because the minister's views were in a broad sense Liberal, and were seldom shared by the Queen, who, with better reason, objected to his habit of action without her prior approval, and his tendency to interpret too freely the approval

---

[44] Described by Mr. Baldwin in the Commons, December 10, 1936, 318 *H. C. Deb.* 5 s., 2176–2186.

[45] Mr. Disraeli's purchase of Suez Canal shares was on his own initiative with royal approval, and he had hard work to persuade his Cabinet: *Letters of Queen Victoria*, 2 s., ii. 363, 427 f., 434; Fitzmaurice, *Granville*, ii. 157 f. For war-time examples of the same procedure see Spender, *Lord Oxford*, ii. 125.

that she might happen to have accorded to lines of action.[46]   Lord John Russell was urged to watch his proceedings, and freely amended his despatches, finally going to the extreme length of demanding that they should be submitted for his approval before going to the Queen, though this was not repeated later.[47]   He had, of course, the excellent excuse that otherwise he would be the recipient of vehement protests from his irate sovereign, prompted, no doubt, by Prince Albert.   But this drastic procedure did not prevent indiscretions, which ended Lord Palmerston's tenure of that office, as has been noted above.   After that the rule was rather close co-operation, and consultation on all matters of importance not too vital to demand Cabinet concurrence.   This is attested of Lord Aberdeen's Cabinet and of Lord Palmerston's ministries,[48] and Mr. Gladstone used to arrange matters with Lord Clarendon and then with Lord Granville, and finally with Lord Rosebery,[49] so that, when issues came before the Cabinet, they appeared in the almost incontrovertible form of policies agreed upon by the essential experts.   Lord Beaconsfield was less happy in the essential issue of the Russian attack on Turkey, for Lord Derby proved hard to handle, and the Prime Minister resorted to employment of an agent of his own behind his Foreign Secretary's back, while he was able to rely on royal aid to impress the Cabinet.   Lord Derby at last showed his resentment of being reduced to the status of an Under-Secretary by resignation, being replaced by the then more complaisant Lord Salisbury.[50]   Lord Salisbury, himself normally as Foreign Secretary, controlled foreign policy, but otherwise he deprecated undue interference by the Prime Minister.[51]   On the other hand he advocated that, so far as possible, the Foreign Secretary should settle issues with the Prime Minister and the Queen to the exclusion of the Cabinet.[52]

Lord Salisbury's view seems to have been followed in his own practice, at least in so far as he managed much business with the

---

46 Bell, *Palmerston*, i. 423, 434 ff., ii. 39.
47 One note to Baron Koller on the attack on Haynau caused particular offence and involved the intervention of the Prime Minister: *Letters of Queen Victoria*, 1 s., ii. 319 ff.
48 Argyll, *Autobiography*, i. 445.
49 Marquess of Crewe, *Lord Rosebery*, i. 277.
50 *Letters of Queen Victoria*, 2 s. ii. 583 ff.; Monypenny and Buckle, *Life of Disraeli* (1929 ed.), ii., p. 1119.
51 Lady Gwendolin Cecil, *Life of Salisbury*, iii. 313-4.
52 *Letters of Queen Victoria*, 3 s., i. 45, 48, 211.

approval of the sovereign alone. This tendency, followed by Mr. Balfour and his Foreign Secretary, who worked most harmoniously, was exemplified in the conversations with French military experts, which were approved in 1905 without formal Cabinet advice. They were renewed and extended to Belgium after the formation of the Liberal ministry by accord between the Prime Minister, Sir E. Grey, and Mr. Haldane, while Lord Ripon, who then spoke for the Foreign Office in the Lords, was duly informed.[53] It is easy to understand how this accord seemed at the time sufficient to give assent, and it must be remembered that from the outset the conversations were marked out as essentially technical, though it might certainly have occurred to the ministers concerned that the result of such conversations must be to convey to France the impression that the principle of co-operation in the event of a German attack on France was accepted as valid. It remains obscure why the other ministers were not given the means of knowing of these conversations. It has been suggested that this was a case of accidental oversight, but Mr. Asquith appears to have realised their existence in 1911, when he felt that they involved danger.[54] It must, however, be remembered that these were busy years, and that ministers often fail to study even the papers circulated to them. Mr. Spender is evidence for the ignorance of Lord Loreburn on matters with which every well-informed journalist was acquainted, and on the whole it may be deemed proper to hold that ministers were mainly ignorant, but that this ignorance was partly their own fault, especially in the case of those who attended meetings of the Committee of Imperial Defence. At any rate the searching investigation of defence issues, which was carried out in connection with the Imperial Conference meeting of 1911, and the visit of the Canadian Premier in 1912, led to fuller knowledge, and the Cabinet in the latter year properly secured from the French Government a formal agreement that the conversations imposed no obligation to aid on the British Government.[55] What is surprising and what shows the Cabinet in rather a foolish light, is the view that the situation could really be treated in this way. Moreover, France had in reliance on Britain, concentrated from 1912 her fleet mainly in the Mediterranean, with

[53] Viscount Grey, *Twenty-five Years* (1925 ed.), chap. vi.; Spender, *Campbell-Bannerman*, ii. 252 ff.; Halévy, *Histoire du Peuple Anglais*, Epilogue, ii. 184 ff.
[54] Spender, *Lord Oxford*, i. 179, 348 f. See also Grey's admission, *Twenty-five Years*, i. 86. [55] Grey, *Twenty-five Years*, i. 96 ff.

the obvious result that Britain must tacitly be deemed to have undertaken the defence of the French coast.[56] The Cabinet should plainly have faced the fact that its action must compel support of France in the event of attack. In 1914 the complementary step of conversations with Russian representatives received Cabinet approval, and once more the ministry should have faced frankly the implication of its action.[57]

In the ultimate issue this failure to appreciate the position proved damaging. In 1914, at the crisis between Austria and Serbia, followed by strained relations between Russia and Austria, which inevitably involved Germany and France, it was impossible for Sir E. Grey to give the necessary assurance to France or warning to Germany, and the issue fell to be decided only by the action of Germany in invading Belgium which brought all the Cabinet round to the necessity of war, with the exceptions only of Lord Morley and Mr. J. Burns.[58] Earlier Mr. Lloyd George and Sir J. Simon had been firm against intervention. The actual refusal on July 30, 1914, to accept the German terms for British neutrality was despatched by accord between the Prime Minister and Foreign Secretary, and approved immediately afterwards by the Cabinet;[59] the decision to send an ultimatum to Germany never came before the Cabinet;[60] but the ministers concerned acted in accordance with a policy which had been accepted by the Cabinet. The episode illustrates admirably the controlling power of the Cabinet. It is impossible to blame Sir E. Grey for his inability to deal more effectively with the crisis by making it clear that Britain must succour France. He had no authority thus to pledge his country, and he could not have obtained it prior to the violation of Belgian neutrality which affected a principle so dear to British diplomacy that Mr. Gladstone had been prepared in 1870 to intervene with armed force if France or Prussia had violated Belgian territory.[61] The *fons et origo mali* was the failure of the Cabinet earlier to grasp the implications of the situation and of

[56] Churchill, *World Crisis*, i. 112–113. For the agreements in 1913, see Halévy, *Histoire du Peuple Anglais*, Epilogue, ii. 594–598.

[57] Grey, *Twenty-five Years*, i. 285; 63 *H. C. Deb.* 5 s., 458; Halévy, *Histoire du Peuple Anglais*, Epilogue, ii. 598–603.

[58] Churchill, *World Crisis*, 203 ff.; Spender, *Lord Oxford*, ii. 86 ff.; *Twenty-five Years*, i. 308 ff.; ii. 1 ff.; Halévy, *Histoire du Peuple Anglais*, Epilogue, ii. 644 ff.

[59] Grey, *Twenty-five Years*, i. 327 ff.

[60] Churchill, *World Crisis*, i. p. 220; but Spender, *Lord Oxford*. ii. 92, suggests a Cabinet just before.

[61] Guedalla, *The Queen and Mr. Gladstone*, i. 248 ff.; Fitzmaurice, *Granville*, ii. 32 ff.

the inevitable consequences of the conversations they had approved without evidently understanding what they were doing.

War begun, control of foreign policy became bound up with military and naval operations and the heads of the Admiralty and War Office necessarily shared with the Foreign Secretary and the Prime Minister the burden of planning policy, which, as Sir E. Grey has often insisted, was vitally determined at every step by the success or failure of British arms and the actions of the allied powers. Even so, final control rested with the Cabinet, to which were submitted for confirmation the decisions reached by the ministers who came to act formally as a War Committee.[62] These discussions naturally caused delay, and, for good or evil, Mr. Lloyd George, in sympathy with Mr. Bonar Law, formed the conclusion that it was essential to constitute a Committee with wide executive authority. Mr. Lloyd George's aim undoubtedly was to secure the removal from immediate connection with the direction of the war of the Prime Minister whose capacity he doubted. The result was the resignation of Mr. Asquith, and the creation of the War Cabinet, which gave Mr. Lloyd George full scope. The Foreign Secretary was not included in that select body, and Mr. Lloyd George became supreme in foreign policy. The Armistice was followed by his period of negotiation at the Peace Conference; we are assured that he often consulted Lord Balfour,[63] but also that he did not deem it essential to do so, still less to obtain his concurrence for the line of action proposed. The fate of Lord Curzon after Lord Balfour's retirement was much worse, for, while Mr. Lloyd George had respect and liking for his late Foreign Secretary, he had no love for Lord Curzon, and his settlement at London and St. Remo of the principles of the abortive treaty of Sèvres was far from acceptable to the latter. The gravamen of the Foreign Secretary's complaint was unanswerable; he did not deny the right of decision of the Prime Minister, but he did deny the propriety of a system by which he maintained in his garden at 10, Downing Street, virtually a second Foreign Office, whose doings were communicated sporadically and partially to the Foreign Minister. It is difficult not to feel that in the circumstances the decision of Lord Curzon to countenance the revolt against the Prime Minister was excusable,

---

62 Cf. Spender, *Lord Oxford*, ii. 186 ff. ; Lloyd George, *War Memoirs*, ii. 973 ff. ; Churchill, *World Crisis*, ii. 393.

63 Dugdale, *Arthur James Balfour*, ii. 263 ff. For Balfour's views on the inevitability of friction, see p. 292.

even if his *modus operandi* was open to the accusation of bad faith.[64]

The fall of Mr. Lloyd George restored relations to normal, while in 1924, foreign policy remained in the hands of the Prime Minister. In the ministry of 1924–29 the position of Mr. A. Chamberlain was satisfactory, for the Prime Minister placed high confidence in him, especially after the success of Locarno which gave him the Garter, and the Foreign Secretary resumed a reasonable discretion, subject to consultation with the Prime Minister and the general control of the Cabinet.   The Prime Minister's control was decidedly increased in the Labour government of 1929–31, for Mr. MacDonald was anxious to resume his activities in the field of foreign affairs, and for this reason his relations with Mr. Henderson lacked cordiality and paved the way for their abrupt parting in 1931.   With Sir John Simon in office in the National government, the Foreign Secretary's position manifestly grew stronger, for the Prime Minister obviously continued to play that rôle, not by virtue of popular approval, but through the support of his Conservative and Liberal allies.   The change of Prime Minister in 1935 rather strengthened than otherwise the position of the Foreign Secretary, but the shock produced by the Hoare-Laval agreement, which necessitated the hasty resignation of the Foreign Secretary, could hardly have been possible if the Prime Minister had been sufficiently alert in supervising the Foreign Secretary's work.   It may, indeed, fairly be deduced from Mr. Baldwin's very unconvincing apologia that he had been permitting Sir S. Hoare too much freedom.[65]

On the other hand, Mr. Eden's policy appears to have been much more effectively dictated by the Cabinet, because his attitude in regard to the abandonment of sanctions was inconsistent with his past line of action, and was evidently dictated by a Cabinet decision which represented the views of Mr. N. Chamberlain, announced indeed in public prior to any indication by the Prime Minister of his determination to violate the obligations imposed on Britain by the League Covenant.[66]   The subsequent policy of the ministry of Mr. Chamberlain seems to have been more and more

[64] Ronaldshay, *Lord Curzon*, iii. 259 ff., 271 ff., 314 ff.; Dugdale, *Arthur James Balfour*, ii. 291 ff.; Nicolson, *Curzon: The Last Phase*, pp. 23 ff., 57 ff., 173, 213–214, 280.   For the merits and demerits of the secretariat in Council business, see Fitzroy, *Memoirs*, ii. 764 f.   [See *ante*, p. 60, n. 20.—Ed.]

[65] For a severe criticism of Mr. Baldwin, see Arnold J. Toynbee, *Survey of International Affairs*, 1935, ii. 314 ff.

[66] June 10, 1936; Toynbee, *op cit.*, ii. 443 ff.

determined by the Premier until, bowing to what Mr. Eden and Lord Cranbourne regarded as an ultimatum, Mr. Chamberlain determined to open negotations with Italy, and thus compelled Mr. Eden to resign on February 20, 1938.[67]

In regard to other departments of State the activity of the Prime Minister is mainly concerned with emergencies or with inter-departmental conflicts. The war crisis of 1914 necessitated immediate action to relieve the Bank of England from its obligations to pay cash under the Bank Charter Act, and following the precedents of 1847, 1857, and 1866, this took the form of an authority signed by the Prime Minister and the Chancellor of the Exchequer; this and other action was speedily legalised by the Legislature.[68] In these and other cases the Prime Minister acts with the full assent of the department and often at its request. It is a different thing to interfere without such request, though the Prime Minister has an obvious right to ask for and obtain whatever information he may wish from ministers, and to lay down for their guidance the class of papers which he desires to see.[69] But the danger of intervention was neatly shown when the Queen's anxiety to secure the Bombay command in the army in India for the Duke of Connaught, induced her to send a communication to the Viceroy through the then Prime Minister.[70] The Secretary of State, Lord R. Churchill, tendered his resignation, and only withdrew it when the Prime Minister explained that he only telegraphed because the Viceroy had not the Queen's cypher and that there was no intention of pressing him to make the appointment. In fact, on a rather thin excuse, it was refused.

The Prime Minister is on stronger grounds when one department appeals against the attitude of another, as when, in 1907, Mr. Haldane induced Sir Henry Campbell-Bannerman to insist on the submission to the Committee of Imperial Defence of a document which the Admiralty was unwilling to put before that body.[71] Clearly the Premier had in such a case not merely the right, but the duty to insist on the production of the paper. Mr. Lloyd

---

[67] Feiling, *Life of Neville Chamberlain*, p. 338; Winston Churchill, *The Second World War*, i. pp. 200, 206–7.
[68] Lloyd George, *War Memoirs*, i. 103 ff.
[69] Cf. Lord Palmerston's efforts to control Panmure: Bell, *Palmerston*, ii. 121–125.
[70] *Letters of Queen Victoria*, 2 s., iii. 689 f.; 703.
[71] Mr. Balfour's memo. on invasion; Esher, *Journals and Letters*, ii. 246 ff.; for his evidence, 316 ff.

George, in like manner, induced Mr. Asquith to arrange for the transfer to his care as Minister of Munitions of responsibility for the design of shells, which lay normally in the province of the War Office,[72] and in the same year, 1915, he himself tells us that he successfully intervened with Mr. Asquith to thwart the intention of the War Office to send home from Russia an officer whose reports were deemed too pessimistic.[73] Later in the war, in 1917, the Shipping Controller suggested that the Transport Department of the Admiralty should be transferred to him. He consulted the Prime Minister and, although the Admiralty objected to the change, the Shipping Controller had his way when the matter was referred to the War Cabinet.[74] On the other hand, according to Sir H. Wilson, the Prime Minister's attempt in 1921 to remove the officer commanding a home district who had dealt unsatisfactorily with a request for information was modified by the remonstrances of the Secretary of State for War.[75] In most cases, however, the influence of the Prime Minister, whether within or without the Cabinet, is devoted to conciliation and the effort to arrange a compromise.

During war, of course, the Prime Minister and the Cabinet are vitally concerned with the conduct of the war and the ministers in charge of the departments neither can nor do expect to be given a free hand. The question was discussed during the Crimean War how far the Prime Minister could push his views regarding the General to be employed in charge of the forces, but Lord Panmure proved extremely firm in the support he gave to General Simpson, nor was Lord Raglan recalled despite his very moderate capacity and his difficulties in co-operating with the French forces.[76] In the Great War difficulties were incessant, especially between Lord Kitchener and Mr. Lloyd George, with the Prime Minister keeping the peace,[77] and Mr. Lloyd George was so dissatisfied with Mr. Balfour's control of the Admiralty that he forced him to resign, and though he accepted his co-operation outside his War Cabinet, removed him to the Foreign Office.[78] Mr. Lloyd George was, until February, 1918, engaged in efforts to secure the acceptance of

---

[72] Rt. Hon. C. Addison, *Four and a Half Years*, i. 146 ff., 296–297; Spender, *Lord Oxford*, ii. 136 ff.
[73] Lloyd George, *War Memoirs*, i. 457. [74] *Ibid.*, iii. 1224–1226.
[75] Callwell, *Wilson*, ii. 285.
[76] Fitzmaurice, *Granville*, i. 114 ff. Lord Panmure increased the pay of the expeditionary force without Cabinet authority, but it was felt necessary to keep him in office: Bell, *Palmerston*, ii. 121 ff.
[77] Spender, *Lord Oxford*, ii. 139 f. [78] Dugdale, *Balfour*, ii. 182.

his ideas of how the war should be conducted as opposed to the objections of Sir W. Robertson, Chief of the Imperial General Staff, and Sir D. Haig.[79] The former he drove to resignation of that post, but the latter he dare not dismiss. Lord Derby throughout could play but a secondary part, and Mr. Balfour was charged only with a quite futile attempt to induce Sir W. Robertson to remain in an unsuitable post.[80] The difficulties of the conflict in these cases are inevitable, even if on this occasion they were aggravated by the temperament of the Prime Minister.

The resignation of Lord Fisher,[81] succeeded in forcing a coalition Government, which fatally delayed the possibility of saving the position at the Dardanelles by effective action, but the new First Lord on the removal of Mr. Churchill, was himself opposed to evacuation, and supported the idea of maintaining the position;[82] he did not, however, attempt to influence the Sea Lords to accept the advice of Admiral Wemyss to use the naval force to penetrate the Dardanelles and save the situation. The Cabinet also concurred, and a decision to evacuate was taken, which is probably open to the condemnation of it made by Mr. Churchill.[83] It seems clear that the decision of Mr. Balfour to replace Sir J. Jackson at the close of 1916, just before the formation of the new coalition, was one pressed by the Prime Minister.[84] His own preference seems to have been for asking Sir J. Jellicoe to accept a special office in the Admiralty for work against submarine attack. The case is of interest, because Sir E. Grey was moved by the success of the submarines to suggest to Mr. Balfour, despite his reluctance to express views on other ministers' departments, the grave importance of a more effective counter-campaign on the submarine.[85] No doubt the desirability of placing in the ministry a First Lord of great determination was the motive for Mr. Balfour's supersession, but Sir E. Carson was certainly not a success in the task.

The limited information at present available suggests that, during the Second World War, major disputes between Ministers,

---

79 Sir W. Robertson, *Soldiers and Statesmen*, i. chap. iv., vii.; ii. chap. xiii.
80 Dugdale, *Balfour*, ii. 239 f.; Duff Cooper, *Haig*, ii. 223 ff.
81 Churchill, *World Crisis, 1915*, pp. 358–365. Lord Fisher refused to obey the written order of the Prime Minister in the name of the King to resume duty which he threw up at a moment's notice, and was even less willing to serve under Mr. Balfour: Spender, *Lord Oxford*, ii. 164, n. 1: Oxford, *Memories and Reflections*, ii. 90–94.
82 Dugdale, *Balfour*, ii. 153–155.   83 Churchill, *World Crisis*, 1915, pp. 503–505.
84 Dugdale, *Balfour*, ii. 163–165.   85 *Ibid.*, ii. 163.

or between Ministers and Service advisers on the higher direction of the war, were avoided. This was achieved partly, from May, 1940 onwards, by the assumption by the Prime Minister of the office of Minister of Defence. The Service Ministers were not included in the War Cabinet and 'rapidly and almost imperceptibly ceased to be responsible for the formulation of strategic plans and the day-to-day conduct of operations.'[86] Secondly, the already highly organised Chiefs of Staff Committee, with its sub-committees, was placed under the direction of the Prime Minister. By the testimony both of the Prime Minister, and of those who served with him, this committee—and the Defence Committee—provided an adequate and ever ready means for that pooling of ideas, of information and of differences of opinion which necessarily preceded the adoption of an agreed policy for the strategic conduct of the war.[87]

It remains to note a very curious incident, which shows Lord Salisbury not unwilling to shelter behind actions of a colleague, which he had been informed of in advance, and which he had in substance sanctioned.[88] The attempt of Lord Carnarvon, in substantial degree successful, to establish a working arrangement between Mr. Parnell and the Conservatives could not finally be homologated by his chief, and, when the matter leaked out, Lord Salisbury's account of it to the Queen can only be described as disingenuous.[89] The truth, of course, was that as the matter had not succeeded, though it gave the Conservatives a good many Irish votes at the general election, Lord Salisbury was only too anxious to conceal from the Queen actions which he would not have ventured to ask her to approve in advance, knowing as he did her bitter dislike of Mr. Parnell. It is more easy to admire Lord Salisbury's skill than his sense of candour or fairness to a colleague.[90]

3. THE REMOVAL OF MINISTERS

MINISTERS, as we have seen, are appointed by the King on the advice of the Premier, and they can be removed on like advice,

---

[86] Churchill, *The Second World War*, ii. 15–16.
[87] *Ibid.*, Gen. Sir L. Hollis, *R.U.S.I. Journal*, November, 1950; 378 *H. C. Deb.* 5 s., 40–42; *ibid.*, 379, 5 s., 796.
[88] Gladstone, *After Thirty Years*, pp. 387–423.
[89] *Letters of Queen Victoria*, 3 s., i. 147.
[90] For an apologia, see Lady G. Cecil, *Life of Salisbury*, iii. 147–164.

unless, of course, the Crown is prepared to refuse assent and to find a ministry to replace that existing. Removal, of course, is always a strong step. It is seldom that a minister has not some following in the Commons, some support in the Cabinet itself, some popularity outside the House. Removal, therefore, indicates defective judgment in placing the minister in office, or suggests error of policy on the part of the Premier. These considerations explain abundantly the fact that ministers of very poor calibre may remain in office long after it would seem desirable that they should be honourably retired with, if need be, a peerage to soften the blow. An alternative to removal is transfer to another office.

Technically, formal dismissal is hardly known, since Pitt gave the King the choice between him and Thurlow in 1792. It could take place only on the advice and responsibility of the Premier. Queen Victoria, according to Prince Albert, had contemplated in the controversy in 1851 dismissing Lord Palmerston on her own initiative, but shrank from using the power of the Crown, as her action would have been criticised without the possibility of making a public defence.[91] Patently such action would have been wholly unconstitutional; her right was to urge action on her Prime Minister. On the other hand there is little doubt of the right of the Premier to ask a colleague to resign, and it is undignified of a minister to hesitate to resign if asked. The minister can sometimes take his revenge by opposition in the Commons.

The powers of the Premier, and the dangers of their use, are illustrated in the classic case of Lord Palmerston. Queen Victoria disliked from 1848 the Liberalism of his policy, as well as his methods of giving effect to it, and she would gladly have seen him in another office. She complained of his sending despatches before she had seen them, and of his departing from policies which she had approved. But Lord Palmerston refused to leave his office, except by resignation, based on a request by the Queen or the Cabinet, and Lord John Russell was too dependent on his subordinate's support in the House of Commons to be able to press for resignation, especially after Palmerston's great Parliamentary success in vindicating his action in the Don Pacifico affair.[92] All

91 *Letters of Queen Victoria*, 1 s., ii. 416, n.
92 *Ibid.*, 1 s., ii. 289–290, 309–312, 313–314; Bell, *Palmerston*, ii. 29 ff.

that could be done was for the Queen to lay down principles for Palmerston's guidance, which he duly accepted :[93]

> 'She requires: (1) that he will distinctly state what he proposes in a given case, in order that the Queen may know as distinctly to *what* she has given her royal sanction; (2) having *once given* her sanction to a measure, that it be not arbitrarily altered or modified by the Minister; such an act she must consider as failing in sincerity towards the Crown, and justly to be visited by the exercise of her constitutional right of dismissing that Minister.   She expects to be kept informed of what passes between him and the Foreign Ministers before important decisions are taken, based upon that intercourse; to receive the Foreign Despatches in good time, and to have the drafts for her approval sent to her in sufficient time to make herself acquainted with their contents before they must be sent off.'

In 1851 Lord Palmerston offended seriously by his desire to receive Kossuth on his arrival in exile, and yielded not to the Premier's request, but to the decision of the Cabinet.[94]   He followed this up by receiving deputations, whose addresses, with more accuracy than courtesy, described the Emperors of Russia and Austria as 'odious and detestable assassins,' but not even this moved the Cabinet to action.[95]   But Lord Palmerston betrayed himself to his enemies by his rashness in expressing to the French Ambassador approval of Louis Napoleon's *coup d'état* after the Queen had urged, and the Cabinet had decided on, an attitude of neutrality on the issue.   Even then Lord John Russell, while informing the offender—whose evil deed had been revealed officially in a despatch from the British Ambassador at Paris, who had learned of his indiscretion when he communicated the official attitude on Lord Palmerston's instructions to the French Government—that the conduct of foreign affairs could no longer be left in his hands with advantage to the country, softened the blow by offering the Lord Lieutenancy of Ireland with a British peerage if desired.   Lord Palmerston preferred resignation, duly accepted by the Queen on the Premier's advice, while the Cabinet also approved his action.[96]   Lord Palmerston, of course, defended his

---

[93] *Letters of Queen Victoria*, 1 s., ii. 315.   This was suggested (March 12, 1850) by Baron Stockmar (*ibid.*, 282).

[94] *Letters of Queen Victoria*, s. 1, ii. 392; Spencer Walpole, *Life of Lord John Russell*, ii. 134 ff.

[95] *Letters of Queen Victoria*, 1 s., ii. 394 ff.; Spencer Walpole, *Life of Lord John Russell*, ii. 137.

[96] *Letters of Queen Victoria*, 1 s., ii. 412 ff.

action in the Commons, while admitting the right of the Premier to ask for his resignation.[97] But his revenge on Lord John Russell was not long delayed, for in 1852 he brought down the ministry on the issue of the militia bill.

The precedent was not such as to encourage imitation. Mr. Gladstone had no love for Mr. Ayrton, but in 1872 he explained to the Queen, who had suggested removal two years earlier, that it was necessary to make out a case intelligible to the public for removing him.[98] Action was delayed until 1873, when the occurrence of irregularities in the post office business caused Mr. Gladstone to transfer Mr. Lowe from the Exchequer to the Home Office, and to make Mr. Ayrton Judge Advocate-General, while the resignation of Mr. Monsell was simply accepted.[1] Mr. Gladstone also solved the problem of the unpopularity of Mr. Bruce as Home Secretary by making him Lord President of the Council, while in 1867 Mr. Walpole was induced to resign without being formally removed from the Cabinet. Mr. Disraeli, however, in 1875 found that the removal of Sir C. Adderley from the Board of Trade, and the consequent rearrangement of offices, would be too difficult, and dropped the project.[2] In 1884, Mr. Gladstone wished to remove Lord Carlingford from the office of Lord Privy Seal in order to make room for Lord Rosebery. Although Lord Carlingford did resign at the end of the year, he was at first reluctant to surrender his office and Mr. Gladstone was, at that point, dubious as to the propriety of carrying the matter further. Writing later about this, Sir William Harcourt reported that Mr. Gladstone entertained 'great doubts as to the right of a Prime Minister to require a Cabinet Minister to resign. I know that he tried it in one case for convenience of reconstruction: he was point blank refused, and acquiesced.'[3]

One episode akin to dismissal is famous for its tragic sequel. In 1886 the resignation of Lord Randolph Churchill, as a result of the refusal of the Cabinet to support his objections to the estimates, resulted in Lord Salisbury's determination to place Mr. Goschen in

97 119 *H. C. Deb.* 3 s., 112.
98 *Letters of Queen Victoria*, 2 s., ii. 225; Guedalla, *The Queen and Mr. Gladstone*, i. 229–230.
1 *Letters of Queen Victoria*, 2 s., ii. 270–276; Guedalla, *The Queen and Mr. Gladstone*, i. 420–426.
2 W. S. Childe-Pemberton, *Life of Lord Norton*, p. 222.
3 Gardiner, *Life of Sir William Harcourt*, i. 508, ii. 610,

the office of Chancellor of the Exchequer. Mr. Goschen objected to Lord Iddesleigh remaining at the Foreign Office, and Lord Salisbury decided to assume that department himself, arguing that it was necessary to leave the post of First Lord of the Treasury vacant for Mr. W. H. Smith, as leader of the Commons. Lord Iddesleigh then learned from the press of his supersession, and his death shortly after could not be disconnected from his unfortunate treatment.[4] Lord Salisbury shrank from dismissing his Home Secretary, Mr. Matthews, in 1890, and the matter was decorously settled by the grant of a peerage. Writing of this episode to the Queen, Lord Salisbury said :

> 'At present Lord Salisbury does not think that a bare dismissal would be admissible. It would be looked upon as very harsh and would beget numberless intrigues. . . . There is no instance of dismissal; and it would require some open and palpable error to justify it.'[5]

Mr. Balfour was confronted in 1903 with a greater difficulty, for he was anxious to rid himself of his free trade colleagues, and they were by no means eager to leave office if they could be assured that the Prime Minister did not intend to yield to the demands of Mr. Chamberlain. Eventually, and by a trick, Balfour allowed them to resign office in ignorance of the fact that Mr. Chamberlain had already resigned. On this occasion Lord George Hamilton, himself one of the sufferers, commented:

> 'A Prime Minister has an undoubted right to request any of his colleagues, whose presence in his Cabinet is, in his opinion or judgment, prejudicial to the efficiency or policy of the Government, to resign his office.'[6]

In 1911 it was thought desirable that the Admiralty should accept reforms modelled on those already undertaken at the War Office by Mr. Haldane, and Mr. McKenna, the First Lord, stood firmly in support of his Admirals in opposition to this scheme. Some change was necessary, despite Mr. McKenna's important work at the Admiralty, but the replacement of him by Mr. Haldane would have appeared to be like a vote of censure. Therefore

---

[4] Lady Gwendolin Cecil, *Life of Lord Salisbury*, iii. 339 ff.; Esher, *Journal and Letters*, i. 134–135.
[5] *Letters of Queen Victoria*, 3 s., i. 646.
[6] Bernard Holland, *Life of the Duke of Devonshire*, ii. 351 ff.; Fitzroy, *Memoirs*, i. 149–158; Dugdale, *Arthur James Balfour*, i. 355 ff.

Mr. Churchill was moved to the Admiralty and Mr. McKenna took his place at the Home Office.[7]

One instance, in 1922, is interesting because of the case of the word 'dismissal' in connection with it. The Khalifat Committee in India asserted that Britain proposed to furnish further aid to Greece against Turkey and, to counter this, the Viceroy asked leave to publish a declaration indicating sympathy with Turkish aspirations. Mr. Montague, then Secretary of State for India, gave permission without consulting the Cabinet, and publication took place on March 4, 1922. Lord Curzon, the Foreign Secretary, was enraged and, on this occasion, was supported by the Prime Minister. Writing to Lord Curzon, Mr. Lloyd George commented that 'The dismissal of Montague will make an undoubted impression both in Paris and Angora.'[8] In form, Mr. Montagu resigned.

From the time of his appointment as Prime Minister in May, 1937, Mr. Neville Chamberlain was in disagreement with his Foreign Secretary, Mr. Eden, over the policy of appeasement. Finally, in February, 1938, Mr. Eden resigned, giving differences of opinion about the negotiations with Italy as his reason. Mr. Chamberlain's biographer, however, tells us that this resignation was preceded by action on the Prime Minister's part which made it clear to the Cabinet that the alternative might be his own resignation from office.[9]

In January, 1940, Mr. Hore-Belisha resigned from his post as Secretary of State for War. Although this was formally a resignation, it is clear that the Prime Minister initiated the move, covering it with an offer of the Board of Trade, which Mr. Hore-Belisha felt unable to accept. On that occasion Mr. Hore-Belisha gave it as his view that:

> 'A Prime Minister is free, in the exercise of his impartial judgment, to make what appointments may seem good to him.'

Mr. Chamberlain claimed that,

> 'Every Prime Minister must from time to time review the allocation of offices among his various colleagues and consider whether that allocation still remains the best that can be effected.'[10]

---

[7] Churchill, *World Crisis*, i. 59 ff., 82 ff.; Fitzroy, *Memoirs*, ii. 466; Spender, *Lord Oxford*, i. 346.   [8] Nicolson, *Curzon: The Last Phase*, p. 268 n.
[9] K. G. Feiling, *Life of Neville Chamberlain*, p. 338.
[10] 356 *H. C. Deb.* 5 s., 32–35.

It has been stated that, during the course of the Labour administration formed in 1945, Mr. Attlee has exercised a clear power of dismissal.[11] Whether this is so, or not, it is difficult to say. In September, 1947, on rearranging the government, Mr. Attlee wrote of his 'distasteful' duty in asking Mr. Greenwood, one of his senior colleagues, to retire on grounds of age.[12] In May, 1949, four Parliamentary Private Secretaries were asked to resign their offices because they had voted against the Government on the Committee stage of the Ireland Bill, a fifth having resigned already in anticipation of such action.[13] If it be claimed that the dismissal of junior ministers is hardly a case in point, then it must be remembered that collective responsibility has usually been considered to be less binding on junior ministers than on their senior colleagues. Whether, however, the power of dismissal is increasing with increased party discipline and the concentration of power at the top, it is as yet too early to say.

Normally, the time when Ministers can be changed is on the coming into being of a new Government. Mr. Asquith, when he succeeded Sir Henry Campbell-Bannerman, in 1908, was able to remove Lord Elgin and to transfer Lord Tweedmouth from the Admiralty.[14] Mr. Baldwin took advantage of his accession to power in 1935 to make changes in his ministry, including the supersession of Lord Londonderry and of Lord Sankey. In 1937 Mr. MacDonald, Mr. Runciman and Lord Monsell resigned. Such changes, of course, are not to be compared with those which almost inevitably take place on the formation of a coalition government, when the sharing of places is a problem of some magnitude.

On the subject of dismissal, therefore, the conclusion would seem to be that the Prime Minister is entitled to ask a colleague to resign or to accept another office, and that only so can the Prime Minister's control of his Cabinet be maintained. Normally there is no need to use the Crown's power of dismissal, although it is theoretically possible for the Prime Minister to advise the King to dismiss a difficult minister.

> 'Under all ordinary circumstances,' Sir Robert Peel said, 'if there were a serious difference of opinion between the Prime Minister and one of his colleagues, and that difference could

---

11 Francis Williams, *The Triple Challenge*, p. 61.
12 *The Times*, September 30, 1947.
13 *The Times*, May 19, 1949.   14 Spender, *Lord Oxford*, i. 198.

not be reconciled by an amicable understanding, the result would be the retirement of the colleague, not of the Prime Minister.'[15]

The proper form for resignation by a minister is clearly an intimation to the Prime Minister, who then submits it for royal acceptance. Only then is publication proper. The Crown, of course, has no real power to refuse to accept a resignation, as opposed to the right to dissuade it, which it has at times employed. In 1855 the Aberdeen ministry, on the defection of Lord J. Russell, was anxious to resign, but the Queen protested against their proposal, and on reconsideration they stayed until actually defeated in the Commons on Mr. Roebuck's motion for an enquiry into the conduct of the war.[16] In 1866 she endeavoured to prevent the resignation of Lord Russell's ministry, but in vain.[17]

---

15 *Report from the Select Committee on Official Salaries* (1850), p. 36.
16 *Letters of Queen Victoria*, 1 s., iii. 90 ff. Lord John sent to the Queen a copy of his request to the Premier to submit his resignation.
17 Guedalla, *The Queen and Mr. Gladstone*, i. 43.

CHAPTER 4

THE WORKING OF THE CABINET SYSTEM

1. The Functions of the Cabinet

The Cabinet is historically a body of Privy Councillors, who possess the particular 'confidence' of the King. By modern usage that confidence is due to the fact that they enjoy the support of the major portion of the House of Commons, and thus for a time at least of the major portion of the electorate. The great majority of the members are necessarily the heads of the administrative departments, though ministers with portfolios of no great complexity, or even without portfolio, may be included for the sake of their advice, and their ability to find time easily to serve on Cabinet committees. Common to all members is the fact that they have been duly sworn of the Privy Council, pledging themselves to faithful service and secrecy on Cabinet business. There is no other condition for membership of the Cabinet than membership of the Council, and the invitation of the Prime Minister, but the King is, as a matter of course, informed of the decision of the latter to add to his Cabinet. Mention has already been made of the fact that the list of offices which are normally held by members of the Cabinet, has been in some degree stereotyped by the Ministers of the Crown Act, 1937, but there is still no binding rule to compel a Cabinet thus to be constituted.

The size of the Cabinet is determined by the function of government, and the Cabinet has thus grown with the incursion of government into many new fields. Sir R. Peel in 1841 was content with thirteen members, Mr. Disraeli in 1874 tried as few as twelve. But the reduction did not avoid ill-luck, for Sir C. Adderley, the President of the Board of Trade, had a Merchant Shipping Bill to carry, and, largely no doubt because he was not in the Cabinet, he failed to secure its support for the measure which had to be dropped. [1]

[1] Childe-Pemberton, *Life of Lord Norton*, p. 220. Mr. Disraeli would have liked to dismiss him (p. 222).

It is probably true to say that Peel's cabinet of thirteen was the smallest possible, consistent with efficiency, at that time. Since then the Cabinet has tended steadily to grow, until recent times. The principle is clear that any department which has not a representative in the Cabinet is likely to be denied a fair consideration, not from any inherent defect of the members of the Cabinet, but for the simple reason that intimate knowledge of any subject is necessary if its claims to the consideration of the Cabinet and Parliament are to receive full recognition. On the other hand, there may come a time when, with the increase of the functions of the State, the number of new ministers produces a Cabinet of unwieldly size. At that point it may be advisable for the sake of efficiency, to divide ministers into those inside, and those who are outside the Cabinet. Such a situation was within sight before 1939, when the Cabinet consisted normally of twenty-one or twenty-two members. The further growth of departments during the Second World War, with a consequent increase in the number of ministers, has meant, since the end of the war, that about a dozen ministers have normally been excluded from the Cabinet. This subject will be referred to again later in a discussion of Cabinet reform.

In the selection of ministers the Prime Minister must have regard to many considerations, including skill in debate, as not less important than administrative capacity, while popularity cannot be ignored, and ability to get on with colleagues and members of Parliament alike counts. These considerations must be borne in mind when the apparent deficiency of a Cabinet in the qualities best suited for the functions which it must perform is criticised. Premiers often doubtless recognise the deficiencies of their colleagues, but feel that they can do no better under the conditions.

An authoritative statement of the functions of the Cabinet was given by the Machinery of Government Committee, 1918.[2] They comprise (a) the final determination of the policy to be submitted to Parliament; (b) the supreme control of the national executive in accordance with the policy prescribed by Parliament; and (c) the continuous co-ordination and delimitation of the authorities of the several departments of State. A profound change has taken place since the first third of the nineteenth century, for legislation is now incumbent on any ministry as its mode of meeting public sentiment,

2 Cmd. 9230, p. 5.

and a ministry which, like that of Mr. Balfour, in 1905, has no serious legislative programme to propose, feels itself unfitted to face the electorate.[3] Administration, of course, is also of fundamental importance, and the Cabinet has fuller control over the departments than over Parliament. In legislation, however, its control over the members of the ministry is complete, for no Bill can be promoted, except with its sanction, and the Legislation Committee or, as it has sometimes been called, the Home Affairs Committee of the Cabinet, has the duty of considering at the commencement of each session what Bills the ministry is to bring forward, for there are always more available under present conditions than can ever be carried in one session through the Houses, and there is an honourable and natural rivalry between ministers to secure the opportunity for publicity and public favour won by successful handling in Parliament of a great enactment.

All matters of importance in the administrative sphere, including, of course, departmental reorganisaton, such as the momentous reconstitution in 1904 of the War Office and the less important readjustment of the Air Ministry in 1938, as a result of the report of the Cadman Committee, should be brought before the Cabinet as a matter of loyalty, and the Cabinet has just ground for dissatisfaction if this rule is ignored. The rule is equally binding on the Premier himself, and it is patently unfair to his colleagues if he commits them without prior consultation, for he thus confronts them with the unpleasant alternatives of accepting action which they would not have approved, had they been permitted an option, or of having to resign office with their chief. Few instances of disregard of this obligation of honour are formally recorded. Lord John Russell, however, committed his Government to legislation against the assumption of territorial titles by the Roman Catholic hierarchy in 1850, so that they had to acquiesce in the passage of an Act, which proved quite useless, though it had royal approbation.[4] Mr. Disraeli occasionally accepted amendments of substance without asking Cabinet accord, and Mr. Gladstone, in accepting a motion for a committee of enquiry on the negotiations with Mr. Parnell in 1882, disregarded a Cabinet decision, for which error he

---

[3] Dugdale, *Balfour*, i. 428 ff., suggests that Mr. Balfour thought resignation rather than dissolution was technically sound in these circumstances.
[4] Bell, *Palmerston*, ii. 34 ff.; Gooch, *Later Correspondence of Lord John Russell*, i. 223–33.

offered the excuse that he was carried away by a fit of temper.[5]
Much more important was the action of Sir H. Campbell-Bannerman, who deliberately threw overboard the elaborately safeguarded
concessions to trade unions in the matter of legal liability worked
out by his Government, and gave them the immunity of the Act of
1906, and it was he who allowed domestic servants to be included
in the scheme of workmen's compensation.[6] Mr. Lloyd George,
however, went further; his famous decision to summon an Imperial
War Conference in 1916 was taken after consultation with the
Secretary of State for the Colonies, and announced to Parliament
before it was reported by him to the War Cabinet, which had to
make the best of the business by accepting a series of meetings of the
War Cabinet, augmented by Dominion representatives.[7] It has
sometimes been supposed that Mr. Baldwin in 1923 appealed to the
country on tariff reform without first consulting the Cabinet. It is
probable, however, that although Mr. Baldwin forced his Cabinet
to consider tariff reform, the appeal to the country was made with
a divided and not an ignorant Cabinet.[8]

It is clear that the ex-Premier may in effect by pre-election
declarations seriously affect the freedom of action of the ministry
subsequently formed, and that these declarations may be made
without the benefit of consultation with colleagues. Similarly, by
statements in opposition, a leader may virtually bind himself and
his party to a line of action which he has not submitted for the
assent of his colleagues. Neither the disestablishment of the Irish
Church nor the project of Home Rule for Ireland were submitted
for approval by Mr. Gladstone to the ex-members of the Cabinet.
With modern development of the idea of the ex-ministers forming
a Shadow Cabinet when in opposition, there is, perhaps, less room
for the taking by the ex-Prime Minister of an individual line of
policy. What, however, is clear is that fairness and loyalty to
colleagues do make it desirable that great political projects should
be fully discussed with them all before responsibility for them is
assumed by the former Premier.

It is true that certain issues, despite their importance, cannot
consistently be brought before the Cabinet, because matters are

---

5 Gwynn and Tuckwell, *Life of Sir Charles Dilke*, i. 489.
6 Spender, *Life of Sir Henry Campbell-Bannerman*, ii. 278, 280.
7 Lloyd George, *War Memoirs*, iv. 1731–1735.
8 Feiling, *Life of Neville Chamberlain*, pp. 108 ff.

urgent. This point is especially applicable to foreign affairs, but the Cabinet is given the possibility of constant criticism by the rule of circulation of the important despatches, both in and out. The practice is of ancient lineage, and its propriety is beyond dispute, though it is, of course, no excuse for the failure of the minister to bring matters deliberately before his colleagues. We have seen Lord Palmerston's reluctance to discuss issues with the Cabinet, as with the Queen and Premier, and Lord Salisbury was quite clear that business should be disposed of with the Queen and Prime Minister without Cabinet intervention, but he admitted in 1887 the necessity of discussion if members of the Cabinet noted any point of a telegram on the Bulgarian issue on which the Queen had strong personal views.[9]   Lord Rosebery offended Sir W. Harcourt deeply, by marking as not to be printed for circulation, a decision which extended British commitments in Uganda[10]; the imperialistic character of his action naturally raised as much wrath as the *modus operandi*, which was declared to amount to a setting aside of the decision of the Prime Minister and the Cabinet. It is not, however, at all clear that so firm a view is justified. It is also doubtful if Sir W. Harcourt was just in reproaching Lord Rosebery, as Prime Minister, with refusing to call a Cabinet at his request, and that of the Foreign Secretary to discuss the issues between Britain and Nicaragua.[11]   Much more serious is the accusation of Mr. Lloyd George that from 1906 to 1914 there was a reticence and secrecy that shut out three-fourths of the Cabinet from the chance of making any genuine contribution to the discussion of foreign politics.[12]   The fact probably is that Sir E. Grey did not welcome incursions into the field of foreign politics by those who were not careful students of these issues. Of deliberate concealment it seems impossible to talk, having regard to the circulation of papers, and Mr. Lloyd George admits that questions were answered with civility if not encouraged.

From the scope of Cabinet decisions certain matters are excluded by custom, for reasons of differing character and importance.

(1) One of these is the annual budget statement. This includes the proposals of new taxation, and accordingly it has been usual

9 *Letters of Queen Victoria*, 3 s., i. 211.
10 Gardiner, *Life of Sir William Harcourt*, ii. 315 f.
11 *Ibid.*, ii. 331 f.; but see Crewe, *Rosebery*, ii. 450.
12 Lloyd George, *War Memoirs*, i. 46 ff.

to restrict disclosure to the Cabinet to an oral statement made shortly before actual presentation. In 1936, despite the secrecy so carefully preserved, a tribunal of enquiry found that there had been disclosure by the Colonial Secretary, Mr. Thomas, to another member of Parliament, Sir A. Butt, both of whom resigned from the Commons as the result. The enquiry also disclosed that the Chancellor's budget proposals are not circulated to the Cabinet, but are announced orally a few days before the Budget speech in the House of Commons. The announcement to the Cabinet usually takes place four or five days before that to the Commons, but it may be longer.[13] There are clear disadvantages in this procedure, necessary though it may be in the interests of secrecy, in so far as the Chancellor is allowed to prepare his plans without the valuable aid which is naturally provided by examination by a committee of the Cabinet. These objections were shown to be very real in the case of Mr. N. Chamberlain's budget in 1937, when he proposed a National Defence Contribution to be based on the rate of expansion of profits arising from rearmament contracts.[14] The result was that the scheme was vitally remodelled, after the new Chanellor, Sir J. Simon, who took the office on Mr. Chamberlain's appointment as Premier, had been allowed in an able speech (May 31) to prove that it was both inherently admirable and workable. In any case, this practice is determined by convenience and therefore may vary at the Cabinet's discretion. In 1860 the Cabinet asked for details of Mr. Gladstone's Budget a month before it was announced, although, in the end, Mr. Gladstone was able to give them only a week.[15] In the case of estimates, on the other hand, the Cabinet is well accustomed to settling disputes, especially those raised by the demands of the defence departments. It was as a result of Cabinet disputes on the estimates that Lord Randolph Churchill resigned in 1886,[16] and Mr. Gladstone in 1894.[17] At the risk of the resignation of the Chancellor of the Exchequer the Cabinet can, of course, overthrow a Budget altogether, or modify some of its terms after they have been made public in deference to Parliamentary or public opinion.

---

13 *Budget Disclosure Enquiry* (1936), *Minutes of Evidence,* p. 25.
14 Feiling, *Life of Neville Chamberlain,* p. 292.
15 Guedalla, *Gladstone and Palmerston,* p. 162.
16 *Letters of Queen Victoria,* 3 s. i. 229; Esher, *Journals and Letters,* i. 131
17 Morley, *Gladstone,* iii. 506 ff.

(2) The Cabinet again does not normally consider issues of the exercise of the prerogative of mercy.[18] It is felt that sound administration demands that the issue should be dealt with deliberately and in the fullest sense of final responsibility by the Home Secretary, and that any effort to weaken this responsibility is to be deprecated.   This does not exclude occasional consideration of cases which raise questions of public feeling of unusual character. When Sir R. Casement was found guilty of treason by inciting Irish prisoners of war to join the German forces, there were various considerations which rendered full Cabinet consideration desirable.[19] There have been other cases in which it is believed that the Cabinet has been consulted. But the general principle is quite clear.

(3) Similar considerations apply in general to criminal prosecutions which, so far as the State intervenes, are under the normal control of the Attorney-General, whose subordinate is the Director of Public Prosecutions. It is clearly desirable that these officers should proceed regularly with full personal responsibility. But it cannot be held that the Cabinet is precluded from decision, for instance, in respect of the policy of prosecution for sedition or incitement to mutiny. The necessity of upholding the law is plain, but the law of sedition is of venerable antiquity and covers many acts which may be of minor importance, nor is it desirable to repress minor actions which may be capable of being held to be seditious. None-the-less it is undesirable that the Cabinet should intervene freely, for that is capable of being regarded as interference with the course of impartial justice.[20] Lord Birkenhead, when Attorney-General, seems to have resented pressure as to prosecutions by the War Cabinet,[21] while in the case of Sir G. Hewart instructions as to prosecutions for sedition were only given, because he asked the advice of the Home Secretary, which was clearly within his rights.[22] Sir P. Hastings' action in the case of Mr. Campbell, in 1924, is less easy to judge. As the public saw the situation, after the Attorney-General had ordered a prosecution for incitement to mutiny, as a result of questions in Parliament, the Prime Minister intervened, had the issue discussed by the

---

[18] In the Denshawi case in 1906 in Egypt, Sir E. Grey had only time to consult Sir H. Campbell-Bannerman and Mr. Asquith, and decided not to intervene: Grey, *Twenty-five Years*, i. 135–139.

[19] G. K. A. Bell, *Life of Archbishop Davidson*, ii. 786–789.

[20] See the debate, 177 *H. C. Deb.* 5 s., 581–704.

[21] *Ibid.*, 614–615.   [22] *Ibid.*, 598–599.

Cabinet, and Sir P. Hastings then authorised the asking of the magistrate's leave to withdraw the prosecution. The Government preferred to be defeated, rather than accept the way out in the form of an enquiry suggested by Mr. Asquith. In defending himself and the Attorney-General the Prime Minister, Mr. Ramsay MacDonald said:

> 'Every Law Officer who is undertaking a prosecution in the interests of the State must possess himself not only of guidance on technical law, but must possess himself of guidance on this question, whether if a prosecution is instituted the effect of the prosecution will be harmful or beneficial to the State in whose interests it has been undertaken.'[23]

This proposition, whether or not it was sufficient cover for the action of the Cabinet on this occasion, would seem to be incontrovertible.

(4) Appointments do not normally come before the Cabinet, though there is no absolute rule. The Cabinet has been consulted from time to time as to the mode in which vacancies should be filled, though no doubt this sort of enquiry is best made privately. In the case of the Viceroy of India the question has on several occasions, according to Mr. Gladstone[24] and Mr. Asquith,[25] been raised in the Cabinet; this post, of course, is of quite special importance. The employment of a member of the royal family as Governor-General is the kind of issue which might thus be dealt with.[26] In the case of Mr. Sinha's appointment to the Council of the Governor-General the Cabinet was consulted, but for special reasons. The King objected to the principle of appointing to that Council any Indian, and only agreed to the appointment when the Cabinet unanimously advised that the appointment should be made as part of the reform scheme in India.[27]

(5) As regards honours, it is natural that the Cabinet should normally be content to leave the matter to the Prime Minister and the Crown.[28] It would, in view of the frailty of Cabinet secrecy,

23 177 *H. C. Deb.* 5 s., 629.
24 *Letters of Queen Victoria,* 3 s., ii. 349, cf. Lord Lieutenant (1882), *ibid.,* 2 s., iii. 271.
25 Lord Oxford and Asquith, *Fifty Years of Parliament,* ii. 194; it must have been Sir C. Hardinge *versus* Lord Kitchener; Lee, *Edward VII.,* ii. 710 f.
26 Cf. discussions of work for the Prince of Wales to do: Guedalla, *The Queen and Mr. Gladstone,* i. 351 ff.
27 Lee, *Edward VII.,* ii. 383–389.
28 Lord Curzon's speech, March 7, 1923: 53 *H. L. Deb.* 5 s., 286–7.

be undesirable if such issues were freely debated in a large body. But the claim of Queen Victoria that all such discussions would be unconstitutional could not stand for a moment. In respect to the Queen's desire to offer a dukedom to the Marquis of Lansdowne on the latter's retirement from the Viceroyalty of India, Mr. Gladstone explained that he felt he was fully entitled to consult the Cabinet, which was cognisant of that officer's services as Viceroy and also ultimately responsible for his administrative acts, but that he had refrained from doing so in the absence of the Secretary of State, and in deference to her views.[29]

One case remains to be noted, because it exhibits very interestingly the interaction of Queen Victoria and Lord Beaconsfield and the elasticity of Cabinet records.[30] In May, 1879, the project of sending Prince Albert Victor and Prince George of Wales for a six months' cruise in the *Bacchante* was approved by the Queen, but Mr. Smith, who learned of it, was afraid that, if anything happened to the princes when together, the Government would be held deeply to blame, and the Cabinet therefore urged that the proposed voyage should be confined to one prince. The Queen was very angry, and insisted that the matter should never have come before the Cabinet. Lord Beaconsfield was deeply apologetic, and excused himself on the score that the matter came up at the end of a long Cabinet, and that he had acted without due consideration, accepting full responsibility for the error in lieu of Mr. Smith. He explained that he would withdraw the matter from the Cabinet, and, as there were no records of Cabinet Councils, would address a letter to the Lord President, assuming the whole responsibility.

2. THE DOCTRINE OF COLLECTIVE RESPONSIBILITY

IT is essential to the modern Cabinet system that responsibility should be collective. Lord Salisbury expressed this clearly:

> 'For all that passes in Cabinet each member of it who does not resign is absolutely and irretrievably responsible, and has no right afterwards to say that he agreed in one case to a compromise, while in another he was persuaded by his colleagues. . . . It is only on the principle that absolute responsibility

[29] *Letters of Queen Victoria*, 3 s., ii. 347–351.
[30] *Letters of Queen Victoria*, 2 s., iii. 22 f.

is undertaken by every member of the Cabinet who, after a decision is arrived at, remains a member of it, that the joint responsibility of Ministers to Parliament can be upheld, and one of the most essential principles of parliamentary responsibility established.'[31]

Matters are discussed in Cabinet, and a decision taken. It then becomes binding on every member of the Cabinet, and, of course, on every minister outside the Cabinet. He must vote for the Government's view if a vote is taken in Parliament, he must, if called upon, defend the decision, he must not excuse himself on the score that he was outvoted. If he does not consent to take responsibility, he must resign, as did Lord John Russell in 1855, Mr. Forster in 1882, the opponents of Home Rule in 1886, the free trade ministers in 1903, and again in 1932, and Lord Morley and Mr. Burns in 1914, because they could not approve of the decision to go to war.

The theory is clear, but in practice there are relaxations. The most obvious is to leave certain issues open questions, and this may be the only way to have an effective ministry for the time being, leaving matters to ripen to a decision. The early history of the corn laws is the classic instance; the ministry of 1831–34 treated it as an open question,[32] and as late as 1841 Lord Melbourne was bitterly opposed to sweeping away protection, while his colleagues in the Commons were strongly in favour.[33] In 1873 the extension of the country franchise was left open,[34] and in 1905 a weak Cabinet could not decide on army reform, and the rather absurd spectacle was afforded of the War Minister presenting his own ideas as such to the Commons.[35] Clearly on matters of this kind, divided counsels are injurious to any Government. It was rather different in the case of female suffrage, which cut across party divisions. The Governments of Mr. Asquith and Mr. Lloyd George were willing to leave it open for the moment, but the issue was settled in 1918.[36] Prayer Book revision in 1928 was looked upon as a non-political question, and one which did not require a Cabinet decision.[37]

---

31 Lady Gwendolin Cecil, *Life of Lord Salisbury*, ii. 219–220.
32 This was later disputed; 45 *Parl. Deb.* 3 s., 585–586.
33 Spencer Walpole, *Life of Lord John Russell*, i. 324–326.
34 Wolf, *Life of Lord Ripon*, ii. 376–378.   35 Lee, *Edward VII.*, ii. 205.
36 Spender, *Lord Oxford*, i. 358 ff.; Lee, *Edward VII.*, ii. 653; Ronaldshay, *Life of Lord Curzon*, iii. 191–3.
37 H. A. Taylor, *Jix—Viscount Brentford*, p. 253.

After the fall of the Labour ministry in 1931 an appeal to the
people was decided upon, and in default of agreement it was based
on asking for general authority, a 'doctor's mandate,' to adopt such
methods as might seem necessary to restore the position. The
Conservative plea for a request for a mandate for protection was
laid aside, as the coalition included a substantial body of Liberal,
though a bare handful of Labour supporters. The election over,
a Cabinet Committee concluded in favour of protection, with the
result that the Liberal ministers felt under a clear obligation to
resign. At the urgent request of the Prime Minister, who claimed
that, if they did so, the difficulty of his position would be patent,
they refrained from this action on the basis of an understanding,
suggested by Lord Hailsham, 'that some modification of usual
ministerial procedure is required,' and 'that ministers who find
themselves unable to support the conclusions arrived at by the
majority of their colleagues on the subject of import duties and
cognate matters are to be at liberty to express their views by speech
and vote.'[38] The position was anomalous and was ended in less
than eight months by the resignation of the ministers in question
in view of the Ottawa agreements. These they criticised as
fixing a system of imperial preference on the country, which would
tend to render difficult the extension of external trade generally,
and would hamper the essential purpose of appeasement in
economic issues in Europe.

The failure of the experiment was really inevitable. The essence
of Cabinet government is the party system, and the existence of
parties divided by principles. Ministers may differ on minor issues
without serious disadvantage, and accept majority decisions thereon
with propriety, but a ministry made up of men without common
principles, held together by little more than the desire for office,
would speedily lack power and cohesion. The Conservatives lost
nothing by the departure from the ministry of men who did not
believe in its fundamental principle, while their continued presence
in the ministry weakened their own party.

The principle of collective responsibility involves that a Cabinet
minister must vote with the party, if he is not paired or if he is not
unavoidably absent when any important vote is taken. Writing
of the action of Sir Charles Dilke, Mr. Bright, and Mr. Chamberlain,

[38] See Snowden, *Autobiography*, ii. 1010; and cf. Lord Hailsham, 83 *H. L. Deb.*
5 s., 551 f.

who in 1881 failed to vote for the Government's proposal for a memorial for Lord Beaconsfield, Mr. Gladstone gave it as his opinion that 'Undoubtedly members of the Cabinet are bound to vote in every case—apart from accidental absences.'[39] Sir C. Dilke in 1883 was reproved by Lord Hartington for failure to vote against a female suffrage amendment to the Reform Bill, but was not actually asked to resign, the matter being of minor importance.[40] On the other hand the duty of refraining from any declaration of policy, contrary to that accepted by the Government, is clear. Lord Palmerston impressed on Mr. Gladstone the necessity of compliance with this principle.

> 'A member of the Government,' he said, 'when he takes office necessarily divests himself of that perfect freedom of individual action which belongs to a private and independent member of Parliament, and the reason is this, that what a member of the Government does and says upon public matters must to a certain degree commit his colleagues, and the body to which he belongs if they by their silence appear to acquiesce; and if any of them follow his example and express as publicly opposite opinions, which in particular cases they might feel obliged to do, differences of opinion between members of the same Government are necessarily brought out into prominence and the strength of the Government is thereby impaired.'[41]

In the course of time Mr. Gladstone repeated this to his colleagues.[42] Queen Victoria was sadly vexed at the lengths to which Mr. Chamberlain went under Mr. Gladstone, who was driven to the admission that he had power to call his ministers to book if they spoke unadvisedly on matters affecting duty to the Crown, or attempted to commit their colleagues.[43] But Mr. Chamberlain found a way out. With Sir C. Dilke he devised the doctrine that for ministers to use public platforms to expound their ideals of future policy, as distinct from current Cabinet issues, was in true accord with modern democracy, and did not offend against official propriety.[44] When in alliance with the Conservatives, but disappointed of the succession to the Premiership, he adopted a like licence of public propaganda, thus creating a position of much

[39] Guedalla, *The Queen and Mr. Gladstone*, ii. 156.
[40] Gwynn and Tuckwell, *Life of Sir Charles Dilke*, ii. 9.
[41] Guedalla, *Palmerston and Gladstone*, p. 288.
[42] Morley, *Life of Gladstone*, iii. 113 f.
[43] *Letters of Queen Victoria*, 2 s., iii. 433 ff.; 526 ff.; Guedalla, *The Queen and Mr. Gladstone*, ii. 292–294.
[44] Garvin, *Life of Joseph Chamberlain*, i. 559 ff.

embarrassment to Mr. Balfour, which ended only with Mr. Chamberlain's resignation in order to obtain the fullest freedom to air his propositions.[45]   On the other hand, when Mr. Lloyd George made his famous speech in 1911, he had the authority of both Mr. Asquith and Sir E. Grey, and was merely declaring a principle, which was self-evident, though his choice of language was well adapted to give special weight to his announcement.   It was quite different, when in 1916 he advocated in an interview the policy of the Knock-out Blow without the assent of the Foreign Secretary.[46]   Sir E. Grey had earlier had occasion to instruct both Mr. Churchill and Mr. Lloyd George regarding the obligations of moderation of language in dealing with foreign affairs.[47]   But Mr. Joynson-Hicks' action in 1927 on a private member's bill in announcing the intention of the Government to concede equal suffrage was clearly an expression of the decision of the Prime Minister, who was beside him, although the Cabinet had not yet come to a decision.[48]   As has been seen, the Prime Minister is apt to claim for himself a freedom of speech on issues not yet settled by the Cabinet, which is justified by the fact that it is normally impossible for his colleagues to do anything except homologate his action with such good grace as is proper.

In 1931, introducing the Sunday Performance (Regulation) Bill, Mr. Clynes, then Home Secretary, claimed to be speaking as an individual advocate of the measure and in no sense committing his colleagues either officially or personally.[49]   Most of the Cabinet voted in favour of the second reading of this Bill, but the then Foreign Secretary, Mr. Arthur Henderson, voted against. In 1948, a more interesting case occurred.   A proposal, introduced as an amendment to the Criminal Justice Bill, to suspend the death penalty for a period of five years was opposed by the Home Secretary, on behalf of the Government, but found a good deal of support among Labour back-benchers   A private meeting of the Parliamentary Labour Party took place before the debate began, and the position of ministers in the forthcoming debate was discussed at some length.   The Government had already decided to permit a free vote of their party on this issue, and the rank and file of the

---

45 Lee, *Edward VII.*, ii. 173 ff.
46 Lloyd George, *War Memoirs*, ii. 856 f.   47 Lee, *Edward VII.*, ii. 655.
48 Taylor, *Brentford*, pp. 279 ff.; Birkenhead, *Life of the First Earl of Birkenhead*, ii. 291–292.
49 251 *H. C. Deb.* 5 s., 633.

party now demanded that Ministers should be given the same freedom. The Government refused to agree to this demand.

> 'Their view was that Ministers must be prepared to accept collective responsibility for policy decisions. It was recognised, however, that some Ministers have long held and have publicly expressed strong views against capital punishment, and in the special circumstances, the Government made it known that such Ministers would be excused from voting, on grounds of conscience, and permitted to abstain. But it was not agreed to permit Ministers to vote against the Government.'[50]

In the event, no member of the Government voted for the new clause.

The rules which apply to Cabinet ministers are not quite so absolute as regards minor ministers, though even in their case they are probably now more stringent than in Mr. Gladstone's time. Non-Cabinet ministers have, in Mr. Gladstone's words, 'only a secondary and derivative share in the higher responsibilities.'[51] He had to explain away successively the failure of Mr. Bright, Sir C. Dilke, and Mr. J. Chamberlain to vote for the motion in favour of the erection of a statue to Lord Beaconsfield in 1881[52]; Sir C. Dilke's refusal to vote for the annuity to Prince Leopold on his marriage[53]; and his failure and that of two minor ministers, Mr. Fawcett and Mr. L. Courtney, to oppose the amendment in favour of female suffrage above referred to. In 1856, however, the Queen told Lord Palmerston to 'make it quite clear to the subordinate members of the Government that they cannot be allowed to vote against the Government proposal about the National Gallery tomorrow, as she hears that several fancy themselves at liberty to do so.'[54] It is dubious if much independence would now be displayed, so strict are the rules of party loyalty, and so active the whips. The dismissal of four junior ministers, and the resignation of a fifth, who voted against the Government in the Committee stage of the Ireland Bill in May, 1949, is probably a truer guide to future practice than Mr. Gladstone's view.

It must be remembered that in private members' bills there is normally no compulsion as to voting, though it is now expected,

50 *The Times*, April 15, 1948; see also 449 *H. C. Deb.* 5 s., 979–1094.
51 Gladstone, *Gleanings*, i. 224.
52 Guedalla, *The Queen and Mr. Gladstone*, ii. 156.
53 *Ibid.*, ii. 183–185. Mr. Fawcett also refrained.
54 *Letters of Queen Victoria*, 1 s., iii. 249.

it seems, that ministers will seldom actually vote against a Bill which is blessed by the minister whose department covers the subject-matter of the Bill, as in the case of the Caledonian Power Bill of 1937, but in 1938 this rule was not kept. Like treatment was accorded to the Church Measure enacting the revised form of the English Prayer Book when brought forward in 1927 and 1928. The ministry were divided in opinion, and the *coup de grâce* was administered by the Home Secretary, despite the unpopularity of his stand for the maintenance of the religion of the Church of England against the encroachment of doctrines of Papistic tendency foreign to the Reformation settlement.

Collective responsibility would be impossible if it were not that the members of the Cabinet from the circumstances of their selection are men naturally of like mind on essential issues, and therefore divergences on fundamentals are comparatively rare. There may be differences on tactics; men who agree on the merits *in abstracto* of a line of action may honestly disagree as to the party wisdom of presenting this as their policy to the electorate. The Cabinet normally, it is clear, arrives at unanimity much as does a village panchayat in India. Views are discussed, differences smoothed out, and a compromise result achieved, which all can accept without dishonour. Where it is impossible thus to agree, voting may take place, although, by tradition, the taking of votes is exceptional. Lord Granville argued: 'that it was absurd to count heads in assemblies in which there was such a difference in the contents of the heads,'[55] and Lord Oxford and Asquith stated that: 'It is not, or was not in any other Cabinets, in which I have sat, the custom (unless in exceptional cases not always of the first importance) to take a division.'[56]

Mr. Gladstone, however, carried the decision to arrest Mr. Dillon by his casting vote in 1881, and the issue of the removal of the statue of the Great Duke from Hyde Park Corner was decided in 1883 by a show of hands.[57] The Education Bill of 1901 was the subject of several divisions[58] and according to Mr. Churchill the

[55] Gwynn and Tuckwell, *Life of Sir Charles Dilke*, i. 370.
[56] Lord Oxford, *Fifty Years of Parliament*, ii. 196.
[57] Gwynn and Tuckwell, *Life of Sir Charles Dilke*, i. 528.
[58] Fitzroy, *Memoirs*, i. 63–67.

naval estimates of 1913, which excited an acute division of opinion, were the subject of discussion at fourteen Cabinet meetings, until the decision was reached.[59]   Overruling of the view of the Prime Minister is not unknown.   Lord Salisbury seems to have acquiesced occasionally in defeats,[60] and Mr. Bonar Law allowed himself to be voted down on the issue of accepting Mr. Baldwin's settlement of the American debt.[61]   With this we may contrast the vehemence with which Mr. Disraeli wrestled with the various views of his small Cabinet, in which at one time there were seven divergent opinions,[62] and later he insisted on securing the acquiescence of the Cabinet in the desire of his Colonial Secretary to retain Sir Bartle Frere in the Cape.[63]   Mr. Gladstone's resignation followed his finding himself in a minority on the issue of defence estimates.[64]

It is easy enough to understand that, even when there is voting, those defeated do not resign.   The issues are usually on points not of essential importance to most of those who vote, and resignation is an *ultima ratio*.   Will it be possible to secure success thereafter? A minister who resigns may, if he is to achieve later success, either have to form his own party or join the Opposition.   Lord R. Churchill's fate remains a warning.   Lord John Russell in 1855 deserted his colleagues on Mr. Roebuck's motion regarding the conduct of the war, and only ten years later on the death of Lord Palmerston did the veteran secure a brief tenure of the Premiership.   Lord Derby, disgusted with the foreign policy of Mr. Disraeli, found a welcome in the ranks of the Liberals, and the Liberals who deserted the leader on Home Rule gradually formed a firm alliance with the Conservatives.   Mr. Addison resigned in 1921, because he considered that the Cabinet had not kept faith with him as regards the housing policy he had been instructed to promote, and his future proved to lie with the Labour Party.   The changes of Mr. Winston Churchill's career have been followed by periods of waiting for office.   Mr. Eden's dramatic resignation in 1938 was

---

59 Churchill, *World Crisis*, i. 172.
60 In 1890, he was angry and only yielded to the Commons' members' view that the resolutions on procedure could not go on because he did not want to dissolve: *Letters of Queen Victoria*, s. 3, i. 618 f.   He and the Queen disliked greatly the dropping of the Education Bill, 1896: *ibid.*, 3 s., iii. 54–56.
61 Taylor, *Bonar Law*, pp. 270 ff.
62 Monypenny and Buckle, *Life of Disraeli* (1929 ed.), ii. 1066.
63 Lady V. Hicks-Beach, *Hicks-Beach*, i. 130.
64 Morley, *Gladstone*, iii. 506 ff.

accompanied by declarations by many Conservatives, that they hoped to see him again in office, and the ex-minister was punctilious in embarrassing as little as possible the Government, to whose principles he asserted in general his firm adherence. In such a case the minister probably looks forward at some later, but not distant date, when the immediate issue is disposed of, to re-employment. On the outbreak of war in September, 1939, Mr. Eden was able to return to office as Secretary of State for Dominion Affairs.

An interesting light on the process of Cabinet adjustment is thrown by Viscount Grey. The difference of opinion is first set out and stoutly maintained in Cabinet. If the conflict is so severe as to suggest resignations, individual ministers of divergent views may undertake private talks with one another outside the Cabinet. In this way the strength of conflicting contentions is tested, and the amount of concession each person can make is ascertained. Finally, the Cabinet again meets with the knowledge that it is going to agree on some solution. This, however, presupposes that the difference of opinion is really about the merits of the question and is not a pretext put forward for a personal or political object; in such cases the procedure is much less pleasant and the prognosis less favourable. This summary shed some light on the manner in which it proved possible to adjust the famous controversy over four, six or eight dreadnoughts, and the regular annual dispute over the military estimates.[65]

That the Cabinet may most efficiently reach Cabinet decisions of the kind mentioned, it is clearly desirable that its members should have the character of good colleagues. The characteristics demanded by Viscount Grey are clearly of universal application. Members should work heartily for Cabinet decisions, should not press personal views unduly on matters not essential, should contend for substance, not form, and each should consider without *amour propre* how his own opinion can be reconciled with that of others. Subject to the qualification of not sacrificing what he regards as essential to the public interests, he should not contend for victory, but work for agreement in the Cabinet. Secondly, when a Cabinet decision is attained, he should accept full responsibility for it. Thirdly, resignation should never be talked about or threatened

---

[65] Grey, *Twenty-five Years*, i. 200 f.

except on a matter of vital importance, and then only when resignation is really intended.[66]

3. COALITION GOVERNMENTS

IT follows from these facts that a coalition government is essentially anomalous in Britain, because it contradicts the fundamental principle that a Cabinet represents a party united in principle. The comparatively rarity of coalitions is due to this inherent difficulty, and the operations of the coalition of 1852–55 have normally been judged by the effect. The ministry was one of many talents, but their minds worked in very different ways, as might be expected from all that is known of the Premier, of Lord John Russell, and of Lord Clarendon. The evidence suggests that the result was a series of compromises which gave effect neither to the views of those who desired to maintain the peace, nor to those who thought an active offensive would serve best British interest, and the country blundered ultimately into a war whence no great profit could be expected and the minimum advantage was derived. Mr. Gladstone, indeed, and the Duke of Argyll can be cited for their admiration of the smooth working of the ministry, but it must have been the smoothness which is produced by sedulous avoidance of realities.[67]

No other coalition occurred until 1915, for Lord Salisbury and the Conservatives absorbed the Liberal Unionists, who soon became imbued with most of their principles. The coalition of 1915 must be regarded as having wrought more injury than good; whatever chance there might have been of saving the situation at the Dardanelles was lost while the new ministers were adjusting themselves to their colleagues, and the effort was being made to weld into a unity men whose chief concern was the question of the reception which their party would give to the decisions taken.[68] All chance of rapid and clear-cut decisions was gone, and it is impossible to disagree with Mr. Churchill, himself a *pars mali*, that it would have conduced far more to the welfare of the nation, which both parties professed sole anxiety to further, if one or other had yielded place and allowed a definite policy to be pursued

[66] Grey. *Twenty-five Years*, i. 67 f.
[67] Cf. Bell, *Palmerston*, ii. 61–105; *Camb. Hist. Brit. For. Policy*, ii. 340–376; Morley, *Gladstone*, i. 495; *English Historical Review*, ii. 288–289.
[68] Churchill, *World Crisis*, ii. 393 f. (three weeks delay). For the conscription deadlock, see Spender, *Lord Oxford*, ii. 208 ff.

without the delays and doubts occurring to many able minds.
Commenting on the shortcomings of this coalition he writes :

> 'Whereas practically all the important matters connected with
> the war had been dealt with in the late Government by four
> or five ministers, at least a dozen powerful, capable, distin-
> guished personalities who were in a position to assert themselves
> had to be consulted. . . . At least five or six different opinions
> prevailed on every great topic, and every operative decision
> was obtained only by prolonged, discursive and exhausting
> discussions. Far more often we laboured through long delays
> to unsatisfactory compromises.'[69]

It is quite easy to believe that the vital change of the creation of
the War Cabinet had the merit of lessening the disadvantage of
the existence of Liberal and Conservative points of view. The close
of the war and the re-introduction of the normal Cabinet system
saw little of a true coalition left, and the Government did not long
survive the peace settlement.

The coalition of 1931 had in its initiation the character of a
coalition between Conservatives and Liberals with a few Labour
representatives. From the retirement of the Liberal ministers in
1932 and their subsequent passing into formal opposition, the element
of coalition disappeared, for the ministers who claimed rank as
Nationals of Liberal type differed in nothing from their Conservative
colleagues, and the National Labour representatives clearly were
without any right to bear that title. The result was doubtless inevitable. The country cannot be governed effectively without clear
party divisions and a National Government might, if seriously constructed, well prove fatal to the maintenance of individual liberty.

The coalition formed in May, 1940, was a true National
Government; all parties were included. But its sole aim was the
successful prosecution of the war and it failed to survive the defeat
of Germany by more than a few weeks. At that point, disagreements about post-war reconstruction proved more fundamental
than the common wish to go on to defeat Japan.

4. The Procedure of the Cabinet

It is clear that in the earlier days of the Cabinet a simple procedure
sufficed.[70] The Premier was informed by his colleagues of any

[69] Churchill, *World Crisis*, ii. 384.
[70] Its genesis can be interestingly traced in Turner, *Cabinet Council*, 1622–1784,
ii. 101 ff., 304 ff.

points which they desired to raise, and any minister who so desired could order the circulation to the Cabinet of a memorandum setting forth his views. Naturally, any member who received such a memorandum could circulate a counter-memorandum, as did Lord Balfour and Mr. Ritchie when Mr. Balfour circulated his meditations on possible modification of the free trade system in 1903. The meeting was summoned in the name of the Prime Minister by his secretary, normally once a week. It was also open to any member of the Cabinet to ask the Prime Minister to summon a meeting to discuss matters connected either with the general policy of the Government or with his own department. This was a right inherent in the Cabinet system from the beginning.[71] It would be open to the Prime Minister, however, to refuse such a request, as did Disraeli when asked by Lord Carnarvon to summon a Cabinet to consider the situation after the publication of Gladstone's pamphlet on the Bulgarian atrocities;[72] but this situation is very unlikely to arise nowadays when meetings are held regularly and when a request of this sort would almost certainly raise matters of as much urgency to the Prime Minister himself as to his colleagues.

At earlier meetings the Prime Minister controlled the proceedings; the Foreign Secretary made his observations on any important incidents and answered questions arising thence or out of the Foreign Office papers which had been circulated.[73] Then the Premier allowed the several ministers to put their questions before the Cabinet, guided the discussion to some final or provisional conclusion, recorded the result and then called on another minister to open his subject and so on. There was neither Secretariat nor a regular record other than the letter from the Premier to the King, a copy of which was kept by the Premier's private secretary. Much play has been made with the informal character of the procedure, and Mr. Asquith has been accused of special carelessness in recording decisions, but there is abundant evidence of doubts arising earlier.[74] The occasions have all the same characteristic. They

---

71 *Parliamentary Papers*, vol. ix, part iii., 290 ff. (Reports of the Sebastopol Committee, 1854–5), Evidence of the Earl of Aberdeen; Esher, *The Influence of King Edward*, p. 139.

72 Sir A. Hardinge, *Life of Lord Carnarvon*, ii. 336.

73 Cf. Lord Salisbury's practice: *Letters of Queen Victoria*, 3 s., i. 211, where he held a special Cabinet arising out of dissent to a telegram on the Bulgarian issue duly circulated.

74 For a summary of such occasions, see Lord Hankey, *Diplomacy by Conference*, pp. 60–69.

were due to long and confused discussions ended rather by passage
to another topic than by a definite result, as was natural in the
muddled deliberations in the ministry in 1876–78 on the Russo-
Turkish issue.[75]   In the next ministry we have the amusing
anecdote of the inability of Sir W. Harcourt and Mr. J. Chamberlain to agree as to what happened at the Cabinet of the day before.
'There must have been some decision,' wrote Lord Hartington's
private secretary to Mr. Gladstone's, 'as Bright's resignation shows.
My chief has told me to ask you what the devil *was* decided, for he
be damned if he knows.   Will you ask Mr. G. in more conventional
and less pungent terms?'[76]   Lord Lansdowne complained when he
was called to account for his publication of the Spion Kop dis-
patches, which annoyed the Queen very greatly, that Cabinet
decisions were not always very distinctly intimated to those who
had to carry them out, and Lord Salisbury with his usual
insouciance doubted whether the traditional practice of not
recording decisions was a wise one.[77]   It is, of course, plain that
it was his duty to have recorded the result definitely, in which case
the mistake could not easily have occurred.   On the same occasion
Lord Lansdowne admitted that 'our decisions are not always very
distinctly intimated to the ministers who have to carry them out.'[78]
It was easy enough for ministers to carry away wrong impressions if
the decision was not precisely summed up by their chief, for the
taking of notes was distinctly banned by men so different as
Mr. Asquith and Lord Salisbury.   One may sympathise with Lord
Derby's claim to be entitled to take notes in Lord Beaconsfield's
Cabinet on the understanding that they would later be destroyed.[79]

At the same time the Cabinet on occasion could put its advice
in the form of a formal minute.   This was done by the Grenville
Ministry in 1807;[80] as regards the creation of peers in 1832, and
the precedent was followed in 1910, as regards the promise to the
King that advice as to the creation of peers would not be tendered
until the occasion arose, and the later request for an undertaking
from the Crown to create peers in certain circumstances.[81]   Queen

---

[75] Monypenny and Buckle, *Disraeli* (1929 ed.) ii. 967, 1070, 1145 ff.
[76] Cited 86 *H. L. Deb.* 5 s., 529.   For Mr. Balfour's Cabinet's misunderstanding
  on tariff policy, 1902, see Dugdale, *Arthur James Balfour*, i. 339 ff.
[77] *Letters of Queen Victoria*, 3 s., iii. 533, 536, 538, 541.
[78] *Ibid.*, 3 s., iii. 541–2.
[79] Cf. Anson, *The Law and Custom of the Constitution* (ed. Keith), vol. II, i. 120 ff.
[80] *Peel Papers*, iii. 496–8.
[81] Spender, *Lord Oxford*, i. 273, 296 f.

Victoria in like manner had insisted on a formal minute before she exercised her powers under the Act of 1809 of revoking the warrant permitting the purchase of army commissions.[82] As the Lords had refused to accept legislation to this end, her insistence on formal procedure was clearly right. A formal minute was drawn up regarding the acquisition of a naval base in the Mediterranean in 1878.[83] Although this had been a fairly frequent practice under Fox and Grenville it does not appear to have been much used after 1832.

The outbreak of war in 1914 unquestionably necessitated a more effective system, and it was found ready to hand in the Secretariat of the Committee of Imperial Defence, which had been created in very modest form late in 1902.[84] This secretariat was augmented under the Liberal regime,[85] and was given the duty of framing the agenda, taking minutes, both of plenary committee meetings and of the ever-growing number of sub-committees, and of communicating the findings to the departments concerned. In special, through the activities of the secretariat, proper arrangements were made for the preparation and dissemination to the numerous authorities concerned in the United Kingdom and overseas of the War Book, which was relied upon for guidance in the early days of the Great War.[86] The War Council set up in November, 1914, naturally used the secretariat, as did the Dardanelles Committee, and the War Committee into which it grew.[87] Hence, in 1916, when the War Cabinet was created by Mr. Lloyd George, it naturally took over the secretariat, and after the war the system continued.[88] The Cabinet secretariat was presided over by Sir M. Hankey who was also Secretary to the Committee of Imperial Defence, when revived in full form, and Clerk of the Privy Council. Obviously the combination of posts was largely personal, but the advantages of having one secretary for the Cabinet and the

---

82 *Letters of Queen Victoria*, 2 s., ii. 152 ff.
83 Monypenny and Buckle, *Disraeli*, ii. 1018.
84 There was a very rudimentary secretariat, almost certainly supplied *ad hoc* by departments when the Committee was set up in December, 1902; the permanent secretariat did not begin until eighteen months later, set up by a Treasury Minute of May 4, 1904 (see Hankey, *Diplomacy by Conference*, p. 84).
85 For Sir H. Campbell-Bannerman's acceptance of it, see Esher, *Journals and Letters*, ii. 128. Cf. 114 ff.
86 Lord Hankey, *Government Control in War*, chap. ii.
87 *Ibid.*, pp. 36–40.
88 See Cmd. 9230, p. 6, for the approval of the Machinery of Government Committee. See also Cmd. 9005; Cmd. 325; 155 *H. C. Deb.* 5 s., 213 ff.

4*

Committee of Imperial Defence was, probably, for a certain time desirable. The Cabinet secretariat was vastly expanded during the war, and, as we have seen, rivalled at times the Foreign Office; under Mr. Bonar Law its abolition was mooted, but wisely all that was done was to reduce it to due dimensions and to define and limit its functions.[89]   It serves now to compile the agenda for meetings of the Cabinet and its committees, under the direction of the Premier or the chairman; to circulate the memoranda and other documents requisite for discussion; to issue summonses to meetings; to record and circulate to ministers the conclusions arrived at by the Cabinet or its committees, and to draw up the reports of such committees; and to keep the Cabinet papers and conclusions.   The war-time practice of recording the discussions of issues is now abandoned; there is recorded in lieu the substance of documents submitted or statements made, the general character of the arguments, and the conclusions reached. It is, in fact, believed to be an instruction to the Secretary to the Cabinet to avoid recording individual expressions of opinion, unless a minister specifically asks for that to be done.   Each Cabinet minister receives a copy of the conclusions or minutes, and non-Cabinet ministers receive, on the authority of the Premier, extracts of conclusions on matters affecting their departments. It lies with the minister to carry out the decision fully and loyally if something unexpected has turned up; he can, of course, refer for guidance to the Prime Minister, but alteration without authority can be excused only by such urgency as exists in war, and must be reported to Prime Minister and Cabinet.   A copy of the minutes goes to the King.

It rests with the Prime Minister to decide on the calling of Cabinets; a weekly meeting may in emergency be supplemented, while during the holiday season, after Parliament has risen, as few Cabinets as possible are summoned.   Normally, as we have seen, the Premier will defer to any request by a Cabinet minister for a meeting, but Mr. Balfour insisted on delaying a Cabinet on fiscal issues[90] pending the return of Mr. J. Chamberlain from Africa to England.   On the other hand, orderly consideration of matters to be dealt with is furthered by rules of modern application.   It is

---

[89] 155 *H. C. Deb.* 5 s., 213 ff.
[90] Dugdale, *Arthur James Balfour*, i. 341.   Cf. Mr. Chamberlain's successful request for a Cabinet: Garvin, *Joseph Chamberlain*, iii. 461.

provided that draft Bills shall not be circulated until the law officers have had a chance of expressing their views, that matters affecting more than one department should be submitted only after discussion, and in special, since 1919, that issues affecting finance shall not be circulated until the sanction of the Chancellor of the Exchequer has been obtained, which means, it is presumed, that the matter must be held over to permit the preparation of a financial memorandum.[91] Not until the Premier is satisfied that these principles have been observed, or can be waived, is circulation of documents permitted. If the papers affect departments not represented in the Cabinet, the documents may, by permission of the Premier, or the minister who supplies them, be sent to the ministerial heads. Items of business usually appear on the agenda not earlier than five days after circulation, to allow of full consideration and preparation and circulation of counter memoranda. It is clearly desirable that the issues should be as fully defined in the papers submitted, which normally become permanent records in the Cabinet Office. The Premier decides the order of the items on the agenda, which includes, as in pre-war days, a statement by the Foreign Secretary on which questions can be asked, and it is communicated to ministers, who thus reach the Cabinet fully prepared, if they have taken the trouble to master the documents supplied, to engage in rapid discussion and decision.[92]

The changes referred to have simplified Cabinet discussions by helping to eliminate issues which can be disposed of by interdepartmental discussions, if necessary with the arbitration of the Premier; by ensuring that discussion takes place on definite issues; and by securing that the financial implications of each proposal are clearly set out. The practice of referring matters to committees saves discussion of issues not yet ripe for settlement. Contentious bills normally have been carefully considered by the law officers. Moreover, matters are sometimes dealt with before the Cabinet discussion by individual ministers, who can present their colleagues with an agreement which the others will not care to attack.[93]

---

91 T. L. Heath, *The Treasury*, pp. 58 f. It is believed that much of this procedure became standardised during the 1924 Labour Government as a result of complaints from the Attorney-General, Sir Patrick Hastings. Treasury approval goes back well beyond this date.

92 Often they do not: Spender, *Lord Oxford*, i. 348.

93 Cf. the older usage under which matters were matured for decision by a Cabinet in a meeting to which not all were summoned: Lord Cranbrook, 185 *Parl. Deb.* 3 s., 1348.

Cabinets, no doubt, may be overworked, though that is not normally the case, unless in time of war, as in 1914–19, or of financial strain, as in 1930–32, or of international unrest on a grandiose scale, as in the period 1935–39. The incident of the Hoare-Laval terms in December, 1935, is an example where undue haste allowed the Cabinet to homologate a policy ruinous to the status of the League, and the surrender of Mr. Chamberlain to the Italian ultimatum on negotiations on February 20, 1938, suggests strong failure on the part of the Cabinet to deal adequately with grave issues on the score of the excessive burden of urgent problems. In normal times the growth of rules of Cabinet procedure assisted by the services of an independent organisation, the Cabinet Office, with the increasing use of Cabinet committees, have made it possible to continue a much criticised tradition whereby ministers carry not only extensive departmental duties, but also responsibility for the formulation of general policy in the Cabinet as a whole.

Especially when the Cabinet is overburdened, it is natural that the leading ministers should take to the practice of settling issues, as far as possible, by consultations *inter se* in anticipation of, or even in substitution for, full examination by the whole Cabinet. This will happen, even if there is no extreme pressure of work, if, as is normal, the Cabinet is composed in part of mediocre and perhaps inexperienced politicians, leavened by a few men marked out by ability, or force of personality, or long experience and mature judgment, or some share of these qualifications. Although in theory all Cabinet ministers are equal the Cabinet, like any similar group, will often be led by the few it respects. 'In most Governments,' wrote Mr. Lloyd George, 'there are four or five outstanding figures who by exceptional talent, experience, and personality, constitute an inner council which gives direction to the policy of a ministry. An administration that is not fortunate enough to possess such a group may pull through without mishap in tranquil season, but in an emergency it is hopelessly lost.'[94] In 1878 the issue was complicated by the disagreement between Lord Beaconsfield and his Foreign Secretary. Hence, in regard to the measures to be taken to safeguard Constantinople the Prime Minister, Lord Salisbury, and the weighty Lord Cairns constituted

[94] Lloyd George, *War Memoirs*, iii. 1042; 304 *H. C. Deb.* 5 s., 363.

themselves an informal committee, which determined on a policy likely to please the Queen, and then presented it to the Cabinet, in which naturally they bore down the resistance of Lord Derby and secured Cabinet approval for the telegrams to be sent to British representatives from the Foreign Office.[95] It is not surprising that Lord Derby resigned. In 1898 when Sir A. Milner, wholly underestimating the power of resistance of the Boers, proposed a policy contemplating as a possibility actual war,[96] Mr. J. Chamberlain communicated it only to Mr. Balfour, then acting Prime Minister, the Duke of Devonshire, the Chancellor of the Exchequer, and the heads of the Admiralty and the War Office, and his reply was sent without consultation of the Cabinet.[97] In a similar spirit Mr. Balfour was in close touch with Mr. Chamberlain over the conduct of foreign affairs.[1] In 1914 the Foreign Secretary and Prime Minister acted as regards the German bid for British neutrality in anticipation of Cabinet sanction.[2] The interesting decision to attempt to save Antwerp by the despatch thither of the naval brigade was taken by Lord Kitchener, Mr. Churchill, the moving spirit, and Sir E. Grey, the Prime Minister not at the moment being immediately available.[3] At the dangerous moment after the retreat from Mons, when it seemed as if Sir J. French might retire beyond the Seine, the decision to send Lord Kitchener to give him Cabinet instructions to the contrary, was taken by some ministers, whose action, of course, received Cabinet endorsement.[4] The further development of the doctrine held by Mr. Lloyd George that super-men are needed to act in a crisis was his creation of the famous War Cabinet.[5] But Mr. Lloyd George's conception of an inner ring was shared by the Labour ministries; Lord Snowden definitely tells us that in the second ministry of Mr. MacDonald, Mr. Henderson, Mr. Thomas, who had, as Lord Privy Seal, in theory the duty of devising a solution of the Labour question,

---

[95] Lady G. Cecil, *Life of Lord Salisbury*, ii. 209.
[96] Garvin, *Joseph Chamberlain*, iii. 364 f. This letter showed Lord Milner determined to bring on war.
[97] *Ibid*. 366–368. He wisely insisted on the pursuit of peace.
[1] Dugdale, *Arthur James Balfour*, i. 266–272.   [2] Grey, *Twenty-five Years*, i. 325 ff.
[3] Churchill, *World Crisis, 1911–14*, pp. 338 ff.
[4] Spender, *Lord Oxford*, ii. 107–109, 125. Sir J. French's indignation at Lord Kitchener's appearance in uniform was ridiculous: Churchill, *World Crisis, 1911–14*, pp. 277 ff.
[5] Mr. Balfour in 1915 thought the Cabinet with prior consultations among certain members would be better than a War Committee: Spender, *Lord Oxford*, ii. 187.

Mr. Snowden, as Chancellor of the Exchequer, and the retiring Mr. Clynes, then Home Secretary, and closely in touch with the party, used to meet weekly for a general conversation on the state of the party and parliamentary business.[6]   Three of these men shared in the formation of the National Government and the destruction of the Labour ministry, so that the case is not a very good example of the value of inner Cabinets, if the members thereof forget the mentality of the rank and file.   The Labour Government of the years since 1945 also seems to have had a group of four ministers, the Prime Minister together with Mr. Bevin, Sir Stafford Cripps, and Mr. Herbert Morrison, 'who have all the strings of policy in their hands.'[7]

It is clear that this idea of an inner Cabinet is not without dangers.   It is not always easy for members of the Cabinet to accept the pre-eminence of a few out of their number.   They must all agree that the Prime Minister stands in a place of his own; there is probably sometimes agreement as to the member of the Cabinet on whom his mantle must fall, if for any reason he is anxious to leave office.   But beyond that opinions will differ, and more resentment than profit may result from any effort to make the Cabinet feel that it meets only in matters of high importance to ratify decisions arrived at by an inner group, self constituted. There is a much more satisfactory and regular mode of aiding the Cabinet to decide, the regular committee system.

5. CABINET COMMITTEES

(a) *The Committee of Imperial Defence and the Defence Committee.*

OF all committees, that on defence is the most important and has had the longest history.   It is essentially a production of the present century, though it had a faint precursor in the naval and military committee of the Cabinet created by Lord Salisbury under Lord Hartington in 1890, who had in 1888 undertaken the work of presiding over a Commission on the War Office.[8]   But that committee, and the Defence Committee of Lord Salisbury's third administration which sat under the chairmanship of the Duke of

---

6 Snowden, *Autobiography*, ii. 924 f.

7 Francis Williams, *The Triple Challenge*, p. 42.

8 Cmd. 5979. See Anson, *The Law and Custom of the Constitution*, vol. II (ed. Keith), i. 148 f.; ii. 185, 245 ff.; Hankey, *Diplomacy by Conference*, chap. iv.; Esher, *Journals and Letters*, ii. 34 ff.; Dugdale, *Arthur James Balfour*, i. 364 ff.

Devonshire, had no effective existence until it was reconstituted in December, 1902, by authority of Mr. Balfour.[9] In 1904, as a result of the advice of the important Esher Committee on the re-organisation of the War Office, it was made a permanent body, as the Committee of Imperial Defence, with a small permanent secretariat.[10] Commenting on the mistakes of the early months of the Boer War and on the lack of preparation for war which made those mistakes inevitable, the report of the Esher Committee said:

> 'The British Empire is pre-eminently a great Naval, Indian and Colonial Power. There are, nevertheless, no means for co-ordinating defence problems, for dealing with them as a whole, for defining the proper functions of the various elements, and for ensuring that, on the one hand, peace preparations are carried out upon a consistent plan, and on the other hand, that, in time of emergency, a definite war policy, based upon solid data, can be formulated.'

To achieve these purposes it considered essential to have not merely a top-level committee presided over by the Prime Minister such as the Committee of Imperial Defence of 1902 was already, in principle, but also a permanent secretariat or department to serve the needs of the Prime Minister and the committee, and to preserve that continuous treatment of defence problems which was desired.[11]

Mr. Balfour desired elasticity in the committee's composition, and thus the Prime Minister was held to be the only permanent member of the body, but naturally the essential ministers were regularly summoned, at that time the Lord President, the Secretary of State for War, the First Lord of the Admiralty and the First Sea Lord, and the Commander-in-Chief, with the heads of the Naval and Military Intelligence Departments as joint secretaries, and a Foreign Office clerk to keep the minutes. Sir H. Campbell-Bannerman, on mature consideration, approved the idea, and expanded the activities of the committee. Sub-committees became important and numerous, the Overseas Defence Committee, the Home Ports Defence Committee, and so on. Mr. Asquith added a standing sub-committee representing all departments likely to be concerned in the event of the outbreak of war, the Co-ordination

---

[9] Hankey, *Diplomacy by Conference*, p. 84; 139 *Parl. Deb.* 4 s., 617.

[10] Cmd. 1932, *Report of the War Office (Reconstitution) Committee*, Pt. 1, p. 3; 139 *Parl. Deb.* 4 s., 601 ff.; 8 *H. C. Deb.* 5 s., 1381 ff.

[11] Cmd. 1932, Part 1, pp. 1–3.

Committee, while, in accord with the conversations with French representatives consequent on the entente of 1904, plans were matured for the despatch, in case of need to France, of an expeditionary corps.[12]   Moreover, as we have seen, the committee was responsible for the famous War Book, which proved invaluable in the crisis, for naturally there was no other source available envisaging the innumerable points which had at once to receive attention, not merely in Britain, but in each Dominion and colony.   The War Book 'was designed to show every Department, not only what it had to do itself, but what other Departments were doing in the matter.   Every piece of legislation; every set of instructions; every order, letter, cable, telegram, including those to the fleets, military stations, the Dominions, India and the Colonies . . . was drafted and kept ready for issue. . . . The whole was kept continuously up to date by a small standing body to meet the changes and additions required from time to time.'[13]   It was at a meeting of the committee, during the Imperial Conference of 1911, that the Prime Ministers of the Dominions were given full information for the first time of the whole character of British foreign policy, and of the defence issues therewith bound up.[14]

It is clear that through the Committee of Imperial Defence the inner Cabinet obtained a very real, but duly authorised existence, for the ministers engaged in defence and foreign affairs were necessarily deeply concerned with the issues then of greatest importance to the future of the country.   It is hardly likely, however, that from their association with military and naval authorities, professionally keen to test in practice their plans, and prepared to use the Opposition to put pressure on the Government, the ministers who served on the committee imbibed any eagerness to go to war. That was imposed upon them by the logic of events and the feeling of the country, especially when the violation of the neutrality of Belgium became known.   Moreover, ministers were too deeply immersed in the affairs of the internal administration of the country, and above all, the Irish problem, to have any desire to be plunged into hostilities.   But they should be given credit for their readiness to consider the plans of the technical experts summoned to the

---

[12] For accounts of this work see Hankey, *Government Control in War*, chap. ii., and Asquith, *The Genesis of the War*, chap. xv.
[13] Hankey, *Government Control in War*, p. 27.
[14] Keith, *Responsible Government in the Dominions* (1928 ed.), ii. 874 f.; Asquith, *The Genesis of the War*, chap. xvi.

meetings, which resulted in Britain being far better prepared for war than any one would have expected.[15]   The despatch of four divisions to France, on the one hand, and the hasty carrying through Parliament of the Defence of the Realm Act, and other measures for meeting the difficulties immediately created by the declaration of war, attested the completeness of the foresight displayed by the committee.

The outbreak of war caused the committee to be transformed in November formally to a War Council, and it was only after peace was restored that the committee began to revert to type.   By the summer of 1921 the work of the Committee of Imperial Defence was again in full swing.[16]   The idea that there should be effective co-ordination of the services under a Minister of Defence had naturally gained strength from the allegations that there had been defective co-operation in the war between the different arms, and from the embittered controversy which had raged regarding the control of the Air Force, which had gradually succeeded in acquiring its status as a distinct arm.   Plainly, to place both the Army and the Air Force under one Secretary of State, as in 1921, when Mr. Churchill was in charge, was inadequate, and the Committee on National Expenditure of Sir E. Geddes declared in favour of the plan of a single ministry, with subordinate ministers not in the Cabinet.   This much discussed plan raised so many difficulties that the Cabinet decided instead to concentrate on the Committee of Imperial Defence as an effective instrument for continuous study of defence co-ordination.   It must be remembered that the coming of peace had reduced the urgency of preparations for war, and owing, perhaps, to this the Prime Minister, from 1920 to 1924, did not act as chairman.   In the case of Mr. Lloyd George this was natural enough, for Lord Balfour was willing and available; Mr. Bonar Law was glad to depute Lord Salisbury, Mr. Baldwin in his first ministry relied on Lord Curzon, while Lord Haldane acted for Mr. MacDonald.[17]   In 1924 a sub-committee under Lord Salisbury reported on the whole question[18] and advocated *inter alia* the creation of a Chiefs of Staff Committee, and the appointment of a minister to preside over the Committee of Imperial Defence as deputy for

15 Asquith, *The Genesis of the War*, ch. xiv–xvii.; Spender, *Lord Oxford*, ii. 62 f. For the inner Cabinet, see Fitzroy, *Memoirs*, ii. 539; for the effective working in August, 1914, *ibid.* 560 ff.
16 Hankey, *Diplomacy by Conference*, p. 97.
17 287 *H. C. Deb.* 5 s., 1321.   18 Cmd. 2029.

the Prime Minister, but rejecting the idea of a separate Minister of Defence in place of the existing Committee.[19]

The report of Lord Salisbury's Committee on National and Imperial Defence remained, with some alterations to suit changing needs, the basis of the work of the Committee of Imperial Defence down to 1939. We will examine the results of its recommendation of a Chiefs of Staff Committee later.[19] For many years its recommendation that a separate minister should preside over the committee instead of the Prime Minister was not acted upon, for Mr. Baldwin definitely decided that he should preside. His arguments in favour of his decision are important;[20] they are reminiscent of those which caused Mr. Asquith in 1916 to refuse to be removed from the War Committee. The Prime Minister should take part in arriving at decisions, which are certain to be of high importance, and which the Cabinet ought normally to homologate without meticulous criticism; he ought to be *au fait* with all important developments of defence problems; and he cannot well decide the thorny questions which arise as to the sums to be allocated to the several claimants in the estimates, unless he is cognisant of defence questions. Undoubtedly, it is easier and more effective for him to study these matters at first hand in committee, instead of merely listening to reports, even from a deputy.

The position thus asserted by Mr. Baldwin, and maintained by subsequent Prime Ministers, naturally did not go uncriticised. In 1928 and again in 1934 there were major debates in the House of Commons on this subject.[21] The 1934 debate showed clearly the fundamental arguments on both sides. Those who demanded a Ministry of Defence were doubtful, firstly, whether a committee whose work was and always had been purely consultative and advising, could overcome the 'particularisms and . . . the vested interests—the innocent and respectable vested interests—of the various Services.'[22] Secondly, they considered that the Prime Minister had neither the time nor the technical experience to control the work of Service co-ordination.

In 1936 the repeated demands for the appointment of a Minister of Defence drove the Government to take action, though it rejected that suggestion as absolutely as it had been rejected twelve years earlier. The grounds for its rejection were strong. The Minister

19 *Post*. p. 117.
21 See, *e.g.*, 215 *H. C. Deb.* 5 s., 1013 ff.
20 215 *H. C. Deb.* 5 s., 1028.
22 287 *H. C. Deb.* 5 s., 1242 ff.

of Defence would have to hold the scales even between three
subordinate ministers, a task very difficult for any single man.   It
would, further, be difficult to find any person whose talents would
seem to others sufficient to justify the subordination to him of other
able ministers, and the subordinate posts would not attract men of
the highest capacity.   There would be risk of friction and intrigue,
and the function of co-ordination, it was argued, could be carried
out in a more satisfactory manner by the creation, not of a Minister
of Defence, but of a Minister for the Co-ordination of Defence.
For that office the Attorney-General, Sir T. Inskip, was held out
as having the necessary characteristics for a post where patience and
skill in securing that men should work effectively and harmoniously
together were the prime desiderata.[23]   To him the Prime Minister
delegated the general supervision and control of the whole organisation and activity of the Committee of Imperial Defence; the co-
ordination of executive action and of monthly progress reports to
the Cabinet, or any committee appointed by it, on the execution of
the reconditioning plans; discernment of any points which had not
been taken up, or were being pursued too slowly, and of appropriate
measures for their rectification.   In the Prime Minister's absence
he was to act as chairman of the Committee of Imperial Defence,
and of the Defence Policy and Requirements Committee of the
Cabinet.   He had the duty of personal consultation with the Chiefs
of Staff, and, while he did not normally preside over their meetings,
he might at his discretion convene the Chiefs of Staff Committee.

In some ways the new departure was preferable to the scheme of
a permanent chairman of the committee other than the Prime
Minister.   But the new scheme was essentially a compromise and
one which clearly favoured those who supported the Committee of
Imperial Defence rather than those who wanted a Ministry of
Defence.   The duty of the Minister for Co-ordination of Defence—
a specialised *alter ego* of the Prime Minister in this respect—was to
try to ensure that the committee did its work satisfactorily.   And
yet it was an unsatisfactory compromise.   The work of the new
minister was made almost impossible from the start by the lack of
any department of his own by means of which he could co-ordinate
the work of those departments theoretically in his general charge.
The war later amply proved that supervising ministers without
departments find it almost impossible to supervise at all.   Secondly,

23 Cmd. 5107, p. 14; 309 *H. C. Deb.* 5 s., 653 ff., 1827 ff.

the new minister took over not only a general responsibility for strategic planning, but also the responsibility for the supply work of the Committee of Imperial Defence which would more properly have come, as it did in 1939, under a Minister of Supply.[24]   By the spring of 1940 it was realised that, especially in war-time conditions, the office of Minister for Co-ordination of Defence had become redundant, and it was not filled again after Lord Chatfield's resignation in April.[25]

The personnel of the committee remained from 1924 as under the original scheme of 1904, the Prime Minister and such other members as he might summon in view of the nature of the matters to be discussed.[26]   The essential figures were, beside the Prime Minister and later the Minister for the Co-ordination of Defence, the Chancellor of the Exchequer, the Secretaries of State for Foreign Affairs, Home Affairs—air defence being essentially under his control, Dominion Affairs, the Colonies, War, Air, India and Burma, the First Lord of the Admiralty, the Parliamentary Under-Secretary of State for Foreign Affairs, the three chiefs of staff, and the Permanent Secretary to the Treasury, as the head of the Civil Service.[27]   Other ministers were added, as was Mr. R. MacDonald during his membership of the Cabinet as Lord President, after his retirement from the office of Prime Minister.[28]   Members of the Opposition might be invited to attend, as was Mr. Balfour in 1908[29] and 1914,[30] and again the Labour Government in 1930–31 acted similarly.[31]   Dominion representatives were invited to be present, if any business of interest to them happened to be under discussion.

The other major recommendation of the Salisbury Committee must be considered now.   While rejecting all plans for a Minister of Defence, the committee agreed that 'the existing system of co-ordination by the Committee of Imperial Defence is not sufficient to secure full initiative and responsibility for defence as a whole and requires to be defined and strengthened.'[32]   Initiative

---

[24] Churchill, *Second World War*, i. 536–7.
[25] *Ibid.*, p. 463.
[26] Treasury Minute, May 4, 1904; 191 *H. C. Deb.* 5 s., 1527.
[27] Maj.-Gen. (later Lord) Ismay, *R.U.S.I. Journal*, May, 1939.
[28] Lord Esher was made a permanent member by Mr. Balfour; *Journals and Letters*, ii. 122.
[29] *Ibid.*, ii. 316 f., on his invasion memorandum.
[30] Dugdale, *Balfour*, ii. 125; this time he was made a regular member.
[31] 299 *H. C. Deb.* 5 s., 998.
[32] Cmd. 2029, para. 36.

lay with Government Departments and the Prime Minister, and no
authority except the Prime Minister—and he had too little time to
devote to defence questions—was responsible 'for the initiation of a
consistent line of policy directing the common action of the three or
any two of the three Services, taking account of the reactions of the
three Services upon one another. It recommended that day to day
initiative in defence matters be entrusted to a committee of the three
Chiefs of Staff, acting as a sub-committee of the Committee of
Imperial Defence. The three Chiefs of Staff, in addition to their
function 'as advisers on questions of sea, land or air policy respectively to their own Board or Council,' were to have 'an individual
and collective responsibility for advising on defence policy as a
whole, the three constituting, as it were, a Super-Chiefs of a War
Staff in Commission.'[33] This recommendation was immediately
adopted.

The Chiefs of Staff Committee was charged under the decision
of 1924 with the consideration and investigation, whether by
reference or on its own initiative, of the problems of imperial
defence as a whole, and of the co-ordination of the three services;
The Prime Minister might preside, but this was not regularly done.
the Chiefs of Staff reported their collective opinion to him, or to his
deputy, whose special function it was to supplement their activities
and initiative by guidance and initiative of his own, in order to
ensure that every aspect was fully considered, and that difficulties
and differences were frankly faced. It is plain that such functions
were far from easy to carry out. The views of the three services
were inevitably far from accordant, and the effort to compel the
Chiefs to merge their individual predilections in a single policy
was an ambitious task, but one fully achieved during the Second
World War if not sooner.[34]

The Chiefs of Staff Committee presented annually a report to
the Committee of Imperial Defence, wherein defence was related to
foreign affairs in their constant flux, and proposals made.[35] The
report was examined by the committee and sent on with its findings
to the Cabinet, where the ministers who served on the committee
could normally count on ready acceptance of those things on which

[33] Cmd. 2029, para. 36.
[34] For the work of the Chiefs of Staff Committee and its sub-committees before
1939, see Ismay, *R.U.S.I. Journal*, May, 1939.
[35] Cmd. 5107, p. 15.

they were in principle agreed.   The policy was thus decided, and this was done in time for the estimates, the total of which as regards defence thus rested on the consideration given to this side of the problem by the Committee of Imperial Defence.[36]   Plainly this *modus operandi* diminished the risk of the repetition of the former unedifying struggles between the departments of defence and the Treasury for funds.

The committee had sub-committees, which varied from time to time in number and in importance.   Most important of these was the Joint Planning Committee, which originally consisted of the Directors of Plans of the three departments, who, in their joint capacity (and they still retained their separate Service responsibilities as well) were appointed from 1927 'to examine and report on plans for combined action by the three Services as directed from time to time by the Chiefs of Staff Committee.' They were strengthened in 1936 by adding three officers, one from each service, graduates of the Imperial Defence College, which had been created in 1925.[37]   As members of their departments they collected information for the use of the committee which they assisted.   Its plans then went to the Committee of Imperial Defence.   In 1936 the pre-war Chiefs of Staff organisation was completed by the addition of a Joint Intelligence Sub-Committee, consisting of the Deputy Directors of Intelligence at the Admiralty, War Office, and Air Ministry, reinforced when necessary by representatives of other departments.

During the inter-war years the Committee of Imperial Defence not only greatly strengthened its organisation on more particularly military and strategic matters, it also developed a whole series of sub-committees to deal with matters which, neglected before 1914, had revealed serious gaps in our preparations.   The most important of these were a Supply Group, consisting of the Principal Supply Officers Committee, the Food Supply Committee and the Oil Board; a Man-Power group to deal with the allocation of man-power in war; and a miscellaneous group of sub-committees engaged in problems of scientific research.[38]   All these bodies were, like the parent Committee of Imperial Defence, entitled to

[36] Cf. the discussions in the Commons, March 21, 1934; 287 *H. C. Deb.* 5 s., 1231 ff.
[37] The Imperial Defence College secures the training of defence and civil experts in all aspects of preparation for war, and is open to Dominion officers : Canada, Australia, and New Zealand use it freely.
[38] Ismay, *R.U.S.I. Journal*, May, 1939.

draw upon all sources of assistance, whether official or otherwise, and the work of all was ultimately bound together by the permanent secretariat of the committee.

At the outbreak of war in 1939 the Committee of Imperial Defence was absorbed into the War Cabinet. Those of its sub-committees which served a merely preparatory or peace-time use were discarded, the rest, and particularly the Chiefs of Staff Committee and its sub-committees, becoming a part of the permanent War Cabinet organisation.[39] The secretariat of the committee amalgamated with that of the peace-time Cabinet to form the War Cabinet Secretariat.[40]

At the end of the war the future organisation of the Cabinet for consideration of defence matters again had to be faced. The accumulated experience of forty years co-ordination in matters of defence, and particularly the now obvious weaknesses of the earlier Minister for Co-ordination of Defence, and the great success, during the war, of the co-operation between the Prime Minister as Minister of Defence and the Chiefs of Staff Committee, had at length indicated the lines along which a Minister of Defence, with a Department of his own, could work. Later in 1946 a Minister of Defence was appointed,[41] assisted no longer by the Committee of Imperial Defence, which was not revived, but by a Defence Committee of the Cabinet. The major changes introduced were, firstly, that the new minister had certain defined functions in defence and a certain control over the Service Departments arising out of those functions. Secondly, for those matters now under his control the new minister was directly responsible to Parliament, as the Minister for Co-ordination of Defence had never been. One further result was that, for all normal purposes, the Minister of Defence alone was a member of the Cabinet; the other Service Ministers attended only occasionally. The Chiefs of Staff Committee and its sub-committees continued as before, though now with special responsibility to the Defence Committee of the Cabinet, and to the Minister of Defence as deputy-Chairman of the Defence Committee. The Prime Minister was to be the committee's chairman.

---

39 For the fully grown war-time Chiefs of Staff organisation, see Cmd. 6351, *The Organisation for Joint Planning.*
40 For the War Cabinet, see *post*, pp. 127 ff.
41 For a full account, see Cmd. 6923, *Central Organisation for Defence.*

(b) Other Cabinet Committees

It is natural that from the earliest period of its existence the
Cabinet should have been ready to refer to committees of its own
number, special issues for discussion and report, just as in earlier
times issues were referred to committees of the Privy Council,
and approved at meetings of that body under the Sovereign.   One
interesting committee was that which drafted the Reform Bill of
1832, and, as under the Privy Council procedure, it was not deemed
essential that all members of the committee should be members of
the Cabinet.[42]   The Cimean War saw the use of committees, one
of which was set up to deal with coast defences,[43] for danger from
France was long an obsession with British ministries.   But most of
these committees have had but a temporary existence, being created
for definite purposes, such as the Finance Committee,[44] which on
the tardy re-appearance of the normal Cabinet system in October,
1919, was appointed to aid the Chancellor of the Exchequer; the
position was wholly exceptional, for the enormous defence forces
and the civil service alike required to be reduced to reasonable
dimensions, and the budget had to be placed on a new footing.

The Home Affairs Committee had a different origin.[45]   It
arose as a palliative of the disorganisation of the War Cabinet
period, when that body had no time to deal properly with those
issues affecting home administration, which in the pre-war period
would, as a matter of course, have been dealt with by the Cabinet,
and dates from June, 1918.   Its modern form has restricted functions.   It considers at the beginning of the session, with the aid of
the Parliamentary Secretary to the Treasury, who is the Chief
Whip, and therefore can speak of conditions in the House of
Commons, which of the Bills the Government desires to promote
can be dealt with in the time available, having regard to the
projects announced in the King's speech, and the claims of the
departments for legislation.   Secondly, it considers Bills in their
technical aspect, with the aid of the Parliamentary counsel to the
Treasury; points of drafting, of delegation of legislative power, of
mode of enforcement, and so on, as distinguished from matters of

---

[42] *Memoirs of Earl Spencer*, p. 292.
[43] Cf. Palmerston's War Committee, 1859; Bell, *Palmerston*, ii. 239.
[44] 120 *H. C. Deb.* 5 s., 744 f.
[45] This committee is now called the Legislation Committee.

principle fall within its sphere. In both of its activities the committee may be assisted by such officials as it thinks fit, and this point is important when Bills affect more than one department, for the matters at issue between departments can thus be dealt with, and so far as possible adjusted, without causing trouble to the Cabinet as a whole. The law officers lend their services, and thus something is done to reduce difficulties as to drafting, and to minimise the possibility of discussions on these heads in Parliament. The work of this committee, now presided over by the Lord President of the Council who is also Leader of the House of Commons, obviously assumes even greater importance during a period of intense legislative activity such as there has been since 1945.

Most other Cabinet committees before 1939 were appointed *ad hoc*. This did not mean that they necessarily broke up after reporting to the Cabinet; many continued in existence for some time to follow up the results of executive action taken upon their original conclusions. Since 1945 the number and scope of standing Cabinet committees has been considerably extended. In addition to the Legislation (formerly Home Affairs) Committee, there are a Defence Committee, an Economic Policy Committee and a Production Committee.[46]

Committees are flexible in composition, containing necessarily the ministers whose business is chiefly concerned, including, therefore, in many cases the Chancellor of the Exchequer, whose business it will be to find the funds; ministers who have scant or no duties of an administrative kind can serve, and if of judicial habit of mind can aid in adjusting the contending views of departments, but they cannot take the place of the departmental heads, for they alone are in immediate touch with their staffs, and sufficiently cognisant of the issues to be dealt with. The Financial Secretary to the Treasury, however, has here the opportunity to deputise for the Chancellor of the Exchequer, and this is one of the reasons why this minister ranks so high in the hierarchy below the Cabinet, and stands forth as normally to be promoted to a vacancy in the Cabinet. If the committee reaches a compromise conclusion, still more if there is a broad measure of agreement, acceptance of its recommendation by the Cabinet is assured, or at least probable. The time of ministers spent on committees, substantial as it is, is partly

---

[46] Sir G. Campion and others, *British Government Since 1918*, pp. 48 ff.

compensated for by the fact that the system enables the Cabinet to confine its meetings within reasonable dimensions, for much time there is saved by the assumption that the questions dealt with have been fully envisaged, and that a minister should not wantonly re-open the matters debated.

The Secretary to the Cabinet, or his deputy, acts as secretary to all Cabinet committees with, if convenient, a joint secretary taken from the department chiefly concerned, and minutes, fuller in character than those of the Cabinet, are usually kept.

One important aspect of Governmental action was for long not dealt with by a committee of the Cabinet. Economic planning was in 1925 facilitated by the establishment by Mr. Baldwin of a Committee of Civil Research,[47] which his successor in 1930 transformed into the Economic Advisory Council.[48] The latter had the Prime Minister as chairman, and included the Chancellor of the Exchequer, the President of the Board of Trade, the Minister of Agriculture and Fisheries, the Secretary of State for Dominion Affairs, and such other ministers as may be invited, together with distinguished experts. It was under the general control of the Prime Minister, and was placed on the Treasury vote. Its functions was to study all aspects of economic affairs, whether local, Commonwealth, or international in their bearing on the welfare of the country, to consider developments, and to advise as to possible uses of the national resources. Subject, of course, to the permission of the Prime Minister, it might hold enquiries with a view to reporting and advising as to possible legislation. Contact with Governmental departments and the outside world was maintained, and two standing committees deal with economic information and scientific research. Other sub-committees are set up for special purposes, such as the consideration of the cotton industry. But its functions were essentially advisory, and it made no attempt to formulate a comprehensive policy for the approval of the Cabinet and Parliament as a planning scheme for British development.

The work of the Economic Advisory Council although not in the strict sense a Cabinet committee, does throw some light on some of the conditions necessary for good committee work. The Council, as a planning organisation for national development both in a period of depression and then in the rearmament period, failed, and

[47] Cmd. 2440 (May 28, 1925).
[48] Cmd. 3478 (January 27, 1930). Cf. Finer, *Modern Government*, ii. 901–904.

for two reasons. In the first place, 'the work of the Council was not effectively integrated with that of the departments affected.' In the second place it had no effective minister in charge.[49] A Cabinet committee, to work realistically, must relate its work to that of interested departments. To work effectively it must work under the regular control of a minister who will form the link between its deliberations and the executive action that should follow from the approval of the Cabinet.

6. The Secrecy of Cabinet Proceedings

It is inherent in the position of Cabinet ministers that they should maintain the confidential character of their proceedings. They are charged with the duty of confidential advice to the Crown on the conduct of affairs of the most vital public importance, and they have collective responsibility. It would be impossible for any ministry to carry on, if it were known that there were divisions of opinion in the Government, and that a decision was merely that of a small majority. No doubt hints of division do leak out, but that is a very different thing from open admissions. As Lord Melbourne is alleged to have said at the conclusion of his ministry on the issue of the corn laws:

> 'What are we to say? Is it to make out corn dearer, or cheaper, or to make the price steady? I don't care which: but we had better all be in the same story.'[50]

The Privy Councillor's oath imposes an obligation not to disclose information, and the Official Secrets Act imposes a further restriction with publication of all official documents. But these are, in practice, unimportant restrictions compared with the combined need for common action and free statement of opinion which any Government must satisfy.

A difficulty obviously arises when a minister feels bound to resign on the score that he cannot continue to accept responsibility for the policy which the Government has determined to adopt. It would be absurd to refuse permission, for a man's honour is involved in such a case, and it was already regarded by Lord Melbourne as settled in principle that the permission must be obtained from the King through the Prime Minister. For the King to act direct

---

49 Sir John Anderson, *The Organisation of Economic Studies in Relation to the Problem of Government*, p. 16.
50 Walpole, *Russell*, i. 369. Cf. *Letters of Queen Victoria*, 2 s., i. 563.

would be subversive of the constitutional principles of government.[51]
Lord Derby in 1878 duly received permission, at the time of
resignation, but unquestionably the Queen was right in asserting
with, of course, the full accord of her Prime Minister, who no doubt
inspired her attitude, that the right to explain applies merely to
the occasion, and gives no licence to make further disclosures.[52]

> 'Her Majesty,' General Ponsonby wrote, 'expects that, when-
> ever a Privy Councillor makes any statement in Parliament
> respecting proceedings in her Majesty's Council, the Queen's
> permission to do so should first be solicited, and the object
> of the statement made clear; and that the permission thus
> given should only serve for the particular instance, and not be
> considered as an open licence.'

The conclusion to be drawn is that at the time the minister should
justify himself as fully as possible. It is natural that the extent of
the revelation should be viewed very differently from opposing
angles. Mr. Gladstone held that Mr. Chamberlain had exceeded
permissible limits in his explanation of his resignation in 1886, and
that he must ask for further authority from the Crown. The
Queen, who was delighted at Mr. Chamberlain's action, held that
the authority given amply covered the statements actually made.[53]
Lord Salisbury in the same year refused permission to Lord
R. Churchill to publish his letter of resignation.[54]

As a rule, a minister who retires gives a fairly full exculpation
of his conduct, but his attitude is necessarily affected by his feeling
as to future co-operation with his party, and the more serious
question of the degree of injury to the public interest which indiscreet disclosures may involve. Mr. Montagu's explanation of his
departure from office in March, 1922, was no doubt less effective
that he could easily have made it, but he was influenced by the
desire not to agitate public feeling in India against the Government
by making patent the disregard for Indian views which characterised
Lord Curzon all his life, and was exemplified most clearly in his
partition of Bengal. It is impossible to read Mr. Eden's apologia
on February 21, 1938, without recognising that he deliberately
withheld what must have established beyond doubt his belief that

51 *Melbourne Papers*, pp. 215 f.
52 *Letters of Queen Victoria*, 2 s., ii. 631 f., 634. In 1888, the Queen objected to
Mr. Gladstone revealing a memo. of 1882 on release of Irish prisoners, and
he dropped the idea: Guedalla, *The Queen and Mr. Gladstone*, ii. 429 ff.
53 *Letters of Queen Victoria*, 3 s., i. 100–5.
54 Winston Churchill, *Lord Randolph Churchill*, ii. 256 f.

in determining to negotiate with Italy Mr. N. Chamberlain was yielding to an ultimatum from Signor Mussolini; he deliberately declined in the public interest to press for the papers, which might have proved his case, on the ground that he was anxious not to prejudice any possibility of success in the negotiations so undertaken. The immediate fruit of the latter was the annexation of Austria by Herr Hitler, who recognised that the will to resistance of the British Prime Minister had broken, and that he must submit, when warned that he must not attempt to intervene.

The secrecy of Cabinet proceedings was deliberately violated after the war of 1914–19 in the interests of propaganda. In view of the controversy over war guilt most countries published, with more or less accuracy, the records of Governmental proceedings in the critical years before hostilities, and thus we have had copious revelations of such proceedings, including assertions as to what happened in Cabinet. What is not unnatural is that the liberty then assumed for a definite important end was rather too widely interpreted. Mr. Churchill and Mr. Lloyd George alike, in their discussions, used material in the shape of Cabinet memoranda, and their action has been criticised. Exception might be taken, either on the score that such use is a violation of the Privy Councillor's oath of secrecy, or on the more effective ground that such publication is a breach of the Official Secrets Acts, 1911 and 1920. In the case of Mr. Edgar Lansbury in 1934, his action in publishing a memorandum drawn up by his father for submission to the Labour Cabinet of 1929–31, resulted in a prosecution and a fine. Moreover, there is a certain difficulty in regarding as worthy of punishment the publication of the *ipsissima verba* of what a Cabinet minister recommended to a former Cabinet. He could not be prevented from stating what his views of policy at the time were, and adding that, of course, he made them known to his colleagues. The law, it may be feared, is not always administered with discretion. The present restrictions are palpably hard to observe, and in 1931, when the Labour Government resigned, the actors in the drama made statements of remarkably contradictory character, which a full examination of the Cabinet records would presumably have cleared up decisively. Mr. Lloyd George, with some justification, contended that, if a minister in or out of office published an account of a transaction, which was one-sided, it should be permissible to give the whole of the facts, declaring that the existing position which made publication in effect depend on the will of the Prime Minister of the day was unfair, as the latter must be affected in his attitude by considerations of party advantage; but very naturally in the circumstances the Prime Minister preferred to retain a check on what might otherwise have been very embarrassing revelations.[55]   That the information will indefinitely be suppressed is not probable; after a lapse of time publication in the memoirs of eminent statesmen will prove safe, though possibly if the new rule prevails that documents may not be taken away, there will be less material available.   But no doubt a minister has always his own copy of a Cabinet memorandum prepared by himself,[56] and nothing can prevent one who wishes his memory to be vindicated later on from having Cabinet documents copied in secrecy.   It must be added, however, that at present the rule of secrecy is carried so far that the records of the proceedings of one Cabinet are held not to be open to the scrutiny of another,[57] except by agreement between the past and present Prime Ministers. Naturally this prohibition must be confined to the motives for decisions, so far as revealed in the minutes, as opposed to the actual decisions taken, which must be regarded as an essential part of the *res gestæ*, and therefore must be known to a succeeding ministry.

The rules of secrecy apply to Cabinet deliberations and to proceedings of Cabinet ministers. In pre-war days the rule precluded the presence of any non-Cabinet minister; disapproval was voiced by purists when Lord Cawdor, appointed First Lord of the Admiralty, was summoned and attended as a Cabinet minister before he had been sworn of the Privy Council.   Lord Lansdowne's defence of his action, as analogous to the attendance of a law officer, was clearly insufficient, for he was not summoned as such.[58]   In 1907, on the other hand, Mr. McKenna, when appointed President of the Board of Education, did not receive a summons as a Cabinet minister until duly sworn, though at one meeting he attended for a short time to answer questions on a matter affecting his department.   It is clear, that in the latter proceeding, there was nothing irregular, though the practice had become rare in the nineteenth and twentieth centuries before the war, when, as Mr. Asquith records, 'no stranger (unless specially summoned to give information

55 238 *H. C. Deb.* 5 s., 2205 ff.
56 See, *e.g.*, for such cases, Dugdale, *Arthur James Balfour*, i. 265 ff., 353 f., 357 f.
57 261 *H. C. Deb.* 5 s., 1163 f.
58 Anson, *The Law and Customs of the Constitution*, vol. II (ed. Keith), ii. 123.

on a particular matter) was ever admitted, and when a message came
from outside the door was always opened and shut by a minister,'
a rule illustrated by the treatment of the Parliamentary Under-
Secretary of State for the Colonies during the absence of Joseph
Chamberlain in South Africa. During the period of the War
Cabinet a vast number of outsiders were called to its meetings,
248 in its first year alone.[59] For the most part these were ministers
and departmental heads from the defence and the civil departments,
with outside experts at the discretion of ministers, and the procedure
was manifestly necessary to keep the War Cabinet in touch with
the rest of the administration which otherwise would have been
dangerously divorced from contact with it. Since the war, no
doubt, this process is rarely necessary, but the presence of the
Cabinet Secretary is an abiding token of the changed conditions
under which the Cabinet operates as compared with pre-war
action. During the war of 1939–45 many visitors either from the
Dominions or from allied countries, particularly the United States
of America, regularly attended meetings of the War Cabinet, as
did the Chiefs of Staff or their substitutes.

7. THE WAR CABINET

(a) *The War Cabinet*, 1916–19

THE deeds of the War Cabinets of 1916–19 and of 1939–45 are
of interest mostly because they present an attempt to devise an
effective means of carrying on war by a democratic country on the
principle of civilian control on the ultimate issue of the operations
of the defence forces of the Crown, and partly because they suggest
some possible reforms in normal peace-time Cabinet organisation
and procedure.

For the first few months after the outbreak of war in August,
1914, the ordinary Cabinet and departmental system continued to
work. The carefully prepared plans of the Committee of Imperial
Defence[60] carried the country from peace into war, and though
decisions of major importance had to be taken there was no attempt
to draw a line between an inner Cabinet and the normal Cabinet of
all major departmental ministers.[61]

Occasionally decisions were taken by a small group of ministers,

---

59 Cmd. 9005 and Cmd. 325.
60 See *ante*, pp. 111 f.   61 Spender, *Lord Oxford*, ii. 123–4.

as in the case of the despatch of the Naval Division to help defend Antwerp,[62] but these decisions were always subsequently ratified by the full Cabinet. This phase lasted so long as the plans of the Committee of Imperial Defence remained to be implemented. When the first German onslaught was halted, and the preliminary plans were worked out, it gradually became clear that some closer central control and preparation of policy was needed.

After October, 1914, the Committee of Imperial Defence suffered transmutation into a War Council, composed of the Prime Minister, the Secretaries of State for Foreign Affairs, War, and India, the First Lord of the Admiralty, the Chancellor of the Exchequer, Mr. Balfour, whose connection with the Committee of Imperial Defence has been noted above, and experts. Lord Haldane and Sir Arthur Wilson were added in 1915.[63] The essential differences between the new body and the committee were that it had a measure of executive authority, though it is not the case that only under it were formal notes of decisions circulated to the departments.   But the Cabinet retained control of all essential matters, the choice of the objectives to be secured by the forces, the raising of men, the production of munitions, and finance.   Military details it left alone, except for special cause, as in the original decision not to send troops to hold the line to Antwerp, a decision hastily modified in anticipation of Cabinet assent by the ministers immediately concerned. Munitions early caused difficulty, for the prodigal use in modern warfare had never been provided for, and a Munitions Committee was set up in October to be replaced by another in April, 1915, but the problem remained unsolved, and Mr. Lloyd George tackled it as Minister of Munitions.   It is not clear that the Cabinet system in the interim was functioning badly; the Dardanelles attack was duly considered and recommended by the War Council, which was certainly competent enough in structure and personnel, and blame for it must fall in large measure on those responsible for defective Staff organisation in the defence department and particularly for their neglect to provide any machinery for joint planning.[64] The Cabinet struggled, not without success, with the issues of neutral rights, involving relations of extreme delicacy with the United States, with the effort to bribe

62 Spender, *Lord Oxford*, ii. 125.
63 *Ibid.*, ii. 126 ff.
64 Hankey, *Government Control in War*, p. 37.

Italy sufficiently to desert her allies, and with the possibility of mobilising support in the Balkan States.[65] The reproach of Mr. Lloyd George that the War Council did not meet from April 6 to May 14 is meaningless, unless it can be shown that any work necessary was being neglected.[66] In fact the Cabinet was approving all necessary action. On the other hand, later experience suggests that some day to day control of the war situation by the War Council might have provided some insurance against the risk of omission or mistake, whereas the Council did, in fact, meet only 'when serious questions involving new departures in policy or joint strategic operations arose.'[67] It was natural that the Opposition should resent the shortage of shells, especially as Sir J. French secretly inspired them to overthrow the ministry he was serving, while the failure of the naval attacks in the Dardanelles from mid-February to mid-March, and the resignation of Lord Fisher, compelled the formation of a coalition Government in May, 1915.[68]

The result of coalition was probably gravely injurious to the purpose it was intended to serve, the effective carrying out of the war. The War Council became in June the Dardanelles Committee, which was overmanned with the Prime Minister, Lord Kitchener, Lord Crewe, Mr. Lloyd George, Mr. Churchill for the Liberals, Mr. Balfour at the Admiralty, Mr. Bonar Law, Sir E. Carson, Lord Lansdowne, Lord Curzon and Lord Selborne for the Conservatives. Such a galaxy of talent failed to produce efficiency in decisions, and, so far was their collective judgment from impressing the Cabinet as a whole, that questions were raised again in the whole body. Whatever chance there remained of success at the Dardanelles was smothered in the talk and delays of this unfortunate body, which in November, 1915, was renamed more suitably the War Committee.[69] The defects of the Dardanelles Committee further sign-posted the way to some effective means of central control in war. In the first place, it was an attempt to divide the war into compartments. During its later days the Committee did pay at least as much attention to operations in the west as in the east, thus proving by its own behaviour that the

---

65 The promise of Constantinople to Russia was agreed on in consultation with the Opposition: Spender, *Lord Oxford*, ii. 129; Grey, *Twenty-five Years*, ii. 181.
66 Spender, *Lord Oxford*, ii. 160 ff.
67 Asquith, *Memories and Reflections*, ii. 87.   68 Spender, *Lord Oxford*, ii. chap. xlii.
69 For the Dardanelles Committee see Spender, *Lord Oxford*, ii., chap. xliv; Churchill, *World Crisis*, ii. 384; Hankey, *Government Control in War*, p. 37.

conduct of the war could not be divided into sections. Secondly, it was much too large for rapid or effective decisions. Thirdly, its members were already partly occupied with departmental and parliamentary duties. The War Committee also became too large, and it seems that it was not loyally served by the departments, which were accused of having withheld essential information of technical character, and of having delayed and obstructed the execution of its decisions.[70] It seems also that it was over-burdened with duties, which minor bodies could well have disposed of. Mr. Lloyd George felt himself hampered, and in communication with Mr. Bonar Law decided to press for the creation of a War Committee with full executive powers, from which the Prime Minister would be excluded, while having the right to refer to the Cabinet any matter he thought necessary. The Prime Minister rejected this suggestion, and after rather unsatisfactory intrigues resigned, to be succeeded by Mr. Lloyd George.[71] His solution took the shape of a small War Cabinet of five or six ministers, whose members should be freed from departmental duties, and who could thus employ their time in considering the questions involved in the prosecution of war. The Cabinet remained accessible to ministers and their experts, but it claimed the right of dealing direct with the latter, and directed that they were to speak freely without regard to the opinions of their political chiefs. The secretariat of the War Council was duly taken over, and the Foreign Secretary, the First Sea Lord and the Chief of the Imperial General Staff attended regularly to give information. The Cabinet deliberated on policy, but necessarily much of its time was devoted to dealing with proposals of ministers and with inter-departmental discussions. It referred minor issues to its members, or to committees of ministers, either with powers to decide or merely to report. There were, in fact, committees on war priorities, with sub-committees of labour, works construction, and industries *inter alia*; on eastern affairs, on economic defence and development, and home affairs.[72] The Prime Minister's task was, first, to create the new ministers necessary to deal with the increasing range of war business, a task facilitated by the fact that more ministers no longer

---

[70] Spender, *Lord Oxford*, ii. 253.
[71] A full account of this period is given in Lord Beaverbrook, *Politicians and the War*; see also Thomas Jones, *Lloyd George*, pp. 83–88.
[72] Lloyd George, *War Memoirs*, ii. 982 ff.; Cmd. 9005; Cmd. 325 (Official War Cabinet reports for 1917 and 1918).

meant a larger Cabinet; and, secondly, to create, within the aegis of the War Cabinet, committees to co-ordinate the work of the growing number of departments.

A useful purpose was served by the decision to invite the Dominion Prime Ministers to take part when in England for the Imperial War Conferences of 1917 and 1918, in meetings of the War Cabinet. These meetings served to give the Dominions the feeling that, in determining the great issues of the war, they were not being ignored. The Dominion Governments had placed their forces at the disposal of the British Government, so far as their navies and their oversea contingents were concerned, and except by the device of the War Cabinet they might have resented their position of being without control of the mode in which their units were employed. The Cabinet thus enlarged was, of course, wholly anomalous. It was as Sir R. Borden, Premier of Canada, declared, a Cabinet of Governments in which there was no Prime Minister in the true sense, for all the Prime Ministers were equal in status, each owing allegiance to his own Parliament. All decisions were thus subject to approval, and, if approved, to execution by each Government, but the situation was simplified by the fact that the British War Cabinet members, being in full control of the Dominions forces, could act at once on any decision agreed to as to the conduct of the war, for the Dominions, in handing over control of their forces, necessarily left to the British Government the decision how they were to be used. It was not necessary, therefore, that decisions on these heads should be dealt with in Dominion Parliaments. In all other matters, as for instance, the economic regime to be applied to enemy and allied countries after the war, the Dominion ministers could only assent *ad referendum*.[73] When the armistice resulted, in 1919, in the transformation of the Imperial War Cabinet into the British Empire Delegation to the Peace Conference at Paris, the distinct position of the Dominions was also claimed and conceded, as they were naturally unwilling to appear in a position inferior to that of the minor powers, which had made no comparable contribution to the achievement of victory, and thus the Dominions were allowed delegations of their own, beside the Empire delegation, in whose deliberations they took part.

It was agreed that, while the Dominion Prime Ministers were not in England, they could be represented by representatives

73 Keith, *War Government of the British Dominions*, pp. 29 ff.

chosen by them, for discussions similar to those of the Imperial War Cabinet, but little came of this suggestion, which would have been difficult to carry out. But General Smuts was invited in 1917 to become a member of the British War Cabinet, as an individual specially qualified. His position was anomalous, and some exception was taken to it, as he was not a peer or a member of the Commons, but the proposal was duly carried out, with most satisfactory results, as it was again during the war of 1939–45.

Of the work of the War Cabinet not much can be said without controversy. Its merits were strongly supported by Mr. Lloyd George, but it is dubious if his eulogies are all deserved. The lessons to be deduced from the experiment are not of great novelty. Palpably in war-time the Cabinet system has to be modified in some degree so as to secure the existence of a body which is in a position to take swift decisions without fear of their being disturbed. The obvious mode of such action is the creation of a Cabinet committee empowered to act, on which the Prime Minister would sit. Such a solution of the problem would probably have proved more satisfactory in the war than that actually tried, which was too much dominated by a man whose eagerness to win the war was not equalled by his ability to plan consecutively and consistently, and whose colleagues showed no remarkable skill or capacity; it is significant that no one of them left any impression on the country by reason of his service thereon. But it is also clear that the business of the country requires a Cabinet in which sit the heads of the great departments, so that they share in responsibility for all decisions. Under the War Cabinet system the responsibility is alleged to have appertained to the War Cabinet alone,[74] with the heads of the departments at liberty to advocate their views without regard to counterclaims by other departments; for, it is claimed, they had for them no jot of responsibility, and they were impelled by every consideration of departmental interest to press without stint the views of their own interests, since otherwise they might find them neglected through the superior insistence of another head.

No clear conclusion can be drawn from the War Cabinet in support of the suggestion of the Machinery of Government Committee in favour of reducing the number of Cabinet ministers and of

[74] Beaverbrook, *Politicians and the War*, ii. 323. [See, however, *post*, p. 140—Ed.]

enabling a small body to consider problems and to plan for the nation without being overburdened with departmental duties.[75]   It is one objection, and by no means unimportant, that the workings of the Parliamentary system are sometimes inimical to the presence in the Commons, at least, of men of the requisite character and ability to plan for national development.   The qualities which produce such characters are not such as are likely to lead to desire for, or success in, efforts to reach membership of the Commons or office.   It is a further difficulty that the nature of politicians is not such as to encourage the belief that men would be found to be willing to act as non-Cabinet ministers in such a régime as is contemplated.   Men are seldom willing to admit the superiority of others in the degree requisite to work any such plan.   It must be remembered also that, in order to deal with the practical problems of government, experience of administration is extremely desirable.   It is important in the highest degree that the men in the Cabinet should have served an apprenticeship of considerable duration, and even more so in all probability that they should still be in direct touch with the activities and problems of a great department.   A Cabinet may well be aided by ministers who are not burdened by administrative duties, but they will be most valuable if they have had experience of such and are still in touch with the issues which come before the Cabinet.

Neither the War Cabinet nor its predecessor arrived at any effective solution of the problem of the true relation between the civil control of actions in war and the position of the heads of the services.   The war brought with it a special difficulty in the fact that Lord Kitchener, as Secretary of State, dominated his department, and the Imperial General Staff virtually disappeared.[76] After the formation of the coalition in 1915, during which the supersession of Lord Kitchener was actually considered,[77] it was increasingly difficult for ministers to work with him, and in September, 1915, the decision was taken by the Cabinet to re-constitute the Staff and to appoint to its head Sir William Robertson.   Sir W. Robertson was anxious to effect two ends, to secure that the War Council or Committee should be so constituted as to be able to take rapid decisions without reference to other authorities; and to provide that the execution of policy should be entrusted to the Chief of the General Staff, who was on this head to

75 Cmd. 9230, paragraphs 5–11.   76 Spender, *Lord Oxford*, ii. 127 f.
77 Churchill, *War Crisis, 1915*, pp. 273–275, 374.

become the channel of advice for the War Committee.[78]   Technically, he secured that without interference with the constitutional position of the Secretary of State or the Cabinet, all orders for military operations should be issued and signed by the Chief of the Imperial General Staff 'under the authority of the Secretary of State for War, and not under that of the Army Council.'   This precluded the possibility of the War Committee, acting through the Secretary of State and the Army Council, a body of mixed composition and of administrative functions, issuing orders which had not been submitted to the expert criticism of the General Staff, and at the same time Sir W. Robertson was accorded direct access to the War Committee, which thus could receive a purely military view. This arrangement worked well in 1916,[79] and Mr. Asquith strongly upheld the doctrine that, while the Cabinet must decide on objectives, they should homologate without debate all decisions on current operations recommended by the General Staff working in conjunction with the generals at the front.

Mr. Lloyd George, on the other hand, had very strong views on the proper method of conducting the war.   Hence the decision of the War Cabinet, in February, 1917, to place the British army under the command of the French Commander-in-Chief.[80]   It was arrived at in the absence, deliberately arranged, of Sir W. Robertson, and was successfully whittled down by Sir D. Haig. But the interpretation placed on the agreement at Calais by Gen. Nivelle met determined resistance on the part of Sir D. Haig, and at London, on March 14, his position was more effectively explained, and any idea of subordination to Gen. Nivelle removed.[81]   Later in the year the two had to fight against the Premier's desire for a campaign based on Italy.[82]   In October the policy of Sir D. Haig, supported by Sir W. Robertson, was fiercely attacked by the Premier, who invited the views of Lord French, whom Mr. Asquith had had to supersede, and Sir H. Wilson.[83]   Sir W. Robertson then desired to resign, but was dissuaded by Sir D. Haig, who remained convinced that no officer should resign unless the Government declared his services no longer required.   But these officers, though ready to criticise, could not recommend any attempt to change the essential theatre of war.   They supported, however, the Premier in

---

[78] Spender, *Lord Oxford*, ii. 189 f.   [79] Sir F. Maurice, *Governments and War*, p. 139.
[80] Duff Cooper, *Haig*, ii. 46 ff.
[81] *Ibid.*, ii. 70 ff.   [82] *Ibid.*, ii. 123 ff.
[83] *Ibid.*, ii. 180.

his idea of setting up an inter-allied body for the supreme control of
operations. But in November, at Rapallo,[84] an agreement was
made by the Premier for the creation of a Supreme War Council,
at whose meeting, on February 1, 1918, Sir W. Robertson disagreed with the Premier's proposals as to Turkey. The decision
was reached by the Premier that a general reserve should be created,
and that orders regarding the use of the British forces included
therein could be given by an executive committee of the Council,
thus creating an unconstitutional position, and superseding the
authority of the Army Council.[85] The solution was then
suggested of the reduction of the position of the Chief of Staff to
what it was before 1915, and the stationing at Versailles of a deputy
as military representative and member of the Army Council, with
authority to give orders as to the use of the reserve.[86] The latter
post was offered to Sir W. Robertson, who declined, and also
declined to remain as Chief of Staff with diminished status. Sir H.
Wilson took his place, but Sir D. Haig made it clear that he
accepted no responsibility for the new position, but accepted the
constitutional possibility of receiving orders through a member of
the Army Council. Fortunately the placing at Versailles of
Sir H. Rawlinson minimised the dangers of the new position, for
he realised the position of Sir D. Haig and successfully prevented
his having to yield divisions for the reserve. In the event, unity of
command was asked for by Sir D. Haig[87] when, on March 24, he
found that Gen. Pétain was not prepared to keep in effective touch
with the much battered British army. His appeal to Lord Milner
and Sir H. Wilson to secure the appointment of Marshal Foch
was successful, and the Commander-in-Chief began effective
resistance, leading ultimately to victories in whose planning he
had a decisive voice.[88] But none the less, intrigues by Sir H.
Wilson for his removal went on,[89] and efforts were made by the
Premier to conceal the fact that the portion of the line in France
to be held by the British army had been increased by a decision
in which Sir D. Haig had not concurred,[90] while it was asserted
that the army in France was considerably stronger on January 1,
1918, than on January 1, 1917. When Sir F. Maurice categorically denied the assertions of ministers on these points, Mr.

84 Duff Cooper, *Haig.*, ii. 214.   85 *Ibid.*, ii. 223 f.   86 *Ibid.*, ii. 224 ff.
87 *Ibid.*, ii. 254 ff.   88 *Ibid.*, ii. 330 ff.
89 Callwell, *Wilson*, ii. 99; Duff Cooper, *Haig*, ii. 300, 328 f.
90 Duff Cooper, *Haig*, ii. 286, 300 f.

Bonar Law proposed an enquiry by two judges, but, when on May 9 Mr. Asquith proposed instead, investigation by a Select Committee, the Premier made a vehement appeal to his followers to support him, ignoring entirely Mr. Bonar Law's admission that enquiry was necessary, and carried the day.[91]   It is, however, clear that the problem of civilian and soldier was far from solved.

(b) *The War Cabinet,* 1939-45

When war broke out again in September, 1939, the transition from a peace-time Cabinet to a War Cabinet took place immediately. Much thought had been given to the details of this change-over, and many had argued that the Lloyd George model of a small War Cabinet of non-departmental ministers should be followed.   In fact, Mr. Chamberlain's and, later, Mr. Churchill's War Cabinets obeyed one of those conditions only in part, and one not at all. Mr. Chamberlain's War Cabinet consisted of nine ministers, including himself, and included five ministers with departmental responsibilities.   The change from plan, as Mr. Chamberlain's biographer points out, is because 'history . . . suggests that every Prime Minister, and each set of circumstances, work out their own way.'[92]   Whatever the theoretical demands of the situation, personalities do count, often a very great deal, and the main object is to construct a Cabinet that will work harmoniously and successfully. And so Mr. Chamberlain included the three Service ministers. together with the Foreign Secretary and the Chancellor of the Exchequer.

When he took office in May, 1940, Mr. Churchill did not greatly change the ways of his predecessor in this particular respect. Although he began with a War Cabinet of only five members, including himself,[93] he gradually included more until, for most of the rest of the war, it continued with a membership of eight or nine.[94] Compared with a pre-war Cabinet of 23 that was a very substantial reduction and, in that respect, confirmed the experience of the First World War and the faith of those who argued that a Cabinet of the pre-war size was too large for the efficient conduct of business. In the second respect, that of the nature of the ministers included, Mr. Churchill copied Mr. Chamberlain's practice, not only from force of circumstances but also on principle.   Describing the

[91] Spender, *Lord Oxford,* ii. 299 ff.   [92] Feiling, *Neville Chamberlain,* p. 421.
[93] Churchill, *Second World War,* ii. 13.   [94] For example, *ibid.,* ii. 287.

ministerial changes effected early in 1942, he writes, 'In direct contrariety to a strong current of opinion, I had now given full effect to my view that War Cabinet members should also be the holders of responsible offices and not mere advisers at large with nothing to do but think and talk and take decisions by compromise or majority.'[95]   In other words, the Prime Minister of the Second World War deliberately, and for a variety of reasons, decided against a War Cabinet of ministers without portfolio and to that extent, and because it is impossible at this stage to be clear whether or not their efforts would have succeeded sooner had they decided otherwise, provided a strong argument against those who advocate such a non-departmental Cabinet for normal use.[96]

In several respects the procedure of the War Cabinet of 1939–45 differed from that of the years 1916–18.   In the first place, there was no Imperial War Cabinet or Imperial War Conference during the second war.[97]   The explanation of this difference is two-fold. Firstly, Dominion ministers, and particularly Prime Ministers, were more closely tied to their own domestic scene.   Secondly, the normal methods of contact, *e.g.*, through the Dominons Office, High Commissioners, and such war-time creations as the Pacific War Council, were more highly developed between 1939 and 1945 than they had been before and, to a large extent, obviated the need for a special imperial policy-making body.   There was, however, a meeting of Dominion Prime Ministers in London in May, 1944, and Dominion representatives, while visiting this country, frequently attended meetings of the War Cabinet.

In the second place, the problem of joint control of war by civilians and soldiers was, it seems from the evidence at present available, solved much more satisfactorily in the second war than in the first.

'The fundamental changes in the machinery of war direction,' writes Mr. Churchill, 'were more real than apparent . . . The existing organisms remained intact.   No official personalities were changed.   The War Cabinet and the Chiefs of Staff Committee at first continued to meet every day as they had done before.   In calling myself, with the King's approval, Minister of Defence, I had made no legal or constitutional

95 Churchill, *Second World War*, iv.
96 For a description of the War Cabinet in the middle of the war, see the Prime Minister's statement, 378 *H. C. Deb.* 5 s., 36 ff.
97 Churchill, *Second World War*, ii. 758–60.

5*

change. I had been careful not to define my rights and duties. I asked for no special powers either from the Crown or Parliament. It was, however, understood and accepted that I should assume the general direction of the war, subject to the support of the War Cabinet and of the House of Commons. The key change which occurred on my taking over was of course the supervision and direction of the Chiefs of Staff Committee by a Minister of Defence with undefined powers. As this Minister was also the Prime Minister, he had all the rights inherent in that office, including very wide powers of selection and removal of all professional and political personages. Thus for the first time the Chiefs of Staff Committee assumed its due and proper place in direct daily contact with the executive head of the Government, and in accord with him had full control over the conduct of the war and the armed forces.'[98]

That control, Mr. Churchill claimed, involved no friction with the Service ministers and relieved the War Cabinet of much work that it had to do in 1916–18.[99] Moreover, he claimed that, whatever the control, the arrangement left the professional heads of the Fighting Services with a freer hand and more direct influence than they had ever had before.[1] Whatever the causes of dissatisfaction, these arrangements did not always go uncriticised, and particularly Mr. Churchill's retention of the office of Minister of Defence. But he considered that essential to his being Prime Minister.[2]

Thirdly, the gradual relieving of the War Cabinet from the day to day direction of the strategic aspects of the war left its members free, in turn, to relieve the Prime Minister of almost the whole weight of home and party affairs.[3] This, in turn, led to a development within the Cabinet which marks yet a further departure from the practice of the first war. With the worst dangers of invasion over in the autumn of 1940, the Prime Minister turned his mind to the best use of our economic resources, a matter which had already aroused some public criticism. With this in mind, in January, 1941, among other changes directed towards the same end, he directed the Lord President of the Council, Sir John Anderson, to assume personal direction of the larger economic issues, through

---

[98] Churchill, *Second World War*, ii. 15.   [99] *Ibid.*, 16–18.
[1] 378 *H. C. Deb.* 5 s., 40–42; 379 *ibid.*, 796. His view of the satisfactory nature of the system is borne out by General Sir L. Hollis in *R.U.S.I. Journal*, November, 1950.
[2] Churchill, *Second World War*, iv. 78 ff.
[3] *Ibid.*, ii. 18.

the medium of the Lord President's Committee.[4] Although it
would be quite wrong to liken the work of the Lord President in
civil affairs to that of the Prime Minister in military matters, none
the less this 'steering committee' did assume a general responsibility
for economic issues and also co-ordinated an enormous amount of
work in the civil conduct of the war by providing a forum wherein
ministers, who were chairmen or members of other high-level or
War Cabinet committees, could and did thrash out their common
problems.

It is, therefore, true to some extent to argue that, whereas the
first war witnessed a transition from War Committees to a War
Cabinet, the second war, starting with the accepted doctrine of a
War Cabinet, thenceforward saw the devolution of much of the
daily conduct of the war, both at home and abroad, to one or two
high-level ministerial committees.

One important development during the war should be mentioned here, since it was closely connected in many ways with the
work of the Lord President's Committee. We have seen already
that, in the inter-war years, Governments attempted to solve the
increasing problem of economic planning first by means of the
Committee of Civil Research, and then through the Economic
Advisory Council.[5] These attempts failed. Then, in the summer
of 1939, the Prime Minister asked a small group of leading
economists, under the chairmanship of Lord Stamp, to undertake
the work of correlating the activities of departments and industry
in the general planning of the country's resources.[6] The 'Stamp
Survey' continued in existence after war began to assist the
Ministerial Economic Policy Committee. Out of its work, and
with the increase in staff there grew, by the end of 1940, first a
Central Statistical Office, and, second, the Economic Section of the
War Cabinet Secretariat, the latter working under the Lord
President of the Council as Chairman of the Lord President's
Committee.[7] This Economic Section was the counterpart in
economic affairs of that secretariat for the continuous study of

---

4 *The Times*, January 7, 1941, 368 *H. C. Deb.* 5 s., 81–150; Churchill, *Second
World War*, iii. 102.
5 *Ante*, p. 122.
6 Sir John Anderson, *Organisation of Economic Studies in Relation to the Problems
of Government*, p. 12. (Stamp Memorial Lecture, 1947.)
7 *Ibid.*, pp. 14–15. (These bodies were in addition to the Prime Minister's
Statistical Section under Professor Lindemann, later Lord Cherwell, which
ended with the end of the war.)

military problems in the widest sense which had been given to the Committee of Imperial Defence in 1904. Its establishment was announced as a permanent measure in the White Paper on Employment Policy of May, 1944, and it continues to work, as part of the Cabinet Secretariat, under the general supervision of the Lord President of the Council.[8] It would appear, at least for the present, to provide a satisfactory answer to those who for long have demanded an 'Economic General Staff.'[9]

A fourth feature of Cabinet government during the war period must be noted. With the growth in the number of departments, and with the peculiar war-time need to co-ordinate the work of several departments, often at short notice, there grew up, in some degree, the practice of 'supervising ministers.' The Minister of Defence, the Minister of Production, the Lord President of the Council and the Home Secretary and Minister of Home Security, all, at one time or another, devoted a good deal of attention to co-ordinating the work of a number of departments with a range of common problems. In no case, except perhaps that of the Minister of Production,[10] was this function of 'supervision' exactly defined as with the post-war Minister of Defence, nor were the methods of achieving it standardised. A Ministerial Committee under the chairmanship of such a minister was the most common method, but the Prime Minister himself worked in an even more direct and personal fashion. In no case, moreover, was the responsibility of a departmental minister infringed.

Both Mr. Lloyd George in the first war and Mr. Churchill in the second, claimed that the institution of a War Cabinet limited collective responsibility in the strict sense to the members of that body only.[11] It is clear that the separation of a small number of ministers who are given the general responsibility for planning the conduct of a war means that they will normally answer, on matters of general policy, to Parliament and the public. On the other hand, the existence of a supreme authority in the War Cabinet, of which they were not members, involved no derogation from their

[8] Cmd. 6527. See also Mr. Morrison's statement in the House of Commons, 419 *H. C. Deb.* 5 s., 2136–9.

[9] In addition to Sir John Anderson's Lecture, see D. N. Chester, *Lessons of the British War Economy*, chaps. ii. and iv.

[10] Cmd. 6337 and 378 *H. C. Deb.* 5 s., 36 ff.

[11] Beaverbrook, *Politicians and the War*, ii. 323; Churchill, *The Second World War*, ii. 12.

responsibility to Parliament for other ministers within their own departmental sphere. Moreover, since in both wars, ministers not in the War Cabinet were regularly summoned to attend its meetings when matters affecting their departments were under consideration, there were constantly occasions when ministers outside the War Cabinet were deciding together with members of it. On these occasions it is difficult to see how a non-member, if attending the War Cabinet, could avoid sharing responsibility for decisions exactly as if he had been a member.

This view about limited collective responsibility arises only if a War Cabinet—or a small Cabinet in time of peace—is looked upon as something more than an administrative convenience, an effective way of conducting Cabinet business. Is it really to be supposed that, if in either war, the House of Commons had passed a vote of censure upon the Government's conduct of the war, only the members of the War Cabinet would have resigned? Since a Government, whether in peace or war, is essentially a group of ministers supporting the same policy and owing common loyalty to the Prime Minister, any censure on him or his closest colleagues must affect all ministers in some degree. And if, as is almost certain, some ministers in a defeated coalition Government return to form part of the next coalition, that, too, is no more than an inevitable peculiarity of war-time conditions. The corollary of the view of limited collective responsibility is that ministers outside the Cabinet enjoy the relative freedom Mr. Gladstone once thought proper to junior ministers. A Government by War Cabinet might well find it extremely difficult to carry on in those conditions.

8. THE CABINET SINCE 1945

THE history of the Labour Government since the general election of July, 1945, illustrates the impact of war-time experience and peace-time theorising upon the conduct of Cabinet business. It has long been a theme of some writers that the pre-1939 Cabinet was too large, and that the growing range of Government business with the consequent increase in the number of departments renders desirable the appointment of 'supervising' ministers.[12] Before the war Mr. Attlee had published a work, 'The Labour Party in

12 For statements of the need for change, see the Haldane Committee Report, Cmd. 9230, and L. S. Amery, *Thoughts on the Constitution;* for a recent presentation of the case for an adaptation of existing methods, see Sir John Anderson, *The Machinery of Government*, Romanes Lecture, 1946.

Perspective,' which discussed these problems. In it he wrote, 'The Cabinet as now constituted sins against the first principle of good administration, in that it does not distinguish between the function of planning broad strategy and making decisions as to the detailed execution of plans.'[13] He went on to argue that it was necessary to distinguish between the functions of ministers and to appoint a small number with the faculty of directing broad issues of policy to be in charge of particular fields of policy instead of single departments. The stage, in 1945, was thus set for change.

There was one obvious and immediate change. Beginning with a Cabinet of twenty members, Mr. Attlee soon reduced it in size and, for most of the time, had a Cabinet of about seventeen ministers. Outside the Cabinet was a further group of ten or eleven ministers of non-Cabinet rank.[14] Within the Cabinet were the Prime Minister himself, the Foreign Secretary, the Chancellor of the Exchequer, the Lord President, the Lord Chancellor, and the Minister of Defence, with a group of eight or nine senior departmental ministers. Below these, and outside the Cabinet was a group of about twelve heads of departments who, although formally of Cabinet status and paid the same salary as Cabinet Ministers, were not members of the Cabinet itself and attended the Cabinet only when specifically invited by the Prime Minister to deal with matters concerning their departments. Whether this reduction to seventeen is the correct one, it is too soon to say. It does look, however, as though a strong precedent has been set for the future division of ministers into those with and those without membership of the Cabinet, a division observed by Mr. Churchill in his 1951 administration.[15]

In the matter of division of functions among ministers, what has happened since 1945 is not quite so clear. In the first place, the Cabinet itself, although reduced in size, is far from solely composed of non-departmental ministers. Secondly, apart from the Minister of Defence, no supervising minister with an exactly defined range of powers and stated group of subordinate departments has been appointed. It is true, on the other hand that, partly as a legacy of the war years, and partly as a result of the proliferation of departments, departments have in practice tended

[13] C. R. Attlee, *The Labour Party in Perspective* (1949 ed.), p. 128.
[14] For the original Cabinet of 1945, see *The Times*, August 6, 1945. For the Cabinet as at March, 1950, see House of Commons Report, March 27, 1950.
[15] For a full list of Mr. Churchill's ministerial appointments see *The Daily Telegraph*, November 8, 1951.

to form themselves into groups and key departments, with an interest in the work of several others, have emerged as the leaders of those groups. Thus the Foreign Office under Mr. Bevin developed some leadership of the Colonial and Dominions Offices; the Treasury a close connection with the Board of Trade, the Ministries of Supply, Food, Fuel and Power and others; the Lord President an interest in the work of all departments concerned with scientific research. But this is a grouping rather under pressure of events than by deliberate planning, and the groups do not always hang together quite in the manner advocated by the Haldane Report. Moreover, and this is perhaps the most important point, what has, so far, bound these groups together is not the carefully defined powers of supervising ministers but an extension of the system of Cabinet committees. In addition to the Defence Committee, and the Legislation Committee (of which Mr. Morrison, Leader of the House of Commons was chairman) there emerged an Economic Policy Committee, the heir of the war-time Lord President's Committee. This was concerned with the formulation of general economic policy under the Prime Minister as chairman, with the Chancellor of the Exchequer, the Lord President, the Foreign Secretary, and the Lord Privy Seal as its other members. Then there came a Production Committee, 'the executive arm of the Prime Minister's Economic Policy Committee,' with the Chancellor of the Exchequer as chairman, with the Ministers of Supply, Works, Labour, Fuel and Power and the President of the Board of Trade as members. It is interesting to note that no Cabinet policy committee on external relations as a whole appears to have developed.[16]

This brief summary should indicate that, perhaps with the exception of the association between the Chancellor of the Exchequer and the President of the Board of Trade, departmental ministers are more guided by Cabinet committees than by supervising ministers. There has been a development of minor Cabinets rather than of super-ministers and, in that, the practice of the War Cabinet, rather than the recommendations of the Haldane Report, have so far been followed.

[16] See Williams, *The Triple Challenge*, chap. v.; D. N. Chester, *Development of the Cabinet, 1914–1949*; *Economist,* January 21, 1950. In his 1951 administration, Mr. Churchill made the Lord President a co-ordinator of food and agricultural policies and a new Secretary of State responsible for the co-ordination of Fuel, Transport and Power, *Economist*, December 1, 1951.

CHAPTER 5

THE MINISTRY

1. The Extent and Character of Responsibility for Administration

British governmental activity at present covers great areas of human life, and authority is exercised in most varied forms. Historically, this is a creation of a Victorian era, which saw a wide expansion of the functions of the State. At an earlier date governmental activities were reduced to little more than the necessities of defence and preservation of the country from hostile aggression, the maintenance of a measure of internal order, and the furtherance of trade and agriculture. Such local government as existed was carried on largely by close corporate bodies in the borough and by magistrates, holding commissions as justices of the peace in the country, acting in the main under statutory authority and controlled chiefly through the Courts. The advance of democracy has meant a complete change; new subjects, such as education, public health, labour conditions, social welfare, have claimed the attention both of the central and the local authorities, while the latter have been virtually recreated on the basis of responsibility to local electorates, and at the same time the needs of co-ordination and control have been met by placing power of guidance and supervision of their activities under law in the hands of central authorities.

The powers which are exercised in central and local government in the newer spheres of activity are derived from statute, not the prerogative, but the older departments of State still exercise large portions of the prerogative, though extended or restricted by statute in many ways. None the less, the prerogative of the Crown in foreign affairs is exercised with Cabinet approval by the Secretary of State with very slight statutory intervention, and much of the work of the Secretary of State for the Colonies must be traced to the same source. The Home Secretary has many statutory functions, but he advises also as to the exercise of various old prerogatives, and all the statutory regulation of the defence forces does not touch such essential questions as the control of their disposition or the making of war or peace.

Local authorities act under statutory powers and the control of the central government over them is statutory. Hence the central departments owe responsibility to Parliament not for whatever the local authorities do, but for the mode in which they exercise or fail to exercise the control which they have power to exercise. Responsible government, that is to say, is restricted to cases where it can be truly asserted that the ministry had power to act, and did not. A simple test of responsibility is provided in Parliament by the rule that the Speaker will not allow questions to be asked where there is no responsibility, and if a question passes his scrutiny, the minister can at once dispose of it by this contention, and his answer must be accepted.

In certain cases, with increasing frequency of late years, Parliament has handed over important functions to statutory authorities which are not, like local bodies, subject to periodic approval by a popular electorate, nor controlled by the central Government in the normal exercise of their functions. The motives in such cases vary. Strongest among them is the desire to relieve the ministry of responsibility for matters which, since they are assumed to be 'specialised' or 'technical,' are also considered best dealt with without being subjected to that interference based on political considerations, which might arise in the course of constant parliamentary inspection and criticism. The British Broadcasting Corporation is a chartered body, with a defined constitution, under which certain paramount rights of interference in the interests of the State are conceded and exercised through powers of control given to the Post Office.[1] It is held, however, that the devising of programmes, and the securing of prudent restraint in respect of matter broadcast, are best left to a body carefully chosen for intelligence and impartiality, so that the minister can answer complaints about the cancellation of broadcasts or similar matters with the reply that the matter is one which Parliament has seen fit to entrust to the Corporation. The establishment of an Unemployment Assistance Board, with power of control on the part of the Minister of Labour carefully defined, served the purpose of preventing daily interpellations of the minister in respect of individual cases. In some instances the plan is adopted of providing

[1] Cmd. 5091 (Committee Report), 5329 (Charter), 5088, 5207.

for control of marketing by producers, as in the case of the numerous Marketing Boards, or the Herring Industry Board; by this means the producers are enabled to apply to the whole mass of producers rules which are supposed to be valuable for the common interest, while the minister is relieved of main responsibility and can parry questions by referring to the autonomy given by the relevant legislation.[2] Other examples of technical issues entrusted to semi-autonomous public corporations are the London Passenger Transport Board, the Central Electricity Board, and the Forestry Commission.[3]

But there are difficulties in giving independence, as well as advantages. The attitude of the London Passenger Transport Board on the question of facilitating the employment of its workers in the territorial army proved so obstructive and hostile as to annoy deeply the War Office, and brought about the curious incident in March, 1938, of the adjournment being successfully moved by a private member on the second reading of a Bill promoted by the Board in order that conversations should take place with its members to arrange a compromise, as later happened. In the case of the Unemployment Assistance Board[4] the power to produce regulations was given to it, subject to approval by both Houses of Parliament. The first set produced in 1935 was duly so approved, but in working such difficulties developed as to render members of the Conservative Party, as well as of the Opposition, acutely uncomfortable. The regulations, however, could not be changed, except on the initiative of the Board. Therefore, advantage had to be taken of a supplementary estimate for the expenses of the Board, and the appeal tribunals under it, for a general criticism. The Minister of Labour represented the views of the House to the chairman, with the result that the Board duly asked Parliament to suspend the operation of the regulations which it had made, so that after further consideration a fresh set could be submitted and duly approved.[5] In other

2 265 *H. C. Deb.* 5 s., 1449–50; 299 *H. C. Deb.* 5 s., 808, 1198.
3 For some accounts of public corporations see W. A. Robson, *Public Enterprise*; E. Davies, *National Enterprise*, and *The Public Corporation*, three articles published in *The Times* on January 20, 21 and 22, 1947.
4 Now the Assistance Board.
5 Unemployment Assistance (Temporary Provisions) Acts, 1935 (cc. 6, 22). 297 *H. C. Deb.* 5 s., 50, 79, 197, 968–970. By the Ministry of National Insurance (Unemployment Insurance and Assistance) Order, 1945, most of the functions of the Minister of Labour under the Unemployment Insurance Acts and the Unemployment Assistance Acts were transferred to the Minister of National Insurance.

words, no purely constitutional or administrative device is likely to prevent criticism of a Government's policies and, particularly when estimates are presented, administrative questions are likely to be raised even though the minister answering them has no direct responsibility. Fully controlled Government departments and semi-autonomous public corporations working side by side present a problem in administration which has yet to be solved. The constitutions of the Coal Board, set up under the Coal Industry Nationalisation Act, 1946, of the British Overseas Airways Corporation, of the Transport Commission and of other similar bodies projected or actually set up since 1945, indicate that the present trend in such public corporations is towards greater rather than less ministerial control.

In such cases, as in the matters of local government, ministers are responsible to Parliament only in a limited manner, based on the powers accorded. It is normally undesirable to seek to press them to exercise further authority; if the system works badly, then they can be pressed to take extra legislative powers, for this is superior to usurping authority. Moreover, undue interference has the bad result of weakening the responsibility of such bodies, and therefore spoils their work.

In certain cases the responsibility is still more attenuated. The Exchequer and Audit Department is intended to secure the control of Parliament over the expenditure of the public money which it votes, and it is clearly desirable that the Comptroller and Auditor-General should be free from ministerial control. In the Constitution of Eire he is chosen by the Dáil. In the United Kingdom the ministry appoints, but he is secured from dismissal without parliamentary initiative, and the only matters in which he is controlled have reference to the need of Treasury sanction for the numbers and pay of his staff, and the Treasury may lay down regulations for his guidance regarding certain types of account.[6] These restrictions are unimportant; if the Treasury tried to restrict his staff unduly he would report the fact to the Public Accounts Committee, and Parliament would no doubt intervene. Ministers again are not responsible for the staffs of the Houses of Parliament, which are controlled by a Select Committee of the Lords, and a Statutory Committee, presided over by the Speaker, for the Commons. The

[6] Royal Commission on the Civil Service (1929), Minutes of Evidence, p. 1191.

Royal Household and the Lord Great Chamberlain's Department, the offices of the Duchy of Cornwall and the County Palatine of Durham, the College of Arms, the Irish Heralds' College, and, in Scotland, the Court of the Lord Lyon, are not subject to ministerial responsibility. The Charity Commission is represented in the Commons by a commissioner appointed by the Crown, and so matters regarding it can be dealt with, but the member is not a minister. There is, however, a vote on the estimates, and to this extent Treasury control. The Forestry Commission, which expends considerable sums of public money, is also represented by a commissioner without ministerial rank. The Church Commissioners, formed in 1948 by the amalgamation of Queen Anne's Bounty and the Ecclesiastical Commissioners, are represented in the House of Commons by the second commissioner. He is appointed by the Crown and answers questions in the House, but there is no estimate.

Over the Courts the control of ministers is minimal, even in the case of the Lord Chancellor as regards the Royal Courts of Justice. In a similar position are such tribunals as the Coal Mines (Reference) Committee, the Land Values Reference Committee and the Patents Appeal Tribunal. The General and Special Commissioners of Income Tax, though associated with the Board of Inland Revenue, are controlled only by the Courts; and the Railway and Canal Commission is similarly controlled, although associated with its own 'parent' department. In Scotland the Law Courts enjoy like immunity.

Over many other departments it is not necessary to set political heads, because it suffices to secure due responsibility by subordinating them to a minister in charge of a major department. The Treasury is naturally placed in control of the Boards of Customs and Excise, the Commissioners of Inland Revenue, the Civil Service Commission, the Mint, the Treasury Solicitor's Office, the Parliamentary Counsel's Office, the National Gallery and the National Portrait Gallery, the British Museum, Wallace Collection, Record Office, the Stationery Office, the *London Gazette* Office, the Development Commissioners, and the Meteorological Office, which for administrative purposes is under the Ministry for Air. The control of the Treasury extends to the Paymaster-General's Office, and in Scotland to the Office of the King's and Lord Treasurer's Remembrancer at Edinburgh. Questions on the proceedings of any of these bodies can therefore be put in Parliament, and will be answered normally by the Financial Secretary to the Treasury.

2. THE FUNCTIONS OF MINISTERS

IT is the duty of the minister to accept responsibility for the work done by his department, and by any departments subject thereto. Responsibility means that he must satisfy two rather different authorities. He has been placed in charge of the portfolio by the Prime Minister, and therefore he must so conduct himself in office as to give his chief no reason to regret that he made the selection, and that normally involves that he must prove acceptable to the rest of the Cabinet. But he must also secure the favour of the House of Commons, and succeed either in justifying clearly any action on the part of his department which is called in question, or in apologising gracefully for any slip, and conveying the impression that there will be no repetition of the blunder impugned. A minister who seeks to defend the indefensible may be appreciated by his office as loyal to his subordinates, but from the governmental point of view such an attitude is probably a mistake. If he cannot keep the confidence of the Commons, it is clearly desirable that he should resign, and thus save his colleagues from the difficulty of defending him or the unpleasantness of removing him. Theoretically, of course, mere retirement is not the sole penalty available. The right of the Commons to impeach a minister is legally intact, however improbable its use may be.[7] Moreover, a minister guilty of misfeasance in office may bring himself under a penal law, as has happened in the Dominions, even of comparatively late years. It was, however, decided not to take any legal proceedings in the case of Mr. J. H. Thomas's revelation of facts about the budget in 1936, and there would always be reluctance to proceed further against a minister who resigned, as in that case, both office and membership of Parliament. If the latter step were not taken, expulsion would, of course, be possible and might easily be resorted to. In Mr. Thomas's case his name was not removed from the Privy Council, which naturally seemed rather curious to the public who could not quite understand how a man should be regarded as unsuitable to remain in the House of Commons, but yet should

---

7 Ridges, *Constitutional Laws of England* (ed. Keith), pp. 215 f.

continue sufficiently honourable to appear in public as a member of that august body.[8]

The nature of the functions of the minister explain the apparent anomaly that the head of a department is normally far inferior in knowledge of the matters with which it deals, to the chief permanent officials. He serves as the link between the House of Commons and the department, and secures that neither encroaches on the sphere of the other, that the department shall administer and devise new proposals, but always subject to the principles which the Commons has approved or will homologate. His ability to do so is largely derived from the fact that he has served in Parliament, usually in the Commons, for a period of years, and that before attaining to the head of the department he has learned something of the conduct of business from service. A young member may secure the post of parliamentary private secretary which is unpaid, but which allows him to become familiar with the mode in which his chief handles public business; he will, if he makes himself useful, have a reasonable chance of promotion to a minor office, one of those now classed as Under-Secretaryships of State. If he shows competence therein, and if his chief is in the Lords, he will have a real chance of doing so, then he may reasonably expect an office, quite possibly of Cabinet rank, though ministers may serve quite long periods, with considerable apparent success, before that position is accorded; Lord Winterton's very long parliamentary career only brought him into the Cabinet as Chancellor of the Duchy in 1938, because of Mr. N. Chamberlain's desire to avoid having to remove Lord Swinton from the Secretaryship of Air, in which office he was held by many Conservatives to have failed to show the requisite driving power to cope with the necessity of rapid re-armament. Sometimes, of course, ministers succeed very early in their careers in obtaining high preferment, but that was more usual in the past in less democratic days. The careers of Lord Hartington and Mr. A. J. Balfour are eloquent instances of the opportunities open to men connected with great families with traditions of public service, and it would be absurd to ignore the advantage of such connections even at the present day.[9]

It is, on the whole, uncommon and in the nature of an accident

---

[8] Sir C. Dilke was not removed in 1886: *Letters of Queen Victoria*, 3 s., i. 168; nor C. Rhodes in 1896: Garvin, *Chamberlain*, iii. 123.

[9] Cf. Dugdale, *Arthur James Balfour*, i. 88 ff.; Holland, *Life of the Duke of Devonshire*, i. 56.

when a minister proves to have had earlier experience as an official. In such cases that experience will probably have been in a subordinate capacity, as with Lord Passfield, who was once a second division clerk in the Colonial Office. The recent example of Sir John Anderson, however, who was at one time Permanent Under-Secretary of State at the Home Office and later returned to it as its political chief, is an important exception and not the only recent one.

The advantages to a minister of an apprenticeship are plain and amply justify Mr. Gladstone's re-affirmation of Sir R. Peel's view that it was undesirable to make a man a Cabinet minister without some such experience. The difficulties of the Labour ministry in 1924 were patently much increased by the lack of men with experience, and the construction of an effective ministry would probably have been impossible without the aid actually accorded by politicians hitherto without Labour leanings in politics. The essential qualification of a minister is that he can form an effective judgment from the papers presented to him and the conversations of the heads of the permanent staff or junior officials specially expert, and can persuade others, in the Cabinet or Parliament, of the soundness of his judgment. That is an art not easily learned; the mass of work in any Government office is enormous, and to grasp essentials is a knack which must be acquired if a minister is not to succumb to the temptation merely to follow the lead of his staff without effective criticism. A minister ought not to fail in making a contribution to the views of his department; it is essentially his duty to foresee the reaction of the Commons or Cabinet, and make it clear to his officers how far they must modify their proposals to meet this consideration. According to one minister, 'The value of the political heads of departments is to tell the permanent officials what the public will not stand.'[10] A minister may often admit quite frankly that the departmental view is ideal, but must add that under parliamentary government it is often necessary to aim not at the best, but at such approximation thereto as is most likely to be accepted by Parliament. It is this fact that renders of minor importance the transfer of ministers at fairly rapid intervals from post to post. Variety of experience is not a bad thing for a minister, whose views must be so much moulded by parliamentary considerations. The introduction, however, of much similarity in scales of salary by the Ministers of the Crown Act, 1937, will

[10] Gardiner, *Life of Sir William Harcourt*, ii. 587.

remove the desire for change which used to be associated with the
illogical differences between salaries, and there is no doubt an
advantage in a minister remaining long enough to acquire the
necessary technical knowledge to be really helpful to his department, and to be able to meet successfully departmental arguments,
which at first sight seem unanswerable.[11] To help on Post Office
re-organisation in the manner of Sir Kingsley Wood needs a
reasonable time, a fact which explains why many Postmasters-
General have left singularly little trace that they ever held that
office.

The supreme test of ministerial ability is the skill shown in
dealing with divergent views of experts, especially in those departments, such as the defence departments, where the difference
between an expert and a layman is peculiarly obvious.   Here the
difficulties are serious.   A minister, of course, can often rely on
the permanent head of the department; in the Colonial Office, for
example, the minister will necessarily feel reluctant to depart from
the advice tendered by a man who has been for years cognisant of
the issues which arise.   But there is always the temptation that he
may be carried away by extraneous influences.   It is difficult, for
instance, to suppose that the palpable error of introducing Chinese
on semi-servile conditions into the Transvaal would have been
committed, if the minister had followed the traditional outlook of the
Colonial Office[12] in these matters in preference to the promptings of
the financial interests concerned, not with the permanent advantage
of South Africa, but with immediate opportunities of profit-making
for themselves.   Mr. Balfour's famous policy[13] of establishing a
National Home for the Jews was clearly not based on departmental
advice, and it is plain that the unfortunate muddle in policy which
was made by the Labour Government in 1930 was due to the fact
that a very carefully thought out scheme, doing justice to the Arabs,
as well as the Jews, was disturbed and confused by the sentimen-
talism of the Prime Minister, who was induced to send to Dr.
Weizmann a letter which was irreconcilable with the policy
deliberately adopted.   For good or bad, these and many other

---

11 See Taylor, *Brentford*, pp. 163 ff.   Mr. Joynson-Hicks, as Home Secretary,
had long enough to make good.   The return of Lord Morley to the India
Office temporarily, *vice* Lord Crewe, who was ill, was awkward for the Council
and staff, who had minuted against his views after his withdrawal in 1910:
Fitzroy, *Memoirs*, ii. 438.   12 Cf. H. L. Hall, *Colonial Office*, pp. 53, 84 f.
13 Dugdale, *Arthur James Balfour*, ii. 213 ff.

instances illustrate the contribution made by the minister to direction of policy in the shape of compelling decisions based on considerations of a kind which lie outside the scope of departmental policy, in the Transvaal case the influence of high finance in the City and the Rand on the Government, in the case of Palestine the influence of the Zionist movement, strengthened no doubt later on by the hope that the creation of a Jewish régime in that area would constitute a valuable reinforcement of British power in the Mediterranean.

In the case of India, again, it is reasonable to suppose, as all the evidence available suggests, that the minister led the way in the matter of progress towards reform of government, and that the development was more rapid than would have been approved, and not on the lines which would have been suggested by the Council of India or the permanent staff.[14] In such cases, of course, the inevitable tendency is in further appointments and promotions to select men whose views are likely to march with those of the minister, just as in India, when the reform scheme had been determined upon, appointments were most properly made with due regard to this consideration.   There is patently nothing wrong in such action; a ministry which has a policy is fully entitled to select for advancement those who show readiness not merely to carry it out, but to do so in full sympathy.   In like manner, movements of heads of departments may be inevitable, if the minister feels that he is constantly meeting with tacit obstruction, for the work in Parliament of a minister is so difficult that he must not have to contend with a reluctant office.   It is, of course, plainly the duty of the permanent staff to accept loyally the new views of ministers.   On a change of government, no doubt, this is not easy for men devoted to the former régime to carry out.   But a really sound civil servant will adapt himself to circumstances, as did Sir Robert Morant, when in 1906 he was concerned with the Bill by which the Liberal Government sought—vainly as it proved through the resistance of the House of Lords—to undo part of the Education Act of 1902 for which that officer was very largely responsible.[15]

At the present day the duty of civil servants to advise on issues, as opposed to the mere presentation of facts and arguments for and against any course, is beyond question.   It can be seen from the

14 This appears clearly from Mr. Montagu's *Diary*.
15 For the Bill see Lee, *Edward VII.*, ii. 455 ff.

information published regarding the Colonial Office that the practice was recognised early in the Victorian epoch.[16] In the Foreign Office, however, Lord Salisbury quite patently had no desire whatever to be advised by civil servants, and it was only after full consideration of the practice of other offices including the Colonial Office, that there was adopted the common sense rule that papers go to the minister with advice so far, of course, as that lies within the scope of a department.[17] Departments, of course, have traditional points of view, many of which can be seen in the proceedings of the Colonial Office. The Commonwealth Relations Office, in the tradition of the Colonial Office, may be assumed to favour the two doctrines of concession of any demand made by a Dominion Government, and reluctance to take any step which can be represented in any way as putting pressure on a Dominion Government. The pre-war Treasury was finally bound to the support of the policies of Sir R. Peel and Mr. Gladstone,[18] and it maintained this attitude after the war until it was inevitably modified to meet the change of views on the part of the ministry. There is a widespread belief, encouraged by the publication of a mass of Foreign Office minutes in the post-war disclosures of the trend of governmental policy, that the Foreign Office staff, especially Sir Eyre Crowe, looked with special favour on close co-operation with France, and therefore was hostile to projects for closer co-operation with Germany as apt to injure the principle of working with France.

But it is not in the relations of civil servants to ministers that difficulties as to loyalty arise.[19] No one supposes that the Colonial Office officials of Conservative habit of mind had any desire in 1905 to thwart the policy of the new ministry as regards South Africa, still less that they would have in any way encouraged the opposition in resistance to it; such an attitude of mind was inconceivable to them. It is different with some military officers. Difficulties may arise here partly because loyalty and discipline between military and naval officers may cut across loyalty to their political colleagues, and partly because, at the highest rank, loyalty from the military officer to the politician in control may not

---

[16] H. L. Hall, *Colonial Office*, chap. iv.
[17] Sir J. Tilley and S. Gazelee, *Foreign Office*, 139 ff.
[18] Cf. Garvin, *Chamberlain*, iii. 611.
[19] For Sir E. Grey's difficulties with Sir A. Nicolson due to the extraneous issue of Ulster, see Nicolson, *Lord Carnock*, pp. 401 f.

be as rigidly observed as it normally is lower down the service scale. This latter difficulty is clearly exposed in Sir H. Wilson's *Diaries*. He gives with naive pride, proof that from 1912–14, when serving on the War Office staff, he was in frequent touch with Opposition leaders, both as regards the crusade for conscription repudiated by his department, and as regards the attitude of officers of the army to the Home Rule question and the possible need of enforcing it by movement of troops.[20]   Moreover, he asked the Opposition leaders to urge the Government to enter into war, and to send the expeditionary force over to France.[21]   In the same spirit of frank disloyalty he took the opportunity, when on leave from France, of seeing Opposition leaders and the editor of the *Morning Post*, and played his part in the intrigues which brought about the fall of the first coalition Government in 1916.[22]   His subsequent career, now as working with, now as working against, Mr. Lloyd George,[23] is candidly set out in his own narrative, with complete indifference to elementary considerations of what most men deem honourable conduct, and it must be feared that this activity had not even the redeeming merit of having in any way advanced the interests of Britain, though one must believe that he genuinely thought that he was justified in conduct, *primâ facie* unscrupulous, by the public interest.

Unhappily for his reputation, the *Life* of Lord Ypres reveals him in a less obviously discreditable, but still unsatisfactory light. It is a minor matter that, when commanding at Aldershot, he used his friendship with Lord Esher to induce the Secretary of State to prefer his advice to that of the Army Council; instances of this sort of thing are not, it is understood, infrequent.[24]   But it is clear that he acted disloyally to the ministry under which he served in giving information to the correspondent of *The Times* after the second battle of Ypres, and in sending home staff officers to interview Conservative leaders.[25]   This deliberate attack on his political

---

20 Callwell, *Wilson*, i. 114–147.
21 *Ibid.*, i. 154–156.   22 *Ibid.*, i. 200 f.; for 1916, pp. 298 f.
23 For his intrigue against Haig and his disloyalty to the Premier, see Duff Cooper, *Haig*, ii. 300, 328, 329; for his complete failure to understand the military position in July, 1918, *ibid.*, pp. 326 f.
24 Hon. G. French, *Life of Field Marshal Sir John French*, p. 140.
25 The exposure of Lord French in Spender, *Lord Oxford*, ii. 141–151, is crushing in its citation of his letter to the Premier of May 17, 1915; he, no doubt, desired to excuse his own grave errors: Beaverbrook, *Politicians and the War*, i. 90 ff.: Lloyd George, *War Memoirs*, i. 199–200.

chiefs may be explained charitably by deep conviction that the Government had failed to supply the necessary munitions, and had thus injured the cause of the country, but it cannot be excused. His conduct contrasts strongly with the absolute loyalty shown by Sir D. Haig to the ministry despite the intrigues which were used in the hope of driving him from office. He saw well what was desired, but, convinced as he was rightly, that he was bound to maintain his post unless deliberately removed thence, he made no effort to retaliate, even when he could have furnished conclusive evidence to destroy the claim of Mr. Lloyd George that he had not failed to provide necessary reinforcements.[26]

A minister, of course, owes no obligation to his subordinates in his department not to go outside for advice, and still less is he bound to follow the advice of his highest officers. In civil business the minister is clearly not bound to acquiesce in only such advice being put before him as the head of his staff approves; the best practice supplies him with the judgments of several officers, and, though the practice of writing minutes to order is not unknown, a competent minister can easily counteract it, as did Mr. Lloyd George.

> 'I have never taken the view,' he tells us, 'that the head of a Government Department is forbidden by any rule of honour or etiquette from sending for any person either inside or outside his office, whatever his rank, to seek enlightenment on any subject affecting his administration. . . . Freedom of access to independent information is quite compatible with order and due respect for the hierarchy, if that liberty is tactfully and judiciously exercised by the minister and wisely acquiesced in by the service.'[27]

A complaisant minister will not bother to investigate for himself, or to read long minutes of discrepant character, and he may acquire the habit of simply taking what his private secretary sums up for him. In defence issues there is a more serious difficulty, in that while civil officers are not required by the rules of the service to subordinate their opinions to those of their seniors, there is much reluctance on the part of subordinate military officers, even of high rank, to criticise the decisions of high commanding officers. Hence during the war it became necessary for ministers to take the otherwise distasteful step of referring to independent advisers.

[26] Duff Cooper, *Haig*, ii. 180.　　　[27] Lloyd George, *War Memoirs*, iii. 1171.

Mr. Asquith invited the opinions of Lord Roberts, Lord Kitchener, and the high military commanders, in a Council of war on August 5, 1914,[28] when in doubt whether to accept as sound the views of the Chief of the Imperial General Staff and Sir J. French, and Mr. Lloyd George used Sir H. Wilson and Lord Ypres to counter that of Sir W. Robertson and Sir D. Haig.[29] No objection could possibly be taken to this procedure. What can be criticised in Mr. Lloyd George is his failure to realise that in Sir W. Robertson he had a far more trustworthy guide than Sir H. Wilson, a conclusion forced upon us by the published works of the two men, and by impartial historians of the war.

Difficult questions are presented to those departments which have to control Governors overseas, especially where there is a change of ministry and to some extent of policy. Modern practice seeks to avoid such friction as occurred in the famous instance of Sir Bartle Frere,[30] by securing that telegraphic instructions are given so fully and freely as to prevent serious misunderstandings. Thus, Lord Selborne was able to remain as Governor of the Transvaal despite the advent to office of a Liberal Government. A case of friction was seen in the treatment of Lord Lloyd, who had to leave the office of High Commissioner when the Labour Government adopted a change of policy towards Egypt.[31] Unfortunately the High Commissioner failed to receive from Mr. Chamberlain and Mr. Baldwin the Parliamentary defence to which his account of the proceedings showed him to be fully entitled, when Mr. Henderson tried to justify his supersession by the theory that the previous Government had been dissatisfied with his conduct of affairs. It is plain, as Lord Lloyd pointed out, that it is as proper for a new Government to make a change if it thinks it necessary as it is incumbent on a Government, which does not make a change or intimate dissatisfaction, to defend the conduct of an officer in Parliament when it is impugned. It is not now the practice lightly to change officers in the diplomatic service on a change of ministry, though exchanges of office may sometimes be promoted on this account.

28 Churchill, *World Crisis, 1911–14*, pp. 231–233. On this date, after consultations with some colleagues, Mr. Asquith decided to appoint Lord Kitchener Secretary of State. See Haldane, *Autobiography*, pp. 277 f.
29 Duff Cooper, *Haig*, ii. 180 f., 232; Lloyd George, *War Memoirs*, iv. 2367.
30 *Letters of Queen Victoria*, 2 s., ii. 644; iii. 22, 24 f., 64, 99, 109, 124.
31 See Lord Lloyd, *Egypt since Cromer*, vol. ii. (1934), ch. xviii.

Diplomats, of course, from their special position owe the changing heads of departments a distinctly difficult duty. If they have been carrying on one line of policy, to advocate another, possibly very discrepant, cannot come easily to them, and they may be forgiven if in making the change they cannot be wholly discreet in their comments to the Governments with which they deal. But the tradition is one of loyalty, though there are notorious exceptions, such as that of Lord Normanby to Lord Palmerston, when the former helped in the overthrow of the latter, who had probably given him cause for resentment by various marks of discourtesy.[32] The question was discussed at length in 1880, when the new ministry decided to make a change at Constantinople and recalled Sir A. H. Layard.[33] The Queen naturally protested, as the minister had been active in carrying out her late Premier's policy, and she felt it objectionable to make a change merely because a change of Government had occurred. The Cabinet, however, persisted. It was pointed out by Lord Granville that Lord Derby recalled the Liberal peers who had diplomatic posts, though Lord Howard de Walden had saved his by changing his politics, and originally it was the regular practice, as regards Paris, and sometimes St. Petersburg and other Courts. For twenty years this had not been necessary, but Lord Beaconsfield had recalled Sir H. Elliot, apparently because of complaints of his lack of interest in the Christian subjects of the Porte. Lord Salisbury himself had intended to make a change, and Germany and France were hostile to his retention. He was impulsive, indiscreet, saw only one side of a question, and his attitude had been so pro-Turkish as to render him unsuitable for the Governmental policy of pressing hard for the carrying out of the terms of the Treaty of Berlin. There was also the fact that he had supplied material to the *Daily Telegraph* for an attack on Mr. Gladstone, and, though the Premier desired that this issue be ignored, the ministry doubted whether there could be full confidence between him and the ministry. The Queen acquiesced, but Lord Granville, to his regret, found it impossible to secure the post at Rome for Sir A. H. Layard.[34]

---

32 Bell, *Palmerston*, ii. 47–49. He was removed by Lord Granville soon after (Fitzmaurice, *Granville*, i. 33–35), as he was hopelessly hostile to the new régime in France. Cf. Greville, *Memoirs*, 1837–52, iii. 441 f., 445.

33 *Letters of Queen Victoria*, 2 s., ii. 92–94.

34 Fitzmaurice, *Granville*, ii. 199 f. Granville's own father retired on the change of ministry in 1841.

There seems no later case really comparable, though clearly a change of post may sometimes be due to political considerations.

Ministers may naturally enough desire to secure in new undertakings the aid of men, whose time has been given to these questions, but who are not in the civil service. This can easily enough be arranged in the case of fresh undertakings, but it is more difficult in other cases, for the rules of the civil service require, except in a limited number of circumstances, a certificate from the Civil Service Commissioners of the suitability of the person proposed for any post. The exceptions, apart from promotions of officers in the service, refer mainly to certain very high posts, filled by appointments made in the name of the Crown, or to officers transferred under Act of Parliament. But the Commissioners, though not subject to political pressure in any vulgar sense, are not unamenable to legitimate suggestion. The existence of this check, however, is doubtless one of the causes of the high standard maintained by the civil service, whose members are not subjected to the disappointment and irritation caused, for instance, in Canada,[35] by the introduction over their heads of ministerial protégés of minor capacity. It would be absurd to suppose that political or purely personal influence on appointments or promotions is non-existent; there are no doubt a certain number of cases where appointments to the higher offices in departments can be explained only on some such ground, in view of their moderate suitability, but the grossest forms of patronage are certainly absent. Whether this tradition can be maintained among the staffs of these organisations called into existence by a policy of nationalisation of major industries, remains to be seen. In the selection of overseas Governors political influence has obviously its place, but it seldom happens that it has any untoward results. An essential merit of the present system is the rule that civil servants hold office, nominally at pleasure, in fact during good behaviour, so long as even a very modest capacity is exhibited. There must be few cases, if any, where removal from the service can properly be attributed to political motives. Naturally, such considerations may have some effect in inducing ministers to encourage early retirement on pension in order to vacate posts for protégés, but civil servants regard that as an inevitable and not very objectionable part of the system.

Ministers, like civil servants, obviously must not risk any

[35] R. M. Dawson, *The Civil Service of Canada* (chap. ix).

interference of private interest with their public duty, and that raises some difficulties. A civil servant undertakes what he knows to be a whole time occupation, and he realises from the outset the limits set upon his other activities thereby. But a minister is in office for an uncertain period, and he must remember the necessity of making a living while not in power.

The point received greater importance when the days of democracy brought forward ministers who had no inherited means to rely upon, to tide them over periods when their country was endeavouring to subsist without their services. Lord Birkenhead's case caused much embarrassment to Mr. Baldwin's Government, for he was in the habit of writing articles on many subjects at high rates of pay, and he contemplated leaving the Government if this source of income was stopped. In 1925 the Conservative Government 'decided to re-affirm the principle that ministers of the Crown, while holding office, should refrain from writing articles for publication in any way connected with matters of public policy.' Lord Birkenhead was allowed to finish his existing contract, writing, of course, nothing about India, his official charge.[36] In 1927 the Government reformulated its policy, as excluding any form of journalism, but as consonant with writings of a literary, historical, philosophic, scientific, or romantic character, for which there were numerous and respectable precedents.[37] But a warning was given that confidential matter acquired during tenure of office should not be published without the permission of the Government of the day. On the other hand, the Government did not forbid the continuation of Mr. Churchill's book, *The World Crisis*, or the appearance in advance, in the Press, of Lord Birkenhead's articles, intended for later book publication. Similarly, in 1936, Mr. Baldwin held that extracts from *Haig* by Mr. Duff Cooper, then Secretary of State for War, which were published in advance in a newspaper, were not within the prohibition.[38] A new angle of the position was raised by the desire of Labour ministers in the National Government to expound their faith in *The News Letter*, and Mr. MacDonald found that this was not professional journalism, but political propaganda.[39] The rule, however, of the Government in 1927 still stands as the expression of the sound principle.

36 184 *H. C. Deb.* 5 s., 1735 f.; 185 *ibid.*, 791.
37 203 *H. C. Deb.* 5 s., 559, 839; 216 *ibid.*, 356.
38 308 *H. C. Deb.* 5 s., 1957. 39 265 *H. C. Deb.* 5 s., 1279.

In the interests of sound administration, it is plain that a minister should have no business appointments or directorship which might interfere with complete regard for his duties, and that he should never have any commercial dealing of a kind which may give rise to the suggestion that he is preferring personal advantage to State interest. It is true that Lord Palmerston had raised no objection to ministers holding directorships or other employment, 'provided that employment can be carried on without prejudice to the Queen's service, which has a paramount claim.'[40] The law officers of the Crown were, similarly, for long allowed to engage in private practice. The briefing of the Attorney General for *The Times* in the Parnell Enquiry led to some changes. The Cabinet decided that no private practice should be undertaken by the law officers in future; and the principle was then adopted that directorships should be dormant, as regards attendance at meetings and emoluments alike, during tenure of office.[41] In 1906 the ministry required resignation of directorships, except honorary directorships in philanthropic undertakings and directorships in private companies, where the interest of the director was similar to that of a partner in a private firm.[42] The Labour Government reaffirmed the rule in application to trade union officials,[43] and it now stands clearly valid. Further, a minister, who is pecuniarily interested in any way in a matter of public business, should, whether in the Cabinet or in the Commons, either refrain from taking part in the proceedings or explain clearly the character and extent of his interest; ministers, it is clear, may have holdings of shares in public companies which have Government contracts, but they should be careful not even to appear to be acting in their own interest.[44] In the first National Government of 1931, one which was clearly due for early reconstruction after the forthcoming general election, ministers retained their directorships but did not accept fees.[45] Otherwise, these rules have remained in force since 1906.

A painful instance of public doubt as to the integrity of ministers arose in 1913 in respect of investments in Marconi shares made by ministers who had knowledge of the course of negotiations then in progress with regard to the development of wireless telegraphy.

---

[40] Hon. E. Ashley, *Life of Lord Palmerston*, i. 130.
[41] *Letters of Queen Victoria*, 3 s., ii. 171.
[42] *Parl. Deb.* 4 s., vol. 154, 234.   [43] 169 *H. C. Deb.* 5 s., 735.
[44] 198 *H. C. Deb.* 5 s., 85–154 (1926); 307 *ibid.*, 727 (1935).
[45] 256 *H. C. Deb.* 5 s., 1967.

While the attacks made on Mr. Lloyd George and Sir R. Isaac were strengthened by personal feeling, it was not wholly easy for Mr. Asquith to defend the action of his colleagues. He asserted that ministers must not use official information for the private profit of themselves or friends; they must not be put in a position to be tempted to use official influence in support of any contract in which they had an undisclosed private interest; they must not accept any kind of favour from persons seeking to enter into contractual or pecuniary or proprietary relations with the State; and they should scrupulously avoid speculative investments in securities as to which, from their special means of early or confidential information, they may have an advantage over other people in anticipating market changes. He also advocated the avoidance of any conduct which might suggest that these obligations were being violated as a rule of prudence.[46] It must be added, however, that both among civil servants and ministers instances of neglect of these principles have occurred. The leakage of budget information through Mr. Thomas, established by the report of a judicial committee of enquiry,[47] necessitated his resignation of his office and of his membership of the Commons, while a civil servant has been removed for speculation in foreign exchange, and another for negotiations with the late Sir E. Geddes, contemplating acquisition of a position of importance, on retirement from the governmental service. The motive in that case seems to have been rather desire for a more important sphere of utility than private profit, but the propriety of the dismissal, after careful investigation by a committee of civil servants, was not questioned.[48]

3. The Treasury and the Departments: Co-operation and Control

The organisation of departments is largely due to historical considerations, wholly unconnected with logic, a fact illustrated by the miscellaneous character of the work of the Home Office, which

---

46 Asquith, *Memories and Reflections*, i. 207 ff.; Spender, *Lord Oxford*, i. 361–365; 54 *H. C. Deb.* 5 s., 391 ff., 543 ff. Cf. J. Burns' view: Fitzroy, *Memoirs*, ii. 514.

47 Cmd. 5184. He had in 1935 taken out a policy securing him a sum if a dissolution took place before January 1, 1936, which thus placed him in an ambiguous position, even if the decision were regarded as resting with the Premier. For an innocent giving away of information, cf. Fitzroy, *Memoirs*, ii. 516.

48 Cmd. 5254, 5255 (1936).

remains in charge of various fragments of prerogative power and possesses certain statutory power for no better reason than its age. Here and there a little planning has been done, as when, on the occasion of the transformation of the Local Government Board into the Ministry of Health, some effort was made to deal on a logical basis with its powers. The creation of the Ministry of Transport permitted the transfer from the Board of Trade of miscellaneous powers regarding railways and ports, but the cut made was not quite clean. The relations between the Ministry (formerly Board) of Education and the Ministry of Health have been far from simple. It required in 1914, for example, a conference under Lord Haldane to arrange for an inter-departmental committee to control the question of medical assistance to children under school age, who may be regarded as needing continuation of the services rendered as part of its maternity work by the Ministry of Health, or in their aspect as prospective members of school classes provided by the Ministry of Education. It took a prolonged and unedifying contest to secure the creation of a separate Air Ministry, without which the development of air defence would have been gravely retarded;[49] it took further contests in 1937–38 to obtain for the Admiralty control over the aircraft essentially bound up with naval defence.

Co-ordination of effort is necessary in many cases; thus the relief of unemployment requires activity by the Ministries of Labour, Health and National Insurance. The Board of Trade and the Ministry of Agriculture and Fisheries affect substantially by their policy the actions of the Minister of Labour. The Home Office controls approved schools, substituted for the old reformatories, though education belongs primarily to the Ministry of Education. In defence, the need for co-ordination between the Service Departments has been the subject of repeated debate within and outside Parliament since the Esher Report of 1904. A variety of methods of achieving this end culminated, in 1946, in the setting up of a Ministry of Defence with a Minister to whom, assisted by a Defence Committee of the Cabinet, were allocated certain supervisory powers over the three separate service ministries.[50] But the Ministry of Defence remains in many ways an exception to normal

---

[49] See the *Report on National and Imperial Defence*, Cmd. 2029, for some later stages in this story.
[50] Cmd. 6923, p. 7.

practice. While co-operation between departments seems obvious in theory, the disease of departmentalism is not easy to eradicate, and the practical difficulties of formal amalgamation or grouping by some such device as 'supervising ministers' are very great.[51] The matter of statistics involves co-operation by all important departments, and this is now effected through the medium of the Central Statistical Office.

Of primary importance is the actual control exercised as well as co-operation given by the Treasury in respect of the other departments of State. This control is exercised in two ways—by general supervision and control of the Civil Service, and by control over finance. The first method will be dealt with later.[52] The second and far more effective method is exercised by the Chancellor of the Exchequer in consultation with the Prime Minister and subject to the ultimate control of the Cabinet. It is derived from the responsibility of the Chancellor of the Exchequer for the financial policy of the Government. The pre-eminence in the modern system of the Treasury is due to the activities of Sir R. Peel as a reformer in the sphere of financial administration, and its powers steadily increase up to the outbreak of the Great War.[53] They had, however, suffered a certain weakening in principle under the new régime of social expenditure, which is associated with the name of Mr. Lloyd George. Hitherto, the Treasury had been mainly engaged in seeking to limit expenditure, while assuring the adequate performance of the primary duties of a State; it was now required to find monies for social ends, which in the opinion of those who promoted them could properly make almost unlimited drafts on the resources of the State, because the interests affected transcended the mere maintenance of orderly life and supplied the instrument for a fuller life for the people. It is easy to understand the difference of outlook; when estimates for defence were narrowly scanned to secure the minimum waste, because their ends were negative if necessary, it was much more difficult to raise objections to expenditures for such obviously beneficial objects as labour exchanges, development, old age pensions, unemployment insurance, national health, housing, education, and so forth. This change in the

[51] Sir J. Anderson, *The Machinery of Government.* (Romanes Lecture, 1946.)
[52] *Post*, p. 173.
[53] Sir T. Heath, *The Treasury*; A. J. V. Durell, *Parliamentary Grants;* F. W. Hirst, *Gladstone as Financier and Economist;* 194 *H. C. Deb.* 5 s., 322.

controlling position of the Treasury, apparent before 1914, has been greatly hastened by the social security schemes of the inter-war years and of the period since 1945. With the open use of the Budget as a means of spreading the national income according to party policy, the Chancellor of the Exchequer tends to become more an agent for the provision of money than a control on the spending of it. But side by side with this weakening of control, in principle, by the Chancellor, there remains a detailed and constant check by the Treasury on spending by departments.

The functions of the Treasury are to assure the collection of the revenue, through the Boards of Customs and Inland Revenue, the Post Office, and the Commissioners of Crown lands; to secure the imposition of new taxation and its adjustment; to control public expenditure, especially in the form of preparing the estimates or supervising their preparation; to provide the funds required from day to day for the public service, borrowing extensively for this purpose; to initiate and carry out measures affecting the public debt, currency and banking; and to prescribe the manner in which the public accounts shall be kept.[54]

The control of the Treasury over the estimates is exercised in different forms. It has been seen that one of the rules regarding Cabinet practice is that no proposals involving substantial increases in expenditure shall be circulated until they have been seen by the Chancellor of the Exchequer, and his consent to circulation obtained, when they will be accompanied by a memorandum setting out the implications. But that does not mean that approval of the proposals in principle carries with it all further Treasury concurrence; the Treasury still supervises details, in accordance with practice, reinforced or modified from time to time by decisions, based on reports of the Public Accounts Committee, or the Select Committee on Estimates.[55] Proposals of a lesser and more strictly departmental character do not need to go to the Cabinet, but they must still receive Treasury sanction. It is proper and desirable that any department which wishes to increase its expenditure on existing services, or to start a new service, should communicate in advance of the time for sending in estimates with a view to ascertaining the attitude of the Treasury, and equally in the case of a

54 Report of the Machinery of Government Committee (1918), Cmd. 9230, p. 16.
55 Epitome of the Reports from the Public Accounts Committee, 1918, pp. 587–8; Exchequer and Audit Departments Act, 1921, s. 1 (3).

department desiring to spend money on works exceeding £1,000, it is requisite that the proposal should go in detail for Treasury sanction, and this even if the principle of the expenditure is already approved by the Treasury itself and Parliament. This special rule is a relic of older usage, but to judge from the number of disputed purchases made it is not clear if the plan produces much security. As regards contracts it would be impossible to apply the rules as to works; departments must comply with the general rules laid down, and must apply for sanction if deviation therefrom, as regards form of contract, omission of tenders, or so forth, is requisite. No doubt attention to these principles is of value; the South African War revealed appalling waste of money, caused by disregard of such rules of commonsense, both in Britain and South Africa, and in the buying in the Great War, where the rules could not be made effective, there was on every side wholesale waste, and inevitably bound up therewith, corruption. Further, on one issue, Treasury control is firm; questions of the number or classification of the staff of any department, or of its conditions of service, are essentially to be dealt with by the Treasury, which *a priori* used to object to any additional staffs, and to suggest temporary expedients. Matters are now in considerable measure ameliorated by reason of the acceptance by the Treasury of the principle that expenditure of public money is not *primâ facie* an evil thing.[56]

The estimates which are presented to Parliament cover all the sums which that body is to be asked to deal with by the Appropriation Act, as opposed to those sums which are by existing Acts charged on the Consolidated Fund, and therefore need not be voted; the latter include one enormous sum, the cost of the management of and interest on the public debt, a substantial sum for Northern Ireland, the royal civil list, the salaries of judges, of the Comptroller and Auditor-General, and of some other officers and a few other miscellaneous charges, such as the pensions of ex-Prime Ministers under the Ministers of the Crown Act, 1937. The other estimates, covering what are known as the 'Supply Services,' include the Army, Navy, Air Force, the civil estimates, and the three great revenue collecting departments, the Boards of Inland Revenue and of Customs and Excise, and the Post Office, whose position, however, is differentiated from the others by the fact that only a

---

[56] Contrast the former attitude to all colonial expenditure: Hall, *Colonial Office*, pp. 32 ff.

fixed sum now goes automatically to the Exchequer as a contribution to general expenditure. There is a certain difference between the treatment of the estimates. Those for the services are presented by the minister in charge (or his subordinate if he is in the Upper House), or by the Minister of Defence, the others by the Financial Secretary to the Treasury. There is unquestionably a difference in the effectiveness of Treasury criticism of service estimates, arising from the difficulty of any criticism of technical details and the control over the details of sub-heads is plainly less; the great question of total expenditure and division between the services is decided by the Cabinet, after prior consideration and report by the Defence Committee, and the Chiefs of Staff.[57]

The estimates reach the Treasury from the departments normally in November, new issues having, as mentioned above, been disposed of in correspondence or in the Cabinet before the estimates are sent in. Control is necessarily comparatively limited; many increases in civil estimates are automatic, following on decisions already taken, *e.g.*, old age pensions and grants for health services, but the Treasury records enable that department to raise points where in detail excess expenditure seems to be proposed. If the total of all the estimates presented proves too great, it may be necessary to ask ministers to accept reductions, and the Cabinet may have to decide if there are disputes; items which have been provisionally included with Treasury prior assent may have to be cut out and so forth. There are many possibilities of reduction in detail where it is made clear some money must be saved, for a department is often astute in changes which diminish efficiency but little, yet save cash, if it is definitely told that there must be a cut. Officials, once they know that the minister has agreed to some figure, will find ways and means to make the necessary reduction without doing much harm to the departmental plans. It seems clear that it is much more effective for the Treasury to demand a total reduction rather than attempt itself to suggest reduction in details. This is perhaps particularly true of the military Services estimates, where it is more than usually difficult for the Chancellor to argue on technical details. Viscount Snowden gave it as his opinion that the only effective policy for a Chancellor to pursue, for example with the Admiralty, is to say, 'I can only afford to give you so much money. Take this and use it in the best

[57] Cmd. 6923.

way you think. If in your opinion additional expenditure is necessary for a building programme then you must make equivalent economies in other directions.'[58]   Sir M. Hicks-Beach,[59] who enjoyed a really terrifying reputation as a watchful guardian of the public purse, concentrated on the mode of total reduction, and on his right to criticise all fresh proposals for additional expenditure, the result being that departments were reluctant to put forward proposals, in the knowledge that a refusal more or less complete would follow, and that, if the matter were to be carried further, the minister himself would have to be prepared to attack the Chancellor, whose formidable character in this regard was matched by his appearance.   On the other hand, we have evidence of the tendency of ministers who knew his propensity for reducing estimates to send in draft estimates rather inflated on the sound theory that, while cuts would be made, they would be acquiesced in sufficiently to make the policy profitable.[60]

Struggles in the Cabinet over estimates, when the influence of the Prime Minister has failed to bring appeasement, are often bitter; Lord Randolph Churchill, Mr. Gladstone, Sir W. Harcourt, Sir M. Hicks-Beach, Mr. Lloyd George, all suffered defeat.   Most amusing of all was the settlement of the struggle over the navy estimates of 1909,[61] for to the man in the street the result seemed to be that after hard fighting by the Treasury, with the aid of information supplied by the school of naval thought which did not succumb to Lord Fisher's blandishments, the Cabinet decided to fix at eight the number of Dreadnoughts as opposed to half that figure advocated by the Treasury and six claimed by the Admiralty. It is in the Cabinet that the influence of the Chancellor of the Exchequer, and through him that of the Treasury, is really exercised. Mr. Gladstone gave it as his opinion that though the Chancellor 'has no right to demand the concurrence of his colleagues in his view of the estimates, he has a rather special right, because these do so much towards determining budget and taxation, to indicate his own views by resignation.'[62]   It may however, be gathered

---

[58] Snowden, *Autobiography*, ii. 623.
[59] See Lady V. Hicks-Beach's *Life of Sir Michael Hicks-Beach*, ii. 151, 178 f.
[60] Lord George Hamilton, *Parliamentary Reminiscences*, i. 304.
[61] Spender, *Lord Oxford*, i. 252 f.   Mr. Churchill was opposed then.   In 1913–14, with Mr. Asquith's aid, he carried his programme against Mr. Lloyd George after discussion in fourteen Cabinets: *World Crisis, 1911–14*, pp. 172–178; Spender, *Lord Oxford*, ii. 73–75.
[62] Morley, *Gladstone*, iii. 365.

with considerable confidence that, under recent conditions, the Treasury has less than its former ability to control expenditure, though probably economy in small things is yet possible.

Control over the expenditure of the sums voted or other expenditure is shared by the Treasury with the Comptroller and Auditor-General, and *ex post facto* the Committee of Public Accounts. The Parliamentary grants are placed at the disposal of the Treasury by a royal order signed by the King, and countersigned by two Lords of the Treasury.[63] The issue of sums from the Consolidated Fund Account at the Bank of England is authorised by the Comptroller and Auditor-General after a requisition has been made to him by the Treasury, and the Treasury then instructs the bank to what account the sums approved shall be placed in its books. The duty of the Comptroller and Auditor-General is to satisfy himself that funds have been duly voted, and he maintains an effective audit which is directed to ascertain that sums are applied only as approved by Parliament, in which duty he is entitled to the fullest support of the accounting officers for each department, who are personally and pecuniarily responsible for irregularities, unless a protest has been duly made to the minister and overruled; in such a case the accounting officer—in most cases the head of the department—can communicate his protest to the Treasury and the Comptroller and Auditor-General.

It is obvious that, if Parliamentary control is to be formally possible, the House of Commons must have before it full details of the proposed expenditure. Estimates therefore are submitted in votes, with sub-heads, and items therein. While one vote may cover the needs of a civil department, the service estimates are divided up into a number of votes. The necessary expenditure for each year has to be provided in part before the financial year begins on April 1, so that a Consolidated Fund Act must be passed before that date to permit expenditure for a period of some months[64] on the various services. Other such Acts may become necessary to carry on until the close of the session sees the passing of the Appropriation Act. That Act serves to appropriate to the purposes approved by the House of Commons in Committee of Supply all the sums granted since the last Appropriation Act, either to cover

---

63 See Anson, *The Law and Custom of the Constitution*, vol. II (ed. Keith), ii. 181 ff.; E. Hilton Young, *System of National Finance*.
64 Usually four and a half.

6*

supplementary estimates for the preceding year, or those provided for the current year, whether by the earlier Consolidated Fund Act, or Acts, or by the Appropriation Act itself, which deals with the major portion of the expenditure for the year. But in the Act the sub-heads and items are not given, so that expenditure which does not fall outside the total of a vote is not illegal. But it is clearly not desirable that there should be any wide departure from the estimates laid before Parliament, on the strength of which, in theory, the vote has been accepted by the Commons, and still less is it desirable that a department should be tempted to spend money at its discretion without Treasury control. Hence, while the Treasury has authority to permit virement, that is transfer between sub-heads, without ratification by Parliament, the action of the Treasury is itself limited by principles which the Committee of Public Accounts has approved. A new service, or the extension of an existing service, necessitating a new sub-head to be opened, or an existing sub-head to be exceeded, will be sanctioned only if the Treasury does not feel that the amount or nature of the service is such as to render Parliamentary approval proper, and any large item or important new work would clearly not deserve approval. It expects in every case that expenditure should not be incurred prior to the grant of permission, and it may refer the issue to Committee of Public Accounts for an opinion before action. Though the Treasury can decide the issue, it must be remembered that the matter may be reported by the Comptroller and Auditor-General, and criticised by the Committee of Public Accounts.

As regards items within a sub-head, Treasury control is less strict, but it extends to any increase of an establishment, of salary, or of cost of a service, or to any additional works or new services which have not been specifically provided for in Parliamentary grants. This rule serves the double purpose of maintaining the Treasury control over salaries and establishment, and of preventing the effort to evade Treasury control by treating as items matters which should be placed as new sub-heads.

In the case of the army, navy, and air estimates, which are divided into several votes, the powers of the Treasury extend to permitting transfer between votes, so that any surplus realised on one vote, whether by under-spending, or by extra receipts beyond those allowed for as appropriations in aid (*i.e.*, payments made in respect of services rendered by the department), may be applied to make up deficiencies in such appropriations in another vote, or to defray expenditure not provided for, postponement of which might be detrimental to the public service. But this power is temporary; the appropriation accounts presented to Parliament of the expenditure of the current year in which transfers have been sanctioned must be accompanied by a statement showing the transfers and the reason for their being made, and the necessary approval must be obtained from the Committee of Supply, and confirmed in the Appropriation Act. Moreover, the Comptroller and Auditor-General reports in the normal manner on these sanctions to the Public Accounts Committee. Nor is sanction lightly given; if it is deliberately proposed to over-spend, sanction should be asked for in advance; if over-expenditure is incurred without previous intention, it should be reported as soon as the excess is realised. Excesses, it must be remembered, are hard to avoid when a department has many distant spending agencies, whose accounts take time to come in.

If it proves impossible for a department to meet its expenditure from a vote or sub-head in the case of those which have but one vote, and virement is not possible, either for lack of funds, or because the Treasury feels that the case is not appropriate for such procedure, there must be a supplementary estimate, and the Treasury, which dislikes such estimates, since *inter alia* they may interfere with the surplus which it would like to show, can insist on having full explanations made of the necessity. Such estimates are drawn up like ordinary estimates, showing the excess on any sub-head, thus permitting full examination by Parliament if desired. If after the close of the financial year an excess is discovered, it has to be provided for by an excess vote, which is duly included in the next Appropriation Act.

Naturally in war it is impossible to insist on proper Treasury control, and a vote of credit is asked for, without detailed estimates. In the Great War the Treasury asked departments to submit estimates to it, but not to Parliament,[65] and a certain measure of authority was given by placing the votes at its disposal. In peace the Treasury cannot control grants in aid, if placed under a department to expend without liability to surrender any balance, nor can it prevent departments taking action, which may result later in

[65] H. C. Paper, 1932–33, No. 140, p. xii.

inevitable expenditure, provided that it is not immediately necessary.

Treasury control of expenditure is clearly, taken in conjunction with the work of the Audit Department and the Public Accounts Committee, effective in seeing that the formal rules of expenditure are respected. It is, of course, clear that the Treasury has not the necessary means or authority to secure that expenditure is well directed, or even that the most economical and effective use is made of the sums provided for the departments in the estimates. But no method to secure this result in a reasonably practical manner has yet been suggested. The Geddes Committee on Public Expenditure,[66] in recommending miscellaneous economies failed on the whole to show any general principle to guide to more satisfactory results, and the total outcome of consideration of estimates selected year by year by the Select Committee set up in the Commons is not impressive. Moreover, the House of Commons cannot be said to take any real and lasting interest in economy. Reports by the Public Accounts Committee may contain important material, but the Commons does not normally discuss them, and they serve essentially as texts upon which the Treasury may deliver homilies to erring departments with an authority which the Chancellor of the Exchequer could not assume without the risk of causing needless irritation and friction.

Cases may arise where no provision exists for meeting expenditure and sums are immediately needed. The Treasury has for such cases the Civil Contingencies Fund, but sums so defrayed must be duly approved by the House of Commons, and it must authorise the reimbursement of the fund. This should, it appears, be carried out without undue delay. It is clear, of course, that by this means the control of the Commons may be reduced to a mere farce, as when the *Codex Sinaiticus* was acquired for the nation, with the aid of a payment, thus in part defrayed.[67] It was duly criticised *ex post facto*, but the existence of the fund had relieved the ministry of the inconvenience of coming to Parliament to ask aid for a purchase, whose importance takes more imagination to appreciate than is possessed by the average taxpayer. It is a little difficult to imagine such a payment under a pre-1914 régime, but the Treasury naturally has changed in spirit with the times, and that it aims at all at

[66] Cmd. 3920.
[67] Anson, *The Law and Custom of the Constitution*, vol. II (ed. Keith), ii. 191 n. 3.

economy is probably to be explained by the fact that it has to devise the means of finding the necessary funds with which to carry on.

In one sphere Treasury control has been retained, and has even inclined to grow stronger. The civil service has been brought more effectively within the ambit of its authority, partly, no doubt, as the necessary result of the wholesale increase in size of the service with the undertaking by the State of a vast area of social work.[68] Since 1919, the existence at the Treasury of a department charged with establishments is a sign of the new position, and establishment officers have been appointed in the departments who are in touch with the Treasury, and who co-operate with it in seeking to secure the maximum efficiency without unfairness to the staffs. In 1920, the rule that the Prime Minister was interested in the appointments to the highest staff offices was reinforced, so that his consent is now required for the appointment of the permanent heads, deputy heads, principal financial officers and principal establishment officers.[69] The Permanent Secretary to the Treasury is recognised as head of the civil service, and his advice is available for the guidance of the Prime Minister and the minister in charge of the department in respect of the selection of a suitable head. These arrangements help to ensure that senior posts go rather to the best men available than simply by departmental promotion, and help to create a sense of unity throughout the civil service.

As already noted, the Treasury exercises over the departments a considerable amount of control by reason of the fact that it determines the classes of officers to be employed therein, and the scale of salaries. The details of these estimates set out these facts, and over them the Treasury exercises real watchfulness. If a minister is dissatisfied, he must persuade the Chancellor to overrule his staff. Further, the Orders in Council, which regulate certain aspects of civil service conditions, including hours of work and leave of absence, are issued by Treasury authority; and the Treasury exercises the discretionary power to award pensions and gratuities by the Superannuation Acts without control by any Court. Regulations of general character regarding restrictions on activities of civil servants are determined, of course, after due discussion with

68 Report of the Royal Commission, 1927–31, Cmd. 3909, and Intr. Memoranda.
69 149 *H. C. Deb.* 5 s., 1565 f.; Royal Commission on the Civil Service (1929), Minutes of Evidence, p. 1269.

the departmental heads, by the Treasury. The salaries and conditions of service of many grades of civil servants are now determined by negotiation with recognised associations or, failing accord, by determinations of the Industrial Court; effect is given to the financial results by Treasury circulars, which are the authority for adopting the new terms, for which parliamentary authority will be obtained formally later on.

In other words, 'as a result of its special constitutional position the Treasury . . . has come to be charged with the duty of acting on behalf of His Majesty's Government in matters affecting the civil service as a whole and with responsibility for the general supervision and control of the civil service.' The actual constitutional power rests with the Lords of the Treasury, of whom the Prime Minister, as First Lord, himself is the most important.

Subject to the general rules laid down by the Treasury, each department may make its own regulations, for matters relative to the civil service depend either on contract or on the royal prerogative which any minister may control. Dismissal for misconduct rests with the minister in the last resort, except, no doubt, in the case of officers appointed with the consent of the Prime Minister, when his authority would clearly be necessary.[70] It is exercised in virtue of the royal prerogative, which can be limited by statute alone, to dispense with the services of any servant of the Crown.[71]

[70] *E.g.*, in 1936: Cmd. 5255.
[71] Anson, *The Law and Custom of the Constitution*, vol. II (ed. Keith), ii. 335.

CHAPTER 6

CABINET AND PARLIAMENT

1. CABINET CONTROL AND THE HOUSE OF COMMONS

THERE was, no doubt, a time when the House of Commons had definitely a position of strength as opposed to the ministry of the day. Bagehot's classical treatise, representing the view of an acute observer in 1867, treats the Commons as the centre of political power, and of political influence, as forming political opinion.[1] Moreover, it is only if we understand the constitution in the light of this point of view, that the history of Lord Palmerston becomes really intelligible. The electorate was deferential; the ten-pound householder held that his representative, from superior education and experience of affairs, was better able to devise policy than he, and so was content to follow in his lead. The Commons, thus composed of men who were not subject to any excessive need for placating electors, was independent; it was not sent from the country to choose a Prime Minister at its bidding, but given a freedom of choice. It could dismiss Lord Aberdeen in 1855, but equally Lord Palmerston in 1858. Moreover, government was based on full discussion by serious men, discussion in which the results were not determined beforehand, but which might lead to changes in the feelings of members and of the public, which looked up to Parliament for reasoned guidance, not for enactment of measures determined upon *ab extra*.

The passage of time has seen vital changes in this attitude, and has completely altered the position of the Commons, changing incidentally the attraction once possessed by mere membership, so that an ex-Cabinet minister may well prefer to be an active member of, for example, the London County Council, than a private member of Parliament. The same cause helps to explain how few young men of promise now, as compared with earlier times, devote their talents to a political career, taking their talents instead to finance or commerce. That the House still has attractions is

[1] W. Bagehot, *The English Constitution* (1st ed., 1867; 2nd ed., 1872).

due in part to the fact that ministerial office has high advantages, and that ministerial posts, great and small, are remarkably numerous, offering possibilities to any young men of ability, in part to the fact that barristers in practice find it possible to combine that work with membership of the Commons.

A further sign of the diminished respect in which the House is held, is seen in the tendency to favour extra-Parliamentary action for the attainment of ends which should manifestly be sought by Parliamentary means. The tendency was seen in the Great War, when Mr. R. MacDonald lent some measure of support to the plan of setting up workers' and soldiers' councils to secure, in the Russian manner, an end of the war; in 1920,[2] when it was proposed by a Council of Action to promote a general strike in order to thwart the Governmental policy of sending munitions and other aid to the Polish Government, which was striving against the Bolshevists; in 1921, when it was endeavoured to organise miners, railwaymen and transport workers, so as to force the Government to accept the demands of the miners[3]; in 1926, when long smouldering hostility to Parliament manifested itself in the general strike, the solid disapproval of vast masses of the people, and the grave doubts of many of the workers, who were precipitated into action menacing to the common welfare, and inspired by hostility to orderly progress.[4] A grave ebullition of the same temper, this time in the navy, manifested itself in 1931, at the time when Britain was forced off the gold standard, in the mutiny at Invergordon.[5] This recalled the deplorable events of 1914, when officers at the Curragh manifested their disloyalty to the State. There is little left of the deference of the electorate. A member finds it exacting and pertinacious in its demands on his time and services, and singularly ungrateful.

It follows, therefore, that the constituencies have changed their attitude. The electorate has suffered enormous additions in 1884, in 1918, and in 1928, and with the growth of the electorate it has developed a readiness to vote not for principles of any definite sort, but for personalities. It is, of course, true that the

[2] D. C. Somervell, *King George the Fifth*, pp. 218 ff.
[3] April 15 was 'Black Friday,' when the railwaymen and transport workers held back.
[4] Somervell, *King George the Fifth*, pp. 351–68, 380 f.; Spender, *Lord Oxford*, ii. 261 ff.
[5] Keith, *The King and the Imperial Crown*, pp. 344 f.

circumstances of the day, in a measure, render it easier for the electorate to form definite opinions on public issues, for literature of all sorts is more easily available, and political propaganda of an educational character is steadily carried on throughout the year, especially on the part of Labour.   But against this must be set the fact that a very large number of electors are young, and, especially if women, indifferent to the issues raised.   They tend, therefore, to vote for personalities, and to trust leaders rather than programmes. This tendency was early in development.   Mr. Gladstone and Mr. Disraeli aroused strong loyalty and repulsion, and the victory of 1892,[6] imperfect as it was, was won mostly on personal grounds. On the fall of Lord Rosebery's ministry, it clearly lacked any leader with an appeal equal to that of Lord Salisbury, who had carried on the government from 1886 to 1892, and had definitely established himself in the public eye as a solid statesman.   But the victory in the 'khaki' election of 1900 was largely due to Mr. Chamberlain's personality.[7]   Mr. Balfour in 1905, in resigning office, effectively doomed his party to extinction for the time being.   Palpably a minister, who dare not go to the country, proclaims his lack of personal magnetism.   Neither victory in 1910 would have been possible if Mr. Asquith had not established himself in the public mind as trustworthy, and not likely to abuse a fresh term of office. The election of 1918[8] was won on the personal appeal of the states-man, who was believed, on his own valuation, to have won the war, and it was the unpopularity of that statesman, through his seeming recklessness of facing the possibility of a renewal of the war with Turkey in 1922, which proved his undoing in the election of 1922. Mr. Bonar Law's appeal was put clearly as that of a solid statesman, who had provided the guiding spirit in the coalition ministry prior to his retirement, and who could be counted upon to bring things back to normal after the conclusion of Mr. Lloyd George's régime. Mr. Baldwin's appeal in 1923, on the other hand, was definitely one of principle, for the electorate had little knowledge of the new leader, whose chief feat was that of securing the recent settlement of the debt to the United States.[9]   This appeal, an attempt to persuade the country of the need for some degree of tariff reform,

6 Morley, *Gladstone*, iii. 490 ff.   The dissensions among the Irish owing to the split over Mr. Parnell (d. 1891), helped to render British voters reluctant.
7 Garvin, *Joseph Chamberlain*, iii. 571 f., 582 ff.
8 Spender, *Lord Oxford*, ii. 311 ff.
9 Against Mr. Bonar Law's advice; Taylor, *Brentford*, pp. 272–74.

failed, partly because such an appeal still ran counter to the conviction of many Conservatives.[10]   On the other hand, the Labour débâcle of 1924 was deeply influenced by Mr. MacDonald's apparent interference with the course of justice in the Campbell case, and probably even more so by the Zinovieff letter, whose authenticity, much disputed, none the less may probably be accepted.[11]   Mr. Baldwin, in contrast, stood out as the moderate and sound man.   But his ministry proved uninspiring, its interference with the system of local government, towards its close, evoked resentment, as did its insistence on equalising the franchise in 1928, and the error was made of appealing to the electorate in the pictorial form of a rather unflattering likeness of the Premier with a caption 'Safety first.'[12]   It is not surprising that Mr. MacDonald proved to have a stronger appeal to the younger voters. The election of 1931 saw both leaders united, with the Liberal chief, in a joint appeal for the restoration of financial equilibrium, which was irresistible in its effect.   On the other hand Mr. MacDonald's popularity was so manifestly on the wane by 1935 that his retirement in June was no doubt timely in permitting the appeal to the electorate taking place under Mr. Baldwin's auspices.[13]

Programmes therefore are inseparably bound up with personalities, and members of Parliament find themselves returned as followers, not only of a party, but also of the party leader.   Nothing can be more significant than the attitude adopted in February and March, 1938, over the foreign policy of Mr. Chamberlain.   The appeal made was very largely not to reasoned defence; no doubt that was present, but the average elector was asked simply to put trust in the leader, and to sympathise with him in his heavy burden of responsibility, and in the main the support then accorded by public feeling was expressive of this point of view.   It is essentially bound up with the fact that the public, as represented by the average elector, does not feel well equipped to decide on policy, but does believe itself a good judge of a man to trust and follow. It would be vain to believe that the people are excellent judges of policy, as Mr. Gladstone once recklessly claimed,[14] and it would be

---

10 Feiling, *Neville Chamberlain*, pp. 108–110.
11 Keith, *International Affairs*, 1919–37, i. 106 ff.
12 Somervell, *King George the Fifth*, pp. 396–402.
13 Feiling, *Neville Chamberlain*, pp. 260 ff.
14 W. E. Gladstone, *Speeches*, ix. (1886–88), 133 f.; Emden, *The People and the Constitution*, pp. 292, 310.

premature to believe that they have yet attained the ideal envisaged by Lord Bryce,[15] of 'a sound perception of the main and broad issues of national and international policy, especially in their moral aspect— a perception sufficient to enable them to keep the nation's action upon right lines.' Modern methods of propaganda, moreover, tend to accentuate personal appeal, at any rate on the part of leading figures.

In these circumstances it would be idle to expect that the members of the Commons should feel free to make or break ministries, or even to deal, with independent judgment, with the policies submitted by ministers. It remains to consider the mechanism by which the new order of things, since Bagehot's day, is made operative.

2. THE MECHANISM OF CONTROL : THE PARTY SYSTEM AND THE WHIPS

THE organisation of parties existed in Bagehot's day, but it had not assumed anything like its modern strength or effectiveness. Parties, themselves divided on real issues, in a sense became real only over reform in 1831.[16] In the pre-reform era voters were too few in most boroughs, and too few and too scattered in the counties, for organisation to seem requisite. But the Act of 1832, not merely created a relatively numerous electorate, adding 217,000 voters, but prescribed registration as a condition of voting. It had already been found necessary by the Whigs to raise funds to finance candidates who advocated reform, and for a short time the Parliamentary Candidate Society had existed to co-ordinate action and to recommend suitable candidates to constituencies. The Conservatives naturally rallied from the effects of the Act of 1832, and set about seeking to regain power; hence for the election of 1834–35 a central fund was raised, and a party organiser appeared for Sir R. Peel, in the person of Lord Granville Somerset, who adapted to modern conditions the activities of Burke on behalf of Lord Rockingham. Local registration societies[17] sprang up among Whigs and Conservatives alike to bring on to the register those likely to support their views; gradually canvassing voters was added to their activities, and persuasion to poll followed, but nomination of candidates was slow to develop; would-be members

---

15 Lord Bryce, *Studies in History and Jurisprudence*, ii. 31.
16 Emden, *The People and the Constitution*, pp. 98–108. After 1846 there was confusion to 1868; Greville, *Journal, 1852 60*, i. 180 f.; Morley, *Gladstone*, i. 621.
17 Emden, *The People and the Constitution*, *op. cit.*, pp. 133 ff.

were left to submit themselves, or were put forward by influential leaders, acting individually or in concert.

A fundamental development was seen in the introduction under Mr. J. Chamberlain of the caucus system, which had been working in America.[18]

Under it the supporters of the Liberal Party in each ward of the city of Birmingham were brought to co-operate in choosing a ward committee, and a central convention was added, to which representatives were sent from the ward committees. This proved of conspicuous value in the general election of 1868, for the reforms of 1867 had devised the plan, in the interests of minority representation, of creating multi-member constituencies in which the voters were authorised to vote for one less than the number of seats. The general committee of the central association undertook the work of nominating the candidates and advising the electors how to vote, so that the party captured the three seats vacant, and in like manner it secured control of the city council and the school board. The new principles of general associations, as opposed to small registration societies, and of their selection of candidates, were thus finally asserted. In 1877 Mr. Chamberlain secured the establishment of the National Liberal Federation, based on agreement of representatives of local associations to co-operate, and he impressed upon the movement the right to select candidates, and to enunciate programmes which their leaders would be induced to homologate. In this way in 1883 the federation meeting adopted resolutions in favour of female suffrage and the extension of household suffrage to the counties. There were clearly difficulties in this procedure, which it was sought to check by the appointment in 1887 of Mr. F. Schnadhorst, the first secretary of the federation, to be honorary secretary of the Central Liberal Association, thus giving the leaders of the party the opportunity of exercising through him a moderating influence on the exuberance of the federation, whose members naturally were without any of the responsibilities of carrying through Parliament the wide schemes of reforms for which they joyfully voted at the annual conference.[19] Mr. Schnadhorst,

---

[18] See Garvin, *Joseph Chamberlain*, i. chap. xiv., for his hero's contribution. For a general account of the growth of party organisation after 1830, see A. L. Lowell, *The Government of England*, pt. ii.

[19] For criticisms, see Gardiner, *Harcourt*, ii. 407; Crewe, *Rosebery*, ii. 595. For the curious episode of Mr. Rhodes' donation of £5,000 in 1891, see Spender, *Campbell-Bannerman*, i. 202 ff.

however, was quite unable to prevent the adoption, with the reluctant acquiescence of the party leaders, of the grandiose Newcastle programme of 1891, with its declaration in favour of Irish Home Rule, the rule of manhood suffrage, the disestablishment of the Church of England in Wales and the Church of Scotland, local veto, the creation of parish councils, and compensation to workers for injury. Unquestionably so elaborate a programme was certain to prove most embarrassing to the ministry of 1892, with its majority of forty but barely sufficient for moderate legislation, and with the solid opposition of the House of Lords to reform. The lesson was not wholly wasted. The business for the annual meeting of the Council, which Mr. Chamberlain had planned to be the informal Parliament of Liberalism, was given in 1896 to an Executive Committee to frame, and the Council thus came to perform the part desired by Mr. Schnadhorst of homologating great policies which the leader had determined to be suitable for party support, with a reasonable prospect of being able to carry them into effect if and when the electorate gave power.

The comparatively restricted sphere of the federation side by side with the Central Office has remained unaltered in essentials through the many vicissitudes of the party since the war, which have resulted in changes in detail in organisation, partly due to the necessity of co-operation with Mr. Lloyd George, whose political fund, collected during the period before the breaking up of the coalition Government, was only put in part at the disposal of the party for electoral purposes under conditions securing a measure of control by its holder.[20] In 1936, however, the federation was re-constituted by the Liberal Party Convention as the Liberal Party. The system is of the form suggested in 1877; local constituency associations,[21] in substantial measure autonomous, districts with area federations to foster joint action, and the federation, renamed the Liberal Party, with its Council and Assembly. The control of the selection of candidates is vital, it rests in part with the constituency, in part with the central or whip's office, whose approval is essential if the candidate is to be aided wholly or in part towards the payment of his election expenses. The party funds were in the period of free trade supplied in some measure

[20] C. Mallet, *Lloyd George*, pp. 246 ff.
[21] Other bodies may be affiliated and allowed representation on Council and Assembly.

by firms and others interested in the maintenance of that system.[22] Since the decline of free trade, and since the fortunes of the party have fallen on evil days, this source of supply has been mainly cut off, and an effort has been made with some success to induce local associations to finance their own expenses, and to build up a fighting fund for elections. Few candidates now forthcoming are fortunate enough to be able and willing to meet their own expenditure, a fact which explains the dependence at the election of 1929 of the party on Mr. Lloyd George's support for the funds necessary to permit of putting enough candidates in the field to render an effective contest practicable. With the growing decline in the fortunes of the party and the separation from it in 1931 of the Liberal Nationals, who created an organisation of their own on parallel lines, but with slight support of the rank and file, the prospect for the party fortunes reviving, steadily diminished. The federation has a counterpart in Scotland, which is in close association though not dependent upon it, in the Scottish Liberal Federation, and the special aspects of Liberalism, which appeal to women, are catered for in the Women's Liberal Federation. The League of Young Liberals provides an organisation for youth.

The National Union of Conservative and Constitutional Societies was the outcome of the addition of a million new voters by the Reform Scheme of 1867, and its progress was stimulated by the contemporary success of the caucus scheme in Birmingham. But its expansion in authority was delayed until a re-organisation in 1885–86, which created a regional organisation intermediate between the Union and the local associations. The plan of passing resolutions on policy dates thence, but at no time, down to the present, has the annual Conference of the Union possessed much importance as an exponent of independent views.[23] Its support

---

22 Peers and M.P.'s to the number of 114 were expected in December, 1879, to pay up an average of £500 apiece; Esher, *Journals and Letters*, i. 65. Cf. the attempt in 1925 to raise a million fund; *Sir Robert Hudson: a Memoir*, pp. 172 f. Each constituency is now expected to raise funds for its own expenses and for the general election; the Council also raises funds, and is in touch with the whip's office, and encourages constituents to find candidates. It works through four Standing Committees. The Executives of the League of Young Liberals and the Women's Liberal Federation rank as Committees.

23 It was, however, the fear of hostility at the National Union meeting of November 13, 1922, that decided the loyal coalition ministers to dissolve before then and appeal to the electorate as a coalition; this led to the secession of Lord Curzon and the break up of the ministry; Nicolson, *Curzon*, pp. 276 ff.

of preferential trade was ignored prior to Mr. Chamberlain's conversion, its advocacy of female suffrage went unheeded, its more recent pleading for the reform of the House of Lords has received no homologation from Mr. Baldwin's or Mr. Chamberlain's régimes, and only on India was the division of opinion regarded as sufficiently strong to induce the Prime Minister to lend his weight to efforts to secure that the Union should not, either at a Council meeting or at the annual Conference, definitely reject the scheme. It is rare for the Conference to carry any resolution against the views of the ministers who attend to encourage it to walk in safe paths; surprise was widely felt when in 1937 a grievance of ex-servicemen elicited a demand for an enquiry protested against by the minister responsible.[24]

Funds are readily available for Conservative purposes: from landowners, financiers, industrialists, bankers, those engaged in the manufacture and distribution of intoxicants and others, for the party is naturally regarded as still the stronghold of property, and as essential to defend those who enjoy it from the assault of communism or socialism. Even so, there has been a movement to seek to secure that local associations shall adopt the plan of raising funds for their own expenses, and to aid in the payments of expenses of candidates who otherwise could not stand. One difficulty of the party has long been the fact that constituencies are eager to select candidates who can normally be trusted to defray all the expenses of their election and the maintenance of the local party agent, to the exclusion of young men of promise but without resources. This fact hampers the effectiveness of the party, and produces, what is at times, but not often, embarrassing, a number of members who may not be wholly amenable to the party whips. It has therefore been decided that candidates, while chosen primarily by the chief constituency associations, shall also be approved by a Standing Advisory Committee. The proposal was criticised on March 24, 1938, on the score that it might give too much power to the central office, but it was defended on the ground that the Committee commanded general confidence and understood its function to be to aid associations in finding suitable candidates, not to impose candidates upon them. The alternative would no doubt be to leave the decision in effect to the Chairman of the Central

[24] Effect to it was definitely refused by the Premier in April, 1938.

Office,[25] who is the nominee of the Prime Minister as head of the party and in immediate control of the party funds, whose wise employment for propaganda is an essential factor in organising victory.

The Labour Party presents a different aspect to the older parties, and one undoubtedly more democratic. In its inception, indeed, it was essentially a class body; the organisers of the Labour Representation Committee of 1900, and the controllers of the early form of the party, were imbued with the idea that the workers were manual workers par excellence, and the party constitution was based on a federation of trade unions, trades councils, socialist societies, and some local Labour parties. In 1918, with the passing of the Representation of the People Act, giving manhood suffrage, a wider policy prevailed, and the Nottingham Conference opened the way to membership of the party, not merely by affiliated organisations, but also by individual men or women who were members of local Labour parties and accepted its constitution and programme, it being made clear that work included brain work as fully as manual labour.[26] This was followed by the constitution of many local parties, together with the reconstruction of those already existing, to allow of effect being giving to the new views. In 1927 an important accession of strength was secured through the acceptance of a formal alliance by the Congress of the Co-operative Union. In October, at the Blackpool Conference, the Executive Committee was authorised to prepare a statement of Labour objectives, and its elaborate pronouncement, *Labour and the Nation*, was accepted by the Birmingham Conference in 1928. The failure of the Labour Prime Minister in 1931 to hold fast to the doctrines thus promulgated at his own original suggestion and with his consent strengthened, not weakened, the determination of the party to secure that its policy shall be carried out. The party executive therefore framed rules to control the action of the leader of the party in the formation of a Cabinet and in recommending a dissolution of Parliament.[27] Further, since 1929, affiliated

---

[25] The great importance of this office in the hands of Sir G. Younger was seen in his influence on the 'coupon' election of 1918 (Spender, *Lord Oxford*, ii. 314 ff.), and on the Unionist desertion of Mr. Lloyd George in 1922.

[26] *Labour and the New Social Order* (prepared in 1917). The party now became definitely socialist in creed. A striking demonstration of the new nature of the party, of its all-class basis, was given in the General Election of 1945; the Parliamentary party then returned to power was representative of all classes, professions, and trades in the community.

[27] Finer, *The Future of Government*, p. 87, n. 15.

associations have been required to accept the principles and policy of the party, to conform to its constitution and standing orders, and to submit their rules to the executive of the party. This principle has caused serious dissension, because a section of the Labour Party, while not desiring to incur the unpopularity of adopting Communism, with its denial of democratic government and its enthusiasm for a dictatorship of the proletariat, is anxious to co-operate, as far as possible, with Communists. This led to the disaffiliation of the Independent Labour Party in 1931,[28] but the contest was renewed in 1936–37, because of the activities since 1934 of the Socialist League, whose leading spirit was Sir S. Cripps, and which on the analogy of the Popular Front in France, formed by Radicals, Socialists, and Communists after the election of 1936, desired to secure a common front of the Labour Party and Communists against capitalism. In 1937, however, this effort was defeated by a very decisive vote of the Conference, though the vote was softened by the contemporaneous adoption of an important reform in the manner of constituting the executive committee. Since 1945, and despite the re-casting of the constitution of the Labour Party in 1932–3 in order to impose a large measure of control over the parliamentary leadership of the party, an interesting feature of Labour Party history has been the ease with which party leaders have been able to dominate the annual party conference. Whatever the party constitution, this is always likely to be the result of the far greater responsibility and knowledge possessed by those who actually hold office.

The Executive Committee of the party was, under the early constitution, composed of sixteen members elected by the annual Conference, eleven representing the trade union movement. In 1918 the number was increased to twenty-three, of whom thirteen were assigned to the national affiliated societies, five to local parties, four to represent women, and the Treasurer *ex officio*, nominations being made by societies and constituency organisations respectively, and election being determined by the full Conference. This arrangement was naturally attacked by the *intelligentsia*, as restricting unduly their influence on the executive, and the number of members open to election to represent the local parties was increased, after a somewhat close vote, to seven, Sir S. Cripps becoming at once a chosen member. In that capacity, however, he had to cease

28 Mr. MacDonald and Mr. Snowden had resigned in 1930.

co-operation on platforms with Communists, while the Socialist League came to an end. The pro-Communist elements of the party obtained a wider sphere of operation from within the party itself, which accords with the tactics enjoined by the Third International.[29]

The executive committee performs like functions to those carried out by the Conservative and Unionist Central Office. It controls the Central Office of the party, and it takes care to secure that the party is represented in each constituency by an organisation, if at all possible; it gives effect to the decisions of the Conference, interprets both constitution and standing orders in case of dispute, subject to appeal to the Conference, and expels individuals and disaffiliates organisations if they offend against the constitution. It promotes the activity of a large number of organisers of men and women alike, and supervises research in the fields of information on labour topics, in international relations, promotes publicity in various forms, and shares with the Trades Union Congress a department for legal advice. The research department is prolific of information on public finance, health, education, justice, local government, land and agriculture, and propaganda is largely provided in the form of pamphlets. The former policy of seeking to run a party newspaper, the *Daily Herald*, has been departed from in favour of entrusting the control to a skilled newspaper organiser, with excellent results. The central organisation exercises a definite influence on the selection of candidates, a stronger influence, in fact, than is exercised in either of the other two parties. The initiative of the local constituency is essential, but the final approval of the executive is necessary. It is requisite that a would-be candidate should stand simply and solely as a Labour candidate, and that in his election address he should include the issues which have been approved by the executive as proper to be stressed at the moment, while, if elected, he must agree to act in accordance with the constitution and standing orders. A problem of special difficulty presents itself with regard to the selection of candidates in areas where a certain trade union is strongly represented, for the union is apt to claim that its nominee should be chosen, especially as the unions are the source whence most of the funds of the party are derived. The system secures a revenue from contributions of

---

[29] In 1938 the executive denounced any idea of forming a Popular Front with Liberals or any others.

unions, socialist and co-operative societies, Labour parties, and trades councils, but the only large returns are from the unions, which were permitted by the Trade Union Act, 1913, to collect a political levy from all members stating their willingness to contribute.[30]   But, though the unions frequently secure the choice of their protégés, this is by no means always the case.   As in the case of the other parties, it is customary to raise by special appeals a fighting fund for a general election, a consideration which gives special weight to the views of the unions.

The control of the executive over a candidate once elected is indirect.   But the desire of the party to maintain solidarity is seen in the system under which the executive co-operates with the executive chosen by the Parliamentary party and the General Council of the Trades Union Congress in the National Council of Labour.   Thus, on March 25, 1938, after a conference in London of these bodies, a manifesto was issued condemning the attitude of Mr. Chamberlain in the matter of Czechoslovakia and the League of Nations, and demanding an immediate meeting of the League Assembly.   In the same spirit of democracy, when Labour is in office, a consultative committee is appointed to keep the rank and file in touch with the ministry, and, when not in office, an executive committee determines the party policy in those minor issues which do not fall under the general principles of the party.[31]   In the case of the Conservatives and Liberals, on the other hand, the control remains with the ex-Prime Minister, who normally consults with the members of his last Cabinet, to whom on occasion other men of promise may be added.

Thus, a summary sketch of the organisations indicates clearly how little independence is left to the average candidate for Parliament.   In almost every case to seek a seat without party backing is mere waste of time and money.   A candidate therefore has to pledge his support to the party, or more specifically to the Prime Minister, or Leader of the Opposition, as the case may be.   Moreover, his chance of success will largely depend on the strength with which he is believed to hold the faith.   The average member elected thus is, normally by habit of mind and profession, a strict party man.

---

30 Modifications to the Act of 1913, or earlier Acts, introduced by the Trades Disputes Act of 1927, were reversed by the Labour Party immediately after taking office in 1945.

31 Any accord in regard to bargaining in constituencies for electoral purposes would need the assent of the National Executive.

Once elected, he falls under the control of the party whips, governmental or opposition, whose business it is to see that the members do not stray from the party fold, and that they vote regularly, except when with due permission they are paired. No doubt the extent of the discipline exercised varies from time to time. If the majority is large, it is impossible to avoid slackness in attendance, and members will absent themselves unpaired. But they must rally if the summons is specially urgent, and failure to obey an urgent summons is considered a breach of loyalty towards the party. Such disobedience, or frequent failure to obey the 'whip' on even minor occasions, almost certainly means loss of party support at the next election. The whips, of course, are aided in their task by many considerations, in addition to the personal appeal which men like Mr. Akers-Douglas, Mr. Marjoribanks, or the Master of Elibank could exercise by dint of character and psychological insight. Men have many motives to be loyal. They feel a definite obligation to their constituents; Mr. Mason in 1932 did not deny the right of his constituents in East Edinburgh to criticise his opposition to Protection, but insisted that he had made his retention of the right to oppose clear during the electoral contest when Conservatives had voted for him; in 1935, however, he was relegated to the bottom of the poll. In March, 1938, a hot controversy was carried on between Mr. Charles Emmott and the executive committee of the East Surrey Unionist Association, which demanded his resignation apparently, because, while he proved a loyal supporter of the ministry, he was not afraid to express his own sentiments. It is interesting to note that the committee[32] was not willing, in his opinion, to give him adequate facilities for his defence.

A further consideration of weight is the interest a member naturally feels in either public or private legislative proposals, which may suffer if he proves recalcitrant to the orders of the whips. A private member has indeed a chance by the luck of the ballot to secure a second reading for a Bill, but, when it passes committee, it often has no chance of passing a third reading unless the Government will prove helpful. Thus the Matrimonial Causes Act, 1937,

---

[32] These bodies are nearly always composed of a small body of stalwarts who hold together and secure re-election at meetings of the Constituency Associations, which normally are poorly attended, by mutual support. Hence the frequent choice of unsatisfactory candidates, especially those commended by the Central Office.

promoted by Mr. A. P. Herbert, received its chance only through governmental favour, which would not have been accorded to a *persona ingrata*. Members again may be interested in procuring for themselves, or others, honorary distinctions, or office, ministerial or other, or be anxious to serve on royal committees, and such favours are not for recalcitrant members, who cannot look to enthusiasm if they seek to promote the interests of their constituency or individuals therein with any government department, whereas a minister will accord unusual complaisance to the member who comes to him with a suggestion from the chief whip, that he would be glad if anything can be done for so and so, who is such a loyal supporter.

Yet another consideration weighs heavily with the recalcitrant member. If he falls from grace the whips will report his activities to his constituency association, and he will be refused their imprimatur if he seeks re-election. Without it very few members can hope for a new term of membership, and few men are eager to fight an election at their own cost and with scant prospect of success. To those who depend in any measure on their salaries for their living the issue is one of grave importance, and loyalty becomes almost automatic.[33] It is this consideration which renders so effective a hint that, if the Government is not supported on some issue, it will dissolve Parliament. The member who hears this threat is conscious that he may very well be a sufferer from hastily induced action, and may speedily find it possible to reconsider his views. The day is certainly gone when members could face a threat of this sort with equanimity, and the hold of the ministry is thus greatly increased. It may be that Labour members are specially tied to obedience, but it is not clear that, in fact, either Conservative or Liberal members are in a much better case. In opposition, of course, there is less severity of pressure,[34] but here also it is very far from being the case that freedom is widely granted. Where the party seeks, for instance, to secure a snap vote against the ministry, punctual obedience is demanded.

The force of these considerations appears fully in the fact that so few members dissociate themselves from their party on vital

[33] The gradual increase of Parliamentary and Cabinet salaries has accentuated the position.
[34] Cf. Sir E. Grey's detachment (1895–1905); *Twenty-five Years*, i. 57 f. But such cases grow rarer.

issues. The abandonment of sanctions in June, 1936, was plainly an action incompatible with the obligations of the Crown deliberately undertaken in the Covenant of the League of Nations, and many Conservatives were certainly resentful that the policy on which the election of 1935 had in part been won should thus be reversed. But Mr. H. Macmillan alone resented the *volte face* sufficiently to cease to desire the party whip, and even so favourably situated a member felt it necessary, in order to participate in useful activities in Parliament, to apply, when Mr. Chamberlain took office, for its resumption. Not less striking was the fact that Mr. Eden's enforced resignation, rather than treat with Italy under an ultimatum, did not produce any serious defection from the party loyalty, when on February 2 the Prime Minister defended his attitude. Moreover, Mr. Eden himself declined in any way to embarrass his party or to encourage a schism, a most significant proof of the bonds of party loyalty, even when he felt that the Prime Minister was endangering national interests by his excursion into the field of foreign politics.[35] His reward is clearly presaged in the insistence of ministers, such as Mr. Elliot, on the probability of an earlier return to office. Later that same year, Mr. Duff Cooper alone of the Cabinet stood out against the terms of Munich and resigned his office in consequence; while the small band of Conservative members who also disapproved those terms registered their disapproval by abstention from the critical vote, not by voting against the Government.[36]

Independence can be shown, and sometimes become effective, by less obvious means than open revolt against the party leaders. From the autumn of 1945 onwards the left wing of the Parliamentary Labour Party attempted to swing the foreign policy of the Government towards the left, using as one of their chief means the newly established External Affairs Committee. This attempt was defeated only by the Foreign Secretary's demand in March, 1946, for what was in effect a vote of confidence at a party meeting. The influences thus thwarted achieved some success the following year, when the Minister of Defence was forced to retreat upon the issue of conscription. On the whole, however, the experience of

[35] For a criticism of the Treaty of April 16, 1938, see Keith, *The Scotsman*, April 19, 1938. The Duchess of Atholl alone in April, 1938, renounced the party whip, because of the Government's failure in duty towards Spain. Cf. Commons Debate, May 2, 335 *H. C. Deb.* 5 s., 533 ff.
[36] Churchill, *The Second World War*, i. 256.

the Labour Party since 1945 has confirmed the tendency in all parties to extend party discipline over back benchers in the interests of their leaders.

Devotion to party, it must be remembered, is not irrational. Party is, as matters stand, the essential mode of working the British constitution. It is, in fact, merely an application in the political sphere of the essential characteristic of human co-operation for common ends. In this way only can there be effective propaganda and dissemination of views, only thus can public opinion be organised and educated along definite lines. The selection of suitable candidates for Parliament can best be secured on the basis of co-operation between a local and a central body, and it is party organisation which provides ministers and leaders of the opposition, which are the necessary condition of the successful working of British democracy. No doubt the party organisation does not operate so as to provide guidance for the formation of policy, which must largely be left to other agencies, but it does keep the ministers in useful touch with the feeling of the party, as well as the party with ministerial projects, and thus secures solidarity of feeling and action.

It is easy to understand the working of the party system where two parties alone exist or where, if parties are in form distinct, there are causes resulting in their functioning as one. Thus the Liberal Unionists, from the nature of things, were soon compelled so wholly to function with the Conservatives that there could be no doubt of the support of Conservative doctrines by Unionists. The way, therefore, lay open for the composite ministry of 1895, and ultimately for the merger of the Unionist organisation with that of the Conservatives. It was only in 1912 that union was consummated, giving the National Union of Conservative and Unionist Associations: it worked smoothly from the first. 'The astonishing thing is that it should have been necessary to maintain the distinction so long after a united Government had been formed, in view of the strength of the prejudice for and against the old party names.'[37]

In the case of the Irish Nationalist party, which afforded for so long support to the Liberals, it was dominated by the aim of achieving Home Rule by this alliance, and, despite the fact that

[37] Austen Chamberlain, *Politics from Inside*, pp. 405, 417 ff., 475–79.

its members were hardly at all of orthodox Liberal views, the party's loyalty was amazingly maintained in the period 1906–14. In 1910, indeed, when the general election had made the Liberals dependent on Irish support, the objections of the Nationalists to the raising of the spirit duties nearly led to a clash fatal to the ministry, especially as the Nationalists were anxious to delay the budget until the proposals of the Government for dealing with the obstruction offered by the Lords to the passage of Home Rule had been passed. Only with much difficulty was the issue accommodated.[38]

Neither of these parties thus affected the general working of the party system in any substantial measure. The advent, however, of the Labour Party, and its rapid rise to the position of the second party in the State, as shown by the elections of 1922, 1923 and 1929, considerably affected the position by creating the possibility of the emergence of a three-party system. For a time it seemed that important effects might thus be produced on the operation of Cabinet Government. The dictatorial power of the Prime Minister would obviously be undermined if he did not command a majority in the Commons. It would become necessary for him to seek collaboration with the other parties to endeavour to pass such measures as commanded general support, or, at least, the support of another party, and he could no longer expect to be able to hold over his supporters the threat of a dissolution, for in this state of things he could not always claim the right authoritatively to advise the Crown to dissolve.[39] In the same way it would be necessary for the Government of the day to leave issues so far as possible open. The Government whips could not be put on unless the matter was clearly vital. The Commons would thus resume the power it enjoyed in Bagehot's time of selecting Governments.[40]

During the nineteen thirties this danger steadily decreased. In the first place there were overwhelming majorities for National-Conservative Governments of 1931 and 1935, and, secondly, the Labour Party had by now replaced the Liberal Party as the second major party. The split of the Liberals in 1932–33 reduced the number of Liberals as an independent group—as distinct from

---

[38] Spender, *Lord Oxford*, i. 270 ff., 278; Chamberlain, *Politics from Inside*, pp. 201 ff. 206 f., 254. The Conservatives were anxious not to defeat the Government themselves, as they did not wish to take office.

[39] See Mr. Asquith's arguments in 1923, *The Times*, December 19, 1923.

[40] See Ramsay Muir, *How Britain is Governed*, for an argument for three parties.

Liberal-Nationals who were virtually a subordinate branch of the Conservative Party—to an almost negligible figure, 21 in all in 1935. The general election of 1950, however, raised the possibility of a decisive third party, in a slightly different form. The unusually even balance between Labour and Conservative members returned on that occasion made even a minute Liberal Party of 9 members a force to be reckoned with in critical divisions.

The connection between the party leader and the Premiership has been referred to above; it remains to consider how the rank of leader is achieved. The power of the party is shown in the fact that it is its members in Parliament, who in one way or another virtually select the leader, and they, of course, take into account the feeling of the supporters of the ministry in the country, as well as the views of those concerned immediately in the Parliamentary sphere. In earlier times any formal selection as leader was unknown. Sir R. Peel was tacitly followed in his leadership of the Conservatives by Lord Stanley and Lord George Bentinck. In 1875 Lord Hartington seems to have been chosen leader of the Commons, but it does not appear that he was adopted in any way as leader of the party as a whole.[41] Mr. Gladstone, though he had in a sense retired from that position, obviously remained in the background as the inevitable head, when, thanks largely to his Midlothian campaign, it achieved victory in 1880.[42] The selection of Lord Rosebery as Prime Minister was preceded by consultations among the Parliamentary members of the party, which resulted in showing that he must be regarded as the real successor to Mr. Gladstone in their view, but the Queen also acted on her own decision.[43] On February 6, 1898, the pre-eminence of Sir H. Campbell-Bannerman was preluded by his election to lead the Liberal Party in the Commons.[44] This gave him a position, whence no intrigues availed to move him during the following years, and assured his acceptance as Prime Minister. The position

---

[41] *Letters of Queen Victoria*, 2 s., ii. 378; Fitzmaurice, *Granville*, ii. 134 ff.
[42] Fitzmaurice, *Granville*, ii. 182 ff.; Morley, *Gladstone*, ii. 587 ff.
[43] *Letters of Queen Victoria*, 3 s., ii. 337, 371, 373.
[44] Lord Rosebery resigned October 6, 1896. At the election of 1895 there had been no real co-operation with Sir W. Harcourt, but a hollow truce was patched up. In December, 1898, Sir W. Harcourt also resigned leadership; Spender, *Lord Oxford*, i. 113–25. The subsequent attacks of the Liberal League failed and destroyed Lord Rosebery's chance of office (*ibid.* 141 ff.). See Gardiner, *Harcourt*, ii. 488. Lord J. Russell in 1849 spoke of Mr. Disraeli as leader in succession to Bentinck; *Letters of Queen Victoria*, 1 s., ii. 216.

still was as defined by Sir A. Chamberlain in 1911 ;[45] either house
must select its own leader, and which of the two would become
leader of the party would be left unsettled until the time came for
the taking of office by the party, when the King would settle it by
his decision as to whom he would ask to form a ministry.

Mr. Balfour's resignation on November 8, 1911, of his leadership
of the party, was not voluntary, in so far as it was the outcome of a
prolonged campaign demanding that 'Balfour must go.'[46] The
position then called for a selection, and the obvious candidates
were Mr. A. Chamberlain and Mr. Walter Long. The latter,
a Conservative of long service, was definitely hostile to Mr.
Chamberlain, who was still a Liberal Unionist, had only joined
the Carlton Club a short time before, and had, by his recent
attitude to the question of the Parliament Bill, caused some resentment. Ultimately, when Sir E. Carson's refusal to stand was
known, Mr. Chamberlain's offer to stand down if Mr. Long did
likewise, let Mr. Bonar Law in as leader. The selection was
decisive of Mr. Chamberlain's future, and probably it was an error
from the party point of view, but the decision was definitely
accepted by the party. Later, health reasons induced Mr. Bonar
Law in May, 1921, to withdraw from the party leadership, which
fell to Mr. Chamberlain, but the adherence of the latter to the
fate of the coalition ministry, when the decision was taken by the
party meeting at Carlton House[47] to go to the next election as an
independent party, rendered his resignation inevitable. Mr. Bonar
Law, in accepting provisionally the royal mandate to form a
Government, took care to have his position, as head of the party,
affirmed by the approval of a meeting of party supporters in both
Houses.[48] Mr. Baldwin, his successor, likewise received approval
in like manner on May 28, 1923, at the Hotel Cecil, and when he
gave way to Mr. N. Chamberlain, the election of the latter as head
of the party was declared by acclamation at a meeting to which
were summoned not only all members of both houses who accepted
the party whip, but also approved candidates and the executive
committee of the National Union of Conservative and Unionist

---

[45] *Politics from Inside*, pp. 380, 383, 386–96; Taylor, *Bonar Law*, pp. 150–55.
[46] Dugdale, *Arthur James Balfour*, ii. 83–92. He notified the King formally.
[47] October 19, 1922. See Taylor, *Bonar Law*, pp. 257 ff.; Dugdale, *Arthur James
   Balfour*, ii. 355 ff.; Somervell, *King George the Fifth*, pp. 299 ff.; Nicolson, *Curzon*,
   pp. 276 ff.
[48] Lords, 152; Commons, 220; Parliamentary candidates, 67.

Associations.[49]   The addition of this body which is elected by the twelve divisional organisations of England, and those of Scotland and Northern Ireland, is a significant proof of the growing importance of the party organisation in the choice of leader.   When Mr. Churchill became Prime Minister in May, 1940, Mr. Neville Chamberlain remained Leader of the Conservative Party.   The latter retained that position until he resigned both Cabinet office and party leadership on grounds of ill-health, in October of the same year; at that point Mr. Churchill was unanimously adopted as the new party leader.[50]

The Liberals have fared less satisfactorily.   Lord Oxford held in 1925 that a leader, once appointed Prime Minister, in opposition retained his leadership until he determined to lay it down.[51]   But his defeat at the election of 1924 undermined his position, as it opened the way to the selection by the party in the Commons of Mr. Lloyd George to be their chief, and his position was immensely strengthened by his control over his political fund.   Though he had given a handsome contribution for the 1923 and 1924 elections, he had done so without giving up control, and the effort of the National Liberal Federation in January, 1925, to secure an independent fund, naturally failed of success, when it was known that another fund actually existed, for the reasons which rendered it difficult to utilise it were essentially based on the desire of Mr. Lloyd George to use the fund as the means of securing his hold of the party.   The issue came to a head in May–June, 1926, when Mr. Lloyd George chose to dissociate himself from the attitude of Lord Oxford and the rest of the Shadow Cabinet on the subject of the general strike.   It is clear that Mr. Lloyd George saw in the episode an opportunity to blot out his coalition activities, and the injury then inflicted on the party, by standing out as a sympathiser with Labour aspirations, denied just consideration by the Government.   The position of the leader of the party thus became hopeless, and Lord Oxford resigned rather than take part in any squabble.   For some time the position of official Leader of the Liberal Party remained unfilled, later being occupied by Sir Archibald Sinclair.   The latter, although not officially a member of the Coalition War Cabinet from 1940–45 in fact, attended many of its meetings in virtue of his party position,

[49] May 31, 1937.   See Keith, *The King and the Imperial Crown*, pp. 159 f.
[50] Churchill, *The Second World War*, ii. 439.
[51] Spender, *Lord Oxford*, ii. 358–71.

particularly when fundamental political issues or important party matters were involved.[52]

The Labour Party adopted the plan of an annual election of a leader in the Commons,[53] and the choice of the King therefore fell in 1924 on Mr. MacDonald, as the due head of the party in that House. This leadership thus confirmed, it remained unquestioned, and led to his second term of office in 1929–31, when he broke with his party, and the plan of electing a head was again resorted to.[54] As has been seen, the selection of a head is now virtually binding on the Crown, when the issue of choosing a Prime Minister arises, for the party naturally expects that its selected representative shall receive the royal summons.

With the development of the party was bound up the use of the Press for the dissemination and formation of political opinion. It is significant of the early days of Lord Palmerston's activities that Whigs held that his unpopularity with *The Times* and other papers was a good reason for not having him at the Foreign Office.[55] Under Melbourne's ministry (1835–41) Palmerston worked hard to secure editorial favour, while more Liberal Whigs in 1835 set the *Morning Chronicle* on its feet; though it came under more Radical control in 1839, Palmerston still kept in touch with it as with the Whig *Globe*, thus countering *The Times* and *Morning Post*.[56] His connection with the *Chronicle* enabled him to maintain his views while in opposition against the grave errors of Lord Aberdeen's foreign policy, despite Lord John Russell's remonstrances.[57] On the other hand, Lord Aberdeen had in *The Times*, under Mr. Delane, a warm admirer of his foreign policy, and a recipient of much valuable news.[58] In 1848 the Peelites acquired the *Chronicle* to Palmerston's disadvantage, but in 1850 he secured support from the *Morning Post* which, Conservative in other aspects, admitted his foreign policy.[59] Backing Palmerston and Protection, the *Post*

---

52 Churchill, *The Second World War*, ii. p. 11.

53 The intellectuals, pacifists and younger trade unionists from Scotland and Wales decided after the 1922 election gave the party 142 members to substitute Mr. MacDonald for Mr. Clynes; cf. Somervell, *King George the Fifth*, pp. 325 ff.; Clynes, *Memoirs*, i. 329 ff.

54 Mr. Henderson was elected on August 28, 1931, by the Parliamentary Labour Party, on Mr. MacDonald becoming Prime Minister on August 25.

55 Bell, *Palmerston*, i. 194, 200. On the power of the Press at this time cf. Greville, *Memoirs*, 2 s., i. 75.

56 Bell, *Palmerston*, i. 256 f., 309.

57 *Ibid.*, i. 330.   58 *Ibid.*, ii. 32 f. 117.

59 *Ibid.*, ii. 33 f.

came to have a circulation inferior only to *The Times*.   Later he won some support from *The Times* itself.   Naturally other parties aimed equally at Press support, and from the first we learn of management of the Press by members of the ministry.[60]   The necessity of keeping closely in touch with the Press was recognised by Mr. Lloyd George when he acquired the *Daily Chronicle* when fighting for his own hand.   The power of the Press was used with deadly effect against Mr. Asquith during the war; he pointed out on May 2, 1916,[61] how all the errors and defects with which the ministry was charged had been brought against the ministry of Mr. Pitt and against the Duke of Wellington, but he forgot that the essential difference between that period and his own was that the Press had an enormous circulation and necessarily deeply affected public opinion.   He himself on March 11, 1918,[62] pointed to two essential facts, the process by which many newspapers fell under one ownership and the substitution of proprietors for editors in the control of the policy of the Press.   Moreover, his difficulties through failure effectively to keep in touch with the Press were accentuated by the existence of the curious personalities of Lords Northcliffe and Beaverbrook, with their personal ambition to determine policies. It is, however, plain from his experience that the weight of the Press in moulding opinion is serious.[63]

It must not, of course, be over-estimated.   The fact that the Press has been mainly anti-Labour has not prevented the progress of that party, and, though *The Scotsman*, the most distinguished of Scottish newspapers, in 1885 deserted the Liberals on the Home Rule issue, that did not prevent its readers remaining in large measure Liberal down to the war period.   But the increase of the electorate presents a wide field for the activity of the Press by suggestion, and suppression of unsuitable facts.   A very large proportion of the electorate never reads any newspaper where the issues are carefully balanced and both sides of questions fairly presented, and such papers have become even rarer than in the

---

[60] In 1839 the Secretary to the Board of Trade and the Under-Secretary for Ireland were thus engaged; Bell, *Palmerston*, i. 257.   Cf. under Peel, G. Kitson Clark, *Peel and the Conservative Party*, p. 216.

[61] Spender, *Lord Oxford*, ii. 229–31.

[62] *Ibid.*, ii. 232 n. 1.   Lord Melbourne had likewise neglected to conciliate the Press.   Sir C. Dilke and Mr. Chamberlain used in 1880–85 their Press connections to maintain their positions.

[63] Beaverbrook, *Politicians and the Press;* Kennedy Jones, *Fleet Street and Downing Street*.

past. One effect unquestionably of the Press is to strengthen the tendency to make personalities more important for party allegiance than principles, and this aspect of the position is further strengthened by the practice of broadcasting, which brings a very small number of persons, mainly the actual heads of the party, into a direct touch with the ever-increasing mass of electors.[64] The effect of the inculcation of political principles in simplified and convincing form by leaders already popular is doubtless to strengthen in their allegiance those who have already some affiliation, and to make that allegiance more and more dependent on admiration for the leader. On persons not already tending to any political attachment the result may be negative.

An important aspect of the party system is the existence of research departments now possessed by all parties alike. Their importance is enhanced by the recent practice now being energetically extended by the Conservatives, late comers in this field, of intensive tuition at summer and Easter schools for those interested in politics. Their instruction is intended and is no doubt effective in giving them a definitive impetus to propagate their newly acquired knowledge orally. It is now widely admitted that continuous oral exposition, such as was initiated by the Labour Party, in informal meetings, is the most effective way to keep a party together and that the mere issue of electioneering literature before an election, and the holding then of meetings, is quite inadequate for effective purposes.

3. THE EXTENT AND CHARACTER OF CABINET CONTROL

IT must be remembered that the members of the Commons have only limited opportunities of attacking effectively the policy of the Cabinet. The King's speech at the opening of Parliament affords one opportunity; twenty to twenty-three days are devoted to supply, when criticism is possible, of the matters covered by the votes put down, which are usually selected as desired by the Opposition; on four occasions, when the House goes into committee to consider the three sets of defence and the civil estimates, motions may be brought

---

[64] The widespread effect of broadcast political speeches can sometimes be a decisive feature in an election campaign. Mr. Snowden's broadcast in 1931 was widely held to have done great damage to the Labour Party; while Mr. Churchill's general election speeches in 1945 were held to have injured the prospects of his own party.

forward if the ballot favours the mover, as when in 1937 foreign policy was debated on the civil estimates. On the motions for the Easter and Whit-Sunday adjournments issues can be raised, as they can be each night when the House is about to adjourn, and in cases of urgency, approved by the Speaker, a motion for the adjournment may be accepted and brought on at 7.30 p.m. A motion of censure by the Opposition will certainly receive a due allocation of time, for a Government which shirks facing such a motion would lose standing in a very marked degree. Finally, legislative proposals afford a constant opportunity for criticism, both in principle and in detail.

But this list of opportunities leaves after all comparatively little scope for members to raise issues other than those which the Government finds it necessary to submit to the Commons. When the ministry can act without legislation the opportunities for criticism are reduced, and in the operation of prerogative or statutory powers a ministry has a very free hand. The essential feature of the exercise of these powers is that the ministry may take decisions, and then confront the Commons with a *fait accompli*. In these circumstances it is inevitable that the Commons should feel bound, if members of the Governmental party, to support the ministry in a much higher degree than in the case of legislation, which, in principle, no doubt, they must accept from the Government, but which in substantial detail they must claim the right to amend.

(1) Of the freedom of action by the Government in external relations affecting the Dominions and colonies there is abundant recent evidence, as well as much of older date. The Cabinet, despite the grave differences among the ministers, imposed on the Commons its South African policy in 1876–80, and Mr. Gladstone, after accepting from his predecessors the acquisition of the Transvaal, retroceded it after Majuba.[65] The Commons was confronted by the results of Mr. Chamberlain's diplomacy and that of the Cabinet in the case of the South African war of 1899.[66] Again, in 1906, the decision to grant responsible government to the Transvaal was taken without Parliamentary control, and the use of the prerogative to establish any form of government in a conquered colony enabled the ministry to evade the obstacle of the House of Lords, which else

[65] Morley, *Gladstone*, iii. 37 ff.   [66] Garvin, *Joseph Chamberlain*, iii. 400 ff.

would have prevented the carrying of the measure in question.[67] The Irish surrender in 1921 was arranged by the Cabinet, and presented as a *fait accompli* for acceptance, though in theory the measure was one which should have been impossible of acceptance by the ministry.[68] In the same year Malta was granted self-government by letters patent, not by Act of Parliament, as desired by the island, partly because of the delay which that procedure would have involved. Later, in 1932 and 1934, the constitution, which had been misused to the profit of Italy by the Italian leaders of the Government, with Papal support, was suspended, and then abandoned with merely formal acceptance of the necessary Acts by the Houses. Southern Rhodesia was likewise added by prerogative Order in Council and letters patent in 1923 to the Empire as a responsible Government colony, while the annexation of Kenya was likewise a prerogative act. More striking still the vital decisions, which conferred on the Dominions a status of equality in internal and external affairs alike with the United Kingdom, were taken without the slightest reference to Parliament, though by this action the whole established system of imperial control of foreign relations and internal government was swept away. The Report of the Imperial Conference of 1926, epoch making as it was, was never brought before the Commons for approval, and, when after further Conferences in 1929 and 1930 the finished result was presented in the Statute of Westminster, 1931, the Commons were told that the measure represented an agreed text which could not be varied without Dominion assent, so that all efforts to change it were voted down. Thus, even when legislation was necessary, it became so only at a stage when it was impossible to amend. Thus the control which the Commons can exercise even now over legislative proposals, of a strong Government, by modification, disappears.

The position is interestingly illustrated by the decisions announced in the agreements with Eire of April 25, 1938.[69] The British Government therein sacrificed all its rights in respect of defence in Eire, which had been regarded as essential in 1921, and it did so without receiving the slightest assurance that Eire would forbid any enemy occupying her territory, or using her waters as a base of attack on Britain. This accord was concluded without any

---

[67] Lee, *Edward VII.*, ii. 481 ff.   [68] Pakenham, *Peace by Ordeal.*
[69] Cmd. 5728; A. B. Keith, *The Scotsman*, April 27, 1938.

prior hint of such a surrender being made, and Parliament had no option but to accept, or to eject the ministry from office.

(2) Nor is the position different in the sphere of external affairs. The foreign policy of Lord Palmerston and Lord John Russell was no more controlled by Parliament[70] than that of Lord Beaconsfield with regard to Russia and Turkey.   It was essentially the dramatic interlude of the death of Gordon which suddenly brought about a bitter attack in the Commons and which threatened to shake the party majority.[71]   That it failed to do so is significant of the power even then of the Cabinet.   The Commons accepted meekly the decisions of Lord Salisbury in the difficult period of the reconquest of the Sudan and the French Treaty of 1899,[72]   and his attitude of concession in the Russian adventure in China, which was but feebly countered by the acquisition of Wei-hai-wei to match Port Arthur.   In the same way the accord reached with Japan in 1902 was a Cabinet decision, and the remarkable entente concluded with France in 1904 was equally unexpected.   Unlike the Japanese alliance the necessity of making some territorial changes led to the submission of a Bill to Parliament.[73]   The ministry thus set its seal on the precedent set in 1890 with the disapproval of Mr. Gladstone in the case of the surrender to Germany of Heligoland, and thus limited ministerial exercise of the royal prerogative as regards surrender of British territory.   Lord Palmerston earlier pointed out that Parliamentary approval of such engagements compels the Government to state its terms in precise form.[74]   The precedent was duly followed in 1925, when Jubaland was surrendered to Italy, and in 1934, when the Dindings was handed over to Johore, but it is significant that in 1935 the Cabinet clearly held that a transfer of protected territory might be arranged without any intention of legislation.[75]   The Liberal Government in 1907 formed an accord with Russia without consulting Parliament, and the conversations with French officers, which committed Britain in effect to aiding France in the Great War, were not even communicated to Parliament.   The Cabinet further had to determine

---

[70] In 1857 Palmerston on defeat successfully dissolved on his Chinese policy; in 1858 his defeat was due to a curious coalition; Bell, *Palmerston*, ii. 167 ff., 182ff.

[71] *Letters of Queen Victoria*, 2 s., iii. 610, 614 ff.

[72] Garvin, *Joseph Chamberlain*, iii. 202 ff., 224 ff.

[73] Lee, *Edward VII.*, ii. 252.

[74] Ashley, *Palmerston*, ii. 103.

[75] A. B. Keith, *Current Imperial and International Problems*, 1935–36, pp. 139 ff.

7*

on declaring war in 1914, and to confront the Commons with a decision already final. In like manner the Commons neither was given, nor demanded, any control over the negotiations in the course of the war, including the offer of Cyprus to Greece, and the secret treaties of 1915, and, while it was asked to vote the Treaty of Peace Act, 1919, there was no possibility of it dealing with the terms of the peace. The Locarno Pact of 1925 was, indeed, submitted for approval, but only when it was final, and there remained no possibility of declining acceptance. The policy of disarmament was accepted and put into effect without any hint by the Cabinet that in 1934 it realised that it was leaving the country seriously underarmed.[76]

The plenitude of Cabinet power is illustrated, even in what is often justly cited as an instance where public feeling compelled for the moment a change of policy. When in December, 1935, the terms of the proposals, devised by M. Laval and Sir S. Hoare, for the settlement of the Ethiopian issue became known, there was so much indignation in view of their complete departure from the obligations of the League Covenant,[77] that, though the Cabinet had hastily approved his suggestions, he himself realised that he had forfeited the confidence of the great body of public opinion in the country, and the proposals were dropped. But the apparent victory of public feeling was rendered illusory, when in June, 1936, it was found that Sir S. Hoare was back in the Cabinet in the important office of First Lord of the Admiralty, which gave him a powerful position in advocating a policy of retreat, and that Mr. Chamberlain was determined to destroy sanctions.[78] It was plain, therefore, that, while the Cabinet had yielded, it had done so merely the better to carry out its policy of conciliating Italy. What must be severely condemned is the failure of the ministry to make it clear to Ethiopia that it would not secure an oil sanction, and that its support would never go so far as to shut out the possibility of maintaining cordial relations with Italy.

The helplessness of Parliament was well illustrated by the abandonment of sanctions, which was plainly a breach of a clear international obligation and involved some degree of national

---

[76] A. B. Keith, *International Affairs*, ii. 175 ff. (Mr. Baldwin at Glasgow, November 18, 1936).

[77] Feiling, *Neville Chamberlain*, pp. 273 ff.; Finer, *The Future of Government*, p. 97.

[78] Toynbee, *Survey of International Affairs*, 1935, ii. 466 ff.

dishonour.[79]   In like manner the ministry determined the attitude of Britain towards the Spanish civil war, and the non-intervention agreement.   Aware in full measure of the complete disregard of the Government of Italy and Germany for the accord, and that its own refusal to allow the supply of munitions was serving to further the views of these two powers and to undermine the position of Britain in the Mediterranean, it persisted in its policy and enforced it by the application of full pressure to the party members.   Finally, on February 21, 1938, the ministry secured a triumphant majority for the policy of negotiating with Italy, though the Foreign Secretary and his Under-Secretary resigned rather than consent to accept an Italian ultimatum.[80]   In like spirit the ministry enunciated on March 24 its acceptance of the German annexation of Austria, and declined to give any promise of aid to Czechoslovakia if attacked by Germany.   It is, however, fair to add that on this occasion Mr. N. Chamberlain used language which might be construed into a much needed warning that his process of retreat before the aggression of the dictators was not without possibility of modification, and it is quite probable that this modification of an original tendency to complete surrender was due to murmurings in the ranks of Conservative members.   None the less the power of the Cabinet can hardly be exaggerated, when it is remembered that the ministry of 1935 had won the election on the strength of promises to support the League of Nations and collective security, which were now being deliberately violated in the Anglo-Italian agreement of April 16, 1938.

Later that same year the power of the Cabinet, and particularly of the Prime Minister over Parliament, was amply demonstrated in the Munich crisis.   Parliament did not sit between July 29 and September 28.   On the latter date it met for a short special session to hear from the Prime Minister a statement on the European situation, and learned for the first time the details of those negotiations which had already committed this country to yet further appeasement, this time in the Sudetenland area of Czechoslovakia.[81] Parliament was confronted with a series of accomplished facts, its approval of which did nothing to lighten the charge that it should have been consulted and not merely informed.[82]

[79]   Keith, *Current Imperial and International Problems,* 1935–6, pp. 182 ff.
[80]   Churchill, *The Second World War,* i. 200, 206–7.
[81]   339 *H. C. Deb.* 5 s., 5–26.
[82]   R. W. Seton-Watson, *From Munich to Danzig,* pp. 94–100, 147–150.

As it is the Cabinet which decides, it matters little whether or not it formally consults Parliament. The decision of the Labour Government in 1924 to lay all treaties before the Commons and to delay ratification for twenty-one days,[83] a plan not followed by any save the Labour Government of 1929–31,[84] was no doubt a gesture to show its submission to the judgment of Parliament, but the Government was a minority one, and to carry through such a treaty as that with Russia,[85] which it prepared, necessitated action by Parliament, which could clearly not be relied upon.

Secret treaties stand in a different light; even before the Covenant of the League of Nations declared treaties not binding until duly registered with the League,[86] the binding character of a secret treaty was manifestly doubtful. The accords with Portugal and Germany regarding the future of the Portuguese colonies in 1898–99 were hardly consistent,[87] but the Foreign Secretary in 1913 was clear that, if a new accord were achieved, it must be made public, and in 1906[88] he took the sound view that an alliance with France could only be concluded if it were to be accepted by Parliament, for the British system did not allow one ministry to bind a subsequent ministry by arrangements without Parliament sanction. It is true that difficult questions of law might arise if such a treaty were made, but the constitutional principle is so notorious that no foreign power would be well advised if it sought to place any reliance in a treaty of alliance not sanctioned by the Legislature, or at least by the Commons. Lord Salisbury made this difficulty clear in his comments on the proposal to include England within the bounds of the Triple Alliance in 1901.

> 'The impropriety of attempting,' he wrote, 'to determine by a *secret contract* the future conduct of a Representative Assembly upon an issue of peace or war would apply to German policy as much as to English, only that the German Parliament would probably pay more deference to the opinion of their Executive than would be done by the English Parliament. . . . It would not be safe to stake any important national interest upon the fidelity with which, in case of national exigency,

---

[83] 171 *H. C. Deb.* 5 s., 2001 ff. Mr. Baldwin dropped the practice: 179 *H. C. Deb.* 5 s., 565. [84] 230 *H. C. Deb.* 5 s., 408. [85] Cmd. 2216, 2261.

[86] Art. 19. The secret clauses of the Treaty of 1904 with France are made light of by Grey, *Twenty-five Years*, i. 50, but Lord Newton, *Lansdowne*, pp. 290 f., admits this view to be untenable.

[87] Garvin, *Joseph Chamberlain*, iii. 307 ff.; Grey, *Twenty-five Years*, i. 45.

[88] Grey, *Twenty-five Years*, i. 80 ff. Cf. A. Chamberlain's views in 1912 (*Politics from Inside*, pp. 425 f., 485 f.).

either country could be trusted to fulfil the obligations of the Alliance, if the Agreement had been concluded without the assent of its Parliament.'[89]

Similarly, when suggestions were made for a formal alliance with France in 1906, Sir Edward Grey gave it as his opinion that 'it was too serious a matter to be kept secret from Parliament. The Government could conclude it without the consent of Parliament, but it would have to be published afterwards. No British Government could commit the country to such a serious thing and keep the engagement secret.'[90]

(3) In other spheres also the Cabinet acts with definite authority. The movement of troops at all times is at its discretion, as is its disposal of the naval forces, effectively used by Mr. Churchill to prepare for immediate action on the outbreak of the Great War. It can give orders in emergency, secure of ratification by Parliament *ex post facto*, as when in 1847 and 1857 the Bank of England was authorised to disregard the terms of the Bank Charter Act, and in 1931 to refuse to pay out gold;[91] in the Great War action often preceded, though but shortly, approval. Even in the field of the chief activity of Parliament, legislation, the tendency is more and more for the Cabinet to decide and the Commons to confirm. In April, 1938, secret purchases for defence purposes of wheat, oil and sugar were indemnified readily. There is, no doubt, some room for independence, and on occasion the ministry yields even on important points. In 1934 the protests of all kinds of people, from Conservative lawyers to Communists, created so strong a body of criticism that the Incitement to Disaffection Bill was severely remodelled before it passed Parliament.[92] But it must be noted that the attack was largely based merely on too wide drafting; it is open to doubt if in effect the ministry sacrificed anything more than some of its dignity in the process. It is more common for issues of property and taxation to invoke serious trouble, and the reason is simple. The Conservative Party is pledged to support the interests of capital and private property, and inroads thereon strike definitely at this essential doctrine. It is easy, therefore, to understand that Mr. N. Chamberlain's National Defence Contribution Scheme in 1937 came in for such serious objections on the

89 British Documents on the Origins of the War (ed. Gooch and Temperley), ii. 69.
90 Spender, *Campbell-Bannerman*, ii. 255.
91 Gold Standard (Amendment) Act, 1931 (21 & 22 Geo. V. c. 46).
92 24 & 25 Geo. V. c. 56.

part of members and outside organisations that the whole principle of drawing extra revenue from those companies which were to make extra profits from re-armament was abandoned, and the burden placed equally on those who made no profits. It may be fairly be claimed that in their action the Commons showed themselves definitely more sympathetic to profiteering than might have been expected. An earlier occasion, when Mr. Churchill had to drop a petrol tax, was likewise marked by much lack of sound consideration; it proved, however, popular for members to represent themselves as opposing the taxation of the simple necessities of the poor, however fallacious the idea was. The power of capital over a Conservative Commons and a ministry is excellently shown in the discussions of 1938 on the Bill to provide for compulsory concentration of the coal-mining industry. The demand conceded by the Ministry that the matter of any compulsory scheme should be brought before a Parliamentary Committee was essentially based on the claim that otherwise private property might be affected without due consideration for the rights of owners. On the other hand, the successful steps taken in 1937 to limit the freedom of the executive to require the giving of certain statistical information in regard to marriage and births, was largely due to the ease with which an agitation can be worked up against any interference with the privacy of members of the public.

In no case, however, is a Government, under normal conditions, prepared to concede anything that it does not really approve as a desirable change, or accept as a graceful and popular concession. A ministry, it must be remembered, wins approval and admiration, not merely by strength, but by gracious consideration for the popular feeling. Moreover, ministries are not guiltless of the tactical cleverness shown in including in measures matters which they do not really desire to carry, but which they can make a virtue of conceding, while they secure thus the acceptance of clauses which, put forward by themselves, might easily have produced serious controversy.

4. The Cabinet and the Electorate: Dissolution and Mandate

The essential connection between the Cabinet and the electorate, already seen in the party system, becomes formally complete at each dissolution of Parliament, when the ministry seeks approval of its policy by the electors, and the Opposition seeks likewise to secure for its rival proposals endorsement, and for its leaders office. If a Government is not prepared to dissolve, it confesses, as in 1885, 1895, and 1905, that it has no policy for which it can claim approbation, and so admits that it would be idle to return it to power.

(a) Dissolution or Resignation

The view of Queen Victoria that a dissolution was an appeal to the people to strengthen by its approbation the Government favoured by the Crown, which Lord Melbourne no doubt shared, was even then out of date. It rested on a failure to appreciate the vital change introduced by the Reform Act, shown clearly in her statement in 1846, that 'the Queen strongly feels that she made a mistake in allowing the Dissolution in 1841; the result has been a majority returned against her of nearly a hundred votes.'[93] Since Sir R. Peel's time this view has died out. The attitude of the people to the Crown normally is wholly divorced from elections, whose object it is to allocate power to one party or other equally devoted to the interests of the country, and equally loyal, but differing in their view of the policy best calculated to serve the public interest at the moment.

(1) The termination of Parliament, by efflux of time, demands since 1911 that there shall be an election every five years at least, in lieu of the seven years of the Septennial Act, 1716. This means, no doubt, that an election will normally fall after the end of the fourth annual session of Parliament. It is not possible to regard, as wholly convincing, the arguments by which Mr. Baldwin settled the suitable time for the election of November 14, 1935, but there was no doubt some substance in his view that November is a convenient month, falling as it does before the epoch of Christmas shopping, which should not be affected by the existence of political movements. Moreover, it gives the ministry an uninterrupted session in the following year, when it is certain to have very important

---

[93] *Letters of Queen Victoria*, 1 s., ii. 108. For the expression of similar views by ministers, see *ibid.*, 1 s., i. 369, and Peel, *Memoirs*, ii. 295. But the Queen in 1892 was wholly unwilling to accept the results of the election as determining her outlook; *Letters of Queen Victoria*, 3 s., ii. 127, 132, where she records her utter disgust at the change.

business to transact.   The general election of 1945, however, an
exceptional one as regards the length of life of the administration
it ended, took place in mid-summer; that of 1950 took place in
February.   In the first case, a general election was inevitable as
soon as the Coalition Government broke up; in the second case,
the Labour Government had work to do in the winter session
before it asked for a dissolution.

Dissolutions, however, based mainly on efflux of time, are few
and far between.   Lord Palmerston dissolved in 1865, virtually on
an appeal for the return of himself and his ministry on grounds of
personal respect.   In 1874 Mr. Gladstone had the consideration
that the end of the period of Parliament was drawing near, as an
additional incentive to appeal, and this consideration was reinforced
by others.[94]   The House of Lords had shown itself inclined to
reject his proposals, no doubt in part, because his mandate of 1868
was growing stale, and by-elections had been running against him.
It is significant that in 1841 a different view of the conclusion to be
drawn from adverse by-elections was drawn by Sir R. Peel,[95] for
he urged that the fact that sixteen out of twenty by-elections in the
current Parliament had gone against Lord Melbourne, indicated
that he ought to resign; he did not draw what later seemed obvious,
that the sign thus afforded of popular disapproval of the ministry
should be regarded as demanding an appeal for a popular verdict.
In 1905 Mr. Balfour defended, on the basis of all precedent, all
law, and all common sense, the doctrine that it was for the Commons
alone to determine whether a Government should remain in office,
and denied that by-elections were, or ought to be, accepted as a
test of public feeling.[96]   This intransigent attitude is characteristic
of its author; the value of by-elections as a test of public feeling is
often alluded to by Sir A. Chamberlain, and what is decisive, is the
confession on November 12, 1936, of Mr. Baldwin, that the fatal
delay in 1934 in British re-armament, which sealed the fate of
Ethiopia, Spain and Austria, was due to adverse by-elections, and
the fear that their number would be augmented if the Government
attempted to add to armaments.   It was then that Mr. Baldwin
enunciated the famous doctrine of the 'time lag' in the preparations

94 Morley, *Gladstone*, ii. 484–87; *Letters of Queen Victoria*, 2 s., ii. 303.
95 58 *Parl. Deb.* 3 s., 817 f.
96 141 *Parl. Deb.* 4 s., 160 ff., 181 f. So in 1904; 132 *ibid.*, 1015 f. For his
     amazing tactics in 1905 in walking out to avoid defeat, see Dugdale, *Arthur
     James Balfour*, i. 410 ff.

of democracies,[97] ignoring entirely the fundamental question whether ministers, who alone have full information on defence issues, are entitled to withhold information from the people, because they fear political disadvantages thence. If this doctrine, which seems to have excited remarkably little protest, is adopted, the dangers for democracies are patent and most grave. Rather, it seems that the plenitude of Governmental knowledge imposes on the ministry an immediate and most important obligation to impart such vital knowledge to the electorate. What is striking, is that when Mr. Baldwin did go to the people in 1935 he showed in his manifesto little appreciation of the gravity of the position, as it must have appeared to him and his colleagues. Subsequently in debate Mr. Baldwin admitted with 'appalling frankness' that, had he gone to the country in 1935 admitting that Germany was rearming and that, therefore, this country must rearm too, nothing would have been more likely to lose him the election.[98]

In 1892 Lord Salisbury's appeal to the people was in part influenced by consideration of time, but his appeal was partly on the record of his ministry, partly on the desirability of securing a message of hope, not of ruin, to the people of Ireland in condemning Home Rule. So wholly did he fail to realise the essentials of the Irish situation.

(2) A more frequent cause of dissolution is defeat in the Commons on an issue deemed vital, the alternative being resignation, discussed below. The dissolution of 1831 on the Reform Bill was consequent on the fall of the Duke of Wellington's ministry in view of its failure to promise reform which, though not a direct issue at the election of July, 1830, had been widely canvassed in the country consequent, in part, on the French revolution. The failure of the Commons to accept the scheme of Earl Grey, who thus entered upon office to press for reform, resulted in the election of April, 1831, when the appeal to the people was not merely to return the Government, as in the case of Pitt's appeal in 1784, but to approve reform, and that too in the special form proposed by the ministry.[99] In 1841 Lord Melbourne was driven to dissolution by a direct vote of

---

97 Cf., Keith, *International Affairs*, ii. 175 ff. Lord Newton's censure (*Lansdowne*, p. 113) of Mr. Asquith before the war falls very aptly against the ministry of 1931–35. For an apology for Mr. Asquith see Grey, *Twenty-five Years*, ii. 47–61.
98 317 *H. C. Deb.* 5 s., 1144.
99 Duke of Wellington, 7 *Parl. Deb.* 3 s., 1193; Emden, *The People and the Constitution*, pp. 201 f.

no-confidence, and in 1857 Lord Palmerston dissolved on his defeat on his Chinese policy, and won as a sturdy imperialist a distinguished victory.   Lord Derby, however, failed to win when he dissolved in 1859, and a like fate befell Mr. Disraeli in 1868, Mr. Gladstone on Home Rule in 1886, and Mr. MacDonald in 1924.

Two further points should be noted.   Firstly, defeat on a vital issue can be followed either by resignation or by a request to the Crown to dissolve.   Resignation will almost invariably, however, as we shall see, involve subsequent dissolution.   Secondly, and making full allowance for the strength of convention, what defeat a Government will treat as of sufficient importance to involve dissolution or resignation is primarily a matter for the Government itself.

(3) A dissolution is normally necessary if, on the resignation of its predecessor, a new Government is formed.   In theory it may be held, as Sir R. Peel did in 1841, that the endorsement of the electorate is not essential for the change, and in the Dominions retirement of ministers, without a dissolution, has been held not to require a dissolution by their successors.   But this has been due to considerations irrelevant under actual British conditions.   It has been due to the existence of less effective party opposition through the existence of groups, which can coalesce to provide a ministry with an effective support in Parliament, so as to allow postponement of an election until the early expiration of Parliament, which has often had no more than three years' duration, rendering dissolutions so frequent that an extra dissolution, with its serious cost, is unpopular.[1]   Under modern British conditions such a result could be contemplated only if a three-party system of a serious and lasting character came into being.   It would then be possible to argue, as Lord Oxford argued in 1923,[2] that the Sovereign should not, in the event of the defeat or resignation of a ministry, grant a dissolution to it or to its successor, if it were possible to arrange a working agreement to carry on in the Commons.   But that condition of things manifestly did not exist in 1924, and the objections to denying the electorate a voice are of very great strength.   A refusal would normally be possible only if there were general agreement within and without the Commons that an election should be delayed pending further developments of the situation.   Where

[1] Keith, *Responsible Government in the Dominions* (1928 ed.), i. 146 ff.
[2] *The Times*, December 19, 1923.

the view of the people can be gathered without a dissolution it would be absurd to insist upon it.[3]

Of dissolutions on the appointment of a new ministry there is that of 1847 accorded to Lord John Russell,[4] because patently having taken over power a year earlier, because of Sir R. Peel's loss of Conservative support, owing to his attitude to the corn laws, he needed additional authority; moreover, the time element spoke in his favour. Lord Derby in 1852[5] had a clear case, for it was plainly impossible to carry on effectively, unless he could be reinforced, and his dissolution undoubtedly strengthened his ministry, though the opposition sections coalesced to defeat it on the budget. In 1885 Lord Salisbury dissolved on Mr. Gladstone's resignation, but only after some delay, due to the fact that redistribution was then in process of being carried out, and a dissolution before it was complete would have been regarded as an effort to defeat an important reform finally agreed upon after royal intervention.[6] He was, therefore, entitled to ask for pledges from Mr. Gladstone for facilitating financial business, and the Queen finally persuaded him to accept those proffered, which proved to be adequate in fact if not in theory. In 1895, after a vain attempt to urge that Lord Rosebery should dissolve, Lord Salisbury took the commonsense decision to do so, and Sir H. Campbell-Bannerman followed his example in 1906, with excellent results. In 1931 the issue arose whether there should be a dissolution, which naturally had no attractions for the Labour Party, whose trusted leaders had led it into disaster, whence they had emerged with office, leaving their quondam associates discredited; but the ministry was clearly entitled to appeal to the electors and, indeed, bound to do so. A complete change of the political position, without the assent of the electorate, would have been wrong, even if the ministry could have been assured by the Opposition that it could rely upon it to support its essential policies, and that the Opposition clearly had no right to do.[7]

The resignation of a Prime Minister in war time, followed by the virtual break-up of his Government, is not necessarily followed

---

[3] For further discussion on this point see below, pp. 231 ff.
[4] *Letters of Queen Victoria*, 1 s., ii. 142 f. He deprecated frequent elections as making members subservient to electors. It was now that Macaulay was defeated on his vote for the Maynooth grant.
[5] *Letters of Queen Victoria*, 1 s., ii. 447 ff. [6] *Ibid.*, 2 s., iii. 669 ff.
[7] Keith, *The King and the Imperial Crown*, pp. 172 ff.

by a dissolution. The break-up of the Aberdeen coalition, and the assumption of office by Palmerston, involved no dissolution of Parliament. In December, 1916, Mr. Lloyd George became Prime Minister and re-formed the administration without appealing to the country, and so did Mr. Churchill in May, 1940. It is not impossible, however, that criticism of the conduct of a war might lead to the defeat and resignation of a government without it being possible to form a new government on the basis of an agreed policy. In that case, dissolution and an election would almost certainly follow.

(4) In other cases a dissolution has been necessitated by the emergence of new issues of fundamental importance. In 1909 the rejection of the ministry's financial scheme of taxation raised definitely the question of the relations of the two Houses, and demanded a readjustment. The dissolution of November, 1910, was equally necessary to afford ground for asking the new King to agree to override the opposition to the Parliament Bill of the House of Lords. In 1923 Mr. Baldwin felt it necessary to ask for a mandate for Protection, and in 1931 the need for a fresh mandate was, as we have seen, unquestionable.

(5) In other cases the dissolution must be ruled as largely inspired by tactical reasons. In 1880 Lord Beaconsfield seems to have held[8] that an appeal would be successful, and in 1900, with much better judgment, Lord Salisbury[9] seized the opportunity of successes in South Africa to go to the country for the return to power of the victorious Government, though, in fact, nearly two years were to pass before the peace terms of Vereeniging gave a real settlement, after many painful vicissitudes and heavy losses. The dissolution of 1918 was, of course, destined to obtain full authority for the men who won the war to make the peace, but it was long overdue, for Parliament had been in being since the beginning of 1911, and its existence had been prolonged by special legislation,[10] which was clearly not to be repeated when no longer justified by the urgency of the war.

---

[8] By-elections at Liverpool and Southwark were favourable; *Letters of Queen Victoria*, s. 2. iii. 61.

[9] Garvin, *Joseph Chamberlain*, iii. 579, 589, 603 ff. For Lord Salisbury's views, *Letters of Queen Victoria*, 3 s., iii. 586. He was reluctant, apparently, because he thought the law of the pendulum should bring a reverse : Austen Chamberlain, *Politics from Inside*, p. 262.

[10] 5 & 6 Geo. V. c. 100; 6 & 7 Geo. V. c. 44.

It is interesting to note the complete contrast between present-day ideas and those of Sir R. Peel on the issue whether it is wise to have dissolutions in time of high feeling in the popular mind.[11] He objected in 1841 to the idea of Lord Melbourne not resigning, but instead seeking a new mandate by dissolution on the score that the ministry was inflaming the mind of the people on a dangerous issue like food. Macaulay gave the effective reply that agitation was created of and by the people, the issue being one which touched them essentially.[12] Peel was rigid, however, on this head, and disliked the idea of appealing, even on the issue of the corn laws. But the temptation to make use of popular excitement, and even to stimulate it into activity, is natural; as early as 1807 the Portland ministry worked up the 'No popery' cry to secure additional strength by a dissolution, which under the views then prevailing was unnecessary, and in 1900 an appeal to patriotism was peculiarly in place, when the state of popular feeling is remembered. On the other hand, there are cases where tactical use of this weapon has, with some magnanimity, been refused. Certainly in 1878, after the seeming triumph of the Congress of Berlin, and the attainment of Peace with Honour, Lord Beaconsfield could have risked an election with very reasonable prospect of success, but the Cabinet decided against it as unjustifiable, when the majority in Parliament was secure, and Mr. Baldwin in 1926 certainly could have capitalised the unpopularity of the General Strike, and the accompanying disunion among the Liberals, to have won a complete victory. But it must be remembered that Parliament had only been elected in 1924, and that his action would have been politically unadvisable, since to add an election to the gravely disturbed condition of public feeling in the country would have been a decidedly provocative step. Instead, the Premier endeavoured to embark on a course of conciliation and appeasement, exemplified in the influence brought to bear on the railway companies to make terms with their employees, whose action throughout had been gravely discreditable. As against Mr. Baldwin's forbearance on this occasion may be set, in the view of some critics, his opportunism in November, 1935, in taking advantage of the favourable conditions created by the Peace Ballot for appealing to the country on a policy of strict adherence to the League of Nations

11 4 *Parl. Deb.* 3 s., 891 f. Cf. William IV. in 1831; *Correspondence of William IV. and Earl Grey*, i. 179 ff.   12 58 *Parl. Deb.* 3 s., 817 ff., 850, 887.

Covenant, and to the doctrine of collective security. Mr. Chamberlain in 1938, like Lord Beaconsfield in 1878, chose not to use a popularly acclaimed stroke of foreign policy as an excuse for a dissolution, although there can be little doubt that an appeal to the electorate soon after Munich would at least have confirmed the Prime Minister's strength in the House of Commons. The Prime Minister denied the charge that a general election, at such a time, would be 'constitutionally indecent,' but stated that he had no wish to make party capital out of the prevalent feeling of thankfulness, or to magnify differences of opinion as a general election must do.[13] In most cases, it may be feared, expediency will prevail.

The British system is essentially opposed to that of France,[14] where dissolution is now in practice obsolete, and the Legislature lasts its normal period of four years. It is noteworthy that, even in the crisis of the war, Mr. Bonar Law[15] seems to have contemplated using the power to dissolve in order to secure a subservient party, though Mr. Churchill denounced this as 'the most terribly immoral thing he had ever heard of,' and Mr. Law was afraid that Mr. Asquith might use the power to solve in his own favour the crisis of November—December, 1916, which that statesman was not inclined to do.[16] The absence of the power to dissolve has no doubt largely accounted for the power of control over ministers of Parliamentary committees in France,[17] though there are other causes, such as the strength of the Senate, and the absence of the British rule confining financial initiative to the ministry alone. The idea of fixed dates is sometimes commended on the score that, given a definite term of office, a ministry can plan definitely for some time in advance, but the argument is of little weight. Moreover, the system of fixed elections does something to destroy continuity of public interest. The Presidential election, in particular, in the United States creates a great mass of political activity in the preceding months, to be followed by a considerable period of indifference. To the outsider it sometimes appears that the frequency and fixity of Congressional elections reduces the effective life of any House of Representatives to little more than twelve

[13] 339 *H. C. Deb.* 5 s., 548.
[14] H. Finer, *The Theory and Practice of Modern Government*, i. 665 ff.
[15] Beaverbrook, *Politicians and the War*, ii. 106, 124.
[16] Spender, *Lord Oxford*, ii. 273, 311 n. 1.
[17] Finer, *The Theory and Practice of Modern Government*, ii. 872 ff.

months.   To restrict the right of dissolution, by some constitutional principle, so as to lessen control over the Commons by the Cabinet, has been vaguely discussed, but no project has received serious backing.   Other means of lessening Cabinet domination will be denoted below.

It rests, therefore, with the Government to decide what issues it shall treat as vital, and as demanding that it must resign or dissolve if it is denied support thereon.   It is, however, more and more the practice for ministries to restrict the freedom of the members, by insisting on making the vote a matter of confidence. The days are gone when the Melbourne ministry suffered repeated defeats with equanimity, and dissolved only when an actual vote of no-confidence was carried by a majority of one, after it had refrained from resignation on a defeat on the sugar duties.[18]   The coalition ministry in 1853 accepted minor defeats without serious difficulties. Lord Rosebery's ministry treated a defeat on the Address in 1894 with calm,[20] but the vote was a snap one, and though such votes discredit a ministry, or at least suggest that its members are slack in their allegiance, or the Whips rather below par, still resignation is by no means essential.   On this occasion the Government subsequently secured the rejection of the amended Address and the passage of the original version.[21]   In June, 1895, the same Administration was defeated on an amendment in Supply reducing the appropriation for the Parliament buildings.   The vote was small and the Government remained in office.   But when they were defeated again, a week later, on the Army Estimates they resigned.   This second vote was also a snap vote, but appears to have been taken seriously, not on its own merits, but because it came at the end of a period of very small majorities.[22]   It was more striking, when in 1905 Mr. Balfour was defeated on an Irish issue in Committee of Supply, without resigning or dissolving.[23] The position, of course, is different when a Government is distinctly a minority Government, as in 1886, when Lord Salisbury advised Lord R. Churchill to make it clear that the Government would not treat private members' bills as raising issues of confidence.[24]   But

[18] 58 *Parl. Deb.* 3 s., 817 ff., 850 ff., 1212 ff.; 59 *ibid.*, 77 ff.
[20] Crewe, *Rosebery*, ii. 445; *Letters of Queen Victoria*, 3 s., ii. 382 ff.
[21] 22 *Parl. Deb.* 4 s., 257 ff.
[22] Crewe, *Rosebery*, ii. 507; Spender, *Campbell-Bannerman*, i. 161 ff.
[23] 150 *Parl. Deb.* 4 s., 49 ff.
[24] Winston Churchill, *Life of Lord Randolph Churchill*, ii. 136.

he did not suggest indifference to the fate of governmental proposals. On the other hand, Mr. MacDonald in 1924 announced that his Government would not go out—or, we may presume, dissolve—on defeats, not on principle, but would do so if a vote of no-confidence was carried.[25]   In fact it was defeated ten times between January and August, and the defeat, which it deemed decisive, was one on a comparatively minor issue, which the Liberals were most anxious not to treat as one demanding resignation or dissolution.[26]

It is, of course, clear that a vote of no-confidence is decisive. A ministry which remained in office thereafter would gravely embarrass the Crown, which would be placed in the dangerous position of continuing to act on the advice of ministers disapproved of by Parliament.   Moreover, Parliament could refuse further supplies,[27] and thus paralyse expenditure of essential funds.   It would, no doubt, block all legislation and petition the Crown for the dismissal of the unworthy ministers, and menace them with impeachment, for a breach of essential convention would justify the adoption of any means to eject the Government.   But such formal votes are few.   In 1841 Lord Melbourne dissolved on such a vote; in 1859 Lord Derby was so defeated and resigned; in 1924 a like fate awaited Mr. Baldwin; in these cases the electorate had just decided.   More often the defeat comes on a substantive issue; the ministry of 1846 fell on an Irish Coercion Bill, though its offence was on the corn laws; in 1852 the Whigs were defeated on the Militia Bill and resigned.   The ministry of Lord Derby in 1852 resigned on defeat on the budget after a dissolution.   Lord Aberdeen resigned in 1855 because the House carried Mr. Roebuck's demand for enquiry into the Crimean war.   Lord Palmerston dissolved when defeated on his policy in China, and won in 1857; in 1858 he fell on the Conspiracy to Murder Bill, and resigned.   Lord Russell's ministry in 1866 resigned on defeat on reform.[28]   Mr. Disraeli was defeated in 1868 on the Irish Church issue, and dissolved; when unsuccessful, he resigned without meeting the new Parliament.   In 1851[29] the Whig Government was defeated on a franchise motion in a small House; the impossibility of securing an alternative Government compelled it to remain in office.   In 1873[30]

---

[25] 169 *H. C. Deb.* 5 s., 749 f.   [26] Spender, *Lord Oxford*, ii. 344 ff.
[27] Cf. Austen Chamberlain, *Politics from Inside*, pp. 256, 258, 266.
[28] *Letters of Queen Victoria*, 2 s., i. 323–332.
[29] *Ibid.*, 1 s., ii. 345 ff.
[30] *Ibid.*, 2 s., ii. 233, 246, 298, 318; Morley, *Gladstone*, ii. 446 ff.

Mr. Gladstone, defeated on the Irish University Bill, resigned, but had to resume office for a like cause; next year defeated at the general election he resigned forthwith. Mr. Gladstone's fall in 1885 was on the budget; in 1886 he was defeated on the Home Rule issue, and dissolved, resigning after a general election. In 1895 a defeat on the vote for cordite ended the life of Lord Rosebery's ministry. In 1924 Mr. MacDonald dissolved on defeat on the Campbell prosecution issue, and resigned when the electorate gave its decision against him. There can be little doubt that Mr. Attlee would have treated a defeat on the Steel Bill, in September, 1950, as sufficient cause either for resignation or for dissolution. An interesting case occurred in 1944. On March 28, Mr. Churchill's Coalition Administration was defeated by one vote (117–116) on an amendment to the Education Bill, moved in Committee on the floor of the House.[31] The amendment was designed to ensure that there should be no differentiation, on grounds of sex, in fixing scales of pay for teachers, and was carried against the Government. On the following day Mr. Churchill announced that, on resumption of the Committee Stage of the Bill, the amended clause would be deleted and that the Government would regard the motion to delete as an issue of confidence.[32] The next day the Government's motion was supported by a majority of 425 to 23.[33]

To sum up, the occasions on which action has been deemed imperative by the ministry have differed in character. The defeat of 1895 was of such a character that the ministry's resignation was clearly a matter due to the disintegration of the party, largely through internal dissension between the Prime Minister and the leader of the Commons. The budget defeat of 1885 stood in a different position,[34] for, as Mr. Gladstone insisted, precedent dictated that resignation was proper in such a case, but the ministry was also in other ways in process of disintegration.[35] In the other cases the issues were equivalent to a vote of censure; no doubt that of 1873 might have been treated otherwise, but Mr. Gladstone had made it clear that the issue was one of confidence. Thus, although

---

[31] 398 *H. C. Deb.* 5 s., 1264 ff. [32] *Ibid.*, 1452.
[33] *Ibid.*, 1654 ff.
[34] *Letters of Queen Victoria*, 2 s., iii. 664 ff.
[35] Tories and Nationalists combined to defeat the ministry. Lord R. Churchill's Tory democracy, like Mr. Chamberlain's radical programme, recognised the importance of the Irish issue; Morley, *Gladstone*, iii. 202 ff. Both appreciated the effect of the extension of the franchise in 1884, which added 1,762,000 voters.

there are instances of Governments surviving defeat on the Budget or the Address, there has been no occasion since 1832 when a Government has failed to regard a vote of no-confidence, if carried, as decisive.

Whether a Government shall resign on a decisive vote or ask the Crown to dissolve is a matter for it to decide in the light of all the circumstances. It is impossible to claim that dissolution is in any sense obligatory, and, indeed, the suggestion, which was made energetically in regard to the resignation of Lord Rosebery in 1895,[36] and of Mr. Balfour in 1905,[37] is incapable of serious support. The idea must be that the Government is in office because of a mandate from the electorate, and that, when it finds that it cannot give it effect, it ought to restore to the electorate the right to pronounce what policy it desires to see adopted. So far the contention can be given weight, but the counter-argument is conclusive. To appeal to the electorate means to ask it to homologate some policy, and a ministry which is not prepared to ask for a mandate cannot properly appeal. In 1895 it was plainly impossible for the ministry to present to the electorate any definite scheme, for its members were far from united in spirit or aims.[38] Thus, it was plainly better that the appeal should be made by those who had defeated the ministry, and who *ex hypothesi* had plans of their own to further. In like manner, when Mr. Balfour refused to dissolve in 1905, it was because he had no policy for which he could ask a mandate. No doubt, in both cases, the results of the dissolution, which the incoming ministry secured, were very unfavourable to the outgoing Government, but that merely shows that a party without a declared policy will always be at great disadvantage compared with one which has a policy. Its preparedness, in this respect, was one considerable advantage enjoyed by the Labour Party at the general election of 1945. It is reasonable to say that it is very unwise politically for a party to have merely to resign, but it is impossible to say that there is any constitutional obligation upon it to dissolve.

In one matter of interest the waning importance of the Commons is plainly to be traced. In 1841 despite patent defeat at the polls, the ministry met Parliament, to be there ejected. In 1868, however, Mr. Disraeli innovated, and the Queen concurred

---

36 *Letters of Queen Victoria*, 3 s., ii. 525 f.
37 Lee, *Edward VII.*, ii. 186–91; Esher, *Journals and Letters*, ii. 120.
38 *Letters of Queen Victoria*, 3 s., ii. 316 ff., 322 ff.

in the view, that the dignity of the ministry and the public interest were best served by resignation without meeting Parliament.[39] The reasons are plain: the new Government should be formed as early as possible, and should frame the royal speech to intimate the course of legislation. The presence of a discredited Government in Parliament can serve no purpose, and may in time of foreign crises be a positive danger. In 1874 Mr. Gladstone hesitated to follow Mr. Disraeli's example, arguing that 'It is Parliament, not the constituencies, that ought to dismiss the Government, and the proper function of the House of Commons cannot be taken away from it without diminishing somewhat its dignity and authority,'[40] adding that dismissal by Parliament itself was more conformable to precedent. To this the Queen's answer was that 'whatever advantage there may be in adhering to usage and precedent, it is counterbalanced by the disadvantage of nearly three weeks' delay for the country and the public service.'[41] The example set was followed by Lord Beaconsfield in 1880, by Mr. Gladstone in 1886, by Mr. MacDonald in 1924, and by Mr. Churchill in 1945. In all these cases the verdict of the electorate was clear. In 1886 Lord Salisbury met Parliament, but there was certainly room for doubt as to whether he could be defeated, and the actual vote was on an amendment to the address, which advocated the famous policy of 'three acres and a cow.'[42] In 1892 it certainly seemed clear that Mr. Gladstone would be supported by the Irish party, but the margin, even in that event, was so small, that the decision to wait for a vote by the Commons could not seriously be questioned, and it was given on a no-confidence amendment.[43] In 1923 it was not altogether clear that the Liberals would support the Labour Party against Mr. Baldwin, and to retain office until actually ejected on a no-confidence motion was perfectly in order.[44] A different situation existed in 1929, for although the Government might have hoped to secure support from the small Liberal Party, which had fared so badly in the Labour régime of 1924 that it might well hesitate to put Labour once again in power, yet the Conservatives were not, as they had been in 1923, the strongest

---

39 *Letters of Queen Victoria*, 2 s., i. 556 f.; Morley, *Gladstone*, ii. 252–3.
40 Morley, *Gladstone*, ii. 492–3; *Letters of Queen Victoria*, 2 s., ii. 316.
41 *Ibid.*, 2 s., ii. 317.
42 *Ibid.*, 2 s., iii. 706 ff.; for Mr. J. Collings' amendment, *ibid.*, 3 s., i. 21 ff.; Morley, *Gladstone*, iii. 288 f.
43 *Letters of Queen Victoria*, 3 s., ii. 128 ff.   44 Spender, *Lord Oxford*, ii. 342 ff.

single party.   But Mr. Baldwin was not in the least inclined to seek
Liberal support, and instead decided that the verdict of the electorate meant 'that whether they wanted the hon. members opposite
or not, they certainly did not want me, and I was going to get out
as soon as I could.   My colleagues agreed with me.'[45]   It must be
remembered that the election had deliberately been fought by the
party on the personality of their chief, rather than on any very
reasoned programme, and this explains his personal feeling of
rejection.

In certain cases, of course, a Government may admit that
censure is just without resignation or dissolution following.   But
these are wholly exceptional, being based on the fact that, while a
minister normally commits his colleagues by his laches, it remains
possible for them to dissociate themselves from his errors.   There
is a classic instance in Lord Ellenborough's resignation, when he
wrongly authorised publication of a severe despatch to the
Governor-General of India in 1858, and when in dealing with the
vote of censure thereon based, the ministry did not justify his action,
though it found excuses for it.[46]   The censure by the Commons in
1864 of the Education Department for withholding parts of the
reports of the inspectors resulted in the resignation of Mr. Lowe,
who would, had he wished, have been defended by the ministry;
he demanded an inquiry, which exonerated him, and the vote was
then rescinded.[47]   Lord Westbury next year resigned on a resolution finding laxity in dealing with an appointment in the Bankruptcy
Court at Leeds.[48]   In later instances actual censure has been
evaded, as when in 1873 Mr. Gladstone effected an exchange of
ministries, consequent on irregularities regarding the practice of
accounting in the Post Office.[49]   Prompt resignation by Col. Seely
in 1914,[50] ended the crisis induced by his apparent surrender of
principle in regard to the claims of the officers in Ireland to be
allowed to attach conditions to their obligation of obedience to

[45] 261 *H. C. Deb.* 5 s., 535.
[46] Martin, *Prince Consort*, ii. 221–32; Fitzmaurice, *Granville*, i. 304–8; Bell,
Palmerston, ii. 188 ff.
[47] Martin, *Sherbrooke*, ii. 226.   Lord Granville resigned, but withdrew resignation
later; Fitzmaurice, *Granville*, i. 431.
[48] Fitzmaurice, *Granville*, i. 479 ff.   The Lord Chancellor had already been
attacked on the Edmunds' case.
[49] Guedalla, *The Queen and Mr. Gladstone*, i. 420 ff.; Morley, *Gladstone*, ii. 461 ff.
[50] Spender, *Lord Oxford*, ii. 44.   Mr. Birrell resigned on the Irish rebellion issue
(April, 1916; *ibid.*, pp. 213 f.), but not Sir G. Cave on the London police
strike, though he offered to do so (Mallet, *Cave*, pp. 20, 216 f.).

orders. The unfavourable comment of the Mesopotamian Royal Commission on the conduct of the campaign resulted in Mr. A. Chamberlain's resignation in July, 1917, as a gesture, asserting the principle that the head of a department is responsible for defects of a subordinate Government; in 1938 Mr. Ormsby Gore admitted his technical responsibility for misgovernment in Trinidad, but no one thought of his resignation; the tragic horrors of the Mesopotamian case differentiate its treatment. Mr. Montagu in 1922[51] relieved the ministry, by hasty resignation, from attack based on his error in permitting publication of a protest from the Government of India against the Turkish policy of the British ministry. The resignation of Sir S. Hoare has been noted; it clearly saved the ministry from the difficult position of having to face an attack which had the sympathy of a large number of members of the Government party, whose views were moulded or strengthened by those of their constituents. Very occasionally a minister may incur censure and yet involve neither the resignation of the Government nor his own. In November, 1949, the Minister of Civil Aviation, Lord Pakenham, issued what even he admitted to be a precipitate and indiscreet observation on the report of an enquiry into an accident at Prestwich airport in October, 1948. There were full debates of the Minister's action in both Houses of Parliament, but the Opposition did not press their criticism to the point of challenging the Minister's competence and he did not, as seemed at one stage possible, resign.[52]

It is also possible to escape serious attack by the device of arranging for enquiry. There is the famous episode of Mr. Roebuck's motion as regards the Crimean war, which brought down the Aberdeen ministry on Lord John Russell's defection. Lord Palmerston accepted it as unavoidable, but it cost him forthwith Mr. Gladstone, who was convinced that such an enquiry was an abuse of the powers of the House, and might prove dangerous.[53] This is clearly an exaggerated view, though there is something to be said for the opinion,[54] that the wiser plan is to appoint a Royal

---

[51] Nicolson, *Curzon*, pp. 267 f. For Wyndham's resignation in 1905 see Dugdale, *Arthur James Balfour*, i. 415 ff.

[52] 165 *H. L. Deb.* 5 s., 1125–1199; 470 *H. C. Deb.* 5 s., 1335–1346, and 470 *H. C. Deb.* 5 s., 2109–2190.

[53] Bell, *Palmerston*, ii. 115; Morley, *Gladstone*, i. 537 ff.

[54] The Select Committee on the Jameson Raid failed to elicit vital papers, and thus has left it open to believe that Mr. J. Chamberlain was privy to the Raid, a point which ought to have been cleared up. As it is, the issue cannot be decided. Cf. Garvin, *Joseph Chamberlain*, iii. 95–125, who unconsciously makes grave admissions; Esher, *Journals and Letters*, i. 193–8, 211.

Commission, as was done during the Great War in respect of the Dardanelles and Mesopotamian fiascos. Alternatively, a tribunal of enquiry under statute has great advantages. This was illustrated conspicuously in the case of the leakage of budget information in 1936, for the report of the judicial body appointed laid blame on Mr. J. H. Thomas, whose immediate resignation relieved the ministry from any attack.[55] On the other hand in 1918, the ministry, after first promising a judicial enquiry into the truth of certain allegations brought by Sir F. Maurice against statements of Mr. Lloyd George, as to the strength of the British forces in France, withdrew the proposal, and saved itself by an energetic exertion of its Cabinet authority, doubtless because it realised that such an investigation was certain to disclose unpalatable facts, for the minister had undoubtedly given information to the Commons, which conveyed a false impression, and concealed his own action in refusing to give Sir D. Haig the necessary reinforcements.[56]

The precedent of the J. H. Thomas case was followed in 1948 when Parliament set up a judicial tribunal, under the Chairmanship of Mr. Justice Lynskey, to enquire into allegations of corruption against certain Ministers and other public servants. The tribunal issued its report in January, 1949.[57] This criticised the actions of a junior minister, Mr. Belcher, and of a Director of the Bank of England, Mr. Gibson, and both subsequently resigned, the former from Parliament as well as from his ministerial post. All others, Ministers and civil servants, whose names had been mentioned in this connection were completely exonerated.

In yet other cases the ministry may appeal to the House to forbear from investigation or demands for information on the score that it is not in the public interest that disclosures should be made. Hence the ministry is not questioned on the expenditure of secret service funds, and the amount demanded is voted without discussion. Most striking of all, it has been agreed by the Commons not to question the use made of the enormous sum placed under Governmental control as the Exchange Equalisation Fund. Moreover, on details of defence preparations the ministry is permitted to preserve complete silence, as is shown by the replies of Sir T. Inskip to all

[55] Cmd. 5184.
[56] Spender, *Lord Oxford*, ii. 303 ff. Mr. Asquith's objection to a judicial enquiry, and preference for a Select Committee was characteristic, as in the case of Mesopotamia in 1917; ii. 294 f. Cf. Fitzroy, *Memoirs*, ii. 675.
[57] Cmd. 7616.

efforts in 1937–38 to extract from him encouragement as to the effectiveness of new British armaments, or types of aeroplanes. The ministry in like manner escapes severe pressure regarding its detailed plans for defence; whatever the degree of scepticism felt as to their efficiency, the Commons will not press a minister to go beyond his statements of what it is safe to reveal. Hence from time to time the suggestions made that the Commons should hold a secret session to discuss such issues as the state of the air defence scheme, but the proposal, which was occasionally acted on during war,[58] has never in peace been adopted. The Opposition may comment on the vital change from Mr. Baldwin's view of the necessity of equality with Germany in the number of first line aircraft to Mr. N. Chamberlain's insistence that other factors must be taken into account, such as reserves, productive capacity, and quality of airmen, but even Mr. Churchill had to rest content with the assurance that all matters relevant had fully been weighed. No doubt many Conservatives share his doubts as to the soundness of British policy in this regard, but it would have been wholly contrary to precedent to question the issue further in the Commons. Only in the case of domestic action has the issue been pressed as regards troop and ship movements, as it was in the famous controversy over Mr. Churchill's attitude towards the means to be taken to suppress any attempt in Ulster to resist, by armed force, the authority of the Crown during the controversy over Home Rule.[59]

(b) The Mandate

The precedents and logic alike make it clear that the electorate should be asked to decide on any vital steps in policy, external or foreign, and it is interesting to trace the manner in which this doctrine has been established, and the extent to which it receives effect. It is clear that before the Reform Act of 1832, and the operation of the modern party system, dissolutions were merely in form appeals to the scanty and artificial electorate. Lord North's advice to dissolve in 1774,[60] like that of Lord Grenville in 1806, was palpably intended not to elicit popular sentiment, but to add to the majority of the ministry by an adroit appeal. The opposition to reform was countenanced by W. Pitt, as he developed from the

58 April 25 and 26, 1916, on compulsory service; Spender, *Lord Oxford*, ii. 210.
59 Churchill, *World Crisis*, 1911–14, p. 181; Spender, *Lord Oxford*, ii. 42.
60 *Correspondence of George III. with Lord North*, i. 219 (ed. W. B. Donne).

broader sentiments of his younger days, while Fox became more and more conscious of the failure of the existing system to express the views of the public. The famous victory of Pitt in 1784 cannot any longer be regarded as the result of an appeal to the people to decide principles. The decisive factor therein was the hostility of the East Indian influence to the projects of Fox and North, the wholehearted aid of the King's 'friends,' who might number a hundred, and the loss of support for Fox due to his rather unprincipled alliance with Lord North.[61]

A real issue was presented in principle, and even in some detail in the election of 1831, when the electorate was asked to give a vote for a special form of reform definitely indicated by the fate of the Reform Bill in the Commons. The logical result of the reform was to render inevitable the gradual increase of popular sovereignty, though the course of advance was slow, and further progress waited until 1867, to be carried further in 1884-85, and extended to the full as late as 1918 and 1928. Moreover, until the Ballot Act of 1872, voters with open voting could easily be intimidated, and bribery flourished, until checked by Acts of 1854 and 1883, and only in 1868 were election petitions consigned to decisions by the Courts.[62] But the election of 1834 brought forth from Sir R. Peel a manifesto addressed to the electors of Tamworth, his seat, but published for general guidance, which gave the principles, and even some details, of the measures he intended to carry, while a contemporary electoral tract by E. L. Bulwer brought home to the electorate that they were being asked to vote for principles, not men only. Sir R. Peel soon repented of his attitude, and denied in 1841 the propriety of Lord Melbourne appealing to the people on principle, and in preparing in 1845 for the repeal of the corn laws, he deliberately declined to appeal to the electors because he did not think it proper, thus to excite a bitter conflict between different classes of society, in lieu of allowing dispassionate consideration by the Commons.[63] Mr. Disraeli at once attacked him bitterly for his failure to let the people decide instead of inducing a Parliament, the majority of which was elected to defend Protection,

[61] Emden, *The People and the Constitution*, pp. 196–98; Laprade, *Parliamentary Papers of John Robinson* (Camden Society, 1922); Laprade, *Public Opinions and the General Election of 1784, English Historical Review*, xxxi., 224 ff.

[62] St. Alban's merited disfranchisement by £24,000 bribery from 1832–54. Cf. Disraeli's boast of £40,000 spent at Maidstone; Parker, *Peel*, ii. 487. See Lord Askwith, *Lord James of Hereford*, pp. 60 ff., 117 ff.

[63] Peel, *Memoirs*, ii. 163 ff.

to adopt Free Trade,[64] but Sir R. Peel showed no sign of accepting this contention, though he admitted that, if he had failed to carry Free Trade, he would have dissolved, rather than accept the *status quo*. But that did not prevent him from issuing a manifesto of policy for the election of 1847, a plan adopted also by Lord George Bentinck for the Protectionists and Lord John Russell for the Government.

Mr. Disraeli was destined to violate the principle he had upheld against Sir R. Peel. In 1866 he defeated Mr. Gladstone's Reform Bill on the score that it went too far, but, on Lord J. Russell's resignation against the advice of Mr. Gladstone in favour of dissolution as the more constitutional course, he himself carried in 1867 a much wider measure, certainly without mandate. In 1868, however, on his defeat on the Irish Church issue, he decided to dissolve to test the will of the electorate, while Mr. Gladstone was driven to urge resignation as appropriate, an untenable doctrine, ill-based on the events of 1846. The election thus came to turn in a manner almost unique on a single issue, which did not deeply affect in any material way the interests of the electors in Great Britain. Yet neither protagonist in the controversy of 1873 over the issue of the duty of Mr. Disraeli to take office on Mr. Gladstone's resignation on the defeat of the Irish University Bill,[65] which ended in the refusal of Mr. Disraeli to accept office, took the obvious point that it was proper to give the electors the opportunity of deciding the policy of the country, which could not be safely left in the hands of a ministry severely discredited by a vital defeat. Mr. Disraeli was naturally chiefly moved by the consideration that his rival was in serious difficulties of several kinds, that by-elections were going against him, and that it was safe to assume that, if he were compelled to carry on in these circumstances, the time would shortly come when a dissolution would be forced on him, when the electors would have their chance to turn to himself for guidance.

A further advance in the doctrine of mandate was made in 1872 by Lord Salisbury.[66] He was moved to it by the Ballot Bill, which was certain to diminish the power of landlords to intimidate

[64] 83 *Parl. Deb.* 3 s., 122.
[65] Paul, *Modern England*, iii. 310 ff.; 214 *Parl. Deb.* 3 s., 1931 ff.; Emden, *The People and the Constitution*, pp. 218, 253; Morley, *Gladstone*, ii. 442 ff.
[66] 211 *Parl. Deb.* 3 s., 1494 f.; Lady Gwendolen Cecil, *Life of Lord Salisbury*, ii. 23–8. Cf. Gladstone's reference to opposition in 1874; *Letters of Queen Victoria*, 2 s., ii. 303 f.

their tenants, and urged that the Lords should assume the duty of ensuring that the Commons should not transgress its mandate from the electors. In 1884 he renewed the same specious attack in regard to the Reform Bill, which was to add to the electorate some two million voters, about the same number as that due to the Acts of 1832 and 1867, and which would widely extend the possibility of Liberal victories in the country areas.[67] The position was obviously open to the accusation that it sought to give to the Lords the right to force a dissolution, and in the result, as the prospects of such a dissolution appeared dubious, and as the Queen intervened, the issue was amicably settled, a Redistribution Bill being agreed upon to accompany the enactment of the Representation of the People Act. In 1886 Lord Hartington took up the cudgels for the mandate.[68] In opposing the Home Rule Bill he said:

> 'Although no principle of a "mandate" may exist, there are certain limits which Parliament is morally bound to observe, and beyond which Parliament has, morally, not the right to go in its relations with the constituents. The constituencies of Great Britain are the source of the power at all events of this branch of Parliament, and I maintain that, in the absence of an emergency that could not be foreseen, the House of Commons has no right to initiate legislation, especially immediately upon its first meeting, of which the constituencies were not informed, and of which the constituencies might have been informed, and of which if they had been informed, there is, at all events, the very greatest doubt as to what their decision might be.'

Lord Hartington's attack was based on the charge that Mr. Gladstone's Home Rule scheme was not made an issue at the general election, where he had apparently stood for nothing more than enlarged powers of local government. It is impossible to regard Mr. Gladstone's defence of his position as convincing, and, in fact, on the defeat of his Bill, two months later, he readily dissolved and appealed for a mandate for Home Rule.[69]

The issue of the mandate, which thus seemed well established, was revived after the election of 1900, when the Education Act of 1902 introduced, with the doubting discouragement of Lord

[67] 290 *Parl. Deb.* 3 s., 468 f.
[68] 304 *Parl. Deb.* 3 s., 1241 ff.; Holland, *Life of the Duke of Devonshire*, ii. 141–2.
[69] 304 *Parl. Deb.* 3 s., 1547; Emden, *The People and the Constitution*, pp. 223 f.; Morley, *Gladstone*, iii. 313 ff., 337 ff.; Gladstone, *Speeches*, ix. 128 ff. In 1893 the Duke of Devonshire went so far as to demand a mandate for an actual Bill; 17 *Parl. Deb.* 4 s., 30 f.

Salisbury, the principle of placing on the rates the maintenance of denominational schools, and thus evoked a bitter religious controversy. There was also grumbling with legislation as to liquor licences, which gratified that industry by giving a valuable interest in place of a tenancy at pleasure. But on the issue of tariff reform the doctrine of mandate was accepted by both sides, as well as by Mr. Chamberlain (May 15, 1903). Indeed, Mr. Balfour ingeniously dwelt on it as precluding action in the current Parliament, and finally advanced to the extreme doctrine that a general election should precede discussion of tariff reform with the colonies, and a second election its being made operative. Finally, Mr. Balfour resigned, refusing to dissolve, and the Liberals received a clear mandate of a wide character from the electorate.[70]

At this point, however, the House of Lords revived the doctrine of Lord Salisbury in 1872 regarding the necessity of a clear mandate for legislation. It rejected the Education Bill and the Plural Voting Bill,[71] and naturally the Conservatives denied absolutely the validity of the claim made in June, 1907, that the power of the Lords to alter or reject Bills 'should be so restricted by law as to secure that, within the limits of a single Parliament, the final decision of the Commons shall prevail.' The Prime Minister most emphatically repudiated the idea of the referendum, mandate, or plebiscite, and seemed to claim that a Parliamentary party, successful at an election, should be able to pass such legislation as it thought fit. In this doctrine he was no doubt sincere, for he had denied in 1900 that the Government of the day needed a new mandate to make peace; moreover, his doctrine was shared by Lord Morley, who in 1902 had dissented from the argument of his colleagues that a mandate was necessary for the Education Act, and who, on the Finance Bill of 1909 and the Parliament Bill of 1911, was again to deny the validity of the doctrine.[72] It would plainly have been far more reasonable to allege that the mandate actually received covered educational reform and the abolition of plural voting, and to take the view that anything reasonably brought before the people at the general election or arising then should be admitted as proper. The dangerous nature of the wider

[70] For admissions see 123 *Parl. Deb.* 4 s., 178; 131 *ibid.*, 678 f.; 141 *ibid.*, 120 f., 190, 338.
[71] Lee, *Edward VII.*, ii. 458 ff.; Newton, *Lansdowne*, pp. 456 ff., who admits the cynical opportunism with which the Lords accepted the Trade Disputes Bill.
[72] 4 *H. L. Deb.* 5 s., 1142; Emden, *The People and the Constitution*, p. 301.

claim was properly stressed by Sir W. Anson, and the Government itself respected the self-limitation of its action as regards Home Rule imposed by its electoral appeal.[73]

In 1909, however, the Lords insisted on refusing a second reading to the Finance Bill until it had been submitted to the judgment of the country, which raised definitely the right of the Lords to compel a dissolution.   As Lord Courtney pointed out, its earlier action did not compel a dissolution, but intervention in finance did, but Lord Curzon insisted that the Lords must have the right to reject, and so compel reference to the electors on any Bill in flagrant conflict with the expressed will of the electors, or which had never been brought before them.[74]   The issue was ultimately settled, so far as the Lords was concerned, by the Parliament Act, 1911, and the loss of power to deal with finance measures was no doubt just, for the claim of a wealthy hereditary House to dictate financial policy is one repugnant to moral and political common sense.

In 1910 prior to the election resolved upon to secure a mandate for the Parliament Bill, the election of January, 1910, not having been fought directly on this issue, the text of the Bill was circulated, though it could not be discussed.   The claim made by Mr. Asquith, Lord Loreburn, and Lord Haldane that a complete mandate had been obtained was really unanswerable, and the counter-arguments of Mr. Balfour, Sir W. Anson, and Lord Curzon will not stand examination.[75]   The contention that the Conservatives had not had time to criticise was frankly absurd, for the Bill was brief and clear, and that the issues were not simple, followed obviously from the fact that there was a general election.   Lord Salisbury had discounted the Liberal mandate in 1892 on this ground.[76]   Nothing can make that fought on any one issue; to put it at the lowest, an unsatisfactory candidate will lose what a sound man would hold as of course.   The real point was that the Liberal majority rested largely on the Irish Nationalists, who were voting in order to secure Home Rule, whereafter the British constitution would mean little to them, but for the Conservatives the fatal logical difficulty was that they demanded the retention of Union, and that being so they could not object to a majority, however much it rested on Irish

[73] 176 *Parl. Deb.* 4 s., 911, 918, 1002.   See also Anson, *Law and Custom of the Constitution; Parliament*, vol. I (ed. Gwyer), p. 329.
[74] 4 *H. L. Deb.* 5 s., 731 ff., 1139, 1260.
[75] They are fairly summed up by Emden, *The People and the Constitution*, pp. 233–34.
[76] Lady G. Cecil, *Life of Lord Salisbury*, iv. 403.

votes. Any argument based on this fact is therefore untenable.[77] The further vehement claim that the ministry had, despite the passing of the Parliament Act, 1911, no mandate to pass a Home Rule Act is equally untenable. No person in his sound senses but knew in 1910 that the Irish Nationalists and the Liberals were co-operating to pass the Parliament Act as the indispensable condition of proceeding to Home Rule.[78] To demand that the detailed proposals should be laid before the electorate, as the Duke of Devonshire had done in 1893, was to misunderstand the function of Parliament and the electorate. The duty of the electors must be to approve principles, of Parliament, to give shape to the principles. Otherwise every change of substance could be seized upon and a further reference to the electors demanded.

The doctrine of mandate suffered in the Parliament of 1918, when female suffrage was carried, though certainly the issue had not been conceded in 1910. It may be said that the conversion of many opponents, such as Mr. Asquith,[79] and wide approval of thus rewarding women for their work in the war, might be deemed to approve the step taken. But the action of the Government in 1921 in departing abruptly from all earlier doctrines, and in conceding Dominion status, with absolute control of tariffs to the Irish Free State, could claim no mandate.[80] It was also hotly disputed among Conservatives whether the grant of equal suffrage in 1928 was justified, for the electorate certainly had not been conscious in 1924 that it was being called upon to homologate this step. But it appeared that the Prime Minister considered himself bound by what he had said prior to the election.

In 1923, however, Mr. Baldwin explicitly emphasised the necessity of a mandate for a policy of protection, and declined to proceed in any other manner than a straightforward appeal to the electors. In his ministry of 1924–29 he declined to introduce protection because he had not asked for any mandate. The ministry of 1931 asked for a 'doctor's mandate' to do whatever seemed to them best designed to correct the adverse balance of trade, and it is quite possible to hold that they were justified in introducing wholesale protection on the strength of it. But

[77] Apparently accepted by Emden, *The People and the Constitution*, p. 234.
[78] Spender, *Lord Oxford*, i. 355 f.; ii. 13 ff.
[79] *Ibid.*, ii. 297.
[80] Asquith had urged Dominion status in 1920; *ibid.*, ii. 332; Keith, *Letters on Imperial Relations*, 1916–35, pp. 18 ff.

the ministry of 1935,[81] in asking for a mandate based on the maintenance of the League Covenant and the doctrine of collective security, prepared serious trouble for itself. In a brief period the flagrant violation of the Covenant involved in the Hoare-Laval terms for Ethiopia resulted in a wide protest among its own supporters, and for the moment the resignation (December 18) of the minister primarily responsible seemed to show respect for the mandate. But in June, 1936, Mr. N. Chamberlain denounced the régime of sanctions and forced their withdrawal, thus clearly violating the Covenant. In 1938, matters went from bad to worse in this regard, for Mr. N. Chamberlain agreed to negotiate with Italy on the basis of the recognition *de jure* of the conquest of Ethiopia, in flat defiance of the League Covenant, and acquiesced in the annexation of Austria as soon as his firm protest had been firmly rebuked by Herr Hitler. That such steps should be taken without according reference to the electorate, as claimed by the leaders of the Labour Party,[82] is certainly a remarkable assertion of the right of a party elected on a definite mandate to ignore it. That Labour did not press still further its protest was, perhaps, due to appreciation that this precedent would enable it, when it secured power, to go at will beyond the terms of the mandate without any possibility of effective Conservative protest. It must be doubted whether it is compatible with elementary principles of political morality to obtain power on the strength of one policy, and thereafter to disregard utterly the doctrines on which office was obtained. The protests of Lord Halifax that it could be shown that the action taken was consistent with the promises given suggest a casuistry whose adoption was damaging to the Conservative cause. The further allegation that the attitude of the Government had popular approval suggested the unanswerable proposal that the Government should undertake to appeal to the people as to the acceptance of such terms as it might arrange with Italy.[83] To confront a country with a *fait accompli* in foreign affairs is a policy fraught with the gravest danger to the State, and destructive of national security.

The doctrine of the mandate is a very loose and vague constitutional concept. On the other hand, it can be a useful part of the political game. If used to suggest that a Government is

[81] Toynbee, *Survey of International Affairs*, 1935, ii. 50 ff., 65.
[82] House of Commons, April 4, 1938; 334 *H. C. Deb.* 5 s., 30 ff.
[83] Cmd. 5726. See Commons, May 2, 1938; 335 *H. C. Deb.* 5 s., 533 ff.

entitled to do nothing that has not received specific electoral approval it has little value, and might well do much harm by paralysing the freedom of government to respond to changing conditions. If employed to suggest that Government is using its majority dishonestly by departing from that vague 'contract' which public acceptance of any party at a general election must involve, then both the charge and the defence against it should, through discussion, maintain that connection between electorate and Parliament which is an essential part of the political process.

5. THE FORMULATION OF ISSUES.

IT is with the Reform Act of 1832 that the question of formulation of issues really begins. Isolated examples of criticism of prospective policy are earlier known, as the election of 1701 on William III.'s policy of war with France, and the Tories sought ineffectively in 1722 to condemn the Whigs for the passing of the Septennial Act, 1716, with its deprival of the electors of their then due right to pronounce on the ministry. Even after 1832 the Duke of Wellington could advise Sir R. Peel to go to the country on the issue whether he should remain Prime Minister, though Peel himself thought free trade and the destruction of protection was the true issue.[84] In 1857 Lord Palmerston virtually asked for a vote of confidence in himself,[85] and Lord Derby in 1859 deliberately made the issue a personal one. Lord Palmerston, who protested, himself did likewise in 1865. Lord R. Churchill, with some exaggeration, but also substantial truth, regarded the election of 1886 as a personal appeal of Mr. Gladstone for a vote of confidence in him.[86] This was natural, for the Irish issue was already dividing deeply his party.

Confused issues are obviously inevitable, for both ministry and Opposition can appeal to past successes or mismanagement and to future policy. In 1837, the Whig ministry extolled its past, the Opposition suggested the evils it would do; in 1841 the ministry denounced the protectionist character of the Opposition, while the Opposition concentrated on the bad record of the ministry. In 1874, Mr. Gladstone stressed the possible removal of the income tax, Mr. Disraeli denounced his blunders and failures. The

[84] Peel, *Memoirs*, ii. 295. [85] Morley, *Gladstone*, i. 564.
[86] Churchill, *Lord Randolph Churchill*, ii. 495.

position is characteristic of the two men, for the Liberals were in the nature of things bound to activity in reform, the Conservatives to insistence on the merits of their administration, or the demerits of their opponents. But in 1880 Lord Beaconsfield devised a new tactic; his record had been chequered and was ignored, but he curdled the blood of the electors by denouncing the destructive character of Home Rule as the disintegration of the realm.[87] As Mr. Gladstone was far from having adopted Home Rule then, he was perfectly justified in condemning this new device, and insisting that it was a complete innovation to make an election turn on the demerits of a supposed policy of the Opposition.[88] On the other hand, after 1886, the policy of Lord Salisbury in 1892 in appealing on his record and on hostility to Home Rule was plainly just.

Necessarily, with the extension of the electorate and the change in the British attitude towards social services, evinced best in the Liberal ministry of 1906, the appeals of all parties are rich in suggestions of direct benefit to the people. Those of 1923 all strike that note, for the Conservatives promised to enrich national life by tariff reform, Labour a national levy for social betterment, and the Liberals a credit system, while the Labour and Liberal parties denounced tariff reform unsparingly.[89] In 1929 it proved fatal to the success of Mr. Baldwin that he could not hold out any panacea for unemployment, while the opponents stressed their rival schemes in this regard. In 1931 and 1935 alike the parties each stressed the social advantages of their plans, and the importance attached to maintenance of the social services is shown by the fact that the budget of 1938, despite the enormous burden of defence expenditure, cheerfully added generously to the already colossal total of social services, the ministry, no doubt wisely, recognising that to stint the latter in favour of the former would be the best way to accumulate unpopularity. In 1945 the Labour Party went to the electorate with a very detailed programme, both of improvements in the social services and measures of nationalisation.[90] The electoral temperature of February, 1950, however, was much cooler; promises were rather to retain what had been given than of further grants, and on this occasion there was little or no attempt at out-bidding. The modern habit of soliciting votes by wide promises of gain is,

[87] Emden, *The People and the Constitution*, p. 248.
[88] Gladstone, *Speeches in Scotland*, ii. 21 f.
[89] Spender, *Lord Oxford*, ii. 342 ff.; Snowden, *Autobiography*, ii. 572.
[90] R. B. McCallum and A. Readman, *British General Election of 1945*.

of course, a commonplace in the Dominions, but even there it is often productive of harm, nor does it seem that its adoption in Britain is likely to add to the standard of public life. It must be added that in the actual electoral combats candidates show often the most singular generosity in interpreting the intentions of their leaders, and lend themselves deliberately or accidentally to the propagation of the most far-reaching promises. On the other hand, Opposition candidates will freely exaggerate the promises made by their adversaries with the aim of discrediting them, either as impossible or as destined to bring upon the country the disasters from which it was saved only by the self-sacrifice of the Prime Minister in 1931 in consenting to form a national Government.

Difficulties naturally present themselves in the way of framing policies in the case of a ministry which takes office on the resignation of an earlier ministry, but they can be exaggerated out of all reason, as they were in the classical instance of Mr. Disraeli's arguments to justify his refusal in 1873 to take office.[91] He held that without experience in office he could not formulate his policy on such issues as the position in Central Asia, the new rules of international law arising out of the Alabama controversy, the treaty of commerce with France, and local taxation. Plainly, however, in this case it was simply a tactical advantage which produced this attitude, and under modern conditions the Opposition is possessed of a body for regular consultation, the 'shadow Cabinet,' and has expert advice in abundance.[92] Lord Salisbury, no doubt, wanted Lord Rosebery in 1895 to dissolve, but he found no difficulty in adopting a programme, and Sir H. Campbell-Bannerman made no bones about doing likewise in 1905. No doubt a ministry, in these circumstances, may have to be more sketchy in its proposals, but that means little.

An Opposition naturally will state its proposals in bold outline, as Mr. Gladstone insisted in 1885 when asked by Mr. Parnell to state fully his views on Ireland; but later, of course, it can be expected to be more precise after its proposals have been long under consideration, as Mr. Chamberlain urged on Home Rule in 1892. On the other hand, the Liberals in 1905 justly declined the demand that they should formulate their policies on education,

91 214 *Parl. Deb.* 3 s., 1931 ff.
92 For references to the 'Shadow Cabinet,' see Austen Chamberlain, *Politics from Inside*, pp. 350–1; Churchill, *The Second World War*, i. 27; *post*, p. 241.

8*

licensing and Chinese labour. A ministry is always well advised to stress its positive merits, as well as to produce a definite policy; the Opposition may concentrate on criticism, but equally it should adduce something definite. What will become the real issue can never be safely predicted.

Mention has already been made of the influence of the party organisations in inducing the ministries to place items on their programmes. The response of ministers varies; the Conservatives have shown little readiness to accept dictation, but the Liberal Party is less exclusive in its attitude. The Labour position has often been more affected by the party control although, as we have already seen,[93] that control has been strongly resisted since 1945. In other cases private organisations are effective; the Anti-Slavery Society and the Anti-Corn Law League played an honourable part in securing the emancipation of slaves by the Act of 1833, and the abolition of taxation of corn.[94] In more recent times, with the multiplication of associations and the ever expanding activities of Government, influences are brought to bear on ministries and oppositions to promote or support legislation. The trade unions, the co-operative societies, the chambers of commerce, manufacturers' associations, the shipping interest, societies to promote free trade or tariff reform, the local authorities and their associations, municipal officials and civil servants, societies for the promotion of interests connected with art, music, films, theatres, public health, education, sanitation and other subjects, have access to members of Parliament and the Government, and can press their claims for attention.[95] Thus the efforts of advocates of physical fitness bore fruit in the Physical Training and Recreation Act, 1937, but it must be remembered that their efforts might have failed but for the temptation offered to the ministry, to secure indirectly a higher standard of physical fitness in possible recruits for the defence forces. Legislation is often based on reports of Commissions, as in the case of cinematograph films in 1938, and administration, as well as legislation, may be suggested in like manner, as in the case of the changes in air administration, based on the report of the

---

93 *Ante*, p. 185.
94 For the failure of the Chartists, see Emden, *The People and the Constitution*, pp. 84 f., 92 f.
95 Thus the Early Closing Association secured in 1928 the Shops (Hours of Closing) Act, 18 & 19 Geo. V. c. 33; Taylor, *Brentford*, pp. 275 ff. The case of the supporters of female suffrage is also conspicuous, and that of the Divorce Law Reform Union.

Cadman Committee on Civil Aviation. The ministries are also filled with eager experts, in close touch with the outer world, from whose brains and experience come forth large numbers of legislative projects, more than sufficient to occupy the whole time of ministries, apart from major legislation. The success of ministers depends largely on their skill to make the best use of the vast possibilities of legislative activity presented to them, and of Oppositions on their capacity for taking up popular proposals and urging them on the electorate. It is significant that in 1937 the Labour Party decided to pledge itself to the provision of a living rate of pension to workers retiring at age sixty-five, despite the enormous sums required to finance so ambitious a scheme. Such an issue obviously presents a fruitful source of advocacy of Labour and its denunciation, as seeking, by reckless promises of public funds, to win unfairly the favour of the electorate.

The attitude of individual ministers to projects not yet adopted by the ministry presents difficulties. In the earlier days there was more room for individual activity, and, while in 1865[96] Lord Palmerston eschewed the issue of Parliamentary reform, Mr. Bright pressed the topic. Mr. Chamberlain caused much annoyance to the Queen, under Mr. Gladstone in 1880–85, and annoyed his leader by promulgating an unofficial programme,[97] including payment of members, free education, and housing reform, while his faithful henchman, Mr. Jesse Collings, won immortality with his doctrine of 'three acres and a cow.' Naturally these projects were aired at the election of 1885, though not adopted formally by the leader. Lord R. Churchill was not much less annoying to his venerable chief, for he urged land reform, improvements in local taxation, and the provision of allotments as counter-attractions, without troubling to secure his chief's concurrence. But it was left for Mr. Chamberlain in the ministry of 1903 to start the demand for tariff reform, and to make the question a definite issue in the election of 1906.[98] If the decision went against the late ministry, the fact remains that of those elected a very large proportion were definitely in favour of the tariff reform programme, as compared to those who followed the much less clear attitude of Mr. Balfour.[99] This was comparatively innocuous since the party was in opposition,

---

[96] Cf. Emden, *The People and the Constitution*, pp. 243, 260.
[97] Morley, *Gladstone*, iii. 173 f.
[98] Dugdale, *Arthur James Balfour*, i. 338, 347 ff.
[99] Of 157 elected 102 were claimed as his supporters.

but it meant weakness, just as was the fate of the Liberal opposition in 1895, when the leaders would not even agree on a cause to make the central issue, for Lord Rosebery desired to grapple with the Lords, Sir W. Harcourt to stress local option, Mr. Morley clung to Home Rule, and others declared for the Newcastle programme of 1891, which after Home Rule had been held out by Mr. Gladstone to be his policy. The modern tendency is to make the appeal as wide as possible, and therefore to unite as many personal policies as possible in the general appeal. But it remains true that no minister must advocate any item which has not been approved by the Cabinet.[1] Opposition leaders have inevitably a greater freedom, but they have to bear in mind that, if successful at the election, they will be confronted by demands for fulfilment of pledges, which may be gravely embarrassing. The rank and file of the party are entitled to expect their leaders to carry out policies announced by any of them, and under the modern system of a Shadow Cabinet policy should be agreed, and then announced in unanimity by the leaders.

The mode of announcement of policies at dissolutions began historically with the royal speech at the close of the existing Parliament, which from the time of Queen Anne came to be recognised as the work of ministers, not a personal declaration by the Crown.[2] The proclamation of William III.'s anti-French policy in 1701 had, however, few successors, for that of 1784 was of formal, rather than real, importance. That of 1831, however, intimated a definite appeal to the electors on a well-defined issue, reform of a defined kind. But Sir R. Peel's Tamworth manifesto of 1834 heralded a more direct approach to the electors, and the speech from the throne ceased to be used to any substantial extent for this purpose, though occasional exceptions are noted, as in 1886 and 1923. Sir R. Peel's innovation was repeated in 1847 by himself, while the Whigs took a published speech by Lord John Russell as their manifesto, and the protectionists accepted a manifesto letter to their leader's constituency. The practice was established by 1865, according to Mr. Disraeli's own account, when in the Lords he substituted for it, in 1880, a letter to the Lord Lieutenant of Ireland, which served equally well. The more direct method of

---

1 Taylor, *Brentford*, pp. 279 ff., shows that Mr. Baldwin pledged himself to equal suffrage before the election of 1924, and that Mr. Churchill's effort to impose responsibility on Lord Brentford was wholly unfounded.

2 Emden, *The People and the Constitution*, pp. 281 ff.

platform appeals, before an election, was due to Mr. Gladstone, who as early as 1857 had started the practice of pre-election oratory outside his own constituency. In 1879 his Midlothian campaign, which, in effect, was an address to the whole body of electors,[3] definitely inaugurated a new régime, to be followed in the shape of speeches outside his constituency in 1886 by action as Prime Minister in support of Home Rule. The Queen remonstrated at the innovation, which Mr. Disraeli had eschewed, but the Premier pointed out that Lords Salisbury and Iddesleigh had forced him to action by speaking frequently since 1880 outside their own constituencies.[4] In 1892 Lord Salisbury innovated, by addressing a manifesto to the electors of the United Kingdom; this was followed by the coalition Government of Mr. Lloyd George and Mr. Bonar Law in 1918, and, though Mr. Baldwin preferred an election address to his constituency in 1924, he resorted thereafter to the system of an address to the electors. It must be added that broadcasting has added a fresh mode of appeal, for the leaders of the parties are now permitted to make a direct application to the electorate in this way, though this cannot supersede the address.

6. His Majesty's Opposition

It is an essential feature of the British party system that the parties should be agreed on fundamentals, in special on the principle of majority rule under a democracy, and the reason of the degree of success attained in its operation lies simply in this consideration. In foreign countries, where the British model has been copied, it has worked only where a like guiding doctrine is accepted, as in Holland, Belgium and the Scandinavian States. Where the doctrine has received only lip service, the result is that the system does not work, as in the case of the troubled history of Spain, ending in the savage hostilities of 1936–39. Its success in the Dominions confirms the view that, for a true democracy, the system has excellent results, and so far there is promise in its operation in India. It is this realisation that Communism and the doctrine of revolution by violence are fatal to democracy that has induced the Labour Party in Britain to decline to form a popular front with the Communists. So far as at any time they may do so, it must be admitted that

[3] Gladstone, *Speeches in Scotland*, i. 211.
[4] Morley, *Gladstone*, iii. 344.

they are striking a serious blow at democracy, and that the British system of government is really in danger.

As matters stand, as both great parties, as well as the Liberals, still cling to democracy, there are definite limits which they must respect. The Opposition seeks power to effect the changes it desires, but it does not seek power by means which deny democracy. There are standards of fair dealing which are normally respected, and which, if any party should violate, it endeavours to prove still in reality intact. It follows, therefore, that in many matters there must be co-operation, above all in arranging the business of the House. It is not the right of the Government to stifle criticism; it must, therefore, put down for discussion such financial items as the Opposition wishes to discuss. It must find time for a discussion of a vote of censure. On the other hand, it expects reasonable aid from the Opposition in dealing with normal non-contentious business, and in arranging the use of Parliamentary time. It is entitled to be free from meaningless obstruction intended simply to waste the session; when the Irish Nationalist party practised this amusement,[5] it was because it denied that the principles of democracy allowed them to be forced to remain in a British Parliament, and by seeking to destroy its operation they hoped to show that they must be conceded Home Rule. A like attitude by an Opposition party today would suggest its deliberate hostility to democracy, which implies essentially that the majority shall govern, and that the Opposition shall criticise, but shall yield, so long as the majority remembers the fundamental fact that it is but a temporary mandate, of a more or less definite character, and that to exceed it is to deny democracy, just as much as if the Opposition should set about to render government difficult by obstruction. Hence every occasion on which by brute violence, such as repeated disorder and noises, the Commons is prevented from functioning, marks the breakdown for the moment of democracy, and the offenders are so conscious of this that they always seek to justify their action by the allegation that the Government has itself broken the convention that it shall not misuse its power. But there are few more discreditable incidents than that of November 12, 1912, when the Opposition shouted down speaker after speaker, and the Speaker,

5 See Gladstone's account, *Letters of Queen Victoria*, 2 s., iii. 189–92, of the measures taken on February 3–4, 1881, to introduce the closure and the suspension of Irish members *en masse*, and J. Redlich, *Procedure of the House of Commons*, pt. ii., chap. ii.

after fruitlessly adjourning the House for an hour, was compelled
to terminate the sitting, which ended with Mr. Ronald McNeill's
assault on Mr. Churchill.[6] It is significant that on July 24, 1911,
a most important speech of Mr. Asquith on the Parliament Bill
could not be delivered for incessant tumult.[7]

The measure of co-operation must vary with the occasion. It
is closest in time of war or threat of war,[8] and even then may be
imperfect. It is true that in 1914–15 there was a measure of
co-operation between Opposition and the Government, that Mr. A.
Chamberlain gave aid in finance, and that Mr. Balfour served on
the Imperial Defence Committee. But that did not prevent their
combining with Sir J. French to compel a coalition on the threat of
attack, based on alleged shortage of munitions. On the other hand,
the concurrence of the Opposition leaders was necessary when so
grave an undertaking was to be entered into, as the grant, as part
of the spoils of war, of Constantinople to Russia, or the accord
with Italy.[9] The existence of such co-operation in matters of
defence is always more or less in evidence. The Labour Government in 1929–31 invited certain forms of co-operation,[10] and the
Labour leaders in 1937–38 were careful not to attack the ministry
on the ground that they were kept at arm's length on defence
matters. Similarly, in the special session of September, 1950, the
Opposition supported the Government's defence proposals, particularly the decision to extend the period of compulsory national
service from eighteen months to two years.[11]

Co-operation is also sought when issues approach such a crisis
that inaction seems dangerous to the public welfare. There are
obvious cases in the repeal of the Test Act, 1828, and the more
radical general relief to Roman Catholics of the following year,
in the repeal of the Corn Laws in 1846, and in the final franchise
settlement of 1867. Mr. Gladstone thus secured his disestablishment of the Irish Church in 1869, his Education Act in 1870, and
his Ballot Act in 1872.[12] Years after, with the aid of the Queen
also proferred in the Irish Church issue, he secured the Acts for the

---

6 See Austen Chamberlain's defence, *Politics from Inside*, pp. 491–4.
7 Spender, *Lord Oxford*, ii. 314–20.
8 *E.g.*, in the Agadir crisis in 1911, Austen Chamberlain, *Politics from Inside*, p. 347.
9 Spender, *Lord Oxford*, ii. 129; Beaverbrook, *Politicians and the War*, i. 59;
  Churchill, *World Crisis, 1915*, pp. 198 f.
10 299 *H. C. Deb.* 5 s., 998.   11 478 *H. C. Deb.* 5 s., 1259–1399.
12 Morley, *Gladstone*, ii. 367 ff.; *Letters of Queen Victoria*, 2 s., ii. 223; Wolf, *Life of
  Lord Ripon*, i. 226–8.

extension of the franchise and redistribution of seats, while it was
by agreement between Government and Opposition that the
Speaker took his famous decision to terminate the debate of
January 31–February 2, 1881; and that the subsequent steps to
counter the obstruction of the Irish party were carried.[13] But he
failed to induce the Opposition to share with him a solution in
1886 of the Irish question, a result most unhappy for Britain, for
from it sprang the Constitution of Eire, in which the name of the
Crown never occurs, and under which all British subjects in Eire
are aliens, if they are not Irish nationals.   In 1906, also, despite the
King's goodwill,[14] it proved impossible to secure agreement on the
Education Bill, and not even a conference under royal auspices
enabled accord to be reached on the Parliament Bill in 1910,[15] nor
on the Government of Ireland Bill in 1914.[16] On the other hand
the Liberal leader refused co-operation in bringing pressure to
bear on President Kruger to accept the British terms for a settlement of the demands of the Uitlanders for fairer treatment in the
Transvaal.[17] But both Liberals and Conservative leaders took
part in consultations with the Labour Government in 1931,[18] and
were apparently willing to afford it assistance if it would only
consent to make such economies and to impose such taxation as
would give a reasonable assurance of security for the stability of the
finances of the country.   In the end they agreed to a coalition or
National Government, rather than seek mere party advantage by
destroying the Labour ministry out and out.   There is no reason to
doubt their sincerity in seeking an accord, which would not have
driven the Labour Party into an embittered opposition.

More curious was the situation during the Palmerstonian
régime from 1859–65.   Lord Derby, though head of the late
ministry, and therefore also of the Opposition, had really no desire
to succeed in ousting his rival, and accordingly virtually supported
his retention of office, thus curbing radical elements in his party,
disliked by both leaders alike, but in this case the co-operation was
not avowed to the younger Conservatives, lest dissatisfaction with
the attitude of their leader should drive them into mutiny.[19]

[13] *Letters of Queen Victoria*, 2 s., iii. 188 f.; Esher, *Journals and Letters*, i. 79 f.
[14] Lee, *Edward VII.*, ii. 458 ff.; so in 1908; *ibid.*, 658 f.; Bell, *Randall Davidson*,
   i. 726 ff.
[15] Spender, *Lord Oxford*, i. 285 ff.   [16] *Ibid.*, ii. 53 ff.
[17] Spender, *Campbell-Bannerman*, i. 233 ff.
[18] Snowden, *Autobiography*, ii. 879–89; J. H. Thomas, *My Story*, p. 195
[19] Cf. Guedalla, *Gladstone and Palmerston*, p. 150; Bell, *Palmerston*, ii. 260, 280 f., 340 f.

Co-operation is greatly facilitated by the maintenance in opposition of cohesion among members of the late Government. The Shadow Cabinet normally contains the members of the late administration, if they remain loyal to their late chief, but it may be supplemented by other members of promise.[20] We know a good deal of the difficulties of the working of such bodies from Mr. A. Chamberlain's references to the Unionist position in the years from 1906,[21] and Mr. Asquith finally parted company with Mr. Lloyd George through disagreement on the latter's abstention from attendance at the Liberal Shadow Cabinet on the occasion of the discussion of the party's attitude towards the General Strike of 1926.[22] In January, 1931, Mr. Churchill finally parted company from Mr. Baldwin's Shadow Cabinet, or Business Committee, objecting to the support the Opposition gave to the Labour Government's India policy.[23] The attitude of the leader of the Opposition party to the Government is strikingly illustrated by the overtures made by Mr. Lloyd George in October, 1910, to Mr. Balfour, with a view to the formation of a coalition ministry, which would solve the Irish question on federal lines, study impartially tariff reform, give colonial preferences, and arrange national training.[24] Mr. Balfour's rejection of the plan seems to have been based on the advice of Mr. Akers-Douglas, Chief Whip under Lord Salisbury and Home Secretary under Mr. Balfour, as regards the feeling of the party and his own determination not to become another Robert Peel, who 'twice committed what seems to me the unforgivable sin. He gave away a principle on which he had come into power—and, mind you, neither time had an unforeseen factor come into the case.'[25] It is clear that the negotiations were from the first known to Mr. Asquith, that later the Cabinet was informed, and that the various Unionist leaders were initiated into them in various ways. Mr. Chamberlain shows also that the final decision to break off negotiations with the Government on the settlement of

---

20 See *ante*, p. 233, n. 92.
21 Austen Chamberlain, *Politics from Inside*, *e.g.*, on Mr. Balfour's Albert Hall pledge (1910) of a referendum on the budget (pp. 306 ff.) ; Lord Milner's position (pp. 368–70).
22 Spender, *Lord Oxford*, ii. 358–71.
23 Churchill, *The Second World War*, i. 27.
24 Lloyd George, *War Memoirs*, i. 32 ff. ; Dugdale, *Arthur James Balfour*, ii. 72–80 ; Spender, *Lord Oxford*, i. 287 f. ; Austen Chamberlain, *Politics from Inside*, pp. 191–3, 283–94.
25 Dugdale, *Arthur James Balfour*, ii. 75. Mr. J. Chamberlain was no less censorious of Peel before his own action in 1886.

the relations of the two Houses in 1910 was taken at a meeting of some twenty leaders of the party meeting at Lansdowne House.[26] There were further soundings as to co-operation in 1913[27] and 1914, and it is easy to see how simple relations of this informal kind are, and how both parties, even in these times of very violent opposition, were brought close to each other by considerations of common interest in securing national defence and preparedness.

The formal work of co-operation in getting business arranged falls, of course, on the Government Whips on the one hand and those of the Opposition on the other; the latter are appointed by the Leader of the Opposition, as are those of the Government by the Premier. It is, perhaps, in the day to day work of Parliament, and in its normal procedural arrangements, that the relations of Government and Opposition best illustrate the essential give and take of democratic discussion. The Government will arrange for a debate on some specific aspect of policy chosen by the Opposition and the Opposition, in return, agrees that a Government Bill be given time for a further reading. Again, during Supply days, the Opposition chooses certain 'votes' for discussion, thus securing a general debate on particular aspects of policy and administration. The rules of procedure for the passage of legislation through both Houses are designed to allow time for the Opposition, and the public, to consider its attitude to the measures proposed. These rules, it is true, can be departed from in an emergency and by a Government with a large majority. That occurred notably during the Labour Administration of 1945–50. Very strong criticism was made, for example, of the use of the 'guillotine' on the Transport and Town and Country Planning Bills in 1947. But even then, on the whole, the Labour Government provided fair opportunities for discussion by arrangement with the Opposition, and later returned to some of the rules it had temporarily suspended.

The principles underlying the work of His Majesty's Opposition were well stated by the then Leader of the Opposition in debate on March 8, 1937:

> 'This House has never been a mere assembly for registration; it has never been a mere debating society. . . . This House has always taken an active share in legislation. . . . Although

---

[26] Austen Chamberlain, *Politics from Inside*, p. 296.
[27] *Ibid.*, pp. 576 f. For Churchill's anxiety to effect an early coalition, cf. in 1915, *World Crisis, 1915*, pp. 198 f. Mr. Asquith always doubted the value of coalitions; Spender, *Lord Oxford*, i. 287.

it is the Government's Bill, it has been framed by the co-operation of Members of this House. Where certain Members oppose the Bill in principle, they take an active part in trying to make it workable. Therefore, every Bill that goes through the House becomes in that way the work of the whole House. The importance of that procedure is that the experience and ideas of the Members of the House are brought into the common pool. That is the traditional British method and the democratic method.'[28]

The essential position of the Opposition, as part of the mechanism of the State, is marked by the fact that the settlement in 1937 of salaries of ministers was accompanied by the grant of a salary of £2,000 a year to the Leader of the Opposition, that is the larger opposition party, if there is more than one. The Speaker decides any question as to the proper recipient of the sum, which is charged on the Consolidated Fund, and is not therefore open to challenge, as are ministers' salaries.

It is worth noting that Mr. Balfour, on formally resigning the party leadership in November, 1911, was careful to intimate the fact to the King, so that he might not learn of his retirement from the Press.[29] It is not known whether this practice has always been followed, but clearly with the grant of a salary the action would be proper.

7. THE CABINET AND THE HOUSE OF LORDS

THE relations of the Cabinet and the House of Lords have consistently presented difficulties, which, modified by the Parliament Acts of 1911 and 1949, are yet very imperfectly solved. That the Lords could control a Government by refusing assent to measures which it deemed so vital that it was prepared to ask the Crown to swamp the Upper House was denied emphatically by Earl Grey in the great dispute over the Reform Bill of 1832,[30] and when in 1910–11 the issue became critical through a conflict between the Commons, resolute and backed by the majority of the electorate, the Lords only claimed the right, not to thwart the will of the people, but to ensure that in fact the people had declared its will in the sense asserted. In the early days of the new system the

[28] 321 *H. C. Deb.* 5 s., 815.
[29] Dugdale, *Arthur James Balfour*, i. 89 f. For Gladstone's action in 1875, see Guedalla, *The Queen and Mr. Gladstone*, i. 453.
[30] See Viscount Esher, *Influence of King Edward*, pp. 82 ff.

Lords' views were regarded with considerable respect; thus in 1839 the demand by that House for a Select Committee on Ireland, though within its powers, elicited from the ministry a demand from the Commons of a vote of confidence.[31]   Sir R. Peel demurred on the ground, in itself quite plausible, that the proper attitude to be adopted was to judge of the attitude of the Lords by their treatment of the legislation submitted to them, and not by abstract declarations.[32]   Even in 1850 the disapproval by the Lords of the action of the ministry in regard to the exaggerated claims of Don Pacifico on the government of Greece was countered by a demand for a vote of confidence in the Commons.[33]   This, however, reflects an older attitude, one quite incompatible with the sovereignty of the electorate as established in germ in 1832, decisively by the extension of the franchise from 1867 to 1928.

Despite the terms of the Parliament Act, 1911, the power of the Upper Chamber to hold up legislation for a minimum period of two years remained a very definite check on the power of a Labour or Liberal Cabinet, and gave the Lords the power of securing effectively that no measure should be passed finally without ample opportunity of consideration.   Moreover, the period mentioned secured that the ministry, which had any drastic measures to pass, must put them forward while fresh in office, and thus in enjoyment of a recent mandate.   It was impossible for a Government to bring forward in the latter period of its tenure of office any legislation of a vehemently controversial type, even if it grew immediately out of a position which had only emerged during the progress of events in that Parliament.   It remained, therefore, open to the House of Lords to insist that nothing should be brought before it without a clear mandate, unless it was adduced early in the life of the Commons.   Moreover, the power of delay might doubtless be used against almost any measure, even if it had figured at the last election as a major issue, for the character of general elections admittedly renders it almost impossible to hold that a clear mandate has been given for any one item.   It is clear, therefore, that, however energetically a Labour opposition might strive at an election to secure a mandate, which the Lords should accept as requiring the immediate passing of legislation, it would

[31] 47 *Parl. Deb.* 3 s., 4 ff.
[32] *Peel Papers*, ed. C. S. Parker, ii. 386.
[33] 111 *Parl. Deb.* 3 s., 1293 ff.; 112 *Parl. Deb.* 3 s., 102–8; Greville, *Memoirs*, 2 s., iii. 342–4.

always be open to the Lords to contend that they are not satisfied that there is any such mandate. It was, therefore, not altogether surprising that the Labour Government elected in 1945, faced not so much with actual opposition from the Lords as with the possibility of opposition as the Government proceeded to the more controversial items of a major legislative programme, decided to curtail the power of the Lords yet further. By the Parliament Act of 1949 the Lords' veto is now reduced to one year. The composition of the House of Lords was not changed. The measure was less remarkable for what it did than for what it failed to do, coming from a party which had for years taught that the House of Lords should be abolished.

The position would doubtless be open to comparatively little objection if the Upper Chamber were impartially constituted, but it is idle to suppose that any measure sent up by a Conservative majority in the Commons would be denied acceptance, even if details might be modified, normally in the direction of greater Conservatism, by the Lords. It is this essential consideration that renders it impossible to accept the Lords, as at present constituted, as a satisfactory Second Chamber. The functions of such a body, as defined by the Bryce Committee,[34] presume that the Upper House is a body free from the acute partisanship which marks the existing House. Its functions should be (1) to revise the legislation sent up from the Commons, a task often neglected by the Upper Chamber, including the law lords. (2) Minor Bills should be more freely introduced in the Upper House, where there is time for full examination, impossible in the Lower House. (3) The House should have the power of delay of any measure, in so far as might be just adequate to enable the opinion of the nation to be adequately expressed upon it, *e.g.*, constitutional changes, fundamental innovations, or issues on which opinion was evenly divided. (4) Full and free discussion in a House, whose views do not determine the fate of the Government, on large and important questions, such as those of foreign affairs. Such discussions have often in the past been of considerable interest, but with the growing importance of the Commons such issues must be discussed there first, leaving them later to be debated in the Lords. The moderation of the Act of 1949 is perhaps an implied admission, even on the part of the Labour Party, that these functions are to some extent already

[34] Cmd. 9038.

fulfilled, and that the Lords' share in legislative work does save valuable time to the Commons.

To deal with such issues it is clear that a hereditary House cannot be entirely suitable. The Chamber must be open to all classes, must represent the will of the people, not of a certain class, must not contain a perpetual preponderance of one party, and should permit of the membership of men of ripe mind and mature experience, whose presence in the Commons would be hard to obtain owing to the exigencies of electioneering. The Bryce Report suggested election of 246 members by panels of the Commons in thirteen districts by proportional representation, and of eighty-one from the hereditary peers in the first instance by a joint standing committee of the two Houses; later, non-peers might be elected, but a minimum of thirty peers was essential; the law lords, and princes of the blood royal if peers. Tenure was to be for twelve years, with quadrennial retirement of a third. The decision of what were money bills was to be transferred from the Speaker to a committee of seven members of each House, elected for the duration of each Parliament, while for deadlocks on other Bills an elaborate procedure by conference was adumbrated. The scheme was still-born, and its determination to maintain a hereditary element unacceptable to all democrats. [35]

The coalition attempt in 1922 to deal with the issue was half-hearted and abortive, [36] and Lord Birkenhead in 1925 and Lord Cave [37] in 1927 adumbrated proposals. The proposal of 1922 suggested part election of hereditary peers by peers, other members elected from outside, and some nominated by the Crown. In 1928 Lord Clarendon suggested 150 peers elected by peers, 150 nominated in proportion to the strength of parties, and a limited number added by the Crown, in the latter case for each Parliament only. In 1932 the Unionists interested suggested 150 elected by the peers, 150 by local authorities, and in 1935 Lord Rockly urged the creation of life peerages as a mode of strengthening the Chamber, while Lord Rankeillour sought wider powers for it. In 1937 Mr. Williams suggested that differences between the Houses might

---

[35] Cf. H. B. Lees-Smith, *Second Chambers in Theory and Practice*, pp. 216–35.
[36] See 51 *H. L. Deb.* 5 s., 524–72, 642–82, 783–815, 963–96; 52 *ibid.*, 261–88.
[37] He desired exclusion of constitutional issues affecting the Crown or the Lords, and reference of the point as to money bills to a joint standing committee. Hereditary peers were to select a number for twelve years, and some were to be nominated. See Mallet, *Cave*, pp. 301 ff.

be settled by votes of members of the local authorities. All these devices were intended to secure power for the Upper Chamber against democracy, and the Labour Party argued that a Second Chamber was merely mischievous. If a Chamber must be preserved, it should be confined purely to revising purposes, and should only have power to delay a Bill for a single session, or for such time as is ruled necessary by the Speaker for adequate discussion.[38] To give such powers only would rule out election by the people or by local authorities, and would suggest selection by the Commons by proportional representation. It is easy to doubt if such a body would have serious merits, and in Queensland no Second Chamber has existed since 1922, nor has its restoration secured any substantial popular feeling, while in Canada one province only, the Conservative Quebec, has a Second Chamber. But it must be pointed out that the work of these Legislatures in federations is not comparable in importance with that of the British Second Chamber.

Should, however, the Second Chamber be abolished, there would be need for some safeguard against misuse of the power of the Cabinet. It might be possible to provide that constitutional changes must be introduced into the first session of one Parliament and become law only if passed by the next Parliament after a general election. It would also be possible to shorten the duration of Parliament to three years, as in the Australian Commonwealth and New Zealand, though that time would be rather inconveniently short. In either case the difficulty would arise of the limitation of the powers of Parliament by its own action, the possibility of which Bacon denied energetically,[39] for that which is sovereign cannot limit its sovereignty. It might be necessary to invoke the intervention of the Crown to safeguard the constitution.[40]

8. THE LIMITATION OF CABINET AUTHORITY

THE system of British government is doubtless open to attack on many grounds. One is that revealed very clearly in 1938, when

---

[38] Cf. Lees-Smith, *Second Chambers*, pp. 247–49.
[39] Cf. Ridges, *Constitutional Law of England* (ed. Keith), p. 14. In the Union of South Africa the Parliament now has unlimited power; Keith, *The King, the Constitution, the Empire, and Foreign Affairs, 1936–7*, pp. 11, 72.
[40] It must be noted that Evatt, *The King and his Dominion Governors*, while asserting the need of safeguards, has no concrete suggestions of value; cf. Keith, *Current Imperial and International Problems, 1935–6*, pp. 81 ff.

the ministry was found using an authority, derived in 1935 in large measure from its professions of fidelity to the League, for the purpose of departing wholly from the principles of the League and negotiating under an ultimatum with Italy. Yet that power had successfully violated the League Covenant in Ethiopia, and was devoting its efforts to bringing Spain under its protectorate as one step in its policy of establishing Italian hegemony in the Mediterranean, and replacing Britain in control of Egypt and the Suez Canal. If this is to be taken as a precedent, then any Government can feel fully entitled boldly to ignore, if in power, any limitation imposed upon it by the terms of its election promises. Whether the danger of serious detriment to British welfare from this source is grave must remain in doubt.

A second danger of the system is that a Government may be based not only on the support of a small majority, or even a minority of electors (this point will be examined shortly) but also that, once in power, it is subject to no Parliamentary limitation on its power except the current rules of procedure, and even these may be altered by its majority. In these circumstances a Government may be strongly tempted to 'steam-roller' its measures through both Houses. This danger was much discussed during the tenure of office of the Labour Government of 1945–50. In its first session of about fifteen months the Government secured the passage of 84 Public Bills, not a record in number for one session, but certainly a record in scope and complexity of legislation. In 1947 the pace was kept up, and a climax of criticism that the Government was pushing its programme too fast came when the guillotine was applied to the proceedings on the Transport Bill and the Town and Country Planning Bill, both in Standing Committee and in subsequent stages in the House of Commons. This was the first time in the history of the House of Commons that the guillotine had been applied to proceedings on a Bill in Standing Committee. As a result, 37 Clauses and 7 Schedules of the Transport Bill were not discussed at all in Standing Committee, and the discussion on several more was cut short by the guillotine. In the case of the Town and Country Planning Bill, about 50 Clauses and 6 Schedules were not discussed at all in Committee. On the Report Stage the guillotine was applied again.

This procedure naturally aroused bitter complaint, all the more understandable when it is remembered that at the time the guillotine fell on the Report Stage of the Town and Country Planning Bill the House had discussed only 13 of the 130 pages of amendments, and that 175 Government amendments were put and carried without discussion.   On the other hand, it should be remembered that the Transport Bill was considered in a total of 31 sittings (Committee included) for a total of about 77 hours; while the Planning Bill was considered at a total of 25 sittings.

It is not easy, at this range, to see these episodes fairly in a long-term setting. There were other faults besides these of shortened discussion. What is clear, however, is that a Government with a large majority is limited in its legislative programme only by its own good sense and its respect for those rules of debate which generations of men in all parties have agreed upon.

A further serious ground of criticism is the fact that the enormous power of the Cabinet may be founded on the support of a small majority only of those electors who have polled their votes at a general election, and the objection to this position is enhanced if the election is of distant date.   There is in theory a very great danger in the misuse of power by a ministry with a distant mandate; that it has been avoided in the past may be assigned to that essential moderation, which is the chief political asset of the British people. But whether that moderation will endure is uncertain, and it is legitimate to consider how often the apparent authority of the ministry, as reflected in the number of seats it claims in the Commons, differs from the actual authority as represented by the votes of the electors.   Such calculations, of course, offer difficulties as regards exactness, but the general facts are beyond serious doubt.

It seems that in 1900 the majority of 134 won by the war election would more justly have been sixteen, in which event the education and licensing legislation of Mr. Balfour would never have been passed, and the unhappy blunder of Chinese labour in South Africa might have been avoided. The colossal Liberal majority of 1906, 336,[41] was unwieldy and the more normal figure of ninety would have given a better Commons, and have avoided the crudities of the Trade Disputes Act, 1906. The election of 1918 gave 478 seats to the coalition Government out of the new total of 707, but the votes in the 600 contested seats were 5,180,257 for the ministry, 5,608,430 for non-coalition candidates, and the most optimistic view could only suggest a total Governmental vote of 7,346,286 to

[41] Liberals, 377; Labour, 43; Irish, 83; Unionists, 167.

6,527,289. In 1922 the total of seats fell to 615, with the elimination of those of the Irish Free State, and the Conservatives with 5,500,382 votes secured 344 (347) seats, the National Liberals, with 1,673,240, 53 seats, the Liberals, with 2,516,287, 61 seats, Labour, with 4,241,383, 142 seats; a Conservative member thus represented 17,900 votes, a National Liberal member 29,100, a Labour member 30,800, and a Liberal no less than 46,200 votes. In 1923, while there was little addition to the total vote, the results were amazingly dissimilar; the Conservatives with 5,538,824 votes received 258 seats, the Liberals with 4,311,147 secured 159, Labour with 4,438,508 had 191, thus incidentally definitely establishing itself in the position of the second party in the State. If the Protection proposals of Mr. Baldwin thus received a definite set-back, the capital levy of Labour was even more decisively rejected. In 1924, on the other hand, the Conservatives with 7,854,523 votes secured 412 (415) seats,[42] the Liberals, with 2,928,747, only forty (44), and Labour, with 5,489,077, 151. Thus the Government was in an actual minority of votes as against the two opposition parties, and while a Conservative represented 19,000 votes, a Labour man 36,000, a Liberal stood for 73,000. In 1929 the results were no more satisfactory as a representation of the electorate, for the Conservatives secured 260 seats with 8,658,910 votes, the Liberals 58 (59) with 5,305,123, and Labour 289 (287) with 8,384,461. In 1931 the results underlined these discrepancies, as was inevitable in an election fought under the strain of severe reaction against the apparent danger to national security in finance, and the majority for the National Government on any reckoning must have been enormous. But on proportional voting the figures would have been less impressive; in lieu of 473 members the Conservatives would have had 270, in lieu of 68 Liberals 110, and in lieu of 13 National Labour would have claimed 50, and the composition of the Commons would thus have differed vitally from that actually achieved. In 1935 there was a slight return to normality, the Government secured Conservatives 387, Liberal Nationals 33, National Labour 8, with three Nationals sans phrase, a total of 431, while Labour had 154, Liberals 21, the Independent Labour party four, and there were four Independents and a Communist. The contested seats gave the Government 405 seats for some 11,789,575

---

[42] Seven members elected as Constitutionalists adhered to Conservatives and Liberals.

votes, Labour 141 for 8,325,446, and Liberals 21 for 1,443,112. Thus the members represented roughly 29,000, 59,000, and 69,000 votes. In the southern counties of England with 79 seats some 836,573 Labour voters found themselves without a single representative, while 2,068,323 Conservatives were rewarded by 77 seats. Yet 760,000 voters in the London area obtained 22 seats, and Labour won 24 seats in the West Riding, with about the same number as in southern England.[43] In 1945 Labour gained 391 seats with 11,992,292 votes, Conservatives 218 seats with 9,944,378 votes, and Liberals 10 seats with 2,245,319 votes, members representing roughly 30,600, 45,600, and 224,532 votes respectively.[44] In 1950, with a very high poll, the results were more even, at any rate as between Labour and Conservative. Labour gained 315 seats with 13,266,498 votes, Conservatives 298 seats with 12,503,010 votes, and Liberals 9 seats with 2,621,489 votes. Labour and Conservative members were returned at roughly 42,000 votes each, while on this occasion it took 291,600 votes to return a single member of the Liberal Party.

The result of an election is much too capricious to be regarded with complete satisfaction. No doubt the present scheme is not the object of violent protest,[45] but the reason is the unsatisfactory one that the party, which may reasonably look for power, feels convinced that in due course the turn of chance will give it a majority equally disproportionate to that of its rival, and that by constitutional usage it will be entitled to expect from the opposition respect for its authority without regard to the numerical proportions of voting.

(a) Proportional Representation

Of the remedies for this state of affairs the most obvious is proportional representation. It is true that it has been used in a full form but little in the British Empire, and that it is not possible to argue very satisfactorily from conditions in Holland, Belgium, Sweden, Norway, Denmark, Switzerland or elsewhere.[46] But in Tasmania it is adopted and operated with general accord; in the

---

[43] J. H. Humphreys, *The General Election, 1935, and Constitutional Reform* (1936).
[44] R. B. McCallum and A. Readman, *The British General Election of 1945.*
[45] The Liberal Party has for a long time advocated some scheme of proportional representation but has failed, so far, to convince either of the other two parties of the strength of its case.
[46] P. R. Pamphlet No. 81, May, 1937.

Union of South Africa it has operated without difficulty for the election of Senators, in the Irish Free State it has greatly mitigated the bitterness of faction, and has probably operated essentially in the interests of peace, order and good government; in the Constitution of Eire it remains enshrined.[47]   In Northern Ireland its operation was not seriously open to exception, and its repeal was dictated by reasons which were purely based on political passion. The report of the Royal Commission in 1910 was hostile, but not very convincing,[48] and the Speaker's Conference in 1918 pronounced in favour of the scheme in all multi-member constituencies to be created under the redistribution impending.[49]   The Lords were strongly in favour of the project, and a bitter controversy raged thereon with the Commons, which quite naturally could not see that it lay in the hands of the Lords to dictate to it such a theme.[50] In the end the Representation of the People Act, 1918, made optional, if decided by Parliament later, an experiment with a hundred seats arranged in groups of from three to seven.   There never was any chance of action being taken under the authority thus accorded, and all that was saved was proportional representation for the Universities in which it has played a very insignificant part. The Conservatives in the Commons were strongly hostile, and the official party attitude is against the change.   Labour since 1918 had committed itself to the doctrine that minorities should be given their proportionate, and no more than their proportionate, representation, but the experience of the election of 1923 had convinced it that there was advantage to be gained from the existing system, and therefore it did not support a private Bill promoted for the Liberals, converted now to the idea, in 1924, and it was defeated by 238 to 144 votes.   In the Parliament of 1929–31 the Liberals were anxious to secure the system of at least the minor boon of the preferential vote, and negotiations with the ministry were carried on, and it was hoped to secure by another Conference, between all parties, an accord on the principle of some change.[51]   In face, however, of the established interests of the larger parties it was not to

---

47 P. R. Pamphlet No. 81, May, 1937.
48 Cmd. 5163.   Cf. J. H. Humphreys, *Proportional Representation;* H. C. Morris, *Parliamentary Franchise Reform in England from 1885 to 1918;* F. Williams, *The Reform of Electoral Representation.*
49 For Mr. Asquith's conversion, see Spender, *Lord Oxford,* ii. 297 f.
50 Cf. Mallet, *Cave,* pp. 197–99.   The Lords turned down the alternative vote.
51 The result was negative, and the Bill was not passed before the fall of the ministry; Somervell, *King George the Fifth,* pp. 421 f., 424 f.

be expected that any real accord could be attained, and the prospect for proportional representation cannot be regarded as bright.

The arguments for the system are clear, and it is idle to ignore their force or their existence.[52] (1) Democracy is based on the prevailing influence of numbers; it is, therefore, logical that the electorate should be so represented as to present in the Commons the proportionate strength of parties. To prefer to this the haphazard results of the present system argues a certain disbelief in democracy, and a desire to curtail artificially its effective working. In fact, many people who do not really accept democracy approve the present mode of election because it is not democratic. (2) At present many voters are in the unfortunate position that they have only a choice of evils; they know that only a Conservative or a Labour man can succeed, that a Liberal or Independent is hopeless, and thus are compelled to vote for a man whose policy they distrust, if they are to have any chance of polling a useful vote. There is really no answer to this contention. The large proportion of unpolled votes at any election is due to many causes, but too little attention is given to the fact that in many cases voters abstain not from apathy or indifference, still less from acceptance of the Government, but simply because they have no candidate for whom they can vote with any pleasure. (3) It should be possible for voters to support a man of character and independent outlook, as contrasted with the average candidate bound slavishly to accept the policy of a political party, and though this would not be easy to arrange under proportional representation it would not be impossible, as it is virtually at present. (4) The system would probably diminish the undue importance which now attaches to the margin of unattached voters, who are easily swayed by emotion to one side or another. In single-member constituencies these voters certainly have a great strength, which might be diminished in the case of five- or seven-member constituencies.

The arguments against the system are in part clearly untenable. (1) That based on the difficulty of voting for the ignorant elector and from the number of spoiled votes is without serious importance, so long as voting for more than one candidate is not made essential. Moreover, experience shows that spoiled votes are few after the

52 They are underestimated by Finer, *Theory and Practice of Modern Government*, ii. 920 ff., in the interests of the driving power for socialisation possible to a Government which is disproportionately strong.

system is once put in operation. (2) It is argued that the system severs the possibility of close connection between member and constituents, and imposes on members impossible difficulties in canvassing. But, in fact, the enormous extension of the electorate has made personal connection very slight, and constituencies do welcome candidates chosen from outside in a rather striking manner. (3) It is contended that the system would increase the power of the political party organisation, which would have to undertake the work of arranging for the members who were to stand, and of instructing the electors how they should mark their papers, so as to secure the return of all, or of as many as possible of the candidates of the party. But it is not clear that this would in effect mean that candidates of independent character would be ruled out as liable by their very character to affect injuriously the voting for party candidates in general. It is possible to argue in the opposite sense, that, by allowing an independent-minded candidate to stand along with docile representatives, the chances of all would be improved. The arguments are purely guess work.[53] (4) It is contended that the system would encourage the creation of numerous small parties, and the splitting up of the country into cliques, with resulting disadvantage to the coherent character of Governments. But the argument seems extremely far-fetched. If in any constituency there exists a sufficiently strong body of opinion on any subject to secure the return of a candidate, it is probable that there would be in many other constituencies a like tendency, and that the idea of a large number of small parties would never be realised in practice. There is not room really in British politics for more than three, or possibly four parties, and it is idle to consider objections resting on mere improbable hypotheses. (5) A fairer argument is based simply on the desire for a strong Government, with an exaggerated majority, as making for continuity and decision of rule. It is thought that, though logically it cannot be counted upon, it is not probable that the custom of single-member constituencies with a simple majority decision will result, as it might do, in producing weak ministries liable to be upset by any chance vote. If that became common, the question would be reconsidered; at present the situation suffices is probably a very general view. (6) The difficulty of working the system at by-elections is stressed and unquestionably is real, but it is quite

53 In many constituencies, as it is, the local body is all powerful.

unnecessary to take so minor a point seriously, just as it is a matter of indifference that any suitable scheme of multi-member constituencies must always leave a considerable margin of inaccuracy of representation. It is quite clear that the Irish scheme, as it now works, gives sufficiently accurate results for all human needs. (7) A further contention suggests that the control of the people on the policy and choice of Governments would diminish. There would be groups, which would assort and re-assort themselves without the necessity of a dissolution, for, as we have seen, the standing principles regarding dissolution could not survive under the new order of things. But the answer obviously is that it is quite impossible to say that this would really mean a genuine loss of control. As matters stand, a bare majority, or a minority of electors, may send into power a Government, which thereafter may depart widely from their wishes, and which in any case probably is wholly unacceptable to the supporters of the Opposition. The more probable outcome of the system would be that ministries would endeavour to legislate and administer in manner less extreme than at present, and the country might gain greatly by continuity of a moderate policy in place of possible violent vacillations from one aspect to another, which are made tolerable only at present by reason of a sense of political moderation in the electorate.

It must be added that in Ireland the result of the general election, held together with the referendum on the constitution in 1937, was a clear disappointment to Mr. de Valera, who on December 2 was moved to state that, while he was a supporter of proportional representation, none the less if the system were to fail to give strong Governments he would be compelled to reconsider the position. It happened that the voting gave exactly equal numbers to the Government and the non-Government parties, a result which, though embarrassing to Mr. de Valera, was regarded by others as securing the country from any rash moves on the part of their leaders.[54] In a democratic country, it is fair to say, what is most valuable is a Government which owes its strength and moral authority to the support of a maximum number of the electors, rather than one given power by accidents of distribution

---

[54] In the June election, 1938, Mr. de Valera intimated his intention to repeal proportional representation if he did not secure a clear majority, but that was given.

of votes. The necessity of redistribution in 1937 was, indeed, so patent, as a result of changes in the distribution of population, consequent on economic conditions, that the ministry readily admitted that redistribution should be undertaken. That has done something, but probably not very much, to improve the present position as regards numerical representation of the views of the electorate.

Little likely, as it is, that proportional representation shall now be adopted, the case for the alternative vote favoured in 1930–31 by the Liberals in their negotiations with Labour on reform is far more dubious. It is not rare in Australia, but its operation is always far more capricious than that of proportional representation, the supporters of which accordingly have little sympathy for an inferior scheme. The second ballot is still less in favour; in New South Wales[55] it was hastily abandoned after trial, and will not easily be restored. As in France, the manœuvres of parties to secure support in the second ballots are most unedifying, and the results are seldom likely to prove in any way satisfactory to supporters of movements for better representation.

(b) The Referendum

A very different proposal suggests the use of the referendum to decide contested issues. The question naturally arose in connection with the position of the House of Lords during the controversies of 1909–11. The claim of the Upper House to dictate a dissolution could not seriously be accepted by the Liberals, nor would it have been accepted by Conservatives if the Chamber had been of Liberal complexion. But the Unionists felt that they might meet the demand of the Liberals that the will of the Lower House must prevail in one Parliament by the offer of a referendum.[56] Mr. A. Chamberlain was prepared to go so far as to make a tariff reform budget subject, when first proposed, to a referendum, but as no accord was reached, he desired to drop the matter,[57] only to find that Mr. Balfour had pledged himself to this expedient, generally as a sop to free trade feeling.[58] In 1912, however, it was found possible to rid the party of the pledge, though there was still

---

[55] Keith, *Responsible Government in the Dominions* (1928), i. 415. For its defects in France, cf. Finer, *Theory and Practice of Modern Government*, ii. 913.
[56] Austen Chamberlain, *Politics from Inside*, pp. 249 ff.
[57] *Ibid.*, pp. 194 f.
[58] *Ibid.*, pp. 302–7, 310 f.

uneasiness on the score of the food taxation, which was deemed necessary by the tariff reformers as part of their scheme of imperial preference.[59]   Mr. Balfour's apologia for the project is interesting; he urged its superiority to a general election, because at the latter issues must be mixed; only in 1831 had there been a single issue, a statement broadly sound, though 1868 can fairly be added, so dominant then was the question of the disestablishment of the Irish Church.   In 1900 there was, perhaps, no very clear issue, save the successful termination of the matters arising out of the alleged victory in South Africa, but in 1906 the voters were moved by education, preferential trade, and Chinese labour as leading features.[60]   In 1910 there were two definite issues, the merits of the budget and the constitutional powers of the Lords, for a certain number of voters disliked the complicated and muddled land taxation scheme, but disliked more the intrusion of the Lords in a spirit of selfish anxiety to protect wealth from bearing a fair share of the additional burdens imposed on the country in part by defence, in part by the social schemes promoted by Mr. Lloyd George.   Lord Curzon also defended the referendum on this ground of the possibility thereby of eliciting a definite affirmative or negative to a clearly formulated question.[61]

A second advantage claimed for the referendum was that by isolation of issues due attention would be paid to those submitted, and a real opinion elicited.   The classical instance of confusion cited in support of this theory is the famous election of 1892, which saw the Liberal Party provided with the Newcastle programme. The electorate thus voted in such a way as to render it quite impossible to say whether it approved municipal reform, which no doubt attracted London voters; employers' liability, desired by artisans; parish councils, dear to agricultural labourers still without local self-government; the eight hours' Bill, approved by the miners; the disestablishment of the Church in Wales, long an object of Welsh endeavour; or Home Rule, Mr. Gladstone's own choice. Thirdly, it is claimed, the referendum eliminates faction, and enables the electorate to determine questions without the alien considerations of the personality of the opposing local candidates, or of the rival leaders.   Fourthly, the verdict on the referendum leaves ministers

59 Austen Chamberlain, *Politics from Inside*, pp. 432 ff.
60 21 *H. C. Deb.* 5 s., 1752.
61 6 *H. L. Deb.* 5 s., 945.   See also Spender, *Campbell-Bannerman*, ii. 351–5.

unaffected, and permits them to continue their official work, without the grave interference involved by the necessity of campaigning at a general election.

On the other side there must be set serious considerations. In the first place the isolation of issues is specially difficult in practice, if not in theory. Mr. A. Chamberlain candidly recognised this difficulty,[62] and it was stressed by Mr. Asquith,[63] who pointed out that in fact when the referendum was on the parties would exercise their whole electioneering power, and the decision would really be given on a party vote. This view was shared from study of the working of the Swiss referendum by Mr. MacDonald,[64] and there is the remarkable case of the attempt in 1929, in the Australian Commonwealth, to treat the general election then arranged as a referendum on the desirability of the federation vacating in the main the field of industrial arbitration in view of the interference of the decision of the Commonwealth Court of Conciliation and Arbitration with the working of industrial authorities, whether Courts or wages boards, in the States, and the solid disadvantages of double control. While both parties were agreed in theory on dealing only with this issue, it proved, in fact, that the election was fought very much on ordinary lines, with all the confusion due to extraneous personal and political considerations.

A second objection, accepted as valid by the Bryce Conference on Second Chamber reform, is that it would not work in the case of a large area like the United Kingdom, for different parts of which special legislation might be requisite. The electors, that is to say, would be confronted with a request for a decision on an issue which had little application to their special circumstances, and might give a negative reply, when the merits of the case demanded an affirmative or *vice versâ*. This argument is valid so far as it goes, but not of first-class importance. Thirdly, the referendum might diminish, as held by Mr. Asquith, the importance of elections, and thus the latter would come to be no more than a verdict on past administration and on personalities, while important issues would fall to the referendum. In view, however, of the great importance of personalities in human psychology, this danger seems hypothetical. Fourthly, it is objected that the referendum would reduce the sense of responsibility of members of Parliament, and

[62] Austen Chamberlain, *Politics from Inside*, p. 194.
[63] 15 *H. C. Deb.* 5 s., 1173 ff.   [64] 21 *H. C. Deb.* 5 s., 1770.

that they might pass legislation on the basis that there remained the control of the referendum if they had acted unwisely. On the other hand it is contended by Lord Curzon, among others, from Swiss experience, that, instead, the fact that a referendum may be claimed on legislation compels legislators to concentrate on the quality of their legislation, conscious that it will come under the scrutiny of the electorate, or at any rate may so do, and that the likeliness of such a contingency will be enhanced by careless drafting, or rash proposals of substance. Clearly, both results are possible, and it is out of the question to predict what in fact would be the result in Britain. Fifthly, would the referendum detract from the authority of Parliament? Both Mr. Asquith and Mr. A. Chamberlain, experienced Parliamentarians, thought that it would, the former contemplating that it would degrade the Commons to the level of a talking club, and Lord Bryce's Conference held that it would tend to lower the authority and dignity of Parliament. More vaguely, but portentously, it is accused of tending to imperil the principle of representative government. Lastly, it is contended that the position of a ministry must suffer if a referendum should go against it, even though it is not directly affected. There is truth in that. The Commonwealth ministry of Mr. Fisher lost prestige and authority, when in 1910 its referenda were rejected, and in 1937 the loss of the referenda on control of aviation, in all aspects, and of marketing schemes, did somewhat weaken the position of the ministry of Mr. Lyons.[65]

In the event of opinion turning more favourably to the referendum the obvious mode of using it would be when the House of Lords, and say a third of the membership of the Commons, were agreed against any measure, whether of a constitutional or ordinary type. No doubt finance measures would have to be excluded in general; there is force in Mr. Morley's view that a budget cannot well be submitted, and Mr. A. Chamberlain, from a very different standpoint, evidently concurred. To restrict the proposal only to constitutional Bills seems unsound, and a more general application would be wise. It is worth noting that it has been ingeniously conjectured that, if proportional representation ever were adopted, the chance of the referendum being adopted might be increased. In fact there would be a considerable incentive in such a case to

[65] For various criticisms and foreign experience, see Finer, *Theory and Practice of Modern Government*, ii. 929 ff.

have a simple way of ascertaining the country's real mind, and with the party system, as altered by the system of proportional representation, it is quite possible that party feeling would affect the operation of the referendum in a markedly minor degree.

Foreign experience in working the referendum is afforded largely by Switzerland, both in the federation and the cantons, and by the States of the United States. In the British Dominions it is embodied as part of the apparatus for amending the Commonwealth constitution, and experience there has been such as to suggest that any far-reaching proposal is apt to fare badly at the hands of the electors. One fundamental change alone has taken place, the acceptance of the transfer to the Commonwealth of the State debts, which involved the grant of a further legislative power. This has had the unexpected result of enabling the Commonwealth to enforce payment of instalments of interest on debt by a recalcitrant State, involving so serious a breach of sovereignty as to render further concessions of legislative power by the States suspect.[66] For conscription in the Commonwealth the proposal failed in 1916 and 1917 alike.[67] It has been used freely enough for decisions on limitation of the use of alcoholic liquors, and occasionally for other matters, but these referenda have simply taken place under special legislation, and the referendum to settle disputes between the Houses of Parliament exists only in New South Wales.

(c) Parliamentary Committees

One proposal stresses the possibility of rationalising the exercise of Cabinet power by the device of appointing Parliamentary committees to co-operate with the ministers.[68] The committees would be attached to the important departments, and would be duly constituted with reference to the strength of parties in the Commons. Purely party committees are not suggested, for many reasons. They would result in a breach of continuity on a change of Government; their members would be under the thumb of the Whips; there would be clear advantage in giving to the Opposition a fair share in co-operation, especially since many subjects are not really party in character, *e.g.*, betting, religious education, liquor

---

66 Keith, *The Dominions as Sovereign States.*
67 Keith, *War Government of the British Dominions*, pp. 88–93.
68 Cf. W. I. Jennings, *Parliamentary Reform* (1934); Finer, *Theory and Practice of Modern Government*, ii. 884–6.

licensing, and so on; and in any case Opposition members of real capacity could often help. Such committees would be able to examine proposed legislation on the subjects dealt with by the department to which each was attached, they could consider suggestions for the amendment of legislation, and could watch general tendencies in the field with which they were concerned, and publish any results of their labours which they deemed expedient. Co-operation between parties would thus be effective in moulding legislation, and the procedure could be applied in the case of the exercise of the delegated legislative powers of departments to good effect. A permanent financial committee might serve to obtain information to examine carefully the audited accounts and the report of the Comptroller and Auditor-General; to investigate the general principles of financial policy, the issue of the gold standard or any substitute therefor, the effect of taxation in its relation to individuals and the country in general, and the measures to be taken to prevent rings of industrialists levying undue profits from the country, for example, by recommending State production in lieu of reliance on private enterprise. Such a body might replace effectively the Public Accounts Committee and the Select Committee on Estimates, which annually examines some selected accounts, but which has little decisive power, and produces results of no great value. In Parliamentary business it would replace the Committees of Ways and Means and of Supply, whose work it would much more efficiently perform, and with its aid a division would be made each year between the matters to be put in a Taxation Bill and a Financial Administration Bill, which would thus be examined more efficiently and satisfactorily. A drafting committee would serve to revise this aspect of Bills.

This scheme has some claims to consideration, but it runs counter to the essential preference of all Governments for wide powers to be exercised by ministers, free from such control as a committee would accord. There are some objections to the introduction in Britain of the demerits of the system of committee government in France, with the resulting lack of a strong Government. The answer, no doubt, is not wholly relevant.[69] The French system rests on a variety of factors, which have no British

---

[69] *Manchester Guardian*, March 25, 1934. Queen Victoria feared the tendency of the Commons to invade the sphere of the executive, but on the issue of the recall of Sir B. Frere, Mr. Gladstone showed that this was no innovation; Morley, *Gladstone*, iii. 6 f., 23 ff.

parallel, the absence in binding practice of a dissolution,[70] the power of the Senate, the lack of any rule that appropriations and taxation must emanate from the Government, and so on. But the fact that the proposal is likely to diminish the autocracy of ministers is unquestionably a grave obstacle to its acceptance in a country where ministerial office is the legitimate object of the ambition of every normal member of the Commons. On the other hand it is easy to point out that much of the work of the Government is badly done, and that a committee system might easily avail to improve it, as in the case of such issues as town and country planning, unemployment, agricultural marketing schemes, and so forth.

No solution of this kind has been adopted in Britain since the Second World War. On the other hand, there has been an extension of the Standing Committee system of the House of Commons, though not to provide a check on the executive but simply to help in the increased pressure of work in the House itself. Until 1945 there might be up to five Standing Committees. It was then decided that there might be any number and, in fact, six have in practice been used. Further, the available working time of such Committees has been approximately doubled. These reforms are, however, very limited in relation to the problem. And the problem, seen as the need for continuous committee work, is becoming much more serious with the creation of numerous Public Boards whose relationship to the Executive is as yet unsatisfactorily defined, and whose conduct is bound to be increasingly a matter for Parliamentary attention.

(d) Devolution: Regional or Functional

From another point of view relief might be obtained from Cabinet domination by handing over to other authorities a substantial area of work, thus leaving ministers with the time necessary to justify their legislation and administration to the Commons, in lieu of merely enforcing their decisions by party control. Unfortunately the difficulties of effective action in this regard appear on examination more and more serious. The idea of devolution to local authorities was alive when the Local Government Act of 1888 was framed; matters might be handed over to

---

[70] It is, as yet, too soon to say whether the dissolution provisions of the constitution of the Fourth Republic will introduce, in practice, a fundamental change.

the new authorities popularly elected, and the Commons might be spared the necessity of investigation of administration and discussions on certain aspects of finance. The grave difficulty which arises is that the whole trend of economic and social conditions is towards an ever increasing integration of the country. Large scale production tends to replace local industries, communications have become so rapid and easy that the existence of local feeling is affected, and the Governmental devotion to great schemes of social benefit render the parcelling out of control very difficult.

It is natural, therefore, that the most recent advocates of devolution admit that the county units of local government are not a sound basis for such action, and should instead suggest that large, more or less, homogeneous units should be created, such as London, the South-East, Wessex, Wales, Cumberland, Westmorland, Lancashire, Cheshire, Northumberland, Durham, York, East Anglia, and Mercia.[71] To them could be assigned agriculture and fisheries, public health, housing, education, local government, order, police, prisons, and their various policies might be subject to control of their legislation by the Home Office, or by the Houses of Parliament, or the Upper Chamber, if reconstituted on the basis of election by the provincial legislatures. The Commons would thus be relieved, centralisation diminished, new life introduced into localities, and the rather chaotic conditions of local government under the existing county boundaries would be remedied. The obvious difficulty of the scheme is its lack of any clear-cut scheme of finance. But the further objection must be made that agriculture and fisheries cannot be severed from tariff policy, protection, bounties and subsidies, that unemployment insurance and national health insurance cannot conveniently be divided from public assistance; housing depends largely on trade policy and distribution of population thence affected. It is difficult to contemplate the division of control of education, and there would have to be central action to provide for the position of children on transfer from one region to another, and so forth. Even more serious is the objection that the necessary local patriotism to secure a local activity is lacking.

The position is different with regard to Scotland. There the law and judicial institutions already differ, and there is a tradition

[71] Ramsay Muir, *How Britain is Governed*; for a later discussion of some of these points see G. D. H. Cole, *Local and Regional Government*.

of a separate Parliament, which is still potent. Moreover, the steady decline of Scots prosperity and population already apparent is increasing with the systematic transfer to the south, especially to the London area, of the control of Scots undertakings. The railways are now merged in concerns vitally English, shipping, banking, many industries and broadcasting are under a more or less complete English control, and the English Press magnates have invaded the Scots sphere with resulting deterioration of the Scots character. Moreover, under the present régime, the social and religious unity of Scotland is being undermined by the steady influx of Irish Roman Catholics hostile to Scots ideals. Further, the Speaker's Conference on Devolution favoured the possibility of some concession, and sources of revenue have been considered, such as licences, taxation of land values, entertainment taxation, inhabited house duties, and a share in income tax. The existence of a Scottish National party is noteworthy, and the necessity of some concession has been seen in the steady removal to Edinburgh of large sections of departments hitherto housed in London, with the result of much delay and expense in communications through delegations, which now can conveniently be interviewed by the Secretary of State in Edinburgh. It has also been proposed that Scots estimates should be studied in detail by the Scottish Committee of the Commons, which includes all members for Scottish constituencies, reinforced by from ten to fifteen others, and considers all Scottish Bills. Such a change, however, has little chance of acceptance in the present state of feeling in England, and support for Scottish self-government is hampered among the wealthier classes by fear lest power should fall into the hands of advanced Socialists, such as are prominent in the west of Scotland, where they enjoy full support from the immigrant and settled Irish community.

The movement in Scotland, however, suffers also from a wide divergence in view as to the proper objectives between the supporters of some form of Home Rule. Thus a section of opinion is eager to secure Dominion status on the model of the original Irish Free State, under the monarchic constitution before the extrusion of the sovereign from any authority. Stress is laid by the supporters of this point of view on the advantage of having representation on international bodies, and developing interest in foreign policies, acting as a force making for peace. Other views would accept the great objections to erecting a tariff barrier between the two countries, and would therefore adopt the principle that on tariff questions there should be a common policy to be arrived at through arrangements with England, and in like manner foreign affairs might be dealt with by agreement, provided that the distinct character of Scotland received due recognition. The great difficulties of devising any working scheme are not ignored, but it is thought that they are not insuperable if the problem is approached with good will on both sides.

The Labour point of view is affected by the fact that the great trade unions are very reluctant to allow of anything which might hamper the maintenance of unity as between English and Scottish workers, and, though some sympathy with Home Rule aspirations is regularly expressed, it is not probable that the party would bring forward any serious policy in this regard. It is significant that Labour members voted strongly among the majority which defeated in 1938 the Caledonian Power Bill, which aimed at the development of electric power in Inverness-shire, with a view to the establishment there of a calcium carbide factory. This was, no doubt, due to the desire to secure the concentration of this new industry in Wales. The fact that a great majority of Scots members pressed for the Bill, and that the opposition was mainly that of the town of Inverness and of powerful landowners, who believed that the introduction of industry would diminish the value of their shooting and fishing rights, indicates that the position is not wholly satisfactory.

Those who favour a limited form of self-government would assign to the Scots Legislature and government the maintenance of order, police, prisons and judicature; ecclesiastical affairs; agriculture and land; education; public health and local government generally; control of trades and professions, and of industrial and commercial undertakings.[72] Like treatment might be given to Wales, which has a special bond of nationality in its language.

Even in this limited form the opposition to devolution is strong.[73] It is insisted that, even with such large areas as Scotland or Wales, there are objections to having distinct systems of education, public health, control of transport or labour questions. Moreover, the central control of international relations, trade and customs would

---

[72] Cmd. 692.
[73] Cf. Finer, *Theory and Practice of Modern Government*, ii. 880–2.

9*

interfere with local autonomy, even in matters assigned to the units, as in Australia and Canada, hours of labour cannot be regulated by the federation, and joint action is difficult. The question of finance, it is added, is still without serious solution. England already pays more than its fair share of expenditure, and cannot be expected to continue to do so unless there is unity; it is admitted that Northern Ireland is specially favoured, but there are special reasons for differential treatment in that case. The effort to assign powers would result in increased legalism and references to the Courts, though that could be diminished if the powers of the Imperial Parliament remained unaltered, in scope, as is the case with regard to Northern Ireland, so that the doctrine of *ultra vires* would apply only to local legislation. In Northern Ireland it has been little invoked. Granted the maintenance of the supremacy of the Imperial Parliament there would be no real risk in the abuse of power by the local legislatures, for that could be swiftly countered by Imperial legislation.

It is objected also that there would be extra cost in having elections and a Parliament. The scheme recommended by the Speaker[74] suggested that the members elected for the areas should form a Council of Commons, as well as sit in the Imperial Parliament, while a Council of Peers would be added; but this would be inconvenient, and add too much to the duties of members, and a distinct single-chambered Legislature would be demanded by most supporters of devolution. But it is plain that neither in Scotland nor Wales is there sufficient driving power to force the issue into practical politics for the present. The application of any such system to England, contemporaneously with Scotland and Wales, is still less in demand; devolution, however, restricted to Scotland and Wales would mean little decrease of the work of Parliament, and if accepted would rest on other grounds than the saving of work for Parliament in order that it might more effectively control the ministry.

Functional devolution would relieve Parliament by aiding it in the performance of its tasks. The classical exposition of a full scheme is that of the Webbs,[75] who suggest the creation of two Parliaments, one charged with foreign affairs, imperial relations,

---

[74] His scheme and that of Mr. Murray Macdonald are set out in Cmd. 692.
[75] Sidney and Beatrice Webb, *A Constitution for the Socialist Commonwealth of Great Britain* (1920); *A New Reform Bill* (Fabian Tract No. 236).

justice and police, the other with the whole field of economics and social services. Both would be popularly elected, but could be differently constituted as regards constituencies, franchise, period of office, time of session, etc. Combined action of both would set up a constitution, which would be enforced by the Courts. The financial legislation would fall to the economic legislature, but the political estimates approved by the other would have to be accepted by it *en bloc*, with decision by a joint session if a deadlock arose. No doubt this duplication would *primâ facie* be objectionable, but the authors contend that single chamber government is not fair, either to ministers or members, and that the idea of one Parliament to express a single general will is a chimera. It must be admitted that the Labour Party has displayed no enthusiasm for the plan, which is generally regarded as open to the fatal objection of destroying unity of action and planning.

Other schemes are based no doubt on the German Federal Economic Council,[76] as it worked under the Weimar Constitution in the days when Germany had constitutional government, and some slight approach to democracy. In Britain in 1919, a National Industrial Conference was held, and in 1928 the Conference on Industrial Relations, favoured by Lord Melchett and others, suggested some endeavour to secure co-operative planning by employers and employed. The idea took a concrete shape in 1933, when it was suggested that a body might be set up composed of forty members of the Commons, twenty peers, 100 representatives of capital, 100 representatives of trade unions, and forty experts, nominated by the Government, which would have referred to it for consideration all Bills involving economic issues, discuss economic questions fully with expert knowledge, and examine the possibility of extending conciliation in the regulation of relations between employers and employed. It is clear that this project took due account of the desirability of having a really representative body, and of permitting full discussion of financial and economic questions, for which Parliament has no time, and many members thereof insufficient appreciation or understanding. The Economic Advisory Council filled none of these purposes, for its membership was restricted, and its deliberations private and without public criticism. But it remains doubtful whether it is possible to construct any satisfactory body. There must be great difficulty in selecting a

[76] Finer, *Theory and Practice of Modern Government*, ii. 888–901.

really representative body, and still more in having one in which the interests of consumers would be fully borne in mind. The experts, if impartial, would hardly be popular with any side, and, if there were any effort to make the body fully representative, it would have to be made unduly large. Hence, though Mr. Churchill has toyed with the idea in an academic way,[77] the chance of action being taken seems small. Yet the whole of the proceedings on such a measure as the Coal Mines Bill in 1938, or the Cinematograph Films Bill, suggests that the grave issues concerned would have been the better considered if they had been submitted to full examination by a body more competent to go into the vital details than was the House of Commons.

[77] Winston Churchill, *Parliamentary Government and the Economic Problem* (Romanes Lecture, 1930); L. S. Amery, *Thoughts on the Constitution*, pp. 66 ff.

CHAPTER 7

THE CABINET AND THE CROWN

1. THE EVOLUTION OF THE POSITION OF THE CROWN

IT was the inevitable result of the Reform Act of 1832 that it rendered obsolete the old conception of the sovereign as essentially concerned with the fate of his ministry, and made the duties of the occupant of the throne those of an impartial head of the State, bound to conduct himself towards any ministry in such a manner that, while he should give it the fullest support, he should not be precluded by any attitude of his from rendering exactly the same services to a subsequent ministry, should the will of the electorate so decree. This was, of course, a novel idea. George III. had pursued a personal policy, and even after he had sacrificed the American colonies he was ready to dismiss Fox and Lord North in 1783, and to replace them by Pitt. In 1807 he had driven the Grenville ministry from office. Under the Regency and George IV. it was admitted that the monarch could determine the complexion of the ministry according to his favour, and the disappointment of the Whigs at his failure to give them power was very great. It was a signal achievement when he was compelled to yield on Catholic emancipation, and no doubt this marks the beginning of the end of the power of the sovereign.[1] William IV. was reluctantly compelled to realise the strength of ministers, but his success in getting rid of Lord Melbourne, on the strength of a half-hearted offer to resign, shows how strong the sovereign still was. When not even his favour could induce the electorate to give Sir R. Peel a majority, his hostility to the Whigs was so well known that Queen Victoria's accession was regarded as invaluable,[2] since it would help them against the Tories, while she in turn would gain from the fact that they would serve faithfully the only member of the royal family, save the Duke of Sussex, who would wish to have them in office. The Queen was generous in

[1] Sir T. Erskine May, *Constitutional History of England*, i. 91 f.
[2] *Letters of Queen Victoria*, 1 s., i. 95 ff.

manifestation of her regard for Lord Melbourne[3]; her refusal to meet
Sir R. Peel's views regarding the ladies of the bed chamber, though
it had the approval of the retiring Cabinet,[4] was, as she recognised
in later life, inconsistent with her constitutional position. It was
in entire harmony with this view that she regarded the grant of a
dissolution as essentially an appeal to the electorate to strengthen
her ministry, so that a defeat would be a personal rebuff, a view
shared by Lord Melbourne, who, because he held it was most
reluctant—quite rightly—to risk the dissolution of 1841.

That the Queen should not openly take sides, however, was
recognised by her, under the influence of Prince Albert, from 1841,[5]
and therewith starts the observation of the rule that criticism of the
sovereign is forbidden, not merely in Parliament, but also in the
Press. This means, of course, that for every royal act of official
character, responsibility must be accepted by a minister of the
Crown, and throughout the whole reign of the Queen, and ever
since, that doctrine has been loyally and completely maintained.
Moreover, it has every warrant to be upheld, for the claim that it
is a fiction is incapable of being seriously sustained.[6]

It is true that the Stuarts saw the enforcement by the people
of responsibility for their governmental acts on Charles I. and
James II., and that it was firmly established that ministers who,
like Strafford and Danby, acted in their master's interest and
with royal approbation, might none the less suffer or run the risk
of suffering severe punishment. The ministers responsible for the
Treaty of Utrecht, despite the assent of their sovereign, were at
once placed in jeopardy, and Bolingbroke had to seek safety in
exile. William III. was unquestionably, in large measure, his own
Prime Minister, but Lord Somers was impeached for his action in
affixing the great seal to full powers to treat and instruments of
ratification of treaties. Under the Hanoverian dynasty, therefore,
the position was plain enough; the King could not, by any normal

---

3 B. Newman, *Lord Melbourne* (1934).

4 *Letters of Queen Victoria*, 1 s., i. 215 ff.

5 Theodore Martin, *Prince Consort*, i. 110.

6 W. I. Jennings, *Cabinet Government* (2nd ed.), pp. 415–417. [When, however,
an action of the King arises from the exercise of the personal prerogatives, it is
difficult to see how any minister or Government can accept 'responsibility.'
Nor is there any reason to suppose that, in such a case, the Crown would be
protected from that criticism against which it is one of the functions of ministerial
responsibility to guard it. This section of the book has been left in its original
form, but in it the author does not consistently make any such distinction. See
Jennings, *op. cit.*, pp. 415–417.—ED.]

procedure, be brought to book, though rebellion might drive him from his realm, but ministers held office, subject to the risk that the process of impeachment might be employed against them by their enemies, and, though the King could pardon after condemnation, he could not prevent the impeachment proceedings, for the Act of Settlement, 1701, was emphatic on that. If, therefore, ministers were to be held responsible, they must also become in reality responsible, else the position would be intolerable. The doctrine prevailed in the reign of George I. and George II., and in part, at any rate, it was connected with the retirement of these Kings from participation in the framing of policy in Council with ministers. We can see in the case of the action of the British naval forces in the Northern War the restrictions placed on the action of George I. by the fact that his British ministers were answerable to Parliament, though he was absolute in his electorate.[7] He could, therefore, render only by indirect, though not ineffective, means aid to the alliance against Sweden, the opportunity of doing so being afforded by the injuries inflicted on British shipping by Swedish action in the war, which served as a sufficient excuse for reprisals so conducted as to do considerable damage to the Swedish cause. But the King did not ask ministers to assume further responsibility than they were prepared to undertake. Moreover, whereas Queen Anne had insisted on her right to select her ministers independently of party and Parliament,[8] and had by her choice in 1702 and 1710 considerably affected the political complexion of the ensuing Parliaments, George II. found that he had little choice in the selection of ministers, as when the Pelhams virtually dictated to him the parting with Cartaret.[9] Even George III. had some difficulty in evading Whig dictation, and was lucky in 1770 in finding Lord North ready to undertake the burden of supporting a policy whose pursuit is a standing example of the danger of hereditary rule. In the triumph of Pitt in 1784, however, Parliament seemed to give approbation to the independent right of the King to choose his ministers, although it must be remembered that Pitt fought this general election with the enormous advantage, in eighteenth-century conditions, of being already in office. In 1801 he strengthened the royal position by his yielding to the

---

[7] Wolfgang Michael, *England under George I.*, i. 287 ff.

[8] *Historical MSS. Commission, 9th Report, App.*, pp. 471 f.; Emden, *The People and the Constitution*, p. 102.

[9] Jenks, *Parliamentary England*, pp. 158–61.

wishes of the sovereign on Catholic emancipation and by his emphatic declaration that the King had the sole right of nominating his ministers, and that the House had no right to form any resolution till their conduct came to be judged of by the acts of their administration.[10] There could be no more emphatic assertion of the doctrine that no minister was responsible for the royal choice of a Prime Minister, and his emphasis is the more striking, because his words show clearly that for other acts of administration ministers must take full responsibility, a doctrine enunciated as early as 1711 by Lord Rochester in the striking words that 'according to the fundamental constitution of this kingdom the ministers are accountable for all.'[11]

It must, however, be remembered that Pitt in his defence of the King was dealing with a ministry, many members of which unquestionably agreed with the royal policy, and from which he had parted chiefly for personal grounds.[12] In 1807, on the occasion of the enforced retirement of the Grenville ministry and its succession by the Portland ministry, Sir Samuel Romilly laid down the doctrine that it was of the greatest importance to His Majesty that the doctrine of responsible advisers should be strictly maintained.[13] Lord Howick also supported the motion, expressing regret on the late change, on the ground that, while the King's prerogative of choice was admitted, the Commons had the privilege of expressing its views on the fitness of the new ministry for its position. This view, it will be seen, does not touch directly on responsibility, but it goes definitely further than Pitt had done. Spencer Perceval, on the other hand, repudiated the doctrine of responsibility; if a ministry were dismissed out of caprice, were those approached to take their places to refuse, and to allow the government of the country to come to a standstill? George Canning also refused responsibility of the new ministry for acts done some weeks before they obtained office. Neither seems to have seen the danger of leaving the King open to attack in the country and in the Press, as must be the case, if there were no responsibility to be

---

[10] 35 *Parliamentary History*, 962.

[11] 6 *ibid*., 972, 1083; cf. Duke of Argyle, 1739 (10 *ibid*., 1138); Sir J. Barnard, 1741 (11 *ibid*., 1268). Contrast Fox, 1778, who said the King was his own unadvised minister (Todd, *Parliamentary Government*, i. 175).

[12] J. Holland Rose, *William Pitt and the Great War*, chap. xx.

[13] 9 *Parl. Deb.* 1 s., 327 ff., 345, 471 ff., 552, 629 f. Lord Selkirk pressed for responsibility (*ibid*., 335, 381).

assumed by ministers.   Yet the election which followed, *inter alia*, asked for support of the King in exercising every prerogative of the Crown.   In 1812 Canning had another opportunity of expressing his views, when on Perceval's death a motion prayed the Prince Regent, who was not hastening the formation of a new ministry, to take steps to form a strong and efficient administration.[14] Canning then admitted the prerogative of choice, but pointed out that the House was a council of advice, as well as of control, and it might be proper to advise the Crown in advance, regarding the character of a ministry, which would be acceptable in lieu of defeating it later on.   Here he advances to much the position of Lord Howick in 1807, and still disclaims the idea of responsibility.   Perhaps his attitude on this head explains his being given the Premiership in 1827 instead of Wellington or Peel, whom the King had reason to suspect of the intention more or less clearly to dictate to him.[15]

But the views even of Canning became obsolete once reform took effect, for the Crown could no longer secure a ministry a majority in Parliament, and Sir R. Peel had the sense to accept the position frankly when he took office after the retirement of Lord Melbourne, and the interim action of the Duke of Wellington in holding a variety of offices pending Peel's arrival.   The Duke would have nothing to do with the idea of responsibility, the change of ministry was definitely settled before he was called in, and he maintained this doctrine in the Lords, when the issue was pressed against him by Lord Melbourne.   Lord Brougham properly insisted that the King could only act through responsible advisers, and that those who took office after a dismissal must be held responsible.   Peel himself was clear; on the assumption of a dismissal he denied the personal responsibility of the King, adding 'I am responsible for the assumption of the duty which I have undertaken, and, if you please, I am, by my acceptance of office, responsible for the removal of the late Government.'[16]   The declaration is the more striking, because he confessed that his absence in Italy had prevented him in fact giving the advice for dismissal.[17]

There is no doubt of the soundness of this doctrine.   It means that there cannot be any occasion on which a ministry can say

---

14 23 *Parl. Deb.* 1 s., 249 ff., 267.
15 Emden, *The People and the Constitution*, p. 146, n. 2.   16 Peel, *Memoirs*, ii. 31 f.
17 See 26 *Parl. Deb.* 3 s., 76 ff., 215 ff., 257.   [It is at this point that the distinction suggested in p. 270, n. 6, becomes important.—ED.]

that such and such an act was done by the King, that they do not approve of it, and that they will not take responsibility for it, but that they will carry on the Government. The objection to such an attitude is that they would be admitting that the people were not sovereign, but that the King had a right to dismiss a ministry on his own authority, and that therefore personal rule existed. This would be to deny the validity of the revolutionary settlement of 1688 and the developments of the constitution under the House of Hanover. It would be wholly unconstitutional for a ministry to take this action, and to do so would be peculiarly foolish, because it would expose itself to the attack of all those who put principles above other considerations. It would further be of grave danger to the monarchy. No doubt the Speaker would prevent direct criticism in the Commons, but in the country the King's action would be canvassed vehemently,[18] and a direct incentive would be given to bitter attacks on the monarch, and to demands for the removal of all personal discretion, or for the abolition of the monarchy. There can hardly be conceived any concatenation of circumstances which would induce a ministry to place itself in so utterly false a position. Suppose that Edward VIII., in December, 1936, had insisted on his marriage project, and that his ministry had as a result resigned, could any ministry have attempted to take its place with the intention of pleading that it did not approve the royal decision, but that the government of the country must be carried on, and that it would therefore proceed with business? The answer is plainly in the negative; if there were would-be ministers like Lord Marley, who were prepared to approve the royal view, and to take responsibility for it, the position would have been quite constitutional. But the King, of course, accepted in precise terms at the outset the view that, either he must find a *modus vivendi* with his existing ministry, or that he must abdicate, a position of the most unimpeachable propriety.

A further consideration must be borne in mind. The King, in rejecting the advice of a ministry, or in dismissing it, would in fact only act because he had reason to know that there were ministers who would accept responsibilities for his decision. Granted that William IV. acted without actually communicating first with the Duke of Wellington, or the distant Sir R. Peel, no one suggests that he was not influenced decisively by the just assurance that he

[18] Cf. what happened in 1914; E. Legge, *King George*, i. 77 ff.

had those who would hasten to support the *fait accompli*, even if, as in Peel's case, they would not have advised the action taken. *Fieri non debuit, factum valet.* It is significant that in the discussions, at such length, regarding the policy which the King ought to adopt towards the question of the appointment of peers in 1910–11 and the treatment of the Government of Ireland Bill in 1914, the Opposition leaders were perfectly clear that they must at once undertake the burden of defending the royal action, and that they could not for a moment shelter behind the King.[19] Needless to say in the decisive days of 1931, the Opposition attacked the Prime Minister in the National Government for its formation, and not the sovereign. The objections to the latter course were patent, as they must always be. The King is certain nowadays of a vast body of unreasoning support, which would rally to him instinctively,[20] and against which arguments would be vain, with the result that critics would sooner or later be driven to determined efforts by vilification of royalty and denunciations of expense caused by it to start a definitely republican movement. The existing feeling to the sovereign is essentially based on recognition of the fact that the sovereign takes no sides in politics, that he acts by the advice of ministers, and that for all he does a minister will take responsibility. The fact that this is the constitutional rule can be attacked only at the expense of injuring an essential part of the fabric of government.

It is, of course, true that impartiality is a maxim of perfection, which is hard to attain. A sovereign, moreover, is not by British constitutional practice expected to be merely the formal head of the State, accepting with equal indifference or approval all proposals put by every ministry. That role could historically not be expected, for responsible Government developed from a position in which the King had a personal policy of marked character, and used ministers to effect, rather than to fashion his purposes. But the essence of the constitutional change of the period from 1832 was to alter the character of the royal position. Power passed definitely to ministers, resting on the support of the Commons later, rather on that of the electorate as enlarged in 1867, but the sovereign retained the right to exercise influence. This means, of course, that the sovereign must be kept informed of the course of all important business; that the sovereign must be allowed to express

19 Cf. Austen Chamberlain, *Politics from Inside*, pp. 246 ff., 256 ff.
20 Cf. T. P. O'Connor's view in Chamberlain, *op. cit.*, p. 249.

opinions thereon before vital decisions are taken; and that ministers must give the most careful consideration to whatever the sovereign brings before their notice.   But what they advise finally thereafter must be accepted by the sovereign unless he is prepared to take the decisive step of replacing ministers by a fresh ministry, if they decline to yield and resign, or in lieu of resignation are dismissed. The latter contingency can no doubt be ignored for normal purposes, and credit given to Mr. Asquith's summary of the situation:[21]

> 'We have now a well-established tradition of two hundred years, that, in the last resort, the occupant of the Throne accepts and acts on the advice of his Ministers.   The Sovereign may have lost something of his personal power and authority, but the Crown has been thereby removed from the storms and vicissitudes of party politics. . . . The rights and duties of a constitutional monarch in this country in regard to legislation are confined within determined and strictly circumscribed limits.   He is entitled and bound to give his Ministers all relevant information which comes to him; to point out to them objections which seem to him valid against the course which they advise; to suggest (if he thinks fit) an alternative policy. . . . But in the end the Sovereign always acts upon the advice which Ministers, after full deliberation and (if need be) reconsideration, feel it their duty to offer.   They give that advice, well knowing that they can, and probably will, be called to account for it by Parliament.'

Mr. Asquith qualified the absolute character of the above by an allusion to the fact that William IV.'s exercise of the power to change his advisers in 1834 was the act of one of the least wise of British monarchs that, even so, he took advantage of a hint of Lord Melbourne, 'but the proceedings were neither well advised nor fortunate. . . . The authority of the Crown was disparaged, and Queen Victoria, during her long reign, was careful never to repeat the mistake of her predecessor.'   Nor, it may be added, was the precedent of William IV. followed, either by Edward VII. or George V., despite the many difficulties of their reigns, which caused a revival of discussions of the right of dismissal.   This issue is of such importance, as regards responsible government, that its consideration is far from academic.

One point may first be noted.   How can a sovereign be regarded as acting on ministerial advice when a new Prime Minister is selected?   We have actually on record the fact that Queen

21 Spender, *Lord Oxford*, ii. 30.

Victoria carefully avoided asking Mr. Gladstone's advice before choosing Lord Rosebery in 1894,[22] and that Mr. Bonar Law gave none in 1923,[23] when Mr. Baldwin was preferred to Lord Curzon. Must there not be responsibility here?   The answer here is that the resposibility rests with the new Prime Minister; for whatever reason he happens to receive the royal invitation to form a ministry, he is wholly at liberty to decline to do so,[24] and he ought so to decline if constitutional propriety under the British system does not mark out his appointment as right and proper on the part of the sovereign.   When, therefore, he accepts office, he assumes therewith the duty of defending the formation of the new ministry, and no criticism of the Crown would be permitted in the Commons by the Speaker, even if any member were so lacking in sense of constitutional propriety as to make it.   It must be added that in most cases the duty of the sovereign under modern usage is perfectly plain, and that any discussion of what is done can hardly arise; where it does, as in the events of 1931, the responsibility of the Prime Minister has been emphasised in the Commons, and in the country generally the constitutional position has been readily understood in the Press, and in public discussion.

Of these principles there are abundant illustrations from Dominion practice, though in the earlier days of responsible government, and even now in the States of Australia and the Provinces of Canada, dismissal or refusal of advice of ministers is easier to defend than in Britain, with its closer adherence to political regularity, while the Governor may err in judgment without affecting seriously the position of the Crown.

The abdication of Edward VIII. illustrates admirably the character of Cabinet responsibility.[25]   Despite a rather inexplicable conspiracy of silence on the part of the British Press, it had become known, in part through foreign papers, that the King was anxious to marry a United States citizen, who had obtained one divorce already, and who in order to contract marriage must obtain another, this time in England.   It was obvious to the Prime Minister, who at first acted alone, that grave difficulties would arise if the King

22 Morley, *Gladstone*, iii. 512.
23 Dugdale, *Arthur James Balfour*, ii. 360, asserts that Mr. Bonar Law's health forbade consultation.   But he seems to have thought consultation not customary; Ronaldshay, *Curzon*, iii. 350.   But it is common.
24 See Lords Hartington's and Granville's action in 1880; Fitzmaurice, *Granville*, i. 193 f.
25 For a brief account of this, see Churchill, *The Second World War*, i. 170–1.

married a lady who had twice obtained divorces, and that she would not be acceptable as Queen. The Cabinet, when consulted, concurred in this view of the Premier, and like opinions were held by the Dominion Governments, which were necessarily consulted, and which, in addition to advising the King through the British Government, also communicated direct in the hope that the sovereign would find it possible to abandon his project of abdication, if marriage were otherwise ruled out. A suggestion to save the situation by the equivalent of a morganatic marriage was mooted for the King, but necessarily negatived, as wholly out of keeping with British ideas of marriage and the relation between the spouses thence resulting, though such a marriage might have evaded the difficulties arising as regards Dominion action in the event of abdication.[26]

The King, therefore, persisted in abdication, and for that decision on him there rested moral responsibility of a serious kind, as the Archbishop of Canterbury stressed in a broadcast immediately after the completion of the abdication. Plainly he was not advised to take this step by the ministry, which had no desire whatever to have the position of the monarchy, and the prestige of the country, adversely affected. The Cabinet, however, had no alternative but to assume responsibility for the abdication *ex post facto*, by promoting and carrying the necessary legislation to give it effect.[27] There was, indeed, a suggestion for a moment that their position might be challenged on the score that they had advised the King that the marriage contemplated would not be acceptable, and had made it clear that they would not remain in office if he insisted on remaining on the throne, and contracting the marriage. There is no doubt whatever that they were responsible for this attitude, but it was speedily obvious to those who tried to attack them that it would be wholly impossible for Mr. Churchill, or any other person who might sympathise with the King, to form a ministry if the Government resigned. In the result, therefore, the action taken was not questioned seriously, and His Majesty's Declaration of Abdication Act, 1936, was duly enacted to provide for the passage of the Crown to George VI. as on a demise of the Crown, and to exclude the ex-King and any offspring from any claim to the succession.

---

[26] Mr. Baldwin, 318 *H. C. Deb.* 5 s., 2175–2196. Cf. Keith, *The King, the Constitution, the Empire, and Foreign Affairs, 1936–37*, pp. 3–13.

[27] His Majesty's Declaration of Abdication Act, 1936 (1 Ed. VIII. c. 3).

At the same time the ex-King was excluded, as well as any offspring, from the operation of the Royal Marriages Act, 1772, being thus enabled to contract marriage without the assent of the sovereign. He was also, no doubt on the recommendation of the Prime Minister, given the rank of Duke, and later that of His Royal Highness was recognised as appertaining to him, but not to his wife or children.[28] In this case, no doubt, the King must have acted on ministerial advice, so as to avoid any criticism of the sovereign on the ground of the novel differential treatment of the wife, as if her marriage did not place her in the normal position of equality to her husband. It does not seem that any precedent existed for the differentiation. The Countess of Inverness, the title given by the Queen in 1840 to the second wife of the Duke of Sussex, whose first marriage was pronounced void under the Act of 1772,[29] was in a completely different position, as she had never in law been married to the Duke, from whom his first wife parted after the decision of George III. not to recognise the marriage, and who therefore was really rather in the position of a so-called morganatic wife.

2. MINISTERIAL RESPONSIBILITY AND THE DISMISSAL OF MINISTERS.

NEVER since 1783 has actual dismissal of ministers taken place, but the resignation of the Grenville ministry in 1807[30] was enforced by the demand of the King for an assurance that it would not tender him advice in regard to Catholic emancipation, and that it could not properly have given. The case of the Melbourne ministry in 1834, though long regarded as one of dismissal, cannot now be treated in that light, because Lord Melbourne, when Lord Althorp became no longer available to lead the Commons on the death of his father, frankly gave the King complete liberty of action in a written communication, and though at an interview he suggested that Lord J. Russell—a *persona ingrata* to the King— might succeed Lord Althorp, it does not appear that he made any attempt to urge the King, or that he recanted his earlier advice.[31]

---

28 See Keith, *The King, the Constitution, the Empire, and Foreign Affairs, 1936–37*, p. 6, n. 1.
29 *The Sussex Peerage Case* (1844), 11 Cl. & F. 85.
30 See *ante*, p. 272.
31 *Melbourne Papers* (ed. L. C. Sanders, 2nd ed.), pp. 220 ff.; Gladstone, *Gleanings of Past Years*, i. 231.

It is, therefore, impossible to regard the royal action as a case of dismissal, nor does it matter much that the King was influenced by the inability of the ministry to secure support in the Upper House, a consideration now irrelevant, or that he disagreed with his ministry as to its chance of keeping a majority in the Commons. Sir R. Peel held the King's act bad, and Mr. Gladstone ruled it rash, while Mr. Asquith's observation has been cited above. Perhaps these dicta are a little severe. The King might well think that the ministry was not particularly capable or energetic, apart from his dislike of its doctrines.[32]

An interesting discussion of the right of a Governor-General to dismiss a ministry arose in 1873 on the famous issue of the Pacific Railway scandals in Canada. The Conservative ministry of Sir J. Macdonald had compromised itself by its dealing with a railway magnate and others, and the issue arose of the extent to which the Governor-General ought to use his authority to secure the resignation of the ministry. The Governor-General in fact told Sir J. Macdonald that:

> 'He did not consider it his duty to intervene until Parliament should have dealt with the matter, but that inasmuch as the decision of Parliament might itself be partially tainted by the corruption disclosed, he should hold himself free to require the resignation of his Ministers in the event of their winning by anything short of a very commanding majority.'[33]

The attitude of the Commons subsequently induced Sir J. Macdonald to retire.

The Queen's interest was aroused by what she thought was a suggestion by the Colonial Secretary, Lord Kimberley, that the Governor-General would be bound to accept as conclusive a vote of the Dominion Parliament on this issue, as against the view of the Governor-General himself that he would be justified in putting 'gentle pressure' on ministers to induce them to retire. The Queen appears, on the whole, to have agreed with the Governor-General, adding that 'Her Majesty . . . has always respected the obligations which exist between the Queen and her Ministry, but these obligations are mutual and honorable. . . .'[34] Nor is it clear that the Queen was not right in her view, for the approval of the Commons implies that the members who approve are not

[32] For the King's view of the Parliamentary position, see *Memoirs of Baron Stockmar*, i. 329–335.
[33] *Letters of Queen Victoria*, 2 s., ii. 288–9.   [34] *Ibid.*, p. 292.

themselves implicated in wrongdoing. There is on record a statement by Sir C. Tupper that in fact the Governor-General had meant to dismiss the Premier, but was persuaded by him not to take this step, as it would place him in the fatal position of being accused of political partisanship.[35] That, of course, is the essential risk, which renders caution necessary. But Lord Kimberley did not dispute the right to dismiss, and in 1878 both Mr. Gladstone[36] and Mr. Disraeli[37] treated it as beyond question. The latter made an interesting point in his allocution; he insisted that, as his ministry had a majority in both Houses, it could not properly resign, but it could be dismissed, although he did not explain, in any way, the likely consequences of dismissal.

In 1893 the Queen was much perturbed at the possibility of Mr. Gladstone raising an agitation against the Lords on the rejection of the Home Rule Bill therein, and through Lord Rowton, whom she had learned to trust as Lord Beaconsfield's secretary, she asked for Lord Salisbury's advice as to whether she could force a dissolution, *e.g.*, if approached after the rejection of the Bill in the Lords by a numerously signed petition, or an address from the Lords, asking for a dissolution.[38] Lord Salisbury had the good sense to point out that, if ministers refused to dissolve, and were compelled to resign, they would go to the country with the intention of criticising the mode of exercise of the royal authority, if not as actual opponents of it. 'No one can foresee what the upshot of such a state of things would be! It might be good; or it might be bad! But there must be *some* hazard that, in the end, such a step would injure the authority of the Queen.' It was, therefore, undesirable to act without urgent reason, which did not exist. The legislation proposed by the Government on disestablishment in Wales or Scotland, or on local option, would do them no good, and by next year the errors, if any, of his administration would be forgotten, and the Government much more unpopular. In 1894 the issue was revived in a peculiar form.[39] The Queen was very anxious, as usual, that nothing should be done against the Lords, and Lord Rosebery on this subject was suspect. She maintained against him two propositions, one that he should not announce a new policy until he had obtained for it the approval of the Crown,

[35] H. B. Keith, *Imperial Unity*, pp. 113 f.
[36] Gladstone, *Gleanings of Past Years*, i. 230 ff.
[37] Monypenny and Buckle, *Disraeli*, ii. 1118.
[38] *Letters of Queen Victoria*, 3 s., ii. 279 ff., 297 ff. [39] *Ibid.*, 3 s., ii. 431 ff.

and, secondly, that before moving resolutions regarding the relations of the Houses there should be a dissolution of Parliament. Lord Salisbury's advice, on both heads, was in favour of the royal doctrines.   But his opinion was counteracted by the views of Sir Henry James, who was ultimately supported by the Dukes of Devonshire and Argyll, and Mr. Chamberlain and Mr. Balfour.[40] Lord Rosebery's contention was evidently based on the common-sense view that there was nothing improper in a Prime Minister moving resolutions, which, of course, could have no immediate effect or importance.   On the other hand, while the right of the sovereign to insist on a dissolution was clear, the *modus operandi* must be either by the accord of the Prime Minister or, if he refused, by accepting his resignation and dissolving on the advice of a new ministry.   In other words, the Queen in her correspondence with Lord Salisbury was in fact asking whether she would be justified in dismissing her ministers, and Lord Salisbury obviously assumed that, if the Queen persisted, the Government would be compelled to resign and that, moreover, at a time suitable for the Conservative opposition.

This subject was revived when the struggle over the Parliament Bill became acute.   In April, 1910, we find Mr. Balfour contemplating that Mr. Asquith would endeavour to place the King in an impasse by approaching him at a time when funds were running short, and asking him for a pledge to create 500 peers, or at least a dissolution now, or in January.[41]   The King would, on refusal, be confronted with resignation, and when Mr. Balfour was asked to form a ministry he would find it impossible to do so, in view of the hostility of the House and the financial position.   Mr. Balfour, however, was inclined, in such an event, to take office if the financial difficulty could be got over, which Mr. A. Chamberlain thought was possible; the difficulties, as he saw them, were the penalties for illegal use of funds and the attitude of the Comptroller and Auditor-General.   But while Mr. Balfour recognised that the dissolution, which he would at once advise, must be final, Mr. A. Chamberlain was prepared to argue that, if the majority for the opposition were 80, 50, 30 instead of 120, the King would still be bound to refuse to accede to Mr. Asquith's demands, and should recall Mr. Balfour and allow him a fresh dissolution.[42]   It is

[40] *Letters of Queen Victoria*, 3 s., ii. 442–44.
[41] Austen Chamberlain, *Politics from Inside*, pp. 256 f., 262, 266.   [42] *Ibid.*, p. 264.

remarkable that so unconstitutional a doctrine should have been placed on record. To act thus would be a complete betrayal of the duty of the Crown, and in effect a revolution. Happily, the King's death saved Mr. Balfour the trouble of a decision. It seems from Lord Esher's record of a Lambeth Palace meeting on April 27 that Mr. Balfour, though guarded in expression, was inclined to think that the King should refuse to give a contingent undertaking to create peers, and was prepared, if he did so, to take office and dissolve. But whether the King would have agreed with this view remains unknown.[43]

George V. decided on November 16 to give the contingent promise asked for,[44] dependent on the result of the election in December; but this fact was not published. Lord Morley is recorded on December 12 as expressing the view that the King might refuse to create 500 peers if the occasion arose, in which case the ministry would resign, and Mr. Balfour would take office, and by dissolving might obtain a majority from a fatigued electorate.[45] It is impossible to understand this expression of opinion in the circumstances, and Mr. Balfour himself on December 27, in writing to Lord Lansdowne, held that a further dissolution, in view of the electoral result, must be regarded as impossible.[46]

The issue arose once more over the Government of Ireland Bill. That measure, the last chance of preserving the name and authority of the Crown in Ireland, erred undoubtedly in its—apparently tactical[47]—insistence of treating Ireland as a unity, though the error was one which Conservatives could not logically censure, for they had obstinately insisted in preserving intact the union, in face of the fact that it was deeply resented in Southern Ireland, where it was never forgotten that the Union had been secured by bribery and corruption, and that it had never operated, as had the Union with Scotland, essentially in the economic interest of the country. Resistance to the Government's proposal led unhappily to the determination of men like Sir E. Carson and Mr. F. E. Smith to raise an organised force in Ulster to defy the authority of the Crown.[48] The Government refused to take legal proceedings

[43] Esher, *Journals and Letters*, ii. 456 f.
[44] Spender, *Lord Oxford*, i. 296 f.
[45] Fitzroy, *Memoirs*, ii. 427.
[46] Newton, *Lansdowne*, p. 407; Dugdale, *Arthur James Balfour*, ii. 63 ff.
[47] Churchill, *World Crisis, 1911–14*, pp. 181 f.
[48] For an *apologia* for the Government see Spender, *Lord Oxford*, ii. 22–24.

against the Ulster volunteers, with the result that a rival force of National Volunteers soon sprang up. An effort was made by the ministry to solve the issue before it was too late.[49]   It was proposed to allow contracting-out of the Act by counties, Belfast and Londonderry ranking in this category for the purposes of the Act; exclusion was to be for six years, a period allowing for further Parliamentary decision after a new election, and after actual experience of the operation of the constitution. But the proposal was rejected, nominally because of the time limit, really, no doubt, because of the fact that five counties and Londonderry itself might well be willing to remain under the Act. The negotiations, which followed, were long and confused, and an amending measure presented to the Lords on June 23 suffered severely at its hands. On July 21–24, a conference,[50] summoned by the King on Mr. Asquith's advice, sought to settle the issue; Mr. Asquith was aided by Mr. Lloyd George, the Conservatives were Lord Lansdowne and Mr. Bonar Law, Ulster and the Nationalists had two members apiece. The result was failure, for agreement could not be reached on the question of the exclusion from the Act of Tyrone and Fermanagh or parts thereof, for these areas were by no means clearly anti-Home Rule; the time limit question was not settled, but might have been accommodated. In the result the Government decided to propose on July 30, on receiving the Lords' amendments, to proceed with county option, but without a time limit for its operation, but instead, as suggested by Sir E. Carson, with a facultative optional inclusion, if counties so desired. The outbreak of war rendered a satisfactory settlement impossible, for the Conservatives could not see the importance of conciliating Ireland if her aid were to be fully assured in the war, and the ministry therefore had to carry the Act over the head of the Lords, but accompanied by an Act suspending its operation for a year, or until a later date, if the war was not over. At the same time assurances were duly given that Parliament would have an amending measure before it, while the Act was still suspended, and that force would not be countenanced for the compulsion of Ulster.

During this period the most remarkable views found free expression. Mr. Balfour unquestionably thought that the King should have insisted on a fresh mandate for the coercion of Ulster,

---

[49] Spender, *Lord Oxford*, ii. 16 ff., 34 ff.; Halévy, *Histoire du Peuple Anglais au XIXe Siècle*, Epilogue, ii. 533 ff.   [50] Spender, *Lord Oxford*, ii. 55–57.

no doubt on the score that this resistance had not been before the
electorate;[51] no doubt the obvious reply is that to accept such an
argument would be to put a premium on rebellion organised by the
Opposition.   But he thought that, if the King shared his view, he
should not refuse assent to the Bill, which might seem unconstitutional, but should require a dissolution (to test the electorate) and
thus almost certainly compel the resignation of his ministers.   The
King should then send for Lord Rosebery, or himself, to hold
office merely for the taking of the expression of the will of the
people.   The scheme was plainly Utopian, and does not seem to
have been urged publicly.   On the other hand, he took up the
position that, while the King could do nothing if he were opposed
to the ministry's plans, if he sympathised with them, or were
impartial, he could properly insist on an election to clear the air.[52]
Lord Lansdowne insisted that the passing of the Parliament Act,
by destroying the power of the Lords to force reference to the
people, placed the duty on the King.[53]   He might, therefore,
demand from his ministers either a dissolution or a referendum.
He declared that there was nothing to be feared from South
Ireland if the Bill were rejected, and contracting out was dismissed
as 'absurd and impracticable.'   Mr. Bonar Law asserted the right
of the King to dismiss, and to give a dissolution to a new ministry.
But he recognised that this meant personal responsibility and risks,
for against the attacks of the extreme supporters of the Government
must be set the bitter and lasting resentment of the people of
Ulster and their sympathisers.   If coercion were tried before the
electors had decided, the Conservatives were pledged to give every
support, and he doubted if the army would act.   But, if the election
went for the Government, the party would give Ulster no support,
while, if the Opposition won, they would reduce by half the number
of Irish members, and hear no more of Home Rule.   Lord Rosebery
held that refusal of assent to a Bill would be definitely unconstitutional, and urged the holding of a conference, which would not
satisfy Ulster, but might satisfy the conscience of Ulster and Britain.
Mr. Cave urged the King to use his prerogative of dissolution,[54]
while others urged him to refuse assent to the Bill.   Sir W. Anson,
while clear that the King had a right to insist on a reference to the
people, pointed out that he could dissolve only by persuading his

[51] Dugdale, *Arthur James Balfour*, ii. 99, 100.   [52] Spender, *Lord Oxford*, ii. 26.
[53] *Ibid.*, ii. 25.   [54] *The Times*, September 6, 1913.

ministry, or by dismissing them and securing an alternative ministry, which would be prepared to take responsibility.[55] Professor Dicey upheld the same view. ' I entirely agree,' he said, 'that the King can do nothing except on the advice of ministers. I totally disagree with the doctrine drawn from this principle that he can never dismiss ministers in order that he may ascertain the will of the nation. Of course, the incoming ministers must, like Sir Robert Peel, except responsibility for the change of ministry.'[56] Lord Hugh Cecil stressed the essential doctrine that the King could refuse ministerial advice in such cases, and those only, in which he could find ministers prepared to undertake to defend his action.[57]

The reply of Mr. Asquith to these contentions was the only one possible. The Lords had claimed the right to force reference to the people at their discretion, and the result had been a constitutional crisis, ended by the denial of their claims by the Parliament Act, 1911. It was most undesirable that the position of the King should be raised in the same way. If once he was asked by a Conservative opposition to refer a matter, he would equally be asked by a Liberal or Radical opposition, and his action would be involved in the case of every important Bill. Moreover, at a dissolution after an intervention necessitating dismissal of ministers, the Crown would become the football of contending factions, a contingency which should be most carefully avoided. ' Every Act of Parliament of the first order of importance, and only passed after acute controversy, would be regarded as bearing the personal *imprimatur* of the Sovereign. He would, whether he wished it or not, be dragged into the arena of party politics. . . . This is a constitutional catastrophe which it is the duty of every wise statesman to do the utmost in his power to avert.'[58]

Mr. Asquith further stressed the dangers of offending the feelings and disappointing the hopes of Southern Ireland, which would become ungovernable if the Bill were not passed. The idea of an election would solve nothing, for Sir E. Carson and his friends would not abate their resistance, whatever that decided, nor could it be otherwise, if men really held their liberty and religion to be in jeopardy. If the Government were defeated, the verdict would not

---

55 *The Times*, September 10, 1913.
56 *Ibid.*, September 15, 1913; cf. Colvin, *Carson*, ii. 240.
57 *The Times*, September 10, 1913.   58 Spender, *Lord Oxford*, ii. 30 f.

really be on the Bill, but, as in the recent by-elections on the Insurance Act, the Marconi contract, and a score of other issues. Again, the election would destroy the whole purpose of the Parliament Act, which was framed simply to prevent the recurrence of the power of the Lords to force a dissolution. On the other hand, it would be possible to arrange that there should be a general election before the Act was brought into operation. This last point affords unquestionably the answer to the much discussed question whether the Governmental attitude was sound, and such as could be accepted by the King. His one right to act was based on the possibility that the ministry had ceased to speak for the people, and the Prime Minister's proposal offered the necessary assurance on that head by making it plain that the people would at an early date be consulted, before the position had been stereotyped. This point is important, for, if the proposal had really been to alter matters so radically that the matter could not be reconsidered, the issue would have presented different aspects.

No doubt it is a very serious matter for the King to determine that the ministry does not really represent the will of the people, so that he is justified in insisting on a dissolution, which normally would mean removing ministers; enforced resignation or dismissal is a point of no real importance.[59] The difficulty is that it is so hard to know what the people will do, and there is always one grave fact to be faced. The dismissed ministry will make a point of the fact, that by constitutional usage, its advice should have prevailed. That consideration may result in the electorate disregarding the issue first involved, and voting instead in whole or in part, on the score that the dismissal was not constitutional. Nor is this mere hypothesis; in 1926, in the electoral contest in Canada, which ensued on Lord Byng's refusal of a dissolution to Mr. Mackenzie King, followed by a grant of one to Mr. Meighen on Mr. King's resignation, no serious doubt can be felt that the issue was largely determined by the skill with which Mr. King raised the constitutional issue.[60]

There are further difficulties in the way of the King obtaining information. He has open to him, of course, the views of the Press, which are singularly difficult to evaluate, especially as under

[59] Keith, *Responsible Government in the Dominions* (1928), i. pp. xxi. f., 146–52.
[60] For some discussion of this episode see H. V. Evatt, *The King and His Dominion Governors*, chap. vii.

modern conditions newspapers fall under the control of 'Press lords,' who normally show little flair for the opinion of the people. He has the evidence of by-elections, but no one can say precisely how much these mean; local considerations are often decisive in such cases, and a seat won at a by-election often reverts to its previous holders at the general election following. He has the views of his entourage, which may be supplemented by those of leaders of the Opposition obtained by discussion with the sanction of the Prime Minister, or offered spontaneously, or learned through his private secretary, or otherwise. We must not under-rate the importance of such material, nor can we say that the King must accept on such a question the opinion of the ministry, but plainly it is requisite that the case should be very clear before the King deliberately takes a step, which may endanger gravely the prestige and future powers of the Crown.

It is not, however, sufficient to say that the Government have a mandate for a policy, as the Liberal Party certainly had one for the Home Rule legislation. On that occasion there had intervened a very serious issue, which was not originally foreseen, the extent of preparations for resistance in Ulster,[61] and the effect on the British army. Few things are more depressing from the constitutional point of view than the record of the participation of Unionist leaders in preparation to defy the sovereignty of the Crown, and to destroy its forces, but even more deplorable is the record of high officers of the army. It is known[62] that Mr. Bonar Law discussed with Sir Henry Wilson, the Director of Military Operations, desperate measures to save a desperate situation, and that the same officer discussed the position with Lord Milner, Dr. Jameson, and Sir E. Carson, their common interest being the organisation and training of forces in Ulster, against whose resistance would be shattered any attempt to put in operation an Act of Parliament to which the royal assent had been given. No excuse can be made for these persons or their associates, but the severest condemnation, of course, must fall on Sir Henry Wilson for his treachery to those he served. On the other hand there is little excuse to be found for

---

61 The Ulster Unionist Council started resistance in September, 1911, and a Covenant was opened for signature in September, 1912. Gun-running took place at Larne (April 24–25, 1914), unpunished. The Nationalists raised volunteers and ran guns at Howth (July 26), with some loss of life. In neither case was justice done; Spender, *Lord Oxford*, ii. 49, 55.

62 Callwell, *Wilson*, i. ch. viii., ix. Cf. Austen Chamberlain, *Politics from Inside*, pp. 624 ff.

the attitude of the Secretary of State for War and the Army Council,[63] for in December, 1913, Sir Arthur Paget, Commander-in-Chief in Ireland, was allowed to permit officers domiciled in Ulster to 'disappear' without prejudice to their prospects, if the army was called upon to deal with disturbances in Ulster. This was followed by an incredible piece of blundering by the War Office, and Sir A. Paget in March, 1914, when officers at the Curragh were given the impression of being asked forthwith to commence operations against the Ulster volunteers, or of refusing and being dismissed, save those of Ulster domicile. It must be remembered that all that was then being considered was the provision of adequate security for police barracks and depots of arms and ammunition in Ulster, an elementary duty of the Crown and of the army. The raising of a question of crushing resistance in Ulster in these circumstances was foolish, so much so that it is not surprising that bad faith was at the time suspected by those who did not realise the essential limitations of the military mind, which were so shortly to be revealed so generously in the disasters of the Great War. As it was, General Hubert Gough and fifty-seven officers of the 3rd Cavalry Brigade expressed preference for dismissal. Their action caused a painful sensation, the Opposition leaders supported them, as they could hardly avoid doing, and the leaders of the malcontents were ordered to report themselves to the Adjutant-General at the War Office, where the duties expected of them were properly explained. As set out in an Army Order issued soon after, the principles are in brief that (1) no officer or soldier should in future be questioned by his superior officer as to the attitude he will adopt, or as to his action, in the event of his being required to obey orders dependent upon future or hypothetical contingencies. (2) An officer or soldier is forbidden in future to ask for assurances as to orders which he may be required to obey. (3) In particular, it is the duty of every officer and soldier to obey all lawful commands given to them through the proper channel, either for the safeguarding of public property or the support of the civil power in the ordinary execution of its duty, or for the protection of the lives and property of the inhabitants in the case of disturbance of the peace. This action should have ended the

---

[63] Spender, *Lord Oxford*, ii. 41 ff.; J. E. B. Seely, *Adventure*, pp. 166 ff.; Halévy, *Histoire du Peuple Anglais au XIXe Siècle*, Epilogue, ii. 546 ff. For Sir E. Carson's advice to the King, see Repington, *The First World War*, i. 69.

matter, but by a blunder which has never been explained, Colonel Seely added to the memorandum giving, in substance, the above rulings an assurance that the Government had no intention of taking advantage of the right to use the forces of the Crown to crush political opposition to the policy or principles of the Home Rule Bill. Plainly, Colonel Seely's action was completely inconsistent with the principles laid down; if it were not right to ask an officer what he would do in a hypothetical contingency, still less could it be right for an officer to ask the Government to give him any such assurance, and General Gough, at whose request Colonel Seely had acted, was informed that the assurance must be deemed cancelled. Colonel Seely's action was indefensible, while the Conservatives lent themselves to support the intrigues of Sir H. Wilson, who consulted Mr. Bonar Law, and from the War Office primed Opposition leaders with questions intended to embarrass the Government. Mr. Churchill committed an indiscretion by orders for naval movements, which afforded the basis for an absolute unfounded rumour that the army and navy were to engage in combined action against the Ulster volunteers, and the capture of their headquarters by a *coup de main*.[64] In the Commons feeling ran high, when on March 23, 24 and 25 the issue was debated, for many, besides Liberals, realised that, if the claims put forward were admitted, the Government and the House of Commons would be put at the mercy of the army and navy. The Labour members pointed the moral that, if officers could refuse to serve, the rank and file would follow their lead if called upon to deal with other forms of civil disorder than those feared in Ulster, and Mr. John Ward quoted a syndicalist leaflet just distributed, asking soldiers to remember that officers had exercised an option in obeying orders, and calling upon them to resolve never to fire on their own class.

Colonel Seely had already resigned, and Mr. Asquith himself on March 30 took the seals of the War Department, thereby rendering himself ineligible for Parliament until re-elected. On April 4 at Ladybank he reminded his constituents of the doctrine of the elder Pitt in 1745: 'The right of inquiring what measures may conduce to the advantage and security of the public belongs not to the army, but to this House. . . . Our armies have no better right to determine for themselves than any other body of

64 Churchill, *World Crisis, 1911–14*, p. 184. Cf. Fitzroy, *Memoirs*, ii. 542–546.

them, nor are we to suffer them to prescribe laws to the Legislature, or to govern those by whose authority they subsist.'

The attitude of the Conservative Party in taking advantage for political purposes of the unrest in the ranks of the officers, and their relations with Sir H. Wilson, establish a precedent for supporting disloyalty in the army, just as their sympathy with preparations in Ulster to resist the Crown established a precedent for preparations for civil war. To ignore these facts is useless, and the Crown must now always take into consideration in regard to action on advice of ministers, the possibility of such advice producing a mutiny in the defence forces. That mutiny in such a case is constitutional was definitely the view of the Unionist leaders in 1914, and none of the comments, since published by them, depart from that position.[65]

There is, therefore, no possibility of assuming that the Crown can safely adopt the rule that the advice of ministers must always be accepted, and the Curragh incident was rendered the more unsatisfactory, because of the negligence of the ministry in failing forthwith to report to the King the events in question, which he learned first from the Press.[66] His distress, or indignation, was most natural, and his insistence that no further instances of such negligence must happen. The idea that matters of this kind can take place without the fullest consultation with the King is intolerable, and the sovereign would have been in a very strong position had he chosen in the event to dismiss ministers for this failure of duty.

Even those who hold most strongly that the sovereign should act on advice have to admit that this cannot be insisted upon to the extent of accepting the destruction of the essential principle of responsible government, the periodical appeal to the people. If, indeed, the idea of automatic action were to be pressed, it would have to be accompanied by safeguards that the power of a ministry should not be abused, for example, by requiring that a reference to the people in some form should be necessary if a certain proportion of the Commons demanded it. As matters stand the King could not properly assent to any measure to extend the life of an existing Parliament, unless there were general assent, as, no doubt, existed

[65] Cf. Lord Brentford's advocacy of civil war in 1913–14; Taylor, *Brentford*, pp. 127 f.
[66] Spender, *Lord Oxford*, ii., 47. Allegations of unconstitutional initiative by the King were decisively denied by Mr. Asquith on March 25; Legge, *King George*, i. 113 ff.

for the extension of the life of Parliament during both World Wars. But could he assent to a measure of franchise reform, which deprived a large section of the franchise, or gave additional votes to a section, or which effected an unfair redistribution of seats? In such cases very grave issues might easily arise, for it is most unlikely that any ministry would put forward proposals so obviously unjust as to make it easy for the King to refuse assent to a Bill, or as would be preferable, to change his ministers before the matter went so far. The issue might again arise in such a case as the approval of a treaty, whether with or without legislation. Could the King accept a compact which violated the principles on which the ministry had obtained office at the preceding general election?

These questions are not academic, for the Hoare-Laval agreement, 1935, as to a possible settlement of the Ethiopian issue was so manifestly incompatible with the terms of the Covenant of the League of Nations that, had they been persisted in, the King would have been placed in a very awkward position. As matters stood, the Commons reacted to the widespread protests among electors, and the policy was for the moment dropped. Moreover, it is plain that royal intervention is always *primâ facie* undesirable, and should be resorted to only as an *ultima ratio*. These considerations explain why in April, 1938, it was not widely felt proper to petition the sovereign to disapprove the Anglo-Italian agreement of April 16, though that agreement contemplated the recognition of the Italian conquest of Ethiopia *de jure*, an act which involved George VI. in a deliberate violation of George V.'s solemn undertaking, under Article 20 of the League Covenant, not to enter into any agreement contrary to the provisions thereof.[67] The failure of the ministry to keep to the principles, on the strength of which it attained support from the nation at the election of 1935, marks, no doubt, a definite abandonment of the exclusion from party strife of foreign politics, and may render difficult in future the royal position.

A further case, where the Crown is deeply concerned, is the maintenance under the constitution of law and order. The royal assent is necessary to a proclamation of emergency, and clearly cannot be given without the adduction of evidence that it is essential, as plainly was the case in 1926, during the dangerous conspiracy against the security of the realm in the form of the general strike,[68]

[67] A. B. Keith, *The Scotsman*, April 19, 1938; Cmd. 5726.
[68] Taylor, *Brentford*, pp. 192 ff.

which was defeated by the encouragement afforded to the loyal population by the steps taken by the ministry to vindicate the elementary rights of the subject. Here, as usual, it is possible, as a rule, for the Crown merely to exercise negative influence; in the period when the Ulster and the Nationalist volunteers were defying law in Ireland the sovereign was not able effectively to intervene to demand ministerial action to enforce the law; no doubt the blame for failure rests largely on Mr. J. Redmond's urgent objections against any action against Sir E. Carson and his supporters, but the fact remains that the lawlessness of these two bodies was inevitably the precursor of the Irish rebellion, and the elimination of the sovereign from the Irish constitution. Yet to dismiss a ministry on such a ground would have been impracticable.

One point remains to be considered. Has the King a right by threat of abdication to force ministers to yield to his wishes? The abdication of a sovereign, it may be thought, as a result of ministers insisting on a line of policy disapproved by him, would injure their position so much that ministers might rather yield than dispute. Queen Victoria occasionally uttered a threat; thus, on August 10, 1871, she intimated that, unless ministers enabled her to leave for Balmoral before prorogation, she could not go on, and must give her heavy burden up to younger hands, a statement which it must have been difficult to take seriously.[69]   In the Russo-Turkish crisis, however, in 1876–78 the Queen used more seriously this dangerous weapon,[70] but it is reasonable to suppose that in this, as in the rest of her curious activities at this period, she was acting very much on the instigation of her Prime Minister, who was certainly clever enough to use this method of securing his own way with the Cabinet, though Lord Carnarvon was put out by her interventions. On May 17, 1885, a more just note is struck, in writing to Lord Hartington against the Governmental policy of evacuating the Sudan: 'The Queen writes strongly, but *she* cannot resign if matters go ill, and her heart bleeds to see such shortsighted humiliating policy pursued, which lowers her country before the whole world.'[71]   To this attitude she appears to have adhered for the rest of her reign.

---

[69] Guedalla, *The Queen and Mr. Gladstone*, i. 300.   Cf. Mr. Gladstone's comment, taking reluctantly responsibility, 303 f.

[70] Monypenny and Buckle, *Disraeli*, ii. 1017, 1020, 1089, 1117 (June 14, 27, 1877; January 10, February 9, 1878).

[71] *Letters of Queen Victoria*, 2 s., iii. 646.

Abdication seems occasionally to have occurred to Edward VII., but rather as a mode of relieving himself from a position rendered irksome by ill-health and worry, due to the bitterness of contending parties, than as a means to enforce his personal views of policy. Of George V. we have the assertion that 'nothing could be further from the truth than the story repeated in after days, that he lost his self-control and threatened to abdicate.'[72]   His efforts to secure a compromise settlement of the issue of Home Rule were unceasing, but they were not reinforced by the suggestion of abdication.   To have made it would have been definitely to take sides against the Government or the Opposition, which is precisely the thing which a King should never do.

The attitude of Edward VIII., elsewhere described, turned not on public business, but on a private issue, though one affecting public interests.[73]   Abdication, therefore, may fairly be ruled out as a legitimate instrument of the Crown.   If the threat were made and failed, the King would either have to give way, which would seriously affect his dignity and future influence, or he would have to resign, with the resulting necessity of legislation to regulate the succession, a matter now involving serious dangers to the cohesion of the Commonwealth.   In the long run the monarchy would probably suffer, even if in some cases the use of this weapon should prove successful.

The point has naturally been raised,[74] whether the position of the King in respect to the Dominions might not enable him to put pressure on ministers, by pointing out to them that if he were driven to abdicate by their pressing undesired counsel upon him, there would be created a dangerous position, involving the maintenance of Imperial unity. But after the abdication of Edward VIII. the issue has probably lost any serious importance.   Dominion autonomy is so complete, that it has to be admitted that British autonomy is in like case, and that ministers could not give up any essential policy in view of such a threat.   Unimportant issues will always find them prepared to make concessions, as in the case of the rather interesting question of the contents of the royal speech from the throne.

---

[72] Spender, *Lord Oxford*, ii. 28.
[73] See *ante*, pp. 277 ff.
[74] Cf. Mr. Balfour's view, quoted November 19, 1909, by Esher, *Journals and Letters*, ii. 421.

The question of the constitutional right of Queen Victoria to have her own way on the speech from the throne was discussed with much warmth in 1881, when it was decided by the ministry to withdraw from Kandahar, as part of the business of clearing up the muddle of Afghanistan.[75] Sir W. Harcourt and Lord Spencer were present, and were in great difficulties, as the Queen was insistent on change, while Mr. Gladstone was equally firm in the other sense. At last the Queen gave way with infinitely bad grace, and the speech was approved in Council. Ministers 'impressed upon Sir H. Ponsonby that the Speech from the Throne was in no sense an expression of Her Majesty's individual sentiment, but a declaration of policy made on the responsibility of her Ministers.' The doctrine that the speech was really the speech of ministers was naturally impressed on the Queen; it had been recognised in 1710 by Swift, asserted by Wilkes in No. 45 of the *North Briton*, as perfectly well understood, and the same doctrine had been laid down by Lord John Russell in 1841.[76] But Lord Beaconsfield laid down that no such principle was known to the British constitution that the speech should be approved in Council, and for that purpose should be submitted well in advance for the royal approval.[77] But it should be noted that Lord Beaconsfield did not then speak as a responsible adviser. Approval in Council was in fact normal at that time; it was only in 1921 that it was held that when in Scotland the royal approval could be given by the sign manual simply in order to save the necessity of holding a formal Council, and that was due to special conditions.[78] The point, of course, of the controversy was simple enough. The nature of the speech really makes it clear that it must represent the policy of the Government, and that it need not be wholly satisfactory to the Crown personally, so that the sovereign is recognised as being detached from its pronouncements in any personal way. But, on the other hand, the sovereign has clearly the right to object, so far as he thinks it worth while. In 1881, if the Queen had persisted, the ministry would have resigned, and that at the moment of the opening of Parliament would have been revolutionary. On the other hand are ministers usually willing to consider seriously any suggestion of

[75] *Letters of Queen Victoria*, 2 s., iii. 178 ff.; Sir H. Ponsonby. *Sidelights on Queen Victoria*, pp. 144 ff.; Gardiner, *Harcourt*, i. 598–600.
[76] *Annual Register*, 1841, p. 198.
[77] *Letters of Queen Victoria*, 2 s., iii. 181–2.
[78] Fitzroy, *Memoirs*, ii. 756 f.

change? Thus in 1864, the Queen secured the deletion of a paragraph in the royal speech on the score that it was needlessly bellicose in tone, and might precipitate a war with Germany. In 1893, Mr. Gladstone agreed to modify reference to a Bill for the better government of Ireland, to a Bill to amend the provision for the government of Ireland.[79] In the speech for February, 1910,[80] some changes were made to meet royal criticisms, and deliberately, without suggestion from the King, the last paragraph was so worded by the insertion of the phrase, 'in the opinion of my advisers,' as to make it plain that the King was not being involved personally in the proposal to regulate the relations of the two Houses. On December 13, 1921,[81] a grave inelegance of diction was duly detected and corrected, with the assent of the two ministers present, with the concurrence of a hereditary master of English in the person of Lord Lytton.

At the close of 1902,[82] the speech was influenced by the desire of the King for the insertion of something in the nature of an eirenicon on the Education Act. The Lord Chancellor is then said to have asserted that he received two copies of the speech, one from the Prime Minister, one from the President of the Council, and that they very rarely agreed, but it mattered little, for the Press derived their information from a third, which generally differed from both!

Insistence on alteration of the speech at the prorogation of Parliament is interestingly attested in 1907,[83] when ministers at first desired the King to express regret at the failure of the Lords to pass the Bill for the creation of small holdings in Scotland. Edward VII. demurred to the 'covered thrust' at the Lords thus implied, and also objected to an expression of regret, and in the ultimate issue the whole reference was deleted. This is a very clear case where a substantial concession was made to the royal wishes. On the other hand, in the speech on the opening of Parliament in 1894 the reference to disestablishment of the churches in Wales and Scotland was modified at the last moment to meet the Queen's wishes.[84] Apparently she had misunderstood what had been

---

[79] Guedalla, *The Queen and Mr. Gladstone*, ii. 462.
[80] Lee, *Edward VII.*, ii. 699 f.
[81] Fitzroy, *Memoirs*, ii. 771.
[82] *Ibid.*, i. 115.
[83] Lee, *Edward VII.*, ii. 476 f.
[84] *Letters of Queen Victoria*, 3 s., ii. 378 ff.

agreed upon with Mr. Gladstone before the retirement of the latter.[85]

3. THE CROWN AND THE DISSOLUTION OF PARLIAMENT

THE prerogative of the Crown to dissolve Parliament is undoubted. The manner of dissolution does not, as often said, strictly speaking involve the aid of ministers, for the King could still present himself in the House of Lords, and by word of mouth, dissolve the Parliament. But in practice dissolution takes place by a proclamation under the great seal, which is based on the advice of the Privy Council, for whose summons the Lord President accepts responsibility; and which refers to an Order in Council requiring the issue of the writs for the meeting of Parliament for which the Lord Chancellor accepts responsibility. No ministry which did not wish to dissolve would give the necessary aid, and, therefore, a forced dissolution is impossible, though one induced by royal pressure is perfectly in order. But it must be remembered that a Government which dissolves must make a good case for dissolution, and, therefore, a ministry, which was itself not unwilling to meet a royal suggestion might be precluded from doing so by the consideration that it could not comply with this condition. Instances where ministries did not wish to dissolve, though royal sanction could have been had, have already been mentioned in 1866, 1873, 1885, 1895, and 1905.

The problem as it arose in 1913 over the Government of Ireland Bill was, as we have seen, really one of dismissal rather than dissolution. These Unionists who claimed that the Liberal Government had received no mandate for such a measure in 1910, and who realised that Mr. Asquith was unlikely to advise a dissolution for that purpose, then went on to discuss the power of the King to dissolve without advice. One of them argued that the King had an undoubted right to dissolve Parliament and that he should exercise the right on this occasion to satisfy himself that the House 'does indeed represent the democracy of today.'[86] Sir William Anson and others admitted that the advice of Ministers was constitutionally necessary, and that if the Government was unwilling

---

[85] There was an interesting exchange of views regarding the speech of June 7, 1859, between Lord Derby and the Queen; *ibid.*, 1 s., iii. 435 ff.
[86] Mr. George Cave, *The Times*, September 6, 1913.

10*

to give such advice then the King would have to ascertain, presumably from the Opposition, if they would take office and responsibility instead.[87]   Professor T. H. Morgan insisted that such independent action on the part of the King 'would almost inevitably be equivalent to a dismissal of his ministers,' and, further, that if once dissolution were effected in this way, 'no dissolution would be free from ambiguity, and speculation as to the degree of responsibility of the Sovereign would be a feature of every election.'[88]   In other words, either the King persuades his ministers to advise dissolution or they resign.   There can be royal pressure, but not an enforced dissolution without advice.

An interesting point, however, arises.[89]   If a ministry dissolved at the request of the Crown—for example, Lord Rosebery in 1894— would it be in order for it to make it clear that it had done so for that reason?   Sir H. James on November 5, 1894, pointed out that the Prime Minister would be compelled to explain why that Government had departed from its earlier intention not to dissolve, and that the royal intervention would thus become known, and the election, instead of being a contest on the issue which the Queen desired to have decided, the position of the House of Lords, might turn on the view of the electorate, as to the treatment of the ministry by the Crown.   Plausible at first sight, this seems to assume in the ministry an attitude which would clearly be improper.   If the ministry deferred to her wishes, they must make them their own, and in that case they would act with serious impropriety if they allowed the argument as to their treatment to be raised in the constituencies, and they could destroy it at once, if raised independently, by saying that they took no exception whatever to the royal persuasion.   In fact, no doubt the ministry would not ascribe the change of view solely, or mainly, to royal suggestion, and the occasion for criticism would not arise.

If the Crown cannot, except by persuasion or dismissal of ministers, secure a dissolution, it is clearly not bound to grant a dissolution when asked for, provided that it can obtain other ministers to take responsibility for the royal refusal.   This view was inevitable under the pre-reform constitution; in 1806 or 1807 the Crown could have refused a dissolution to Lord Grenville and the Duke of Portland without hesitation.   In 1831 William IV.

[87] *Ante*, p. 285.   [88] *The Times*, September 10, 1913.
[89] *Letters of Queen Victoria*, 3 s. ii. 431 ff.

would have refused to dissolve if he could have secured a ministry to replace that of Earl Grey. Moreover, the view of Queen Victoria, shared by Lord Melbourne and Sir R. Peel, that a dissolution was a weapon in the hands of the Crown, to be used only in extreme cases, and with a certainty of success, since its use followed by defeat, 'is a thing most lowering to the Crown, and hurtful to the country,' assumed that the Crown preserved full discretion.[90] When the question of the possibility of the Lords rejecting the great Bill to sweep away the Navigation Acts was mooted, Lord J. Russell doubted if the Queen, on sending for Lord Stanley, would be willing to give him a dissolution. In 1851 the resignation of Lord John Russell led to discussion between the Queen and Lord Stanley; Lord John thought that it would involve a responsibility too great for the Crown to refuse an appeal to the country for a new Government, though a decision ought to depend on the peculiar circumstances of the case.[91] Lord Stanley pointed out to the Queen that he would have no chance of success in the Commons if it were thought that the Queen would withhold from him the privilege of dissolving, and the Queen went so far as to allow him to deny, if necessary, that the Queen would not consent to a dissolution, though she would not give any promise, however contingent.[92]

The constitutional position was explained by Lord Aberdeen in 1858 in response to the royal enquiry, as to her attitude in the event of Lord Derby asking for a dissolution.[93] His aim, of course, was primarily to obtain permission to announce that, if defeated, he had royal sanction for a dissolution; this the Queen refused, as an unconstitutional use of her name and authority to coerce the Commons. Lord Aberdeen felt clear that, if asked, she should give a dissolution; it must be assumed that the minister thought it necessary for the good of the country. The Queen could refuse a dissolution—it was one of the very few acts which the Queen could do without responsible advice at the moment, but the new ministry must assume responsibility for the refusal, and defend it in Parliament. There was no precedent for refusal, which would mean the dismissal of Lord Derby, instead of his resignation from inability to carry on the Government. A new minister would have to give

---

90 *Letters of Queen Victoria*, 1 s., ii. 108.   91 *Ibid.*, 1 s., ii. 348.
92 *Ibid.*, 1 s., ii. 366 ff. For the action of Lord Derby in stating he would advise a dissolution, *ibid.*, 465 ff.   93 *Ibid.*, 1 s., iii. 363 ff.

reasons why a dissolution was refused, and no considerations of public business, or the possible bad effect of frequent general elections, would be an effective ground, unless something could be made of the danger of discussing intemperately upon every hustings the proceedings of the Government regarding India.

Lord Aberdeen's statement has been criticised, but it is clearly sound sense. A ministry which asks for a dissolution will insist on resigning if it is refused; Lord John Russell and Mr. Disraeli made that clear in 1866 and 1868 alike. As Lord Salisbury said in 1886, to allow a dissolution is the natural and ordinary course, and would shield the Queen from any accusation of partisanship.[94] It is difficult to understand the alleged dissatisfaction of Edward VII. at Mr. Balfour's statement that the dissolution obtained by Sir H. Campbell-Bannerman was dictated by the Cabinet, and that the House of Commons could force one.[95] A new Cabinet in the circumstances of the case must have a dissolution, and the King knew that perfectly well. The statement that the King on November 16, 1910,[96] refused a dissolution until he was given some proof that ministers were powerless in a Parliament of their own choosing, rests on an assertion of Sir A. Fitzroy, from whom Lord Morley, for whatever reason, had withheld the facts. We know now that the issue between the King and ministers was not that of dissolution, but of the giving of a pledge by the King to swamp the Lords if the dissolution resulted in victory for the party.

In 1923, in view of the appearance of a three-party system, Mr. Asquith affirmed that the King would be at liberty to refuse a dissolution to Mr. MacDonald, if it were asked for.[97] The assertion may have been based partly on the hope that, if that occurred, the King would turn to him to form a new ministry. Serious consideration should have shown that, however, when the occasion arose in the particular political conditions, the King would be under every conceivable obligation to allow the ministry to take the verdict of the country. Mr. Asquith perhaps forgot that a dissolution is an appeal to the political sovereign, and that when it is asked for every consideration of constitutional propriety normally demands that it be conceded. In fact the King did concede it

---

[94] *Letters of Queen Victoria*, 3 s., i. 117.   [95] Lee, *Edward VII.*, ii. 43 f.
[96] Fitzroy, *Memoirs*, ii. 422 f.
[97] *The Times*, December 19, 1923; Evatt, *The King and his Dominion Governors*, chap. viii.

without hesitation to Mr. MacDonald, as had been clear, even to many of Mr. Asquith's sympathisers long before the event took place, and as no doubt he himself recognised in his gallant attempt to save the ministry from a defeat in the Campbell case, which threatened to force it into resignation.[98] If, however, it is admitted that the King could not well have taken any other course in the political circumstances of 1924, it does not follow that his action then in any way surrendered the Crown's prerogative of refusing a dissolution in the future. In the debate on the Education Bill in March, 1944, already referred to,[99] Mr. Churchill stated categorically that although advice to dissolve comes from the Prime Minister, it is only advice and may, in exceptional circumstances, be disregarded. Such an occasion had now occurred. 'This is one of the exceptional occasions,' he said, 'when the Prerogative of the Crown comes into play and where in doubtful circumstances the Crown would refer to other advisers. It has been done on several occasions.'[1]

It is, of course, true that the right to a dissolution is not a right to a series of dissolutions. The King could not, because a ministry had appealed and lost an election, give them forthwith another without seeming to be endeavouring to wear out the resistance of the electors to the royal will. Herein the Crown might have to refuse, and so enforce the retirement of a ministry; indeed, the theory of automatic action by the Crown comes on this point disastrously to grief. But it must be remarked that it would, indeed, be an unwise ministry which asked at once for a fresh dissolution, for probably it would succeed in extinguishing itself. It was considerations of this sort which undoubtedly influenced Mr. Asquith to some extent in 1923, although they were hardly applicable to that particular setting. He argued that the prerogative of the Crown meant that, when a second dissolution was called for very soon after an earlier one, 'the Crown is not bound to take the advice of a particular minister to put its subjects to the tumult and turmoil of a series of General Elections so long as it can find other ministers who are prepared to give contrary advice.'[2] With that view it is difficult to disagree, except on the definition of the word 'series.' Following upon the General Election of February, 1950, it seemed as though some such definition might be called for. With so unusually small a majority in the House of Commons,

---

[98] Spender, *Lord Oxford*, ii. 342 ff.   [99] *Ante*, p. 217.
[1] 398 *H. C. Deb.* 5 s., 1516.   [2] *The Times*, December 19, 1923.

and allowing for the chances of illness, and change in by-elections, it appeared that the Labour Government might very soon be defeated on some important measure and then be faced with the alternatives of resignation or request for dissolution. The rights and duties of the Crown in such a situation called forth some comment in the Press, but nothing was added to earlier expressions of opinion on this subject.[3] In fact, no such defeat took place, and the lengthening life of the Government gradually made further discussion on this subject unprofitable.

How long must elapse before a ministry, returned with a small plurality, or dependent on aid from other groups at one election, can be given another dissolution, depends entirely on circumstances, and defies any attempt at definition. In Canada the plurality given to the Liberal Party by the election of 1925 was too small to allow it to carry on effectively, and one reason for Lord Byng's refusal of a dissolution in 1926 was, no doubt, the fact that Mr. Mackenzie King had had so recently a dissolution without achieving full success, so that another was not proper. The crushing defeat of the new Government of Mr. Meighen in the election following on its advent to office was largely due to the raising of the constitutional issue of the right of the Governor-General to grant a dissolution, and no very exact conclusion can be drawn, except that in all the circumstances, the refusal of a dissolution to Mr. King was an unfortunate error of judgment, since an election was patently necessary to allow an effective ministry to be formed and, that being so, to refuse it to the Premier, and then to give it to his successor, looked like political partisanship, though, in fact, it was not.[4]

It appears that, while there is some divergence of view among the authorities on the question whether the King can refuse a dissolution to a Prime Minister who asks for it, the better opinion is that the power still exists, but that it could properly be exercised only in exceptional circumstances.

It is difficult to imagine circumstances in which the King could properly refuse a dissolution to a Prime Minister with a clear majority in the House of Commons; for, if he did so, the Prime

---

[3] *The Times*, April 24, 25, 26 and 27, 1950. No further dissolution took place until October, 1951.

[4] Keith, *Responsible Government in the Dominions*, i. 146–52 ; H. V. Evatt, *The King and His Dominion Governors*, chap. vii.

Minister would presumably resign and the King would have to send for the Leader of the Opposition who, though he accepted office on the view that the House of Commons had not outlived its usefulness, would 'ex hypothesi' be unable to form a stable government with a majority in the House. The King could hardly grant a dissolution to the second Prime Minister after refusing to the first.

A request for a dissolution seems more likely to be refused to a Prime Minister in a minority in the House of Commons if it appeared that the parties who formed a majority were prepared to join forces to support an alternative Government. Even in these circumstances a dissolution could scarcely be refused unless the Parliament had been in existence a comparatively short time and appeared still to reflect the views of the electorate. If the King were to refuse a dissolution on these grounds and his judgment of the willingness of the other parties to work together proved unfounded, so that the new Government was shortly afterwards defeated in its turn, it seems probable that he would then send for the Prime Minister who had first requested a dissolution and allow him a dissolution in due course.

The right to advise a dissolution was long assumed to belong to the Cabinet, and for this view there is abundant precedent from 1841, when Lord Melbourne's decision to dissolve was due to the Cabinet, which vetoed his desire to resign, based on his doubt whether the result would not be a rebuff for the Crown. In 1868 Mr. Disraeli was criticised for asking for a dissolution without calling a formal Cabinet meeting; the answer was that ten days before the Cabinet had assented to a policy of dissolution, so that the Premier could assume he had the right to act, and, in fact, his request was approved next day by the Cabinet.[5] Mr. Gladstone was so far from dissolving without consulting the Cabinet that on January 21, 1874, he informed the Queen that he would recommend that the Cabinet should advise dissolution, and Lord Granville simultaneously urged the Queen to view the idea favourably; the Cabinet on January 23 took the step unanimously. The Premier, it is true, had consulted only Lord Granville, Mr. Goschen, and Mr. Cardwell, but it was their objections, as heads of the navy and army departments, to Mr. Gladstone's requests for reduction of expenditure in his capacity of Chancellor of the Exchequer, which rendered

[5] Lord Malmesbury, *Memoirs of an Ex-Minister*, p. 639.

matters in the Cabinet decidedly difficult.[6] In 1895 the Cabinet
debated resignation or dissolution, and the accord of Lord Rosebery
and Sir W. Harcourt was sufficiently amazing to carry the day.
In 1900 dissolution was long discussed before Lord Salisbury gave
way. In 1905 Mr. Balfour's position is somewhat obscure, but not
on this point; Mr. Wyndham,[7] indeed, asserted that it lay alone
with him to advise a dissolution, but Mr. Balfour did not in the
slightest agree, and in his final decision to resign, he was acting with
the Cabinet, which had discussed, as in 1895, dissolution or resignation.[8] His view on dissolution, which annoyed the King in some
degree, was that it was in the power of the Commons to decide that
it was necessary, no doubt by ceasing to support the ministry
effectively; the King evidently ascribed a greater measure of
autonomy to his advisers, and to himself, as against the Commons.
In 1906, and in 1910, the Cabinet discussed and decided.[9]

The decision to dissolve now rests with the Prime Minister, and
apparently has done so since 1918. On that occasion Mr. Lloyd
George quite clearly took the lead, although the evidence on which
Mr. Bonar Law justified his behaviour was not historically accurate.[10] Since 1918, although the evidence is not complete, it
seems that no decision to dissolve has been brought before the
Cabinet, and Prime Ministers now assume a right to tender advice
to dissolve on their own account.[11] The present position was made
clearer in 1935. Describing that occasion, Sir John Simon wrote
that, 'the decision, whether there shall be an immediate general
election and, if so, on what date the country shall go to the polls,
rests with the Prime Minister, and until the Prime Minister has
decided, all anticipations are without authority.'[12] The wording
of this statement is not altogether free from ambiguity; it is compatible with the view that the principle of dissolution had been
discussed in Cabinet, but the details left to the Prime Minister.
Mr. Baldwin himself certainly, in justifying the choice of date, spoke
in the Commons as if he had decided the matter, but he did not
actually announce any constitutional principle in clear terms. We

---

6 *Letters of Queen Victoria*, 2 s., ii. 304–6.
7 G. W. Mackail and G. Wyndham, *Life and Letters of George Wyndham*, ii. 505.
8 Lee, *Edward VII.*, ii. 188–91; Esher, *Journals and Letters*, ii. 118–21.
9 Lord Oxford and Asquith, *Fifty Years of Parliament*, ii. 196.
10 110 *H. C. Deb.* 5 s., 2425.
11 M. A. Hamilton, *Life of Arthur Henderson*, p. 25; Clynes, *Memoirs*, ii. 63.
12 *The Times*, October 18, 1935.

are therefore not completely certain to what extent, if any, Cabinet discussion did take place. But Mr. Baldwin undoubtedly tended to magnify his office[13] and, in his first dealing with Edward VIII. on the abdication issue, he did not take any member of the Cabinet into his confidence. If this is so, it is not easy to say that the example he set was advantageous. The other members of a Cabinet are often not much, if at all, inferior in ability or popularity in the party to the Prime Minister, and to assume the right to dictate might prove dangerous in other cases.

There is every reason that the Cabinet should be consulted and decide such an issue, and the fact that the older practice has been departed from, to some degree, is no ground that further departure should take place. It is derogatory to the dignity of other Cabinet ministers, and tends to make them appear in the public eye the servants, rather than the equals, of the Prime Minister. It runs counter to the best aspects of the constitution, the doctrine of collective responsibility and deliberation, and it presumes that for some reason or other, in this vital issue, the Prime Minister has a pre-eminence in other issues denied to him. In the Dominions the doctrine is not accepted. The Prime Minister naturally has the initiative in proposing a dissolution,[14] but the recommendation goes forth from the Cabinet, and in New South Wales the Governor very properly refused to dissolve on the advice of Mr. Lang, not homologated by Cabinet, adopting in lieu the perfectly constitutional procedure of accepting the Premier's resignation, and then appointing him head of a new ministry which would advise dissolution. Dominion practice and early British practice seem sounder than the arrogation to himself of authority by a single mind, not necessarily of outstanding capacity as compared with those of his colleagues.

4. The Cabinet, the Crown, and the House of Lords.

The Cabinet, as we have seen, is dependent solely on the favour of the Commons, and, except when a Conservative Cabinet is in office, it is likely that its policy will find a measure of opposition in the Lords. Criticism and amendment in detail of Governmental measures it is unreasonable to resent, but, as the Upper Chamber has necessarily a strong leaning to Conservatism—whether for good

13 Keith, *The King, the Constitution, the Empire, and Foreign Affairs*, 1936–37, pp. 41–47.
14 Keith, *The Dominions as Sovereign States*, p. 355.

or evil—conflict between it and the Commons is in the nature of things. The one power which the Cabinet possessed, until 1911, to constrain the Lords to accept proposals of the Commons, was the plainly delicate power to add members to the Lords to swamp their resistance. Such swamping has occurred often enough in the Dominions in constitutions permitting thereof, by having nominee Upper Houses without any limitation of numbers.[15] These bodies tend inevitably to disappear under the operation of this process, as in Queensland in 1922, while the House of New South Wales was only rescued from destruction by being placed on a new basis. But to swamping in this way the Lords has always presented a grave obstacle in its hereditary character, no less than in its vast prestige derived from its great strength in past history, and from the wealth and social standing of its members. No doubt the Reform Act of 1832 secured the primacy of the Commons, but it was very long before that primacy was not liable to be thwarted by the resistance of the Upper Chamber.

The power of the Crown over the House of Lords, considerable under the Tudors in view of the disappearance of so many ancient names in the Wars of the Roses, had gradually lessened through new creations, and the right of the Crown to withhold a summons was successfully remonstrated against as early as 1626 in the case of the Earl of Bristol.[16] In the case of the Treaty of Utrecht in 1712 the peers showed sufficient hostility to acceptance of the surrender to a scion of the house of Bourbon of Spain and the West Indies, that twelve peers were hastily added to carry the day.[17] The precedent passed without special notice, but, when in 1830 reform became urgently necessary, the situation had changed.[18] The first Reform Bill introduced in March, 1831, passed second reading by one vote only, and in committee was amended on a vital point; a dissolution followed on April 22, and the second Bill passed in September, to be rejected by the Lords on October 8. The ministry, on receiving promise of royal support, passed another Bill through second reading on December 12, and, in order to secure its accept-ance by the hostile Lords, on January 13, 1832, advised the creation of peers so soon as it was evident that thus only could the measure

---

[15] Keith, *The Dominions as Sovereign States*, p. 250.
[16] Ridges, *Constitutional Law of England* (ed. Keith), p. 69.
[17] *Ibid.*, p. 93.
[18] See Grey, *Correspondence with William IV. and Sir Herbert Taylor*, ii., 96 ff.

be passed, arguing that the creation of peers was the only way to prevent the House of Lords from 'continuing to place itself in opposition to the general wishes of the nation, and to the declared sense of the House of Commons.'[19] The King gave a rather grudging assent, but his reply to the Cabinet's recommendation on March 27 that, if the peers rejected the Bill, a prorogation and creation of peers should follow, was not a categorical undertaking. On April 14 the Bill received a majority of nine on second reading, but was amended on May 7 to postpone consideration of the vital disfranchising clauses. The Cabinet then asked for creation of peers, but without success for the moment, though reinforced by an address to the Crown from the Commons passed by a majority of eighty on their resignation, asking the King to call to his Council those who would secure the passage of the Bill. An effort was made by the King to induce Lord Lyndhurst and the Duke of Wellington to take office in a ministry formed to support moderate but extensive reforms. Sir R. Peel held back and the Duke abandoned the commission on May 15; the King yielded, but sought to secure, by appeal on May 17, to the Duke and others, a declaration of the dropping of their opposition. The Cabinet, however, demanded indisputable security, and obtained it verbally and in writing on May 18, the King now giving a promise to create an unlimited number, though so far as possible the addition was to be made up of the eldest sons of peers and collateral heirs of childless peers, so as to reduce any permanent addition to the peerage.[20] It was, no doubt, this promise which was made public through Sir H. Taylor, the King's Secretary, which secured the third reading on June 4. It is quite unfair to pay any attention to Lord Brougham's doubts of twelve years later as to whether the King would have created peers,[21] if his appeals to them not to resist had proved ineffective; a King is entitled to be credited with good faith, and the whole procedure shows the sovereign being gradually and reluctantly, but ineluctably, drawn towards the logical solution. Whether Lord Esher thought so or not, and his wide knowledge of constitutional episodes was not equalled by his judgment thereon, the precedent was clear.[22]

19 See Grey, *Correspondence with William IV. and Sir Herbert Taylor*, ii., especially 96 ff.
20 *Ibid.*, ii. 434.
21 Lord Brougham, *Political Philosophy* (2nd ed.), iii. 308.
22 Lord Esher, *Influence of King Edward*, p. 78; *Journals and Letters*, ii. 424.

The conclusion to be drawn from this case was not very far-reaching. It established only that the prerogative to add members might be invoked where the Commons had a clear mandate, as shown by a general election, and where government could not be carried on in the face of the view of the Commons. The position, however, of the Commons was strengthened by Mr. Gladstone's success in establishing the supremacy of the Commons in finance by his action in respect of the claim of the Lords to refuse permission for the abolition of the duty on paper in 1860; by including in one measure the whole proposals of the Government next year, he presented the Lords with the alternative of rejecting the whole financial provisions or acquiescing in his project.[23] In other matters the Lords, as in the case of the disestablishment of the Church in Ireland, were accustomed to accept the clear voice of the electorate. The controversy over the franchise and redistribution in 1884–85 was animated, but accommodated fairly enough by securing that both steps were duly taken so as to coincide in effect. In 1906, however, a new note appeared in the Lords, whose ranks had been swollen by former Liberal peers who had deserted that cause on the Irish issue, or from dissatisfaction with the death duties of 1894. Many of them were not willing to acquiesce in the primacy of the Commons, and Lord Lansdowne asserted the claim that the Lords should arrest the progress of measures which they believed to have been insufficiently considered or not to represent the considered judgment of the country. This was a dangerous claim, because it was so indeterminate, for the system of general elections is not such as to give any mandate which cannot be attacked either because so many issues were combined, or that the electors really voted for men not measures, or that the number of seats gained, and of votes cast, was disproportionate, or that the majority included non-homogeneous elements. At any rate the rejection of the Bills for education and plural voting in 1906 elicited the determination of the Government that the powers of the Lords should be so restricted that the will of the Commons should prevail in the period of one Parliament. Steps to this end were forced on the ministry in 1909, when the Finance Bill was rejected by 350 votes to 75,[24] an act denounced by the Premier on December 2 as unconstitutional. It is stated that the Government for a time

[23] Bell, *Palmerston*, ii. 260 ff., 283 ff.; Morley, *Gladstone*, ii. 29 ff.
[24] For admission of the folly of these tactics see Newton, *Lansdowne*, pp. 375–83.

contemplated action in the form of advising the King to place in the hands of the Prime Minister the right to create peers, or, in the alternative, of a Bill accompanied by an intimation that the Crown would create peers to secure its passing if opposed.[25]   Lord Esher regarded this idea, placed before him by Lord Haldane, as inadmissible, and Mr. Balfour insisted that there could be no justification for the King giving a promise to secure the passing of a Bill not so far submitted to the Commons, while he was prepared to take office if the ministry resigned on the refusal of so unjust a request.[26]   Lord Knollys, after a dissolution had been granted without any arrangement, informed Mr. Asquith that the King had come to the conclusion that he would not be justified in creating new peers (say 300) until after a second general election, and that the country should be informed of the project, which would amount to the destruction of the Lords, before such an election.[27]   The ministry on February 11, 1910, in answer to an enquiry from the King about an election speech of Mr. Asquith's which seemed to imply the 'guarantees' to compel the Lords had already been obtained, formally assured the Crown that they did not 'propose to advise or request any exercise of the royal prerogative in existing circumstances, or until they have submitted their plan to Parliament. If, in their judgment, it should become their duty to tender such advice, they would do so when—and not before—the actual necessity may arise.'[28]   On February 21 Mr. Asquith reiterated this position in the Commons, and on April 14, on the first reading of the Parliament Bill, made it clear that, if the Bill were not passed, the Government would resign, or advise a dissolution, but 'in no case will we recommend a dissolution except under such conditions as will secure that in the new Parliament the judgment of the people, as expressed at the elections, will be carried into law.'[29]   Reference has been made above [30] to the Lambeth Palace meeting of April 27, when Mr. Balfour indicated his attitude, but the death of the King on May 6 ended this phase.

The possibility of compromise was afforded thus, and a conference met on June 17 and expired on November 10,[31] largely

---

[25] Esher, *Journals and Letters*, ii. 423–5 (December 1, 1909).
[26] *Ibid.*, ii. 435–7.
[27] Spender, *Lord Oxford*, i. 261.
[28] *Ibid.*, i. 273.   [29] 16 *H. C. Deb.* 5 s., 1548.
[30] See *ante*, p. 283.
[31] Spender, *Lord Oxford*, i. 285–91; Newton, *Lansdowne*, pp. 396–403.

because the Conservatives proved too exigent in their demands, which plainly were based on their essential desire to safeguard themselves from the passing of a Home Rule Bill, as the Government had at the last election rid itself of the limitation of action announced in 1906. On November 11 Mr. Asquith pointed out to the King that the Cabinet had decided on recommending an immediate dissolution, and that it was necessary that, in the event of the Government obtaining an adequate majority in the new House of Commons, the matter should be put in train for settlement. The withholding of summonses to peers would probably be un-constitutional, the creation of peers was indisputably constitutional, and the knowledge that the Crown would use the prerogative would be sufficient to bring about acceptance. On November 15 the Cabinet formally advised a dissolution, but only on the under-standing that 'in the event of the policy of the Government being approved by an adequate majority in the new House of Commons, His Majesty will be ready to exercise his constitutional powers (which may involve the prerogative of creating peers) if needed to secure that effect shall be given to the decision of the country.'[32] It was added that the King would 'doubtless agree that it would be inadvisable in the interest of the State that any communication of the intentions of the Crown should be made public, unless and until the actual occasion should arise.' The advice was repeated by Mr. Asquith and Lord Crewe personaly on November 16, and accepted by the King on the understanding that the Parliament Bill would be submitted to the Lords before the election, which was duly done before the dissolution.[33]

This silence was remarkable and very inconvenient, as was proved, when on January 27, 1911, the King saw, with the reluctant consent of Mr. Asquith, Lord Lansdowne.[34] Lord Lansdowne explained the position of the party in vague terms, but agreed that for Mr. Balfour to win an election would be very difficult at the time. It is not clear what purpose this interview served, but probably the King hoped that, in view of the reluctance he would feel to creating peers, and to the plain fact that, if asked, he could have no alternative, Lord Lansdowne might secure the acceptance of the Governmental proposals, or something near enough to alter

[32] Spender, *Lord Oxford*, i. 296 f.
[33] Newton, *Lansdowne*, pp. 407–411.
[34] *Ibid.*, pp. 409 ff.

the position for him vitally. If so, his hope was not fulfilled. The Lords in Committee from June 28 to July 14 so altered the Bill that on the latter date the Cabinet, denying the possibility of a third dissolution, advised the exercise of the prerogative without doubt that the sovereign would feel it to be his constitutional duty to accept their advice. The royal assent was given on July 17.[35] The fact was communicated on July 18 by Mr. Lloyd George to Mr. Balfour and Lord Lansdowne, and formally on July 20, immediately after the third reading of the Bill, by Mr. Asquith, who insisted that he, as responsible, not the King, should act.[36] Next day it was considered by a meeting of Unionist peers, and Lord Lansdowne saw the King on July 24, learning his anxiety, and that of the Government, to limit the creation. On that date Mr. Asquith was shouted down when he attempted to state the position in the Commons on the consideration of the amendments from that House.[37] On August 7 a vote of censure was moved in the Commons on the unconstitutional advice given to the King, Mr. Balfour suggesting that advantage had been taken of the King's lack of personal experience, while Mr. Asquith insisted on the absolute correctness of his action. On August 8, on a like vote in the Lords, Lord Crewe, with royal sanction, explained the interview of November 16, 1910, but further than that he felt it unwise to do. The King's reluctance had been explained, and the fact that he had no alternative but to accept or dismiss ministers, when an election would have been fought against him personally, was plain. In the Lords, when the Bill was sent back with only one slight change accepted, Lord Morley read with royal sanction the words: 'if the Bill should be defeated to-night His Majesty will assent to the creation of peers sufficient in numbers to guard against any possible combination of the different parties in opposition, by which the Parliament Bill might be exposed a second time to defeat.'[38] The result was that 131 peers gave assent to 117 negatives. The Archbishop of Canterbury, Lord Rosebery, and Lord Curzon helped the victory, as did the Archbishop of York and eleven bishops, while Lord Lansdowne abstained. Some peers voted simply to prevent the creation of rivals. Lord Halsbury and others showed reckless disregard of the unwisdom of resistance.[39]

[35] Spender, *Lord Oxford*, i. 310. [36] *Ibid.*; Newton, *Lansdowne*, pp. 417 ff.
[37] Spender, *Lord Oxford*, i. 314. [38] Morley, *Recollections*, ii. 353.
[39] Fitzroy, *Memoirs*, ii. 457–61; cf. Spender, *Lord Oxford*, ii. 312 ff.

The measure[40] thus passed puts complete power over a money Bill so certified by the Speaker, whose decision cannot be questioned in any Court, in the hands of the Commons, though the Lords must have it before them for a month before the end of the session. Other Bills, except a Bill to extend the duration of Parliament, or to confirm a provisional order, may be passed over the head of the Lords if passed for three consecutive sessions in one or more Parliaments and not accepted, either without amendments or with amendments accepted by the Commons, in each session, the Bill having been sent up at least a month before the end of the session. Two years, at least, must elapse between the second reading in the first session and the date of passing in the third session.[41] The rule is confined to public Bills, but the Commons has full power to decide what shall be passed as a public Bill.

Can the royal prerogative now be invoked to overcome resistance when it is not desired to wait the length of time allowed to the Lords for suspending veto? Sir S. Cripps and other Labour leaders have expressed the view that it can be used, and that it might be necessary to use it to secure the effective working of their plans for immediate socialisation. The position is difficult, because the provision of a deadlock procedure normally means that constitutionally it should be resorted to, and it must be remembered that the powers of constitutional change under procedure of the Acts of 1911 and 1949 are almost unlimited, so that there is no excuse that long delay would be occasioned, even on a proposal to abolish the House itself. No doubt, if the ministry has a very clear mandate for immediate action, the King might have to yield, for in that case to force a dissolution would be unwise in the interests of the Crown as suggesting, not desire to preserve the constitution, but prejudice against Labour. If, however, the mandate were less clear, it would certainly be constitutional to urge strongly procedure by the appointed process, and a Government might well accept, rather than face a hotly contested election fought over action, which would in any case be rather abnormal. One result of the halving of the length of veto by the Parliament Act of 1949, however, is that this difficulty should be much less likely to occur in the future.

It must be remembered that, while the King cannot ultimately defy the electorate, he has a limited power of delaying action. A

[40] 1 & 2 Geo. V. c. 13.   [41] Altered by the Parliament Act, 1949, to one year.

minority Government might be created if a majority denied its request for swamping of the Upper House resigned, and, if the Appropriation Act had been already passed, it might carry on for a time, for the Act gives power to spend, and supplementary sums might be taken from the civil contingencies fund, or borrowed under the terms of the Act. For the rest, the risk might be taken of seeking to borrow more money, but it must be remembered that the assent to expenditure of the Comptroller and Auditor-General is requisite, and he might raise insuperable difficulties.[42] If the Finance Act had been passed, then revenue would be available, but not if that were not the case, for the Provisional Collection of Taxes Act, 1913, permits only levying under resolutions for a fixed time.[43] If the Army and Air Force (Annual) Act had not been passed, the effort of a minority Government to carry on could be destroyed forthwith. On the whole the financial difficulties may be exaggerated, but they are very serious, and a minority Government would probably have at once to make it clear that it merely proposed to carry on for a brief period in order to allow the country quiet reflection and time to recover from the excitement and strain of a general election.

An issue of very substantial importance is suggested by the question of the secrecy observed and maintained successfully regarding the King's promise of November 16, 1910. Lord Morley preserved it, even in his discussion of December 12 with Sir A. Fitzroy,[44] and there is no doubt that the Opposition leaders found it hard to believe that it had been given when the fact was revealed to them. It may be held that the procedure was justified on the score that it obviated bringing the position of the King under party attack during the election of 1910. But this appears to be a very unconvincing argument, hardly to be taken seriously. Candour would seem to have required that the country should have been told quite frankly of the pledge, so that the electors could have cast their votes knowing what the result would be. It must be assumed that the Government, in urging secrecy, thought that this course of

---

[42] Cf. A. Chamberlain, *Politics from Inside*, pp. 258 f.   In 1909–10 the Government carried on without a Finance Act; cf. *ibid.*, p. 218.

[43] Four months from the date of the resolution; 3 Geo. V. c. 3.   The Act was due to *Bowles* v. *Bank of England*, [1913] 1 Ch. 57.   For the solution of the financial difficulties of the rejection of the Finance Bill in 1909, see Spender, *Lord Oxford*, i. 275 n. 1.

[44] Fitzroy, *Memoirs*, ii. 427.   Cf. Dugdale, *Arthur James Balfour*, ii. 63.

action would be of advantage to them; that is, their attitude was merely tactical. It is impossible to see how the position of the King could have been attacked during the election if the fact of the pledge had been known. It would have been clear that the King was taking the perfectly proper course of leaving the people a definite decision to make in full knowledge of what they were doing. The earlier declarations of the Government, it is arguable, should have been taken as making it clear that they were assured that the King would act as they desired in the event of success at the election, but the matter should have been candidly stated. It may be hoped that in any future instance secrecy will not be practised. Though ministers are, of course, responsible for it, it must involve the King in some measure of discredit among those who feel that in such a matter he is entitled to ask, and to insist, that no mystery be made regarding his line of action.

A further point regarding the relations of the ministry and the Lords was raised in the controversy over the Home Rule Bill of 1912–14. An idea was suggested in March, 1914, that the peers should reject the Army Annual Bill, thus depriving the Government of any power to use the forces to coerce Ireland.[45] Fortunately Mr. Asquith was able to secure the bringing of influence to bear to prevent the scheme developing into action; it may legitimately be supposed that the King intimated that he could not approve a step which would have rendered the existence of the whole of the army illegal in the face of the growing dangers in Europe. How far the resistance of the Opposition in 1914 rendered greater the likelihood of Germany going to war in August will never be determined, but that it had some effect is probable.

5. The Participation of the King in the Formation of Policy and in Government

(a) The King's Relations to the Cabinet

THE Cabinet, as we have seen, is a body whose duty it is to decide on policy, which is then carried out by other branches of the Government. Its decisions must have the approval, express or tacit, of the King, and not only are the minutes of the Cabinet

---

[45] Austen Chamberlain shares responsibility for this most dangerous suggestion; *Politics from Inside*, pp. 609, 619–21.

promptly supplied to him, but it is the duty of the Prime Minister
to keep him fully informed of all major matters. The trouble, of
course, is to decide what matters are major and at what stage the
sovereign should be informed.

Prior to the creation of the Cabinet Secretariat, the Prime
Minister was wont to write a note of the decisions of the Cabinet
in his own hand. The date when the practice began is not
recorded, but no doubt it must practically have been contemporaneous with the cessation under George I. of the practice of
the sovereign presiding over the deliberations of the Cabinet.
Edward VII. was by no means prepared to excuse slackness in this
report; he reminded Mr. Balfour that it should be of the old type,
four sides of a quarto sheet, although it may be surmised that
towards the end Lord Salisbury was briefer than desirable.[46]
Under Queen Victoria, not only did the Prime Ministers report on
Cabinet decisions, but, beginning with Sir R. Peel, each night of
Parliament they sent a summary of what had happened in Parliament;[47] some examples are found in the *Letters*. Edward VII.[48]
relaxed the rule; he permitted the Home Secretary to report, and
did not demand that it be sent the same evening. George V.
allowed the practice to lapse: when the Debates were delayed, as
under the Queen, the value of the letter might be asserted; though
the Press gave full information, it might be biased; under modern
conditions of rapid publication of the Debates, the letter is no doubt
less valuable. It is characteristic of Mr. Gladstone that only in his
last ministry did he delegate the work with royal assent to Sir W.
Harcourt, who was less *persona ingrata* to the Queen than he.[49]

The Cabinet is in policy a unity, after discussion, but no one
doubts that there are divergent views, and these are often allowed
to leak out by accident or design. It was obvious in 1938, before
Mr. Eden's resignation, that the Press were not badly informed of
the trend of Cabinet feeling, however wrong in theory this must be.
But how far should the Prime Minister go in revealing the secrets of
Cabinet divisions to the sovereign. It is clearly arguable, as
Mr. Gladstone held,[50] that the Prime Minister should in his

---

[46] Lee, *Edward VII.*, ii. 47.
[47] *Letters of Queen Victoria*, 1 s., i. 405.
[48] Lee, *Edward VII*, ii. 47.
[49] See, *e.g.*, *Letters of Queen Victoria*, 3 s., ii. 222, 224. For the publication of the
Debates, see H. D. Jordan, *Economica*, xi. 437–48.
[50] Gladstone, *Gleanings of Past Years*, i. 74 f., 243.

dealing with the sovereign adopt, with complete loyalty, the decisions of the Cabinet; he should not attempt to counteract the work of his colleagues, to increase his share of royal favour at their expense, or to pursue aims not shared by them. But it must be admitted that this is a counsel of perfection, which has been more often ignored than adhered to. Presumably it is felt that, as no one doubts that there are Cabinet differences, and newspapers refer to them with more or less imaginative detail, it is better for the sovereign to be frankly informed. Nor are there lacking cases where the Prime Minister seems to have invoked the influence of the sovereign to secure from his colleagues acceptance of his views of policy.

There is, of course, no doubt that before 1832 the sovereign was freely informed of dissensions, and we find George IV. deliberately asking Lord Liverpool, in view of Mr. Canning's recognition of the South American republics, for the individual views of the members of Cabinet, whether or not certain principles of policy were to be abandoned. The reply, however, was not in the form desired, for it was given generally and collectively, stating that there had been differences, but there was unanimity that the action taken did not conflict with the principles in question.[51] Under William IV. the Cabinet minute as to creation of peers on which the King was unwilling to act included a dissent by the Duke of Richmond, and later difficulty arose when Lord Grey resumed power, because the King had shown it to the Duke of Wellington when asking him to form a Government.[52] Lord Melbourne, as might be expected, told the Queen freely of differences of opinion. Thus in 1837 he notes Lord Howick's wise desire for conciliation, as well as repression, in Canada, and in 1839 his probably just strictures on the civil administration of the army,[53] while in 1840 the Cabinet decision on Egypt was accompanied by minutes dissenting therefrom by Lords Clarendon and Holland.[54] On the other hand, despite Prince Albert's desire that the practice of William IV. should be renewed, and the Queen be made aware of the course of argument in the Cabinet, ignorance of which he deemed a great weakness of the Crown, Sir R. Peel was reticent,

[51] A. G. Stapleton, *Political Life of George Canning*, pp. 418–20.
[52] Grey, *Correspondence with William IV.*, ii. 395, 424, 431.
[53] *Letters of Queen Victoria*, 1 s., i. 184–5.
[54] Sir Herbert Maxwell, *Life of Lord Clarendon*, i. 193 ff.; Bell, *Palmerston*, i. 301.

even as to the dissent in 1845,[55] as to the Corn Laws, which led to the attempt to form a new ministry.

Lord Stanley naturally explained his views for dissent, and Sir R. Peel explained the extent of the dissent when he had resumed office. Lord John Russell was also in favour of reticence.

But naturally enough under the régime of Lord Aberdeen, which was a coalition, there was free disclosure of divisions, not only by the Prime Minister,[56] but by Lord John Russell[57] and Sir James Graham.[58] On the contrary Lord Palmerston insisted that the Cabinet was always mentioned by him as an aggregate body.[59] Yet in 1865 we find him explaining to the Queen Mr. Gladstone's objections to military and naval expenditure,[60] but he and Mr. Gladstone often had difficulties, such as that already mentioned over the Paper Duties Bill, which his chief encouraged the Lords to reject.[61] On the other hand, the Queen had in Lord Granville a source of information,[62] and received with satisfaction his advice to insist that the foreign policy of the Prime Minister and Lord Russell should be submitted to the whole Cabinet.[63] This emphasises the essential principle that it is the right of the sovereign to insist that she be advised by the Cabinet. Lord Granville again provided in 1868–74 the information which Mr. Gladstone deliberately withheld; we know from him that the Cabinet overruled Mr. Gladstone and Mr. Cardwell when they felt inclined to drop the Bill for the disestablishment of the Irish Church, despairing of the sudden conversion of the Lords, which was finally secured.[64] Mr. Disraeli throughout his career was eager to inform the Crown, undoubtedly thereby adding to his authority in a high degree.[65] Most important of all was his action in the Russo-Turkish discussions of 1877–78 in inducing the Queen, who no doubt fully shared his views, and may in part have inspired them—the interaction of their minds cannot definitely be cleared up—to put pressure on the Cabinet to accept a very strong line of pro-Turkish

[55] *Letters of Queen Victoria*, 1 s., ii. 63; Parker, *Peel*, iii. 234 ff.
[56] *Letters of Queen Victoria*, 1 s., ii. 573–5; iii. 27.
[57] *Ibid.*, 1 s., iii. 26.
[58] *Ibid.*, 1 s., ii. 552–4.
[59] Guedalla, *Gladstone and Palmerston*, pp. 258 f.
[60] *Letters of Queen Victoria*, 2 s., i. 248.   [61] Bell, *Palmerston*, ii. 260 ff.
[62] Fitzmaurice, *Granville*, i. 349 ff., 469 ff.; ii. 123.
[63] *Letters of Queen Victoria*, 2 s., i. 66 ff. (Poland); 180 ff. (Denmark).
[64] *Ibid.*, 2 s., i. 622; iii. 246–7.
[65] Monypenny and Buckle, *Disraeli*, ii. 1024, 1027, 1043–4, 1065–7.

policy.   Lord Derby resigned and Lord Carnarvon is authority for
the fact that at this time the Queen saw ministers personally and
dictated her ideas of policy.

The issue was definitely raised by the Queen in 1880 when,
basing her request on newspaper assertions of dissensions, she
demanded information from Lord Granville, if he could not induce
the Premier to tell her.   Mr. Gladstone's views did not change, and
in 1885 she tried to reinforce her claim by allusions to the precedent
of Sir R. Peel and Lord J. Russell, as well as Lords Melbourne and
Beaconsfield; so far as can be seen, the argument as regards the two
former is untenable.   Mr. Gladstone gave her some information
as to views on the Irish issue,[66] but he never in any degree satisfied
her.   In his last ministry the Queen obtained some information
from Lord Rosebery,[67] especially as regards the strength of the
British forces in Egypt, on which he had the backing of Mr. Bryce,
but he insisted on the fair attitude of Sir W. Harcourt.   He also
invoked and received her aid in pressing his policy in that matter.
Mr. Gladstone, no doubt, knew in 1892 of Lord Rosebery's strong
objection on the issue of Uganda to the trend of the view of the
Cabinet, as being likely to be known to the Queen, when he alluded
to it in one of his rare revelations of divergence of view in the
Cabinet,[68] and he refrained from any statements of differences of
opinion on the Home Rule Bill of 1893.[69]   Lord Rosebery, as
Prime Minister, does not seem to have given much information,
but he did defend himself in his desire to reform the Lords by
reference to the fact that half the Cabinet favoured a single Chamber
only.[70]   Lord Salisbury again reverted to the tradition of Lord
Beaconsfield, at least, in his later days.[71]   He had in 1885 concealed
successfully from the Queen the strange dealings of certain members
of the Government with the Irish Nationalists in their efforts to
obtain Home Rule from the Conservative Party.

Under Edward VII. Mr. Asquith does not seem to have been
anxious to be reticent in this topic.   On February 2, 1909, he
informed the King of disagreement,[72] but when the latter thought
that there had been further discussions of which he had not been

---

[66] *Letters of Queen Victoria*, 2 s., iii. 652 ff.
[67] *Ibid.*, 3 s., ii. 211; she had appealed to him in 1885; see *ibid.*, 2 s., iii. 640.
She appealed also to Lord Granville, 642 ff.
[68] *Ibid.*, 3 s., ii. 160 ff.   [69] *Ibid.*, 3 s., ii. 277 ff.
[70] Cf. his explanation of Sir W. Harcourt's hostility; *ibid.*, 3 s., ii. 398–400.
[71] *E.g., ibid.*, 3 s., i. 10, 201 f., 211, 229.   [72] Lee, *Edward VII.*, ii. 678 f.

informed, he was assured that this was not the case, and full details were given when the Cabinet deliberated and the issue of four, six or eight Dreadnoughts divided the ministry. He did not, however, mention to the King, it seems, Lord Morley's doubts on the issue of the Parliament Bill, which was too radical for that peer's Whig mind.[73] He informed the King of resignations in the Cabinet on the war issue, but only when they became sufficiently mature.[74] He seems also to have kept the King informed of all important dissensions in the War Cabinet[75]; apparently the Retaliation Order in Council of March, 1915, resulted in acceptance by the Prime Minister, Sir E. Grey and Lord Crewe of the views of the majority, headed by Mr. Churchill, but the administration of the Order was much restrained in order to prevent acerbation of feeling in the United States. He also reported the meeting of the Cabinet of June 27, 1916, when an effort was made, despite most remarkable divergences of view, to secure accord on Ireland, an attempt fated to be a failure after an apparent success.[76] Under the new scheme of Cabinet minutes the record shows the divergent arguments adduced, but not the names of those who adduce them. It remains, no doubt, for the Prime Minister, in his dealings with the Crown, to reveal as he may think fit how voices went.

The desire of the sovereign to know of divisions of opinion is quite natural, for it increases his power over the Prime Minister and the Cabinet alike. Yet there are plainly disadvantages. There is the risk of the sovereign becoming a partisan, and definitely taking sides, more probably with the Prime Minister, but possibly with the minority of ministers, which must render relations with the Prime Minister strained. It is rather unfair to dissentient ministers to have the fact brought before the Crown, for it may be prejudiced by representations made *ex parte*. But the case of the Queen's attitude to Lord Randolph Churchill in 1885 was really determined by the latter's speech in the Commons, and the Premier was quite generous in his defence of his attack on Lord Spencer's Irish administration, insisting that Lord Randolph was only adhering to an attitude expressed while in opposition, and was not bound by Parliamentary practice to alter in office an opinion relative to the merits, or otherwise, of past policy.[77] But it does not seem

[73] Esher, *Letters and Papers*, ii. 453–5.
[74] Spender, *Lord Oxford*, ii. 81 ff.   [75] *Ibid.*, ii. 131, 219.
[76] *Ibid.*, ii. 218 ff.   [77] *Letters of Queen Victoria*, 2 s., iii. 688 f.

doubtful that the report by Lord Salisbury of opposition in Cabinet to the efforts of the Queen to obtain restoration to power of Prince Alexander of Bulgaria caused the Queen irritation against the malcontents. It appeared, however, that behind the difficulty in this case there loomed one much greater, the question of maintaining the traditional British policy of hostility to Russian advance in South-East Europe. Mr. Smith, Lord George Hamilton, and Lord R. Churchill were hostile, on the score that it was a futile policy, while Lord Salisbury, who shared the majority view, admitted that the actions of the Turkish Government made efforts to aid it very difficult.[78] It is amusing to find that the Queen was anxious to prevent Foreign Office business being brought before the Cabinet at this time. That was clearly unsound, even if Lord Salisbury could not say so, since he had advised that Lord Rosebery should act in this sense.[79]

It is clear that it is better for the Cabinet to act as a unity, but equally clear that it is impossible to prevent individual members revealing their views to the sovereign. The sovereign must obviously not conceal that this has been done from the Premier; this was admitted by William IV. when Lord Melbourne in 1834 protested against a communication by Lord John Russell. When Lord Melbourne described Lord Russell's action as 'subversive of all principles upon which the Government of this country has hitherto been conducted,' the King replied that he 'had never contemplated for a moment holding correspondence with any of your colleagues, or with anyone, on questions affecting the Government, of the nature and extent of which the individual at the head of the Government should be ignorant.'[80] But, if the Prime Minister cares to reveal differences of view, he can ask the sovereign to aid in smoothing them out. In October, 1840, the Queen wrote to Lord Palmerston, obviously on Lord Melbourne's inspiration, endeavouring to bring him into a more moderate spirit on the issue of relations with France.[81] But more important was her skill in inducing General Peel to remain in Lord Derby's Government in 1867, when desirous of resigning over reform.[82]

Edward VII.'s efforts were chiefly directed to endeavouring to

---

[78] *Letters of Queen Victoria,* 3 s., i. 202.　　　[79] *Ibid.,* 3 s., i. 211.
[80] *Melbourne Papers,* pp. 215 ff.　　　[81] *Letters of Queen Victoria,* 1 s., i. 304.
[82] *Ibid.,* 2 s., i. 399. The Queen urged the Premier to jettison the dissentients if need be.

induce members of the Cabinet to avoid undue violence of speech, and he resented deeply the vehemence of Mr. Lloyd George's attacks on the Upper House, nor would he believe that the Prime Minister could like them.[83]   Even Mr. Harcourt offended by references to 'black hand of the peerage' and 'edicts of assassination' of Governmental measures, on July 15, 1909, but in that case there was the additional aggravation that the King had just been his guest.[84]   Mr. Lloyd George and Mr. Churchill also were offenders in their allusions to foreign policies, and had to receive instruction from Sir E. Grey in the rules of etiquette in this regard.[85]   The King also insisted on having the definite advice, after full consideration by the Cabinet, that an Indian member should be added to the Council of the Governor-General, and when he yielded to that advice, he put his doubts on record.[86]

A very difficult issue presents itself on the point how far it is necessary for the Prime Minister to inform the sovereign of matters which are not covered by his Cabinet reports and therefore known to him.   It is clear that courtesy alone demands that nothing major should be done without information being given.   In the case where the royal prerogative is concerned, apart from the final formal assent, it is necessary that the royal consent to discussion should be obtained before the measure passes either House.   Thus Lord Granville was right in 1863, when he asked the Lord Chancellor to hold over for such consent a Bill to deal with the Crown livings.[87]   When Mr. Gladstone commenced in opposition in 1868 his effort to disestablish the Irish Church, he duly proceeded, by way of address, praying the Crown to place at the disposal of Parliament its interest in the temporalities of that Church,[88] and in the case of the various Bills brought forward for the purpose of affecting the creation of peers, royal permission for discussion has been duly obtained,[89] as also in the case of a measure, the Peace Bill, 1935, in the Commons, intended to limit the authority of the Crown to declare war.   In other cases, however, the propriety of early intimation of legislation is plain, and Lord Melbourne duly

83 Lee, *Edward VII.*, ii. 456 ff.   84 *Ibid.*, ii. 665 f.
85 *Ibid.*, ii. 655.   86 *Ibid.*, ii. 388 f.
87 *Letters of Queen Victoria*, 2 s., i. 77 f.
88 *Ibid.*, 2 s., i. 517; see Fitzmaurice, *Granville*, i. 521–26, for the issue whether he could have acted otherwise.
89 Asquith, *Fifty Years of Parliament*, ii. 95; Keith, *Imperial Relations*, 1916–35, p. 256.

apologised for bringing in a Bill dealing with municipal corporations in Ireland without prior notice to the King, who clearly ought not to have to read the papers to know what legislation is on foot.[90] The Queen also had a good case in 1864,[91] when she took exception to Mr. Gladstone's expressing, when speaking on behalf of the Government, a view tantamount to recognising the eligibility of every person for the franchise, for the policy was not that of the ministry, and in fact deeply shocked Lord Palmerston. On the other hand, her efforts to prevent even the discussion of the Report of the Hartington Commission, which recommended the abolition of the office of Commander-in-Chief, were quite illegitimate,[92] and equally impossible was her demand that Lord Rosebery should not intimate any new policy without consultation with her.[93] Lord Rosebery made an effective and conclusive answer. If his proposals on the House of Lords had been intended to be brought before the Commons, he would, after mature Cabinet consideration, have submitted them to the Queen, but this principle could not well apply to proposals laid before a popular audience. To this it may be objected that, if a Government is to adopt a fundamental change of policy, then the matter should be determined in Cabinet, and then submitted for information to the Queen, who then could have the opportunity of suggesting difficulties, and endeavouring to modify the policy. But this ignores the fact that policy cannot well be formed and determined upon by the Cabinet without some idea of the public attitude thereon, and when it is inchoate a procedure like that on this occasion of Lord Rosebery may be necessary in order to determine whether the time is ripe for action of the kind. But Lord Salisbury went to the length, when consulted, no doubt improperly by the Queen, of contending that, if a Premier submitted a policy, and the Queen did not accept, he must resign. The result would follow that every new policy would be accepted as approved by the Crown, and that the country would be asked to fight against plans which had the royal backing. On the other hand, the Queen had a perfectly valid grievance, when for some unexplained cause, the Spion Kop correspondence was issued without her sanction, and apparently by some blunder of Lord Lansdowne's.[94] Edward VII. had an even better case, for his

[90] *Lord Melbourne's Papers*, pp. 307 ff. [91] *Letters of Queen Victoria*, 2 s., i. 189 f.
[92] *Ibid.*, 3 s., i. 577 ff. [93] *Ibid.*, 3 s., ii. 433 ff.
[94] *Ibid.*, 3 s., iii. 533, 536, 538, 541.

dislike of the terms of the declaration against transubstantiation, which he had to make before reading his first speech at the opening of Parliament, had secured the appointment of a committee to consider the possibility of changing the declaration, and its report was issued without communication to him, much to his indignation, by authority of the Lord Chancellor, who failed when rebuked to show serious repentance.[95]   It must be added that the King had further reason for annoyance, for the Bill, carried by Lord Salisbury through the Lords, was unsatisfactory, and the Government left the whole matter over to be disposed of in 1910 by the Liberal ministry in the inoffensive Accession Declaration Act.[96]   In 1905 another error took place, for the delicate correspondence between Lord Curzon and Mr. Brodrick, regarding the position of the Indian military department and the Commander-in-Chief, was published without his consent.[97]   Moreover, Cabinet decisions were, as Lord Esher pointed out, constantly being taken under Mr. Balfour without any prior information to the King, and he naturally feared that matters would be even worse under a Liberal régime.   In fact, Sir H. Campbell-Bannerman was not fond of sending long communications, and even so important a measure as the Education Bill was intimated to the King inadequately, to his annoyance.[98] The same annoyance was renewed, when during the progress of that Bill on July 17th, 1906, Mr. Lloyd George spoke as if a Minister for Wales had been decided upon, for the King demanded to know why this had not been before him earlier, and it had to be explained that all that was meant was a proposal to have a minister in charge of education for Wales.[99]   Mr. Lloyd George's subsequent attacks on the Lords for their treatment of the Bill, and his demand (December 1), whether the country is to be governed by the King and his peers, or by the King and his people, caused fresh annoyance, but on this occasion the Premier was prepared to defend his minister in view of the provocation given by the peers.[1]   The King was also deeply irritated by later phases of the attack, as above mentioned, and by Mr. Lloyd George's attitude on female suffrage, especially his speech at the Albert Hall on December 5, 1908, but the Premier pointed out that the issue was deliberately left open in

---

95 Lee, *Edward VII.*, ii. 23 f.
96 Ridges, *Constitutional Law of England* (ed. Keith), p. 108.
97 Esher, *Journals and Letters*, ii. 103–7, where an interesting comment on older usage is given.
98 Lee, *Edward VII.*, ii. 455, 460 ff.   99 *Ibid.*, ii. 456.   1 *Ibid.*, ii. 457.

the Cabinet.[2] Mr. Asquith, however, as little as his predecessor complied with the royal standard of the giving of information, and no doubt the sovereign did not feel inclined to adopt Lord Esher's advice to bombard his ministers with demands for information.[3]

There is little evidence how far of late the King has been kept fully informed of Cabinet proposals, and of proposals which may be brought before the Cabinet. There is evidence that he was taken fully into confidence by Mr. Asquith on the various war developments, and his letter of satisfaction at the passing of the first Conscription Act is on record.[4] He was also notified of the necessity of reconstruction in 1916, and his action thereupon has been noted. There is no reason to doubt that Mr. Lloyd George followed the attitude of his predecessor in personal discussions and in communications. Of later practice there may be some more doubt. The affair of the Cabinet approval of the disastrous Hoare-Laval agreement in December, 1935, regarding Ethiopia suggests that the King was not effectively consulted in any way. The account given of the events leading up to the abdication of Edward VIII. suggests strongly that the Prime Minister and his sovereign were not always in close communication. It is as yet too soon to know in any detail the evidence for the present reign. It is clear, however, that during the war of 1939–45 the King himself took a continuous and active interest in his minister's problems, and that the Prime Minister, Mr. Churchill, not only recognised the King's constitutional right 'to be made acquainted with everything for which his ministers are responsible,' but also was 'most careful that everything should be laid before the King.'[5]

It need hardly be said that the sovereign is in no wise bound to await ministerial initiative on any head. Queen Victoria was always ready to suggest the necessity of considering the strength of the defence forces, and had, as we have seen, strong views on Russo-Turkish policy, and on the treatment of Bulgaria and its Prince by the Czar, which she deeply resented. It is recorded that the Prince Consort drafted the instructions for the new volunteer corps, which the Cabinet approved,[6] and that he submitted in 1855 a plan

---

[2] Lee, *Edward VII.*, ii. 653.

[3] For the failure of Mr. Asquith to keep him informed of the proceedings regarding the illegal procession of Roman Catholics on September 13, 1908, see *ibid.*, ii. 659 ff.

[4] Spender, *Lord Oxford*, ii. 212.   [5] Churchill, *Second World War*, ii. 335.

[6] Martin, *Prince Consort*, iv. 437.

for the command of the army in the Crimea.[7] More interesting
is the vehement appeal of the Queen in 1872[8] for steps to increase
security of railway travel and punctuality; no doubt she had felt
the difficulty in the latter respect in her pilgrimages to Balmoral, for
the northern service remained unsatisfactory until long after the
end of her reign.   Of the initiative of later sovereigns there is less
direct evidence, but Edward VIII.'s personal tours of inspection of
depressed areas evidently impelled him to second, or even encourage, energetically the efforts of the ministry to relieve their
difficulties, a matter taken up with satisfactory results under
George VI., whose interest in the promotion of the physical welfare
and recreation of his subjects is also recorded.

The sovereign is naturally entitled to expect that the Prime
Minister shall always be available for consultation except as otherwise arranged.[9]   Hence the royal rebuke to Mr. Gladstone for his
unexpected but quite impromptu visit to Denmark in 1883, which
assumed a serious aspect in her eyes, because he was invited by the
King to meet several royal personages.[10]   But her indignation led
her into writing a letter called 'somewhat unmannerly' by Mr.
Gladstone.   There was much more cause for annoyance in the case
of Mr. Asquith's failure to pay Edward VII. a visit at Windsor, at
the end of January, 1910.[11]   It is clear that the incident was
merely inadvertent, and was not due to illness, and the King was
not prepared to accept an effort by Mrs. Asquith to mitigate his
just annoyance.   Mr. Asquith, however, made due amends, and
immediately on his return from Cannes visited the King at Brighton,
where he obtained not merely his acceptance of the minister's
changes consequent on the appointment of Lord Gladstone to
South Africa, but his aid in ascertaining how far the Opposition
leaders would go in aiding the Government to pass the budget,[12]
then seriously threatened by the probable revolt of the Irish

7 Martin, *Prince Consort*, iii. 381 ff.
8 *Letters of Queen Victoria*, 2 s., ii. 229–30.   She also persuaded (she believed) Mr.
Gladstone and Mr. Acland of the dangers of over-educating the working
classes; *ibid.*, 3 s., ii. 380 f.
9 Sir W. Harcourt, as leader of the Commons, asked leave in 1894; *Letters of
Queen Victoria*, 3 s., ii. 421 f.
10 Guedalla, *The Queen and Mr. Gladstone*, ii. 47, 242–48; *Letters of Queen Victoria*,
2 s., iii. 440, 444.
11 Spender, *Lord Oxford*, i. 270; Lee, *Edward VII.*, ii. 697, n. 1; Esher, *Journals
and Letters*, ii. 443 f.; the versions of this incident can be reconciled by dint of
some interpretation only.
12 Newton, *Lansdowne*, p. 389; Dugdale, *Arthur James Balfour*, ii. 59 f.

members. The result of the King's consultation was mainly negative, but the action taken bears out Mr. Spender's claim that the King's relations with his Premier were satisfactory, despite the annoyance inherent to the sovereign's position therein involved.[13]

(b) The King and the Work of the Departments

As the Cabinet has advisory functions and decides but does not carry out policy, the connection of the King with the actual working of the departments is essential if he is to be able to take a full part in the process of government. It is in the departments or the Privy Council that advice is prepared for acts to be done by the King, and it is also necessary that, even where no action of his is required, he should be familiar with important issues to be decided. It must be remembered that he is always entitled in case of doubt to ask that the decision on a disputed issue shall be taken by the Cabinet.

The department with which in matter of policy the King is most closely connected is the Foreign Office, just as that is the department whose business the Prime Minister normally supervises in special degree. Reference has alrady been made to the disputes between the Queen, inspired by Prince Albert, and advised by Baron Stockmar, and Lord Palmerston.[14] In 1849, Lord John Russell mediated by undertaking to revise drafts of despatches before submission to the Queen, and in 1850 the Queen laid down the conditions above mentioned, her right to have the foreign despatches sent, to consider drafts submitted, and to require that a policy once sanctioned must not be varied.[15] The dismissal of Lord Palmerston in 1851, for disregard of a Cabinet decision not to recognise forthwith the French *coup d'état*, was justified by the Prime Minister, who pointed out that in matters of small importance the Secretary of State must be able to act independently, but not in great.[16] The submission of drafts via the Premier was regarded as unconstitutional by Mr. Gladstone and was dropped,[17] but the Queen consistently objected to the despatch of telegrams without her formal approval, nor did Lord Rosebery dispute her claim in 1893, while explaining that failure to consult in one case was due to the absolute

[13] Spender, *Lord Oxford*, i. 270.　　　[14] See *ante*, pp. 77–78.
[15] As note 14.　　　　　　　　　　　[16] 119 *Parl. Deb.* 3 s., 97.
[17] Gladstone, *Gleanings of Past Years*, i. 86 f.

necessity of advising Lord Cromer that he must not take such drastic steps as he proposed to bring the Khedive to order.[18] It seems clear that Edward VII. expected important despatches to be submitted before despatch;[19] on the other hand, George V. seems not to have been inclined to insist on this special mode of procedure, especially as pressure in the war period rendered immediate action often necessary, just as the decision to send Mr. Churchill to Antwerp was taken without even Cabinet assent.[20] But the Hoare-Laval fiasco suggests that to rush matters through, as was then done without consulting the King formally and full discussion, was a very unfortunate error. Obviously the King must be kept informed, and, as in the past, despatches received and sent must be supplied to him and are printed for immediate circulation to him and the Cabinet, and also for the Dominion Governments. Thus he can intervene at any time to enquire, and the Premier and Foreign Secretary are bound to give him full advice on any issues, either at his request or spontaneously.

In no other department is the connection so close. The Queen indeed proposed to supervise Indian affairs when the Crown took over the government in 1858, asking that the practice of the new Department should be assimilated to that of the Foreign Office; despatches were to be sent for perusal, drafts of instructions submitted, the royal pleasure to be taken before appointments involving the royal name were made, prior sanction to be obtained before important issues were brought before Council, and Council minutes sent.[21] The minutes were sent, but the rest of the arrangement seems to have been negligently carried out; at any rate, in 1898, Lord George Hamilton decided to drop sending minutes, substituting copies of telegrams, and despatches of interest.[22] Other matters, of course, went before the Queen separately, and she corresponded with Viceroys, and took a deep interest in certain aspects of Indian affairs, such as the treatment of the princes and the welfare of the people.

As regards the colonies, and later the Dominions, the rule was early adopted of referring to the Queen only matters of real

18 *Letters of Queen Victoria*, 3 s., ii. 205–8; for a solitary blunder by Lord Salisbury, see *ibid.*, 3 s., ii. 581 f.
19 Cf. Grey, *Twenty-five Years*, i. 203.
20 Spender, *Lord Oxford*, ii. 125.
21 *Letters of Queen Victoria*, 1 s., iii. 380.
22 *Ibid.*, 3 s., iii. 267, 304 f.

importance,[23] and the same principles were adopted under her successors. Thus, the Morley-Minto reform schemes went before the King in detail in 1907–9,[24] and the period of office of Lord Curzon was marked by the King's interest in the Coronation Durbar when he supported ministers against Lord Curzon,[25] and in the dispute between Lord Curzon and Lord Kitchener.[26] In like manner, he was far from anxious to see Lord Kitchener sent to India as Commander-in-Chief, and yielded mainly because of his intention otherwise to drop the service.[27] On the other hand, he would have liked later on to see him Governor-General, but Lord Morley refused, and took advantage of his death to appoint Lord Hardinge. The King was indignant with Mr. Lyttelton in July, 1904, for offering a public funeral to President Kruger without consulting him, and at the terms in which he telegraphed approval in his name of the Chinese Labour Ordinance of 1904, though his financial friends persuaded him to approve the Ordinance itself, and to deprecate the hostility with which it was received.[28] He found severe fault with Lord Elgin in 1906 for the steps taken in this regard without prior sanction,[29] an omission not repeated by that politician, and earlier he had protested against the Prime Minister's announcement on the subject at the Albert Hall. The Clerk of the Council luckily intervened to see that Lord Elgin was available to explain to the King the terms of a draft Order in Council regarding the franchise under the new Transvaal constitution, an interesting example of the mode in which the Crown is enabled to exercise its judgment on issues which have not been earlier submitted.[30]

George V. had to deal with the vast constitutional changes in India marked by the Montagu-Chelmsford reforms, and the still greater changes under the Government of India Act, 1935, and in 1912 he himself visited India for a Coronation Durbar, at which the important decision to transfer the capital of India to Delhi and to undo the partition of Bengal was announced.[31] To the principles of these measures his assent was obtained fully. He was also deeply

---

[23] See her complaint in 1868 of being informed only after a despatch had gone on the issue of Nova Scotia's desire to be released from Canada; *Letters of Queen Victoria*, 2 s., i. 532, and in 1866 of action as regards Fenian prisoners in Canada; *ibid.*, 2 s., i. 363 ff.

[24] Lee, *Edward VII.*, ii. 378 ff., 384 ff.   [25] *Ibid.*, ii. 366 f.

[26] *Ibid.*, ii. 375–80.   [27] *Ibid.*, ii. 82 f.

[28] *Ibid.*, ii. 180.   [29] *Ibid.*, ii. 479.

[30] Fitzroy, *Memoirs*, i. 297 (December 21, 1905).

[31] A. B. Keith, *Constitutional History of India, 1600–1935*, pp. 234 f.

concerned in the vital changes in the structure of the Empire involved in the evolution of Dominion status, and, though he accepted the advice of ministers, it was with some doubt at the wisdom of the system which placed him in direct contact with the Dominions without the advice of the British Government.

In all these departments important appointments continue to be submitted for royal approval, and essential appointments receive full consideration.

The defence departments have also occupied royal attention. The Queen insisted on full information being supplied, and Lord Lansdowne was reproved for alterations in names of regiments without her sanction.[32] Very wisely, he did not attempt to deal with Lord Roberts' suggestion,[33] of special stars for colonial troops, without her views, which were hostile. Edward VII. was indignant with Mr. Arnold-Forster for failing to keep him informed; 'during the late Queen's reign not a step was taken at the War Office, in connection with the army, of the slightest importance without her being informed of what was going on, and the King hopes the same course will be pursued with him,' and specifically he asked for communication of the proceedings of the Army Council, in addition to those of the Imperial Defence Committee already supplied.[34] He then in detail criticised the proposals of his minister. Lord Haldane wisely, in his proposals, took him into his confidence, and secured his full co-operation and help in popularising the territorial army by the presentation of colours, and in other ways.[35]

Of failure to keep the sovereign informed, the most amazing of recent record is the omission to inform him of the Curragh incident, of which he learned from the Press.[36] It is recorded also that the Admiralty caused him just annoyance by their action in deciding on the creation of the rank of lieutenant-commander, without explaining the project, or obtaining his sanction prior to asking for formal approval in Council.[37] The omission was the more surprising, for the King's interest in the navy from his service therein was, naturally, especially great.

---

[32] *Letters of Queen Victoria*, 3 s., iii. 133.   [33] *Ibid.*, 574 f.
[34] Lee, *Edward VII.*, ii. 200. For failure to inform him of the new naval base on the Forth, see *ibid.*, ii. 50 (1903).
[35] *Ibid.*, ii. 500 ff.   [36] Spender, *Lord Oxford*, ii. 47.
[37] Fitzroy, *Memoirs*, ii. 540 (March 9, 1914). The King censured the First Lord and Prince Louis of Battenberg.

In one department the use of the assent of the Crown before it is actually given is regular. The Home Secretary submits his decisions as to pardons to the King for signification of his pleasure, but his conclusions are acted on forthwith.[38] The practice is the more remarkable, because the sovereign on some occasions is really interested. Queen Victoria was not at all happy at the reprieve of Mrs. Maybrick, condemned for poisoning her husband,[39] and Edward VII. was not convinced of the justice of the reprieve of Rayner, the murderer of Mr. W. Whiteley, disliking concession to popular excitement when unjustified.[40] In cases of political importance, of course, he was consulted,[41] and the treatment of Mr. Lynch for rebellion shows his prudent judgment both in according clemency, and in marking none the less the seriousness of high treason. In *Casement's Case* the decision was taken by the Cabinet, and thus the King's position was definitely dissociated from personal responsibility.[42]

It is interesting to note Queen Victoria's action in insisting in anticipation of her Secretary of State's decision that the convict Lee, whose execution had been prevented by accident, should not be again subjected to an effort at execution.[43] She very gladly secured in 1872 the exemption from signing death warrants in the case of criminals in the Isle of Man, which she had received in England, under the legislation passed on her accession.[44]

In many other matters the Home Secretary is in frequent communication with the King, mainly for the purpose of securing signatures to many kinds of instrument, while he is the normal minister to be present on occasions on which the King comes officially into contact with his subjects, as in ceremonials of opening docks, as at Liverpool, or hospitals, or receiving addresses, and so on.[45] A curious question arose in 1928,[46] when the Archbishop

---

[38] Lee, *Edward VII.*, ii. 39; Mr. Akers-Douglas, September 26, 1903.

[39] *Letters of Queen Victoria*, 3 s., i. 527 (August 22, 1889). Cf. in 1880; Gardiner, *Harcourt*, i. 397, on number of remissions.

[40] Lee, *Edward VII.*, ii. 42.

[41] But the responsibility is solely ministerial: cf. Mayor of Cork's case, *The Times*, August 26, 27, 31, 1920. See also Taylor, *Brentford*, pp. 182 ff.; Clynes, *Memoirs*, ii. 144.

[42] Spender, *Lord Oxford*, ii. 214 n. 2.

[43] *Letters of Queen Victoria*, 2 s., iii. 613. She was justly annoyed at the leniency of the sentence on her assailant O'Connor in 1872 (Guedalla, *The Queen and Mr. Gladstone*, i. 344–47), and at the form of verdict in Maclean's case (1882) (*ibid.*, ii. 179 ff., 186 f.).

[44] *Letters of Queen Victoria*, 2 s., ii. 223; 7 Will. IV. and 1 Vict. c. 77.

[45] Taylor, *Brentford*, pp. 203–9.   [46] *Ibid.*, pp. 272–74.

of Canterbury went to the King, then convalescing at Bognor Regis —the appellation was given later—in order to do homage on appointment. The oath on such occasions is properly administered by the Home Secretary, and the Prime Minister's decision to act instead was questioned formally by Mr. Joynson-Hicks as illegal, not, indeed, on the basis of statute, but of established usage. Unquestionably he had a strong case, but in the absence of statute to assert illegality was strictly speaking impossible. Most of the duties, however, of the Home Secretary are rather formal than such as involve issues on which the sovereign would desire to form or express views, as in the case of the granting the fiat to petitions of right, which is a matter dealt with on fixed principles.

In certain questions, however, the Crown takes personal cognisance, above all, those affecting the police force of the metropolis. The post of Commissioner is regularly submitted to the sovereign,[47] but Mr. Monro's appointment in 1898 proved unsatisfactory;[48] he championed the cause of the police against the Government, badly represented by the Home Secretary, Mr. Matthews, and had to be replaced by Sir Edward Bradford, after serious police unrest and rioting, the postmen having chosen the occasion to engineer a strike.[49] The Queen was most anxious that Mr. Matthews should be displaced, and she secured that he should not be included in the ministry of 1895. In 1918 the outbreak of a grave police strike took the ministry by surprise, as it had not been foreseen, and Sir Edward Henry was working for the provision of better terms for the police.[50] The resignation of the Home Secretary was refused, but that of Sir E. Henry accepted, and he was given no opportunity to present his defence.[51] The remarkable appointment by Mr. Joynson-Hicks to the Commissionership in 1928 of Lord Byng, was, no doubt, only rendered possible by the latter's reluctance to refuse a post offered to him with royal approval.[52]

Any failure to submit appointments of importance is, of course, most careless. Mr. Wyndham was severely called to account by

[47] *E.g.*, *Letters of Queen Victoria*, 3 s., i. 452.
[48] Sir C. Warren had resigned and the Cabinet had accepted his resignation as he denied the supremacy of the Home Secretary. *Letters of Queen Victoria*, 3 s., i. 448 f.
[49] *Ibid.*, 3 s., i. 616, 622.　　　　　[50] Mallet, *Cave*, pp. 216 ff.
[51] The treatment of a subordinate in this way seems of dubious justice.
[52] Taylor, *Brentford*, pp. 217–20.

Edward VII. for appointing Sir A. Macdonnell to be his Under-Secretary without prior approval, though in fact the King welcomed the choice made.[53]

(c) *The King and the Opposition*

It is an essential feature of the system of Cabinet government that the sovereign is advised on political issues by the ministry alone. This was asserted clearly by Earl Grey under William IV., when the Duke of Wellington addressed the Crown on the danger of the arming of political societies during the political excitement of the moment.   The King replied, though he did not accept the suggestions made, but Lord Grey pointed out that it might produce inconvenience if His Majesty were to express opinions to any but his confidential servants on matters which might come under their consideration, and the King promised only to acknowledge such communication in future.[54]   There is, of course, no possibility of preventing the tendering of advice by ex-ministers, and a peer still has, in theory, the right to ask for an audience to proffer such advice, but the practice is obsolescent or obsolete, and no reply of substance is made.[55]   That a Privy Councillor as such is entitled to offer advice must be negatived, if by that is meant that his advice is of any more meaning constitutionally than that of any private person who may choose to address the Crown.[56]   Unless and until summoned to the Council or to the Crown, a Privy Councillor is in the position of an ordinary subject, save in so far as he enjoys ceremonial precedence and style.

Relations, therefore, between the sovereign and ex-ministers, or other leaders of the Opposition, be they peers or Privy Councillors, or simple commoners, are necessarily delicate.   It was quite natural in the infancy of the new system that the position of the Queen to Lord Melbourne led to the continuation of their correspondence after he quitted office.   The danger of this action was patent to Baron Stockmar, who strongly deprecated it,[57] and Sir R. Peel made it clear that he would not remain in office if he found that the Queen was taking advice from his rival.   But nothing untoward happened.   Lord Melbourne was not of the temperament to seek to overthrow his opponent by form of intrigue, even if the Prince

[53] Lee, *Edward VII.*, ii. 50.   [54] Grey, *Correspondence with William IV.*, i. 413–24.
[55] *Letters of Queen Victoria*, 1 s., i. 431.
[56] Cf. Keith, *The King and the Imperial Crown*, p. 243.
[57] *Letters of Queen Victoria*, 1 s., i. 415 ff.

had not been there to object, and it is not seriously arguable that the general constitutional instruction, which he imparted, could injuriously affect the Queen's relations with her new ministry. Peel himself, after retirement, continued an innocuous correspondence with Prince Albert.

The same innocence of real harm cannot be predicated of the correspondence of the Queen with Lord Beaconsfield.[58] Unhappily, the Queen by this time had lost confidence in Mr. Gladstone, and, as she had never fully appreciated her duty[59] to support loyally any ministry marked out by the vote of the electorate, she had no hesitation in seeking aid from her late adviser, and in revealing to him the plans of her ministry. Fortunately, serious injury to the position of the Crown was prevented by the early death of Lord Beaconsfield, whose share in the correspondence clearly permits of no excuse. The truth, of course, is that by various means, including certainly exaggerated flattery, the ex-Premier had established with the Queen relations of so close a character that she found it quite impossible to treat her new Premier with fairness.[60] While excuses, no doubt, will be found by ingenious writers for the royal action, the fact that it was unconstitutional is really not open to dispute, and it is not believed that the practice has ever since been revived. The Queen certainly does not appear to have gone so far with Lord Salisbury.

Leaving this case apart, the rules as to communications with the Opposition still present difficulties. There are, however, certain principles to be discerned.

(1) When a ministry resigns, it is right and proper for the Crown to make enquiries in any directions which it thinks fit to secure a new ministry. There was clearly nothing undesirable in the reference made to the Duke of Wellington, to Lord Lansdowne and to Lord Aberdeen above referred to,[61] and there is no reason whatever to suppose that the principle does not still stand good. That there is little evidence of recent usage is due simply to the development of the party system under which normally a leader stands out for selection to head the party. It will be remembered that in 1886 Mr. Goschen declined respectfully to call on the Queen

58 *Letters of Queen Victoria*, 2 s., iii. 127 ff.; Monypenny and Buckle, *Life of Disraeli*, ii. 1414 ff.
59 See Martin, *Prince Consort*, i. 110, for the Prince's recognition.
60 Guedalla, *The Queen and Mr. Gladstone*, ii. 3 ff.   61 See *ante*, p. 33.

to give her advice, because her course was so obviously to send for
Mr. Gladstone that there was no real possibility of him giving other
counsel. [62]   We have, however, a certain reappearance of the right
to secure advice in 1916, when Mr. Lloyd George determined to
exclude Mr. Asquith from effective control of the war.   The
resignation of Mr. Asquith and the Cabinet was tendered on
December 5, 1916, and Mr. Bonar Law, who was sent for by the
King, and on December 6 Mr. Lloyd George, were unable to accept
responsibility.   The King suggested a meeting at Buckingham
Palace, [63] which was held on the afternoon of December 6.   What
happened is uncertain.   Mr. Balfour had first audience, and later
he and Mr. Bonar Law, Mr. Lloyd George, Mr. Asquith, and Mr.
Henderson were those present.   It is alleged by Mr. Lloyd George
that all save Mr. Asquith were willing to serve under Mr. Balfour,
but this is plainly a mistake.   Mr. Balfour records a general
discussion, which, at the royal request, he summed up as leading to
the conclusion that if either Mr. Bonar Law or Mr. Lloyd George
were chosen, Mr. Asquith would not serve, and Mr. Henderson
was in that case doubtful of Labour support for a coalition ministry.
Both the latter, however, pointed out that their views were rather
strongly put, and the final conclusion was that Mr. Bonar Law
should form a Government to include Mr. Asquith, if possible.
That was rejected by the Liberal leader with the solid support of
his party, except Mr. Montagu, and Mr. Bonar Law then declined
to go on with the attempt to form a ministry, and gave instead his
support to Mr. Lloyd George.   Mr. Bonar Law then called upon
Mr. Balfour and offered him the Foreign Office, which he accepted.
When it is remembered that Mr. Asquith had just before refused to
meet the wishes of Mr. Lloyd George to remove Mr. Balfour from
the Admiralty, [64] Mr. Balfour's action cannot be said to stand out
as remarkable for gratitude or chivalry.   But his anxiety for office
was natural, and he seems wholly to have failed to see that his
conduct in this matter fell short of any reasonable standard of
candour.   But the formation of the coalition of 1916 is not an

[62] *Letters of Queen Victoria*, 3 s., i. 27 f.
[63] Spender, *Lord Oxford*, ii. 272 ff.; Dugdale, *Arthur James Balfour*, ii. 175 ff.   We
know now that the King in 1923 deliberately asked Lord Balfour's views on Mr.
Bonar Law's successor; Dugdale, *Arthur James Balfour*, ii. 359 ff.   The views of
Mr. Amery, Mr. Bridgeman, Lord Long, Lord Salisbury, and the Labour
Party seem to have been tendered spontaneously; Nicolson, *Curzon*, pp. 335 f.;
Amery, *Thoughts on the Constitution*, p. 21.
[64] Spender, *Lord Oxford*, ii. 265 f.

episode of which any of those sharing in it could be proud.[65] Mr. Balfour's acceptance of the combination, in the hands of Mr. Lloyd George, of the functions of head of the Government and controller of the War Council, which he had declared to the King impossible, and which had been denounced by Mr. Lloyd George in the case of Mr. Asquith, is clearly without defence. That his removal from the Admiralty was in the national interest cannot be denied. His acceptance of his ejection by Mr. Lloyd George suggests that he felt that he had muddled matters.

In 1931, again, the ministry was conscious of its inability to face the situation caused by the reckless finance for which its leaders were responsible. The final decision of the ministry to resign was followed by a conference between the retiring Prime Minister, Mr. Baldwin, and Sir A. Sinclair, which led to the creation of a National Government. The action of the King in favouring such action was clearly unexceptionable, and has been recognised as such by as impartial and well-informed an authority as Lord Passfield.[66] The propriety of the acceptance of office by Mr. MacDonald, who was largely responsible as head of the ministry for the mismanagement of the affairs by the Government, of Mr. Snowden and Mr. Thomas, is a very different thing, and the bitterness of the Labour Party against these men can easily be understood.

(2) Another class of case allows unquestionably of royal action, the grant of assistance to ministers in seeking accommodation of difficulties. The ways of a peacemaker are hard, but royal mediation has one great advantage, that the King should command courtesy from those he approaches. There is only one recorded case to the contrary, attested by Mr. A. Chamberlain,[67] dealing with the attitude of Mr. Bonar Law to the King on May 4, 1912, on the question of his position in respect to the Government of Ireland Bill. But it must be remembered that Mr. Bonar Law was essentially a new man.

Queen Victoria naturally was ready for action, even without any prompting of the Government. That was natural in cases where some interest of her own of a private character was concerned,

---

65 On Mr. Lloyd George's conduct and the manipulation of the Press in his favour, see Spender, ii. 248–71. Mrs. Dugdale's apologia (ii. 156 ff.) for Balfour is not satisfactory.
66 See *ante*, p. 37; for another interpretation see H. J. Laski, *The Constitutional Crisis*.
67 A. Chamberlain, *Politics from Inside*, pp. 486 f.

as in her approach in 1856 to Lords Derby and Lyndhurst to aid the passage of legislation mooted for dealing with the precedence of Prince Albert, a matter later disposed of otherwise.[68]   Lord Derby in 1863 was asked to favour the project of purchasing the buildings and site of the exhibition of 1851, which was inseparably connected with the Prince's enlightened activity.   The land was purchased, but the maintenance of the buildings was vetoed by the Commons, despite Mr. Gladstone's best efforts, which, Lord Palmerston held, were defeated in part by his lack of caution in showing how utterly wrong his opponents were.[69]   Personal reasons, affecting her own health, explain in part her urgent appeal in 1866 to Lord Derby to come to some arrangement on the issue of reform; Lord Derby proved obdurate, considering the Bill fatal to the constitution, an amusing view, since next year his Government was to pass a much more dangerous measure.[70]   Next year she endeavoured to secure Liberal support for a settlement, and urged Mr. Disraeli not to be led away by the 'tea-room revolt' against Mr. Gladstone, into failing to remember the necessity of conciliation.   Both these demarches were uninspired by the ministry, but innocuous.   Much more important was her action in 1869 in regard to the disestablishment of the Irish Church.   The Queen arranged a meeting between Archbishop Tait and Mr. Gladstone,[71] and later on, when after refraining from voting on the second reading, which thus passed, the Archbishop claimed amendments, she used her influence with her Premier and the Archbishop to secure an agreed settlement.   No doubt Lord Cairns' attitude in this case was important, for he explained to the Lords that this was a case where the verdict of the electors had pointed out the duty of the Upper Chamber, but there is no need to minimise her services.

Naturally the Queen was equally ready to help Lord Beaconsfield in 1877, by offering to use her influence with the Opposition to induce them not unduly to trouble the Government at that critical time by questions regarding its Russian policy;[72] she actually did communicate with Mr. Forster and the Duke of Argyll.   But she also asked Sir S. Northcote and Lord Beaconsfield

[68] *Letters of Queen Victoria*, 1 s., iii. 244 ff.
[69] *Ibid.*, 2 s., i. 89 ff., 97 ff.
[70] *Ibid.*, 2 s., i. 330 f.
[71] Randall Davidson, *Archbishop Tait*, ii. 8 ff.; Guedalla, *The Queen and Mr. Gladstone*, i. 151–56, 159–63, 167, 189–92.
[72] *Letters of Queen Victoria*, 2 s., ii. 532, 534, 538.

to help in 1881,[73] the Governmental plan to counter Irish obstruction, a matter, of course, of common interest, and one on which
negotiations between the parties were in train; and in 1882 Lord
Salisbury, in deference to her, was asked to refrain from pressing a
fatal amendment to the Arrears Bill.[74] It seems clear that he
would not have given way, but the Queen had engaged the aid of
the Duke of Abercorn, who managed to carry other members of
the party, so that Lord Salisbury could only denounce it. In both
cases she acted spontaneously, as also in her criticism of the
Opposition's apparent sympathy with the rebel Arabi Pasha, whom
the Queen heartily disapproved of.

Far more important was her action in 1884[75] over the dispute
between the two Houses over the franchise and redistribution.
She there had the full consent of the Premier, and wrote to Lord
Salisbury to urge him to compromise. He was not willing to do so,
but among further activities she interviewed the Duke of Richmond,
who influenced Lord Cairns and Lord Salisbury, and the invaluable
Sir H. Ponsonby served as intermediary for a long correspondence
between Lord Salisbury and Mr. Gladstone, the net outcome being
that a system of redistribution was agreed upon, and the Representation of the People Act, 1884, was allowed to pass. There is no
doubt of the value of her services in this case. In like manner, in
1885, she mediated between Mr. Gladstone and Lord Salisbury on
the vexed issue of the assurances to be given regarding financial
business by the former, if the latter were to take the burden of
Government at a time when, owing to redistribution, he could not
at once dissolve, and must, therefore, be in some measure dependent
on the goodwill of his opponent.[76]

The precedent of 1869 was followed in 1906 by Edward VII.,
for he urged communications on the Education Bill between the
Premier and the Archbishop of Canterbury. But the attempt to
secure accord proved vain,[77] considerably to the royal annoyance,
which was repeated on the failure of the Licensing Bill. In 1908,
the King urged Lord Roberts, on the suggestion of the Premier, not
to raise the dangerous issue of the possibility of invasion.[78] In

---

[73] *Letters of Queen Victoria*, 2 s., iii. 187.   [74] *Ibid.*, 2 s., iii. 320, 325 f.
[75] Morley, *Gladstone*, iii. 130 ff.; *Letters of Queen Victoria*, 2 s., iii. 515, 518 ff., 537,
542 ff., 577; Fitzmaurice, *Granville*, ii. 320–23, 379 f.
[76] *Letters of Queen Victoria*, 2 s., iii. 670 ff.
[77] Lee, *Edward VII.*, ii. 461 f.; Spender, *Campbell-Bannerman*, ii. 301 ff.
[78] Esher, *Journals and Letters*, ii. 360 f.

1909, he suggested[79] that he might communicate with and bring pressure to bear on the Opposition as regards the Finance Bill, and Mr. Asquith approved such action, stressing the precedent of the royal intervention of 1832, though, of course, the position was not wholly parallel, for then, as in 1869 and 1884, royal intervention had not come until after the Lords had started amending the Bills. Before this, however, he had obtained from Lord Cawdor on October 2, while at Balmoral, a memorandum giving his view on the position of the Lords on the budget, which was naturally entirely opposed to the official view presented by Mr. McKenna in a memorandum of September 27.[80]   On October 12, the King saw Mr. Balfour and Lord Lansdowne at Buckingham Palace, and reported to Mr. Asquith that they had not yet decided the issue. But, in fact, the party was now under the influence of two great driving forces, that of the wealthy party supporters, who feared that they would be hard hit by the budget, and that of the tariff reformers, who were afraid that the budget might prove to solve the problem of the source of the extra revenue urgently needed for the Governmental social policies and defence.   The Lords therefore rejected the budget, and the royal effort to seek some compromise thereafter was ineffective.[81]

A different issue arose after the second election in 1910, for Mr. Asquith was far from anxious to encourage the King to act as mediator.   He suggested a parallel with George III.'s efforts to obtain advice from opposing sides with a view to form his own policy, which had been abandoned after the accession of Mr. Pitt to power.[82]   But, when the King insisted that he sought information, not advice, he reluctantly gave way, and the King saw Lord Lansdowne on January 27, 1911.[83]   There is no doubt that Lord Lansdowne kept within the limits of stating his view of the position taken up by the Opposition, but the whole affair was unreal in so far as the King could not mention his own promise to create peers if the Government had an adequate majority, which by that time had been secured.

In the grave crisis of 1913–14 on the Government of Ireland Bill, the King sought steadily to mediate between the angry com-

79 Spender, *Lord Oxford*, i. 257.
80 Lee, *Edward VII.*, ii. 667, gives the correct order of events.   There is no evidence of Mr. Asquith's consent to this action.
81 Newton, *Lansdowne*, pp. 388 f.
82 Spender, *Lord Oxford*, i. 306 (December, 1910).   83 Newton, *Lansdowne*, p. 409.

batants.   How badly he was treated by Mr. Bonar Law in 1912 has
already been noted, and the Conservatives, it must be admitted,
showed as little readiness to compromise as they had done under
his father.   But he persisted;[84] he asked representatives to Balmoral
so that they could talk matters over; he secured personal contact
between Mr. Asquith and Sir E. Carson;[85] he induced the Government to consider the possibility of excluding Ulster for a definite
period which would secure that it could not be included without a
further election.   He endeavoured to secure by a conference in
July accord,[86] just as he had done as regards the Parliament Bill in
1910.

Obscurity marks the accounts of his share in bringing about
the Irish settlement of 1921.   Undoubtedly, the speech from the
throne on the inauguration of the Parliament of Northern Ireland,
June 22, 1921, contained the germ of subsequent negotiations leading
up to the treaty of 1921.   Responsibility, of course, for the speech
rested with the Premier, but that the King had pressed for it was
then widely believed and has never been rendered unlikely.   The
sovereign, of all people, was the one most anxious to secure the
cessation of a civil war waged without pity or decency by both
sides.

Of the royal mediation in 1931,[87] mention has already been
made.   It is patent that the functions of the sovereign in this
connection are as important as they are delicate.   The obvious
danger is that of seeking to act too early, for that suggests distrust of
ministerial proposals which the King should not feel or at least
manifest.   On the other hand, to delay may result in both sides
having so committed themselves that neither can make the vital
concessions which will secure peace.

With these legitimate interventions must be contrasted the
actions of Queen Victoria in regard to Mr. Gladstone after the
defeat of Lord Salisbury's Government in the election of 1885.
She had then definitely endeavoured to induce the Whig elements to
refuse support to Mr. Gladstone,[88] and, when he took office without
their aid, she endeavoured by communications with Mr. Goschen

84 Spender, *Lord Oxford*, ii. 28 ff.
85 Colvin, *Carson*, ii. 287; A. Chamberlain, *Politics from Inside*, pp. 605–7, 643–45.
86 Spender, *Lord Oxford*, ii. 53 f.
87 For 1916, see *ante*, p. 334.   Cf. Addison, *Four and a Half Years*, i. 270, who asserts
   efforts at intervention by Lord Stamfordham.
88 *Letters of Queen Victoria*, 2 s., iii. 709 ff.; 3 s., i. 5 ff.

and Lord Salisbury to form an alliance of Whigs and Conservatives which would be effective to defeat any attempt at Home Rule.[89] Both these politicians were ultimately agreed in advising the Queen that a dissolution would be advantageous, and should, therefore, be granted to Mr. Gladstone.[90]   Mr. Gladstone, therefore, was gladly given his dissolution, the request for which he supported by reference to the wishes of the Opposition, not knowing that the Queen had already canvassed it.[91]   It certainly does not appear that the Queen was giving away any secrets of the ministry, but her action is quite without defence on the fundamental theory of responsible government that it is the will of the electorate that is to prevail, and that the sovereign must honestly co-operate with each ministry.

There have been noted above the efforts made by the Queen in 1893 and 1894[92] to obtain from Lord Salisbury and others assistance in ejecting Mr. Gladstone and Lord Rosebery from office. All that can be said is that she was now so obsessed by the idea that any action was sound, if it delayed Home Rule, that she did not realise that her action was unconstitutional.   Nor is it unusual to find apologists for her action, who themselves are plainly animated by the same conviction.   How unwise it was, the loss of Eire to the Commonwealth in anything but name, and the fact that British subjects are therein aliens, show clearly.[93]

(d) The King's Sources of Knowledge

Primarily in the nature of things the royal knowledge on which decisions are based rests on the information supplied by the ministers, who suggest also the conclusions to be reached.   But, patently, no king can work without aid, and George III. used Sir H. Taylor in the capacity of private secretary.   George IV. had the aid of Sir W. Knighton, while William IV. recurred to Sir H. Taylor, who is well known from Earl Grey's correspondence with him.   Lord Melbourne undertook the work for Queen Victoria, but mention must also be made of Baron Stockmar, who undertook the task of mentor to Prince Albert and the young Queen.   His

---

[89] *Letters of Queen Victoria*, 3 s., i. 32 ff., 37, 41, 45, 49 f., 79, 90 f., 98, 101, 111 f., 116 f.   [90] *Ibid.*, 128 ff., 131 f., 134 f.
[91] *Ibid.*, 3 s., i. 143.   [92] *Ante*, p. 281.
[93] Social relations with the Opposition leaders are, of course, a matter of discretion. But the formal creation in 1937 of a salaried post of leader renders a royal invitation, such as that of Mr. and Mrs. Attlee to Windsor in April, 1938, peculiarly appropriate.

devotion to both was plain, his erudition considerable, though his constitutional knowledge was rather acridly described by Mr. Gladstone as an English top-dressing on a German soil.[94] To regard him as Victoria's 'guardian angel'[95] requires some imagination. The Prince, himself, had as private secretary the attractive George Anson (1840–47), and from 1849 to his death General Grey served. On his death, no formal appointment of General Grey was made until 1867, and he died in 1870. His virtues are recorded with much distinction of phrase in Mr. Gladstone's farewell to Sir Henry Ponsonby, his successor in 1894. Ponsonby died in 1895, having been praised with equal cordiality by Mr. Gladstone and Mr. Disraeli; his acute judgment is seen in the papers published in *Sidelights on Queen Victoria*. Sir Arthur Bigge took his place; his action in October, 1900, in securing from the Queen unsparing condemnation of the sanitary defects of Windsor is a pleasing testimonial to a kindly disposition.[96] Under Edward VII. Lord Knollys was active, while his predecessor aided the Duke of York and then became secretary to George V. After his death in 1931, Sir C. Wigram took his place, and though a change was made under Edward VIII. he continued to serve George VI., being given the post of political adviser as well as that of Keeper of the Archives given by Edward VIII. The taking on as secretary by George VI. of Sir A. Hardinge marked the fact that the latter was in no way discredited by his service under the former sovereign.[97]

These officers and their subordinates necessarily acquire great masses of information from all sorts of sources, and may be in touch with ex-ministers, as well as ministers, officials, and so forth. No one doubts their competence, of which evidence for Queen Victoria is afforded occasionally by the memoranda included in the publication of her correspondence.

On July 23, 1873, Sir H. Ponsonby[98] gave a singularly warm commendation of Mr. Cardwell's army reforms to the Queen, endeavouring, it is clear, to persuade her that her minister was devoted to the maintenance of the royal prerogative, and was careful of the position of the Commander-in-Chief, who had, at last, been brought under proper subordination to the minister.

[94] Gladstone, *Gleanings*, i. 84.   [95] P. Crabites, *Victoria's Guardian Angel.*
[96] *Letters of Queen Victoria*, 3 s., iii. 607 f.
[97] Sir Alan Lascelles became Secretary in 1943.
[98] *Letters of Queen Victoria*, 2 s., ii. 265 f.

The Queen in 1879 suggested that he should disseminate her dislike of Mr. Gladstone and his policies, referring to similar services rendered by Baron Stockmar and Mr. Anson, which obviated the actual emergence of such difficulties as that of the ladies of the bedchamber in 1839. His Whig friends would enable him to do so effectively.[99] But there is much less authority for the allegation that Lord Stamfordham was hostile to the Government of Ireland Bill in 1914; the pressure of worrying events then filled society with rumours of all kinds. What is clear is that he endeavoured to induce the Conservatives to moderate the ferocity of their language, but without success. Mr. Bonar Law seems never to have quite appreciated that the British tradition, as opposed to the Canadian, deprecated extreme violence of denunciation in Parliament.[1]

Beside ordinary members of the royal entourage must be mentioned Lord Esher, who managed to have himself recognised as a quasi-permanent adviser to the Crown on military and constitutional questions. His service on the War Office Reconstitution Committee provided him with much information, and he was authorised to study and organise the records of royal correspondence.[2] Lord Esher was definitely Conservative in outlook, and his position was decidedly anomalous, but Sir H. Campbell-Bannerman seems to have approved of his services, as had Mr. Balfour, and there is no reason to doubt that his aim was to forward to the utmost of his ability the interests of the Crown and his country.

Other sources of information were naturally available, and the quality varied considerably. Queen Victoria's reliance in ecclesiastical affairs on the advice of Randall Davidson was profound. Lord Palmerston had no effect on her when he criticised her desire to have more than one name submitted for a vacant canonry at Westminster, by suggesting that this involved a reference of 'a recommendation by one of your Majesty's responsible advisers to the judgment of your Majesty's irresponsible advisers in such matters.'[3] The Queen merely insisted on her right to make enquiries regarding the qualifications of persons submitted. No doubt she was greatly influenced by her entourage,[4] but that must not be exaggerated; her action in telegraphing *en clair*[5] to Mr.

99 *Letters of Queen Victoria*, 2 s., iii. 48.
1 A. Chamberlain, *Politics from Inside*, p. 617 ff. Cf. Fitzroy, *Memoirs*, ii. 551; Addison, *Four and a half Years*, i. 28.
2 *Journals and Letters*, i. 292; ii. 56.   3 *Letters of Queen Victoria*, 2 s., i. 236, 240.
4 *Ibid.*, 3 s., ii. 172.   5 *Ibid.*, 2 s., iii. 597 f.

Gladstone, in vehement terms, regarding the position of General Gordon seems clearly enough spontaneous, rather than prompted, and Mr. Gladstone's observation that 'he does not presume to estimate the means of judgment possessed by your Majesty' was sufficient rebuke.   Unluckily, after the split on Home Rule, there is no doubt of the fact that the views of Liberals were hardly represented at all in the circles of the Court, a fact which made it increasingly difficult for the Queen to behave with due impartiality. In any case it was long inevitable that the sovereign should hardly come into effective contact with opinion not of a markedly Conservative or Whig character.   Queen Victoria, no doubt, knew something of the Scottish peasantry from her connection with John Brown and otherwise, as can be seen from *Leaves from a Journal of our Life in the Highlands from* 1848 *to* 1861, and the further volume covering the period to 1882.   She had the advantage of intercourse with Mr. Norman Macleod,[6] a Scottish divine, representing the democratic spirit of the Church of Scotland, as well as with another Scotsman of far different character, a Conservative statesman in political outlook, Randall Davidson.   But it would be difficult to think of a single Liberal in political views with whom she had contact, not essentially official.   Her son, Prince Leopold, was essentially unsound in his views, as when he encouraged her in the belief that the Queen's speech was a matter in which she was personally concerned.   It was only late in her life that she listened much to the views of the Prince of Wales, who, at least, had the advantage that he knew socially a number of highly placed Liberals, and who had the vision to get into touch socially with Sir H. Campbell-Bannerman before the time came for political intercourse.[7]   As regards Labour Party contacts it is plain that even George V. had little connection with members of that party; Lord Snowden tells us that in 1923, he, Mr. Thomas and Mr. Clynes were invited to meet the King and the Queen at a dinner given by Lady Astor, while Mr. MacDonald was invited to Buckingham Palace.[8]   It was noted, no doubt correctly, at the time of the abdication of Edward VIII. that, though he had many acquaintances and a variety of personal friends, he was not in effective contact with a single representative of Labour opinions, a fact which

---

6 *Letters of Queen Victoria*, 2 s., i. 376, 380; ii. 217.
7 For his Conservative leanings see Hardie, *Political Influence of Queen Victoria*, pp. 184 ff.
8 Snowden, *Autobiography*, ii. 661.

no doubt helps to explain his complete failure to appreciate the probable reaction of his matrimonial project. Even the present sovereign, it has been suggested, has an entourage essentially non-Labour in outlook, and the point of Mr. Attlee's suggestion regarding the reduction of royal ceremonial in 1937 was the feeling that the etiquette which surrounds the sovereign inevitably separates him from the vast majority of his people, and prevents his appreciating the standpoint of large sections of his subjects. How far that bias is now counteracted by the activity of the sovereign and his consort in seeking to learn closely of the life of the workers it is difficult to say. Probably the experience obtained by the Duke of Kent in service under the Home Office served to broaden the mind and helped to keep the Court in touch with realities. Nevertheless, men like Sir S. Cripps, while accepting hereditary monarchy as the best type of constitution, have not hesitated to assert that in the event of a Labour Government attaining power, and seeking to carry through the policy approved by the electorate, it would find a steady focus of resistance in the royal entourage.[9] This view, it may be assumed, is pessimistic. George V. certainly accommodated himself remarkably to the spirit of the times, and there is no reason to suppose that George VI. has done differently during the lifetime of the first Labour Governments with a safe majority in the House of Commons.

In matters of defence Queen Victoria was curiously placed, for in her time the tradition of the special position of the Crown with regard to the forces was much alive, and was strengthened by the fact that her cousin, the Duke of Cambridge, was Commander-in-Chief, and that by custom his position was one of imperfect subordination to the Secretary of State. It was, therefore, natural that she should oppose every measure which was not approved by him, and it was only in 1895 that Sir H. Campbell-Bannerman, by a combination of tact and firmness, persuaded the Queen to secure his resignation of an office whose tenure by him would have proved fatal to military reform.[10]

Edward VII. was wont to place great confidence in chosen advisers on technical subjects, and in matters affecting the fleet he relied on Sir J. Fisher from 1904 onwards.[11] The position of this

[9] Ridges, *Constitutional Law of England* (ed. Keith), p. 138.
[10] Spender, *Campbell-Bannerman*, i. chap. ix.
[11] Lee, *Edward VII.*, ii. 327 ff. Cf. Churchill's character sketch: *World Crisis, 1911-14*, pp. 72-79.

officer in relation to the sovereign was regularised ingeniously in making him principal aide-de-camp to the King in addition to his position as First Sea Lord, in which, of course, he could normally not have had any right of direct access to the sovereign, though he might have been deputed to discuss matters with him. Sir J. Fisher, the value of whose services to the navy has probably been exaggerated, was certainly of erratic temperament, and he had no hesitation in tendering to the King advice on political issues, most of which must, to judge from what has been made known of his opinions, have been utterly valueless; the King called them 'effusions.' In military matters he relied on the opinions of his Adjutant-General, Sir T. Kelly-Kenny,[12] but the Haldane reforms found him ready to accord full support, though he insisted on careful consideration of the counter-proposals of Lord Roberts.[13] It is clear that, if the sovereign is to have any useful views on such issues, access to advice of experts, even if not serving the Government of the day, is valuable, and a stimulant in discussions with ministers. No real jealousy of this form of advice can seriously be felt by the latter.

Nor can there be any impropriety in the encouragement given by Queen Victoria to direct communications from the Viceroy,[14] Governors, Ambassadors and military and naval commanders, though doubtless such action requires to be carefully guarded on either side. These communications are essentially informative and personal, and the difficulty arises only when efforts are made to induce royal intervention by such communications. A very bad case of transgression of rules occurred on March 31, 1885, when the Queen communicated with Lord Wolseley, urging him not to retreat from the Sudan, but to hold Khartoum firmly.[15] 'She fears some of the Government are very unpatriotic, and do not feel what is a necessity.' No wonder she asked the recipient to destroy this message, which he loyally did. Contemporaneously Lord Hartington had to suggest that she should telegraph her congratulations to generals in the field through the War Office, and

12 Lee, *Edward VII.*, ii. 86 f.
13 *Ibid.*, ii. 503–5. Lord Roberts wrote to Lord Stamfordham on the Curragh incident; A. Chamberlain, *Politics from Inside*, p. 626.
14 Lord Lansdowne was rebuked by the Secretary of State in April, 1891, for not telegraphing direct to the Queen regarding Manipur; *Letters of Queen Victoria*, 3 s., ii. 21.
15 *Ibid.*, 2 s., iii. 633 f. Cf. her letter to Lady Wolseley, *ibid.*, 619.

not as she had done after the victory of Abu Klea direct.[16]   The
Queen's anger was magnificent; she had always telegraphed direct
to her generals, and always would, but she admitted she usually
sent an official telegram also, but had forgotten or omitted to do so
on this occasion.   'But she thinks Lord Hartington's letter *very
officious* and *impertinent in tone*.   The Queen *has* the *right* to telegraph
congratulations and enquiries to *anyone*, and won't stand dictation.
She *won't* be a *machine*.   But the Liberals always wish to make her
feel that, and she *won't accept it*.'   The tact with which Sir H.
Ponsonby wrote to the minister was perfect; a simple statement of
the Queen's regular practice and of regret at her omission to
telegraph the message simultaneously to Lord Hartington.   Thus
was intercourse between the Queen and her ministers rendered
possible without a breach.

Under Edward VII., an interesting case of the limits of such
direct correspondence is recorded.   Lord Curzon was anxious that
at the Coronation Durbar to celebrate the royal accession there
should be an announcement in the King's name of a remission of
taxation in accordance with oriental precedent.   But the ministry
was hostile, and the Viceroy appealed to the King to overrule it.
The King in no way snubbed this appeal, but explained that he
had discussed the matter with the Prime Minister and other
ministers, and found them unanimously determined against the
policy, and expressed the hope that Lord Curzon would drop the
proposal, which he could not sanction.   But he urged him also to
abandon any idea of resignation of office on this score, and the
Viceroy complied.[17]   In the same way the King received direct
communications from Lord Minto regarding his reform scheme,
and, though he never liked the placing of an Indian in the Viceroy's
Council, he accepted the decision of the Cabinet in its favour,
though not even Lord Minto convinced him of the wisdom of the
step.[18]

India affords a rather curious instance of influence brought
to bear on the Queen from an unexpected source, namely, the
Indian secretary, who in her later days taught her Hindustani and,
in the opinion of Lord Ponsonby, exercised an influence less

16 *Letters of Queen Victoria*, 2 s., iii. 594 f.
17 Lee, *Edward VII.*, ii. 366 f.   The Cabinet resented his action; Dugdale,
   Arthur James Balfour, i. 395 f.
18 Lee, *Edward VII.*, ii. 387-9, 709.

justifiable than that of John Brown. To him may be traced the rather surprising efforts made by the Queen to secure mercy for the ringleader in the murder of the Chief Commissioner of Assam, in Manipur, which happily were resisted firmly by Lord Lansdowne, supported by the Secretary of State.[19] More justifiable was her hostility to the failure of courtesy on the part of residents at Indian courts to the rulers. No doubt she overlooked the moral defects and political incapacity of many of the rulers, which helped to explain the high-handed treatment meted to them by the residents, but Lord Curzon also found that there were grave errors made in this regard, and the Queen would have applauded his views.[20] As in the case of the colonies, she was anxious to have all important despatches from India submitted to her; in this way, as in the case *par excellence* of the Foreign Office, her private communications enabled her more effectively to follow the official despatches.

The Queen had no desire to entertain direct relations with ambassadors. George IV. had already been told by George Canning that, while he would be sorry to do anything unpleasing to the King, it was his duty to be present at every interview between the King and a foreign representative,[21] and Victoria never desired personal contacts, a fact which explains her reluctance to see any increase in the number of ambassadors, because of their formal right to ask for personal interviews. But her correspondence with foreign sovereigns was copious, as was that of Prince Albert, and there is no reason to doubt that, so far as it was political, it was shown to the Prime Minister or Foreign Secretary, or both.[22] There are many instances in her *Letters* of action taken after ministerial advice, as in the case of the unfortunate King of Naples and Sicily, when he sought aid from the attacks of Garibaldi and his sovereign,[23] of her inability to aid the Queen Regent of Spain when assailed by the United States over Cuba,[24] and her efforts to aid Greece when the disastrous war with Turkey took place in 1897.[25] Her famous snub to the German Emperor, when he suggested mediation in the South African War, ran:[26] 'The time for, and the terms of, peace must be left to our decision, and my country,

[19] *Letters of Queen Victoria*, 3 s., ii. 3, 18, 21 f., 25, 27, 29, 42, 55, 60.
[20] *Ibid.*, 3 s., iii. 251.   [21] Stapleton, *Canning*, p. 433.
[22] Martin, *Prince Consort*, iv. 433.
[23] *Letters of Queen Victoria*, 1 s., iii. 505 ff.
[24] *Ibid.*, 3 s., iii. 236, 240, 268, 289.
[25] *Ibid.*, 3 s., iii. 150–62.   [26] *Ibid.*, 3 s., iii. 508 ff.

which is suffering from so heavy a sacrifice of lives, will resist all interference.'[27]

Edward VII. was busied in diplomatic activities in support of the policy of his Government, and interviews with foreign sovereigns were not rare. The rule that either a minister or a diplomatic representative should be present on these occasions was normal, but it did not negative occasional interviews without such support.[28] Thus, on April 14, 1904, at the British legation in Copenhagen, the King conversed for three-quarters of an hour with Alexander Isvolsky.[29] But at all times the King was the agent of a ministerial policy which he cordially approved, not an independent actor in the diplomatic field. Naturally, the changed appearance of Europe has vitally reduced the possibility of the sovereign playing either by correspondence or by personal intercourse an important part in the conduct of foreign affairs.

(e) The Forms of and Responsibility for the King's Administrative Acts

In a few cases the King acts without written record. He could still dissolve or prorogue Parliament in person: he could strike the name of a Privy Councillor out of the list at the Privy Council Office;[30] he could demand that a Secretary of State hand over his seals. But even for such personal acts ministers would be held responsible. Other acts he does in the presence of the Council, as when he admits members to that body or declares the President thereof.[31]

Where written instruments are used, then care is taken to show who is responsible for each. The forms of these instruments are in the main derived from custom, and it is possibly open to dispute how far it is requisite by law that they should be used, except in those cases where there is statutory provision; thus, in the Government of India Act, 1935, the mode of appointment of the Governor-General and of the Commander-in-Chief is specified, and the legality of an appointment made otherwise could be tested in the

---

[27] *Letters of Queen Victoria*, 3 s., iii. 509.   [28] Grey, *Twenty-five Years*, i. 203 ff.
[29] Lee, *Edward VII.*, ii. 283–87. For Lord Lansdowne's diplomatic corrections of over-statement of views by the King, see Newton, *Lansdowne*, pp. 308 ff. He obtained Mr. Balfour's consent.
[30] Procedure by Order in Council is now usual.
[31] See Anson, *The Law and Custom of the Constitution*, vol. II. (ed. Keith), i. 59 ff.

Courts. The absence of a grant in proper form might be taken as invalidating it by the Courts.

(1) Orders in Council, whether prerogative or statutory, are not signed by the King, but he presides in Council, and his having done so and the making of the order are attested by the signature of the Clerk of the Council and by the seal. Responsibility naturally cannot rest with the councillors present, though their names are set out in the formal record of the making of the Order. Only three councillors are essential, and no one of these need be a minister. But the responsibility lies with the minister who requested the making of the Order by application to the Lord President for that purpose, and to make clear his responsibility the request for the making is signed by or on his behalf.

In certain cases the determination in Council may be embodied in a royal proclamation which bears the great seal of the realm. Proclamations are used for the prorogation,[32] dissolution and summoning of Parliament, and for the declaration of war, peace, or neutrality, matters of prerogative, or for declarations as to coinage, under the Coinage Acts, 1870 and 1920, or for a declaration of emergency under the Emergency Powers Act, 1920.

(2) Sign manual warrants are used for a considerable number of appointments, and are countersigned by the responsible minister. Those of stipendiary magistrates are countersigned by the Home Secretary, that of the Paymaster-General by two Lords of the Treasury. Such instruments are used for the pay warrant for the army and air force, or for the grant of pardons, and various other purposes.

But in many cases the warrant is essentially a preliminary step in the issue of instruments under the great seal. Thus the procedure in regard to the issue of letters patent requires the transmission to the King by the Crown Office through a responsible minister of a warrant to be signed and counter-signed by a Secretary of State, the letters patent to be sealed, and a docket explaining the purport of the letters patent and stating by the orders of which Secretary of State they are prepared. The royal signature of the warrant gives authority to affix the great seal, but the King does not actually sign the letters patent. The responsibility rests with the Secretary of

---

[32] For an interesting case of an Order in Council for prorogation, see Fitzroy, *Memoirs*, ii. 760 f.

State, who countersigns. In the case of charters to towns or other corporate bodies an Order in Council is requisite to authorise the preparation of the warrant. This applies also to instruments for the government of colonies and protectorates, and an Order in Council in 1928 and 1936 authorised the issue of a warrant for the commission to the Counsellors of State to act during the royal illness.

Commissions under the sign manual and the signet are used for the appointment of Governors of colonies, Dominions,[33] and of India, while officers in the army and air force receive their first commission under the sign manual and the appropriate secretarial seal.

A royal order, signed by the King and countersigned by two Lords of the Treasury, authorises the release for expenditure of public money appropriated for the year by Parliament.

(3) Letters patent, bearing the great seal, are used for a large number of purposes: to authorise the opening of Parliament or assent to bills by commissioners; to put in commission the offices of Lord High Treasurer and Lord High Admiral; to constitute corporate bodies; to confer judgeships and other offices; to commission judges to hold circuits; to confer dignities such as peerages or baronetcies; to grant permission to a Dean and Chapter to elect a bishop, nominated by the King; and to authorise the making of canons by the Convocations. In most cases the authority for issue is a sign manual warrant duly countersigned, but in certain instances the Lord Chancellor acts without previous signification of the royal pleasure, as in the case of certain circuit commissions, commissions of the peace, and also in the case of writs of summonses to peers to attend Parliament on succeeding to the peerage, and certain judicial writs.

In certain cases the authority takes the form of an Order in Council, as in the case of proclamations. Writs for the election of members of Parliament are in practice issued on the strength of the proclamation summoning Parliament, but an Order in Council is also made directing the Lord Chancellor to issue them.

Instruments of full powers to negotiate and sign treaties and of ratification of treaties are issued under the great seal, authorised by a sign manual warrant countersigned by a Secretary of State. In

33 These are countersigned by Dominion Prime Ministers.

the case of Dominion treaties, where the British instruments are still used as in Canada, Australia and New Zealand, the counter-signature is that of the Dominions Secretary, but his responsibility must be regarded as merely formal. In the case of Eire and the Union of South Africa, there is no British signature involved.[34]

The forms above mentioned are the remnants of an elaborated system devised, and in part made statutory, in 1535, to secure that the King should not lightly make grants without having to secure the co-operation of a number of ministers, each of whom might find himself liable to punishment if Parliament should become hostile. Later the complication grew greater, as in part the temptation to collect fees added to complexities. But the forms were reduced under Queen Victoria, and the use of the privy seal disappeared wholly in 1884, when a sign manual warrant, countersigned by the Lord Chancellor, a Secretary of State, or two Lords of the Treasury became authority for the affixing to any document of the great seal, with a saving for any cases where the fiat, authority or direction of the Chancellor was sufficient.

It will be seen therefore that abundant precaution exists under which ministerial responsibility for each act of administration can be fixed. Behind, of course, the responsibility of each minister, stands that of the Cabinet, which, however, can in effect be relieved thereof by the resignation of the minister responsible,[35] unless the opposition is able to enforce responsibility by defeating the ministry.[36]

[34] See Constitution of Eire, Art. 29; Union Royal Executive Functions and Seals Act, 1934.

[35] *E.g.*, Mr. Birrell in 1916, over Ireland (Spender, *Lord Oxford*, ii. 213 f.); Col. Seely in 1914 (*ibid.*, ii. 44 f.); Mr. Montagu in 1922 (Fitzroy, *Memoirs*, ii. 775–77).

[36] See Anson, *The Law and Custom of the Constitution*, vol. II. (ed. Keith), i. 62–70.

CHAPTER 8

THE KING'S INFLUENCE ON PUBLIC AFFAIRS

1. THE SOURCES AND CHARACTER OF ROYAL INFLUENCE

MANY causes unite to give the King a position of unique character and influence. In a country like Britain heredity counts for much, and the long lineage of the sovereign itself demands respect; even the lest dependent mind is moved by the existence of so striking a link with the past. Moreover, the social prestige of the sovereign is very great, and the influence of 'society' on political feeling is far from negligible. We have the constant experience that elevation to the House of Lords produces rapid alienation from Liberal or Labour sentiments even in a few years, while the next generation in the peerage is normally noted for a distinguished vehemence of Conservative thought.

But those who care for none of these things nevertheless support the monarch for an essential reason. He forms the ideal mode of hypostatising the State, and giving men a living person to whom they can pay the debt of loyalty which they owe the State. The appeal to 'My King and my Country' is far stronger psychologically than that of 'my country' only to the vast majority of minds.[1] If the imperial idea has a strong hold on Britain, it is largely due to the pageantry of the Jubilee celebrations of 1887 and 1897, and the imperial note was also struck in a most effective manner in the Jubilee of 1935 and the Coronation of 1937. Since the development of Dominion autonomy a new importance has more and more come to attach to the Crown, the fact that a common King and a common allegiance form the sole remaining link between the United Kingdom and the Dominions. The importance of this aspect of the Crown[2] is doubtless only in part appreciated by the masses of the people, but it adds a solid consideration in favour of

[1] *E.g.*, Herr Hitler proved far more inspiring than the Republic; contrast Finer, *Theory and Practice of Modern Government*, ii. 1126.
[2] Noted in 1902, after the Queen's death, by Mr. Balfour; Dugdale, *Arthur James Balfour*, i. 317.

the maintenance of monarchy. Nor is there any doubt of the value which attaches in the eyes of students of the constitution to an office which serves so well to provide the State with a formal and cere- monial head and saves it from all the turmoil and excitement almost inevitably involved in the office of President.

Moreover, the King is very wisely brought into immediate connection with many essential features of government and adminis- tration. He is the head of the army, the navy, and the air force, and of the civil service. The administration of justice is carried out in his name, and that fact adds much to the impressive character of judicial process; the judges are his judges. His head on the postage stamps and on the coinage is a perpetual reminder of his existence and a presentation of his personality. It is regarded as a distinction to hold an appointment from the King, as do Regius Professors and various other officials.

Further, the King is the fountain of honour, and in a country like Britain this aspect of the sovereign counts for very much, as could easily be appreciated by the attitude adopted by so many of his subjects on the occasion of the Jubilee celebrations of 1935, the Coronation of 1937 and the marriage of Princess Elizabeth. Nor, though it is widely known that the prerogative of mercy is one essentially in the hands of the Home Secretary, it is unimportant that it is exercised in the name of the King, and that certain docu- ments bear his signature, for the impression is given that remission of punishment reflects the gracious side of royalty.

The value of the Crown is enhanced in many minds by the readiness now shown by the sovereign and the rest of the royal family to take part in the ceremonials of all kinds which are more and more in favour with the emergence of the people from the grimmer toil and aversion to frivolity of the Victorian era. Much aid can be given in this way to the encouragement of worthy ends in education, in public health, and in varied forms of social service.

But the essential factor in giving the King influence in matters political is the history of the monarchy. The King is descended from a long line of ancestors, who were all in greater or less degree concerned with State affairs, and the most dominant feature of modern British constitutional history is the reign of Queen Victoria and her tradition of service. It is perfectly true that for many years of her reign the Queen was far from popular, but the length of her reign and its unique character among the contemporary sovereignties of Europe, together with the efforts to encourage her people in the dreary days of the South African War, succeeded in establishing a tradition, since her death, greatly enhanced by the publication of her *Letters*, which reveal her incessant toil in the field of public affairs.[3]   Edward VII. has been accused of lack of aptitude or desire for business,[4] but this impression seems, on the whole, unjust, having regard to the evidence available of his activities, mainly no doubt in the field of foreign affairs and defence,[5] but also in other directions.   George V., by common consent, set himself the duty of accomplishing a large amount of business, and George VI. continued his father's practice of devotion to duty.[6]

Training in important public affairs from a comparatively early age and length of tenure of office plainly give ripe experience and render a sovereign as time goes on capable of playing mentor to ministers of less standing.   Queen Victoria, in the latter years of her life, formed a living link with the Great Duke and with an epoch which was for some of her ministers merely history, and George V. had been King for thirteen years when he appointed Mr. Baldwin his Prime Minister.   To judge from the evidence so far known, few ministers or ex-ministers have felt able to treat their sovereign with less than deference.   That of Mr. Gladstone, despite his intellectual superiority, was real and profound, that of Mr. Disraeli must have been in substance sincere, and Lord Salisbury never took liberties with the Queen.   Sir A. Fitzroy attests the ability of the King to hold his own against Lord Lansdowne and Mr. Bonar Law—despite the brusqueness of the latter on the one hand, and the Prime Minister on the other, and Mr. Asquith bears testimony to his firmness and appreciation of the different aspects of his own position.   Moreover, it must be remembered that the Crown has access to non-ministerial sources of information of no slight value, which, added to personal experience, place the sovereign in a position to carry on arguments with even a very able minister.   No doubt the distance between the Crown and the facts with which ministers have to deal is often great.   Queen Victoria was patently in her old age unable to

---

[3] This latter aspect of her reign is admirably brought out in Hardie, *The Political Influence of Queen Victoria*.

[4] Cf. Lord Ponsonby's criticisms, *The Observer*, July 1, 1934.

[5] Lee, *Edward VII.*, and Esher, *Journals and Letters*, both stress the great interest taken by the King in foreign policy and defence.   For Grey's comments, see *Twenty-five Years*, i. 204 ff.

[6] Churchill, *The Second World War*, ii. 335.

appreciate the spirit of the new times, as is seen in her attitude to Mr. J. Chamberlain and his modernism.[7] Writing of her later, Lord Gladstone remarked:

> 'Prince Albert and Lord Beaconsfield alike had made her believe that continuity of high responsibility gave her knowledge and experience to which no passing minister could attain. . . . But in fact this continuity on the heights cut her off from all personal contact with the ideas of the people, and relieved her from the necessity of ever going to the roots of big questions by reason and argument. Politicians had to fight these things out in principle and detail on the platform, in the press, and in the House of Commons. . . . Continuity such as the Queen experienced, was a great disadvantage because in its constitutional irresponsibility it was out of touch with forward movements.'[8]

But kings move with the times, and it would be difficult to assert that George VI. is not by experience well equipped fully to understand those difficult social issues which represent the main internal problems of the realm. Foreign policies have always had a distinct fascination for the royal family, and if George V. was not so much concerned therewith as his father, that was due in part to the many other issues which held attention during his reign.

But the influence of the Crown is now wholly different from the ideal set by Lord Beaconsfield when, on September 25, 1879,[9] 'he still trusts that events will show that the sovereign of Great Britain is the arbitress of Europe,' and responded to by the Queen on October 2, with the warning, 'In the Queen's long experience, half measures, temporising with Cabinet and Parliament are *no use*. Don't make promises and declarations to satisfy Parliament, especially *not* when the honour and safety of the country and the great Empire and colonies belonging to it are concerned. They have hampered us in Zululand.'[10] A very different view is presented by Lord Grey,[11] who points out that though in theory constitutional monarchy might be shown to be improbable, the Crown must either be a check on democracy or be reduced to futility. The conditions for success he gives are plain. The monarchy must be hereditary; the sovereign must embody the traditions of the past as well as the practice of the present; his previous life must have

---

[7] *Letters of Queen Victoria*, 2 s., iii. 165, 290, 298, 522 ff., 550 ff., 554, 652.
[8] Lord Gladstone, *After Thirty Years*, p. 375.
[9] *Letters of Queen Victoria*, 2 s., iii. 49; 'dictatress,' on p. 46.
[10] *Ibid.*, 2 s., iii. 50.   [11] Grey, *Twenty-five Years*, i. 208 f.

trained him for the position. He must realise that the Crown is a democratic institution. Each ministry must have his confidence, support and goodwill. However much his influence may be used in favour of his personal opinion about policy or appointments, he must do nothing to weaken or undermine the position of ministers. In return the attitude must be one of respect as well as frankness; they must be careful to protect the monarchy and observe its forms. The performance by the sovereign of the duties and his observance of the limitations of the monarchy must be repaid by perfect loyalty to him. This, he suggests, was the attitude adopted from the first by George V.

The satisfactory evolution of the monarchy explains the failure of republicanism so far to achieve any real hold on British political opinion. Queen Victoria's reign saw for various reasons the development of a spirit of discontent during the period when, after the Prince Consort's death in 1861, she devoted herself to seclusion. In 1864,[12] in addition to growing unpopularity on this score, she was attacked for alleged partiality to Germany in the matter of Schleswig-Holstein. Attacks on her seclusion were marked in 1871,[13] when also complaint was made of her failure to spend on public entertainment her large civil list, and it was suggested that instead she was accumulating a private fortune. Sir C. Dilke, at Newcastle, on November 6,[14] uttered words on republicanism which the Queen never forgave, and Mr. Chamberlain commented on it to the effect that the republic must come, and at the rate at which we are moving it will come in our generation. In 1872,[15] Dilke demanded an enquiry into the civil list, with the result that he was in a minority of 276 votes to two. But the prospect of office induced Dilke on March 13, 1880, to explain that, while, if the country were starting afresh like France after Sedan, a republican constitution would be the best, there was no justification in disturbing constitutional monarchy, a recantation which allowed him to become Under-Secretary of State.[16] In 1872, Mr. Bradlaugh's *Impeachment of the House of Brunswick* attacked the pro-German attitude of the Queen, but did not actually plead for republicanism

---

12 175 *Parl. Deb.* 3 s., 609. In May, 1879, Mr. Dillwyn's attack was on the prerogative rather than the Queen.
13 Hardie, *Political Influence of Queen Victoria*, pp. 205 ff.
14 Gwynn and Tuckwell, *Dilke*, i. 139. He had opposed the grant of £30,000 as dowry for Princess Louise.
15 *Letters of Queen Victoria*, 2 s., ii. 202.
16 Gwynn and Tuckwell, *Dilke*, i. 308.

forthwith. In the next year the last republican conference met at Birmingham, and Mr. Chamberlain was absent no less than Mr. Bright. In 1874 Mr. Chamberlain welcomed the Prince and Princess of Wales to Birmingham. But in 1883 he committed the *faux pas*, in contrasting the jubilee celebration of Mr. Bright with the recent coronation of the Czar, of saying 'the representatives of royalty were absent . . . and nobody missed them.'[17] The Queen was angry with Mr. Gladstone for having induced her to accept such a minister, but he denied any lack of respect.[18] Beyond some occasional grumbling at royal grants,[19] which Mr. Gladstone supported as far as he possibly could, no serious dissatisfaction appeared later. There has been no substantial revival since of attack personally on the Crown. Incidental criticism has been made, especially in respect of acceptance of Mr. MacDonald's change of front in 1931.[20] But the constitutional character of royal action was even then supported by Lord Passfield.[21] The fact is the more surprising because the abdication of Edward VIII. took place in circumstances which would have given an admirable opportunity for a pronouncement in favour of republicanism, if it had existed.[22] As it was, the support of the disappearance of the Crown was voiced only by individual members of advanced Independent Labour views, and the Labour attitude in general was that of full acceptance of the Crown. The continuation of this attitude is doubtless dependent on the acceptance by the sovereign of the definition of his position summarised above from Lord Grey.[23]

2. THE SOVEREIGN AND INTERNAL AFFAIRS

MUCH has already been said incidentally of the influence of Queen Victoria on the course of internal affairs. Her opinions were definitely Conservative, as was natural enough, but they were confirmed in this aspect by the association with Mr. Disraeli in the

---

[17] Garvin, *Joseph Chamberlain*, i. 395.   [18] *Letters of Queen Victoria*, 2 s., iii. 431.
[19] *Ibid.*, 3 s., i. 384, 509, 514, 520.
[20] H. J. Laski, *The Crisis and the Constitution*, p. 34.
[21] *What happened in 1931: A Record* (Fabian Tract No. 237), p. 8.
[22] December 11, 1936: 403 to 5 votes (Mr. Maxton leading); 318 *H. C. Deb.* 5 s., 2203 ff.
[23] The excitement in March, 1914, over the Curragh episode terminated with the formal assertion on March 25 by Mr. Asquith of the King's completely constitutional attitude throughout; see Legge, *King George*, i. 113 ff. Col. Ward had raised the point on March 24: 'What we demand, Mr. Speaker, is the right to make laws absolutely without interference, either from King or Army.'

ministry of 1874–80, and from that date they never varied in substance. Mr. Gladstone, on the other hand, tended steadily towards more advanced democratic views, and, unlike the Queen, his interests were in domestic affairs rather than in foreign policy, to which naturally the Prince Consort had been specially attracted, and in which Mr. Disraeli had been deeply concerned together with the sovereign. It was, perhaps, this difference of interest, as well as divergences of view, which led her later to complain that 'Lord Beaconsfield raised up the position of Great Britain from '74 to '80 in a marvellous manner. Mr. Gladstone and Lord Granville pulled it down again during the five years of their mischievous and fatal misrule.'[24] It is fair also to note the much greater psychological appreciation of the Queen shown by Mr. Disraeli, whose sympathy with her in her bereavement was no doubt real, though his admiration for her intellectual capacities can hardly have been wholly sincere. Mr. Gladstone certainly erred in treating his sovereign as if she possessed his own intellectual subtlety, wide knowledge and enthusiasm,[25] and his failure naturally raised a barrier between them which his, to modern eyes almost exaggerated, loyalty to the throne was powerless to remove. From the moment when, in 1862, Mr. Gladstone found his powers as a popular speaker in his northern tour, he was moving steadily to the Left, and his separation in 1865 from Oxford University set his development free. It is significant that in his old age he could realise the necessity of Home Rule, when Mr. Chamberlain destroyed the possibility of enduring achievement by shrinking from an intellectual advance foreign to his settled convictions of middle age. His susceptibility to new ideas was noted by Lord Rosebery in 1892,[26] and contrasts most interestingly with the imperviousness to such influences of the amiable Lord Granville.[27]

The divergence of opinion between the Queen and Mr. Gladstone was no doubt at first connected with issues of a special kind, the disestablishment of the Irish Church, and the controversy over the position of the Commander-in-Chief.[28] The other bone

---

[24] *Letters of Queen Victoria*, 3 s., i. 196.
[25] L. Stachey, *Queen Victoria*, p. 215. See Hardie, *Political Influence of Queen Victoria*, pp. 46 ff.
[26] Esher, *Journals and Letters*, i. 163.
[27] Hardie, *Political Influence of Queen Victoria*, p. 127, n. 4, cites Mrs. Webb's contemptuous view, but Fitzmaurice's *Life* shows that he had some intelligence.
[28] Cf. Guedalla, *The Queen and Mr. Gladstone*, i. 269, 274 f. The Queen was approached before the Cabinet was consulted.

of discord was significantly enough connected with the Premier's suggestion of further employment for the Prince of Wales and a royal residence in Ireland.[29] But it is clear from Viscount Gladstone's evidence,[30] that the association between the Queen and Mr. Disraeli after 1874 was the essential cause of estrangement, though she had welcomed his victory as showing the existence of a strong Conservative Party. The Queen was accused by Lady Ponsonby,[31] in a letter to her husband as early as 1878, of having been converted by Mr. Disraeli into the belief in the idea of personal government.[32]

But more serious damage to the relations of Premier and sovereign had been caused in 1871 over the issue of the royal determination at seclusion.[33] General Grey, her Private Secretary, who was fully aware of the demands on her time, did not approve it, and encouraged Mr. Gladstone to press her to remain in England until the end of the session, but the threat of abdication resulted, and when the Premier visited Balmoral later he found her manner repellent. It was, of course, plain that this failure to take part in public affairs was a definite danger to the popularity of the throne: 'Worse things may easily be imagined; but smaller and meaner cause for the decay of thrones cannot be conceived.' Still, it was the Gladstonian opposition to the foreign policy of his rival which resulted in the attempt, already mentioned, to keep him out of the Premiership in 1880. But in addition to determination not to reverse that policy, the Queen declared, on April 8, that there must be no democratic leaning,[34] and Lord Hartington tried to console her for the necessity of accepting Mr. Gladstone by the consideration that, if he had to form a ministry, it would have to be more Radical than that of Mr. Gladstone.[35] Compelled to accept Mr. Gladstone, she denied him any serious confidence. But the essential feature now became the royal opposition to any tampering with the

29 Guedalla, *The Queen and Mr. Gladstone*, i. 351 ff., 359 ff., 368 ff., 374 ff., 381.

30 Lord Gladstone, *After Thirty Years*, pp. 320 ff.

31 Ponsonby, *Mary Ponsonby*, p. 144. In 1874, Mr. Disraeli begged for her advice in regard to a living for Dr. Hayman: *Letters of Queen Victoria*, 2 s., ii. 333.

32 Cf. Lord Beaconsfield's hope to make her 'arbitress of Europe' in 1879: *Letters of Queen Victoria*, 2 s., iii. 49.

33 Guedalla, *The Queen and Mr. Gladstone*, i. 66–70, 297 ff. It was one of Mr. Disraeli's greatest feats that she stayed two days for the Czar's reception in 1874.

34 Letter to Lady Ely, *Letters of Queen Victoria*, 2 s., iii. 47 f.

35 *Ibid.*, 2 s., iii. 75 ff; Esher, *Journals and Letters*, i. 69.

constitution; the House of Lords now appeared to her essentially bound up with the monarchy and as necessary to keep the Commons from usurping power, a doctrine which ran wholly counter to the trend of opinion in her Premier's mind. Despite her aid to the Premier in 1884 in the matter of the franchise and redistribution, her own feeling was that the Premier was undermining the position of the Crown and Lords, and she deprecated his refusal to dissolve so as to obtain a verdict from the people on his franchise scheme. She seems, indeed, even to have contemplated forcing a dissolution on the issue. It is significant that Mr. Chamberlain fell under special displeasure on the score of his attitude to the Lords.

It was inevitable that on Home Rule there should be hopeless divergence of view. The Queen, however, took the very reasonable position of suggesting that the new policy had not the support of the majority of her subjects in the United Kingdom, and aimed at one time at creating a centre party under Lord Hartington with moderate Conservatives and Liberals.[36] She claimed that 'this is no party question, but one which concerns the safety, honour, and welfare of her dominions.'[37] Later she aimed at detaching the Liberals, who favoured union, from the main body of Liberals, and in December, 1885, as we have seen,[38] sought to induce Mr. Goschen, who disliked much Mr. Gladstone's eastern policy, to secure such a result. Her attitude now went so far as to endeavour to persuade the Duke of Roxburghe publicly to announce that his wife had refused the offer of the post of Mistress of the Robes on the score of opposition to the Irish policy of her Prime Minister.[39] While he was in office she was sustained by the certainty of his defeat, and consulted Lord Salisbury as to whether in that event it would be convenient to the Conservatives if she allowed him to dissolve.[40] Moreover, she was disappointed at his attitude towards the House of Lords, though he refused to accept Mr. Labouchere's demand for the abolition of the hereditary element. The Queen insisted on (1) the value of a body which was independent and need not, therefore, have to make pledges which proved undesirable to

[36] Gardiner, *Harcourt*, i. 552. Cf. her suggestion to the Duke of Argyll in 1884; *Letters of Queen Victoria*, 2 s., iii. 547.
[37] *Ibid.*, 3 s., i. 102.
[38] *Ante*, pp. 33 f.
[39] *Letters of Queen Victoria*, 3 s., i. 51.
[40] *Ibid.*, 3 s., i. 129.

keep; (2) the fact that any attack on the Lords must affect the stability of the Crown and the Commons; and (3) the necessity of the Lords to combat Radical doctrines.[41]

The Queen's hostility to the election of 1892[42] and to the necessity of facing the 'danger to the country, to Europe, to her vast Empire, which is involved in having all those great interests entrusted to the shaking hand of an old, wild and incomprehensible man of $82\frac{1}{2}$' is painfully recorded,[43] and her hostility to Home Rule was only modified by the certainty of its defeat in the Lords. Her concern to prevent any agitation against the Lords and the idea of forcing a dissolution to prevent this action whether by Mr. Gladstone or Lord Rosebery had already been mentioned.

Of Edward VII. it was not to be expected that he should be other than Conservative in essential outlook. Sir C. Dilke, in 1882, pointed out that he was essentially a Conservative and even more of a jingo than his mother, though more under the influence of the last person with whom he had discussed a matter, and with more sense and more usage of the modern world then his mother.[44] Even Sir S. Lee admits that his Palmerstonian faith never completely reconciled him to the full claims of political democracy.[45] This explains his hostility to Home Rule expressed vehemently in 1886,[46] and never it may safely be assumed relaxed. It is clear that in the matter of the House of Lords he was not in much sympathy with his ministry, but his power of accommodating himself to political necessities is shown in his readiness to consider that change might be requisite. His own plan for the reconstruction of the Lords was decidedly conservative, though not uninteresting. As set out to Lord Crewe on January 30, 1910,[47] it preserved the hereditary principle unimpaired as regards the right to membership and to take part in the debates, but one hundred only, fifty on each side, chosen by the leaders of the Conservatives and Liberals in the House, would be able to vote. This would mean, if moderate men

41 Guedalla, *The Queen and Mr. Gladstone*, ii. 278 ff., 283 ff., 291 f., 298.
42 For the sham character of royal audiences in 1892–94 see *ibid.*, ii. 71; Lord Gladstone, *After Thirty Years*, p. 341.
43 Newton, *Lansdowne*, p. 100. Her desire for a six wecks' close season for tourists in the Highlands being inserted in Bryce's Access to Mountains Bills of 1892 naturally did nothing to increase her welcome for a Liberal ministry; *Letters of Queen Victoria*, 3 s., ii. 112, 114 f.
44 Gwynn and Tuckwell, *Dilke*, i. 500.
45 Lee, *Edward VII.*, i. 518.
46 *Ibid.*, i. 526.   47 *Ibid.*, ii. 695 f.

were chosen, that no Bill would be thrown out if it came strongly endorsed by the Commons on second reading, and that a reasonable compromise would be achieved on third reading. Lord Crewe made the obvious comment that the party leaders would be little likely to accept the duty of nominating moderate men.

The King, however, realised far more clearly than his mother the limits of royal resistance on matters in general, though he bitterly resented Mr. Lloyd George's attacks on the peerage. He seems clearly to have wished compromise by the Opposition on the issue of education,[48] but it does not appear that he cared for the modest Bill to increase small holdings in Scotland,[49] no doubt because opinion among the Scottish aristocracy was, as usual, unfavourable to anything which might affect sporting facilities or their complete control of their estates. Nor is there any evidence of his positive approval of the great social legislation which marked the first ministry really democratic in character, that of Mr. Asquith.[50] His attitude is well illustrated by a sentence from a letter from his private secretary written to the Prime Minister on the subject of the Army reforms of 1905. 'The King cannot withhold his consent from the proposals which he is advised by the Cabinet to approve, but he cannot conceal his strong misgiving.'[51]

Of the attitude of George V. towards internal reforms nothing can be said positively. The impression from his attitude to the great issue of the House of Lords is that he accepted in the fullest sense, though not without natural misgivings, the duty of a constitutional King.[52] This is the more to his credit, because of the grave impropriety of the efforts of Mr. Bonar Law, with the support of Mr. Chamberlain, and even of Mr. Balfour to throw upon him the onus of dismissing a ministry on the very problematic chance that he would, by an appeal to the country, secure a majority against the passing of the Parliament Bill, or later the Home Rule Bill.[53] It is not suggested that either measure appealed to the King. The measure on Irish government, we now know, was framed to cover the whole of Ireland, not from conviction that this was proper, but from reasons of tactics, but this view does not appear

[48] Lee, *Edward VII*, ii. 455–65, 658 f.   [49] *Ibid.*, ii. 476 f.
[50] The King was annoyed at Mr. Balfour's failure to tell him in advance of his proposal to attack (March 4, 1903) Lord Rosebery's theory of a central party, *ibid.*, ii. 50.
[51] *Ibid.*, ii. 206.   [52] *Ante*, p. 311.
[53] For various articles urging royal intervention, see Legge, *King George*, i. 84 ff.

to have been made clear at the inception to the King, nor is it clear that he would have been willing to agree to the promotion of a measure which it was not intended seriously to press forward in the vital matter of the inclusion of Ulster. In this regard it may fairly be said that the sovereign might have had serious grounds of complaint against the ministry for lack of candour to him and also to the electorate. No doubt, the exigencies of placating the Irish vote could be pleaded in palliation, but hardly as a valid excuse.

The movement for female suffrage aroused grave objection on the part of Edward VII., only natural in view of the tactics employed by those who promoted the movement,[54] but it is not probable that the new sovereign found any difficulty in adapting himself either to the change of 1918 or the more far-reaching one of 1928. It is easy to imagine how Queen Victoria or even Edward VII. would have viewed the sweeping away in 1918 of the safeguards which guaranteed a minimum of political capacity in the electors.

3. THE SOVEREIGN AND FOREIGN POLICY

OWING doubtless in large measure to her marriage to Prince Albert and to the influence of the King of the Belgians, Queen Victoria early manifested a deep interest in foreign issues. Marriages extended, in course of time, the sphere of her concern; the end of her reign saw the German Emperor her grandson, the Czar of Russia married to her granddaughter, while four other grand-daughters were destined to become Queens in Greece, Rumania, Norway, and Spain. Mr. Gladstone has testified the value of the contacts which she established with other royalties, and there is no evidence to the contrary. Whether, of course, the existence of family connections is always desirable as between sovereigns may be doubted; if William II. had a considerable respect for his grand-mother, and could acquiesce in very firm language as in the case of her rebuke when he suggested mediation in the South African War, his personal quarrels with Edward VII.,[55] both before and after his accession to the throne, cannot be regarded as wholly unconnected with his growing hostility to Britain.

At first the Queen's relations with Lord Palmerston were cordial, but she was undoubtedly perturbed by his hostility to France in

---

54 Lee, *Edward VII.*, ii. 467 f.; Spender, *Lord Oxford*, i. 243.
55 Lee, *Edward VII.*, ii. 94 f., 117 ff.

1840–41, over the issue of the position of Mehemet Ali in Egypt,[56] and King Leopold, who was most anxious to avoid war, certainly did everything he diplomatically could to alter her confidence in Palmerston. The result, no doubt, was her eventual cordiality to Louis Philippe and her acceptance of the failure of that sovereign to ratify the treaty between the five powers for suppression of the slave trade. Nor did she protest against the Ashburton Treaty with the United States[57] under which that nobleman, whose wife and property interests were largely American, made generous surrender of British territorial claims, while the miseries of African negroes were continued by the surrender of the right of visit, and France was thus encouraged to terminate the agreements of 1831 and 1833 for mutual right of search. The visit of the Queen and the Prince to France in 1843 was secured through the influence of the King of the Belgians.[58] In the period of Palmerston's return to the Foreign Office, for a time the Queen worked wholeheartedly with him in the famous episode of the Spanish marriage plans,[59] the result of which was to show complete dishonesty on the part of the French sovereign in the disgraceful marriage arranged for the young Queen of Spain in the hope of the ultimate reversion of the throne to Louis Philippe's son. The Queen spontaneously rebuked the King in severe terms.

Trouble arose, however, over Palmerston's drastic attitude towards Queen Maria of Portugal, who was oppressing her subjects and endeavouring to suppress the rebels at Oporto. Queen Victoria disliked his harshness to another Queen, and it was only with the aid of Lord John Russell that he was able in 1847 to secure promises of reforms from Maria which justified the grant of British help to subdue the insurgents, whose revolt became unjustifiable when concessions were made.[60] It was from now onwards that the Queen complained of Palmerston's failure to submit despatches to her.[61] He was able to carry the Queen and the Prince with him in 1847–48 in his policy of encouraging moderate reform in Italy, and the mission of Lord Minto[62] may have helped the grant of constitutions in Piedmont, Tuscany and the Papal States, though the project of establishing diplomatic relations with the Vatican

56 Bell, *Palmerston*, i. 306, 312 f., 319 f.   57 *Ibid.*, i. 333–36.   58 *Ibid.*, i. 338 f.
59 *Ibid.*, i. 373 ff.; *Letters of Queen Victoria*, 1 s., i. 432, 485 ff.; ii. 31, 96–109.
60 Bell, *Palmerston*, i. 391 ff.
61 *Letters of Queen Victoria*, 1 s., ii. 132, 143, 153, 202.
62 Bell, *Palmerston*, i. 413–17.

foundered on the demand of the Lords, approved by Palmerston, that the envoy should not be a prelate. The subsequent events in Italy with the attack of Piedmont on Austria produced fundamental divergence of view, for an entente with the French Republic, established through the deposition of Louis Philippe, to drive Austria from Italy, was wholly repugnant to the Queen,[63] who detested also the idea that peoples had the right by universal suffrage to decide their allegiance, though obviously this doctrine was essential to Palmerston's schemes for the creation of a strong Italian kingdom. Palmerston's habit of sending off despatches before she had seen them, and of altering some she had seen, irritated the Queen, who made no allowance for the necessity of greater haste than was possible if she held over drafts for long consideration, but Palmerston was, no doubt, to blame in considerable measure. Moreover, the British envoy at Madrid was summarily dismissed because of the terms of warnings to the ministry to practise moderation given by Palmerston.[64] But a worse step was his reproof to Austria for the atrocious conduct of Marshal Radetzky in Milan, which arrived when Prince Schwartzenberg had just restored full power in Vienna, and resulted in the refusal of Austria to send an archduke to announce to Victoria the accession of Francis Joseph.[65] The Queen was so angry that she allowed Lord Aberdeen to explain to the Austrian chargé d'affaires that she quite understood the Austrian action.[66] As she had vainly tried in September, 1848, to induce the Premier to move Palmerston from his post and to make him Lord Lieutenant of Ireland, it is possible to excuse her annoyance, though not the action of Lord Aberdeen. A worse *faux pas* on her minister's part was undoubtedly his connivance at the withdrawal from a government arsenal of guns, which a contractor desired to provide for the aid of the Sicilian rebels against the tyranny of Ferdinand II.[67] Lord Grey and his colleagues resented this error, and Lord John Russell wished to have an apology offered to the Neapolitan Government, and suggested that he might transfer him to Ireland with an English peerage and the Garter to soften the blow. But he

[63] *Letters of Queen Victoria*, 1 s., ii. 215 f.; Bell, *Palmerston*, ii. 435.
[64] *Ibid.*, i. 439 f.　　　　　　　　[65] *Ibid.*, i. 441–43.
[66] His 'antiquated imbecility' was hinted at by Palmerston in revenge; 107 *Parl. Deb.* 3 s., 810.
[67] Bell, *Palmerston*, i. 443–45; Russell, *Later Correspondence of Lord John Russell*, i. 348 f.; Greville, *Memoirs*, 2 s., iii. 276 f.

declined to move, and all that was settled was to offer an apology
if Ferdinand asked for it, while Palmerston won a distinct success
in the Commons in his own defence.   It is, however, characteristic
of the unsatisfactory character of the whole position that Lord
Ponsonby, the ambassador to Austria, was disloyal to his chief and
working against him behind his back in communication with the
royal entourage.

Differences of opinion were accentuated over the relations of
Prussia and Denmark regarding Schleswig-Holstein,[68] and the
Queen, whose sympathies were Prussian, resented his success in
securing a protocol by the five great powers, asserting the doctrine
of the maintenance of the integrity of the Danish possessions.   She
equally disliked his intervention to urge the Turkish Government to
refuse to surrender the Poles and Hungarians who escaped thither
from the disgraceful treatment accorded to them by Russia and
Austria, and his defence in September, 1849, of the Hungarian
revolution as embodying the principles which had placed the
Hanoverian dynasty on the throne.[69]   But, even so, it is amazing
that the Queen had persuaded herself that all his measures on the
Continent were in favour of a movement, anti-constitutional, anti-
Protestant, and anti-English, and that Prince Albert could believe
that, since Palmerston's return to power, Britain had not had a
single success except perhaps in Switzerland, where the credit
belonged to Stratford Canning.[70]   The removal of Palmerston was
planned in 1850,[71] on the basis of his chief's going to the Upper
House as Foreign Secretary, while Palmerston became Home
Secretary and leader of the Commons, but this plan miscarried.
Palmerston had unwisely supported a very dubious claim against the
Greek Government by Don Pacifico, and the British fleet was used
to enforce surrender, which France helped to mediate.   But
Palmerston postponed notification of the settlement, so that
another accord was made under coercion, and he so annoyed
France that the recall of her envoy was mooted, and the French,
Russian and Bavarian courts were not represented at the diplomatic
celebration of the Queen's birthday.[72]   A combined effort was
made by Lord Aberdeen, inspired by M. Guizot and Princess

[68] Bell, *Palmerston*, ii. 6 ff.   [69] *Ibid.*, ii. 17 ff.
[70] On this episode see *ibid.*, i. 403–7.
[71] *Letters of Queen Victoria*, 1 s., ii. 281 f.; 306 ff.; Greville, *Memoirs*, 2 s., iii. 316 ff.,
    335 ff.
[72] Bell, *Palmerston*, ii. 22–28.

Lieven, to muster the protectionists to procure his fall through Lord Stanley's attack on June 17 in the Lords, but the defence of his foreign policy as a whole by Palmerston on June 25 won him a remarkable success against the hostility of the Crown and the doubts of the Cabinet, as well as the combined denunciations of the protectionists, Peelites and Manchester advocates of economic internationalism.[73]

In August the Queen took the only step open to her, as the minister would not go and could not be dismissed without breaking up the Government, and defined the relations of the Crown and Foreign Secretary by a memorandum already alluded to.[74] Palmerston accepted it, because, *inter alia*, to reject it and resign would have brought the Queen directly into politics. So little did he worry over it that, soon after, he despatched the apology to the Austrian Emperor for the assault made on the infamous General Haynau by brewery men when he visited Barclay's Brewery in London, without giving the Queen the chance of strengthening its terms.[75] Nor could the resignation of the ministry in February, 1851, bring relief, for it was found impossible to secure an alternative Government.[76] Moreover, Lord J. Russell could not move Palmerston to another office for, as he pointed out to the Queen, Palmerston was 'the strength of the Government from his popularity with the Radicals.'[77] At the end of October, the arrival of Kossuth in London, and his announcement of intention to visit the minister, procured an urgent royal command, requested by the Premier, that he should not do so, but in fact it was a Cabinet resolve, not based on the royal wishes, which induced the minister to accept the request to decline a visit. But at once he received delegations, who referred to the Emperors of Russia and Austria as 'odious and detestable tyrants.' The Queen was angry enough to be rude to Lady Palmerston, while, in revenge, the Emperor withheld much longer than usual the reception of the new British ambassador, a slight which maddened the Queen.[78] On December 3 he commented favourably to the French ambassador on Louis Napoleon's *coup d'état*.[79] It seems that Lord John Russell

73 *Letters of Queen Victoria*, 1 s., ii. 299 ff.
74 *Ante*, p. 78.
75 *Letters of Queen Victoria*, 1 s., ii. 319.
76 *Ibid.*, 1 s., ii. 345 ff.
77 *Ibid.*, 1 s., ii. 377.
78 *Ibid.*, 1 s., ii. 392 ff.
79 *Ibid.*, 1 s., ii. 404 ff.; Bell, *Palmerston*, ii. 48–51; Greville, *Memoirs*, 2 s., iii. 433 ff.

had done the same thing, but the Cabinet decision was in favour of absolute neutrality, and the utterly incompetent British ambassador at Paris, who disliked Palmerston, communicated this view to the French Government, only to be told of the opinion of Palmerston. The ambassador was delighted to revenge himself and complained to the minister, who replied with a sufficient defence, but did not, before sending it, communicate the papers to the Queen, who had learned from Col. Phipps, brother of Lord Normanby, of his grievances. She was deeply angry, and Lord John Russell was, as he later admitted, hasty and precipitate enought to demand, on December 19, his resignation. This decision was later approved by the Cabinet and delighted the Queen. She then, with the very disingenuous aid of Lord John Russell, secured the Foreign Secretaryship for Lord Granville, to the exclusion of Lord Clarendon, who denounced the desire of the Queen and the Prince to manage foreign policy through courtiers, even though they had 'suffered such deep humiliation from Palmerston that they now fear an independent-minded man as a scalded dog does cold water.'[80] Lord Granville, who had no great ability, was then required to draw up a programme of policy which after approval was to be adhered to. Palmerston's defence on February 3, 1852, lacked fire, partly perhaps because Lord J. Russell read a memorandum of August, 1850, which was an unexpected and rather discreditable blow. But on February 20 he defeated the weakened and discredited ministry on the militia issue.

In the Aberdeen Cabinet, as Home Secretary, Palmerston was still of vital importance in foreign affairs, winning support from Clarendon and Lord J. Russell, and in some measure unquestionably bearing responsibility for bringing on the war, but his attitude in Cabinet was praised as irreproachable. In 1853 a discreditable intrigue, approved by Lord Aberdeen, extruded Palmerston for a brief period from the Cabinet in view of his attitude towards reform, but the majority of the Cabinet compelled Lord Aberdeen and Lord J. Russell to readmit a man whose ability was such as to make both negligible in comparison.[81] The Prince and the Queen, who had eagerly desired his fall, were soon to admire him as the driving power for effective conduct of war, for which Lord Aberdeen was plainly quite unfitted. When Lord J. Russell broke up the

---

80 Sir Herbert Maxwell, *Life and Letters of Lord Clarendon*, i. 334 ff.
81 Bell, *Palmerston*, ii. 94–101.

ministry by his resignation (January 23, 1855) over Mr. Roebuck's demand for a Parliamentary enquiry into the war in the Crimea, Palmerston's appointment as Prime Minister became inevitable. Moreover, when he was defeated in 1857 as the result of his high-handed policy towards China in the matter of the lorcha *Arrow*,[82] the Queen readily gave him a dissolution by which he effectively rallied the Liberals to his aid.

Nor had the Queen any hand in Lord Palmerston's defeat on February 19, 1858, on the unfair accusation of yielding feebly to the French demand for measures to discourage plots in Britain against the Emperor. After Palmerston became her Premier in 1859, difficulties were frequent, especially on Italian policy. The situation which resulted was remarkably unsatisfactory in a constitutional sense. The Queen and the Prince received information irregularly regarding Cabinet discussions, sought advice outside it, and used their knowledge to influence individual ministers to defeat the plans of the Prime Minister. On the other hand, Lord Palmerston and Lord J. Russell endeavoured to evade Cabinet control by committing the Government in speeches and in diplomatic interviews to policies not approved by the Cabinet, and by sending despatches which they knew the Cabinet would not accept. In July, 1859, Palmerston was eager for intervention on the side of France, but the Queen demanded a Cabinet decision, and this went against the Premier (July 24), who now had Mr. Gladstone as well as Lord J. Russell in general sympathy. The Premier was determined to secure that the terms of the preliminary peace of Villafranca should not become definitive as regards the hegemony in an Italian federation promised to Austria or the return of the rulers of Modena and Tuscany to their territories. Much bitterness ensued, and Prince Albert was guilty of the injustice of accusing Palmerston of disregarding British interests for the sake of revenge on Austria and of inspiring pamphlets against himself and the 'Coburg Influence.' Gradually the policy of the Prime Minister proved effective, for Austria decided not to insist in using troops in central Italy, and thus the duchies were able to join Sardinia. The Queen and the Prince shared their Premier's objections to Napoleon's taking Savoy and Nice as the price of his services to Sardinia. But the Queen was shocked at his proposal to induce

[82] Bell, *Palmerston*, ii. 167 ff.; Morley, *Gladstone*, i. 225 ff.

Austria to sell Venetia to Italy, and prevented the matter being mooted officially, though such action might have affected vitally the future of Austria by saving her from Italian hostility in 1866. She accepted, however, his refusal to help in any way the young King of Naples against Garibaldi and the Italian government.[83]

In relations with the United States the action of the Prince Consort in softening the tone of the British despatch on the *Trent* affair is well known, but Palmerston was a willing party to the change, and the despatch was excused as the work of some fourteen hands.[84] It seems that later in the struggle the Queen used her influence against any project of recognition of the Confederate States,[85] such as Mr. Gladstone would have liked,[86] but Palmerston seems always to have realised the dangers of hasty action.[87] On the other hand, her opposition to any co-operation with France on behalf of Polish rebels in 1863 was dictated by her devotion to German interests, and so in 1864 her steady hostility to any British intervention on behalf of the Danes. In February she used her influence to secure the dropping of the idea of sending a force to counter any Austrian naval action in the Baltic.[88] Here, again, the Queen acted quite unconstitutionally; she used Lord Granville to perform his usual rather contemptible work of reporting on the views of the Cabinet and of stirring up its members to oppose their chief; she sent him correspondence with the Duke of Coburg,[89] which she told him to show to any one of the Cabinet except Palmerston and Lord J. Russell, and she invited Lord Derby's support for the Cabinet views against those of her Premier.[90] Palmerston, unable to make head against her intrigues, which earned severe comment from Lord Ellenborough in the Lords in May, could only reprove her for allowing her personal views to leak out.[91] In fact she had no defence on that score, but her policy of acquiescence in the unjust treatment of Denmark prevailed. Yet it must not be thought that the Queen's influence was decisive. The essential fact throughout was that the majority of the Cabinet was against war, and that the Premier and Foreign Secretary had to support them only Lord Westbury and Lord Stanley of Alderley.[92]

[83] *Letters of Queen Victoria*, 1 s., iii. 450 ff.; Fitzmaurice, *Granville*, i. 352 ff.; Bell, *Palmerston*, ii. 220 ff.

[84] *Ibid.*, ii. 294 f.   [85] Gardiner, *Harcourt*, ii. 611.

[86] Morley, *Gladstone*, ii. 70 ff.; Bell, *Palmerston*, ii. 326–28.

[87] Bell, *Palmerston*, ii. 314 ff., 326 ff.   [88] *Letters of Queen Victoria*, 2 s., i. 174.

[89] Fitzmaurice, *Granville*, i. 468.   [90] *Letters of Queen Victoria*, 2 s., i. 154.

[91] *Ibid.*, 2 s., i. 186.   [92] Morley, *Gladstone*, ii. 118; Fitzmaurice, *Granville*, i. 462 ff.

The Queen, however, changed her attitude somewhat when Prussia began to turn on Austria, and even urged an alliance with France and Austria to counter Prussia,[93] but after Sadowa, she again thought of a liberal united Germany as an ally of Britain,[94] a curious dream inherited from the Prince Consort. She advocated, but in vain, the giving of a definite pledge to Portugal against a Spanish attack in 1869,[95] and urged a thorough understanding with Germany against France from 1867 onwards, in the hope that this alliance would prevent hostilities by France. When war seemed imminent, she consented to write to the Count of Flanders to induce his brother, Leopold of Hohenzollern, to withdraw his candidature for the throne of Spain,[96] and after the defeat of France she tried to induce the King of Prussia to moderate his terms of peace[97]; but Bismarck's influence, of which she now became fully aware,[98] prevented this, just as it had already negatived any possibility of the growth of her husband's ideal, a liberal Germany.

In 1876–78 her initiative appears at its height in her hostility to Russia, whose action she believed instigated the Bulgarian massacres in order to render it difficult to protect the Turks.[99] It is clear that on the whole she was working along the lines indicated by her Prime Minister, but it is also certain that once engaged in this course she proceeded to lengths embarrassing to her Premier, and used upon him the technique of abdication which has impressed the reluctant Cabinet: 'she cannot remain the sovereign of a country that is letting itself down to kiss the feet of the great barbarians.'[1] The policy thus followed was clearly unwise especially when seen in perspective, but probably the villain of the piece was rather the Prime Minister than his mistress. Still she must have the credit, or otherwise, of holding her disbelief in 'any permanent settlement of peace until we have fought and beaten the Russians.'[2]

Later, the royal concern centred in the difficulty of preventing unfavourable results in relations with Germany from the bitter

---

[93] *Letters of Queen Victoria*, 2 s., i. 314.
[94] *Ibid.*, 2 s., i. 364.
[95] *Ibid.*, 2 s., i. 589–92.
[96] *Ibid.*, 2 s., ii. 28.
[97] *Ibid.*, 2 s., ii. 71.
[98] *Ibid.*, 2 s., ii. 75 (Sir R. Morier's report).
[99] R. W. Seton-Watson, *Disraeli, Gladstone, and the Eastern Question*, pp. 197 f. The private mission of Col. Wellesley to the Czar was concealed from the Foreign Secretary.
[1] Monypenny and Buckle, *Disraeli*, ii. 1089 (January 10, 1887); 1020 (June 27); 1017 (June 14); 1117 (February 9, 1878).
[2] *Letters of Queen Victoria*, 2 s., ii. 625 (May 31, 1878).

quarrels between the Prince of Wales and William II., whose conduct to his mother gave just irritation to the aged Queen.[3] The Empress Frederick had indeed an unfortunate life, as her husband succeeded his father in March, 1888, only to die in June, and for years Bismarck, who controlled the old King, had been hostile as well as her mother-in-law, the Empress Augusta. It was clearly unfortunate that feelings ran so high that the British ambassador was asked in 1892 to discourage the Emperor's annual visit to Cowes,[4] and after his telegram to President Kruger after the Jameson raid, the Prince of Wales spoke of his most gratuitous act of unfriendliness, and said he should not come to Cowes.[5] The Queen herself had told him in 1897,[6] with reference to his hostility to Greece, that 'she was astonished and shocked at his violent language against the country where his sister[7] lives.'

Doubtless this personal feeling had something to do with the gradual recognition by the Queen of the desirability of keeping on good terms with Russia, as a means also of keeping France quiet. The fact that Germany behaved so badly was a factor in her acceptance without much indignation of the Russian occupation of Port Arthur: 'It is I think important that the world at large should not have the impression that we will not let anyone but ourselves have anything, while at the same time we must secure our rights and influence.'[8] Her efforts, however, were also devoted to trying to moderate the hostility of tone towards the Emperor in the British Press, and Sir Theodore Martin claims to have been successful even with the editor of *Punch*, whose caricatures 'are not liked by the English public, but must have been very irritating to the Germans.'[9] Hence it is not surprising that in the affair of Fashoda she concurred heartily indeed in the determination to secure the retirement of the French forces, but she was eager to aid in this being effected without discredit to France.[10] Appealed to by the Queen of Spain in regard to the war with the United States, she recognised that Britain could do nothing to help, and the ministry shortly after was unfavourably impressed by Spain continuing to create works which threatened the fortress and the anchorage itself, so that Lord

---

[3] *Letters of Queen Victoria*, 3 s., i. 441 (October 15, 1878).
[4] *Ibid.*, 3 s., ii. 125.   [5] *Ibid.*, 3 s., iii. 7 f.
[6] *Ibid.*, 3 s., iii. 138.   [7] Sophia, Queen of the Hellenes.
[8] *Letters of Queen Victoria*, 3 s., iii. 238 f.
[9] *Ibid.*, 3 s., iii. 224.
[10] *Ibid.*, 3 s., iii. 305, 309.

Salisbury was moved to suggest that it might be necessary to blockade Algeciras. The Queen wrote persuasively to the Queen Regent on the topic.[11] She also accepted the arrangements with Germany of 1898 regarding the possibility of the break up of the Portuguese Empire in Africa and Timor, which amounted to a virtual alliance as regards South Africa in her Premier's view.[12] As Britain was still anxious for the integrity of the Portuguese dominions, it was not technically inconsistent, that in 1899, a fresh treaty with Portugal reaffirmed the obligations of the ancient treaties for the British protection of the Portuguese oversea possessions.[13]

The most characteristic action of the Queen in these years was her determined effort to support Prince Alexander of Bulgaria, who had been appointed by agreement with Turkey Governor-General, also of Eastern Roumelia for five years. The hostility of the Czar secured his kidnapping by military conspirators on August 21, 1886, and his enforced abdication. Public opinion in Europe was shocked, and the Prince was encouraged thereby to return in triumph to his capital. But Russian hostility became more marked, if possible, a wide conspiracy was engineered, and on September 7 the Prince resigned the throne. The Queen had secured efforts to induce the powers to oppose Russia, but following the lead of Prince Bismarck, they had yielded to Russian persuasion and had given no support to the Prince.[14] Lord Salisbury explained to his sovereign the reasons for British inferiority in diplomatic battles.[15] (*a*) Britain was sadly lacking in secret service money, £15,000 a year compared to the funds available in Russia. (*b*) The diplomatic service was inferior. Most who entered were not able, and promotion had to go by seniority. In 1878 he had promoted an officer to be Secretary of Embassy, and a motion of censure in the Commons was the result, which was indeed defeated, but it effectively prevented him from trying the experiment again. To remove a man before the retiring age was almost impossible for like reasons, as in the case of Sir R. Morier.[16] (*c*) The lack of a land

11 *Letters of Queen Victoria*, 3 s., iii. 289.
12 *Ibid.*, 3 s., iii. 263, 267 f. She agreed also to the Samoan surrender, 416 (1899).
13 *British Documents on the Origin of the War* (ed. G. P. Gooch and H. W. V. Temperley), i. 88 ff.; Garvin, *Joseph Chamberlain*, iii.
14 *Letters of Queen Victoria*, 3 s., i. 4, 10, 12, 90, 96, 187, 189, 191 f., 199 f.
15 *Ibid.*, 3 s., i. 193–96.
16 *Ibid.*, 3 s., i. 355, 363; ii. 321, 325, 326.

force capable of meeting even a second-class continental power prevented our diplomatists from threatening, and this circumstance often deprived their words of advice of any weight.   Other causes were 'our precarious Governments, the necessity of adapting our foreign policy to the views of a Cabinet of fourteen or sixteen men, usually ignorant of it and seldom united in their views!' and 'our shifting foreign policy during the last ten years.'   Hence the failures of Her Majesty's servants in foreign affairs.   The Queen, however, rather neatly reminded her sad Premier of Lord Beaconsfield's success in raising up the position of Great Britain from 1874 to 1880 in a marvellous manner, though 'Mr. Gladstone and Lord Granville pulled it down again during the five years of their mischievous and fatal misrule.'   She assured him that all Germany was boiling over with indignation and furious with the language of the co-called official organs of the German Government.   Lord Salisbury, after the final resignation of the throne, had to insist that protests were not much use, since Bulgaria itself was divided in feeling, as a result of the belief that Russian hostility would be implacable while the Prince was on the throne, since Britain had no ally, and since British opinion itself was divided and, on account of distress, timid about the danger of war.   As the Prince would not return, the Queen had to content herself with an abortive project to secure for him the hand of her granddaughter, Princess Viktoria of Prussia, but Bismarck intervened, and the Emperor negatived the project.   In this case the Queen's reasons were plainly rather personal than public, but in her request to the Czar in 1875 to discourage any idea of a preventive war by Germany against France,[17] and in her anxiety in 1887 lest the Boulangist movement might lead to hostilities,[18] she showed her desire to promote peace, as later in the war between China and Japan.[19]   Her acceptance, on the other hand, of the necessity of the South African war was complete and wholehearted, and she distinguished herself by her firm refusal to countenance any idea of German mediation and her resolute assertion at the darkest moment of the war: 'There is no one depressed in this house; we are not interested in the possibilities of defeat; they do not exist.'[20]

It will be seen even from this brief summary that the royal

[17] *Letters of Queen Victoria*, 2 s., ii. 391, 406; Lee, *Edward VII.*, i. 350, n. 2.
[18] *Letters of Queen Victoria*, 3 s., i. 262.   [19] *Ibid.*, 3 s., ii. 418.
[20] Cf. *ibid.*, 3 s., iii. 432 ff.

influence at no time could determine vitally the outlook of British policy. When all is said and done, ministers were the decisive element,[21] but she could aid or hinder as the case might demand, and she unquestionably counted always for something, especially in the issue of intervention in favour of Denmark in 1863–64 and in the Russo-Turkish question in 1876–78. She left a tradition of activity which was to be continued by Edward VII., though with the marked distinction that he was far more in his work the agent than the critic of ministers.

The new King came to the throne well equipped and informed. His mother had needlessly delayed letting him see the foreign despatches[22] and having access to knowledge of Cabinet decisions,[23] but she had at last yielded, and he had, moreover, discussed matters with British ambassadors and ministers, and had corresponded with the Kaiser, the Czar and the King of Greece on public topics. He had learned to like France and to accept republicanism as his mother never did: his dislike of German policy dated at least from the treatment of Schleswig-Holstein and of his father-in-law, and he advocated an entente as early as the eve of the Franco-Prussian War. He had sympathised with his mother's dislike of Russia,[24] and from the outset of his reign he was anxious to take a full share in foreign policy, to exercise his right to inform, to suggest and to criticise the suggestions of ministers. Nor were ministers unwilling to admit his right.

Mr. J. Chamberlain had already preached the desirability of terminating the isolation cherished by Lord Salisbury,[25] and the King approved of a German entente. There were difficulties for the Kaiser's reference to the Government as 'unmitigated noodles' displeased the King as a similar attack on Lord Salisbury had offended Queen Victoria, though, according to Count Hatzfeldt, he admitted that his Premier was not likely to favour the project of closer relations with Germany.[26] An effort to arrange a meeting with the Kaiser in August, 1901, showed the latter adroit to insinuate the necessity of Britain seeking an alliance, since Russia

[21] For her assent as to the surrender of Heligoland, see *Letters of Queen Victoria*, 3 s., i. 549, 611 ff.
[22] Lord Rosebery did so in 1886 (Lee, *Edward VII.*, i. 216 f.), Lord Salisbury modified the position.
[23] In some degree given by Lords Beaconsfield and Salisbury, and Mr. Gladstone (*ibid.*, i. 217).   [24] *Ibid.*, i. 421.
[25] Garvin, *Joseph Chamberlain*, iii. 254 ff.; Dugdale, *Arthur James Balfour*, i. 249 ff.
[26] Lee, *Edward VII.*, ii. 119 f.; Newton, *Lansdowne*, pp. 196 ff.

was seeking closer relations, and France and Germany were on warmer terms. No promise regarding Morocco, where Britain wished no alteration in the *status quo*, was forthcoming.[27] Matters became worse when Mr. Chamberlain, now despairing of an accord, retorted hotly at Edinburgh on October 25, 1901, to attacks on British war methods, to be counter-attacked by Count Metternich for his master and by the Imperial Chancellor.[28] The loss of hope of an agreement resulted in royal support of the alliance of January 30, 1902, with Japan, the King wisely dropping doubts of the wisdom of accord with a non-European race.[29] On February 8, the King explained to Baron von Eckardstein his doubts as to the attitude of Germany.[30] *The Times* continued critical of Germany, and refused, in March, 1903, to modify its tone, despite royal suggestions.[31] On the other hand, the Kaiser, after much consideration, solved a difficult point by declining to receive the Boer generals who visited Europe, while a counter compliment was paid in arranging that the 1st Royal Dragoons, of which the Kaiser was Hon. Colonel, should not leave England before the Kaiser had been given the opportunity to see them for which he had put in a claim.[32]

As regards Persia, the King vainly pressed in 1901 for more effective resistance to Russian influence, and in November, 1902, 'from patriotic motives and a high sense of duty, though with the greatest reluctance,' gave way to the demand that the Garter be bestowed on the Shah, to whom it had been promised, but to whom he had refused to give it in August. He remained, however, firm in limiting distribution of orders to his suite.[33]

On February 8, 1902, Mr. J. Chamberlain welcomed the desire of M. Cambon for an entente with France which he had vainly suggested to Lord Salisbury after the settlement in 1898 of the Fashoda affair.[34] In accordance with the new outlook, the King gave no encouragement to the request of the Sultan of Morocco for

---

27 Lee, *Edward VII.*, ii. 128 ff.
28 *Ibid.*, ii. 132 ff.; Newton, *Lansdowne*, pp. 203 ff.
29 Lee, *Edward VII.*, ii. 140 ff.; Newton, *Lansdowne*, pp. 218 ff.
30 Lee, *Edward VII.*, ii. 144 f.   31 *Ibid.*, ii. 146, n. 3.
32 *Ibid.*, ii. 147–49.
33 *Ibid.*, ii. 156.   The honour had been given to the State in 1873 and to successive Sultans in 1856 and 1867, but was refused to the King of Siam.   The King gave in only when it was clear that Lansdowne must resign, and Mr. Balfour suggested that the Cabinet would also resign; Newton, *Lansdowne*, p. 238.
34 Lee, *Edward VII.*, ii. 217 ff.   It has been alleged that Edward VII. disagreed with Lord Salisbury's foreign policy, but there is no evidence (Legge, *King George*, i. 50).

aid against France in 1902, but only on enquiry from Lord Lansdowne in 1903 did he learn of the proposal of France for the partition of Morocco. In that year the King undertook a visit to Portugal, where he revitalised the ancient alliance,[35] followed by one to Rome. There he forced Mr. Balfour, by steady insistence,[36] to agree to his paying a 'private and informal visit to the Vatican,' which he did from the British Embassy, negativing the suggestion that he should start from the English College. In May he paid a most important visit to Paris, where he won from a reluctant people a cordial regard. In July, the President, with M. Delcassé, returned the visit, and steps were taken to perfect the promise of an entente. In the draft proposals two alterations were made by royal suggestion; mention of a disclaimer of the intention to annex Egypt was omitted, and commercial equality in Morocco became 'absolutely indispensable.'[37] The Cabinet was not as one regarding the surrender of the Los Islands, but the King approved. The convention was signed on April 8, but the King remonstrated that he had been treated with scant courtesy in that Mr. Balfour had announced that it must be approved by Parliament, because of the cession of territory and the financial payments involved.[38] But the Premier stuck to the principle. In Parliament only Lord Rosebery criticised,[39] on the score that the entente would lead to war, and it is significant that M. Delcassé, in 1906, explained to Sir Donald Wallace that Frenchmen had accepted the surrender of Egypt, to strengthen their claim to recover some day the lost provinces of Alsace and Lorraine. Germany showed for the moment, however, no resentment.

The King, who was in cordial accord with ministers in this issue, pleaded vainly for the intervention in the Macedonian revolt to help the rebels against Turkish misrule,[40] but found Lord Lansdowne as lukewarm as Count Goluchowski, the Austrian-Hungarian foreign minister. No doubt, the reason was Austrian indifference. On August 31, 1903, the King visited Francis Joseph, but neither then nor later does this intercourse seem to have effected any political result. He spent many months after in urging on his ministry the taking of stronger measures to bring the Porte

35 Lee, *Edward VII.*, ii. 222 ff.   36 *Ibid.*, ii. 231 ff.
37 *Ibid.*, ii. 246 ff.; Newton, *Lansdowne*, pp. 275 ff.
38 Lee, *Edward VII.*, ii. 252 f.
39 Curiously enough Grey, *Twenty-five Years*, i. 53, forgets this speech.
40 Lee, *Edward VII.*, ii. 258 f., ignored in Newton, *Lansdowne*, pp. 301 ff.

to book, but Lord Lansdowne remained immobile.[41]   More successful was his renewal of cordial relations with Prince Ferdinand of Bulgaria, a Coburg, who had taken in 1887 the place of Prince Alexander, and whose policy the King, as late as 1903, stigmatised as 'double-faced.'   But towards the new monarch in Serbia he remained hostile, for the massacre of King Alexander and Queen Draga on June 10, 1903, deeply shocked him, and it was at his instance that diplomatic relations were broken off.[42]   Efforts by the Russian and Italian ambassadors, who claimed a special audience for the purpose in 1905, were met by a firm negative: 'We should be obliged to shut up our business if we, the Kings, were to consider the assassinations of Kings as of no consequence at all.' Only in 1906, after the leading regicides had been removed from office, in which the British minister would be brought into contact with them, did the King consent to the renewal of diplomatic relations.   His feelings was, no doubt, strengthened by realisation that the new King knew all about the plot to destroy his predecessor. In the same spirit in 1903 the King refused any intercourse with the King of the Belgians, whose infamous government of the Congo is a dark page in the history of the Belgians, whose capital was adorned at the expense of incredible human sufferings.[43]

With regard to Russia, the King's desire for an entente was sincere, but the war between that power and Japan created a difficult position in which the King desired to act so as to prevent any breach with Russia.   Thus he approved, while Lord Lansdowne disapproved, the idea of Russia sending war vessels through the Dardanelles contrary to treaty.[44]   But he approved the British protests against the actual passage, and shared the general indignation at the incredible incompetence of the Russian fleet in its attack on October 21 on fishing vessels on the Dogger Bank.[45]   But he rather hastily decided not to press Russia unduly, and accepted the solution of an International Commission of Inquiry, which awarded £65,000 damages; the callous conduct of the Russian officers in making no effort to succour the victims of their panic was justly rewarded at the crushing disaster of Tsushima, which virtually ended the war.   The King was then anxious to get into touch with

---

[41] Lee, *Edward VII.*, ii. 264–67.   [42] *Ibid.*, ii. 270 ff.
[43] *Ibid.*, ii. 274–77.
[44] Newton, *Lansdowne*, pp. 314 f.; Lee, *Edward VII.*, ii. 289 f.; cf. 297 f. on the illegal seizures of British ships.
[45] Newton, *Lansdowne*, pp. 315 f.; Lee, *Edward VII.*, ii. 301 ff.

Count Witte, Finance Minister of Russia, but that statesman unlike Isvolsky, whose friendship the King had obtained at Copenhagen in 1904, did not believe in an entente, as he feared thence estrangement from Germany.[46]   On the other hand, the Japanese alliance was renewed and strengthened in 1905 so as to cover British interests in India.[47]

In 1905, however, the King was largely concerned with the question of the separation of Sweden and Norway and the selection of a sovereign for the latter.   He was anxious to go rather further than the absolute neutrality favoured by Lord Lansdowne, and to aid the candidature of Prince Charles of Denmark, grandson of King Christian, who was married to his third daughter, Maud, and in this he was encouraged by the Hon. Alan Johnstone, minister at Copenhagen.   The final result was as he desired, but his personal intervention was comparatively ineffective, though he certainly showed great consideration to all concerned, and tactfully secured the Garter for the Swedish Crown Prince, while he welcomed the new King of Norway to London in 1906, and there conferred on him the Garter.   Mr. Johnstone received the K.C.V.O. in token of his personal services to the family.[48]

With Germany, however, things went badly.   The Kaiser determined, on his Chancellor's advice, to resist French penetration of Morocco, conceded by Britain in the treaty of 1904, and his landing at Tangier on March 31, 1905, was followed by a proposal of the Sultan for an international conference to deal with the status of his realm.   Britain was loyal to the compact, but M. Rouvier's Government yielded to an ultimatum and M. Delcassé had to go, an event unparalleled until Mr. Eden resigned in 1938 in deference to Signor Mussolini's demands.   Moreover, on July 24, the Kaiser, at Björkö, induced the feeble Czar to sign a treaty of alliance.   But that was so obviously treachery to France that Lamsdorff, Witte and the Grand Duke Nicholas secured that it never was ratified, and the Conference on Tangier, 1906, at Algeciras, was a complete disappointment for the Kaiser, for British support secured excellent terms for France.[49]   In the same year the marriage of King Alfonso to Princess Victoria Eugenie of Battenberg strengthened relations with Spain, though Protestant feeling disliked the conversion of the Princess.

[46] Lee, *Edward VII.*, ii. 307 f.
[47] Newton, *Lansdowne*, pp. 327 f.   [48] Lee, *Edward VII.*, ii. 315–26.
[49] Newton, *Lansdowne*, pp. 329–45; Lee, *Edward VII.*, ii. 336 ff.; Grey, *Twenty-five Years*, i. 69 ff., 100 ff.

In the case of Greece, the King's interest was unbroken, ever since he had favoured the transfer of the Ionian Islands to that power as an inducement for it to accept the rule of his brother-in-law. In 1906 his influence was exerted to secure the retirement of Prince George from the office of High Commissioner, in which he had supported him so long as he remained popular. Later he agreed with Mr. Asquith on the merits of the union of Crete with Greece, but only in 1913 did it become possible to achieve this end.

In 1907, visits by the King to meet the King of Spain at Cartagena and to Italy were regarded as evidence of a desire to encircle Germany,[50] and in fact the former visit was not unconnected with the conclusion of a treaty with France and Spain for the maintenance of the *status quo* in the Mediterranean, Sir C. Hardinge being in attendance as in 1906, when the Cretan issue was discussed. Later he visited the Kaiser, and discussed politics with Von Bülow, but not with the Kaiser. He followed this up by a visit to the Emperor Francis Joseph at Ischl, which again has been represented as aiming at driving a wedge between Germany and Austria, but clearly without truth.[51] To dispel French uneasiness, he saw M. Clemenceau, President of the Council, immediately afterwards. The Kaiser's visit to Windsor, which took place in November, was marked by a seeming desire on his part to co-operate with France and Russia as well as Britain on the Baghdad railway issue, but the good effect of this demarche was at once ruined by the decision to strengthen the navy, and shortly after difficulties appeared in any rapprochement.

In the meantime the entente with Russia had been concluded.[52] The King in this played a part in reconciling the Government of India,[53] and the India Office to a project which they did not like. The failure to consult the ruler of Afghanistan was deliberately faced rather than cause delay or difficulty, and Persia was divided up into spheres of influence with singularly little consideration for her sovereignty or real interests. Nothing was done to injure Germany, but the close connection between Britain and Russia was

---

[50] Lee, *Edward VII.*, ii. 538 ff.; Morel, *Diplomacy Revealed*, p. 74, gives Baron Greindl's suspicions.
[51] Lee, *Edward VII.*, ii. 549 f.; Grey, *Twenty-five Years*, i. 150 f.
[52] On the difficulty caused by Sir H. Campbell-Bannerman's mot (July 23, 1906), 'La Duma est morte: vive la Duma,' see Lee, *Edward VII.*, ii. 567 f.; Grey, *Twenty-five Years*, i. 154 f.
[53] Lee, *Edward VII.*, ii. 569 f.; Grey, *Twenty-five Years*, i. 163 f.

inevitably resented. But the King's visit to Reval in June next year was marked by Mr. Ramsay MacDonald's denunciation of the Czar as a 'common murderer' and 'blood-stained creature,'[54] and the issue was debated on a Labour motion in the Commons, when the royal action was defended by ministers as their responsibility and accepted by a large majority. Unluckily the King, who had made a bad blunder in asking Mr. Asquith to go to Biarritz to be appointed Prime Minister, now made a more remarkable *faux pas* by withholding invitations from a royal garden party on June 20 from Mr. Keir Hardie, the Labour Party leader, Mr. Grayson, an independent, and Mr. Arthur Ponsonby, just elected at Stirling to succeed the late Premier. To do so was to bring himself into politics, and there was no answer to Mr. Keir Hardie's censure of him on this head. No excuse can be imagined, except failing health and mental robustness, for his mistake. It is, of course, open to doubt whether the ministry in furthering his visit was acting wisely, but it could plead that German hostility was driving it on to closer relations with Russia, whose completely unsound condition was probably not realised by the Government. A further blunder followed: the King at Reval created the Czar an Admiral of the Fleet without ministerial authority, and the Admiralty disliked the action, which it attributed to the mischievous activity of Sir J. Fisher. Obviously, however, a minister should have been in attendance, but Sir E. Grey was no believer in ministerial negotiations abroad. Unluckily his absence, and the fact that the King made no political accords with the Czar, had no effect in diminishing the growing suspicion in the mind of the Kaiser that the King was seeking to drive him into commencing a war.

Relations unfortunately were badly affected in March, 1908, by the revelation that the Kaiser had written spontaneously to Lord Tweedmouth at the Admiralty disclaiming hostility to Britain in his new efforts to accelerate construction of a large fleet,[55] and that Lord Tweedmouth had replied, divulging the British proposals for the estimates which, though decided in Cabinet had not been before the Commons, though this point did not then leak out. The incident was unwisely exploited by *The Times* against the ministry and the difficulties involved at home for the Kaiser, no doubt

---

54 Lee, *Edward VII.*, ii. 587 f.
55 *Ibid.*, ii. 604 ff.; Esher, *Journals and Letters*, ii. 285 ff., whose letter in *The Times* started the trouble.

acerbated his feeling towards Britain.   His ministers seem to have
had some realisation of the advantages of an accord on naval
construction, not so the Kaiser.   Sir E. Grey suggested that the
King at Cronberg, in August, might present a memorandum to the
Kaiser on the topic, but the imperial attitude was such as to render
this unwise.   Then the publication in the *Daily Telegraph* of
October 28 of an interview with the Kaiser, really of December,
1907, both brought on the Kaiser a rebuke from his Chancellor and
irritated him further into the indiscretion of giving next month an
interview to an American journalist, W. B. Hale, in which he was
hostile to Britain and the King.[56]   Efforts to suppress the interview
succeeded, but enough was known to cause further bad feeling.

After failure at Cronberg the King proceeded to Ischl in
August, 1908, and there had his last interview with Francis Joseph,
while Sir C. Hardinge consulted with Baron von Aehrenthal.   Both
concealed from their interlocutors the fact that, following on the
revolution in Turkey, due to the young Turks, it had been decided
to annex Bosnia and Herzegovina, nominally under Turkish
sovereignty, while Bulgaria would proclaim her independence.
The news was broken to the King at Balmoral on October 5, and
was bitterly resented.   For a time British diplomacy sought a
conference to give sanction to the changes thus made in the Treaty
of Berlin, but Isvolsky had promised acceptance of annexation in
return for a promise of freedom for Russia, as regards passage of
the Dardanelles, and Germany backed Austria against Serbia,
which Russia could not support.   Nothing but Sir E. Grey's
firm resistance to a threat of war by Austria produced a comparatively satisfactory settlement, which, however, left it inevitable
that Serbia should arm in preparation for the day when she could
strike back with Russia no longer impotent to aid.[57]   Austria, for
her part, was permanetly estranged from Britain and France, as
well as from Russia, and became subservient in large measure to
the power of Germany.   The King now for the first time realised
the risk of war, and thus in April next raised the issue whether in
framing the budget the Cabinet had taken into consideration the
possible event of a European war.

56 Lee, *Edward VII.*, ii. 620; cf. Esher, *Journals and Letters*, ii. 352.
57 *Ibid.*, ii. 626 ff.; Grey, *Twenty-five Years*, ii. 172–94.   Halévy, *Historie des Peuple
    Anglais au XIXe Siècle, Epilogue*, ii. 365 ff., who explains the German-French
    rapprochement in the treaty of February 9, 1909, and the menace to the
    entente.

In all these activities the King plainly was acting in accord with ministers, and furthering policies which they desired him to under-take.[58] It is clearly absurd to impute to him personally any idea of attempting to isolate and encircle Germany,[59] though von Bethmann-Hollweg accepted this doctrine and pronounced it to the Reichstag in 1915. British political conditions of the time would effectively have negatived any such deliberate policy, had it ever occurred to the King, and the sovereign's one real desire was patently to promote and maintain peace. His talents were unquestionably of the diplomatic character,[60] not constructive, and his attitude to issues presented was never complex.

To assess the comparative importance of his relations to foreign politics with that of his mother is difficult. It has been suggested that his influence fell much below that of her predecessor,[61] and that with the advance of democracy had passed away the power of the Crown to initiate or obstruct the foreign policy of the ministry. This seems to exaggerate the position. The Queen's power, for good or evil, could be exerted only when the Cabinet was divided, as under Lord Palmerston, or as auxiliary to a policy urged by her Prime Minister, as under Lord Beaconsfield. Her apparent control then of the Cabinet was after all no more than her reinforcement by her enthusiasm of the position of her Premier. In all cases where these factors were not present, her power was ineffective. Lord Salisbury did not change his policy at any time to meet her views, nor could Lord Rosebery help Siam against France, however strongly he disliked the actions of that power.[62] The Queen, too, was handicapped in her utility by her refusal to pay State visits, and by her reluctance even to receive royalties. The King enjoyed being host and being guest, his range of friends was large, and he could learn much from them, while he maintained as active a correspondence with ambassadors and others as she ever did, and, unlike her, knew many of them intimately.

No doubt the activities of George V. in foreign issues were on a very different footing. Though the sovereign had followed foreign affairs under his father's régime, and had seen despatches,[63] he had

---

[58] See the very deliberate minimising of his action by Lansdowne's biographer, Newton, *Lansdowne*, pp. 290 f., and by Lord Grey, *Twenty-five Years*, i. 150 f.
[59] Lee, *Edward VII.*, ii. 729 ff.
[60] As recognised by Soveral; Esher, *Journals and Letters*, ii. 460.
[61] A. Cecil, *Cambridge History of British Foreign Policy*, iii. 615.
[62] Crewe, *Rosebery*, ii. 426.   [63] Lee, *Edward VII.*, ii. 290, n. 1.

no desire to imitate his personal diplomacy, and his part therefore seems to have been reduced to that of a spectator and supporter of his ministers rather than that of an independent critic. His help was clearly always available to ministers for formal purposes, such as his welcome to the representatives of the powers in 1913, when the problems of the Balkan States, due to their wars on Turkey, received for the moment a settlement. In the same year he visited Berlin, and the attempts to promote better relations produced an accord with Germany, pointing to her ultimate attainment of further African lands. In June he received M. Poincaré in London, and in May, 1914, paid a successful visit to Paris, with Sir E. Grey in attendance. Sir E. Grey, who had placed on record in November, 1912,[64] the informal relations with France regarding concerted defence, entered into an accord on a like basis with Russia, but explained that no alliance was possible. In the same way, at the critical moment when the issue of war was in the balance, it was impossible for the King to give an affirmative answer to the French President's enquiry if Britain would render aid. The invasion of Belgium and the King's appeal for aid changed the situation and enabled the King to give the necessary assurances. He had exerted his influence before the matter went too far to procure peace, but he had, inevitably, not such weight as would have attached to his father.

The King in the war clearly was equally helpful. He was quite unfairly, it seems,[65] represented as reluctant for the stern treatment found necessary against Constantine of Greece, and was prepared for personal discussions of the possibility of peace with the King of Italy and the French President when the death of Francis Joseph opened up the possibility of negotiations with the new sovereign. He also offered an asylum in England to the Czar, though unhappily his benevolent project failed to achieve success for reasons not wholly clear. In the actual work of treaty making, he does not appear to have taken any active part, nor, indeed, in the circumstances was that possible, but his grant of the Garter to Mr. A. Chamberlain after Locarno, in 1925, was an act of tactful recognition of a very considerable achievement which, if followed up, as at the time Mr. Lloyd George demanded, might have led to lasting appeasement. In the same spirit he presided over the opening of the London Conferences of 1930 and 1935–36 on disarmament.

64 Grey, *Twenty-five Years*, i. 97 f.   65 Legge, *King George*, i. 324.

More recent events suggest that the control of foreign policy had passed more and more completely to the Prime Minister acting with the Foreign Secretary. It appears clear that the idea of securing a settlement in Ethiopia by the offer to transfer to that country a portion of Somaliland was determined upon without due regard either to the necessity of obtaining the royal approval in advance or to the principle that transfer of British rights of protectorate must require an Act of Parliament.[66] The confused answers on this head of the Dominions Secretary are inconsistent with any adequate consideration in advance of the issue and submission to the King. The Hoare-Laval proposals for the settlement of the actual conflict between Italy and Ethiopia were plainly not duly brought before his notice before sanction by the Cabinet.

These proposals, and the complete change of British policy effected in March, 1938, in the decision to accept negotiations with Italy under an ultimatum, suggest the difficulty under which the Crown labours where action must be taken swiftly and where the ministry of the day has a large majority, however obtained. The Crown is in such cases reduced to the necessity of assent,[67] or of finding a new ministry to support refusal to accept the advice of the ministry. The responsibility of refusal of advice in such cases is so serious that it is difficult to see how the sovereign can take it. All that seems possible is pressure to induce the ministry in such a case, where it has to depart from the mandate which it sought when it was elected, to refer the issue to the electors, and the easy answer is to urge, as the Prime Minister urged on April 4, that to plunge the country into the turmoil of an election was unjustifiable. Yet for a Government which in 1935 secured public support by a policy of upholding the League of Nations to decide to abandon that principle without a fresh mandate when challenged by a direct demand from the Opposition is clearly a strong decision.

It would appear that Mr. Chamberlain's action in the Munich crisis of September, 1938, eliminated any real possibility of royal intervention. From the Prime Minister's statements it does not appear that he was in touch with the King regarding his intention to negotiate personally.[68] The *modus operandi* clearly deprived the

---

66 A. B. Keith, *Current Imperial and International Problems*, 1935–36, pp. 139–41.
67 The treaty of April 16, 1938, was no doubt duly thus accepted: the King had seen Lord Perth before he went back to Rome to negotiate.
68 September 28, October 3 and 6.

King of any opportunity of discussion, as opposed to mere assent to a policy in whose formulation he had taken no part. It is significant that the accord which the Prime Minister asked the Fuehrer to sign on September 30, was one between himself and the German dictator, the Royal name being entirely omitted.[69]

It is interesting to add that the question of the possibility of the sovereign having a foreign policy of his own was formally dealt with in the Commons on August 9, 1917, as the outcome of a telegram sent by the German Emperor on August 10, 1914, to the President of the United States containing statements made to Prince Henry of Prussia in relation to the foreign policy of Great Britain and her attitude to foreign powers by the King.[70] Mr. Bonar Law had, naturally, no difficulty in stating that the rule of constitutional practice still obtained, that the sovereign did not take independent action in foreign affairs, and that everything which passed between him and foreign ministers was known to his own ministers, and in asserting that the treatment of letters to and from foreign sovereigns, if they touched on politics, continued to be as under Queen Victoria. Such letters, as we have seen, can have only a limited importance now, but the King of Greece remained on cordial terms with the royal family, and at the outset of his restoration to the throne appeared ready to apply the principles of responsible government to his much harassed country, a decision, however, later seemingly altered, perhaps under the influence of the establishment of dictatorial rule in Rumania and Yugoslavia.

4. THE SOVEREIGN AND THE EMPIRE

IN Imperial affairs Queen Victoria had comparatively little interest, as indeed was not surprising in one whose mind was so occupied with the greater and more immediate affairs of Europe. What she did was mainly formal. She selected the city of Ottawa as capital of the United Province of Canada, on Sir E. Head's advice, but her choice was not at first received with the necessary courtesy, and she showed little enthusiasm in regard to the creation of the Dominion of Canada. But for the caution of Lord Derby, who feared to irritate the United States, the style might have been kingdom and the symbolism of Empire which was to be created by

---

[69] *The Times*, October 1, 1938.
[70] Legge, *King George*, i. 327–35; ii. 9 f.; Cmd. 7860.

Mr. Disraeli in securing for her the title of Empress of India might have been accelerated. The style of Commonwealth for Australia was not attractive to her, but Mr. J. Chamberlain ingeniously explained that it was done so as to distinguish Australia from Canada.[71] Her interest in the extension of the Empire seems to have been moderate, but she quite approved of the assumption of control of British New Guinea because of the probable gain to the natives in whose welfare she had a kindly interest. The name of Fiji she insisted on leaving unchanged with excellent taste. Nor did she refuse in 1897 to give membership of her Privy Council to eleven colonial premiers.

Naturally the Queen's keenest concern was with colonial issues when they impinged on foreign questions. On the subject of Egypt she had firm doctrines which led her somewhat far from the limitations of her position. The case against Britain then holding the Sudan was unanswerable;[72] the effort would have needed 20,000 men at great cost for no purpose of importance to Britain. But the decision to send Gordon to Khartoum was a bad blunder, though the Queen approved of it and Sir Evelyn Baring accepted it. The Queen was anxious throughout the year, and was bitterly indignant at the readiness of ministers to consent to fix a term for the British occupation of Egypt, though this was virtually necessitated by the attitude of Germany and Austria as well as France. On the receipt of the news of Gordon's death, the Queen telegraphed *en clair* to Mr. Gladstone to say: 'These news from Khartoum are frightful, and to think that all this might have been prevented and many precious lives saved by earlier action is too frightful.'[73] It is not surprising that Mr. Gladstone would have resigned, had he found that this view had been made public by leakage in the telegraph department. The Queen had to allow him to be assured that there was no question of censure, but merely of regret, and none of publication, and so the storm subsided. Mr. Gladstone's reply to the Queen was singularly effective, and it is no answer to say, as Lord Cromer did later,[74] that the Nile expedition was sanctioned too late, because Mr. Gladstone was not persuaded early enough of its necessity. Clearly the advice given by Lord

---

71 *Letters of Queen Victoria*, 3 s., iii. 566. His views as to Governors (pp. 576 ff.) of the States received her approval.

72 *Ibid.*, 2 s., iii. 454, 464 ff., 601 ff.

73 *Ibid.*, 2 s., iii. 597 ff.

74 Lord Cromer, *Modern Egypt*, ii. 17. Cf. Fitzmaurice, *Granville*, ii. 379 ff.

Cromer was erroneous; Mr. Gladstone realised that the true course of action was merely to protect Egypt, but this was not accepted there, and the decision to send Gordon should never have been agreed to. Thereafter she pressed unweariedly for the retention of so much of the Sudan as was possible, and urged, privately and unconstitutionally, Lord Wolseley to threaten to resign, if necessary, to secure his own way.[75] But ministers declined for ten reasons of weight to agree to that, while informing the Khedive that he must treat the Commander-in-Chief's authority as supreme. Lord Wolseley's policy at this juncture was an impossible one; he recognised that the connection with the Sudan should be severed, but he wished first of all to destroy the Mahdi and set up a native government. He recognised the danger of locking up British forces in the Sudan when they might be urgently needed for service against Russian or French aggression.[76] At the same time, Russian action on the Afghan frontier, involving the defeat of an Afghan force at Penjdeh, compelled the Cabinet to decide against any forward movement in the Sudan. The Queen vehemently demanded advance, but had to yield to the force of the Cabinet position,[77] which stressed the fact that the expedition would demand stronger forces than could be spared, that the Mahdi was not menacing Egypt, and that the forces in the Sudan could be safely withdrawn. The Queen stormed, but Lord Rosebery pointed out that to send troops to attack the Mahdi would have been folly, that our distraction had enabled France to use menacing language as to Egypt such as Bismarck might address to France, that the danger in Afghanistan was serious, and that any other policy would not have been tolerated by Parliament or the country, so that the ministry could not resign, as Sir R. Peel did in 1845.[78] It is significant that, after the resignation of the ministry, the same policy was preserved. The Queen, however, remained very interested, and in 1893 she again was active in demanding that another battalion should be sent to Egypt, as desired by Lord Cromer.[79] She was, naturally, deeply gratified at the recovery of the Sudan in 1898, and proposed to Lord Salisbury who readily accepted the suggestion, the offer of a peerage to Lord Kitchener.[80]

[75] *Letters of Queen Victoria*, 2 s., iii. 633.   [76] *Ibid.*, 2 s., iii. 630–32.
[77] *Ibid.*, 2 s., iii. 634 ff.; Morley, *Gladstone*, iii. 50 f., 165 ff.
[78] *Letters of Queen Victoria*, 2 s., iii. 640–42.
[79] *Ibid.*, 3 s., ii. 208 ff.   [80] *Ibid.*, 3 s., iii. 275.

In India her interest was keen after the transfer of the control, though it had existed before. The idea of taking a formal title was hinted at by Mr. Disraeli in 1859, and in 1873 was definitely put to Lord Granville, but nothing was then done. In 1876 the Bill was carried through the Commons at her request by Mr. Disraeli.[81] It is clear that the opposition to the Bill was quite widespread, and that the Commons, though it accepted, did not welcome the measure, while Lord Hartington led a stout opposition to it in the Lords. Yet the Bill was sound in principle. It was in the interest of the Crown thus to stand out as definitely associated with India, and it helped to establish a personal relation between the Queen and the Indian princes. In Britain it, no doubt, was a prelude to the sentiment which stresses the position of the sovereign as the link of Empire.

The Queen Empress, as she was duly proclaimed at Delhi on January 1, 1877, never forgot the consideration due to Indian princes. She had already manifested it in the case of the enquiry into the conduct of the Gaekwar of Baroda, who was ultimately deposed in 1875 after a semi-judicial enquiry of the fairest type. It is interesting to note that in 1859 she had expressed the view that this procedure might be adopted. The matter was of high importance, because the cessation under the new régime of the annexation of States to prevent misrule made it imperative to secure the people of the States against chronic misgovernment. She was always ready to show consideration to Indian princes, and was mild even as regards Holkar,[82] whose insolence to the Government of India was marked, and urged that if a political agent were appointed, he should be a military man of high standing, very firm but courteous, 'a *superior* person.' She repeated later to Lord Curzon her views on the necessity of treating princes with due good manners, and he, himself, took the view that princes should become stones in the building of Empire, but also honoured members of society.[83] In one case her partiality outran judgment. The murder of Mr. Quinton and others in Manipur, while on an official mission to place on the throne a new Maharajah and to expel the author of the deposition of the previous Maharajah, demanded retribution, and, after careful consideration of her

[81] *Letters of Queen Victoria*, 2 s., ii. 438, 440; Fitzmaurice, *Granville*, ii. 159–63; Guedalla, *The Queen and Mr. Gladstone*, i. 455 f.
[82] *Letters of Queen Victoria*, 3 s., iii. 386.
[83] *Ibid.*, 3 s., iii. 462, 510, 546, 624.

wishes, the Viceroy decided that the Senapati must be executed for his treason and murder. The Queen's protests were clearly quite unjustified, as was her gratuitous suggestion that Mr. Quinton acted with harshness and ignorance. Fortunately the Secretary of State, fortified by the Prime Minister, Lord Chancellor, and Cabinet, backed Lord Lansdowne loyally. This, however, is a clear case where, had she had the power, she would gravely have misused it, probably from relying on the biased advice of an Indian in her suite.[84]

On the other hand, the Queen's interest in seeing that Indians received a generous share of decorations of the Orders of the Star of India and Indian Empire, was no doubt wise,[85] and in 1897 she insisted on the presence of Indian troops at her Jubilee celebrations, while she started the practice of having Indian officers attached to her household, a proper recognition of India's place in the Empire. But she shared Conservative reluctance to contemplate any introduction of the elective principle in Indian government in 1889,[86] and even in 1892 a minimal step in this direction only was sanctioned.

On Afghanistan her outlook was affected by the fact that it formed part of the Russian question, and the decision of Mr. Gladstone to withdraw thence was the cause of the violent dispute on January 5, 1881, regarding the wording of the royal speech from the throne.[87] She yielded only on clear intimation that to refuse would mean the revolutionary step of turning out the ministry on the eve of meeting Parliament, and complained that 'she had never before been treated with such want of respect and consideration in the forty-three and a half years she had worn her thorny Crown.' Yet the wisdom of the decision was shortly proved to the hilt. She was naturally not pleased at the necessity of yielding to Russia in some degree over the Penjdeh incident,[88] but Lord Salisbury was not able to advise any stronger measures than those of his predecessor, and the incident ended peacefully enough. In the case of Chitral she was reluctant to agree to evacuation in 1895, but for once the Cabinet was unanimous.[89] On the fall of the

[84] Newton, *Lansdowne*, pp. 81–88.
[85] *Letters of Queen Victoria*, 3 s., iii. 449 f., 562.
[86] *Ibid.*, 3 s., i. 524.   [87] *Ante*, p. 295.
[88] *Letters of Queen Victoria*, 2 s., iii. 634, 672; or the wisdom of Mr. Gladstone's policy, see Morley, *Gladstone*, iii. 183 ff.
[89] *Letters of Queen Victoria*, 3 s., ii. 517, 562.

ministry the new Government reversed the policy, and the Queen was satisfied therewith.

One essential improvement in the government of India introduced on taking over direct control in 1858 earned her disapproval, the carrying out of the system of competitive recruitment for the civil service. But ministers could not give way in so important a matter, and the system was soon to be introduced in Britain.[90] It is, on the other hand, pleasant to note that she insisted that her famous proclamation on taking over government should be animated by benevolence, generosity, and religious toleration, and should insist on the benefits to be derived from civilisation, and should stress the equality of Indians with other British subjects, though it must be admitted that fully sixty years were to pass before that principle was fully accepted.[91]

The issue, however, of the Indian army nearly led to the resignation of her Prime Minister.[92] On February 5, 1859, the Queen spontaneously warned Lord Derby of her firm determination 'not to sanction, under any form, the creation of a British army distinct from that known at present as the army of the Crown. She would consider it dangerous to the maintenance of India, to the dependence of the Indian Empire on the mother country, and to her throne in these realms.' Such an army would be free from the constitutional control of the Crown and Parliament, would be hostile to the regular army, and would give an unconstitutional amount of power and patronage to the Indian Council and Government. She also accused, in effect, her minister of systematically, in regard to India, placing her in a false position. He had not formed any judgment on the issue until he had heard the views of the Indian Army Commission and matured a judgment thereon. The Queen, however, had made up her mind, and he would thus be fettered in his advice, knowing that, if it took one form, it would not be accepted, and without sharing his knowledge with his colleagues he could not discuss properly the issues. The Queen then recognised that she had gone too far, and told Lord Derby he could consider her letter as not having been written, unless he preferred to have a communication in different terms

90 *Letters of Queen Victoria*, 1 s., iii. 355, 377; cf. Morley, *Gladstone*, i. 509 ff., 649 ff., ii. 314 f.
91 *Letters of Queen Victoria*, 1 s., iii. 358 ff.
92 *Ibid.*, 1 s., iii. 357 ff., 404.

which could be given to the Cabinet. It is clear that in her attitude she was in effect coming perilously near to the position of George III. in 1807, when he tried to restrict the freedom of the Grenville ministry, as regards constitutional advice on the issue of Roman Catholic emancipation. But too much importance must not be attached to action not pressed. The final settlement of the matter in 1861 did not create a distinct European army in India separate from the royal forces, and therefore coincided with her views, but how far she was responsible for the result is not recorded.[93]

To Edward VII. the affairs of the Empire were of interest, but his pre-occupation with foreign affairs, and the dangers of his absence from proximity to England, precluded in 1906 his acceptance of the urgent invitation of the Canadian Parliament to visit that country, and his acceptance of the invitation to visit Quebec for the tercentenary of 1908, though he sent his son.[94] Curiously enough it required Lord Salisbury's authority to make him adhere to the promise of his mother that the Duke of York should open the first Parliament of the Commonwealth of Australia,[95] possibly he had then reason to suspect his health. On the subject of Chinese labour for the Transvaal the King took a strongly affirmative attitude, which may safely be attributed to the favour extended to the proposal by financial circles with access to the royal ear, and he resented strongly the decision to reverse the policy, ignoring the fact that the election had been in part won by the Liberals on the cry of Chinese slavery.[96] He was not enthusiastic on the grant of responsible government to the Transvaal, and resented the attitude of the Government to the vote of censure moved in the Commons on March 24 regarding the errors of his South African administration. With somewhat doubtful propriety he invited Lord Milner to Windsor, and spoke to him with impatience of the action of the Commons in virtually censuring him by 355 votes to 135.[97] He had the sense, however, despite Lord Milner's advice, which was freely tendered, to recognise that self-government must be conceded to the Transvaal.[98] The King welcomed General Botha to the Colonial Conference of 1907, though declining to

[93] A. B. Keith, *Constitutional History of India, 1600–1935*, pp. 188 f.
[94] Lee, *Edward VII.*, ii. 521 f.   [95] *Ibid.*, ii. 17 f.
[96] *Ibid.*, ii. 178–80, 479 ff.; Spender, *Lord Oxford*, i. 166 f., 177 ff.
[97] Lee, *Edward VII.*, ii. 480 ff.
[98] Halévy, *Histoire du Peuple Anglais au XIXe Siècle, Epilogue*, ii. 30 ff.

make him an Honorary General in the army, on honour conceded in 1912 by George V. There followed on this visit the curious episode of the Cullinan diamond found in 1905, which the Boers desired to present to the King.[99] The English element was stupidly hostile, the Cabinet wavered unaccountably, but in the end the King insisted that it must not throw the responsibility on him, and it then finally advised acceptance, in accord with the advice of Lord Selborne, and of the Prince of Wales. To the Union of 1909 he gave full sanction, provided that the position of the Native Territories, Basutoland, Bechuanaland Protectorate, and Swaziland was fully secured by the maintenance of direct British control, and he warmly consented to receive a Basutoland deputation on March 18, 1909.[1] The subsequent choice of Mr. H. Gladstone to succeed Lord Selborne, and to be first Governor-General, he did not much like, but Mr. Asquith insisted, and the King yielded and gave a viscountcy to the new appointee.

In 1909 he raised the question of due precautions for the safety of the Somaliland tribes, which would be affected by the decision to withdraw the British forces to the coast, and insisted on receiving fuller information from Lord Crewe than that given by his Prime Minister, but, here again, Mr. Asquith, fortified by the support of the Cabinet, remained firm, and the withdrawal, duly approved by the Commons, was carried out in 1910.[2] The policy was no doubt wise, having regard to the difficulties of maintaining peace, but happily it fell to be reversed under George V., when air power was sufficiently developed to render action against disturbers of the peace possible.

In Indian affairs the King was kept fully informed by Lord Curzon, who was most willing to report and to ask for approval. His attitude to the princes was that of his mother. He recognised the disadvantages of too frequent visits to Europe, but thought advice preferable to strict regulation,[3] which, of course, involved a rather delicate assertion of the right of the paramount power. In the same spirit he refrained from permitting Lord Curzon to forbid the absence of the Gaekwar of Baroda from India during the visit of the Prince of Wales in 1905, a stupid piece of discourtesy on the Gaekwar's part. Reference has already been made to his

[99] Lee, *Edward VII.*, ii. 487–90.
[1] *Ibid.*, ii. 490–93.　　　　　[2] *Ibid.*, ii. 44, n. 1.
[3] *Ibid.*, ii. 364 f.

13*

refusal to overrule his ministers on the issue of the announcement to be made at the Coronation Durbar of 1903. He stoutly supported his ministers in the refusal to sanction the terms arranged with Tibet of September 7, 1904, in so far as they provided for the payment of the indemnity of £500,000 for a period of seventy-five years, and the occupation by Britain of the Chumbi Valley during that period. This was contrary not merely to promises given in Parliament, but to assurances to Russia, and Colonel Younghusband unquestionably far exceeded the authority given. But he generously secured him the grant of the K.C.I.E. in recognition of his success in the actual expedition.[4] Nor was anything lacking in his courtesy to Lord Curzon on his arrival home on leave in 1904, after agreeing to stay two more years in India. But he could not support his demand for a stronger line in the negotiations with Habibullah of Afghanistan,[5] who made no concession, and in 1905 obtained instead an increase of his subsidy to eighteen lakhs of rupees. His visit to India in 1907 resulted in no real improvement of relations, and he deeply resented the fact that he was ignored in the Anglo-Russian negotiations, though his position was safeguarded in the treaty concluded. He declined, however, to recognise that instrument, and allowed his subjects to aid the rebels in the Zakkha Khel and Mohmand insurrections in 1908. But the King deprecated any possibility of war. He always held that in these matters the Indian Government must take its line of action from Britain, thus agreeing with Lord Morley that there could not be separate foreign policies in India and Whitehall regarding the proposed entente with Russia.

In the great struggle between Lord Curzon and Lord Kitchener on the control of the Indian army, the King accepted the advice of his ministers.[6] In persuading Lord Curzon to acquiesce on his return home instead of keeping the matter alive, the King undoubtedly helped to permit the continuation of a grave error. But Mr. Morley and the Liberal Government, which maintained the decision of their predecessors, must share blame for a very unfortunate error.

---

[4] Lee, *Edward VII.*, ii. 369–71. Lord Midleton alleges that differences on foreign policy, rather than on army control, caused the breach between the Cabinet and Lord Curzon.

[5] *Ibid.*, ii. 371–73; Dugdale, *Arthur James Balfour*, i. 401 ff.

[6] Lee, *Edward VII.*, ii. 375–80. Lord Kitchener in 1915 had to be forced to allow munitions to pass from his control, just as in India he had engrossed all power: Crewe in Fitzroy, *Memoirs*, ii. 595.

The King used more individual judgment in regard to the great problems which marked the Liberal tenure of office. He urged the necessity of control of the Press as demanded by the Commander-in-Chief, and ultimately steps were taken in 1908 and 1910 to meet the situation.[7] He also pressed for steps against sedition in England, and proceedings were instituted against the printer of the *Indian Socialogist*. On the other hand, the ministry declined to consider a grant of honours to general officers who had fought in the Indian Mutiny as likely to arouse annoyance. But the King shared in the wording of the message of November, 1908, on the fiftieth anniversary of the taking over of direct government.[8]

On the issue of the addition of an Indian member to the Viceroy's Council, the King proved to hold exceptionally strong views, which ran counter to those quite unanimously held by the Cabinet, by the Viceroy, and by a majority of his Council.[9] 'At the last meeting of the Cabinet Council the Government were unanimous on the subject; the King has no other alternative but to give way much against his will. He, however, wishes it to be understood that he protests most strongly at this new departure.' Yet both Lord Minto and Lord Morley stressed the fact that to refuse to put an Indian on the Council was to negative the royal proclamation of 1858 disclaiming any racial distinction. The King would not yield, and insisted that Mohammedans would resent a Hindu being given a place and that there was danger in an Indian taking part in the deliberations of the Council. No doubt in this view, then shared by his son, he was merely showing inability to advance with the times.[10] But his continued interest in the position of the princes was shown in his insisting on the grant of the G.C.B. in diamonds to the Prime Minister of Nepal in 1908, and in seeking to secure a definite list of precedence for the princes, though that attempt was not wholly successful.[11]

To George V. fell the duty of sanctioning far wider developments in Indian government than those which had distressed his father. In 1917 the famous announcement by Mr. Montagu heralded the beginning of responsible government in India. The

---

[7] Lee, *Edward VII.*, ii. 381 f.　　　　[8] *Ibid.*, ii. 750–52.
[9] Lord Curzon and Lord Lansdowne were hostile to the project.
[10] Lee, *Edward VII.*, ii. 382–89.
[11] *Ibid.*, ii. 389 f.; Esher, *Journals and Letters*, ii. 353, was hostile and killed the project as a whole.

King, himself, by his presence at the Delhi Durbar of 1911,[12] had
set a precedent of personal connection with India of high importance,
and had announced far-reaching changes desired by minsters who
were criticised for thus employing his authority to secure approval
of the transfer of the capital of India from historic Calcutta to a new
Delhi, and the virtual cancellation of the partition of Bengal, which
was the most resented of all that Lord Curzon did in India.   But
the move of 1917 was far more important, and was followed up by
the Government of India Act, 1919.   He persuaded the Duke of
Connaught to open the new Legislature of India, when he delivered
a moving appeal for oblivion of the Amritsar massacre.[13]   The
King also sent a message in 1921 for the inauguration of the
Chamber of Princes,[14] and issued a proclamation of December 23,
1919,[15] which forms a worthy continuation of the tradition of
1858 and 1908.   His acceptance of the selection of Lord Reading in
1921 marked a definite break with the tradition of aristocratic
Viceroys, and once more illustrated the fact that the King possessed
a most remarkable and valuable faculty of adapting himself to the
changes of social outlook of the day.

As regards the reform movement of 1930 the King proved
helpful in regard to the activities of the Round Table Conference,
which resulted in the scheme of Indian federation under which the
princes were given the opportunity of entering for certain purposes
into a federation of India.[16]   At the same time in all matters in
which they did not desire to accept federation their direct relations
remained, and their character as such was marked by the fact that
the Governor-General dealt with the States not as such as in the
past, but as representative of the Crown for its relations with the
princes.   This personal connection became of great significance in
the eyes of these rulers.   At the same time the abandonment of the
old system by which the Government of India was vested in the
Secretary of State in Council and vested in the King, brought a
new relationship into play, and secured that more completely than
in the past the relations of the Crown to Indian government were
assimilated to the ordinary type of relations as existing in regard to
the Colonial Empire.   Burma, now a separate possession, came

---

12 Keith, *Constitutional History of India, 1600–1935*, pp. 232 ff.
13 Keith, *Speeches and Documents on Indian Policy*, ii. 335 ff.
14 *Ibid.*, 332 ff.   15 *Ibid.*, 327 ff.
16 Keith, *Constitutional History of India, 1600–1935*, ch. x.; *Letters on Imperial Relations, 1916–1935*, pp. 189–244.

under the new office of Secretary of State for Burma, held concurrently with that for India.[17]

Much more important in their bearing on the position of the King was the change effected in regard to the Dominions by the resolutions of the Imperial Conferences of 1926 and 1930 and the Statute of Westminster. The decision that the Dominons stood on a footing of complete equality in internal and external affairs with the United Kingdom in 1926 was followed by the decision that the King could be directly advised by the Dominion ministries in respect of such acts as he might personally have to perform for them. This decision was acted on by the Irish Free State and the Union of South Africa, in the latter case formally arranged by the Status of the Union Act, 1934, and the Royal Executive Functions and Seals Act, 1934. Later, the Irish Free State in 1936, on the abdication of Edward VIII., deprived the King of all functions of internal concern and restricted him to those of external negotiation and appointment of diplomatic and consular agents only, a situation further emphasised in the Constitution of Eire, 1937.[18] This Constitution made no reference to the Crown. On the other hand, it kept in force the Eire Executive Authority (External Relations) Act of 1936, the significance of which has just been mentioned. In December, 1937, after consulting the Governments of Canada, Australia, New Zealand and South Africa, the Government of the United Kingdom announced that it, and those other governments, had agreed to treat the new Constitution as not effecting a fundamental alteration in the position of Eire as a member of the Commonwealth.[19]

The final break between Great Britain and Eire came eleven years later. In September, 1948, the new Prime Minister of Eire announced that his government were preparing to repeal the External Relations Act of 1936. The new Act, when passed, the Republic of Ireland Act, ended Eire's remaining connection with the Commonwealth and, with it, the part previously played by the Crown in that connection. The Eire government recognised a specially close bond between Eire and the Commonwealth, and the position of citizens of Eire in the United Kingdom remained—as

---

[17] Keith, *The King, the Constitution, the Empire, and Foreign Affairs, 1936–37*, pp. 114 ff.
[18] Keith, *The Dominions as Sovereign States* (1938).
[19] *The Times*, December 30, 1937.

governed by the British Nationality Act, 1948—a privileged one; but 'common allegiance to the Crown' no longer united Eire with other Commonwealth countries.[20]

It is clear that there is no real parallel between the relation of the King to his British ministers and that of his relation to the Dominion ministers. He cannot attempt to exercise any functions with regard to the latter except of formal action on formal advice. The point has raised serious problems. If the King were asked to approve action by a Dominion incompatible with the unity of the Empire, would he be required to assent? In the case of the Union, action could now be taken without his personal intervention if desired. In the case of the accrediting of an envoy to the King of Italy, Emperor of Ethiopia, for Eire in 1938, action by the King personally was requested by Mr. de Valera, disregarding the fact that the King was thus made a King with two faces, and he still recognised the Emperor of Ethiopia as *de jure* Emperor.[21] If, of course, the action proposed amounted to secession, the King might have to ask that he be excused performance, and that it be carried out by the Governor-General under local advice. Whether the King would be entitled or bound to oppose British ministers, if they advocated action which he knew would be resented by the Dominions, is open to discussion. The cause for such right of dissent is plainly not a strong one, for with the doctrine of equality the case for British deference to Dominion claims is greatly weakened. On the whole it seems inevitable that the sovereign must act on the advice of each group of ministers, so far as it is compatible with the maintenance of the existence of the Commonwealth, and nothing but the most serious divergence of action must be deemed incompatible. The tendency thus is for the Crown to become essentially divided, and for the relations between the Dominions and the United Kingdom to approach more nearly the conditions prevailing between Britain and Hanover before the separation of the Crowns in 1837. In the abdication crisis of 1936 both the Union and Eire asserted the doctrine that the Crown was divisible, and had in fact been divided, the reign of Edward VIII.

[20] 458 *H. C. Deb.* 5 s., 1413; Ireland Act, 1949, 12 & 13 Geo. 6, c. 41.
[21] The inconvenience was lessened by the British decision in the treaty of April 16, 1938, to violate its obligations under Articles 10 and 20 of the League Covenant and to recognise the King of Italy as Emperor: see Keith, *The Scotsman*, April 19, 1938.

ceasing on December 10 in the Union, of December 12 in Eire, and on December 11 in the rest of the Empire.[22]

In the case of Eire it must be remembered that the movement for separation was in part the result of the grave failure of Queen Victoria and Edward VII. to keep in touch with the people. It is deeply to the discredit of the Queen that, in the sixty-three years of her reign, she could spare less than five weeks for Ireland as compared with seven years for Scotland. Her visit in 1900 showed how much could be done by personal presence to win loyalty to the throne, and the fact of Fenian activities was wholly insufficient to excuse her consistent neglect. Nor would she consider the establishment of a royal residence there, nor press the Prince of Wales to make a practice of residing there for a fixed part of each year. Both Mr. Disraeli and Mr. Gladstone[23] would have favoured making the Prince her representative in Ireland, but royal jealousy prevented this being done, seconded, no doubt, by the Prince's unwillingness thus to hamper his enjoyment of English social life and foreign travel alike.

On ascending the throne the King, who had systematically neglected Ireland since his visit in 1885,[24] made some amends. He had already concluded that the political office of Lord Lieutenant might go in favour either of the appointment as the deputy of the King of a member of the royal family or of visits by the Prince of Wales from time to time. This scheme, which had not attracted Lord Salisbury, was rejected by Mr. Balfour on the advice of Mr. Lecky, and an opportunity of conciliation was lost.[25] But the King favoured the efforts of Mr. Wyndham at agrarian settlement, and approved Sir A. MacDonnell's appointment as Under-Secretary at Dublin Castle, with a position substantially more important than usual. He postponed a visit to 1903 for rather insufficient reasons, but was greeted with much cordiality, and equal success attended a visit in 1904. But in 1905 disaster greeted the amiable Mr. Wyndham, because his Under-Secretary, assuming his agreement, had gone too far in encouraging the

---

22 Keith, *The King, the Constitution, the Empire, and Foreign Affairs, 1936–37*, pp. 7–13.

23 On finding occupation for the Prince, see Guedalla, *The Queen and Mr. Gladstone*, i. 320 f., 340 f., 351–70, 374–81, 383–85.

24 Lee, *Edward VII.*, i. 245. The idea of an Irish residence was again negatived in 1889 by the Queen.

25 *Ibid.*, ii. 161–63. Lord Salisbury is said even to have opposed the Queen's visit in 1900, but to have been overruled by her; Legge, *King George*, ii. 135 f.

prudent scheme of the Irish Reform Association, headed by Lord
Dunraven, to encourage some measure of devolution in Ireland.
The result was a dangerous revolt in Conservative ranks, the
retirement of Mr. Wyndham on March 7, and the retention of
Sir A. MacDonnell, who never lost the King's confidence in office
until in 1908 he retired with a peerage.[26]   In the meantime, in
1907, the King had paid a final visit to Ireland,[27] which, however,
was not wholly satisfactory, for Lord Aberdeen was not precisely a
persona grata, and the theft of the jewels of the Order of St. Patrick,
which had just occurred, added to royal resentment.

As we have seen, the idea of providing for visits by the Prince
of Wales to Ireland to represent his father had broken down, and
it was not, therefore, given to George V. to influence, by personal
contact with the people, the future of that country.   The alarms
and excursions of his early years of office precluded any attempt to
establish his position in Ireland, and the outbreak of the rebellion
presented the Government with a position whence no successful
effort to extricate itself was ever made.   It remains to the credit of
the King that, whether on his own motion or not, he took the
occasion of his visit to Belfast to inaugurate the opening of the first
Parliament of Northern Ireland to make an appeal for peace,[28]
which preluded the Irish negotiations of 1921 and the creation
thereby of the Irish Free State.

Major developments within the Commonwealth since 1945
have led to a re-statement of the position of the Crown in relation to
the Dominions.   By a series of Independence Acts in 1947 the
Government of the United Kingdom brought to an end its responsibility for the affairs of India, Burma and Ceylon.   India was
divided into the two fully self-governing Dominions of India and
Pakistan, Ceylon also became (in 1948) a fully self-governing
Dominion, and Burma was declared to be both self-governing and
no longer a part of the King's Dominions.   In 1948 India declared
her intention of becoming a Republic and, by a Royal Proclamation of June 22 of that year, the words 'Emperor of India' were

---

[26] Lee, *Edward VII.*, ii. 183 ff.   Lansdowne is credited with part responsibility for
MacDonnell's selection, Newton, *Lansdowne*, pp. 498 ff.   Wyndham is defended in his *Life* by Mackail and Wyndham, and some light is thrown by Mrs.
Dugdale in *Arthur James Balfour*, i. 415 ff.; cf. Esher, *Journals and Letters*, ii. 76 f.
[27] Lee, *Edward VII.*, ii. 472–74.
[28] June 22; on July 29 Mr. Lloyd George asserted the falsity of current rumours
and insisted on ministerial responsibility.   Cf. *ante*, p. 339.

declared to be omitted from the style and titles of King George VI.[29]

On the other hand, India stated her wish to remain a member state of the Commonwealth. This decision to adopt a republican form of constitution, while continuing a member of the Commonwealth, raised a constitutional problem which was not settled until April, 1949, when the Prime Ministers of the Commonwealth met in London for the sole purpose of finding a solution. At the end of those meetings a statement was issued, the relevant parts of which run as follows:—

'The Governments of the United Kingdom, Canada, Australia, New Zealand, South Africa, India, Pakistan and Ceylon, whose countries are united as members of the British Commonwealth of Nations and owe a common allegiance to the Crown, which is also the symbol of their free association, have considered the impending constitutional changes in India.

'The Government of India have informed the other Governments of the Commonwealth of the intention of the Indian people that under the new Constitution which is about to be adopted India shall become a sovereign independent republic. The Government of India have however declared and affirmed India's desire to continue her full membership of the Commonwealth of Nations and her acceptance of the King as the symbol of the free association of its independent member nations and as such the Head of the Commonwealth.

'The Governments of the other countries of the Commonwealth, the basis of whose membership of the Commonwealth is not hereby changed, accept and recognise India's continuing membership in accordance with the terms of this declaration.[30]

Commenting on this statement in the House of Lords Viscount Simon spoke of the 'contribution made by the almost mystical position of the Crown' to the development of the Commonwealth, adding that the solution just described showed once more that the Crown stood above all contending political parties, 'and in discharging its constant and silent service is always an emblem of unity and never the cause of dispute.'[31]

5. THE SOVEREIGN AND DEFENCE

QUEEN VICTORIA was never much interested in the navy, largely, no doubt, not because she did not care for being on the sea, but because

---

[29] *London Gazette,* June 22, 1948.
[30] 162 *H. L. Deb.* 5 s, 126 ff.
[31] *Ibid.,* 129.

she had in army matters the advice of the Duke of Cambridge, who was absolutely conservative in all matters appertaining to the army. Moreover, it must be remembered that the Prince Consort was much more keenly interested from training and tradition in military than in naval issues. There was abundant opportunity of criticism of the defence preparations of Britain; the Queen could point out defects in numbers and equipment, and she gave a cachet to the efforts of Miss Florence Nightingale by royal favour. She came into conflict as often with Lord Palmerston, whom her husband accused of juvenile levity, because he was certain that he was in control of the Indian situation, and that neither France nor Russia could intervene.[32]   In fact she thought that he failed to realise the danger adequately, but he succeeded in giving Lord Canning support of 80,000 European troops within five months of the beginning of the disaster of the mutiny, and it was not found necessary to consider the offer of foreign troops, even by King Leopold.

An interesting question arose when the abolition of army purchase was determined upon.[33]   The idea that the Queen was seriously displeased with Mr. Gladstone on this issue cannot be maintained. She may not have been anxious for the change, but Lord Halifax is authority for her readiness to sign the necessary warrant revoking, under powers given by Act of 1809, the authority for purchase then accorded. The Queen merely required that a Cabinet minute should be recorded, and the requirement was just, because the ministry was, thus, by use of the royal authority—not prerogative—defeating the efforts of the House of Lords to prevent the abolition of a system, which had provided the army with inferior officers, and kept many able men out of it, or prevented their reaching high command. In 1873 she pressed, with success, for the appointment of a commission to consider alleged grievances of officers under the new position.[34]   Her view, however, as regards the vital reforms of Mr. Cardwell, were totally unfavourable;[35] she was certain that he was much disliked by the army, and wished him to be made Speaker, and in 1880, in making clear that she did not intend to have Lord Cardwell again at the War Office, she explained to her Premier, who had not been aware of it, that his plan had broken down.[36]   She demanded 'no mere theorist, but

32 Bell, *Palmerston*, ii. 172–75.   33 Morley, *Gladstone*, ii. 361–65.
34 *Letters of Queen Victoria*, 2 s., ii. 252.   35 *Ibid.*, 2 s., ii. 162.
36 *Ibid.*, 2 s., iii. 76, 82.

someone who will act cordially and well with the Commander-in-Chief,' who could not forgive Mr. Cardwell for his firm assertion of the civil control of the army.

The Hartington Commission on National Defence of 1888–90 caused her deep indignation by its proposal to abolish her cousin's office, and she stigmatised it as 'this really abominable report, which she beyond measure is shocked should have emanated from a Conservative Government.'[37] Sir H. Ponsonby was told that this step could not be allowed for one moment, and that he should take steps to prevent this being even discussed. The position of the Crown, in her view, demanded the right of direct communication with an immovable and non-political officer of high rank about the army. The command, it must be remembered, of the army signified to her a means of maintaining the prerogative of the Crown, and of combating the advance of democracy. Lord Wolseley pointed out, with energy, that the Duke of Cambridge had successfully blocked reform for years, and urged that the Duke of Connaught should be appointed in his place, as the best means of preserving the office of Commander-in-Chief and securing essential reforms;[38] while the Cabinet refused to give the Duke of Connaught the post of Adjutant-General, doubtless in large measure, because it was determined not to place him in a position in which he could claim reversion to the office of Commander-in-Chief, which it had decided to abolish when the Duke of Cambridge could be induced to resign. Not until 1895 did the ministry, through Sir H. Campbell-Bannerman, induce the Queen to persuade her cousin to resign, and even then she was disappointed that her son was passed over.[39] The office, in fact, though held by Lord Wolseley and Lord Roberts on a five years' tenure, disappeared under the re-organisation of 1904. Lord Esher had carefully paved the way for the royal acceptance of the proposal, by insisting that the King should not have in peace the competition in authority of a Commander-in-Chief.[40]

The Queen's attitude towards generals in the field was always cordial,[41] and, as we have seen, she did her best to induce her ministry to follow Lord Wolseley's policy as regards the Sudan.

[37] *Letters of Queen Victoria*, 3 s., i. 582, 600. [38] *Ibid.*, 3 s., i. 627.
[39] *Ibid.*, 3 s., ii. 517–22. [40] Esher, *Journals and Letters*, i. 406 ff.
[41] But not even she could induce Lord Beaconsfield to receive at Hughenden Lord Chelmsford after his return from his chequered command in South Africa; *Letters of Queen Victoria*, 2 s., iii. 40.

Her objections to the weakness of the army were impressed on Lord Beaconsfield in 1879 as regards the operations in Zululand and Afghanistan,[42] and in 1882 she so annoyed Mr. Gladstone in urging objections to the reduction of the army in Egypt that he described her action as intolerable: 'It is my firm intention not to give in, so far as I am personally concerned, for a moment to proceedings almost as unconstitutional as they are irrational; though the unreasonableness of her ideas is indeed such that it is entitled to the palm in comparison with their other characteristics.'[43] In March, 1885, she was most indignant with Lord Hartington and Mr. Gladstone, because of the despatch of a telegram to Lord Wolseley without her permission, and reminded the former of the rule of 1850 as regards Lord Palmerston.[44]   It was explained that her wishes were noted, but that the telegram in question did not bear the interpretation she had put on it.   In the same spirit under a Conservative ministry she was anxious that the wishes of Lord Roberts should, as far as possible, be met.   Her exertions in the South African war to show interest in her armies were continuous, and taken in conjunction with the fatigues of her visit to Ireland, undertaken in the same spirit, doubtless accelerated her death.[45]

In naval matters the chief incident of her reign which illustrates her position was the amusing controversy over the question whether, when the Prince of Wales was present on the royal yacht with the fleet, the evening gun should be fired from his yacht or the flagship of the Admiral in command.   The issue was settled amicably by an alteration in the Admiralty Instructions in 1873, but the questions raised were not uninteresting.   Lord Halifax laid down the sound rule that the Prince of Wales *eo nomine* had no authority to exercise royal powers; else an ambitious Prince might in older days have won strength against his sovereign, while Sir H. Ponsonby insisted that the Queen could never be made subject on her yacht to the Lords of the Admiralty.   Mr. Gladstone may be pardoned for ostentatiously keeping out of this amusing squabble over *The Fatal Gun*, as a contemporary skit named it.[46]

The vital question of the relative position of the Crown, ministers,

[42] *Letters of Queen Victoria*, 2 s., iii. 43.
[43] Guedalla, *The Queen and Mr. Gladstone*, ii. 43 (to Hartington, October 4, 1882).
[44] *Letters of Queen Victoria*, 2 s., iii. 627 ff.
[45] Cf. Askwith, *Lord James of Hereford*, pp. 261 f.
[46] Ponsonby, *Sidelights on Queen Victoria*, pp. 1–45; Keith, *The King and the Imperial Crown*, pp. 360 ff.

and generals in the field regarding responsibility for conduct of war was raised in a very definite form at the close of her life. The Cabinet had authorised instructions to Lord Roberts virtually suggesting removal of Col. Broadwood and General Gatacre in view of their failure in avoiding Boer traps. To Lord Lansdowne the Queen telegraphed that 'Lord Roberts is the only judge of what is necessary, and must really not be interfered with by civilians at a distance who cannot judge the exact state of the case.'[47] With deepest respect Lord Salisbury submitted that under the constitution 'the doctrine that the Cabinet have no control over a general in the field is not practicable. If they have no control, of course they have no responsibility. In the case, which is, of course, possible, that some grave evil were to result from the policy of the general, the Cabinet could not accept the responsibility of what had been done, or be under any obligation to defend him in Parliament; and in case Parliament took an adverse view, a condition of great embarrassment would result.' In the instance under examination, Lord Roberts could make representations which would receive full consideration. In fact he relieved General Gatacre of his command.

Edward VII. was not merely in a position to take more personal interest in his army, but the existence of a tedious war at his accession rendered him especially anxious to press forward its conclusion by urging on the Government every effort to force a finish and full support for Lord Kitchener, despite the criticism of methods of barbarism used by the Liberal leader. He doubted the wisdom of sending Lord Kitchener to India, and only yielded to the urgent advice of the Secretary of State and the Viceroy combined.[48] But he took a severe view of the indiscretion by which Sir Redvers Buller defended himself from attacks on his management of the Natal campaign on October 10, 1901, and refused to disapprove of his compulsory retirement.[49] He was influenced during this period by the advice of Sir T. Kelly-Kenny, and used his influence in 1901 to secure him the post of Adjutant-General in which he maintained him until the reorganisation of 1904, with which he was not in sympathy. He approved cordially the generous terms of peace on May 31, 1902, and the grant to Lord Kitchener of a

---

[47] *Letters of Queen Victoria*, s. 3, iii. 525. The Queen concurred in Cabinet responsibility, but deprecated hasty suggestions to the General on the spot.
[48] Lee, *Edward VII.*, ii. 81 ff.   [49] *Ibid.*, ii. 84.

viscounty, and rank as general, adding himself the Order of Merit,[50] while a peerage in 1901 was conferred on Sir A. Milner.

The Queen had deprecated any enquiry by a Royal Commission into the conduct—clearly unsatisfactory—of the war, and the King protested on June 13, 1902, to the decision to appoint such a body. Lord Salisbury, however, insisted that he could not overrule his Cabinet as suggested, and that it was a question of honourable adherence to a pledge.[51] His criticisms of defects were not spared, and Mr. Brodrick felt that he was unjustly suspected of taking upon himself too much authority, and disregarding the advice of the military side of the War Office and the Commander-in-Chief. It fell, however, to his successor, Mr. Arnold-Forster, to take up reform. The time was now ripe for the appointment by the Prime Minister, with the King's approval, and after consultation with the Secretary of State, of a committee composed of Lord Esher, Sir J. Fisher and Sir G. Clarke to advise on the reconstruction of the War Office.[52] Its report was of great importance, creating the Army Council, and thus abolishing the dualism between the Secretary of State and the Commander-in-Chief of the former system. The King accepted it against the advice of Sir T. Kelly-Kenny. He also approved the appointment of the Duke of Connaught to the new post of Inspector-General, which *pro forma* was offered to Lord Roberts, who ceased to be Commander-in-Chief. The further changes made resulted in some friction with Mr. Arnold-Forster, who failed to send the draft Orders on Decentralisation early enough for his criticism, and the King was annoyed by his insistence, with the backing of the Army Council, that the age of entry to the Guards should not be reduced to eighteen years, and by his refusal of a special salute for the Inspector-General: 'The Secretary of State for War is obstinate as a mule.'[53] Mr. Arnold-Forster then adumbrated his well-known scheme of a dual form of army, long-service and short-service, for consideration by Parliament, the Government not being committed to any definite view. This scheme, as too nebulous, evoked the King's remark: 'The King cannot withhold his consent from the proposals which he is advised

---

[50] Lee, *Edward VII.*, ii. 90.
[51] *Ibid.*, ii. 91 f. The friction on this point, added to disagreements on honours and foreign affairs, may explain his resignation (July 11, 1902). Cf. *ibid.*, ii. 158 f.
[52] Anson, *The Law and Custom of the Constitution*, vol. II. (ed. Keith), ii. 238, 247
[53] Lee, *Edward VII.*, ii. 199.

by the Cabinet to approve, but he cannot conceal his misgivings,' though he accepted the proposals finally made by the ministry.[54] On the question of the new pay warrant, he carried on a struggle with Army Council and Treasury, and refused to sign the new warrant until assured that no officer would suffer financial hardship under the new regulations.[55] No doubt his insistence was aided by the fact that the ministry was in a very feeble position in the Commons. Moreover, his resistance was, no doubt, conditioned by a stupid error on the part of the minister, who on July 25 submitted for immediate sanction an amended army order regarding general officers commanding districts and accountants, through his Private Secretary. The King complained of his treatment to the Prime Minister, and Mr. Arnold-Forster apologised profusely for the oversight.[56] His compliments on retirement were, no doubt, really meant.

Mr. Haldane's famous proposals regarding an expeditionary force and a territorial army were supported fully by the King, whose influence aided their acceptance by the Cabinet.[57] He added to his services by summoning the Lord-Lieutenants to Buckingham Palace, where he asked their support for the county associations, which form an essential part of the territorial scheme.[58] The expeditionary force of 60,000 of pre-South African war times was raised to 160,000, yet army estimates were reduced by two millions in three years to spare funds for the navy. But the King was perturbed at the defects of the territorial artillery dwelt on by Lord Roberts, and, though Mr. Haldane produced much expert authority, the King still felt doubtful whether on mobilisation the artillery would be able to secure six months' training before their services were required. Moreover, he became dubious of the policy of reducing the regular forces when the territorial army was still in the making, especially as the territorials only numbered 106,000 by the end of April 1908, and approached its strength of 300,000 two years later.[59]

On the strength of the South African garrison the King's views were strong. In 1904 and 1905 he deprecated any reduction with

---

54 Lee, *Edward VII.*, ii. 206.
55 *Ibid.*, ii. 210 ff.
56 *Ibid.*, ii. 213 ff.
57 *Ibid.*, ii. 500 ff.
58 Ridges, *Constitutional Law of England* (ed. Keith), p. 328.
59 Lee, *Edward VII.*, ii. 502 ff.

dismay. In March 23, 1906, he stated that Mr. Haldane must 'clearly understand that I cannot give my sanction to the reduction of any garrison in South Africa.' He held that Gibraltar and Malta should be taken over by the Admiralty and the forces in South Africa and Egypt increased, in view of the excellent training grounds they presented. Nothing could, however, be done, and on June 26, 1908, the decision to reduce the South African garrison was duly taken by the Cabinet, a step denounced by the King as a 'most ill-advised and dangerous proceeding.' As always, he yielded to the Cabinet ruling.[60]

His dislike of publicity in army scandals showed itself in 1906 and 1907, when he yielded, with reluctance, to the publication of details of the ragging in the Scots Guards and another episode, discreditable to military honour, but obviously certain to be exaggerated by rumour if the facts were concealed.[61]

The navy also engaged his earnest attention, and throughout he supported the policy of Sir John Fisher in favour of the construction of Dreadnoughts, with economy in other directions, involving cutting down the forces available to show the flag overseas.[62] Lord Charles Beresford's dislike of Sir J. Fisher and his policy led to his lending support to his critics, and after a prolonged struggle Lord C. Beresford was removed from command of the Channel Fleet on March 24, 1909, but the latter made such serious allegations regarding the new distribution of the fleet, and other defects, that a committee was considered necessary, which found finally in favour of Sir J. Fisher's views.[63] The navy estimates in 1909 caused general anxiety; the Admiralty wanted six, later eight, Dreadnoughts, while Mr. Lloyd George, Mr. Churchill, Mr. Harcourt, and Lord Morley demanded four only, on economic grounds.[64] Ultimately, to the satisfaction of the King, eight were arranged for by some obscure process of reasoning, but not until after the ministry had been severely weakened by constant attacks by the Opposition, which, undoubtedly, had a distinct effect on lessening the Governmental majority in the election of January, 1910. Mr. Churchill has candidly admitted that on this occasion he was

[60] Lee, *Edward, VII.*, ii. 484 f.
[61] *Ibid.*, ii. 498 f.
[62] *Ibid.*, ii. 330 ff. Cf. Churchill, *World Crisis, 1911–14*, pp. 121 ff. In 1910 Sir J. Fisher retired with a peerage, as a result of his indiscretions.
[63] Lee, *Edward VII.*, ii. 599 ff.
[64] Churchill, *World Crisis, 1911–14*, pp. 36 ff.; Spender, *Lord Oxford*, i. 252–54.

in the wrong, while in his turn, when transferred to the Admiralty in 1911, he found opposition to his own schemes.

In the Great War the part played by the King was mainly to encourage the forces by his unfailing interest, shared by the Queen and other members of the royal family in their welfare. He, himself, visited the front and consulted with his Prime Minister and others on the question of conscription, in a manner reminiscent of the days when the sovereign actually might sit in Cabinet to discuss questions with ministers;[65] it is interesting to note that the Governor of Newfoundland contemporaneously sat in Council with ministers to devise means of aiding the Empire. The King also appealed to munition and other workers to give unsparingly of their time and efforts to aid their fellows at the front, and undoubtedly appeals from such a quarter had much greater results than those from employers or officials only. His effort to inculcate abstinence from intoxicating liquors for the duration of the war as a means of saving, and of securing a higher standard of efficiency, was unhappily but little followed, even in the highest ranks of society; a King can set fashions only when they are in substantial accord with the wishes of his people.[66]

How far the King was consulted in the course of the war does not very distinctly appear; but we know that he approved the substitution of Sir D. Haig for Sir John French, and that he accorded to the latter firm support in his difficult task, and cheered him by much courtesy.[67] It must be remembered that in vital issues, the sovereign was necessarily bound to accept the decision of the War Cabinet, as in the resolution to get rid of Sir W. Robertson from the office of Chief of the General Staff and to substitute for him Sir Henry Wilson.[68] It may be surmised that the Premier's refraining from deciding to supersede Sir D. Haig was essentially due not merely to the unpopularity of the step, but also to the undoubted reluctance of the King to accept so drastic an action.

The limits of royal action may be noted again in 1934, when the ministry, which by that time had become conscious of the grave deficiencies of British strength in armaments, refrained from its original intention of re-arming, because by-elections seemed to show

[65] Asquith, *Memories and Reflections*, ii. 109, 114 ff.
[66] Lloyd George, *War Memoirs*, i. 317 ff., 328 ff.
[67] Duff Cooper, *Haig*, ii. 14, 63, 69, 72, 129, 161, 392.
[68] *Ibid.*, ii. 223 ff.

that any such policy was unpopular. It is difficult to suppose that the King could have been satisfied with an attitude which, as presented in the Commons on November 12, and at Glasgow on November 18, 1936, by Mr. Baldwin, seems to condemn the democracies to decisive inferiority to the Fascist powers.[69] In the pre-war years the ministry seems to have been in full agreement with the King, that it lay with it, despite all Parliamentary difficulties, to secure that due preparation was made to meet the inevitable war.

6. THE SOVEREIGN AND ECCLESIASTICAL POLICY

To a generation in which ecclesiastical issues count for very little, the steadfast character of Queen Victoria's concern comes curiously. But her views were simple and pertinaciously held. She believed herself head of the Church of England,[70] and even Mr. Disraeli admitted that she was at least supreme governor in all spiritual and ecclesiastical causes, and she was an orthodox Protestant of her period, wholly opposed to extreme tendencies. Her aim was to maintain things unaltered, and she was therefore definitely hostile to anything which menaced it. Already in 1830 examination by the Bishops of London and Lincoln had shown that her mind was being duly trained in orthodoxy as then esteemed.[71] Six years later the King of the Belgians impressed on her the necessity of maintaining good relations with the Church, whose advice she accepted.[72] Naturally she disliked the appearing of Romanising tendencies in *Tracts for the Times*, but Lord Melbourne, in and out of office, was not inclined to take the issue very seriously.[73] But she was not bigoted, and warmly commended Sir R. Peel when he added to the endowment of the Roman Catholic College at Maynooth in 1845; while she would not use the resources of the Church in Ireland for this purpose, she held that the Roman Catholic clergy should be well and handsomely educated, and deplored the bigotry and blind passions shown by the Protestants.[74]

In 1850 the papal brief establishing a Roman Catholic hierarchy in England raised much indignation in certain quarters, including Lord John Russell. The Queen approved of the Ecclesiastical

[69] Keith, *The King, the Constitution, the Empire, and Foreign Affairs, 1936–37*, p. 140.
[70] *Letters of Queen Victoria*, 2 s., ii. 348 f. [71] *Ibid.*, 1 s., i. 19 ff.
[72] *Ibid.*, 1 s., i. 53. [73] *Ibid.*, 1 s., i. 257.
[74] *Ibid.*, 1 s., ii. 43.

Titles Bill,[75] in view of popular feeling, but deprecated abuse of the Roman Catholic religion as unchristian and unwise. She resented, however, quite as much the activity of the Tractarians and the Archbishop's failure to hold out any means by which the laity could protect themselves from Puseyite rituals. Lord Derby in 1852[76] gave her assurances as desired of his intention to keep the Church Protestant against Puseyites and Romanisers, and Prince Albert raised the question of the constitution of a Church Assembly based on Diocesan Assemblies and Vestries exercising local legislative functions. In fact the regular meeting was revived in 1852.

In course of time, the growth of ritualistic practices developed so much that she felt impelled to urge that steps be taken to deal with 'dressings, bowings, &c., and everything of that kind, and, *above all, all* attempts at confession'; the bishops should seek power to put down '*all* these *new* and *very* dangerous as well as absurd practices,' and should give permission, as on the Continent, for other Protestant ministers to preach in their churches.[77] She expressed her fears to Mr. Gladstone, who promised careful consideration for any views as to legislation put forward by the Archbishop of Canterbury, and expressed his own regret at the appearance within the Church of persons who held views inconsistent with the tenets it professed.[78] But it was left to Mr. Disraeli[79] to obey her commands and to carry the Public Worship Regulation Bill in 1874, which the Queen welcomed but which Mr. Gladstone ineffectively attacked. The measure, of course, failed entirely of its main purpose, to put down ritualism, in the public and royal view, but it afforded an effective ground for the Prime Minister to base a claim in 1879 for the Queen's consent to grant preferment to Lord A. Compton,[80] though a High Churchman, on the ground that he had worked assiduously to diminish the resentment against the Government felt by the High Churchmen, who pinned their faith to Mr. Gladstone, and so deserved promotion. With this formal and barren success in the war against ritualism, the Queen had to be content, save in so far as she could still influence opinion in the Church through the royal control of appointments. This

---

[75] *Letters of Queen Victoria*, 1 s., ii. 336. Cf. Greville, *Memoirs, 1837–52*, iii. 366 ff.
[76] *Ibid.*, 1 s., ii. 456.   [77] *Ibid.*, 2 s., ii. 290.
[78] *Ibid.*, 2 s., ii. 302, 306–8. Cf. Morley, *Gladstone*, ii. 514 ff.; Gladstone, *Gleanings*, vi. 141.
[79] *Letters of Queen Victoria*, 2 s., ii. 298, 300, 329, 335, 339, 342, 347, 350 f.
[80] *Ibid.*, 2 s., iii. 51 f.

applies to archbishops, bishops, deans, and some canons, while a number of livings valued at over £20 a year *temp.* Henry VIII. also fall to be filled by the Crown on the advice of the Prime Ministers.

It is not recorded how the Queen came to accept Lord John Russell's unfortunate promotion of Dr. Hampden, which caused much unrest and an attempt to secure a judicial ruling as to his fitness.[81]   But with the passage of time her interest became strong. She claimed the Deanery of Windsor as a personal, not political, appointment, and proposed for it in 1882 Canon Connor.   Mr. Gladstone, without waiving responsibility, settled the point by immediately recommending him, whereupon the Queen formally offered the post through Prince Leopold.[82]   On his death in 1883 the Queen consulted the Archbishop of Canterbury and proposed Randall Davidson, whom Mr. Gladstone accepted, though recognising that in view of the youth of the chosen prelate, some of his critics would be down upon him.[83]   The position is clear; the appointment rests on the Prime Minister's responsibility, though he will naturally defer to royal wishes in a matter so immediately interesting to the sovereign.   The issue was more formally raised as regards the canonries, and Mr. Gladstone stuck firmly to the *status quo*, which gives the responsibility to the Premier, though the sovereign can take the initiative if desired.[84]   This removes any anomaly.

In other cases the Queen was wont to rely on her ecclesiastic advisers, the successive Deans of Windsor.   Dean Wellesley, who died in 1882, had for twenty-five years been in touch with ecclesiastical appointments.   Lord Palmerston, in 1864,[85] commented on the Queen's request for more than one name to be submitted to her for the vacant deanery of Westminster as a reference to irresponsible advisers, but he gave two names with a preference for Dr. Conway whom the Queen accepted, but with a strong defence of her right to consider the merits of persons recommended.   This was, no doubt, in itself not an unsound doctrine, but illegitimate when it came to asking for the right to choose. Moderate views she demanded in her appointments from Lord

[81] *Letters of Queen Victoria*, 1 s., i. 159 ff.; Ridges, *Constitutional Law of England* (ed. Keith), p. 73; Greville, *Memoirs, 1837–52*, iii. 109 f., 114–20.
[82] *Letters of Queen Victoria*, 2 s., iii. 341 f., 345 f.
[83] *Ibid.*, 2 s., iii. 421.   For Mr. Gladstone's general views see Morley, *Gladstone*, ii. 430–33; iii. 95 ff.   He ignored political views.
[84] *Letters of Queen Victoria*, 2 s., ii. 441; 3 s., i. 106 f.   [85] *Ibid.*, 2 s., i. 236, 240.

Derby in 1852,[86] and she exercised strong pressure on Mr. Disraeli to conform to her wishes in matters ecclesiastical. Thus she obtained the appointment of Dr. Tait as Archbishop of Canterbury despite his doubts,[87] and caused much difficulty to her loyal Prime Minister, who had to warn her that the great mass of the Conservative Party viewed with suspicion the Broad Church movement and that votes would be lost if the Government favoured it. Moreover, 'if Church preferment were bestowed on some who are mentioned by name in your Majesty's confidential memorandum, a disruption of the Cabinet would inevitably take place.'[88] He urged on her the grant of a canonry to S. Turner, son of the historian, Sharon Turner, a friend of his father, but found her most reluctant, and received a stern warning on the danger of Romanism and Popery and Atheism and Materialism. Mr. Disraeli, in fact, got himself into much trouble owing to finding a post for Dr. Duckworth, simply to please the Queen, who hoped it would benefit the health of Prince Leopold.[89] She conceded with very bad grace her Premier's pleasing for the Deanery of Chichester for Dr. Burgon,[90] and, only after Canon Lightfoot had refused it, did she give that of Ripon, 'under a narrow-minded diocesan, with an entirely sympathising clergy, and indeed laity,' to Mr. Turner, who not surprisingly resigned the meagre post within a year.[91] She could not obtain from Mr. Disraeli a canonry for her friend, Charles Kingsley,[92] but he received one in 1873, while Mr. Disraeli gave a canonry to Mr. Birch, who had been tutor to the Prince of Wales, who, it may be added, was by no means backward in urging favours for his friends.[93]

Dr. Davidson adopted a moderate view of the royal position. He held that she should exercise the right to reject names, but should not advocate candidates for particular appointments, though she might mention to her Premier in general terms divines whom she deemed meet for promotion.[94] Hence, as in the case of the translation of the Bishop of Exeter to London in 1885, there

86 *Letters of Queen Victoria*, 1 s., ii. 456. Puseyites and Romanisers to be avoided.
87 *Ibid.*, 2 s., i. 545 ff. For the selection of Dr. Benson in 1882 see iii. 381–86; Morley, *Gladstone*, iii. 95 ff.
88 *Letters of Queen Victoria*, 2 s., ii. 370 f., 373 f.   89 *Ibid.*, 2 s., ii. 373.
90 *Ibid.*, 2 s., ii. 422.
91 *Ibid.*, 2 s., ii. 374, 423, 433.
92 *Ibid.*, 2 s., i. 519; ii. 248; Gladstone sacrificed Dr. Miller, but refused to promote Mr. Phipps, brother of Sir C. Phipps, for very good reasons; ii. 281 f.
93 *Ibid.*, 2 s., i. 520, 531.   94 Bell, *Randall Davidson*, i. 164 f.

was a complex interaction of influences, the Dean, the Archbishop, Mr. Gladstone and the Queen all expressing views.[95] In 1888, Lord Salisbury pressed Canon Liddon for the see of Oxford on the Queen,[96] explaining his reluctance to tender her unacceptable advice, but stressing the bad effect of the impression of the royal hostility. But the Dean cleverly secured a way out for the Queen on the score of the poor health of the candidate, whose place was taken by the solid erudition of Dr. Stubbs. Lord Salisbury, however, was quite firm against promoting the Dean himself, to Durham in 1889,[97] and refused him Winchester in 1890,[98] but gave him Rochester. He pointed out that the evangelicals had claims to preferment, which the Queen would not gratify, and that to promote Dr. Davidson, who was not yet known as preacher, author or parish priest, too rapidly would be a blunder, a view which the person criticised had the sense to accept as sound. The Queen again was hostile to Dr. Percival for Hereford,[99] because of his association in her mind with the cause of Welsh Disestablishment, but Dr. Davidson pressed her to accept Lord Rosebery's strong recommendation as necessary to prevent it being thought that only one type of religious view appealed to her.

The influence of the Queen was not sufficient to secure Dr. Davidson preferment in 1896 to Canterbury, Dr. Temple being preferred,[1] but after his appointment to be Archbishop his influence was maintained in effect. He was regularly consulted, would explain the special nature of the vacant see, and suggest names, whence a choice would be made after full consultation between him and his sovereign. It appears that, though he did not always secure the preferment of the candidate whom he favoured, no appointment which he actually disapproved was made. Edward VII. was seemingly responsible for the appointment to London of Dr. Winnington Ingram, an appointment which had considerable effect on the growth of irregularities in that diocese.[2] After 1906,[3] however, his interest in the matter waned, but in 1902,

95 Bell, *Randall Davidson*, i. 166 ff., 173 ff.   96 *Letters of Queen Victoria*, 3 s., i. 426 ff.
97 *Ibid.*, 3 s., i. 539 ff., 553 ff., 558 ff.   Nor did he promote her protégé Bishop Barry.
98 *Ibid.*, 3 s., i. 631 ff.   99 *Ibid.*, 3 s., ii. 467–72.
1 *Ibid.*, 3 s., iii. 94 f., 100, 104, 110.   2 Lee, *Edward VII.*, ii. 52.
3 *Ibid.*, ii. 53.   He tried to persuade Lord Salisbury to promote to the Deanery of Peterborough his son or his brother-in-law, Canon Alderson: but, perhaps, because of his very generous treatment of his relatives in his ministry in 1900 (Garvin, *Joseph Chamberlain*, iii. 614; 88 *Parl. Deb.* 4 s., 375, ' The Hotel Cecil Unlimited') he refused.

he negatived the suggestions of the Bishop of Winchester that colonial bishops might be made canons without dropping the episcopal style and habit, and that royal chaplains should no longer be required to resign on being made suffragan bishops or deans, a pluralism which he deemed unfair to other clergy. Mr. Asquith was especially careful in his ecclesiastical patronage, and always took his own decisions for submission to the King.[4] His own outlook was that of an old-fashioned Protestantism, without leanings to the High Church.

Of later appointments, no doubt, the most remarkable are those of Dr. Barnes, as Bishop of Birmingham, which was made by a Labour Prime Minister, and of Dr. Temple as Archbishop of York.

To the Church of Scotland the attitude of Queen Victoria was very interesting. It was never forgotten by her that the sovereign has a double duty to support the Church of England, in England, and to support the Church of Scotland when in Scotland. Fortunately for her, she was deeply attached to the Church, which she regarded as the real and true stronghold of Protestantism,[5] and she found in Dr. Norman Maclean a typical exponent of its spirit, just as in Dr. Davidson she had a polished diplomatic adviser in the far more difficult questions of the Church of England. She was still young when the great disruption of 1843 took place, and she had to approve the decision of Sir R. Peel that the Government could not accept the claim of the Church to override the right of patronage given by the Act of Anne,[6] and only in 1874 was that Act, which was probably contrary to the Act of Union, repealed. She claimed to be head of the Church,[7] though, of course, as the Lord Advocate pointed out, no such claim was admitted by the Church, but that claim was not meant in any serious sense. While patronage lasted the Crown livings were dealt with, with special care.

The idea of disestablishing the Church of Scotland was wholly foreign to her, and Lord Rosebery found himself exposed to a complete refusal to contemplate such action,[8] though it was alluded

---

[4] Spender, *Lord Oxford*, ii. 378 ff.   The present Archbishop of Canterbury admittedly exercises a wide influence on episcopal appointments, but there is on foot a movement to secure directly for the Church some degree of control.

[5] *Letters of Queen Victoria*, 2 s., iii. 47.   [6] *Ibid.*, 1 s., i. 560 ff.

[7] *Ibid.*, 2 s., ii. 349.   She deprecated any proselytising by the Episcopal Church, and the tendency of Scots upper class families to join that church of dissenters.

[8] *Ibid.*, 3 s., ii. 452 f.

to in the speech from the throne for 1894. She reminded him of
the coronation oath, and certainly it would have been very difficult
to ask a Queen, who was perfectly sincere in her religious convictions, to accept a Bill contrary to that oath. The precedent of the
irreligious and generally worthless George IV. and Roman Catholic
emancipation was far from a cogent argument. Luckily the
issue never became urgent in her lifetime, and in 1921 an Act was
duly passed which opened the way to the reunion of the Church of
Scotland and the United Free Church in a much larger and very
representative body. It is significant of the good will of George V.
to the change that, before it was consummated, he authorised his
High Commissioner to abandon the formality of claiming the right
to dissolve in the royal name the General Assembly contemporaneously with its dissolution by the Moderator of the Church.

To Roman Catholics the Queen was kindly disposed, but her
consent to the disestablishment of the Irish Church was rather due
to her slightness of interest in Ireland than to conviction of the case
for the Roman Catholics. Edward VII. showed the effect of the
development of religious toleration by his objections to the terms of
the declaration, which he was required by statute to make on
accession, repudiating the doctrine of transubstantiation, and the
adoration of the Virgin Mary, and the sacrifice of the mass as used
in the Church of Rome.[9] But his anxiety to induce ministers to
act was foiled by the stubbon resistance of Lord Halsbury, who
published, without consulting the King, the report of a committee
of peers set up to advise as to changes. The King disliked both
failure to consult and the terms of the report, and, when the Government produced a Bill, based on the report, and passed it through the
Lords, his attitude, no doubt, helped to induce the ministry to let
the matter stand over. But, after George V. had had to take the
oath in the old form, the new ministry in 1910 reduced the royal
obligation to that of a declaration that the sovereign was a true
Protestant by the Accession Declaration Act.[10]

The King showed also his desire to treat with respect the head
of the religion professed by so many of his subjects, and therefore
secured ministerial approval for a private visit to the Pope when
visiting Rome as above mentioned.[11] But in 1908 an episode

9 Lee, *Edward VII.*, ii. 22.
10 Anson, *The Law and Custom of the Constitution*, vol. II. (ed. Keith), i. 267, n. 3.
11 *Ante*, p. 377.

occurred, very embarrassing alike to ministers and the sovereign, out of the proposed public procession of the Holy Sacrament on September 13, as 'an act of reparation for the Reformation.'[12] The Protestant Alliance and the Church Association naturally protested and addressed the sovereign, who heard nothing from the Home Secretary, or at first Mr. Asquith. Cardinal Bourne was induced, through Lord Ripon, to omit the host and the vestments from the procession which took place. The King rightly rebuked the Home Secretary for failure to deal effectively with the matter in the first instance, and Lord Ripon was so annoyed at this lack of consideration of the religion to which he had been converted that he resigned, though age and health were given as motives to avoid embarrassing the ministry. In 1910 Mr. Churchill managed to persuade him in advance that a procession in the vicinity of the Westminster Cathedral would not cause difficulty, and it passed off quietly. But it was left to George V.'s reign to see the legal removal of all Roman Catholic grievances[13] and the establishment under stress of war conditions of diplomatic representation at the Vatican.

A point of some difficulty presented itself to Edward VII. in virtue of the proposed marriage between the King of Spain and Princess Victoria Eugenie of Battenberg, daughter of his sister, Princess Beatrice. The marriage necessitated the conversion to Roman Catholicism of the Princess, and the Church Association and the Protestant Alliance, and the more weighty objections of the Archbishop of Canterbury and the Bishop of London had to be considered. Fortunately, however, for the King, it was found that as Princess Beatrice had married into a foreign family, though her husband was later naturalised, under the Royal Marriages Act, 1772, which as a rule requires royal assent for the validity of the marriages of descendants of George II., no action by the sovereign, personally, was necessary, and the marriage duly took place.[14]

Fortunately for the sovereign, the grant of wide legislative power to the Church of England Assembly (Powers) Act, 1919, removes from him, personally, any concern with the tendencies towards Romanising in the Church which would have deeply affected his grandmother, who would have been most reluctant to authorise

---

12 Lee, *Edward VII.*, ii. 659–63.
13 Roman Catholic Relief Act, 1926; Ridges, *Constitutional Law of England* (ed. Keith), pp. 146, 379.
14 Lee, *Edward VII.*, ii. 512 ff.

the Convocations to take action towards amending the Prayer Book in the direction of sanctioning practices which are, strictly speaking, illegal. If future efforts succeed better than those of 1927 and 1928 in securing the assent of the Commons,[15] then the assent of the sovereign would be in the same position as his assent to an ordinary Act of Parliament.

It is still the case that the sovereign does not recognise the territorial appellations adopted by the members of the Roman Catholic hierarchy, and addresses from the members thereof by their territorial styles may not be submitted by the Home Secretary to the King. This was reiterated in 1937, but it is of long standing, in view of the provisions of the Act of 1871, which repealed the prohibitions of the Ecclesiastical Titles Act.[16]

7. Crown Appointments

(1) A LARGE number of offices at home and abroad have always been in the gift of the Crown, though the number has been affected by the removal of the sphere of patronage of a large number of posts in the civil service. The use of offices to reward party supporters was inevitable and natural, but Sir R. Peel struck a new note in determining to consider merit and long and faithful service as prime grounds for preferment. 'The party interests of a Government,' said Peel, 'are in the long run much better promoted by the honest exercise of patronage than by the *perversion* of it for the purpose of satisfying individual supporters.'[17] None the less it is clear that political reasons have power in affecting appointments. The part of the King in this part is clear. He is entitled to secure that those recommended for his approval are worthy; more he cannot well do, for he is seldom in a position to press the claims of others since he cannot normally have better knowledge than his ministers. Where, however, he can form a judgment, he is plainly entitled to maintain it, subject to the usual rule of yielding if the ministry make the matter one of principle.

---

15 Taylor, *Brentford*, pp. 251–67. The issue was treated as open, and Mr. Joynson-Hicks had to contend against the Prime Minister and Mr. Churchill in 1928, when approval was withheld by 266 to 220 votes. On the decline of Protestantism, see Halévy, *Histoire du Peuple Anglais au XIXe Siècle, Epilogue*, ii. 75 ff.

16 See correspondence with Archbishop Vaughan in 1892; *Letters of Queen Victoria*, 3 s., ii. 114.

17 Parker, *Peel*, iii. 414. See Finer, *Modern Government*, ii. 1295 ff.

Naturally, it is only the highest appointments which have to be specially submitted to the Crown, and in most of these cases both the Prime Minister and the minister in immediate charge of the department concerned take counsel together and recommend, for it is established practice that a departmental minister ought not to ignore in any such matter the Prime Minister. On occasion even the Cabinet may be consulted informally; the issue of filling the office of Viceroy of India has thus been dealt with. Normally, where the Prime Minister and the departmental minister are agreed, the sovereign will assent, as in the case of ambassadorial appointments or those of Governor-General, though in the case of the Dominions the appointment is now either formally or in practice in the hands of the Dominion.[18]

An instructive case, showing the Queen's good sense, is that of her attitude to the proposal to appoint Lord Elgin Governor-General of India.[19] She objected that 'he is very shy, and most painfully silent, has no presence, no experience whatever in administration.' The matter was considered virtually in Cabinet and the proposal sustained largely because of the recommendations of his personal friends, Lord Rosebery, Sir H. Campbell-Bannerman, and Mr. Marjoribanks;[20] unquestionably the Queen's doubts were just, for Lord Elgin's strength lay in Scottish local government which ill-fitted him for the cares of India or of the Colonial Office, which was given to him in 1905 at the desire of the Prime Minister, a close personal friend, but whence he was immediately removed by Mr. Asquith.[21] In the case of the proposed appointment of Sir G. Wolseley, later a favourite of the Queen, as adjutant-general in 1881, her objections were based on the Duke of Cambridge's hostility and reinforced by suspicions that Wolseley used the Press to further his military views. In the result, however, Mr. Gladstone secured acceptance of the appointment on terms.[22]

The Queen's interest in diplomatic appointments was connected with her views on foreign policy. She undoubtedly took trouble to

---

18 Union of South Africa has no British action in those cases.

19 *Letters of Queen Victoria*, 3 s., ii. 300 f., 304 f., 315 f. He was not a success as Viceroy, but the position there was very difficult, with plague, famine, and the North-Western frontier expedition (*ibid.*, 3 s., iii. 216 f.).

20 The selection of Sir H. Robinson in 1880 to replace Sir B. Frere at the Cape was made by the Cabinet as part of their policy of recalling Frere; Guedalla, *The Queen and Mr. Gladstone*, ii. 109.

21 Spender, *Lord Oxford*, i. 198.

22 Gardiner, *Harcourt*, i. 415 f.

persuade her ministers in 1864[23] and 1870[24] to recall Sir A. Buchanan and Lord A. Loftus respectively from Berlin, as her daughter, the Crown Princess, warned her that they were not successful in carrying out their mission. Naturally, in 1880, she stood up for Sir H. Layard, when it was decided to recall him from Constantinople, for he had been only an instrument of the policy of her late ministry.[25] She had to accept the explanation that H. Layard was not considered satisfactory and that changes in such offices on change of government were not unusual. She showed appreciation of the vicissitudes of Sir R. Morier's career and pointed out that his unpopularity in Germany was largely due to Bismarck's dislike of his relations with the Queen's daughter.[26]

Edward VII. had naturally strong views on appointments, because he knew many people personally and thus was able to put them forward or criticise proposals to advance them with real knowledge, which in the Queen's latter days was certainly lacking. He regretted the haste to send Lord Kitchener to India, but later would gladly have made him Viceroy but for the refusal of Lord Morley to countenance the suggestion. He approved the appointment of Sir J. D. Poynder to New Zealand,[27] but was not enthusiastic of the peerage demanded for that democratic community, especially as Lord Gladstone, whose appointment to South Africa he approved without enthusiasm, had been given a peerage for much more distinguished services than mere conversion rather late in life to Liberalism. In diplomatic appointments he had quite strong views, and he took much interest in the succession in 1908 to Sir F. Lascelles at Berlin, which proved difficult to arrange, as Sir F. Cartwright proved impossible because of a youthful *jeu d'esprit*.[28] Finally, as the result of a personal interview at Cronberg, Sir E. Goschen was appointed, despite his most natural reluctance to take a difficult post. He had been selected for his former post at Vienna on the royal initiative after the King had insisted on the fixing of a final date for the retirement from that embassy of Sir F. Plunkett on the score of age. He also pressed for promotion for Sir A. Herbert and Sir R. Rodd, with success in the former case.[29]

---

23 *Letters of Queen Victoria*, 2 s., i. 206, 243.

24 *Ibid.*, 2 s., ii. 80, 85. Cf. her action in 1884 in selecting Sir E. Malet for Berlin; iii. 532, 536, 538.

25 *Ibid.*, 2 s., iii. 92 ff.

26 *Ibid.*, 3 s., i. 457 f. For Lord Beaconsfield's cleverness in making an appointment of General Wolseley and then apologising, see *ibid.*, 2 s., iii. 22, 24–26.

27 Lee, *Edward VII.*, ii. 708 f.   28 *Ibid.*, ii. 618 f.   29 *Ibid.*, ii. 180 f.

The King's interest in defence appointments was natural. He encouraged Sir T. Kelly-Kenny to resist efforts to withdraw him from the office of Adjutant-General,[30] and, though not enthusiastic about the new office of Commander-in-Chief in the Mediterranean, he induced the Duke of Connaught to accept it, and was much annoyed when in 1909 he refused to continue in a useless post.[31] He persuaded Lord Kitchener to follow him, most reluctantly, but released him at a last interview on April 28, 1910. He was in regular correspondence with Major-General Haig when he was Inspector-General of Cavalry in India, and gladly promoted his interests on the termination of that appointment. George V. continued the interest felt by his father, and wrote with his own hand to confer on Haig the rank of Field-Marshal, and in 1917 presented him with the Order of the Thistle, which the Duke of Buccleuch had declined to accept until it had been bestowed on the greatest living Scotsman. The King steadily supported Haig throughout with his confidence, and it is interesting to note that on April 8, 1919, they were both in agreement on the unwisdom of the step then taken in depriving the troops of full dress; it has since been realised that as Haig then argued to maintain a voluntary army, it would be desirable 'to clothe troops smartly, pay them well, and amuse them with games, &c.'

Of the non-political appointments filled by the Crown, the most interesting, of course, is the poet laureateship. The death of Lord Tennyson[32] should, no doubt, have been seized upon to afford the opportunity of terminating an office, which it has been only rarely possible, worthily, to fill. Instead Lord Salisbury quite inexcusably preferred to it A. Austin,[33] whose first effusion was the really incredible poem on the Jameson Raid, which was, in his words, 'to the taste of the galleries in the lower class of theatres, and they sing it with vehemence.'[34] The further opportunity of dropping Mr. Austin on the death of the Queen was missed by Edward VII.,[35] who thought wrongly that the post was unpaid.

In other cases Edward VII. showed interest, proposing Mr. Morley as successor to Lord Acton as Regius Professor of History at

---

30 Lee, *Edward VII.*, ii. 86 f.   31 *Ibid.*, ii. 496 f.

32 A. Tennyson was recommended by Lord J. Russell in 1850; *Letters of Queen Victoria*, 1 s., ii. He was offered a baronetcy by Lord Beaconsfield and Mr. Gladstone (1873), and created a baron in 1883; Guedalla, *The Queen and Mr. Gladstone*, ii. 245 f., 248.   33 *Letters of Queen Victoria*, 3 s., ii. 582.

34 *Ibid.*, 3 s., iii. 24.   35 Lee, *Edward VII.*, ii. 53.

Cambridge, as against the more novel suggestion of Admiral Mahan by Mr. Balfour. Ultimately the office went to Professor Bury of Dublin. It is understood that George V., no less than his father, took a real interest in similar appointments. Inevitably political responsibility may have to be faced by the Premier in such cases, as when objections were taken to the appointment, as Professor Gilbert Murray's successor at Oxford in 1936, of one who asserted his right of Irish citizenship.

The Prime Minister is solely responsible for the grant of civil list pensions, which to a total of £2,500 can be granted each year to persons who have rendered public service, or done important work in literature or in science, or, more often, to their dependants. The former total of £1,200 was only raised in 1937 under considerable public pressure.

Judicial patronage, though exercised in the name of the Crown, is essentially a matter in which royal intervention must be limited, for appointments are necessarily made on grounds of technical qualifications, which the sovereign cannot well call into question. The puisne judges are chosen by the Lord Chancellor, who informs the Prime Minister as a matter of courtesy;[36] Lord Brougham actually submitted first to the Queen and then informed the Premier. The other judges, the Lords of Appeal in Ordinary, the Lords Justices of Appeal, the Lord Chief Justice, the Master of the Rolls, and the President of the Probate, Divorce and Admiralty Division, and the members of the Judicial Committee of the Privy Council, are selected by the Prime Minister, who usually informs the Lord Chancellor of his proposals.

The law officers of the Crown used to claim the right to be considered for appointment to the rank of Lord Chief Justice and Lord Chief Baron on vacancies occurring in these offices. This doctrine was solemnly repudiated by the Cabinet after the passing of the Judicature Act,[37] and promotion was to rest on length of service and qualification only, but there is no evidence that this doctrine was ever seriously acted upon. At any rate Mr. Gladstone, in his next ministry, treated Sir H. James as naturally entitled to the offer of a Lordship of Appeal and Master of the Rolls.[38]   But in 1907 Lord Davey's death was not followed by the natural appointment

36 Cf. Mallet, *Cave*, pp. 296 f.
37 *Letters of Queen Victoria*, 2 s., ii. 290.
38 Askwith, *Lord James of Hereford*, pp. 105 ff.

to fill the vacancy of Sir Lawson Walton, the Attorney-General, whose selection was expected on all hands. The Lord Chancellor intervened to secure that the Master of the Rolls should go to the Lords, being succeeded by Lord Justice Cozens-Hardy, the vacancy thus created being filled from the Court below. It is clearly now the normal rule that the law officers should be seriously considered when vacancies occur in the headships of the divisions of the High Court or in Lords of Appeal, but there is no absolute claim, and in 1938 the Lord Chancellor was chosen for judicial distinction, without any record of political service, and the Master of the Rolls in 1937 was without political claims. In Scotland the claim of the Lord Advocate on the other hand is regularly recognised, as in the case of Mr. W. G. Normand, who became Lord President in 1937.

Political considerations, no doubt, sometimes weigh with regard to appointments. In 1915 a serious difficulty arose, because the Conservatives, when forming a coalition with Mr. Asquith, insisted on securing the Lord Chancellorship of Ireland for Mr. Campbell, a proposal abhorrent to Mr. Redmond, whose remonstrances brought from Mr. Asquith the poignant admission: 'Nothing but the most compelling sense of public duty could have induced me to be where I am, and surrounded as I am, and cut off as I am today.'[39] The claim was compromised for the moment, but Mr. Campbell became Attorney-General in 1916, and Lord Chancellor in 1918, ending finally as Lord Glenavy and first Chairman of the Senate of the Irish Free State. More recent instances of political exigencies can be suggested, but royal action is really not involved. It would be difficult to conceive any concatenation of circumstances which would justify assertion of the royal discretion, for no Government would be reckless enough to put forward for judicial office any person not well qualified and of respectable character;[40] the days of men like Sir A. Cockburn, whose moral character was far below their ability, may safely be said to be gone.

In all cases of appointments the same rule applies; while the proposed appointee must necessarily be approached to learn if he will accept, it must be made clear that the offer is subject to the royal approval and that no mention of it must be made until such

---

39 Spender, *Lord Oxford*, ii. 168 f.
40 Mr. Justice Darling's was a purely political appointment, but he was far from incompetent.

approval has been obtained.[41]   No doubt, cases happen where the fact leaks out before approval is given, but that is perhaps inevitable, for ministers and others are far from infallible.

8. The Honours Prerogative

IT is of the essence of honours of any kind that they should appear to be the personal gift of the sovereign, and for this reason all honours are submitted to and formally approved by the sovereign, and whenever possible the investiture with the insignia or other act in connection with its bestowal is performed by the King in person, or at least the royal signature is attached to the instrument conferring it.   But the principle in the great majority of cases of the conferment of honours is that the recommendation to the sovereign goes from a minister, and normally the Prime Minister.[42]   There are certain exceptions in regard to honours for services in certain fields.   Thus, the Order of St. Michael and St. George (1818) is conferred for foreign, Dominion and Colonial services on the recommendation of the Foreign, Dominions and Colonial Secretaries; those for army, navy and air force servants by these departments represented by their political chiefs; Indian services were rewarded by the Star of India (1861) or the Order of the Indian Empire (1877) on the proposal of the Secretary of State.   But the Prime Minister is informed of the recommendations of ministers, though they go direct to the King, and for all other honours he is directly responsible, except in the case of the Royal Victorian Order (1896), which is personal to the King.   The King also controls the Royal Victorian Chain,[43] whose grant is very restricted and distinctly personal, and in the first instance the Order of Merit was to have been a personal order.   Whether that has remained the case is not clear.   At any rate, we may suppose that the King definitely approves those included in it, and does not accept merely formally the suggestions of the Prime Minister.   If, on the other hand, the King desires to confer an award of honour or a baronetcy or peerage

---

[41] In case of household appointments action, of course, without royal sanction is inexcusable; see J. D. Corigan's case in 1847: *Letters of Queen Victoria*, I s., ii. 161.

[42] Cmd. 1789 (Report of Royal Commission).

[43] Lee, *Edward VII.*, ii. 99 f.   It has been only rarely given, *e.g.*, in 1935, to Earls Derby and Cromer, and in 1936 to the Duke of Kent.   The honours of K.G., K.T., and K.P. are largely under royal control by suggestion.

on any person for household or personal services,[44] the Prime Minister must be asked to include the name on his list and thus to take full responsibility for it. The same remark, of course, applies if the King desires a reward to be conferred for public services which is not spontaneously proposed by the Prime Minister.[45]

The only issue, therefore, which is doubtful, is that of the control which the Crown exercises over the grant of honours, and in this case the facts certainly suggest a steady diminution in authority on the part of the Crown. The Queen in 1859 refused a Privy Councillorship to Mr. Bright[46] for his attacks on the institutions of the country, though later she was to regard him with favour. In 1866 a new issue arose, the appointment of peers on the retirement of Lord Russell, the Prime Minister.[47] The practice of giving honours on such occasions was already observed, and the Queen agreed to those desired by Lord Russell except peerages other than that for Lord Monck, for services in Canada. But she stressed the fact that several peerages had been created since Lord Palmerston's death, and that Sir R. Peel, Lord Aberdeen, and probably Lord Derby, had not made such proposals on retirement. But in 1868,[48] with some hesitation, she promised to create peerages for Lord Derby, who had embarrassed her and Mr. Disraeli by delaying his formal resignation because he wished to be in the position as Prime Minister to announce his creations to those thus honoured. In 1869 she declined a peerage to Sir L. de Rothschild as a Jew engaged in banking operations for foreign countries, his speculations she regarded as gambling.[49] In 1881 she objected to the grant of a peerage to Sir G. Wolseley,[50] but conceded it after his successes in Egypt next year. In one matter her attitude commands respect: she consented to give a peerage to Sir A. Cockburn in 1865 only because it had been promised, though without her authority, but asserted her duty of securing that

---

44 *E.g.*, Lord Sydney, Lord Chamberlain, in 1874; Guedalla, *The Queen and Mr. Gladstone*, i. 447. So no doubt the Dukedoms of Fife and Windsor. For Lord Reay, see *ibid.*, ii. 146. Lord Rosebery demurred to reckless bestowal of baronetcies on the occasion of a royal birth; *Letters of Queen Victoria*, 3 s., ii. 412 f. Cf. also *ibid.*, 2 s., iii. 26.

45 Lord Salisbury was delighted to knight musicians as named by the Queen, as he had no musical knowledge; *ibid.*, s. 3, ii. 128 (1892).

46 *Ibid.*, 1 s., iii. 446.

47 *Ibid.*, 2 s., i. 347. She used this precedent in 1868 to justify refusal to create peers to strengthen Mr. Disraeli on the eve of the general election; *ibid.*, 552 f.

48 *Ibid.*, 2 s., i. 498, 501–5.

49 Guedalla, *The Queen and Mr. Gladstone*, i. 207.

50 *Ibid.*, i. 141–51, 158–61 (a very strong refusal).

14*

peerages should be given only to people of good moral character.[51] Her views were narrow in some respects; she would not, even at Lord Salisbury's urgent request, give Sir F. Leighton a peerage in 1891,[52] and that conceded in 1895 only preceded, shortly, his death.   Sir W. Thomson was honoured in 1891, but mainly, it seems, because Lord Hartington urged his claim as an upholder of Unionism in Scotland.   To Mr. Watts she denied, in 1897, a Privy Councillorship as inappropriate, though Professor Max Müller was accorded that distinction.   But earlier he had refused a baronetcy.[53]

In her own desires for honours her most notable struggle was that over a dukedom or the Garter for Lord Lansdowne on his retirement from the Governor-Generalship in India.[54]   Mr. Gladstone was willing to give a G.C.B. (Extraordinary), but rightly held that that nobleman's Indian services were not such as to justify the step proposed, and the Queen resented his argument that, after being Chancellor of the Exchequer, he himself had not resented the offer of an ordinary G.C.B., alleging that political party services could not be compared to great political services to the Queen and country.   It is a melancholy thought that a minister of the Crown can do less for this country than a Viceroy, who, after all at that time was a mere agent of the Secretary of State for India in Council.

Edward VII. was more enlightened, for he was anxious to honour C. A. Abbey and J. S. Sargent not less than H. von Herkomer and W. Q. Orchardson, but the two former were ruled out as not being British subjects.[55]   Lord Curzon he would have been glad to find a place for in the Lords on his return from India, but neither Mr. Balfour nor Sir H. Campbell-Bannerman would agree, the latter inevitably, as he had no responsibility for his Indian work.[56] He was anxious to restrain his Government from excessive generosity in creations.   He accepted ten peerages for the first new year list,[57] and gave with pleasure a Privy Councillorship to Henry Labouchere, the *bête noir* of his mother, but a man of character not dissimilar in some aspects to his own.   For the June honours he tried to fight

---

[51] *Letters of Queen Victoria*, 2 s., 257–62; he took a G.C.B. later; ii. 239.
[52] *Ibid.*, 3 s., ii. 105.
[53] *Ibid.*, 3 s., iii. 167; Guedalla, *The Queen and Mr. Gladstone*, ii. 483, 488.
[54] *Letters of Queen Victoria*, 3 s., ii. 340 f., 343 ff.   He got the Garter.
[55] Lee, *Edward VII.*, ii. 469.   [56] *Ibid.*, ii. 379 f.
[57] *Ibid.*, ii. 451.

against seven peerages and eight Privy Councillorships, and above all against the peerage for Mr. Pirrie, but in vain, for Sir H. Campbell-Bannerman, though full of respect for the King, was firmly convinced of his rights as Prime Minister. Three years later he conferred the St. Patrick on Lord Pirrie with great discontent, accentuated by the fact that none of the other knights would take part in an investiture, which therefore had to be performed privately by Lord Aberdeen,[58] whom the King had no love for, mainly because of his failure to deal effectively with the theft of the jewels of the Order in 1907 just before the royal visit to Ireland, when he did not stay at Viceregal Lodge. The Aberdeens were also suspect on the score of their endeavour to create human relationships between themselves and their servants, both at Ottawa and in Dublin, acts pleasing *per se*, but regarded by the King as *infra dignitatem* of their office.[59] He objected at first to give Ray Lankester the K.C.B. on the score that he had not received the C.B. and had been removed from office at the Natural History Museum, but gave way at once when told that the offer had been as usual in such cases already made privately.[60] He deprecated the grant of the Garter to the Shah of Persia on grounds which were perfectly sound, but was compelled on diplomatic grounds to concede it, but this was done in such a manner as to minimise any good from the grant.[61] To the King of Siam he was steadfast in refusing the honour, but naturally gave it to the Emperor of Japan, and he gave in also to the wishes of ministers regarding the honours to be paid to Prince Fushimi on his visit in 1907 to return the compliment paid in the preceding year by the mission of Prince Arthur of Connaught to present the Garter to the Emperor, though he was reluctant to concede the full ceremonial honours in the case of a sovereign. He secured, however, through the Lord Chamberlain, the withdrawal from performance of *The Mikado* during the Prince's visit, and the military and naval bands were instructed not to perform the music of the opera during that period.[62] One personal appointment of the King outside the Order of Merit and the Royal Victorian Chain, which he endeavoured to render important, was that of Lord Carrington to be a member of the Order of the Garter.

58 Lee, *Edward VII.*, ii. 452.   59 *Ibid.*, ii. 472.
60 *Ibid.*, ii. 470. The King disliked special remainders for peerages, a view shared by George V.
61 Newton, *Lansdowne*, pp. 239 f.   62 Lee, *Edward VII.*, ii. 313 f.

The real difficulty over honours, however, broke out during the reign of George V., as a result of the efforts made by the head of the coalition Government to secure a large political fund.   The use of honours as political awards is naturally ancient; Walpole used it and W. Pitt found it excellent, when Burke's Act, 1782, curtailed the number of places and pensions available to bribe members for their support.   The settlement of the civil list at the accession of Queen Victoria added to the difficulties of providing funds for payment of supporters, and the creation of party organisations by Mr. Disraeli and Mr. Chamberlain established the need of large subscriptions, which were naturally often forthcoming in return for promises of honours.   The system was well recognised;[63] applications were made by individuals or friends to the Patronage Secretary —now Parliamentary Secretary to the Treasury—in the case of M.P.'s, and to the head of the party organisation, who might be, and now is as a rule, different from the Parliamentary Secretary in other cases.[64]   Or the Prime Minister was approached direct.[65] None of these high officials would admit that they had been cognisant of any bargain to give an honour for a contribution, but no one seriously supposes that the minor officials, at least, were not fully aware that there was in fact an understanding.   That this was so was alleged in Parliament, and in 1914 elicited a resolution by the Lords against a contribution being a consideration for a recommendation for an honour; but the Commons did not accept the suggestion of similar action.   It was alleged in the Lords— no doubt correctly—that the Chief Whip was so aware, or at least one of his subordinates, and the view was widely accepted even among Liberals at the time.   No one expected that the Prime Minister was informed, and his denial was categorical.[66]   In 1917 in the Lords it was unanimously demanded that the reasons for conferment of honours, other than royal or service honours, should be stated publicly, and that the Prime Minister should satisfy himself that no payment, or expectation of payment, to a party fund was directly or indirectly associated with the grant, or promise of the grant, of an honour.[67]   Thirty-four peers also voted for a

---

[63] *E.g.*, Legge, *King George*, ii. 15–19.
[64] Cmd. 1789, p. 8.   His list might be submitted to the Patronage Secretary for his observations.
[65] He then made up his mind, with or without further advice.
[66] 15 *H. L. Deb.* 5 s., 252 ff.
[67] 26 *H. L. Deb.* 5 s., 172 ff., 835 ff.; cf. Mallet, *Lloyd George*, pp. 246–54; Jennings, *Cabinet Government* (1951 ed.), pp. 431 ff.

preamble, asserting that honours had been conferred in return for payments, and Lord Selborne testified to spontaneous touting by persons who claimed to be able to influence the conferment of honours. He gave the name of Sir James Gildea, the founder of the Soldiers' and Sailors' Families Association, as having thus been approached, and instanced the case of the Mayor of Lewes, in whose case the Whip had pronounced his claim good, but had demanded a contribution. Lord Knutsford instanced a case where a baronetcy was obtained for £25,000 contribution. Lord Loreburn expressly gave £25,000 as the price of a baronetcy, £15,000 for a knighthood, with a possibility of £10,000 for the latter,[68] full value being allowed for the payment if a baronetcy was wanted later. Lord Curzon, on the other hand, frankly justified a wealthy man giving his money for the benefit of his country.[69] The practice, however, of mentioning why honours were given in a purely perfunctory way was started in January, 1919, but in May the issue was again debated, this time in the Commons, when pointed reference was made to the honours given those connected with the papers loyal to the ministry.[70] But a proposal to require publication of particulars of party funds did not pass. The proposed peerage for Sir J. B. Robinson in 1922 proved disastrous, for the nominee was under a cloud in South Africa, as the result of strictures on his conduct by the Chief Justice, and the Colonial Secretary had not been consulted, while the ex-Governor-General very bluntly denounced the honour as quite undeserved.[71] The peerage was ultimately declined, but the discussions in both Houses drove the Government to the appointment of a royal commission. The further evidence adduced in the debates had shattered the pretence of no sale. The Commission recommended the setting up by each Government of a committee of the Privy Council of not more than three members, not in the Government, for the period of existence of the Government. It receives notice of proposed political honours, and is supposed to satisfy itself that no element of payment is involved, whereupon it reports to the Prime Minister if the person is a suitable person to be honoured. If its report is unfavourable, the Prime Minister must submit it with his recommendation to the

---

68 The price before the war was lower; £5,000 is recorded for 1910; 26 *H. L. Deb.* 847; Legge, *King George*, ii. 18.
69 26 *H. L. Deb.* 200.   70 116 *H. C. Deb.* 5 s., 1334 ff.
71 50 *H. L. Deb.* 5 s., 1126 ff.; 51 *ibid.*, 103 ff., 475 ff.; 156 *H. C. Deb.* 5 s., 1745 ff.

King. This committee was duly accepted, and has since been periodically set up.[72]   Moreover, in 1923, the Honours (Prevention of Abuses) Act was passed, penalising persons who promise to secure honours for payment and those promising to pay. With the reduction of the size of honours lists the issue is less discussed, but there is really no reason to doubt that honours are still used to reward party contributions, though no doubt the whole matter is managed with the quiet decency which marked the business before the creation of Mr. Lloyd George's political fund. One case of grave error was exposed by proceedings in bankruptcy in Scotland, when it transpired that a baronetcy had been conferred for a payment, which was returned on the suicide of the baronet, who had involved himself in heavy losses through his concern with liquor smuggling into the United States. Carelessness in awards was painfully frequent, and the local public opinion was often shocked at honours bestowed on persons whose claims to any distinction were quite invisible.

How far the new rules are efficacious in preventing irregularities is not certain.   The case of *Parkinson* v. *College of Ambulance*[73] throws a painful light on the methods employed to obtain honours, and the prosecution successfully of a trafficker in honours, and civil proceedings in which he was subsequently concerned,[74] proved absolutely the truth of Lord Carson's assertion from personal experience in practice, that brokerage was regularly paid on such transactions. It is not surprising that in Canada since 1919, except under Mr. Bennett's disastrous Premiership, the giving of honours has been stopped as a source of corruption, or that the Union of South Africa adopts the same principle.

The honours list appears on January 1st, and on the date, real or adopted, of the King's birth anniversary.   Large lists are issued at jubilee and coronation celebrations,[75] and for these the leader of the Opposition party—or leaders, if more than one—are usually asked to make some suggestions. The vast majority of those honoured, however, are supporters of the ministry.

---

[72] In 1938 Lord Macmillan, Mr. G. N. Barnes, and Lord Crewe.
[73] [1925] 2 K. B. 1.
[74] *Maundy-Gregory, In re, Trustee* v. *Norton*, [1935] Ch. 65.
[75] Lee, *Edward VII.*, ii. 95 ff.   1,540 honours were given in 1902, 515 in 1911. In 1937 the Queen received the Thistle; Queen Alexandra was given in 1901 the Garter (*ibid.*, ii. 54, n. 2), which was also given to Queen Mary and Elizabeth; the latter is Grand Master of the Royal Victorian Order.

Apart from normal honours are those, as mentioned above, bestowed on the retirement of a Prime Minister. The King, on such occasions, himself offers an honour to the retiring Premier. Mr. Gladstone refused consistently, Lord Salisbury deprecated the offer of a dukedom, Mr. Lloyd George remained a commoner, as did Mr. MacDonald, while Mr. Baldwin accepted the usual earldom and the Garter, and secured a viscountcy for a personal friend. In such cases responsibility rests, no doubt technically, with the incoming Prime Minister. It is clear that in the case of Mr. Asquith's earldom and Garter in 1925, while the offer was made at a time when there was for the moment virtually an interregnum, the responsibility rested ultimately with Mr. Baldwin.[76]

In minor matters of honorary character the sovereign has, no doubt, a comparatively free hand, as in the case of precedence. When ministers desire, it is, of course, regulated as they recommend, as in the case of the place assigned to the Prime Minister, which was decided upon by Mr. Balfour,[77] who was inclined to emphasise the outstanding position of the head of the Government. Similarly in the Dominions precedence is virtually regulated by the Governors-General, unless ministers intervene.

Medals are properly issued only with the sanction of the Crown, and this practice is jealously followed. Queen Victoria disliked even the grant without her approval of a medal to the forces of the East India Company, and in agreement with ministers firmly vetoed the idea of giving colonial forces in the South African war a special star, on the sound ground that all medals issue from the sovereign personally, a rule still respected in the Dominions.[78] But, whereas she had authorised the grant of a local medal in Ceylon, not even that precedent would move Edward VII. to allow one in Hong Kong, despite the special pleading of Mr. Lyttleton, whose amiable character did not give him sufficient force to have his own way with a masterful King.[79] He had definite ideas on the grant of permission to wear foreign medals, and to accept

[76] Spender, *Lord Oxford*, ii. 351 ff.
[77] Lee, *Edward VII.*, ii. 443 f. The Speaker's precedence after the Lord President was given by Order in Council.
[78] *Letters of Queen Victoria*, 3 s., iii. 574 f. Lord Milner wished to make the clasp a special gift from the Queen; on the other hand she insisted on having an Ashanti Star in 1896, because Prince Henry of Battenberg died on service; *ibid.*, 3 s., i. 32.
[79] Lee, *Edward VII.*, ii. 182.

foreign decorations. Though, at first, inclined to allow acceptance freely, as in the case of officials decorated by the German Emperor on his visit to England to grace the funeral of Queen Victoria by his presence, he later realised that the results of the practice were unsatisfactory, and the wearing of such decorations has been restricted with royal sanction.[80]

Types of uniform were of great interest to Edward VII., who took under his special protection the regiments of Guards, and in 1904 critically reviewed the defects of their overcoats. His historic sense showed itself in his success in securing the restoration to the Duke of Cornwall's Light Infantry of the right to wear a red pagri with the foreign service white helmet to perpetuate the gallantry in the field of its predecessor, the 46th Regiment, in 1777.[81] The subject of dress and equipment, as well as of armaments, also interested George V. and his successors.

The King also is consulted personally on all issues of salutes and official visits,[82] as in the case of the recognition to be paid to Indian princes and other rulers of protected territories within the Empire. Coinage designs are regularly submitted for his approval, which is not a formality.

Even on the issue of the name of the Royal Family the principle of ministerial responsibility was duly observed. The King readily recognised as the war continued that public feeling was running against the connection of the Royal Family with Germany, and accordingly, on July 17, 1917, a Council was held to approve a proclamation taking the name of Windsor for the Royal Family and the discontinuance of all German titles.[83] It is significant that the Council included to represent the Empire the High Commissioners for the Commonwealth of Australia and the Union of South Africa as well as General Smuts. Ministers also approved the further step of conferring on those members of the family who abandoned foreign titles the ranks of Marquis of Cambridge,[84]

---

[80] Lee, *Edward VII.*, ii. 101 f.   [81] *Ibid.*, ii. 209.

[82] Edward VII. vainly asked for a special salute for the Duke of Connaught as Inspector-General: 'no go. The Secretary of State for War is as obstinate as a mule' (Lee, ii. 199). The effort to name a battleship in 1912 Oliver Cromwell was negatived by George V.; Fitzroy, *Memoirs*, ii. 500.

[83] Legge, *King George*, i. 293 ff. For the many other grants of precedence, change of designation, &c., see 286 ff., 297 ff. Parliamentary intervention was necessary to deprive the Dukes of Albany and Cumberland and Brunswick of their titles: 7 & 8 Geo. V. c. 47; Order in Council, March 28, 1919.

[84] Formerly Duke of Teck, Prince Alexander of Teck, Prince Louis of Battenberg, and Prince Alexander of Battenberg.

Earl of Athlone, Marquis of Milford Haven, and Marquis of Carisbrooke.

A minor but not important vexation arises as regards the grant of honorary distinctions to foreign sovereigns, to which allusion has already been made. Queen Victoria declined to lavish the Garter, confining its bestowal to special occasions, as after the Crimean War to the Sultan, to the King of Denmark as the father-in-law of the Prince of Wales, and to visiting sovereigns, especially if relatives, as in the case of the Kings of Portugal and the Belgians. She refused, therefore, to send it to the Emperor of Russia in 1866, though advised to do so by Lord Stanley.[85] To William II. she gave the Hon. Colonelcy of the Royals, which greatly delighted him in 1894, and allowed him to have the privilege of conferring honours on two of its officers. This action seems to have been taken without the advice of ministers,[86] and this failure to consult was repeated in 1908 by Edward VII., when, in his desire to please the Czar during his visit to Reval, he created him an Honorary Admiral of the British Fleet.[87] Mr. Asquith immediately pointed out that neither he, nor Sir E. Grey, nor Mr. McKenna, nor the Cabinet, had been consulted. There was no excuse for the King's totally unconstitutional action, and he admitted to all three ministers that he regretted he had, without knowing it, acted irregularly. As was pointed out, had the matter been raised in the Commons, the ministry would have been placed in a most unfortunate position; as already mentioned, the King had already been brought into a sense of his duty to accept ministers' advice by the threat of resignation over the grant of the Garter to the Shah of Persia. He made also a very serious blunder in May, 1905, when he advised the Grand Master of the Order of St. Michael and St. George to appoint as Chancellor the Duke of Argyll. As the appointment was one to be filled by the Colonial Secretary under the statutes of 1877, Mr. Lyttelton properly protested, and only acquiesced reluctantly in the acceptance of the illegal action of the King.[88] Nothing, of course, is more incumbent on the sovereign than obedience to the law, and as advice is always

---

85 *Letters of Queen Victoria*, 2 s., i. 370.
86 Spender, *Campbell-Bannerman*, i. 128.
87 Lee, *Edward VII.*, ii. 593 f.; Spender, *Lord Oxford*, i. 249–51. Lord Knollys pointed out that the King should have had a minister to keep him straight; Esher, *Journals and Letters*, ii. 322.
88 Lee, *Edward VII.*, ii. 523.

available, action of this kind can have no just excuse. Normally, of course, marks of distinction for relatives will be advised without hesitation by ministers, unless some political signification could arise. The matter is now of very minor interest.[89]

As in the case of appointments, the person whom it is proposed to honour ought to be approached in confidence to ascertain whether the proposal is acceptable.[90] Thus, in the case of the services, honours are only conferred after due enquiry. In some cases of distinction in letters, science or art, or otherwise, the honour may be conferred without such enquiry. At least, that alone can excuse the occasional instances in which the issue of an honours list is followed by an announcement that the recipient does not desire it, in which case, of course, the formal steps to confer the honour are not taken. The refusal of a lower honour sometimes is a bar to further advancement; sometimes it has no such effect. Thus Earl Haig had earlier declined a peerage of inferior standing, and it appears that Mr. Barrie declined a knighthood, though, finally, he accepted the rarer honour of a baronetcy, which his means easily enabled him to support. It may be added that the abolition of payment of fees on obtaining honours has simplified their acceptance.

---

[89] For the converse case of foreign honours cf. Queen Victoria's objections and those of ministers to the Prince of Wales accepting a Russian regiment in 1873: *Letters of Queen Victoria*, 2 s., ii. 297.

[90] In the case of Mr. Balfour's K.G. the King pressed the proposed recipient direct, and gave him it at a Cabinet; Fitzroy, *Memoirs*, ii. 775–77. A peerage soon followed.

APPENDIX 1

GOVERNMENTS FROM WILLIAM IV

In 1827, the resignation through ill health of Lord Liverpool terminated a ministry which had lasted since June, 1812. In April, Canning took office with a coalition, but only to die in August, when Lord Goderich maintained a coalition government whose internal dissensions led to his retirement and the advent of a Tory government under the Duke of Wellington in January, 1828. In June, 1830, the demise of the Crown necessitated a general election, but in November, the ministry, defeated on the civil list, resigned rather than face the problem of reform.

1. Earl Grey who now took office in order to carry reform dissolved on that score in April, 1831, and secured the necessary mandate for the passage of the Reform Bill, which finally received the royal assent in June, 1832. In the subsequent General Election the Reformers of all kinds had a majority of 300 over the Tories, but, owing to internal dissensions, the Premier resigned in July, 1834, making way for Lord Melbourne.

2. Lord Melbourne had only a brief tenure of office. He resigned in November in consequence of certain difficulties with the more than ready acquiescence of the King, and was succeeded by Sir R. Peel.

3. Sir R. Peel secured a dissolution, but the results in January, 1935, gave the Tories only 293 as against 365 seats, thus strengthening them greatly but not so as to be able to maintain office. In April, the ministry resigned on defeat on the issue of the revenues of the Irish Church.

4. Lord Melbourne's new ministry held office until August, 1841. The dissolution of 1837 on the demise of the Crown left it with no more than 339 to 319 seats, and May, 1839, saw it driven, by the disappearance of its majority on the issue of the coercion of Jamaica as regards slavery, to resignation.[1] Sir R. Peel undertook to form a government, but the opposition of the Queen on the

---

[1] *Letters of Queen Victoria*, 1 s., i. 193 ff. Greville, *Memoirs*, 2 s., i. 199 ff.

issue of parting with certain ladies of the bedchamber led to his giving up his commission, and Lord Melbourne resumed his precarious tenure of office.[2] In June, 1841, he was defeated on a definite issue of no confidence and against his own judgment dissolved. The voting gave him only 289 to 369 seats, and he resigned in August after defeat in the Commons.

5. Sir R. Peel held office until 1845, when he resigned in December in view of difficulties on the issue of free trade.[3] Lord John Russell, however, failed to form a ministry, for Earl Grey would not accept office if he was to have Lord Palmerston as a colleague in the post of Foreign Secretary, and Sir R. Peel had to resume his post. He succeeded in passing the legislation repealing the corn laws, but only at the cost of deeply splitting his party, with a result that he was defeated and resigned in June, 1846, on an Irish Coercion Bill.

6. Lord John Russell took office in July, 1846, but the general election of 1847 failed to give him a clear majority; though all figures for this period are disputed, he seems to have had about 325 Whig and Liberal votes as against 226 Tories and 105 Peelites; a more favourable view gives him 337 seats, Protectionists 202, and Peelites 116. The position was difficult, and in February, 1851,[4] the ministry was defeated on a franchise motion and resigned. The leader of the Protectionists, Lord Stanley, was most reluctant to take office, and, after prolonged negotiations which failed to clarify the situation in any essentials, Lord John Russell had to resume office. Owing to his quarrel with Lord Palmerston, whom he removed from the government in December, he was defeated on the Militia Bill and resigned in February, 1852.

7. Lord Derby had clearly a most difficult task, and his dissolution in July, 1852, brought him no sufficient support. It is calculated that some 300 Conservatives were returned, 270 Whigs and Liberals, 40 Peelites and 40 members of the Irish party.[5]

2 *Letters of Queen Victoria*, 1 s., i. 204 ff.   Parker, *Peel*, ii. 387 ff; Greville, *Memoirs*, 2. s, i. 201 ff.

3 *Letters of Queen Victoria*, 1 s. ii. 56 ff; Parker, *Peel*, iii. 229 ff., 283 ff.; Greville, *Memoirs*, 2 s., ii. 317–332.

4 *Letters of Queen Victoria*, 1 s., ii. 345 ff; Monypenny and Buckle, *Disraeli*, i. 1101 ff.; Walpole, *Russell*, ii. 123 ff; Bell, *Palmerston*, ii. 40 ff; Greville, *Memoirs*, 2 s., iii. 377 ff.

5 Cf. Lord Derby's figures, December 18, 1852 (*Letters of Queen Victoria*, 1 s., ii. 501): 286 Conservatives, 150 Radicals, 120 Whigs, 50 Irish Brigade, 30 Peelites.

Defeated in December by 19 votes on Mr. Disraeli's budget, the ministry resigned.

8.   Then followed the coalition of Whigs, Liberals or Radicals, and Peelites under Lord Aberdeen with Lord John Russell to lead the Commons.[6]   The resignation of the latter in January, 1855, on Mr. Roebuck's proposed motion for a committee on the Crimean War, so weakened the ministry that, though it was induced by the Queen not to resign forthwith, it succumbed to the motion and then resigned.   Much confused searching for a successor followed, but the inevitable result was the appearance in power in February of Lord Palmerston.[7]

9.   Lord Palmerston, however, lost almost at once his Peelite colleagues on his acceptance of the Roebuck motion, and thus the ministry assumed a predominantly Liberal appearance.   In March, 1857, Conservatives, Peelites, Radicals, acting for very differing motives, defeated him on the issue of his policy in China, but the following dissolution gave him 373 seats to 281.   But in February, 1858, his seeming submission to French threats on the Conspiracy to Murder Bill caused his defeat.[8]   He insisted on resignation, and the Queen sent for Lord Derby, who undertook to form a government when the Queen pressed him so to do.

10.   The Derby ministry survived a severe attack on the unfortunate error committed by Lord Ellenborough[9] in censuring the conduct of Lord Canning as regards Oudh, by the use of the threat of dissolution, which the Queen had reluctantly permitted it to employ, but in 1859 it was defeated on reform.   The dissolution of April increased the Conservative strength but not enough to give them an absolute majority over a united opposition.   In June the ministry was defeated on an amendment to the address in reply to the royal speech and resigned.

11.   Lord Palmerston took office after Lord Granville had made a fruitless attempt at the request of the Queen to form a ministry in which Lord Palmerston and Lord John Russell would serve under him;[10] the former agreed, the latter declined, but was willing

6 Bell, *Palmerston*, ii. 70 ff.; Lady F. Balfour, *Aberdeen*, ii. 171–177.
7 Bell, *Palmerston*, ii. 110 ff.; Lady F. Balfour, *Aberdeen*, ii. 288–296; Monypenny and Buckle, *Disraeli*, i. 1372 ff.; Morley, *Gladstone*, i. 521 ff.
8 Bell, *Palmerston*, ii. 181 ff.; *Letters of Queen Victoria*, 1 s. iii. 335 ff; Monypenny and Buckle, *Disraeli*, i. 1513 ff.; Morley, i. 574 ff.
9 Bell, *Palmerston*, ii. 187ff.
10 *Ibid.*, ii. 202 ff.; *Letters of Queen Victoria*, 1 s., iii. 435 ff.; Fitzmaurice, *Granville*, i. 324 ff.

to serve under Palmerston, who thus became Premier. He dissolved in July, 1865, winning 360 seats to 298 seats, but died in October.

12. Lord Russell took his place,[11] but in June, 1866, was defeated on his Reform Bill by the defection of Mr. Lowe and others, and resigned.

13. Lord Derby took office,[12] as the ministry declined to continue despite the Queen's wish. He and Mr. Disraeli now combined to 'dish the Whigs' and carried a Reform Bill, which increased the electorate from 1,056,659 in 1866 to 1,995,086 in 1869. In February, 1868, Lord Derby resigned from ill health and advised the Queen to send for his obvious successor, Mr. Disraeli.[13]

14. Mr. Disraeli in April, 1868, was defeated on the issue of the Irish Church, but did not resign,[14] expediting instead preparations for a new register of voters, and in November, Parliament was dissolved, giving Liberals 380 to 278 seats.

15. Mr. Gladstone's first ministry took office in December, 1868,[15] and resigned in March, 1873, when defeated on the Irish University Bill. But Mr. Disraeli would not take office[16] and it had to resume, dissolving in January, 1874. The Liberals won 249 seats, Home Rule supporters 51, but Conservatives 352, and the ministry resigned in February without meeting Parliament, as Mr. Disraeli had done in 1868.

16. Mr. Disraeli's ministry dissolved in March, 1880,[17] under the impression that events were favourable, but as a result of its unpopularity on foreign issues the election gave Liberals 350, Home Rulers 64, and Conservatives only 238. The ministry resigned in April.

17. Mr. Gladstone took office after a futile attempt to obtain a ministry under Lord Hartington.[18] This Government passed a

11 Morley, *Gladstone*, ii. 157 ff.; *Letters of Queen Victoria*, 2 s., i. 279 ff.

12 *Letters of Queen Victoria*, 2 s., i. 333 ff.; Monypenny and Buckle, *Disraeli*, ii. 173 ff.

13 *Letters of Queen Victoria*, 2 s., i. 495 ff.; Monypenny and Buckle, *Disraeli*, ii. 316 ff.

14 *Letters of Queen Victoria*, 2 s., i. 521 ff.; Monypenny and Buckle, *Disraeli*, ii. 366; Morley, *Gladstone*, ii. 247 ff.

15 *Letters of Queen Victoria*, 2 s., i. 559 ff.; Morley, *Gladstone*, ii. 249 ff.

16 Guedalla, *The Queen and Mr. Gladstone*, i. 385–410; Morley, *Gladstone*, ii. 446 ff.; Monypenny and Buckle, *Disraeli*, ii. 546 ff.

17 *Letters of Queen Victoria*, 2 s., ii. 315; Monypenny and Buckle, *Disraeli*, ii. 621 ff.

18 *Letters of Queen Victoria*, 2 s., iii. 73 ff.; Monypenny and Buckle, *Disraeli*, ii. 1396 ff.; Morley, *Gladstone*, ii. 616 ff.; J. L. Garvin, *Life of Joseph Chamberlain*, i. 285 ff.

Reform Act in 1884 under which the electorate grew from 2,618,453 in 1883, to 4,380,540 in 1885. It was defeated on the budget in June, 1885, and resigned. Pending redistribution of seats in the House of Commons, which was in progress and increased the total to 670 (England 495, Scotland 72, Ireland 103), Lord Salisbury accepted office with a pledge of tolerance from Mr. Gladstone until a general election could take place.

18. After receiving some assurances as to aid in financial business from Mr. Gladstone, Lord Salisbury took office[19] and dissolved in November. The election gave Liberals 335, Nationalists 86, and Conservatives 249, a number secured by the aid of the Nationalist voters in boroughs given under the belief that the Conservatives would make concessions on Home Rule. The ministry met the Commons in January, 1886, but was defeated on an amendment to the address, and resigned.

19. Mr. Gladstone took office in February, 1886,[20] but in June was defeated on the issue of Home Rule. The dissolution which followed was disastrous to him, giving Conservatives 316, Liberal Unionists 78, Liberals 191, supporters of Parnell 85, and he resigned in July.

20. Lord Salisbury assumed office,[21] failing to form a coalition with the Liberal Unionists although he was willing to serve under Lord Hartington. On the resignation of Lord Randolph Churchill, however, the ministry was strengthened by securing Mr. Goschen as Chancellor of the Exchequer, and was able to hold its own, but the dissolution of June, 1892, gave Conservatives 268, Liberal Unionists 47, Liberals 274, and Nationalists 81. The ministry waited for defeat in the Commons on a vote of no-confidence in August.

21. Mr. Gladstone took office,[22] faced by an impossible task of carrying Home Rule with a quite inadequate majority, and in March, 1894, the failure of his colleagues to support him in economy on defence resulted in his resignation.

19 *Letters of Queen Victoria*, 2 s., iii. 657 ff.; Winston Churchill, *Life of Randolph Churchill*, i. 397 ff.; Morley, *Gladstone*, iii. 200 ff.
20 *Letters of Queen Victoria*, 2 s., iii. 706 ff.; 3 s., i. 5 ff.; Lady G. Cecil, *Salisbury*, iii. 272 ff.; Morley, *Gladstone*, iii. 277; Churchill, *Randolph Churchill*, ii. 1 ff.
21 *Letters of Queen Victoria*, 3 s., i. 161 ff.; Cecil, *Salisbury*, iii. 307 ff.; Churchill, *Randolph Churchill*, ii. 116 ff. For Gladstone's comments on Lord Hartington's position, see Morley, *Gladstone*, iii. 364 ff.
22 *Letters of Queen Victoria*, 3 s., ii. 103; Morley, *Gladstone*, iii. 490 ff.

22. The Queen then chose Lord Rosebery[23] whose tenure of office ended in June, 1895, when a snap vote on cordite supplies was eagerly welcomed as an excuse for resignation, the Premier declining to dissolve as desired by Lord Salisbury, on the ground that the same Commons had defeated him in August, 1892.

23. Lord Salisbury then took office,[24] and dissolved Parliament in July, winning 340 seats, with Liberal Unionists 71, as against Liberals 177 and Nationalists 82. A dissolution cleverly planned on the strength of a supposed cessation of war in South Africa in September, 1900, gave Conservatives 334, Liberal Unionists 68, Liberals 186, and Nationalists 82. In July, 1902, Lord Salisbury resigned through ill-health.

24. Mr. Balfour was his inevitable successor,[25] as Leader of the Commons throughout his ministry. His term was troubled by the dispute on protecton, which led to resignations of great importance in 1903, but he held to office until December, 1905, when the Cabinet finally agreed to resign.

25. Sir H. Campbell-Bannerman took office,[26] and the election of January, 1906, gave Liberals 377, Labour 43, Nationalists 83, and Conservatives with whom the Liberal Unionists had in effect merged since 1895 only 167. He resigned in April, 1908, owing to ill-health, and was succeeded by Mr. Asquith.[27]

26. The rejection of the Finance Bill of 1909 necessitated an election in January, 1910, which gave Liberals 275; Labour 40, Nationalists 82, and Conservatives 273. The issue over the Parliament Bill and the creation of peers necessitated an election in December, which gave Liberals and Conservatives 272 each, Labour 42, and Nationalists 84. In May, 1915, opposition criticism compelled a coalition.

27. The coalition lasted only until December, 1916, when it was converted into a new coalition with a War Cabinet under the premiership of Mr. Lloyd George.[28]

28. The Government of Mr. Lloyd George dissolved in

[23] *Letters of Queen Victoria*, 3 s., ii. 364 ff.; Morley, *Gladstone*, iii. 507 ff.; Marquess of Crewe, *Life of Lord Rosebery*, ii. 437 ff.; Gardiner, *Harcourt*, ii. 258 ff.
[24] *Letters of Queen Victoria*, 3 s., ii. 321 ff.; Holland, *Devonshire*, ii. 216 ff.
[25] Lee, *Edward VII.*, ii. 158 ff.; Holland, *Devonshire*, ii. 279 f.
[26] Spender, *Campbell-Bannerman*, ii. 188 ff.; Lee, *Edward VII.*, ii. 441 ff.
[27] Spender, *Lord Oxford*, i. 194 ff. ; Lee. *Edward VII.*, ii. 578 ff.
[28] For 1915, see Spender, *Lord Oxford*, ii. 164 ff.; Beaverbrook, *Politicians and the War*, i. 90 ff.

November, 1918,[29] when the concession of the franchise to men at age twenty-one and women at age thirty had added thirteen million new voters to the eight million already existing. The election, fought on an appeal to support the man who won the war, gave the coalition 526 seats, Labour 63, Liberals 33, Irish 80, and Independents 5, the total seats having on redistribution been increased to 707 (England 528, Scotland 74, Ireland 105), as opposed to 670 in 1885, and 658 earlier. The ordinary Cabinet system was restored in 1919, and Mr. Lloyd George remained head of a Coalition Government until his resignation in October, 1922.

29. Mr. Bonar Law took office as leader of the Conservative party whose breakaway had destroyed the Lloyd George coalition[30] and dissolved at once, winning 347 seats to Labour 142, and Liberals 114. In May, 1923, he resigned owing to ill-health.

30. His successor, Mr. Baldwin,[31] dissolved again in November in order to secure a mandate for protection, but the Conservatives won only 258 seats to Labour 191, and Liberals 159. He met Parliament in January, 1924, but was defeated on a vote of no-confidence and resigned, and the King sent for Mr. MacDonald as leader of the Opposition.

31. The Labour ministry of Mr. MacDonald[32] held on only until October, when it chose a defeat on a minor issue as a ground of dissolving. It was decisively defeated, in part as a result of the incident of the Zinovieff letter, and resigned; the figures were Conservatives 420, Labour 151, and Liberals only 40, though 18 per cent. of the recorded votes went to them. The instinct for the two-party system thus manifested itself decisively.

32. Mr. Baldwin's Conservative ministry[33] held office from November, 1924, to June, 1929, when he resigned as the result of the election just preceding, which gave Conservatives about 260 seats, Labour 287, and Liberals 59.

33. Mr. MacDonald's second Labour ministry[34] held office until August, 1931, when it fell through internal disagreements on the policy to solve the country's serious financial and economic

29 Spender, *Lord Oxford*, ii. 248 ff.; Beaverbrook, *Politicians and the War*, ii. 208 ff.; Lloyd George, *War Memoirs*, ii. 997 ff.
30 Ronaldshay, *Curzon*, iii. 809 ff.; Taylor, *Bonar Law*, pp. 257 ff.; Mallet, *Cave*, pp. 253 ff.   31 Ronaldshay, *Curzon*, iii. 349 ff.
32 Snowden, *Autobiography*, ii. 589 ff.
33 Feiling, *Neville Chamberlain*, chap. xi.; Mallet, *Cave*, pp. 270 ff.
34 Snowden, *Autobiography*, ii. 754 ff.

problems. Mr. MacDonald was invited to form a National Government, and succeeded with Conservative and Liberal aid in doing so, on the ground that the national financial emergency dictated the dropping of party recrimination. Parliament was dissolved in the autumn and the general election gave the National Government an enormous majority—Conservatives 471, Labour 52, Liberal Nationals 35, Liberals 33, National Labour 13, and Independents 9, with two Irish Nationalists. The total seats had fallen, after the separation of the Irish Free State, to 615.[35]

34. The election over, the Government was reconstituted into a full Cabinet, representing the Conservatives, Liberals, and National Labour, the previous Government having been merely an emergency ministry to meet the immediate situation.[36] The Liberals proper in the new ministry went out of the Government on September 28, 1932, when the acceptance of the Ottawa Conference agreements ended any possibility of a return to freedom of trade, but the ministry continued its coalition character. In June, 1935, Mr. MacDonald resigned and accepted another office, and Mr. Baldwin became Prime Minister.

35. At the ensuing general election the Government majority, though somewhat reduced, still remained very large—Conservatives 385, Liberal Nationals 33, National Labour 8, with 154 Labour and 21 Independent Liberals forming the bulk of the Opposition.[37] The virtually Conservative ministry of Mr. Baldwin lasted until his resignation in May, 1937.

36. In May, 1937, Mr. N. Chamberlain became head of a ministry which, as the figures of the election of 1935 show, depended essentially on Conservative votes. On the outbreak of war in September, 1939, the Ministry remained Conservative, but a War Cabinet of nine Ministers was set up immediately in place of the larger peacetime Cabinet.[38]

37. In May, 1940, in face of growing opposition, Mr. Chamberlain resigned and Mr. Churchill became Prime Minister.[39] The War Cabinet system was retained but the administration now became a coalition, all the major parties participating, and this

---

35 Feiling, *Neville Chamberlain*, p. 196.
36 *Ibid.*, p. 198; Churchill, *Second World War*, i. 52.
37 Feiling, *Neville Chamberlain*, p. 270.
38 *Ibid.*, p. 420; Churchill, *Second World War*, i. 317.
39 Churchill, *Second World War*, i. 525.

Coalition continued in office until the successful conclusion of the war in Europe. In May, 1945, the Labour and Liberal parties left the coalition and Mr. Churchill formed a Conservative 'Caretaker' government until a new Parliament could be elected. There had been no general election since 1935.

38. At the general election of July, 1945, the Labour Party was returned with a very large majority and, in August, Mr. Attlee took office as Prime Minister. In this, the first general election for ten years, Labour gained 394 seats and Conservatives 216, in a total of 640.[40] With such a majority, and with no break-up within the Labour Party itself, the government held office for little short of the normal term of five years.

39. At the General Election of February, 1950, there was a big change in the parliamentary position. Of the new total of 625 seats Labour gained 315, Conservatives 298, and Liberals 9. As the leader of the largest party Mr. Attlee again took office as Prime Minister.[41]

40. In October, 1951, Parliament was again dissolved. In a closely fought general election the Conservatives won 321 seats, Labour 295, Liberals and others 9. Mr. Attlee resigned without meeting Parliament and Mr. Churchill formed a Conservative administration.

[40] R. B. McCallum and A. Readman, *The British General Election of* 1945.
[41] H. G. Nicholas, *The British General Election of* 1950.

APPENDIX 2

EXAMPLES OF CABINETS

(1) Sir Robert Peel's Cabinet of 1841

Prime Minister and First Lord of the Treasury
Lord Chancellor
Lord President of the Council
Lord Privy Seal
Chancellor of the Exchequer
Secretary of State for Home Affairs
Secretary of State for Foreign Affairs
Secretary of State for War and Colonies
First Lord of the Admiralty
President of the Board of Trade
President of the Board of Control
Secretary at War
Paymaster-General
Minister without Office

(2) Mr. Asquith's Cabinet of 1908

Prime Minister and First Lord of the Treasury
Lord Chancellor
Lord President of the Council
Lord Privy Seal
Chancellor of the Exchequer
Secretary of State for Home Affairs
Secretary of State for Foreign Affairs
Secretary of State for the Colonies
Secretary of State for War
Secretary of State for India
Secretary of State for Scotland
Chief Secretary for Ireland
First Lord of the Admiralty
Chancellor of the Duchy of Lancaster
President of the Board of Trade

President of the Local Government Board
President of the Board of Agriculture
President of the Board of Education
Postmaster-General
First Commissioner of Works

(3) Mr. Churchill's Cabinet of 1951

Members of the Cabinet

Prime Minister, First Lord of the Treasury and Minister of Defence
Secretary of State for Foreign Affairs
Lord President of the Council
Lord Privy Seal
Lord Chancellor
Secretary of State for the Home Department and Minister for Welsh Affairs
Chancellor of the Exchequer
Secretary of State for Commonwealth Relations
Secretary of State for the Colonies
Secretary of State for Scotland
Secretary of State for the Co-ordination of Transport, Fuel and Power
Minister of Health
Minister of Labour and National Service
Minister of Housing and Local Government
President of the Board of Trade
Paymaster-General   16

Ministers not in the Cabinet

Chancellor of the Duchy of Lancaster
First Lord of the Admiralty
Secretary of State for War
Secretary of State for Air
Minister of Agriculture and Fisheries
Minister of Education
Minister of Supply
Minister of Food
Minister of Fuel and Power
Minister of Transport and Civil Aviation   19.

Minister of National Insurance
Minister of Works
Postmaster-General
Minister of Pensions
Minister of State for Economic Affairs
Minister of State, Foreign Office
Minister of State, Scottish Office
Minister of State for Colonial Affairs

BIBLIOGRAPHY

Note:—This bibliography does not pretend to be an exhaustive list of even second-ary sources for British constitutional history, but simply a list of those works which have been used in the preparation of the text. The principal omissions of sources which have been considerably used are Hansard's *Parliamentary Debates* and various newspapers and journals, particularly *The Times*.

Addison, Christopher, Viscount. *Four and a Half Years.* 2 vols. (1934.)

Amery, L. S. *Thoughts on the Constitution.* (1947.)

Anderson, Sir J. *The Machinery of Government.* (1946.) *The Organization of Economic Studies in Relation to the Problems of Government.* (1947.)

Anson, Sir W. R. *Law and Custom of the Constitution.* Vol. I, *Parliament,* ed. Gwyer (1922); Vol. II, Parts i and ii, ed. Keith (1936).

Argyll, Duke of. *George Douglas, Eighth Duke of Argyll: Autobiography and Memoirs.* 2 vols. (1906.)

Ashley, Evelyn. *The Life of Henry John Temple, Viscount Palmerston, 1846–1865.* 2 vols. (1876.)

Askwith, Lord. *Lord James of Hereford.* (1930.)

Aspinall, A. *Lord Brougham and the Whig Party.* (1927.)

Attlee, C. R. *The Labour Party in Perspective,* 2nd ed. (1949.)

Bagehot, W. *The English Constitution.* (1872.)

Balfour, Arthur James, first Earl. *Chapters in Autobiography.* (1930.)

Balfour, Frances, Lady. *The Life of George, Fourth Earl of Aberdeen.* 2 vols. (1922.)

Beaverbrook, Lord. *Politicians and the War.* 2 vols. (1928–32.)

Bell, G. K. A. *Life of Archbishop Davidson.* 2 vols. (1935.)

Bell, H. C. F. *Lord Palmerston.* 2 vols. (1936.)

Bibesco, Marthe, Princess. *Lord Thomson of Cardington.* (1932.)

Birkenhead, Earl of. *Frederick Edwin, Earl of Birkenhead.* (1933–34.)

Bolitho, H. (ed.) *The Prince Consort and His Brother.* (1933.)

Butler, J. R. M. *The Passing of the Great Reform Bill.* (1914.)

Callwell, C. E. *Field-Marshal Sir Henry Wilson, His Life and Diaries.* 2 vols. (1927.)

Campbell, Lord John. *Lives of the Lord Chancellors,* 3rd ed. 7 vols. (1848.)

Campion, Sir G. (and others). *British Government Since 1918.* (1950.)

Cecil, Lady Gwendolen. *Life of Robert, Marquis of Salisbury.* 5 vols. (1921.)

Chamberlain, Sir Austen. *Down the Years.* (1935.) *Politics from Inside.* (1936.)

Chester, D. N. (and others). *Lessons of the British War Economy.* (1951.)

Childe-Pemberton, W. S. *Life of Lord Norton.* (1909.)

Churchill, Winston, S. *Lord Randolph Churchill.* 2 vols. (1906.) *The World Crisis.* 5 vols. (1923–28.) *Parliamentary Government and the Economic Problem.* (1930.) *The Second World War.* (1948– .)

Clark, G. N. *The Later Stuarts.* (1934).

Clynes, J. R. *Memoirs, 1869–1924.* (1937.)

Colvin, I., and Marjoribanks, E. *Life of Lord Carson.* 3 vols. (1932–36.)

Crewe, Marquess of. *Lord Rosebery.* 2 vols. (1931.)

Dicey, A. V. *Introduction to the Study of the Law of the Constitution,* 9th ed. (1945.)

Disraeli, B. *Lord George Bentinck: A Political Biography.* (1858.)

Duff Cooper, A. *Haig.* 2 vols. (1935–36.)

Dugdale, B. E. C. *Life of Arthur James Balfour.* 2 vols. (1936.)

Emden, C. S. *The People and the Constitution.* (1933.)

Esher, Viscount. *Journals and Letters of Reginald, Viscount Esher,* ed. M. V. Brett. 4 vols. (1934–38.) *The Influence of King Edward and Essays on Other Subjects.* (1915.)

Evatt, H. V. *The King and His Dominion Governors.* (1936.)

Feiling, Keith. *The Life of Neville Chamberlain.* (1946.)

Finer, H. *The Theory and Practice of Modern Government.* 2 vols. (1932.) *The Future of Government.* (1946.)

Fitzmaurice, Lord Edmond. *The Life of Granville George Leveson-Gower, Second Earl of Granville, K.G.* 2 vols. (1905.)

Fitzroy, Sir Almeric. *Memoirs.* 2 vols. (1925.)

French, G. *The Life of Field-Marshal Sir John French.* (1931.)

Gardiner, A. G. *The Life of Sir William Harcourt.* 2 vols. (1923.)

Garvin, J. L. *The Life of Joseph Chamberlain.* 3 vols. (1932–35.) vol. IV by Julian Amery. (1951.)

George, David Lloyd, first Earl Lloyd George. *War Memoirs.* 6 vols. (1933–36.)

Gladstone, W. E. *Gleanings of Past Years.* 6 vols. (1879.)

Gladstone, Lord. *After Thirty Years.* (1930.)

Gooch, G. P.　*The Later Correspondence of Lord John Russell.*　2 vols. (1925.)

Greville, Charles.　*The Greville Memoirs.*　1st Series, 1820–37. 3 vols. (1874.)　2nd Series, 1837–52.　3 vols.　(1885.)　3rd Series, 1853–59.　2 vols.　(1887.)

Grey, Edward, first Viscount.　*Twenty-Five Years.*　2 vols.　(1925.)

Grey, Henry, Earl.　*Correspondence of William IV and Earl Grey, November 1830 to June 1832.*　2 vols.　(1867.)

Guedalla, P.　*Palmerston.*　(1926.)　*Gladstone and Palmerston.* (1928.)　*The Queen and Mr. Gladstone.*　2 vols.　(1933.)

Gwynn, D.　*Life of John Redmond.*　(1932.)　*Daniel O'Connell,* revised ed.　(1947.)

Gwynn, S., and Tuckwell, G. M.　*The Life of the Rt. Hon. Sir Charles W. Dilke, Bart.*　2 vols.　(1917.)

Haldane, Lord.　*Richard Burdon Haldane: An Autobiography.*　(1929.)

Halévy, E.　*Histoire du Peuple Anglais au XIXe Siècle.*　5 vols.　(1930–32.)

Hall, H. L.　*The Colonial Office.*　(1937.)

Hallam, Henry.　*Constitutional History of England from the Accession of Henry VII to the Death of George II,* 7th ed.　3 vols.　(1854.)

Hamilton, Lord.　*Parliamentary Reminiscences and Reflections.*　2 vols. (1917–22.)

Hankey, Lord.　*Government Control in War.*　(1945.)　*Diplomacy by Conference.*　(1946.)

Hardie, F. M.　*The Political Influence of Queen Victoria.*　(1935.)

Heath, Sir T. L.　*The Treasury.*　(1928.)

Hicks Beach, Lady Victoria.　*Life of Sir Michael Hicks Beach.* 2 vols.　(1932.)

Hirst, F. W.　*Gladstone as Financier and Economist.*　(1931.)

Humphreys, J. H.　*Proportional Representation.*　(1911.)

Jenks, E.　*Parliamentary England.*　(1903.)

Jennings, Sir W. I.　*The Law and the Constitution.*　(1933.)　*Parliament.*　(1939.)　*The British Constitution.*　(1941).　*Cabinet Government,* 2nd ed.　(1951.)

Jones, Thomas.　*Lloyd George.*　(1951.)

Keith, A. B.　*Responsible Government in the Dominions,* 2nd ed. (1928.)　*Constitutional History of the First British Empire.* (1930.) *Constitutional History of India,* 1600–1935.　(1935.)　*The King and the Imperial Crown.*　(1936.)　*The Dominions as Sovereign States.*　(1938.)

Kitson Clark, G. S. R.　*Peel and the Conservative Party.*　(1929.)

Laprade, W. T. *The Parliamentary Papers of John Robinson.* Camden Society. (1922.) *Public Opinion and the General Election of* 1784. English Historical Review, vol. XXXI.

Laski, H. J. *Parliamentary Government in England.* (1938.) *Reflections on the Constitution.* (1951.)

Lee, Sir Sidney. *King Edward VII: A Biography.* 2 vols. (1925–27.)

Lees-Smith, H. B. *Second Chambers in Theory and Practice.* (1923.)

Legge, E. *King George.* 2 vols. (1918.)

McCallum, R. B., and Readman, A. *The British General Election of* 1945. (1947.)

Mackail, G. W., and Wyndham, G. *Life and Letters of George Wyndham.* 2 vols. (1925.)

Mallet, Sir C. *Lloyd George.* (1930.) *Lord Cave: A Memoir.* (1931.)

Malmesbury, third Earl of. *Memoirs of an Ex-Minister: An Autobiography.* 2 vols. (1885.)

Martin, A. P. *Life and Letters of the Rt. Hon. Robert Lowe, Viscount Sherbrooke.* 2 vols. (1893.)

Martin, Sir Theodore. *The Life of His Royal Highness the Prince Consort.* 5 vols. (1877–80.)

Maxwell, Sir H. *The Life and Letters of George William Frederick, Fourth Earl of Clarendon.* 2 vols. (1913.)

Maxwell, W. H. *Life of Wellington.* 2 vols. (1839.)

May, Sir T. E. *A Constitutional History of England Since* 1760. 2 vols. Edited by F. Holland and continued in a 3rd volume to 1911. (1912.) *A Treatise on the Law, Privileges, Proceedings and Usage of Parliament*, 14th ed. (1946.)

Michael, W. *England Under George I*, vol. I (1936); vol. II (1939). [This is a translation of part of the German edition, *Englische Geschichte in Achtzehnten Jahrhundert.* 4 vols. (1920–37.)]

Monypenny, W. F., and Buckle, O. E. *Life of Benjamin Disraeli, Earl of Beaconsfield.* 6 vols. (1910–20.) [References in the text are to the new edition in 2 vols. (1929.)]

Morley, Lord John. *The Life of Richard Cobden.* 2 vols. (1879.) *The Life of William Ewart Gladstone.* 3 vols. (1903.) *Recollections.* 2 vols. (1917.)

Namier, L. B. *The Structure of Politics at the Accession of George III.* 2 vols. (1929.) *England in the Age of the American Revolution.* (1930.)

Newton, Lord. *Lord Lansdowne: A Biography.* (1929.)

Nicholas, H. G. *The British General Election of* 1950. (1951.)

Nicholson, H. *Lord Carnock.* (1930.) *Curzon: The Last Phase.* (1934.)

Oxford and Asquith, Earl of. *The Genesis of the War.* (1923.) *Memories and Reflections.* 2 vols. (1926.) *Fifty Years of Parliament.* 2 vols. (1928.)

Parker, C. S. *Sir Robert Peel from his Private Papers.* 3 vols. (1891.) *Life and Letters of Sir James Graham.* 2 vols. (1907.)

Peel, Sir Robert. *Memoirs of the Rt. Hon. Sir Robert Peel, Bart., M.P.,* published by Lord Mahon and the Rt. Hon. Edward Cardwell. 2 vols. (1856.)

Porritt, E. and A. *The Unreformed House of Commons.* 2 vols. (1903.)

Ridges, E. W. *Constitutional Law of England,* 7th ed. by A. B. Keith. (1939.)

Robertson, Field-Marshal Sir W. *Soldiers and Statesmen,* 1914–1918. 2 vols. (1926.)

Ronaldshay, Earl of. *The Life of Lord Curzon.* 3 vols. (1928.)

Rose, J. H. *Life of William Pitt.* 2 vols. (1912.)

Rosebery, Lord. *Miscellanies, Literary and Historical.* 2 vols. (1921.)

Saintsbury, George. *The Earl of Derby.* (1892.)

Samuel, Herbert, Viscount. *Memoirs.* (1945.)

Sanders, L. C. *Lord Melbourne's Papers,* 2nd ed. (1890.)

Seton-Watson, R. W. *Disraeli, Gladstone and the Eastern Question.* (1935.)

Snowden, Philip, Viscount. *An Autobiography.* 2 vols. (1934.)

Somervell, D. C. *The Reign of King George the Fifth.* (1935.)

Spender, J. A. *The Life of the Rt. Hon. Sir Henry Campbell-Bannerman.* 2 vols. (1923.)

Spender, J. A., and Cyril Asquith. *Life of Herbert Henry Asquith, Lord Oxford and Asquith.* 2 vols. (1932.)

Stanhope, P. H. (Earl Stanhope). *Life of William Pitt.* 4 vols. (1867.)

Stanmore, Lord. *The Earl of Aberdeen.* (1893.)

Stockmar, Baron E. von. *Memoirs of Baron Stockmar.* 2 vols. (1872.)

Taylor, E. *The Taylor Papers.* (1913.)

Taylor, H. A. *Jix—Viscount Brentford.* (1933.) *The Strange Case of Andrew Bonar Law.*

Thomas, J. H. *My Story.* (1937.)

Tilley, Sir J., and Gaselee, S. *The Foreign Office.* (1933.)

Trevelyan, G. M. *Lord Grey of the Reform Bill.* (1920.)

Trevelyan, Sir G. O. *The Life and Letters of Lord Macaulay.* (1908.)

Turner, E. R. *The Privy Council of England,* 1603–1784. 2 vols. (1927–28.) *The Cabinet Council of England,* 1622–1784. 2 vols. (1930–32.)

Victoria, Queen. *The Letters of Queen Victoria.* 1st Series, 1837–61, edited by A. G. Benson and Viscount Esher, 3 vols. (1907.) 2nd Series, 1862–85, edited by G. E. Buckle. 3 vols. (1926–28.) 3rd Series, 1886–1901, edited by G. E. Buckle. 3 vols. (1930–32.)

Walpole, Spencer. *The Life of Lord John Russell.* 2 vols. (1889.)

Williams, E. T. *The Cabinet in the Eighteenth Century,* History, vol. xxii.

Williams, Francis. *The Triple Challenge.* (1948.)

Wolf, Lucien. *Life of the first Marquess of Ripon.* 2 vols. (1921.)

Yu, Wangteh. *The British Cabinet System.* (1939.)

Zetland, Marquess of. *Lord Cromer.* (1932.)

INDEX

453

120 ·2